ISBN 978-0-282-37964-3
PIBN 10032243

English
Français
Deutsche
Italiano
Español
Português

www.forgottenbooks.com

Mythology Photography **Fiction**
Fishing Christianity **Art** Cooking
Essays Buddhism Freemasonry
Medicine **Biology** Music **Ancient
Egypt** Evolution Carpentry Physics
Dance Geology **Mathematics** Fitness
Shakespeare **Folklore** Yoga Marketing
Confidence Immortality Biographies
Poetry **Psychology** Witchcraft
Electronics Chemistry History **Law**
Accounting **Philosophy** Anthropology
Alchemy Drama Quantum Mechanics
Atheism Sexual Health **Ancient History**
Entrepreneurship Languages Sport
Paleontology Needlework Islam
Metaphysics Investment Archaeology
Parenting Statistics Criminology
Motivational

A TREATISE

ON

FEDERAL TAXES

INCLUDING

THOSE IMPOSED BY THE WAR TAX ACT
OF CONGRESS OF 1917

THE INCOME TAX LAW AS AMENDED

AND OTHER UNITED STATES INTERNAL
REVENUE ACTS NOW IN FORCE

WITH COMMENTARIES AND EXPLANATIONS, REFERENCES TO THE RULINGS
AND REGULATIONS OF THE TREASURY DEPARTMENT AND
PERTINENT DECISIONS OF THE COURTS

BY

HENRY CAMPBELL BLACK, LL. D.

AUTHOR OF TREATISES
ON INCOME TAXES, BANKRUPTCY, RESCISSION OF
CONTRACTS, CONSTITUTIONAL LAW,
ETC.

1917
VERNON LAW BOOK COMPANY
KANSAS CITY, MO.

Copyright, 1917
BY
HENRY CAMPBELL BLACK

(Bl. Fed. Tax.)

PREFACE

THE War Revenue Act of Congress of October 3, 1917, not only introduced radical changes and amendments into the existing income-tax law, but, by materially lowering the exemption for the purpose of the war tax, brought within its incidence some millions of citizens who had never before been subject to that particular form of governmental exaction and who had regarded the taxation of incomes as a matter of no concern save to the wealthy few. For both these reasons it seemed necessary to revise thoroughly what I had previously written on the subject of Income Taxes; and the present volume supersedes my work on that subject, since it includes (though in somewhat more condensed form) all the material to be found in the book mentioned, and also the additions and changes made by the act of 1917 and such new rulings, regulations, and decisions as have been made public down to the time when this volume shall issue from the press.

But the scope of this work is much wider. It includes a discussion of all the internal-revenue taxes now in force, that is to say, not only of the income tax, but also of the estate tax, the excess profits tax, the capital stock tax on corporations, the excise taxes on various occupations, the new taxes on transportation and on insurance, the stamp tax, the excise, commodities, and miscellaneous taxes laid by the act of 1917, and general chapters on the assessment, payment, and collection of internal revenue taxes, and on the refunding and recovery of taxes illegally exacted. Care has been taken in each instance, and in the appropriate connection, to .quote the full and exact text of the applicable statute or part thereof, and the text is supported by such comments and explanations as seemed necessary or desirable, and by references to such rulings and regulations of the Internal Revenue Bureau and such decisions of the courts as were available. In the case of some of the forms of taxation now in operation under the laws of the United States, such as the income tax, the estate tax, the capital stock tax, and the stamp tax, the law is now fairly well settled, either tentatively by the regulations and rulings of the Treasury Department, or definitively by the decisions of the courts. In regard to some of the newer taxes, it is naturally impossible at the present moment to lay before the reader much more than the text of the enactment. But this fact is worthy of notice, that the whole internal revenue system of the country is now so co-ordinated that he who seeks a full comprehension of any part of it must needs study the system as a whole. Hence, even in advance of authoritative interpretations of such problems as are presented by the excess profits tax, for example, it cannot but be of advantage to have before one a conspectus of the entire scheme of internal revenue taxation.

It is hoped that the book will be found valuable not only to individual taxpayers and their legal advisers, but also to the financial officers of corporations, to banks and bankers, and to business men and investors generally, since now, for the first time in American history, a system of federal taxation is in force which, in at least some of its aspects, will come directly home to every corporation, every partnership, and practically every individual throughout the length and breadth of the land.

HENRY CAMPBELL BLACK.

WASHINGTON, D. O., 1917.

TABLE OF CONTENTS

CHAPTER II

NATURE, HISTORY, AND LEGAL BASIS OF INCOME TAXES

CHAPTER III

CONSTITUTIONAL VALIDITY OF INCOME TAX LAWS

CHAPTER IV

CONSTRUCTION OF STATUTES IMPOSING TAXES

CHAPTER V

WHAT CONSTITUTES TAXABLE INCOME

CHAPTER VI

PERSONS AND CORPORATIONS SUBJECT TO INCOME TAX

CHAPTER VII

EXEMPTIONS AND EXCEPTIONS

CHAPTER VIII

DEDUCTIONS AND CREDITS IN COMPUTING TAXABLE INCOME

CHAPTER IX

COLLECTION OF INCOME TAX AT THE SOURCE

CHAPTER XII

ESTATE TAX; REGULATIONS AND DECISIONS

CHAPTER XIII

EXCESS PROFITS TAX

CHAPTER XIV

CAPITAL STOCK TAX

CHAPTER XV

OCCUPATION TAXES

CHAPTER XVI

TAX ON FACILITIES FURNISHED BY PUBLIC UTILITIES AND ON INSURANCE

CHAPTER XVII

STAMP TAXES

CHAPTER XVIII

EXCISE. COMMODITIES, AND MISCELLANEOUS TAXES

CHAPTER XIX

ASSESSMENT, PAYMENT, AND COLLECTION OF TAXES

CHAPTER XX

REFUNDING AND RECOVERY OF TAXES ILLEGALLY EXACTED

INDEX

TABLE OF CASES CITED

[THE FIGURES REFER TO SECTIONS]

A

B

BL.FED.TAX.

(xix)

[The figures refer to sections]

V

Vallambrosa Rubber Co. v. Farmer, 155.

Van Brocklin v. Tennessee, 50.

Van Dyke v. Milwaukee, 98, 100, 198.

Vassar's Will, Matter of, 61.

Vedder, In re, 91.

Venable v. Richards, 473.

Vernon v. Manhattan Co., 89.

Vicksburg & M. R. Co. v. State, 61.

Vinton's Appeal, 103.

Violet v. Heath, 375.

Voight v. McKain, 400.

Von Baumbach v. Sargent Land Co., 70, 73, 195, 330.

W

Walker v. Brisley, 242.

Walsch v. Call, 84.

Ward, In re, 75.

Waring v. Savannah, 36, 44.

Warren v. Shook, 345.

Washington Nat. Bank v. Daily, 244.

Watchmakers' Alliance, In re, 226.

Waterbury Gas Light Co. v. Walsh, 330.

Watney v. Musgrave, 170.

Weaver v. Ewers, 472.

Webb v. Outrim, 113.

Weeks, In re, 240.

Weeks v. United States, 244.

Wells v. Shook, 66.

Wentz's Appeal, 73.

Western Express Co. v. United States, 459.

White v. Arthur, 476.

White v. Koehler, 75.

Wilcox v. Middlesex County Com'rs, 53, 66, 86.

Wilder v. Hawaiian Trust Co., 95.

Wilder's S. S. Co., In re, 184.

Wilkes-Barre & W. V. Traction Co. v. Davis, 328.

Williams v. Peyton, 461.

Wilmerding's Estate, In re, 51.

Wilson v. Parvin, 145.

Wiltbank's Appeal, 102.

Wisconsin v. Frear, 462.

Wood, Ex parte, 60.

Wood v. District of Columbia, 463.

Woodruff v. Oswego Starch Factory, 53.

Woolner v. United States, 466.

Worth v. Wilmington & W. R. Co., 44.

Worts v. Worts, 100.

Wright v. Blakeslee, 470, 474.

Wright v. Michigan Cent. R. Co., 400.

Y

Young, Ex parte, 60.

Young, In re, 110.

Z

Zonne v. Minneapolis Syndicate, 330.

FEDERAL TAXES

CHAPTER I

TEXT OF INCOME TAX LAW, AS AMENDED, AND OF WAR INCOME TAX LAW

Introduction.—The Federal Income Tax Law was enacted October 3, 1913. It was revised, considerably modified, and re-enacted September 8, 1916. The War Revenue Act of October 3, 1917, does not repeal the 1916 statute. On the contrary, it imposes an additional tax on incomes, individual and corporate, which is not in substitution of the former income tax, but is cumulative. The tax imposed by the act of 1917 is not expressed to be in force "during the war," or for any other definite period. Hence it should be carefully noted that, as affecting incomes for the year 1917 and every year thereafter until one or other of the statutes shall be repealed, those persons and corporations who are liable will be called upon to pay two income taxes to the United States; one of which may be called the "regular" or "ordinary" income tax and the other the "war" income tax. They will probably both be included in one and the same return to be made by the taxpayer, and will be assessed and collected in the same manner and at the same time. But the two income taxes differ in respect to the amount of personal exemption allowed and in some other particulars, all of which will be fully explained in the succeeding pages of this volume. It is to be observed, however, that the new or "war" income tax "shall not extend to Porto Rico. or the Philippine Islands, and the Porto Rican or Philippine Legislature shall have power by due enactment to amend, alter, modify, or repeal the income tax laws in force in Porto Rico or the Philippine Islands, respectively." (Act Cong. Oct. 3, 1917, § 5.)

But although the act of 1917 did not repeal that of 1916, it amended it in numerous and important particulars. This chapter therefore contains the text of the income tax law of 1916, as amended by the act of October 3, 1917 (the sections of this chapter being numbered concurrently with the sections of the income tax law), with the addition of the provisions of the act of 1917 levying the "war income tax."

§ 1. [a] Normal income tax
There shall be levied, assessed, collected, and paid annually upon the entire net income received in the preceding calendar year from all sources by every individual, a citizen or resident of the United States, a tax of two per centum upon such income; and a like tax shall be levied, assessed, collected, and paid annually upon the entire net income received in the preceding calendar year from

all sources within the United States by every individual, a nonresident alien, including interest on bonds, notes, or other interest-bearing obligations of residents, corporate or otherwise.

[b] Additional tax; income included; provisions relating to normal tax applicable

In addition to the income tax imposed by subdivision (a) of this section (herein referred to as the normal tax) there shall be levied, assessed, collected, and paid upon the total net income of every individual, or, in the case of a nonresident alien, the total net income received from all sources within the United States, an additional income tax (herein referred to as the additional tax) of one per centum per annum upon the amount by which such total net income exceeds $20,000 and does not exceed $40,000, two per centum per annum upon the amount by which such total net income exceeds $40,000 and does not exceed $60,000, three per centum per annum upon the amount by which such total net income exceeds $60,000 and does not exceed $80,000, four per centum per annum upon the amount by which such total net income exceeds $80,000 and does not exceed $100,000, five per centum per annum upon the amount by which such total net income exceeds $100,000 and does not exceed $150,000, six per centum per annum upon the amount by which such total net income exceeds $150,000 and does not exceed $200,-000, seven per centum per annum upon the amount by which such total net income exceeds $200,000 and does not exceed $250,000, eight per centum per annum upon the amount by which such total net income exceeds $250,000 and does not exceed $300,000, nine per centum per annum upon the amount by which such total net income exceeds $300,000 and does not exceed $500,000, ten per centum, per annum upon the amount by which such total net income exceeds $500,000 and does not exceed $1,000,000, eleven per centum per annum upon the amount by which such total net income exceeds $1,-000,000 and does not exceed $1,500,000, twelve per centum per annum upon the amount by which such total net income exceeds $1,-500,000 and does not exceed $2,000,000, and thirteen per centum per annum upon the amount by which such total net income exceeds $2,000,000.

For the purpose of the additional tax there shall be included as income the income derived from dividends on the capital stock or from the net earnings of any corporation, joint-stock company or association, or insurance company, except that in the case of nonresident aliens such income derived from sources without the United States shall not be included.

All the provisions of this title relating to the normal tax on individuals, so far as they are applicable and are not inconsistent with this subdivision and section three, shall apply to the imposition, levy, assessment, and collection of the additional tax imposed under this subdivision.

[c] Normal and additional tax rates applicable to entire income

The foregoing normal and additional tax rates shall apply to the entire net income, except as hereinafter provided, received by every taxable person in the calendar year nineteen hundred and sixteen and in each calendar year thereafter.

§ 2.   [a] Net income of taxable person, how determined

Subject only to such exemptions and deductions as are hereinafter allowed, the net income of a taxable person shall include gains, profits, and income derived from salaries, wages, or compensation for personal service of whatever kind and in whatever form paid, or from professions, vocations, businesses, trade, commerce, or sales, or dealings in property, whether real or personal, growing out of the ownership or use of or interest in real or personal property, also from interest, rent, dividends, securities, or the transaction of any business carried on for gain or profit, or gains or profits and income derived from any source whatever.

[b] Income of estates of decedents and trust estates; indemnity and credit to executors, etc.

Income received by estates of deceased persons during the period of administration or settlement of the estate, shall be subject to the normal and additional tax and taxed to their estates, and also such income of estates or any kind of property held in trust, including such income accumulated in trust for the benefit of unborn or unascertained persons, or persons with contingent interests, and income held for future distribution under the terms of the will or trust shall be likewise taxed, the tax in each instance, except when the income is returned for the purpose of the tax by the beneficiary, to be assessed to the executor, administrator, or trustee, as the case may be: Provided, That where the income is to be distributed annually or regularly between existing heirs or legatees, or beneficiaries the rate of tax and method of computing the same shall be based in each case upon the amount of the individual share to be distributed.

Such trustees, executors, administrators, and other fiduciaries are hereby indemnified against the claims or demands of every beneficiary for all payments of taxes which they shall be required to make under the provisions of this title, and they shall have credit for the amount of such payments against the beneficiary or princi-

(4)

pal in any accounting which they make as such trustees or other fiduciaries.

[c] Gain derived from sale of property, how determined

For the purpose of ascertaining the gain derived from the sale or other disposition of property, real, personal, or mixed, acquired before March first, nineteen hundred and thirteen, the fair market price or value of such property as of March first, nineteen hundred and thirteen, shall be the basis for determining the amount of such gain derived.

§ 3. Taxable income of individual for purpose of additional tax; fraudulent accumulations; statement of gains and profits by corporation, etc.

For the purpose of the additional tax, the taxable income of any individual shall include the share to which he would be entitled of the gains and profits, if divided or distributed, whether divided or distributed or not, of all corporations, joint-stock companies or associations, or insurance companies, however created or organized, formed or fraudulently availed of for the purpose of preventing the imposition of such tax through the medium of permitting such gains and profits to accumulate instead of being divided or distributed; and the fact that any such corporation, joint-stock company or association, or insurance company, is a mere holding company, or that the gains and profits are permitted to accumulate beyond the reasonable needs of the business, shall be prima facie evidence of a fraudulent purpose to escape such tax; but the fact that the gains and profits are in any case permitted to accumulate and become surplus shall not be construed as evidence of a purpose to escape the said tax in such case unless the Secretary of the Treasury shall certify that in his opinion such accumulation is unreasonable for the purposes of the business. When requested by the Commissioner of Internal Revenue, or any district collector of internal revenue, such corporation, joint-stock company or association, or insurance company shall forward to him a correct statement of such gains and profits and the names and addresses of the individuals or shareholders who would be entitled to the same if divided or distributed.

§ 4. Income Exempt from Taxation

The following income shall be exempt from the provisions of this title: The proceeds of life insurance policies paid to individual beneficiaries upon the death of the insured; the amount received by the insured, as a return of premium or premiums paid by him under life insurance, endowment, or annuity contracts, either during the term or at the maturity of the term mentioned in the contract or upon surrender of the contract; the value of property acquired by gift, bequest, devise, or descent (but the income from such property shall be included as income); interest upon the obligations of a state or any political subdivision thereof or upon the obligations of the United States (but, in the case of obligations of the United States issued after September first, nineteen hundred and seventeen, only if and to the extent provided in the act authorizing the issue thereof) or its possessions or securities issued under the provisions of the Federal Farm Loan Act of July seventeenth, nineteen hundred and sixteen; the compensation of the present President of the United States during the term for which he has been elected and the judges of the supreme and inferior courts of the United States now in office, and the compensation of all officers and employees of a state, or any political subdivision thereof, except when such compensation is paid by the United States Government.

§ 5. Computation of Net Income of Citizen or Resident of the United States. [a] Deductions Allowed

In computing net income in the case of a citizen or resident of the United States, for the purpose of the tax there shall be allowed as deductions:

First. The necessary expenses actually paid in carrying on any business or trade, not including personal, living, or family expenses;

Second. All interest paid within the year on his indebtedness except on indebtedness incurred for the purchase of obligations or securities the interest upon which is exempt from taxation as income under this title;

Third. Taxes paid within the year imposed by the authority of the United States (except income and excess profits taxes) or of its territories or possessions, or any foreign country, or by the authority of any state, county, school district, or municipality, or other taxing subdivision of any state, not including those assessed against local benefits;

Fourth. Losses actually sustained during the year, incurred in his business or trade, or arising from fires, storms, shipwreck, or other casualty, and from theft, when such losses are not compensated for by insurance or otherwise: Provided, That for the purpose of ascertaining the loss sustained from the sale or other disposition of property, real, personal, or mixed, acquired before March first, nineteen hundred and thirteen, the fair market price or value of such property as of March first, nineteen hundred and thirteen, shall be the basis for determining the amount of such loss sustained;

(6)

Fifth. In transactions entered into for profit but not connected with his business or trade, the losses actually sustained therein during the year to an amount not exceeding the profits arising therefrom;

Sixth. Debts due to the taxpayer actually ascertained to be worthless and charged off within the year;

Seventh. A reasonable allowance for the exhaustion, wear and tear of property arising out of its use or employment in the business or trade;

Eighth. (a) In the case of oil and gas wells a reasonable allowance for actual reduction in flow and production to be ascertained not by the flush flow, but by the settled production or regular flow; (b) in the case of mines a reasonable allowance for depletion thereof not to exceed the market value in the mine of the product thereof, which has been mined and sold during the year for which the return and computation are made, such reasonable allowance to be made in the case of both (a) and (b) under rules and regulations to be prescribed by the Secretary of the Treasury: Provided, That when the allowances authorized in (a) and (b) shall equal the capital originally invested, or in case of purchase made prior to March first, nineteen hundred and thirteen, the fair market value as of that date, no further allowance shall be made. No deduction shall be allowed for any amount paid out for new buildings, permanent improvements, or betterments, made to increase the value of any property or estate, and no deduction shall be made for any amount of expense of restoring property or making good the exhaustion thereof for which an allowance is or has been made;

Ninth. Contributions or gifts actually made within the year to corporations or associations organized and operated exclusively for religious, charitable, scientific, or educational purposes, or to societies for the prevention of cruelty to children or animals, no part of the net income of which inures to the benefit of any private stockholder or individual, to an amount not in excess of fifteen per centum of the taxpayer's taxable net income as computed without the benefit of this paragraph. Such contributions or gifts shall be allowable as deductions only if verified under rules and regulations prescribed by the Commissioner of Internal Revenue, with the approval of the Secretary of the Treasury.

[b] Credit for normal tax purposes of dividends on stock or net earnings of corporation, etc., taxable upon net income

For the purpose of the normal tax only, the income embraced in a personal return shall be credited with the amount received as dividends upon the stock or from the net earnings of any corporation, joint-stock company or association, trustee, or insurance company, which is taxable upon its net income as hereinafter provided.

[c] Credit for normal tax purposes of normal tax paid or withheld at source

A like credit shall be allowed as to the amount of income, the normal tax upon which has been paid or withheld for payment at the source of the income under the provisions of this title.

§ 6. Computation of Income of Nonresident Alien. [a] Deductions Allowed

In computing net income in the case of a nonresident alien, for the purpose of the tax there shall be allowed as deductions—

First. The necessary expenses actually paid in carrying on any business or trade conducted by him within the United States not including personal, living, or family expenses;

Second. The proportion of all interest paid within the year by such person on his indebtedness (except on indebtedness incurred for the purchase of obligations or securities the interest upon which is exempt from taxation as income under this title) which the gross amount of his income for the year derived from sources within the United States bears to the gross amount of his income for the year derived from all sources within and without the United States, but this deduction shall be allowed only if such person includes in the return required by section eight all the information necessary for its calculation;

Third. Taxes paid within the year imposed by the authority of the United States (except income and excess profits taxes), or of its territories, or possessions, or by the authority of any state, county, school district, or municipality, or other taxing subdivision of any state, paid within the United States, not including those assessed against local benefits;

Fourth. Losses actually sustained during the year, incurred in business or trade conducted by him within the United States, and losses of property within the United States arising from fires, storms, shipwreck, or other casualty, and from theft, when such losses are not compensated for by insurance or otherwise: Provided, That for the purpose of ascertaining the amount of such loss or losses sustained in trade, or speculative transactions not in trade, from the same or any kind of property acquired before March first, nineteen hundred and thirteen, the fair market price or value of such property as of March first, nineteen hundred and thirteen, shall

(8)

be the basis for determining the amount of such loss or losses sustained;

Fifth. In transactions entered into for profit but not connected with his business or trade, the losses actually sustained therein during the year to an amount not exceeding the profits arising therefrom in the United States;

Sixth. Debts arising in the course of business or trade conducted by him within the United States due to the taxpayer actually ascertained to be worthless and charged off within the year;

Seventh. A reasonable allowance for the exhaustion, wear and tear of property within the United States arising out of its use or employment in the business or trade; (a) in the case of oil and gas wells a reasonable allowance for actual reduction in flow and production to be ascertained not by the flush flow, but by the settled production or regular flow; (b) in the case of mines a reasonable allowance for depletion thereof not to exceed the market value in the mine of the product thereof which has been mined and sold during the year for which the return and computation are made, such reasonable allowance to be made in the case of both (a) and (b) under rules and regulations to be prescribed by the Secretary of the Treasury: Provided, That when the allowance authorized in (a) and (b) shall equal the capital originally invested, or in case of purchase made prior to March first, nineteen hundred and thirteen, the fair market value as of that date, no further allowance shall be made. No deduction shall be allowed for any amount paid out for new buildings, permanent improvements, or betterments, made to increase the value of any property or estate, and no deduction shall be made for any amount of expense of restoring property or making good the exhaustion thereof for which an allowance is or has been made.

[b] Credits allowed

There shall also be allowed the credits specified by subdivisions (b) and (c) of section five.

[c] A nonresident alien individual shall receive the benefit of the deductions and credits provided for in this section only by filing or causing to be filed with the collector of internal revenue a true and accurate return of his total income, received from all sources, corporate or otherwise, in the United States, in the manner prescribed by this title; and in case of his failure to file such return the collector shall collect the tax on such income, and all property belonging to such nonresident alien individual shall be liable to distraint for the tax.

§ 7. Exemptions Allowed for Purpose of Normal Tax

That for the purpose of the normal tax only, there shall be allowed as an exemption in the nature of a deduction from the amount of the net income of each citizen or resident of the United States, ascertained as provided herein, the sum of $3,000, plus $1,000 additional if the person making the return be a head of a family or a married man with a wife living with him, or plus the sum of $1,000 additional if the person making the return be a married woman with a husband living with her; but in no event shall this additional exemption of $1,000 be deducted by both a husband and a wife: Provided, That only one deduction of $4,000 shall be made from the aggregate income of both husband and wife when living together: Provided further, That if the person making the return is the head of a family there shall be an additional exemption of $200 for each child dependent upon such person, if under eighteen years of age, or if incapable of self-support because mentally or physically defective, but this provision shall operate only in the case of one parent in the same family: Provided further, That guardians or trustees shall be allowed to make this personal exemption as to income derived from the property of which such guardian or trustee has charge in favor of each ward or cestui que trust: Provided further, That in no event shall a ward or cestui que trust be allowed a greater personal exemption than as provided in this section, from the amount of net income received from all sources. There shall also be allowed an exemption from the amount of the net income of estates of deceased citizens or residents of the United States during the period of administration or settlement, and of trust or other estates of citizens or residents of the United States the income of which is not distributed annually or regularly under the provisions of subdivision (b) of section two, the sum of $3,000, including such deductions as are allowed under section five."

(NOTE. The original subdivision "b" of this section was repealed by the act of Oct. 3, 1917.)

§ 8. [a] Tax computed on income received in preceding calendar year

The tax shall be computed upon the net income, as thus ascertained, of each person subject thereto, received in each preceding calendar year ending December thirty-first.

[b] Returns of incomes; form and contents; extension of time for filing; making by agent

On or before the first day of March, nineteen hundred and seventeen, and the first day of March in each year thereafter, a true and accurate return under oath shall be made by each person of lawful age, except as hereinafter provided, having a net income of $3,000 or over for the taxable year to the collector of internal revenue for the district in which such person has his legal residence or principal place of business, or if there be no legal residence or place of business in the United States, then with the collector of internal revenue at Baltimore, Maryland, in such form as the Commissioner of Internal Revenue, with the approval of the Secretary of the Treasury, shall prescribe, setting forth specifically the gross amount of income from all separate sources, and from the total thereof deducting the aggregate items of allowances herein authorized: Provided, That the Commissioner of Internal Revenue shall have authority to grant a reasonable extension of time, in meritorious cases, for filing returns of income by persons residing or traveling abroad who are required to make and file returns of income and who are unable to file said returns on or before March first of each year: Provided further, That the aforesaid return may be made by an agent when by reason of illness, absence, or nonresidence the person liable for said return is unable to make and render the same, the agent assuming the responsibility of making the return and incurring penalties provided for erroneous, false, or fraudulent return.

[c] **Returns by guardians, trustees, etc.; provisions applicable to**
Guardians, trustees, executors, administrators, receivers, conservators, and all persons, corporations, or associations acting in any fiduciary capacity, shall make and render a return of the income of the person, trust, or estate for whom or which they act, and be subject to all the provisions of this title which apply to individuals. Such fiduciary shall make oath that he has sufficient knowledge of the affairs of such person, trust, or estate to enable him to make such return and that the same is, to the best of his knowledge and belief, true and correct, and be subject to all the provisions of this title which apply to individuals: Provided, That a return made by one of two or more joint fiduciaries filed in the district where such fiduciary resides, under such regulations as the Secretary of the Treasury may prescribe, shall be a sufficient compliance with the requirements of this paragraph; Provided further, that no return of income not exceeding $3,000 shall be required except as in this title otherwise provided.

(NOTE. Subdivision "d" of this section was repealed by the act of Oct. 3, 1917.)

[e] **Tax on partnerships; returns**
Persons carrying on business in partnership shall be liable for income tax only in their individual capacity, and the share of the

profits of the partnership to which any taxable partner would be entitled if the same were divided, whether divided or otherwise, shall be returned for taxation and the tax paid under the provisions of this title: Provided, That from the net distributive interests on which the individual members shall be liable for tax, normal and additional, there shall be excluded their proportionate shares received from interest on the obligations of a State or any political or taxing subdivision thereof, and upon the obligations of the United States (if and to the extent that it is provided in the act authorizing the issue of such obligations of the United States that they are exempt from taxation), and its possessions, and that for the purpose of computing the normal tax there shall be allowed a credit, as provided by section five, subdivision (b), for their proportionate share of the profits derived from dividends. And such partnership, when requested by the Commissioner of Internal Revenue, or any district collector, shall render a correct return of the earnings, profits, and income of the partnership, except income exempt under section four of this Act, setting forth the item of the gross income and the deductions and credits allowed by this title, and the names and addresses of the individuals who would be entitled to the net earnings, profits, and income, if distributed. A partnership shall have the same privilege of fixing and making returns upon the basis of its own fiscal year as is accorded to corporations under this title. · If a fiscal year ends during nineteen hundred and sixteen or a subsequent calendar year for which there is a rate of tax different from the rate for the preceding calendar year, then (1) the rate for such preceding calendar year shall apply to an amount of each partner's share of such partnership profits equal to the proportion which the part of such fiscal year falling within such calendar year bears to the full fiscal year, and (2) the rate for the calendar year during which such fiscal year ends shall apply to the remainder.

[f] Returns to include income derived from dividends on capital stock or net earnings of corporation, etc.

In every return shall be included the income derived from dividends on the capital stock or from the net earnings of any corporation, joint-stock company or association, or insurance company, except that in the case of nonresident aliens such income derived from sources without the United States shall not be included.

[g] Returns on accounts kept on basis other than of actual receipts and disbursements

An individual keeping accounts upon any basis other than that of actual receipts and disbursements, unless such other basis does not clearly reflect his income, may, subject to regulations made by the Commissioner of Internal Revenue, with the approval of the Secretary of the Treasury, make his return upon the basis upon which his accounts are kept, in which case the tax shall be computed upon his income as so returned.

§ 9.   [a] Assessments to be made by Commissioner of Internal Revenue; notice to persons liable; time for payment of tax; penalty and interest

All assessments shall be made by the Commissioner of Internal Revenue and all persons shall be notified of the amount for which they are respectively liable on or before the first day of June of each successive year, and said amounts shall be paid on or before the fifteenth day of June, except in cases of refusal or neglect to make such return and in cases of erroneous, false, or fraudulent returns, in which cases the Commissioner of Internal Revenue shall, upon the discovery thereof at any time within three years after said return is due, or has been made, make a return upon information obtained as provided for in this title or by existing law, or require the necessary corrections to be made, and the assessment made by the Commissioner of Internal Revenue thereon shall be paid by such person or persons immediately upon notification of the amount of such assessment; and to any sum or sums due and unpaid after the fifteenth day of June in any year, and for ten days after notice and demand thereof by the collector, there shall be added the sum of five per centum on the amount of tax unpaid, and interest at the rate of one per centum per month upon said tax from the time the same became due, except from the estates of insane, deceased, or insolvent persons.

[b] Deduction and withholding of normal tax at source; payment to government; personal liability for and indemnity to persons required to deduct; exemptions and deductions where tax is deducted, etc., at source, how obtained

All persons, corporations, partnerships, associations, and insurance companies, in whatever capacity acting, including lessees or mortgagors of real or personal property, trustees acting in any trust capacity, executors, administrators, receivers, conservators, employers, and all officers and employees of the United States, having the control, receipt, custody, disposal, or payment of interest, rent, salaries, wages, premiums, annuities, compensation, remuneration, emoluments, or other fixed or determinable annual or periodical gains, profits, and income of any nonresident alien individual, other

(13)

than income derived from dividends on capital stock, or from the net earnings of a corporation, joint-stock company or association, or insurance company, which is taxable upon its net income as provided in this title, are hereby authorized and required to deduct and withhold from such annual or periodical gains, profits, and income such sum as will be sufficient to pay the normal tax imposed thereon by this title, and shall make return thereof on or before March first of each year and, on or before the time fixed by law for the payment of the tax, shall pay the amount withheld to the officer of the United States Government authorized to receive the same; and they are each hereby made personally liable for such tax, and they are each hereby indemnified against every person, corporation, partnership, association, or insurance company, or demand whatsoever for all payments which they shall make in pursuance and by virtue of this title.

[c] **Normal tax deducted and withheld at source on fixed or determinable annual or periodical gains, profits, etc., from interest on bonds, mortgages, etc., of corporations**

The amount of the normal tax hereinbefore imposed shall also be deducted and withheld from fixed or determinable annual or periodical gains, profits and income derived from interest upon bonds and mortgages, or deeds of trust or other similar obligations of corporations, joint-stock companies, associations, and insurance companies, (if such bonds, mortgages, or other obligations contain a contract or provision by which the obligor agrees to pay any portion of the tax imposed by this title upon the obligee or to reimburse the obligee for any portion of the tax or to pay the interest without deduction for any tax which the obligor may be required or permitted to pay thereon or to retain therefrom under any law of the United States) whether payable annually or at shorter or longer periods and whether such interest is payable to a non-resident alien individual or to an individual citizen or resident of the United States, subject to the provisions of the foregoing subdivision (b) of this section requiring the tax to be withheld at the source and deducted from annual income and returned and paid to the Government, unless the person entitled to receive such interest shall file with the withholding agent, on or before February first, a signed notice in writing claiming the benefit of an exemption under section seven of this Title.

(NOTE. Subdivisions "d" and "e" of this section were repealed by the act of Oct. 3, 1917.)

(14)

[f] License to and regulations concerning persons, etc., collecting foreign payments of interest, etc., by coupons, checks, etc.; penalty for collecting without license

All persons, corporations, partnerships, or associations, undertaking as a matter of business or for profit the collection of foreign payments of interest or dividends by means of coupons, checks, or bills of exchange shall obtain a license from the Commissioner of Internal Revenue, and shall be subject to such regulations enabling the Government to obtain the information required under this title, as the Commissioner of Internal Revenue, with the approval of the Secretary of the Treasury, shall prescribe; and whoever knowingly undertakes to collect such payments as aforesaid without having obtained a license therefor, or without complying with such regulations, shall be deemed guilty of a misdemeanor and for each offense be fined in a sum not exceeding $5,000, or imprisoned for a term not exceeding one year, or both, in the discretion of the court.

[g] Personal returns on gains, profits, and income not included in section; intent of act

The tax herein imposed upon gains, profits, and income not falling under the foregoing and not returned and paid by virtue of the foregoing or as otherwise provided by law shall be assessed by personal return under rules and regulations to be prescribed by the Commissioner of Internal Revenue and approved by the Secretary of the Treasury. The intent and purpose of this title is that all gains, profits, and income of a taxable class, as defined by this title, shall be charged and assessed with the corresponding tax, normal and additional, prescribed by this title and said tax shall be paid by the owner of such income, or the proper representative having the receipt, custody, control, or disposal of the same. For the purpose of this title ownership or liability shall be determined as of the year for which a return is required to be rendered.

The provisions of this section, except subdivision (c), relating to the deduction and payment of the tax at the source of income shall only apply to the normal tax hereinbefore imposed upon nonresident alien individuals.

§ 10. [a] Tax of 2 per cent. on net income of corporations; fiscal year; mode of ascertaining gain or loss from sale or disposition of property

That there shall be levied, assessed, collected, and paid annually upon the total net income received in the preceding calendar year from all sources by every corporation, joint-stock company or association, or insurance company, organized in the United States, no matter how created or organized but not including partnerships, a tax of two per centum upon such income; and a like tax shall be levied, assessed, collected, and paid annually upon the total net income received in the preceding calendar year from all sources within the United States by every corporation, joint-stock company or association, or insurance company organized, authorized, or existing under the laws of any foreign country, including interest on bonds, notes, or other interest-bearing obligations of residents, corporate or otherwise, and including the income derived from dividends on capital stock or from net earnings of resident corporations, joint-stock companies or associations, or insurance companies whose net income is taxable under this title.

The foregoing tax rate shall apply to the total net income received by every taxable corporation, joint-stock company or association, or insurance company in the calendar year nineteen hundred and sixteen and in each year thereafter, except that if it has fixed its own fiscal year under the provisions of existing law, the foregoing rate shall apply to the proportion of the total net income returned for the fiscal year ending prior to December thirty-first, nineteen hundred and sixteen, which the period between January first, nineteen hundred and sixteen, and the end of such fiscal year bears to the whole of such fiscal year, and the rate fixed in Section II of the Act approved October third, nineteen hundred and thirteen, entitled "An Act to reduce tariff duties and to provide revenue for the Government, and for other purposes," shall apply to the remaining portion of the total net income returned for such fiscal year.

For the purpose of ascertaining the gain derived or loss sustained from the sale or other disposition by a corporation, joint-stock company or association, or insurance company, of property, real, personal, or mixed, acquired before March first, nineteen hundred and thirteen, the fair market price or value of such property as of March first, nineteen hundred and thirteen, shall be the basis for determining the amount of such gain derived or loss sustained.

[b] Additional tax on undistributed net income of corporations

In addition to the income tax imposed by subdivision (a) of this section there shall be levied, assessed, collected, and paid annually an additional tax of ten per centum upon the amount, remaining undistributed six months after the end of each calendar or fiscal year, of the total net income of every corporation, joint-stock company or association, or insurance company, received during the year, as determined for the purposes of the tax imposed by such subdivi-

(16)

sion (a), but not including the amount of any income taxes paid by it within the year imposed by the authority of the United States.

The tax imposed by this subdivision shall not apply to that portion of such undistributed net income which is actually invested and employed in the business or is retained for employment in the reasonable requirements of the business or is invested in obligations of the United States issued after September first, nineteen hundred and seventeen: Provided, That if the Secretary of the Treasury ascertains and finds that any portion of such amount so retained at any time for employment in the business is not so employed or is not reasonably required in the business a tax of fifteen per centum shall be levied, assessed, collected, and paid thereon.

The foregoing tax rates shall apply to the undistributed net income received by every taxable corporation, joint-stock company or association, or insurance company in the calendar year nineteen hundred and seventeen and in each year thereafter, except that if it has fixed its own fiscal year under the provisions of existing law, the foregoing rates shall apply to the proportion of the taxable undistributed net income returned for the fiscal year ending prior to December thirty-first, nineteen hundred and seventeen, which the period between January first, nineteen hundred and seventeen, and the end of such fiscal year bears to the whole of such fiscal year.

§ 11. [a] Corporations exempted

That there shall not be taxed under this title any income received by any—

First. Labor, agricultural, or horticultural organization;

Second. Mutual savings bank not having a capital stock represented by shares;

Third. Fraternal beneficiary society, order, or association, operating under the lodge system or for the exclusive benefit of the members of a fraternity itself operating under the lodge system, and providing for the payment of life, sick, accident, or other benefits to the members of such society, order, or association or their dependents;

Fourth. Domestic building and loan association and cooperative banks without capital stock organized and operated for mutual purposes and without profit;

Fifth. Cemetery company owned and operated exclusively for the benefit of its members;

Sixth. Corporation or association organized and operated exclusively for religious, charitable, scientific, or educational purposes, no part of the net income of which inures to the benefit of any private stockholder or individual;

Seventh. Business league, chamber of commerce, or board of trade, not organized for profit and no part of the net income of which inures to the benefit of any private stockholder or individual;

Eighth. Civic league or organization not organized for profit but operated exclusively for the promotion of social welfare;

Ninth. Club organized and operated exclusively for pleasure, recreation, and other nonprofitable purposes, no part of the net income of which inures to the benefit of any private stockholder or member;

Tenth. Farmers' or other mutual hail, cyclone, or fire insurance company, mutual ditch or irrigation company, mutual or cooperative telephone company, or like organization of a purely local character, the income of which consists solely of assessments, dues, and fees collected from members for the sole purpose of meeting its expenses;

Eleventh. Farmers', fruit growers', or like association, organized and operated as a sales agent for the purpose of marketing the products of its members and turning back to them the proceeds of sales, less the necessary selling expenses, on the basis of the quantity of produce furnished by them;

Twelfth. Corporation or association organized for the exclusive purpose of holding title to property, collecting income therefrom, and turning over the entire amount thereof, less expenses, to an organization which itself is exempt from the tax imposed by this title; or

Thirteenth. Federal land banks and national farm-loan associations as provided in section twenty-six of the Act approved July seventeenth, nineteen hundred and sixteen, entitled "An Act to provide capital for agricultural development, to create standard forms of investment based upon farm mortgage, to equalize rates of interest upon farm loans, to furnish a market for United States bonds, to create Government depositaries and financial agents for the United States, and for other purposes."

Fourteenth. Joint stock land banks as to income derived from bonds or debentures of other joint stock land banks or any Federal land bank belonging to such joint stock land bank.

[b] Tax on income of public utility accruing to state or other political divisions; imposition of tax not to impose loss or burden upon state, etc.

There shall not be taxed under this title any income derived from any public utility or from the exercise of any essential governmental function accruing to any State, Territory, or the District of Columbia, or any political subdivision of a State or Territory, nor any income accruing to the government of the Philippine Islands or Porto Rico, or of any political subdivision of the Philippine Islands or Porto Rico: Provided, That whenever any State, Territory, or the District of Columbia, or any political subdivision of a State or Territory, has, prior to the passage of this title, entered in good faith into a contract with any person or corporation, the object and purpose of which is to acquire, construct, operate, or maintain a public utility, no tax shall be levied under the provisions of this title upon the income derived from the operation of such public utility, so far as the payment thereof will impose a loss or burden upon such State, Territory, or the District of Columbia, or a political subdivision of a State or Territory; but this provision is not intended to confer upon such person or corporation any financial gain or exemption or to relieve such person or corporation from the payment of a tax as provided for in this title upon the part or portion of the said income to which such person or corporation shall be entitled under such contract.

§ 12. [a] Mode of ascertaining net income of domestic corporations ¶

In the case of a corporation, joint-stock company or association, or insurance company, organized in the United States, such net income shall be ascertained by deducting from the gross amount of its income received within the year from all sources—

First. All the ordinary and necessary expenses paid within the year in the maintenance and operation of its business and properties, including rentals or other payments required to be made as a condition to the continued use or possession of property to which the corporation has not taken or is not taking title, or in which it has no equity.

Second. All losses actually sustained and charged off within the year and not compensated by insurance or otherwise, including a reasonable allowance for the exhaustion, wear and tear of property arising out of its use or employment in the business or trade; (a) in the case of oil and gas wells a reasonable allowance for actual reduction in flow and production to be ascertained not by the flush flow, but by the settled production or regular flow; (b) in the case of mines a reasonable allowance for depletion thereof not to exceed the market value in the mine of the product thereof which has been mined and sold during the year for which the return and computation are made, such reasonable allowance to be made in the case of both (a) and (b) under rules and regulations to be prescribed by the Secretary of the Treasury: Provided, That when the allowance authorized in (a) and (b) shall equal the capital originally invested, or in case of purchase made prior to March first, nineteen hundred and thirteen, the fair market value as of that date, no further allowance shall be made; and (c) in the case of insurance companies, the net addition, if any, required by law to be made within the year to reserve funds and the sums other than dividends paid within the year on policy and annuity contracts: Provided, That no deduction shall be allowed for any amount paid out for new buildings, permanent improvements, or betterments made to increase the value of any property or estate, and no deduction shall be made for any amount of expense of restoring property or making good the exhaustion thereof for which an allowance is or has been made: Provided further, That mutual fire and mutual employers' liability and mutual workmen's compensation and mutual casualty insurance companies requiring their members to make premium deposits to provide for losses and expenses shall not return as income any portion of the premium deposits returned to their policyholders, but shall return as taxable income all income received by them from all other sources plus such portions of the premium deposits as are retained by the companies for purposes other than the payment of losses and expenses and reinsurance reserves: Provided further, That mutual marine insurance companies shall include in their return of gross income gross premiums collected and received by them less amounts paid for reinsurance, but shall be entitled to include in deductions from gross income amounts repaid to policyholders on account of premiums previously paid by them and interest paid upon such amounts between the ascertainment thereof and the payment thereof, and life insurance companies shall not include as income in any year such portion of any actual premium received from any individual policyholder as shall have been paid back or credited to such individual policyholder, or treated as an abatement of premium of such individual policyholder, within such year;

Third. The amount of interest paid within the year on its indebtedness (except on indebtedness incurred for the purchase of obligations or securities the interest upon which is exempt from taxation as income under this title) to an amount of such indebtedness not in excess of the sum of (a) the entire amount of the paid-up capital stock outstanding at the close of the year, or, if no capital stock, the entire amount of capital employed in the business at the close of the year, and (b) one-half of its interest-bearing indebtedness then outstanding: Provided, That for the purpose of this title preferred capital stock shall not be considered interest-bearing indebtedness, and interest or dividends paid upon this stock shall not be deductible from gross income: Provided further, That in cases wherein shares of capital stock are issued without par or nominal value, the amount of paid-up capital stock, within the meaning of this section, as represented by such shares, will be the amount of cash, or its equivalent, paid or transferred to the corporation as a consideration for such shares: Provided further, That in the case of indebtedness wholly secured by property collateral, tangible or intangible, the subject of sale or hypothecation in the ordinary business of such corporation, joint-stock company or association as a dealer only in the property constituting such collateral, or in loaning the funds thereby procured, the total interest paid by such corporation, company, or association within the year on any such indebtedness may be deducted as a part of its expenses of doing business, but interest on such indebtedness shall only be deductible on an amount of such indebtedness not in excess of the actual value of such property collateral: Provided further, That in the case of bonds or other indebtedness, which have been issued with a guaranty that the interest payable thereon shall be free from taxation, no deduction for the payment of the tax herein imposed, or any other tax paid pursuant to such guaranty, shall be allowed; and in the case of a bank, banking association, loan or trust company, interest paid within the year on deposits or on moneys received for investment and secured by interest-bearing certificates of indebtedness issued by such bank, banking association, loan or trust company shall be deducted;

Fourth. Taxes paid within the year imposed by the authority of the United States (except income and excess profits taxes), or of its Territories, or possessions, or any foreign country, or by the authority of any State, county, school district, or municipality, or other taxing subdivision of any State, not including those assessed against local benefits.

[b] Mode of estimating net income of foreign corporations

In the case of a corporation, joint-stock company or association, or insurance company, organized, authorized, or existing under the laws of any foreign country, such net income shall be ascertained by deducting from the gross amount of its income received within the year from all sources within the United States—

First. All the ordinary and necessary expenses actually paid within the year out of earnings in the maintenance and operation of its business and property within the United States, including rentals or other payments required to be made as a condition to the continued use or possession of property to which the corporation has not taken or is not taking title, or in which it has no equity.

Second. All losses actually sustained within the year in business or trade conducted by it within the United States and not compensated by insurance or otherwise, including a reasonable allowance

(21)

for the exhaustion, wear and tear of property arising out of its use or employment in the business or trade; (a) and in the case (a) of oil and gas wells a reasonable allowance for actual reduction in flow and production to be ascertained not by the flush flow, but by the settled production or regular flow; (b) in the case of mines a reasonable allowance for depletion thereof not to exceed the market value in the mine of the product thereof which has been mined and sold during the year for which the return and computation are made, such reasonable allowance to be made in the case of both (a) and (b) under rules and regulations to be prescribed by the Secretary of the Treasury: Provided, That when the allowance authorized in (a) and (b) shall equal the capital originally invested, or in case of purchase made prior to March first, nineteen hundred and thirteen, the fair market value as of that date, no further allowance shall be made; and (c) in the case of insurance companies, the net addition, if any, required by law to be made within the year to reserve funds and the sums other than dividends paid within the year on policy and annuity contracts: Provided, That no deduction shall be allowed for any amount paid out for new buildings, permanent improvements, or betterments, made to increase the value of any property or estate, and no deduction shall be made for any amount of expense of restoring property or making good the exhaustion thereof for which an allowance is or has been made: Provided, further, That mutual fire and mutual employers' liability and mutual workmen's compensation and mutual casualty insurance companies requiring their members to make premium deposits to provide for losses and expenses shall not return as income any portion of the premium deposits returned to their policyholders, but shall return as taxable income all income received by them from all other sources plus such portions of the premium deposits as are retained by the companies for purposes other than the payment of losses and expenses and reinsurance reserves: Provided further, That mutual marine insurance companies shall include in their return of gross income gross premiums collected and received by them less amounts paid for reinsurance, but shall be entitled to include in deductions from gross income amounts repaid to policyholders on account of premiums previously paid by them, and interest paid upon such amounts between the ascertainment thereof and the payment thereof, and life insurance companies shall not include as income in any year such portion of any actual premium received from any individual policyholder as shall have been paid back or credited to such individual policyholder, or treated as an abatement of premium of such individual policyholder, within such year;

(22)

Third. The amount of interest paid within the year on its indebtedness (except on indebtedness incurred for the purchase of obligations or securities the interest upon which is exempt from taxation as income under this title) to an amount of such indebtedness not in excess of the proportion of the sum of (a) the entire amount of the paid-up capital stock outstanding at the close of the year, or, if no capital stock, the entire amount of the capital employed in the business at the close of the year, and (b) one-half of its interest-bearing indebtedness then outstanding, which the gross amount of its income for the year from business transacted and capital invested within the United States bears to the gross amount of its income derived from all sources within and without the United States: Provided, That in the case of bonds or other indebtedness which have been issued with a guaranty that the interest payable thereon shall be free from taxation, no deduction for the payment of the tax herein imposed or any other tax paid pursuant to such guaranty shall be allowed; and in case of a bank, banking association, loan or trust company, or branch thereof, interest paid within the year on deposits by or on moneys received for investment from either citizens or residents of the United States and secured by interest-bearing certificates of indebtedness issued by such bank, banking association, loan or trust company, or branch thereof;

Fourth. Taxes paid within the year imposed by the authority of the United States (except income and excess profits taxes), or of its Territories, or possessions, or by the authority of any State, county, school district, or municipality, or other taxing subdivision of any State, paid within the United States, not including those assessed against local benefits.

[c] What constitutes payments to reserve funds of assessment insurance companies

In the case of assessment insurance companies, whether domestic or foreign, the actual deposit of sums with State or Territorial officers, pursuant to law, as additions to guarantee or reserve funds shall be treated as being payments required by law to reserve funds.

§ 13. [a] Tax computed upon net income as ascertained; corporations may designate closing day of fiscal year

The tax shall be computed upon the net income, as thus ascertained, received within each preceding calendar year ending December thirty-first: Provided, That any corporation, joint-stock company or association, or insurance company, subject to this tax, may designate the last day of any month in the year as the day of the closing of its fiscal year and shall be entitled to have the tax payable by it computed upon the basis of the net income ascer-

(23)

tained as herein provided for the year ending on the day so designated in the year preceding the date of assessment instead of upon the basis of the net income for the calendar year preceding the date of assessment; and it shall give notice of the day it has thus designated as the closing of its fiscal year to the collector of the district in which its principal business office is located at any time not less than thirty days prior to the first day of March of the year in which its return would be filed if made upon the basis of the calendar year;

[b] **Corporations shall render return of net income annually; form and contents of return; verification; to whom return made; transmission to Commissioner of Internal Revenue**

Every corporation, joint-stock company or association, or insurance company, subject to the tax herein imposed, shall, on or before the first day of March, nineteen hundred and seventeen, and the first day of March in each year thereafter, or, if it has designated a fiscal year for the computation of its tax, then within sixty days after the close of such fiscal year ending prior to December thirty-first, nineteen hundred and sixteen, and the close of each such fiscal year thereafter, render a true and accurate return of its annual net income in the manner and form to be prescribed by the Commissioner of Internal Revenue, with the approval of the Secretary of the Treasury, and containing such facts, data, and information as are appropriate and in the opinion of the commissioner necessary to determine the correctness of the net income returned and to carry out the provisions of this title. The return shall be sworn to by the president, vice president, or other principal officer, and by the treasurer or assistant treasurer. The return shall be made to the collector of the district in which is located the principal office of the corporation, company, or association, where are kept its books of account and other data from which the return is prepared, or in the case of a foreign corporation, company, or association, to the collector of the district in which is located its principal place of business in the United States, or if it have no principal place of business, office, or agency in the United States, then to the collector of internal revenue at Baltimore, Maryland. All such returns shall as received be transmitted forthwith by the collector to the Commissioner of Internal Revenue;

[c] **Returns by receivers, trustees in bankruptcy, or assignees of corporations**

In cases wherein receivers, trustees in bankruptcy, or assignees are operating the property or business of corporations, joint-stock

(24)

companies or associations, or insurance companies, subject to tax imposed by this title, such receivers, trustees, or assignees shall make returns of net income as and for such corporations, joint-stock companies or associations, and insurance companies, in the same manner and form as such organizations are hereinbefore required to make returns, and any income tax due on the basis of such returns made by receivers, trustees, or assignees shall be assessed and collected in the same manner as if assessed directly against the organizations of whose businesses or properties they have custody and control;

[d] Corporations permitted to make return on basis on which their accounts are kept

A corporation, joint-stock company or association, or insurance company, keeping accounts upon any basis other than that of actual receipts and disbursements, unless such other basis does not clearly reflect its income, may, subject to regulations made by the Commissioner of Internal Revenue, with the approval of the Secretary of the Treasury, make its return upon the basis upon which its accounts are kept, in which case the tax shall be computed upon its income as so returned;

[e] Provisions as to deduction of tax from income of nonresident alien individuals applicable to income of nonresident alien firms, corporations, etc., derived from interest on bonds, etc., of domestic and resident corporations

All the provisions of this title relating to the tax authorized and required to be deducted and withheld and paid to the officer of the United States Government authorized to receive the same from the income of nonresident alien individuals from sources within the United States shall be made applicable to the tax imposed by subdivision (a) of section ten upon incomes derived from interest upon bonds and mortgages or deeds of trust or similar obligations of domestic or other resident corporations, joint-stock companies or associations, and insurance companies by nonresident alien firms, copartnerships, companies, corporations, joint-stock companies or associations, and insurance companies, not engaged in business or trade within the United States and not having any office or place of business therein.

[f] Provisions as to deduction of tax from income of nonresident alien individuals made applicable to income of nonresident alien companies, derived from dividends of domestic or resident corporations, etc.

Likewise, all the provisions of this title relating to the tax authorized and required to be deducted and withheld and paid to the officer of the United States Government authorized to receive the same from the income of nonresident alien individuals from sources within the United States shall be made applicable to income derived from dividends upon the capital stock or from the net earnings of domestic or other resident corporations, joint-stock companies or associations, and insurance companies by nonresident alien companies, corporations, joint-stock companies or associations, and insurance companies not engaged in business or trade within the United States and not having any office or place of business therein.

§ 14.   **[a] Notice of assessment and time for payment; immediate payment in case of refusal to make return or making of false return; penalty for nonpayment; refundment**

All assessments shall be made and the several corporations, joint-stock companies or associations, and insurance companies shall be notified of the amount for which they are respectively liable on or before the first day of June of each successive year, and said assessment shall be paid on or before the fifteenth day of June: Provided, That every corporation, joint-stock company or association, and insurance company, computing taxes upon the income of the fiscal year which it may designate in the manner hereinbefore provided, shall pay the taxes due under its assessment within one hundred and five days after the date upon which it is required to file its list or return of income for assessment; except in cases of refusal or neglect to make such return, and in cases of erroneous, false, or fraudulent returns, in which cases the Commissioner of Internal Revenue shall, upon the discovery thereof, at any time within three years after said return is due, make a return upon information obtained as provided for in this title or by existing law; and the assessment made by the Commissioner of Internal Revenue thereon shall be paid by such corporation, joint-stock company or association, or insurance company immediately upon notification of the amount of such assessment; and to any sum or sums due and unpaid after the fifteenth day of June in any year, or after one hundred and five days from the date on which the return of income is required to be made by the taxpayer, and after ten days' notice and demand thereof by the collector, there shall be added the sum of five per centum on the amount of tax unpaid and interest at the rate of one per centum per month upon said tax from the time the same becomes due: Provided, That upon the examination of any return of income made pursuant to this title, the Act of August fifth, nineteen hundred and nine, entitled, "An Act to provide revenue, equalize duties and encourage the industries of the United States, and for other purposes," and the Act of October third, nineteen hundred and thirteen, entitled, "An Act to reduce tariff duties and to provide revenue for the Government, and for other purposes," if it shall appear that amounts of tax have been paid in excess of those properly due, the taxpayer shall be permitted to present a claim for refund thereof notwithstanding the provisions of section thirty-two hundred and twenty-eight of the Revised Statutes;

[b] **Filing returns in office of commissioner of internal revenue; inspection; rules as to inspection; access to returns by state officer**

When the assessment shall be made, as provided in this title, the returns, together with any corrections thereof which may have been made by the commissioner, shall be filed in the office of the Commissioner of Internal Revenue and shall constitute public records and be open to inspection as such: Provided, That any and all such returns shall be open to inspection only upon the order of the President, under rules and regulations to be prescribed by the Secretary of the Treasury and approved by the President: Provided further, That the proper officers of any State imposing a general income tax may, upon the request of the governor thereof, have access to said returns or to an abstract thereof, showing the name and income of each such corporation, joint-stock company or association, or insurance company, at such times and in such manner as the Secretary of the Treasury may prescribe;

(c) **Penalty for failing to make return or for rendering false return; extension of time**

If any of the corporations, joint-stock companies or associations, or insurance companies aforesaid shall refuse or neglect to make a return at the time or times hereinbefore specified in each year, or shall render a false or fraudulent return, such corporation, joint-stock company or association, or insurance company shall be liable to a penalty of not exceeding $10,000: Provided, that the Commissioner of Internal Revenue shall have authority in the case of either corporations or individuals, to grant a reasonable extension of time in meritorious cases, as he may deem proper.

(d) **No recovery of taxes paid in case of false return or fraudulent return; exception**

That section thirty-two hundred and twenty-five of the Revised Statutes of the United States be, and the same is hereby, amended so as to read as follows:

Sec. 3225. When a second assessment is made in case of any list, statement, or return which in the opinion of the collector or deputy collector was false or fraudulent, or contained any understatement or undervaluation, no tax collected under such assessment shall be recovered by any suit unless it is proved that the said list, statement, or return was not false nor fraudulent and did not contain any understatement or undervaluation; but this section shall not apply to statements or returns made or to be made in good faith under the laws of the United States regarding annual depreciation of oil or gas wells and mines. (U. S. Comp. St. 1916, § 5948.)

§ 15. Definition of terms

The word "State" or "United States" when used in this title shall be construed to include any Territory, the District of Columbia, Porto Rico, and the Philippine Islands, when such construction is necessary to carry out its provisions.

§ 16. Amendment of sections of Revised Statutes

Sections thirty-one hundred and sixty-seven, thirty-one hundred and seventy-two, thirty-one hundred and seventy-three and thirty-one hundred and seventy-six of the Revised Statutes of the United States as amended are hereby amended so as to read as follows:

"Sec. 3167. It shall be unlawful for any collector, deputy collector, agent, clerk, or other officer or employee of the United States to divulge or to make known in any manner whatever not provided by law to any person the operations, style of work, or apparatus of any manufacturer or producer visited by him in the discharge of his official duties, or the amount or source of income, profits, losses, expenditures, or any particular thereof, set forth or disclosed in any income return, or to permit any income return or copy thereof or any book containing any abstract or particulars thereof to be seen or examined by any person except as provided by law; and it shall be unlawful for any person to print or publish in any manner whatever not provided by law any income return or any part thereof or source of income profits, losses, or expenditures appearing in any income return; and any offense against the foregoing provision shall be a misdemeanor and be punished by a fine not exceeding $1,000 or by imprisonment not exceeding one year, or both, at the discretion of the court; and if the offender be an officer or employee of the United States he shall be dismissed from office or discharged from employment. (U. S. Comp. St. 1916, § 5887.)

"Sec. 3172. Every collector shall, from time to time, cause his deputies to proceed through every part of his district and inquire after and concerning all persons therein who are liable to pay any internal-revenue tax, and all persons owning or having the care and management of any objects liable to pay any tax, and to make a list of such persons and enumerate said objects. (U. S. Comp. St. 1916, § 5895.)

"Sec. 3173. It shall be the duty of any person, partnership, firm, association, or corporation, made liable to any duty, special tax, or other tax imposed by law, when not otherwise provided for, (1) in case of a special tax, on or before the thirty-first day of July in each year, (2) in case of income tax on or before the first day of March in each year, or on or before the last day of the sixty-day period next following the closing date of the fiscal year for which it makes a return of its income, and (3) in other cases before the day on which the taxes accrue, to make a list or return, verified by oath, to the collector or a deputy collector of the district where located, of the articles or objects, including the amount of annual income charged with a duty or tax, the quantity of goods, wares, and merchandise, made or sold and charged with a tax, the several rates and aggregate amount, according to the forms and regulations to be prescribed by the Commissioner of Internal Revenue, with the approval of the Secretary of the Treasury, for which such person, partnership, firm, association, or corporation is liable: Provided, That if any person liable to pay any duty or tax, or owning, possessing, or having the care or management of property, goods, wares, and merchandise, article or objects liable to pay any duty, tax, or license, shall fail to make and exhibit a list or return required by law, but shall consent to disclose the particulars of any and all the property, goods, wares, and merchandise, articles, and objects liable to pay any duty or tax, or any business or occupation liable to pay any tax as aforesaid, then, and in that case, it shall be the duty of the collector or deputy collector to make such list or return, which, being distinctly read, consented to, and signed and verified by oath by the person so owning, possessing, or having the care and management as aforesaid, may be received as the list of such person: Provided further, That in case no annual list or return has been rendered by such person to the collector or deputy collector as required by law, and the person shall be absent from his or her residence or place of business at the time the collector or a deputy collector shall call for the annual list or return, it shall be the duty of such collector or deputy collector to leave at such place of residence or business, with some one of suitable age and discretion, if such be present, otherwise to deposit in the nearest post office, a note or memorandum addressed to such per-

(29)

son, requiring him or her to render to such collector or deputy collector the list or return required by law within ten days from the date of such note or memorandum, verified by oath. And if any person, on being notified or required as aforesaid, shall refuse or neglect to render such list or return within the time required as aforesaid, or whenever any person who is required to deliver a monthly or other return of objects subject to tax fails to do so at the time required, or delivers any return which, in the opinion of the collector, is erroneous, false, or fraudulent, or contains any undervaluation or understatement, or refuses to allow any regularly authorized Government officer to examine the books of such person, firm, or corporation, it shall be lawful for the collector to summon such person, or any other person having possession, custody, or care of books of account containing entries relating to the business of such person, or any other person he may deem proper, to appear before him and produce such books at a time and place named in the summons, and to give testimony or answer interrogatories, under oath, respecting any objects or income liable to tax or the returns thereof. The collector may summon any person residing or found within the State or Territory in which his district lies; and when the person intended to be summoned does not reside and can not be found within such State or Territory, he may enter any collection district where such person may be found and there make the examination herein authorized. And to this end he may there exercise all the authority which he might lawfully exercise in the district for which he was commissioned: Provided, That 'person,' as used in this section, shall be construed to include any corporation, joint-stock company or association, or insurance company when such construction is necessary to carry out its provisions. (U. S. Comp. St. 1916, § 5896.)

"Sec. 3176. If any person, corporation, company, or association fails to make and file a return or list at the time prescribed by law, or makes, willfully or otherwise, a false or fraudulent return or list, the collector or deputy collector shall make the return or list from his own knowledge and from such information as he can obtain through testimony or otherwise. Any return or list so made and subscribed by a collector or deputy collector shall be prima facie good and sufficient for all legal purposes.

If the failure to file a return or list is due to sickness or absence the collector may allow such further time, not exceeding thirty days, for making and filing the return or list as he deems proper.

The Commissioner of Internal Revenue shall assess all taxes, other than stamp taxes, as to which returns or lists are so made by a collector or deputy collector. In case of any failure to make and file a return or list within the time prescribed by law or by the collector, the Commissioner of Internal Revenue shall add to the tax fifty per centum of its amount except that, when a return is voluntarily and without notice from the collector filed after such time and it is shown that the failure to file it was due to a reasonable cause and not to willful neglect, no such addition shall be made to the tax. In case a false or fraudulent return or list is willfully made, the Commissioner of Internal Revenue shall add to the tax one hundred per centum of its amount.

The amount so added to any tax shall be collected at the same time and in the same manner and as part of the tax unless the tax has been paid before the discovery of the neglect, falsity, or fraud, in which case the amount so added shall be collected in the same manner as the tax." (U. S. Comp. St. 1916, § 5899.)

§ 17.	Receipt for taxes paid; separate receipts to debtor making payments affecting separate creditors; receipts as evidence; surrender of receipts to creditor

It shall be the duty of every collector of internal revenue, to whom any payment of any taxes is made under the provisions of this title, to give to the person making such payment a full written or printed receipt, expressing the amount paid and the particular account for which such payment was made; and whenever such payment is made such collector shall, if required, give a separate receipt for each tax paid by any debtor, on account of payments made to or to be made by him to separate creditors in such form that such debtor can conveniently produce the same separately to his several creditors in satisfaction of their respective demands to the amounts specified in such receipts; and such receipts shall be sufficient evidence in favor of such debtor to justify him in withholding the amount therein expressed from his next payment to his creditor; but such creditor may, upon giving to his debtor a full written receipt, acknowledging the payment to him of whatever sum may be actually paid, and accepting the amount of tax paid as aforesaid (specifying the same) as a further satisfaction of the debt to that amount, require the surrender to him of such collector's receipt.

§ 18.	Penalty for failure to make return or pay taxes; penalty for false return by individual for corporate officer; taxation at source not to be made where tax paid by taxpayer

That any person, corporation, partnership, association, or insurance company, liable to pay the tax, to make a return or to supply information required under this title, who refuses or neglects to pay such tax, to make such return or to supply such information at the time or times herein specified in each year, shall be liable, except as otherwise specially provided in this title, to a penalty of not less than $20 nor more than $1,000. Any individual or any officer of any corporation, partnership, association, or insurance company, required by law to make, render, sign, or verify any return or to supply any information, who makes any false or fraudulent return or statement with intent to defeat or evade the assessment required by this title to be made, shall be guilty of a misdemeanor, and shall be fined not exceeding $2,000 or be imprisoned not exceeding one year, or both, in the discretion of the court, with the costs of prosecution: Provided, That where any tax heretofore due and payable has been duly paid by the taxpayer, it shall not be re-collected from any withholding agent required to retain it at its source, nor shall any penalty be imposed or collected in such cases from the taxpayer, or such withholding agent whose duty it was to retain it, for failure to return or pay the same, unless such failure was fraudulent and for the purpose of evading payment.

§ 19. Verification of returns; notice to show cause why amount of return should not be increased; statement of proof; appeal

The collector or deputy collector shall require every return to be verified by the oath of the party rendering it. If the collector or deputy collector have reason to believe that the amount of any income returned is understated, he shall give due notice to the person making the return to show cause why the amount of the return should not be increased, and upon proof of the amount understated may increase the same accordingly. Such person may furnish sworn testimony to prove any relevant facts, and, if dissatisfied with the decision of the collector, may appeal to the Commissioner of Internal Revenue for his decision under such rules of procedure as may be prescribed by regulation.

§ 20. Jurisdiction of district court to compel attendance of witnesses and production of books

Jurisdiction is hereby conferred upon the district courts of the United States for the district within which any person summoned under this title to appear to testify or to produce books shall reside, to compel such attendance, production of books, and testimony by appropriate process.

(32)

§ 21. Statistics relating to operation of income tax law

The preparation and publication of statistics reasonably available with respect to the operation of the income tax law and containing classifications of taxpayers and of income, the amounts allowed as deductions and exemptions, and any other facts deemed pertinent and valuable, shall be made annually by the Commissioner of Internal Revenue with the approval of the Secretary of the Treasury.

§ 22. Consistent provisions of internal revenue law applicable

All administrative, special, and general provisions of law, including the laws in relation to the assessment, remission, collection, and refund of internal-revenue taxes not heretofore specifically repealed and not inconsistent with the provisions of this title, are hereby extended and made applicable to all the provisions of this title and to the tax herein imposed.

§ 23. Extension to Porto Rico and Philippine Islands

The provisions of this title shall extend to Porto Rico and the Philippine Islands: Provided, That the administration of the law and the collection of the taxes imposed in Porto Rico and the Philippine Islands shall be by the appropriate internal-revenue officers of those governments, and all revenues collected in Porto Rico and the Philippine Islands thereunder shall accrue intact to the general Governments thereof, respectively: Provided further, That the jurisdiction in this title conferred upon the district courts of the United States shall, so far as the Philippine Islands are concerned, be vested in the courts of the first instance of said islands: And provided further, That nothing in this title shall be held to exclude from the computation of the net income the compensation paid any official by the governments of the District of Columbia, Porto Rico, and the Philippine Islands, or the political subdivisions thereof.

§ 24. Repeal

Section II of the Act approved October third, nineteen hundred and thirteen, entitled "An Act to reduce tariff duties and to provide revenue for the Government, and for other purposes," is hereby repealed, except as herein otherwise provided, and except that it shall remain in force for the assessment and collection of all taxes which have accrued thereunder, and for the imposition and collection of all penalties or forfeitures which have accrued or may accrue in relation to any of such taxes, and except that the unexpended balance of any appropriation heretofore made and now available for the administration of such section or any provision thereof shall be available for the administration of this title or the corresponding provision thereof.

§ 25. Income assessed under Act Oct. 3, 1913, not to be considered as income; effect as to fiscal year fixed by taxpayer

Income on which has been assessed the tax imposed by Section II of the Act entitled "An Act to reduce tariff duties and to provide revenue for the Government, and for other purposes," approved October third, nineteen hundred and thirteen, shall not be considered as income within the meaning of this title: Provided, That this section shall not conflict with that portion of section ten, of this title, under which a taxpayer has fixed its own fiscal year.

§ 26. Corporations to report payment of dividends with names and addresses of stockholders

Every corporation, joint-stock company or association, or insurance company subject to the tax herein imposed, when required by the Commissioner of Internal Revenue, shall render a correct return, duly verified under oath, of its payments of dividends, whether made in cash or its equivalent or in stock, including the names and addresses of stockholders and the number of shares owned by each, and the tax years and the applicable amounts in which such dividends were earned, in such form and manner as may be prescribed by the Commissioner of Internal Revenue, with the approval of the Secretary of the Treasury.

§ 27. Brokers to report transactions for customers, with profits and losses

That every person, corporation, partnership, or association, doing business as a broker on any exchange or board of trade or other similar place of business shall, when required by the Commissioner of Internal Revenue, render a correct return duly verified under oath, under such rules and regulations as the Commissioner of Internal Revenue, with the approval of the Secretary of the Treasury, may prescribe, showing the names of customers for whom such person, corporation, partnership, or association has transacted any business, with such details as to the profits, losses, or other information which the commissioner may require, as to each of such customers, as will enable the Commissioner of Internal Revenue to determine whether all income tax due on profits or gains of such customers has been paid.

§ 28. Payments of rent, interest, salaries, etc., of $800 or more a year to be reported

That all persons, corporations, partnerships, associations, and insurance companies, in whatever capacity acting, including lessees or mortgagors of real or personal property, trustees acting in any trust capacity, executors, administrators, receivers, conservators, and employers, making payment to another person, corporation, partnership, association, or insurance company, of interest, rent, salaries, wages, premiums, annuities, compensation, remuneration, emoluments, or other fixed or determinable gains, profits, and income (other than payments described in sections twenty-six and twenty-seven), of $800 or more in any taxable year, or, in the case of such payments made by the United States, the officers or employees of the United States having information as to such payments and required to make returns in regard thereto by the regulations hereinafter provided for, are hereby authorized and required to render a true and accurate return to the Commissioner of Internal Revenue, under such rules and regulations and in such form and manner as may be prescribed by him, with the approval of the Secretary of the Treasury, setting forth the amount of such gains, profits, and income, and the name and address of the recipient of such payment: Provided, That such returns shall be required, regardless of amounts, in the case of payments of interest upon bonds and mortgages or deeds of trust or other similar obligations of corporations, joint-stock companies, associations, and insurance companies, and in the case of collections of items (not payable in the United States) of interest upon the bonds of foreign countries and interest from the bonds and dividends from the stock of foreign corporations by persons, corporations, partnerships, or associations, undertaking as a matter of business or for profit the collection of foreign payments of such interest or dividends by means of coupons, checks, or bills of exchange.

When necessary to make effective the provisions of this section the name and address of the recipient of income shall be furnished upon demand of the person, corporation, partnership, association, or insurance company paying the income.

The provisions of this section shall apply to the calendar year nineteen hundred and seventeen and each calendar year thereafter, but shall not apply to the payment of interest on obligations of the United States.

§ 29. Credit for excess profits taxes assessed

That in assessing income tax the net income embraced in the return shall also be credited with the amount of any excess profits tax imposed by Act of Congress and assessed for the same calendar or fiscal year upon the taxpayer, and, in the case of a member of a partnership, with his proportionate share of such excess profits tax imposed upon the partnership.

§ 30. Exemption of foreign governments from income tax

That nothing in section II of the Act approved October third, nineteen hundred and thirteen, entitled "An Act to reduce tariff duties and to provide revenue for the Government, and for other purposes," or in this title, shall be construed as taxing the income of foreign governments received from investments in the United States in stocks, bonds, or other domestic securities, owned by such foreign governments, or from interest on deposits in banks in the United States of moneys belonging to foreign governments.

§ 31. Meaning of "dividends" as used in income tax law

(a) That the term "dividends" as used in this title shall be held to mean any distribution made or ordered to be made by a corporation, joint-stock company, association, or insurance company, out of its earnings or profits accrued since March first, nineteen hundred and thirteen, and payable to its shareholders, whether in cash or in stock of the corporation, joint-stock company, association, or insurance company, which stock dividend shall be considered income, to the amount of the earnings or profits so distributed.

(b) Any distribution made to the shareholders or members of a corporation, joint-stock company, or association, or insurance company, in the year nineteen hundred and seventeen, or subsequent tax years, shall be deemed to have been made from the most recently accumulated undivided profits or surplus, and shall constitute a part of the annual income of the distributee for the year in which received, and shall be taxed to the distributee at the rates prescribed by law for the years in which such profits or surplus were accumulated by the corporation, joint-stock company, association, or insurance company, but nothing herein shall be construed as taxing any earnings or profits accrued prior to March first, nineteen hundred and thirteen, but such earnings or profits may be distributed in stock dividends or otherwise, exempt from the tax, after the distribution of earnings and profits accrued since March first, nineteen hundred and thirteen, has been made. This subdivision shall not apply to any distribution made prior to August sixth, nineteen hundred and seventeen, out of earnings or profits accrued prior to March first, nineteen hundred and thirteen.

§ 32. No deductions for premiums on insurance on the lives of officers and employees

That premiums paid on life insurance policies covering the lives of officers, employees, or those financially interested in any trade or business conducted by an individual, partnership, corporation, joint-stock company or association, or insurance company, shall not

(36)

be deducted in computing the net income of such individual, corporation, joint-stock company or association, or insurance company, or in computing the profits of such partnership for the purposes of subdivision (e) of section nine.

§ 33. Amounts heretofore withheld at the source, in certain cases, to be released and paid over to taxpayer

That any amount heretofore withheld by any withholding agent as required by Title I of such Act of September eighth, nineteen hundred and sixteen, on account of the tax imposed upon the income of any individual, a citizen or resident of the United States, for the calendar year nineteen hundred and seventeen, except in the cases covered by subdivision (c) of section nine of such Act, as amended by this Act, shall be released and paid over to such individual, and the entire tax upon the income of such individual for such year shall be assessed and collected in the manner prescribed by such Act as amended by this Act. (Act Cong. Oct. 3, 1917, § 1212.)

§ 34. War income tax of 1917

The following is the text of Title I of the Act of Congress of October 3, 1917, levying additional or "war" taxes upon the incomes of individuals and corporations:

Section 1. That in addition to the normal tax imposed by subdivision (a) of section one of the Act entitled "An Act to increase the revenue, and for other purposes," approved September eighth, nineteen hundred and sixteen, there shall be levied, assessed, collected, and paid a like normal tax of two per centum upon the income of every individual, a citizen or resident of the United States, received in the calendar year nineteen hundred and seventeen and every calendar year thereafter.

Sec. 2. That in addition to the additional tax imposed by subdivision (b) of section one of such Act of September eighth, nineteen hundred and sixteen, there shall be levied, assessed, collected, and paid a like additional tax upon the income of every individual received in the calendar year nineteen hundred and seventeen and every calendar year thereafter, as follows:

One per centum per annum upon the amount by which the total net income exceeds $5,000 and does not exceed $7,500;

Two per centum per annum upon the amount by which the total net income exceeds $7,500 and does not exceed $10,000;

Three per centum per annum upon the amount by which the total net income exceeds $10,000 and does not exceed $12,500;

Four per centum per annum upon the amount by which the total net income exceeds $12,500 and does not exceed $15,000;

(37)

Five per centum per annum upon the amount by which the total net income exceeds $15,000 and does not exceed $20,000;

Seven per centum per annum upon the amount by which the total net income exceeds $20,000 and does not exceed $40,000;

Ten per centum per annum upon the amount by which the total net income exceeds $40,000 and does not exceed $60,000;

Fourteen per centum per annum upon the amount by which the total net income exceeds $60,000 and does not exceed $80,000;

Eighteen per centum per annum upon the amount by which the total net income exceeds $80,000 and does not exceed $100,000;

Twenty-two per centum per annum upon the amount by which the total net income exceeds $100,000 and does not exceed $150,000;

Twenty-five per centum per annum upon the amount by which the total net income exceeds $150,000 and does not exceed $200,000;

Thirty per centum per annum upon the amount by which the total net income exceeds $200,000 and does not exceed $250,000;

Thirty-four per centum per annum upon the amount by which the total net income exceeds $250,000 and does not exceed $300,000;

Thirty-seven per centum per annum upon the amount by which the total net income exceeds $300,000 and does not exceed $500,000;

Forty per centum per annum upon the amount by which the total net income exceeds $500,000 and does not exceed $750,000.

Forty-five per centum per annum upon the amount by which the total net income exceeds $750,000 and does not exceed $1,000,000.

Fifty per centum per annum upon the amount by which the total net income exceeds $1,000,000.

Sec. 3. That the taxes imposed by sections one and two of this Act shall be computed, levied, assessed, collected, and paid upon the same basis and in the same manner as the similar taxes imposed by section one of such Act of September eighth, nineteen hundred and sixteen, except that in the case of the tax imposed by section one of this Act (a) the exemptions of $3,000 and $4,000 provided in section seven of such Act of September eighth, nineteen hundred and sixteen, as amended by this Act, shall be, respectively, $1,000 and $2,000, and (b) the returns required under subdivisions (b) and (c) of section eight of such Act as amended by this Act shall be required in the case of net incomes of $1,000 or over, in the case of unmarried persons, and $2,000 or over in the case of married persons, instead of $3,000 or over, as therein provided, and (c) the provisions of subdivision (c) of section nine of such Act, as amended by this Act, requiring the normal tax of individuals on income derived from interest to be deducted and withheld at the source of the income shall not apply to the new two per centum normal tax prescribed in section one of this Act until on and after

(38)

January first, nineteen hundred and eighteen, and thereafter only one two per centum normal tax shall be deducted and withheld at the source under the provisions of such subdivision (c), and any further normal tax for which the recipient of such income is liable under this Act or such Act of September eighth, nineteen hundred and sixteen, as amended by this Act, shall be paid by such recipient.

Sec. 4. That in addition to the tax imposed by subdivision (a) of section ten of such Act of September eighth, nineteen hundred and sixteen, as amended by this Act, there shall be levied, assessed, collected, and paid a like tax of four per centum upon the income received in the calendar year nineteen hundred and seventeen and every calendar year thereafter, by every corporation, joint-stock company or association, or insurance company, subject to the tax imposed by that subdivision of that section, except that if it has fixed its own fiscal year, the tax imposed by this section for the fiscal year ending during the calendar year nineteen hundred and seventeen shall be levied, assessed, collected, and paid only on that proportion of its income for such fiscal year which the period between January first, nineteen hundred and seventeen, and the end of such fiscal year bears to the whole of such fiscal year.

The tax imposed by this section shall be computed, levied, assessed, collected, and paid upon the same incomes and in the same manner as the tax imposed by subdivision (a) of section ten of such Act of September eighth, nineteen hundred and sixteen, as amended by this Act, except that for the purpose of the tax imposed by this section the income embraced in a return of a corporation, joint-stock company or association, or insurance company, shall be credited with the amount received as dividends upon the stock or from the net earnings of any other corporation, joint-stock company or association, or insurance company, which is taxable upon its net income as provided in this title.

Sec. 5. That the provisions of this title shall not extend to Porto Rico or the Philippine Islands, and the Porto Rican or Philippine Legislature shall have power by due enactment to amend, alter, modify, or repeal the income tax laws in force in Porto Rico or the Philippine Islands, respectively.

(39)

CHAPTER II

NATURE, HISTORY, AND LEGAL BASIS OF INCOME TAXES

§ 35. Definitions and General Considerations.
  36. Property Taxes Distinguished.
  37. Excise, Franchise, License, and Occupation Taxes Distinguished.
  38. Income Tax as Direct Tax.
  39. Constitutional Provisions Affecting Income Taxes.
  40. Same; Sixteenth Amendment.
  41. History of Federal Income Tax Laws.
  42. Departmental Regulations.

§ 35. Definitions and General Considerations

An income tax is distinguished from other forms of taxation in this respect, that it is not levied upon property, nor upon the operations of trade or business or the subjects employed therein, nor upon the practice of a profession or the pursuit of a trade or calling, but upon the acquisitions of the taxpayer arising from one or more of these sources or from all combined, annually or at other stated intervals, and generally, but not necessarily, upon only the excess of such acquisitions over a certain minimum sum. It is not a tax upon accumulated wealth, but upon its periodical accretions. It is not a tax upon personal exertion for gain, whether combined with the employment of capital or not, but upon the fruits thereof. An income tax is in effect a tax upon earnings, taking that term in its broadest sense, and irrespective of the question whether the person whose income is taxed has actively earned it or has merely profited by loaning his capital for active employment by another.[1] The definition of an income tax as one which relates to the product or income from property or from business pursuits,[2] is sufficient for the purposes of a practical description, but is not scientifically accurate, since the term "income" may include acquisitions from other sources than those mentioned. For instance, money coming to one by gift or bequest is undoubtedly "income," though it is in the discretion of the taxing power to include it within the incidence of the tax or to exempt it. In the sense that it is imposed upon a limited and selected subject of taxation, an income tax may also be regarded as a special tax, rather than a general tax. Thus, in South Carolina, a general taxing act enacted in 1905 requir-

----

[1] An income tax is a tax at an arbitrary rate, an excise tax, and is not a property tax. That the tax imposed by a statute laying a tax on interest or dividends resembles an income tax in some of its features does not render the tax invalid. In re Opinion of the Justices, 77 N. H. 611, 93 Atl. 311.

[2] Levi v. City of Louisville, 97 Ky. 394, 30 S. W. 973, 28 L. R. A. 480.

ed the proper officers to collect the taxes levied under its provisions, and forbade them to collect any other taxes except such "special tax" as might be authorized under an act of joint resolution of the legislature. It was contended that this operated as a repeal of the income tax law of 1897. But the courts held otherwise, declaring that the income tax was a "special tax" within the meaning of the general statute.[3]

§ 36.   Property Taxes Distinguished

A tax on incomes is not a tax on property, and a tax on property does not embrace incomes. Hence a municipal corporation which has authority by its charter to levy taxes for its own purposes on all "taxable property" does not possess the authority to lay a tax on incomes.[4] For the same reason a tax laid on income is different from a tax laid on the property out of which the income arises, and although a statute may tax land at a different rate from that imposed on incomes, it is not therefore in conflict with a constitutional provision that taxation on all species of property must be uniform.[5]

§ 37.   Excise, Franchise, License, and Occupation Taxes Distinguished

License and occupation taxes, which are payable in respect to the privilege of engaging in or carrying on a particular business, are not income taxes, although the amount of the tax payable by any individual may be measured by the amount of business which he transacts or his earnings therefrom. And conversely, although a person's entire income may be derived from a particular pursuit or trade, a tax on the income as such is not a license or privilege tax.[6] Thus, a person carrying on a certain business (for instance, a dealer in intoxicating liquors) may be subjected to a license tax for the privilege of pursuing that avocation, to a state or municipal tax for general purposes upon his stock in trade, and to a tax upon the income derived from his business, and yet, as all these taxes relate to different subjects and do not overlap or conflict, their imposition affords no legal ground for complaint.

Excise taxes include license fees and also some other forms of taxation, and these also are theoretically distinguishable from income taxes, although the practical difference is very slight in cases

---

[3] Alderman v. Wells, 85 S. C. 507, 67 S. E. 781, 27 L. R. A. (N. S.) 864, 21 Ann. Cas. 193.

[4] City of Dubuque v. Northwestern Life Ins. Co., 29 Iowa, 9.

[5] Waring v. City of Savannah, 60 Ga. 93.

[6] Commonwealth v. Brown, 91 Va. 762, 21 S. E. 357, 28 L. R. A. 110; Ould v. City of Richmond, 23 Grat. (Va.) 464, 14 Am. Rep. 139.

where the excise is measured by the income. It has been said: "Excises are a species of tax consisting generally of duties laid upon the manufacture, sale, or consumption of commodities within the country, or upon certain callings or occupations, often taking the form of exactions for licenses to pursue them. The taxes created by the law under consideration, as applied to savings banks, insurance companies, to building or other associations, or to the conduct of any other kind of business, are excise taxes, and fall within the requirement, so far as they are laid by Congress, that they must be uniform throughout the United States." [7]

But a franchise tax upon corporations is not an income tax, although it may be called an excise tax. And this is so, whether the tax is laid by the state under whose laws the corporation is organized, and is exacted annually for the privilege of continuing its corporate existence, or is imposed by a different state for the privilege of doing business within its limits, or is imposed by an outside power, such as the United States, upon the franchise of transacting business in a corporate capacity. For this reason the tax on corporations imposed by Congress in 1909, being laid specifically upon the carrying on or doing of business in a corporate or quasi corporate capacity, was adjudged not to be an income tax, although the amount of the tax in each instance was measured by the net annual income of the corporation, but an excise tax, not direct, and therefore not invalid because not apportioned among the several states according to population. [8] For the same reason, and as against the charge that they were direct taxes and invalid for want of apportionment, the courts have sustained the constitutionality of the internal-revenue taxes on bankers and brokers, on the business of sugar refining, and on sales of corporate stock and of commodities on the produce exchange. [9]

§ 38. Income Tax as Direct Tax

In general usage, and according to the terminology of political economy, a direct tax is one demanded of the person who is expected to pay it and bear the expense of it without recoupment, while an indirect tax is demanded from one person in the expecta-

[7] Pollock v. Farmers' Loan & Trust Co., 157 U. S. 429, 15 Sup. Ct. 673, 39 L. Ed. 759, concurring opinion of Field, J.
[8] Flint v. Stone Tracy Co., 220 U. S. 107, 31 Sup. Ct. 342, 55 L. Ed. 389, Ann. Cas. 1912B, 1312.
[9] Anderson v. Farmers' Loan & Trust Co., 241 Fed. 322; Real Estate Title Ins. & Trust Co. v. Lederer (D. C.) 229 Fed. 799; Spreckels Sugar Refining Co. v. McClain, 192 U. S. 397, 24 Sup. Ct. 376, 48 L. Ed. 496; Nicol v. Ames, 173 U. S. 509, 19 Sup. Ct. 522, 43 L. Ed. 786; Thomas v. U. S., 192 U. S. 363, 24 Sup. Ct. 305, 48 L. Ed. 481.

tion that he will indemnify himself at the expense of others. When the question of the difference between direct and indirect taxes first came before the Supreme Court of the United States, in connection with the constitutional provision that "representatives and direct taxes shall be apportioned among the several states," it was held that the term "direct," as here used, was to be taken in a narrower sense than that above indicated; and it was ruled that only two classes of taxes could be considered as coming under this designation, namely, taxes on land and capitation taxes.[10]   But these decisions have been overruled, and it is now held that income taxes, whether levied on the issues and profits of real estate or on the gains and interest from personal property, are also direct taxes within the meaning of the constitution.[11]   The Sixteenth Amendment permits the levy of an income tax without apportionment, but does not change the nature of the tax or the correctness of the Supreme Court's decision. It is held, however, that, independently of the operation of the Sixteenth Amendment, the tax imposed by the income tax act of Oct. 3, 1913, upon the product of the working of a mine owned by a corporation, is not a direct tax on property by reason of its ownership, merely because adequate allowance may not be made for the exhaustion of the ore body resulting from such operations.[12]

§ 39.   Constitutional Provisions Affecting Income Taxes

As originally adopted the Constitution of the United States contained the following provisions with reference to national taxation: "Representatives and direct taxes shall be apportioned among the several states which may be included within this Union, according to their respective numbers" (Art. 1, § 2.)   "The Congress shall have power to lay and collect taxes, duties, imposts, and excises, to pay the debts and provide for the common defense and general welfare of the United States; but all duties, imposts, and excises shall be uniform throughout the United States" (Art. 1, § 8.)   "No capitation or other direct tax shall be laid unless in proportion to the census or enumeration herein before directed to be taken." (Art. 1, § 9.)   During the period of the Civil War and for some time thereafter, that is, between the years 1861 and 1870, successive acts of Congress imposed general taxation upon incomes derived from all sources, for the support of the federal government, without any

[10] Springer v. U. S., 102 U. S. 586, 26 L. Ed. 253; Pacific Ins. Co. v. Soule, 7 Wall. 433, 19 L. Ed. 95; Hylton v. U. S., 3 Dall. 171, 1 L. Ed. 556.
[11] Pollock v. Farmers' Loan & Trust Co., 157 U. S. 429, 15 Sup. Ct. 673, 39 L. Ed. 759; s. c., 158 U. S. 601, 15 Sup. Ct. 912, 39 L. Ed. 1108.
[12] Stanton v. Baltic Min. Co., 240 U. S. 103, 36 Sup. Ct. 278, 60 L. Ed. 546.

attempt at apportionment among the states. But it was held by the courts that an income tax is not a direct tax and therefore does not require such apportionment, while the question of the "uniformity" of such acts under the constitutional provision above quoted does not appear to have been raised. But a similar statute enacted in 1894 was adjudged unconstitutional, in so far as it applied to incomes derived from the renting of real property or from the investment of personal property, for lack of apportionment, the court now holding it to be a direct tax, and invalid so far as it applied to income derived from state or municipal bonds, on the ground that Congress had no rightful power to tax those subjects. In so deciding, the Supreme Court advanced the suggestion that if the "ultimate sovereignty" desired to intrust to Congress a general power to tax incomes, it could be done by an amendment to the Constitution.[13]

§ 40. Same; Sixteenth Amendment

Thereafter a constitutional amendment was proposed by act of Congress, submitted to the legislatures of the several states, ratified by the necessary majority, and proclaimed in 1913 as the Sixteenth Amendment. It is as follows: "The Congress shall have power to lay and collect taxes on incomes, from whatever source derived, without apportionment among the several states, and without regard to any census or enumeration."

This amendment is not a grant of power, but only the removal of a constitutional restriction. From the use of the words "from whatever source derived" it might be argued that it was the intention to bring within the taxing power of Congress certain subjects not previously included, such as income derived from the bonded debts of states and municipalities and the salaries of state officers. But this would be a strained construction, because the lack of authority in the federal government to tax the subjects mentioned does not arise from any explicit provision of the Constitution, but from the relation between the states and the Union and the necessity of giving to each an entire immunity from possibly destructive taxation on the part of the other. This was also the understanding of Congress in enacting the income tax laws of 1913 and 1916, as is shown by the fact that they expressly exclude "interest upon the obligations of a state or any political subdivision thereof," and also "the compensation of all officers and employees of a state or any political subdivision thereof."

---

[13] Pollock v. Farmers' Loan & Trust Co., 158 U. S. 601, 15 Sup. Ct. 912, 39 L. Ed. 1108.

On the other hand, the decision of the court in the Pollock Case was confined to the question of the constitutionality of the tax in so far as it bore upon income derived from real estate and from invested personal property. It was not decided that a tax upon income derived from business operations or from the practice of a trade or profession or the receipt of a salary was a direct tax, and this was explained by Mr. Justice Harlan, in his dissenting opinion, as equivalent to a declaration that no apportionment among the states would be necessary in so far as a tax upon incomes might be laid upon those subjects alone. It never was doubted that Congress possessed the power to tax incomes in so far as it could be done without infringing upon the rightful sovereignty of the states. The only question was as to the necessity of apportionment. On this question, the Supreme Court ruled that a tax on income derived from certain specified sources would require apportionment, while a tax on income derived from certain other sources would not. Now the Sixteenth Amendment, which was prompted by the decision in the Pollock Case, and which need not have been proposed and adopted if it had not been for that decision, declares that there shall be no necessity of apportionment among the several states, nor any regard to the census or enumeration, for the purposes of a federal tax on incomes "from whatever source derived." It does not, therefore, enlarge the power of taxation previously possessed by Congress, but merely repeals certain parts of the existing Constitution which imposed a limitation upon the levying of one form of direct taxation, namely, an income tax. And in fact the court has more recently declared that the whole purpose of the Sixteenth Amendment was to exclude the source from which the taxed incomes were derived as a criterion by which to determine the applicability of the constitutional requirement as to the apportionment of direct taxes.[14]

§ 41. History of Federal Income Tax Laws

The first attempt of Congress to levy a tax of this kind was made in 1861, when it was sorely pressed with the burden of providing revenue to carry on the pending war. This act levied a tax upon practically all sources and kinds of income, but at varying rates, viz., three per cent upon incomes generally, one and one-half per cent upon interest on treasury notes and United States bonds, and five per cent on the incomes of American citizens residing abroad.

[14] Brushaber v. Union Pac. R. Co., 240 U. S. 1, 36 Sup. Ct. 236, 60 L. Ed. 493, Ann. Cas. 1917B, 713, L. R. A. 1917D, 414; Stanton v. Baltic Min. Co., 240 U. S. 103, 36 Sup. Ct. 278, 60 L. Ed. 546; Tyee Realty Co. v. Anderson, 240 U. S. 115, 36 Sup. Ct. 281, 60 L. Ed. 554.

Annual incomes below $800 were exempted. The tax was to be levied and collected for only one year, that is, on the income of 1861, and no elaborate system for its collection was provided, administrative details being left to the regulation of the officers of the treasury department. In the following year, 1862, this act was re-enacted, but with very important changes. The exemption was now fixed at $600, and the tax was at the rate of three per cent. on incomes between that minimum and the sum of $10,000, and five per cent on all incomes exceeding the latter amount, as also upon the incomes (irrespective of amount) of American citizens living abroad, except those in the service of the government. Salaries of persons in the employ of the United States, including senators and representatives in Congress, were exempted, and provision was also made for the deduction from taxable income of other taxes paid by the subject and also dividends received from corporations subject to tax. The statute was to be in force until and including the year 1866 and no longer, and taxable persons were required to make returns of their income. In the next year (1863) this act was amended by permitting the taxpayer to deduct from his taxable income rent paid for the dwelling house in which he resided. The income tax law of 1864, as amended in 1865, materially increased the burden of taxation, the exemption remaining as before, but the duty being now fixed at five per cent on incomes up to $5,000, and ten per cent on the excess over that sum. Several new features were now introduced, as, for instance, a partial attempt at "collection at the source" by taxing dividends declared by certain kinds of corporations and then permitting the stockholder to deduct the same from his estimate of income, and a like provision as to persons paid by the government. Now for the first time also we meet the provision that only one deduction of $600 shall be allowed from the aggregate incomes of the members of a family. Salaries paid to persons in the employment of the United States, including the members of Congress, were now subjected to the tax, as also premiums on gold. But the rental value of a homestead owned and occupied by the taxpayer was not to be included. Special provisions were made for estimating the income and the allowable deductions of farmers and stock-raisers. The life of the act was limited to the year 1870. It was amended in details in 1866 and 1867. Again in 1870 a statute was passed, to be in force only for that year and the one following, which imposed a flat tax of two and one-half per cent on income from all sources. These sources were elaborately defined and described, and it may be remarked that they were made to include interest accrued within the year but unpaid, if collectible,

(46)

a stockholder's proportionate share of the undivided profits of the corporation, interest on United States securities and premiums on gold, the salaries of federal officers including members of Congress, and profits realized within the year from sales of real estate purchased within two years previous. The exemptions or deductions included the sum of $2,000 of income and also pensions under the laws of the United States, taxes paid, losses sustained and bad debts written off within the year, "but excluding all estimated depreciation of values," interest paid, and rent and the expenses of business. Consuls of foreign countries were exempted from the payment of the tax, so far as concerned their official emoluments and income from their property in foreign countries, but only in case their governments reciprocated. It is a significant fact that, during all this period, there was no attempt to tax corporations as such, except that the acts of 1862, 1864, and 1870 laid a tax on the dividends declared, and interest paid, by banks, trust companies, savings institutions, insurance companies, and railroads and other transportation companies.

The period of modern activity in income tax legislation was inaugurated by the enactment of the federal income tax act of 1894. This statute was intended to expire by its own limitation in 1900, but in the year following its passage it was adjudged unconstitutional and therefore was not enforced. Allowing an exemption of $4,000, it imposed a tax of two per cent on all income above that amount, from whatever source derived, and a like tax upon the net earnings of all corporations doing business within the United States (not including partnerships), except corporations for charitable, religious, or educational purposes, fraternal benefit societies, mutual insurance companies, and certain kinds of building and loan associations and savings banks. It made some provision for collection of the tax at the source, and covered carefully the administrative features of such a tax, in regard to returns, the method of collection, the imposition and recovery of penalties, and conditions upon the publicity of the returns. But in other respects it did not differ very materially from the last and most elaborate of the earlier acts, that of 1870. The corporation excise tax law of 1909 imposed a tax of one per cent upon the entire net income (over and above $5,000) received in each year by "every corporation, joint stock company or association organized for profit and having a capital stock represented by shares, and every insurance company," whether organized under state or territorial or federal laws, or organized under the laws of a foreign country and engaged in business in any state and territory of the United States. In its main features, this statute very closely resembled that act of 1894, in so far as the latter was applicable to corporations. But the tax laid by the act of 1909 was specifically denominated a "special excise tax," and was declared to be imposed "with respect to the carrying on or doing business by such corporation." This was in reality an income tax very thinly disguised, and restricted to corporations. But the theoretical distinction between a tax on income and a tax on the privilege of dong business in a corporate capacity, as measured by income, afforded sufficient ground for the courts to hold that it was not a direct tax and therefore not in conflict with the Constitution.

In October, 1913, the Sixteenth Amendment having been promulgated, a tariff act was passed, the second "section" or grand division of which contained an elaborate and detailed income tax law, affecting the incomes of both individuals and corporations. This remained in force until September 8, 1916, on which date Congress, finding it necessary to raise and revise the rates of income taxation, took the opportunity to subject the law of 1913 to a complete and thorough revision, in the process of which it was purged of many obscurities and doubtful and even inconsistent provisions, and reenacted in a greatly improved and more scientific form. This statute, as further amended by the Act of Congress of October 3, 1917, is the federal income tax law now in force, and it is printed in full as the first chapter of this volume.

§ 42. Departmental Regulations

All the federal income tax statutes, not excepting the one now in force, have confided to the administrative officers of the government a large measure of authority and discretion in the matter of prescribing rules and regulations for the assessment and collection of the tax, particularly to the Commissioner of Internal Revenue, whose bureau is specially charged with the collection of this tax, as of all other internal revenue taxes. In most instances, however, his regulations must have the approval of the Secretary of the Treasury. This is not considered as an unlawful delegation to these officers of the legislative power of Congress itself, and no objection to the constitutional validity of such a grant of authority has been successfully maintained. But of course it is not within the lawful power of these officers to go a step beyond the limits of the act of Congress under which their authority is exercised. They could neither bring within the purview of the law or of their regulations anything not definitely within the words of the act, nor except from its operation anything not clearly meant to be excluded, nor add to the burden of the taxpayer anything which Congress did not intend to impose upon him. But within the limits of their rightful authority, regulations prescribed by the Commissioner of Internal Revenue, pursuant to statutory authority, with the approval of the Secretary of the Treasury where necessary, in respect to the assessment and collection of internal revenue taxes, or for the government of the officers of the revenue department, have all the force and effect of law, and are as binding as if incorporated in the statute law of the United States; and the acts of the Commissioner are presumed to be the acts of the Secretary.[15] But the construction given to an act of Congress imposing internal revenue taxes by the Commissioner of Internal Revenue, though officially published, is not a construction of so much dignity that a re-enactment of the statute subsequent to the construction is to be regarded as a legislative adoption of that construction, and especially when the construction would make a proviso to the act repugnant to the body of the act.[16]

[15] Stegall v. Thurman (D. C.) 175 Fed. 813; In re Huttman (D. C.) 70 Fed. 699.

[16] Dollar Sav. Bank v. U. S., 19 Wall. 227, 22 L. Ed. 80.

BL.FED.TAX.—4   (49)

CHAPTER III

CONSTITUTIONAL VALIDITY OF INCOME TAX LAWS

§ 43. Requirement of Due Process of Law

In sustaining the validity of the income tax act of 1913, the Supreme Court stated that the "due process of law" clause of the Constitution is not a limitation upon the taxing power conferred upon Congress, unless, under a seeming exercise of the taxing power, the taxing statute is found to be so arbitrary as to force the conclusion that it was not really an exercise of the legitimate power of taxation, but was really a confiscation of property, or unless the statute is so wanting in a proper basis for classification as to produce an inequality so patent and so gross as to lead inevitably to the same conclusion.[1] Again, as applied to the levy, assessment, and collection of taxes, the constitutional requirement of due process of law does not mean that either the validity of the tax or the liability of the particular person or property should be adjudicated by a court of justice. Nor does it mean that personal notice should be given to the taxpayer of each or any step in the proceedings. It is enough if he is informed of the amount for which he is to be charged, and is afforded an opportunity to contest the legality of the tax, the question of his liability to it, or the amount of the assessment, before some board or tribunal empowered to give him all the relief which justice may demand, though it be a board of ad-

[1] Brushaber v. Union Pac. R. Co., 240 U. S. 1, 36 Sup. Ct. 236, 60 L. Ed. 493, L. R. A. 1917D, 414, Ann. Cas. 1917B, 713.

ministrative officers in the first instance, with a final appeal to the courts. As this method of procedure has commonly been prescribed by the income tax laws, their validity has been upheld as against the contention that they deprived the citizen of his property without due process of law.[2]

§ 44. Requirement of Equality and Uniformity

The term "property," as used in reference to taxation, means the corpus of an estate or investment, as distinguished from the annual gain or revenue from it. Hence a man's income is not "property" within the meaning of a constitutional requirement that taxes shall be laid equally and uniformly upon all property within the state.[3] For this reason, no valid objection to an income tax on constitutional grounds can be based on the fact that it may exempt certain classes of persons or corporations while taxing others, or that it may be graduated or progressive, bearing with increasing severity upon the citizen in proportion as his income increases. Whatever force such objections might possess as applied to a general property tax, a tax on incomes is not included in the constitutional requirement.[4] And where the provision of the constitution is broader,—as, that "taxation shall be equal and uniform,"—still it is said, in relation to income taxes, that this requirement is satisfied by such regulations as will secure an equal rate and just valuation, without reference to the method of valuation, and in order to be uniform a tax need not be imposed and assessed upon all property by the same agency or officers.[5] "The uniform rule to be observed in the exercise of the taxing power seems to be so far applicable to the taxes imposed on trades, professions, franchises, and incomes as to require that no discriminating tax be imposed on persons pursuing the same vocation, while varying amounts may be assessed

---

[2] Flint v. Stone Tracy Co., 220 U. S. 107, 31 Sup. Ct. 342, 55 L. Ed. 389, Ann. Cas. 1912B, 1312; Cass Farm Co. v. Detroit, 181 U. S. 396, 398, 21 Sup. Ct. 644, 645, 45 L. Ed. 914, 916; Kentucky Railroad Tax Cases, 115 U. S. 321, 6 Sup. Ct. 57, 29 L. Ed. 414; Davidson v. New Orleans, 96 U. S. 97, 24 L. Ed. 616; Alderman v. Wells, 85 S. C. 507, 67 S. E. 781, 27 L. R. A. (N. S.) 864, 21 Ann. Cas. 193.

[3] Waring v. Savannah, 60 Ga. 93; Glasgow v. Rowse, 43 Mo. 479.

[4] Alderman v. Wells, 85 S. C. 507, 67 S. E. 781, 27 L. R. A. (N. S.) 864, 21 Ann. Cas. 193. But under the Constitution of Massachusetts, all property taxes must be proportional; that is, general taxes must be in proportion to the value of the property, and special taxes in proportion to the benefit received; and it is held that a bill imposing a tax on incomes from intangible personal property, and exempting such property from other taxes, is contrary to this requirement. In re Opinion of the Justices, 220 Mass. 613, 108 N. E. 570.

[5] Commonwealth v. Brown, 91 Va. 762, 21 S. E. 357, 28 L. R. A. 110.

upon vocations or employments of different kinds.[6] And as regards the provision of the federal Constitution that taxes imposed by act of Congress shall be "uniform throughout the United States," it is said that the uniformity here required is a geographical uniformity, which does not require the equal application of the tax to all persons or corporations who may come within its operation, but only that the tax, whatever may be its incidence, shall be everywhere in force throughout the United States.[7]

§ 45. Equal Protection of the Laws

Income tax laws have commonly contained provisions classifying the subjects of taxation, discriminating between individuals and corporations, or between residents and nonresidents, exempting certain classes of companies or those engaged in certain pursuits, allowing deduction of some items and not of others, and altogether releasing from taxation incomes below a certain minimum and imposing a gradually increasing burden upon incomes above that sum. On account of these features they have always been urgently assailed as denying the "equal protection of the laws." But without avail. This provision, it is held, does not prevent such reasonable classifications and distinctions as those mentioned.[8] The constitutional requirement is satisfied if there is no discrimination in favor of one as against another of the same class, and if the method for the assessment and collection of the tax is not inconsistent with natural justice.[9] If the classification is not arbitrary, that is, if it bears a reasonable relation to the purposes to be effected, and if the constituents of each class are all treated alike, under similar circumstances and conditions, the rule of equality is satisfied.[10]

The same principles apply to the validity of any income tax law enacted by Congress. Although the provision against denying the equal protection of the laws applies only to the legislation of the

[6] Worth v. Wilmington & W. R. Co., 89 N. C. 291, 45 Am. Rep. 679.

[7] Brushaber v. Union Pac. R. Co., 240 U. S. 1, 36 Sup. Ct. 236, 60 L. Ed. 493, L. R. A. 1917D, 414, Ann. Cas. 1917B, 713; Flint v. Stone Tracy Co., 220 U. S. 107, 31 Sup. Ct. 342, 55 L. Ed. 389, Ann. Cas. 1912B, 1312. And see Edye v. Robertson, 112 U. S. 580, 5 Sup. Ct. 247, 28 L. Ed. 798.

[8] Peacock v. Pratt, 121 Fed. 722, 58 C. C. A. 48; Bell's Gap R. R. Co. v. Pennsylvania, 134 U. S. 232, 10 Sup. Ct. 533, 33 L. Ed. 892; Magoun v. Illinois Trust & Sav. Bank, 170 U. S. 283, 18 Sup. Ct. 594, 42 L. Ed. 1037; Commonwealth v. Clark, 195 Pa. 634, 46 Atl. 286, 57 L. R. A. 348, 86 Am. St. Rep. 694; State v. Frear, 148 Wis. 456, 134 N. W. 673, 135 N. W. 164, L. R. A. 1915B, 569, 606, Ann. Cas. 1913A, 1147.

[9] Michigan Cent. R. Co. v. Powers, 201 U. S. 245, 26 Sup. Ct. 459, 50 L. Ed. 744.

[10] Alderman v. Wells, 85 S. C. 507, 67 S. E. 781, 27 L. R. A. (N. S.) 864, 21 Ann. Cas. 193.

states, it is probable that other clauses of the Constitution could be found which would stand in the way of any act of Congress containing arbitrary, invidious, or unreasonable discriminations against individuals or classes. But within reasonable limits, "we must not forget that the right to select the measure and objects of taxation devolves upon the Congress, and not upon the courts, and such selections are valid unless constitutional limitations are overstepped. It is no part of the function of a court to inquire into the reasonableness of the excise, either as respects the amount or the property upon which it is imposed." [11]

§ 46. Discrimination Between Corporations, Partnerships, and Individuals

The substantial difference between the rights, privileges, duties, and business methods of corporations and those of individuals engaged in business has been thought to afford a reasonable basis for placing them in different classes for the purposes of taxation. Hence an income tax law cannot be adjudged invalid, as making unjust or illegal discriminations, because it imposes a different rate of taxation upon the income of corporations from that imposed on the income of individuals, or because it exempts the income of the individual below a certain sum, but does not grant a similar exemption to corporations.[12] As to the latter point, in particular, the theory is that an exemption of a minimum income is granted to the individual in lieu of a deduction for personal and family expenses, and that no rule of justice requires a similar allowance to corporations which have no such expenses, a deduction of other necessary expenses being granted in both cases.[13] So, allowing individuals to deduct from their gross income dividends paid by corporations whose incomes are taxed, and not giving such right of deduction to corporations, does not render the tax wanting in due process of law.[14] And limiting the amount of interest which may be deducted from the gross income of a corporation, for the purpose of fixing its taxable income, as is done by the present income tax law, which does not place any limit on the amount of interest paid which an

[11] Flint v. Stone Tracy Co., 220 U. S. 107, 31 Sup. Ct. 342, 55 L. Ed. 389, Ann. Cas. 1912B, 1312; Anderson v. Forty-Two Broadway Co., 239 U. S. 69, 36 Sup. Ct. 17, 60 L. Ed. 152; Stanton v. Baltic Min. Co., 240 U. S. 103, 36 Sup. Ct. 278, 60 L. Ed. 546.

[12] State v. Frear, 148 Wis. 456, 134 N. W. 673, 135 N. W. 164, L. R. A. 1915B, 569, 606, Ann. Cas. 1913A, 1147; Robertson v. Pratt, 13 Hawaii, 590; Flint v. Stone Tracy Co., 220 U. S. 107, 31 Sup. Ct. 342, 55 L. Ed. 389, Ann. Cas. 1912B, 1312.

[13] Robertson v. Pratt, 13 Hawaii, 590.

[14] Brushaber v. Union Pac. R. Co., 240 U. S. 1, 36 Sup. Ct. 236, 60 L. Ed. 493, L. R. A. 1917D, 414, Ann. Cas. 1917B, 713.

individual may so deduct from his gross income, does not open the statute to the objection that it is wanting in due process of law.[15] For similar reasons, there is a sufficient ground for classification between individuals and partnerships in the imposition of an income tax. And the Wisconsin statute was sustained by the Supreme Court of that state against the contention that it made an unjust discrimination in allowing exemptions to individual taxpayers which were denied to partnerships.[16] So, as to the federal statute, the allowance of a deduction of stated amounts to ascertain taxable income does not render the tax wanting in due process of law because of the discrimination between married and single persons, and husbands and wives living together, and those who are not; and no such objection can be urged against the law because it does not compel owners of houses to estimate the rental value thereof, as a part of their income, while those who live in rented houses are not allowed to deduct the rent paid, nor because farmers are permitted to omit from their income products of the farm used by their families during the year.[17]

§ 47. Discrimination Between Residents and Nonresidents.

Very serious objections have been urged against the various income tax laws, on account of the discriminations which they have ordinarily made between residents and nonresidents or citizens and aliens. It has been adjudged that the legislature may put foreign insurance companies in a class by themselves, and tax them at a rate of one per cent on their gross incomes, while other persons and corporations are taxed two per cent on their net incomes and one per cent on their property.[18] But has the United States power to tax the income of a person residing abroad, whether a citizen or an alien? If so, is it unlawful discrimination to grant exemptions to residents and deny them to nonresidents? Or to tax the entire income of the resident and only so much of the income of the nonresident as is derived from sources within the country? And in the latter case, how is the validity of the law affected by differences in the administrative features of the law, in regard to the assessment and collection of the tax, as applied to the two classes of taxpayers?

15 Brushaber v. Union Pac. R. Co., 240 U. S. 1, 36 Sup. Ct. 236, 60 L. Ed. 493, L. R. A. 1917D, 414, Ann. Cas. 1917B, 713; Tyee Realty Co. v. Anderson, 240 U. S. 115, 36 Sup. Ct. 281, 60 L. Ed. 554.

16 State v. Frear, 148 Wis. 456, 134 N. W. 673, 135 N. W. 164, L. R. A. 1915B, 569, 606, Ann. Cas. 1913A, 1147.

17 Brushaber v. Union Pac. R. Co., 240 U. S. 1, 36 Sup. Ct. 236, 60 L. Ed. 493, L. R. A. 1917D, 414, Ann. Cas. 1917B, 713.

18 Robertson v. Pratt, 13 Hawaii, 590.

It cannot be said that these questions have as yet been authoritatively settled by the courts. They were strongly urged upon the Supreme Court of Wisconsin in the case which tested and sustained the constitutionality of the income tax law of that state. But as they were not necessarily implicated in the case, and as the court held that, even conceding the invalidity of the particular features of the law which were objected to, that would not be sufficient ground for pronouncing it unconstitutional as a whole, no positive decision was rendered.[19] But it has been ruled that a federal tax on interest and dividends is not invalid in so far as it affects interest paid by a domestic corporation to nonresident alien holders of its bonds, as being a tax on property beyond the jurisdiction of the sovereign.[20]

§ 48. Federal Taxation of Corporations Created by States

When the constitutionality of the federal corporation tax law of 1909 was attacked before the Supreme Court of the United States, the objection was very strongly urged that, for the federal government to impose a tax on corporations which received their franchises from the states was beyond its rightful authority, inasmuch as it was imposing a burden upon the right of the several states to create corporations, which might be pushed to such an extreme as to destroy that right, and hence an invasion of their prerogatives, and the crippling of a power rightfully belonging to them as separate governments. That act laid a tax on the privilege of engaging in or carrying on business in a corporate capacity, the amount of the tax to be measured by the net income of the corporation. The income tax law taxes the income of the corporation directly and by name. But the same argument, if it had prevailed against the one statute, would be equally potent as against the other. Hence it becomes important to consider the decision of the Supreme Court in which this argument was tested and rejected. The court said: "The cases unite in exempting from federal taxation the means and instrumentalities employed in carrying on the governmental operations of the state. The exercise of such rights as the establishment of a judiciary, the employment of officers to execute and administer the laws, and similar governmental functions, cannot be taxed by the federal government. But this limitation has never been extended to the exclusion of the activities of a merely private business from the federal taxing power, although the power to exercise them is derived from an act of incorporation by one of

---

19 State v. Frear, 148 Wis. 456, 134 N. W. 673, 135 N. W. 164, L. R. A. 1915B, 569, 606, Ann. Cas. 1913A, 1147.

20 U. S. v. Erie Ry. Co., 106 U. S. 327, 1 Sup. Ct. 223, 27 L. Ed. 151.

the states. We therefore reach the conclusion that the mere fact that the business taxed is done in pursuance of authority granted by a state in the creation of private corporations does not exempt it from the exercise of federal authority to levy excise taxes upon such privileges. Nor is the special objection tenable, made in some of the cases, that the corporations act as trustees, guardians, etc., under the authority of the laws or courts of the state. Such trustees are not the agents of the state government in a sense which exempts them from taxation because executing the necessary governmental powers of the state. The trustees receive their compensation from the interests served, and not from the public revenues of the state." [21]

§ 49. Taxation of Income from Non-Taxable Property

It has been broadly stated that there is no constitutional objection to imposing an excise or license tax on a business or occupation, although the property employed in the business is exempt from taxation.[22] And on the same principle, a tax on income could not be held invalid merely because the income was derived from property not subject to be taxed. Also it has been decided that the rule that the power to tax depends upon jurisdiction of the subject-matter of the tax has no application to taxation under the laws of the United States.[23] But in passing upon the constitutionality of the federal income tax law of 1894, the Supreme Court held that, in so far as the act levied a tax on the income of persons or corporations derived from the bonds of municipal corporations, it was invalid, because such a tax is a tax on the power of the states and their instrumentalities to borrow money, and consequently repugnant to the Constitution.[24] A similar question arose under the corporation excise tax law of 1909, but it was held by the same court that the latter statute was not invalid because the income of a corporation subject to the tax might consist in part, or even entirely, of interest on municipal bonds, the ground of the distinction being that the act of 1909 did not impose a tax on the income so derived, but on the franchise or privilege of doing business in a corporate capacity, the income being merely used as a measure of the amount of the tax in the particular case.[25] The acts of 1913

[21] Flint v. Stone Tracy Co., 220 U. S. 107, 31 Sup. Ct. 342, 55 L. Ed. 389, Ann. Cas. 1912B, 1312.
[22] Nunnemacher v. State, 129 Wis. 190, 108 N. W. 627, 9 L. R. A. (N. S.) 121, 9 Ann. Cas. 711.
[23] U. S. v. Bennett, 232 U. S. 299, 34 Sup. Ct. 433, 58 L. Ed. 612.
[24] Pollock v. Farmers' Loan & Trust Co., 157 U. S. 429, 15 Sup. Ct. 673, 39 L. Ed. 759.
[25] Flint v. Stone Tracy Co., 220 U. S. 107, 31 Sup. Ct. 342, 55 L. Ed. 389, Ann. Cas. 1912B, 1312.

and 1916 have reverted to the principle of taxing incomes directly, but they meet the point in question by excluding from taxable income "interest upon the obligations of a state or any political subdivision thereof." It had also been held in an earlier case that the act of Congress of 1864, imposing an income tax, and containing a provision for taxing the interest paid by railroads and some other corporations on their bonded debt, requiring them to pay the tax and deduct the amount thereof from their periodical payments to the holders of the bonds, could not be applied in the case of a municipal corporation owning such bonds, since the municipalities created by the states are entirely beyond the taxing power of the federal government.[26]

§ 50. Taxing Salaries of Federal and State Officers

The income tax law exempts "the compensation of all officers and employees of a state or any political subdivision thereof, except when such compensation is paid by the United States government." (Act Cong. Sept. 8, 1916, § 4 [U. S. Comp. St. 1916, § 6336d].) It would not be competent for Congress to lay a tax upon the salary of an officer of a state. This is an implication from the Constitution itself and from the mutual relation of the federal and state governments, neither being authorized to tax the means or agencies employed by the other in carrying out its governmental functions. And hence it was held that a tax assessed, under the federal income tax law of 1864, upon the salary of a state judge was wrongfully imposed, and if paid under protest could be recovered back.[27] And in a similar case it was held to be immaterial that the judge's salary was fixed by the authorities of a county and payable out of the treasury of a city.[28] So, one's compensation as state's attorney is not liable to the federal income tax, nor can such compensation be applied to the satisfaction of the monetary exemption; it must be omitted altogether from the computation of his income, and the taxpayer must have his exemption out of his income from other sources.[29]

As to the incidence of the income tax upon federal officers, it should be observed that there are some whose salary, while it is to be fixed and appropriated by Congress, is safeguarded from change during their tenure of office by the Constitution itself. As to the President, he is to "receive a compensation which shall nei-

[26] U. S. v. Baltimore & O. R. Co., 17 Wall. 322, 21 L. Ed. 597.
[27] The Collector v. Day, 11 Wall. 113, 20 L. Ed. 122. And see Van Brocklin v. Tennessee, 117 U. S. 151, 6 Sup. Ct. 670, 29 L. Ed. 845; King v. Hunter, 65 N. C. 603, 6 Am. Rep. 754.
[28] Freedman v. Sigel, 10 Blatchf. 327, Fed. Cas. No. 5,080.
[29] U. S. v. Ritchie, Fed. Cas. No. 16,168.

ther be increased nor diminished during the period for which he shall have been elected." (Const. U. S., art. 2, § 1.) And as to the federal judges, they shall "receive a compensation which shall not be diminished during their continuance in office." (Const. U. S., art. 3, § 1.) The income tax laws enacted by Congress during the period of the Civil War contained no such exception, but the justices of the Supreme Court, through Chief Justice Taney, addressed a communication to the Secretary of the Treasury declaring their conviction that their salaries were not legally subject to the tax. Thereupon the Attorney General, to whom the communication had been referred, gave an elaborate opinion, advising the Secretary of the Treasury that the income tax could not lawfully be assessed upon and collected from the salaries of those judicial officers of the United States who were in office at the time of the enactment of the statute imposing the tax.[30] No attempt was made thereafter to assess the tax upon the salaries of the judges. But in the income tax law of 1894, Congress again failed to make an exception in this particular, and the statute was held unconstitutional and void in so far as it attempted to tax the salaries of the judges of the United States courts.[31] But the present statute meets this point by providing that "in computing net income under this section, there shall be excluded the compensation of the present President of the United States during the term for for which he has been elected, and of the judges of the Supreme and inferior courts of the United States now in office." (Act Cong. Sept. 8, 1916, § 4.) And the Treasury Department rules that the salaries of the federal judges who may be appointed subsequent to the date of its enactment, and of judges who have been retired, are subject to the income tax. (T. D. 2090, Dec. 14, 1914.) But as to all the other officers and employees of the United States (including the members of Congress themselves) whose salary or compensation may be fixed and changed in the absolute discretion of Congress, there is no constitutional objection to the incidence of the income tax upon such salaries. Such was the decision made under the act of 1862 in regard to collecting the income tax from the salary of an officer in the United States army,[32] and the rule is equally applicable to all others save those mentioned above.

Finally, an income tax law is not to be pronounced unconstitutional and void in its entirety simply because it lays a tax upon the salaries of certain officers who are constitutionally exempt from

---

[30] 13 Opin. Atty. Gen. 161.

[31] Pollock v. Farmers' Loan & Trust Co., 157 U. S. 429, 15 Sup. Ct. 673, 39 L. Ed. 759, per Field, J., concurring.

[32] Galm v. U. S., 39 Ct. Cl. 55.

such taxation, or fails to make an explicit exception in their favor. The protection of the constitution because of such an illegal provision can be invoked only by one against whom it is sought to be enforced; and even in such a case, if the law in affirmative terms lays the tax on such an exempt income, that portion of it can be exscinded without destroying the rest, while if it merely omits to make the necessary exception, it can be construed as not applying in the particular case.[33]

§ 51. Exemption of Incomes Below a Fixed Sum

It has been held by a great many authorities that a statute imposing taxes on inheritances, legacies, and successions is not unconstitutional because it exempts from its operation estates or inheritances below a certain minimum value,[34] provided only that the exemption is not so excessive as to be entirely unreasonable.[35] On the same principle, an income tax law is not unconstitutional because it wholly exempts from taxation all incomes below a certain annual amount, and the question where the tax shall begin, or where the exemption shall end, is one exclusively for the decision of the legislature.[36]   Such a tax law, making a reasonable exemp-

[33] State v. Frear, 148 Wis. 456, 134 N. W. 673, 135 N. W. 164, L. R. A. 1915B, 569, 606, Ann. Cas. 1913A, 1147; Peacock v. Pratt, 121 Fed. 772, 58 C. C. A. 48; Robertson v. Pratt, 13 Hawaii, 590.

[34] Knowlton v. Moore, 178 U. S. 60, 20 Sup. Ct. 755, 44 L. Ed. 977; Magoun v. Illinois Trust & Sav. Bank, 170 U. S. 283, 18 Sup. Ct. 594, 42 L. Ed. 1037; Colton v. Montpelier, 71 Vt. 413, 45 Atl. 1039; In re Hickok's Estate, 78 Vt. 259, 62 Atl. 724, 6 Ann. Cas. 578; In re Wilmerding's Estate, 117 Cal. 281, 49 Pac. 181; State v. Vance, 97 Minn. 532, 106 N. W. 98; State v. Bazille, 97 Minn. 11, 106 N. W. 93, 6 L. R. A. (N. S.) 732, 7 Ann. Cas. 1056; Black v. State, 113 Wis. 205, 89 N. W. 522, 90 Am. St. Rep. 853; State v. Guilbert, 70 Ohio St. 299, 71 N. E. 636, 1 Ann. Cas. 25; Gelsthorpe v. Furnell, 20 Mont. 299, 51 Pac. 267, 39 L. R. A. 170; State v. Alston, 94 Tenn. 674, 30 S. W. 750, 28 L. R. A. 178; In re Mixter's Estate, 10 Pa. Co. Ct. R. 409; Nunnemacher v. State, 129 Wis. 190, 108 N. W. 627, 9 L. R. A. (N. S.) 121, 9 Ann. Cas. 711. So, a state statute imposing an ad valorem tax is not unconstitutional as denying the equal protection of the laws because it exempts the property of telephone companies whose gross receipts for the year do not exceed $500, at least where, under the classification made by the statute, the companies taxed are mainly those organized for profit, while the untaxed enterprises are mainly not profit-making, but mutual or co-operative. Citizens' Telephone Co. v. Fuller, 229 U. S. 322, 33 Sup. Ct. 833, 57 L. Ed. 1206.

[35] Minot v. Winthrop, 162 Mass. 113, 38 N. E. 512, 26 L. R. A. 259, in which case it was held that an excise tax on inheritances was not so clearly unreasonable, by reason of exempting estates under $10,000, as to render it unconstitutional. But see State v. Ferris, 9 Ohio Cir. Ct. R. 298, holding void an inheritance tax law which exempted property to the amount of $20,000.

[36] Moore v. Miller, 5 App. D. C. 413; New Orleans v. Fourchy, 30 La. Ann. 910; Peacock v. Pratt, 121 Fed. 772, 58 C. C. A. 48.

tion, is not in violation of a constitutional provision that taxes shall be equal and uniform.[37] And if it is at all within the power of a court to adjudge that the exemption granted is so excessive as to invalidate the statute, at least no such decision has ever yet been rendered. On the contrary, the decisions have sustained the income tax laws in this particular. That of Hawaii, exempting incomes to the amount of $1,000, was sustained as against the objection that the allowance was excessive.[38] That of Wisconsin was similarly held valid, although it exempts life insurance to the amount of $10,000, in favor of one legally dependent on the deceased. The court called this a "striking exemption," but said: "While this is somewhat large, we cannot say that it is unreasonable."[39] The income tax act of Congress of 1894 was sustained (by an inferior court) as against objection that the exemption allowed, $4,000. was unreasonably great.[40] The corporation excise tax law of 1909 was assailed on the ground that it exempted incomes of less than $5,000, but the Supreme Court of the United States answered this objection with a mere reference to certain of its earlier decisions concerning similar exemptions in inheritance tax laws.[41]

Finally, when the validity of the income tax act of 1913 was before the Supreme Court, it was urged that the allowance of a deduction of $3,000 (or $4,000) rendered the statute obnoxious to the requirement of due process of law, because persons subject to the supertax, as having incomes in excess of $20,000, were not given the right to deduct such exemption a second time, and because no second right is given to such persons to deduct dividends received from corporations, and also because the right to make such a deduction is given to individuals but not to corporations. But the court refused to consider these objections as valid, and fully sustained the constitutionality of the law.[42]

§ 52. Exemption of Classes of Individuals or Corporations.

It is a conceded principle of taxation, applicable to income taxes as well as to any others, that there is no constitutional objection

[37] New Orleans v. Fourchy, 30 La. Ann. 910.

[38] Robertson v. Pratt, 13 Hawaii, 590.

[39] State v. Frear, 148 Wis. 456, 134 N. W. 673, 135 N. W. 164, L. R. A 1915B, 569, 606, Ann. Cas. 1913A, 1147.

[40] Moore v. Miller, 5 App. D. C. 413.

[41] Flint v. Stone Tracy Co., 220 U. S. 107, 31 Sup. Ct. 342, 55 L. Ed. 389, Ann. Cas. 1912B, 1312.

[42] Brushaber v. Union Pac. R. Co., 240 U. S. 1, 36 Sup. Ct. 236, 60 L. Ed. 493, L. R. A. 1917D, 414, Ann. Cas. 1917B, 713; Stanton v. Baltic Min. Co., 240 U. S. 103, 36 Sup. Ct. 278, 60 L. Ed. 546. And see Pollock v. Farmers' Loan & Trust Co., 158 U. S. 601, 15 Sup. Ct. 912, 39 L. Ed. 1108, dissenting opinions of Justice Brown and Justice Harlan.

to an exemption in favor of those corporations or institutions which serve important public purposes or confer benefits upon the public at large, such as religious, charitable, and educational organizations. Also it is clear that any corporation which bears its due share of the public burden, under a special form of taxation, may lawfully be exempted from the payment of any or all other taxes. Thus, the exemption of insurance companies from an income tax law does not render it invalid as to other corporations which are made subject to the law, where the exemption is made expressly on the ground that such companies are required by another law to pay a tax on the premiums received.[43] But beyond these elementary principles, the subject is not free from doubt. It would be obviously contrary to sound principles of constitutional law to push the power of exemption so far as to make the burden of the tax in reality fall upon a selected class of individuals or corporations. On this point the Supreme Court of Louisiana has said: "It is not necessary for us to decide whether or not, under the Constitution, the legislature has power to levy an income tax. It suffices to say that, if the legislature has such power, it would be an indispensable condition of its exercise that the tax should embrace the incomes of all persons not exempted, and whatever power of classification the legislature might possess as to the subject-matter of taxation, that power could under no pretext be stretched so as to embrace the right to single out a particular class of taxpayers and to require them to pay such a tax, while exempting all others."[44] No such sweeping exemptions have been attempted in recent income tax laws. But they commonly contain exemptions in favor of labor organizations, agricultural societies, savings banks, mutual building and loan associations, mutual insurance companies, fraternal orders and benefit societies (or some of the foregoing), as well as charitable and educational institutions. The validity of such exemptions has been severely criticized. And many thoughtful persons cherish a profound conviction that they are not only economically unsound but entirely contrary to every principle of justice and fairness in the imposition of taxes. Nevertheless, the Supreme Court has fully sustained the validity of the exemptions in the present income tax law in favor of labor unions, agricultural associations, mutual savings banks, etc., and it is probable that the question is now definitely foreclosed.[45]

---

[43] Peacock v. Pratt, 121 Fed. 772, 58 C. C. A. 48.

[44] Parker v. North British & M. Ins. Co., 42 La. Ann. 428, 7 South. 599.

[45] Stanton v. Baltic Min. Co., 240 U. S. 103, 36 Sup. Ct. 278, 60 L. Ed. 546: Brushaber v. Union Pac. R. Co., 240 U. S. 1, 36 Sup. Ct. 236, 60 L. Ed. 493,

§ 53. Double Taxation

Vigorous objections to the validity of income tax laws have been based on the ground that they impose, or at least result in double taxation. And it cannot be denied that this is usually the case. "It may safely be said that the payment of an income tax almost necessarily involves, in some indirect and limited sense, the payment of a double tax. For income, oftener than otherwise, in some way, either directly or indirectly, is derived from or grows out of property subject to taxation." [46] But though double taxation is vicious and unjust in principle, and no statute will be so construed as to impose double taxes if it can reasonably be avoided, yet a statute which produces this result cannot be adjudged invalid on economic principles, nor unless it conflicts with some explicit provision of the constitution. This important point is discussed, in relation to income taxation, by the court in South Carolina, in the following terms: "The next objection to the act is that it results in double taxation. The contention is that plaintiff's income was derived from dividends received upon his stock in corporations chartered and doing business under the laws of the state, and as these corporations had paid taxes on their property, and also on their franchises, a tax on plaintiff's income is double taxation. There is much room for discussion and difference of opinion as to what really amounts to double taxation. But the weight of authority and reason sustains the taxation of shares of stock in a corporation to the holder thereof, notwithstanding the corporation has paid taxes on its property and also on its franchises. The rents and profits derived from real estate, and the products of the farm, may be taxed, though the land from which they are derived has also been taxed. The profits of a business may be taxed though the property in the business, bought on credit, has been taxed to the owner, and the debt he owes therefor has been taxed to the creditor, and the property covered by mortgage may be taxed to the owner, and the mortgage thereon to the mortgagee. These may be instances of double taxation in one sense, yet they are not within the rule of uniformity and equality prescribed by the Constitution, which forbids the taxation twice of the same property for the same purpose, while other property, under similar circumstances and conditions, is taxed only once. There is no constitutional inhibition against such taxation; and in the absence of constitutional restriction, the power of the legisla-

L. R. A. 1917D, 414, Ann. Cas. 1917B, 713; Flint v. Stone Tracy Co., 220 U. S. 107, 31 Sup. Ct. 342, 55 L. Ed. 389, Ann. Cas. 1912B, 1312.
   [46] Lott v. Hubbard, 44 Ala. 593.

ture to tax is limited only by its own discretion and its responsibility to its constituents. It has been said the power to tax is an inherent right of sovereignty, necessary to its existence, and limited only by its necessities. We make out no conclusive case against a tax when we show that it reaches twice the same property for the same purpose. This may have been intended, and, in many cases, at least is admissible." [47] The general weight of authority undoubtedly does sustain the principle that a tax may be levied on income derived from property, in the shape of rent or otherwise, although the property yielding the income is also subjected to taxation, and that this does not violate the rule against double taxation, because the two interests or species of property are distinct and severable. [48] It must be admitted, however, that this doctrine does not pass entirely unchallenged. [49] And in at least one state this very result has been guarded against by a clause in the constitution which provides that "the general assembly may tax trades, professions, franchises, and incomes, provided that no income shall be taxed when the property from which the income is derived is taxed." [50] On the other hand the constitution of another state having an income tax law (Wisconsin) expressly makes a distinction between "property" and "income" and authorizes the taxation of both. And the Supreme Court of that state, in sustaining the income tax, has remarked: "It is claimed with much earnestness and ability that the act violates the provisions of the fourteenth amendment to the federal Constitution. One of the contentions under this head is that the progressive features of the act are discriminatory, if not absolutely confiscatory. Another contention is that the act provides for double taxation, and for both reasons it is claimed that it denies to citizens the equal protection of the laws. It is said in support of this contention that the United States Supreme Court in the Pollock case [51] has held that taxation of income derived from land is in fact taxation of the land itself, hence that the act provides for double taxation, first of the land in specie, and next of the income therefrom. It seems that this claim

[47] Alderman v. Wells, 85 S. C. 507, 67 S. E. 781, 27 L. R. A. (N. S.) 864, 21 Ann. Cas. 193.

[48] Comstock v. Grand Rapids, 54 Mich. 641, 20 N. W. 623; Woodruff v. Oswego Starch Factory, 177 N. Y. 23, 22 N. E. 994; Chisholm v. Shields, 21 Ohio Cir. Ct. R. 231; Memphis v. Ensley, 6 Baxt. (Tenn.) 553, 32 Am. Rep. 532.

[49] See City of New Orleans v. Fassman, 14 La. Ann. 865; Kennard v. Manchester, 68 N. H. 61, 36 Atl. 553.

[50] Const. N. C., art. 5, § 3.

[51] Pollock v. Farmers' Loan & Trust Co., 157 U. S. 429, 15 Sup. Ct. 673, 39 L. Ed. 759.

comes which are already and concurrently taxed under the income tax act of 1916, a question may be raised as to constitutional authority of Congress to impose this form of double taxation. No decisions on this point have been made. But the Supreme Court has ruled that it was within the power of Congress to impose, by the War Revenue Act of 1898, an additional excise upon manufactured tobacco, upon which the excise theretofore imposed by law had been paid, even though the tobacco had passed from the hands of the manufacturer, where it had not reached the consumer, and was, at the time of the passage of the act, held and intended for sale.[59]

§ 55. Validity of Graduated or Progressive Tax

The validity of statutes authorizing the graduation or progressive increase of the income tax has been sustained in various states, as against objections drawn from different features of the state constitutions, and also as against the claim that such a feature denied the equal protection of the laws.[60] The only contrary decision was rendered in Hawaii, where the court decided against the constitutional validity of a graded income tax (enacted in 1896, and much resembling the federal income tax law of 1894) on the ground of its being in conflict with a provision of the constitution that each citizen "shall be obliged to contribute his proportion or share" of the expenses of government. The law in question exempted all incomes below $2,000, allowed an exemption of $2,000 on all incomes below $4,000, and taxed all incomes above $4,000 without exemption. It was held that this was not proportional taxation, but unjust discrimination.[61]

The corresponding provision in the federal acts of 1913 and 1916 has been sustained by the Supreme Court. The progressive rate feature, it was said, could not be held to make the statute wanting in due process of law, unless it caused the tax to transcend all proper conceptions of taxation, and to amount to a mere arbitrary abuse of power, which, in the opinion of the court, was certainly not the case.[62]

---

[59] Patton v. Brady, 184 U. S. 608, 22 Sup. Ct. 493, 46 L. Ed. 713.

[60] Alderman v. Wells, 85 S. C. 507, 67 S. E. 781, 27 L. R. A. (N. S.) 864, 21 Ann. Cas. 193; State v. Frear, 148 Wis. 456, 134 N. W. 673, 135 N. W. 164, L. R. A. 1915B, 569, 606, Ann. Cas. 1913A, 1147.

[61] Campbell v. Shaw, 11 Hawaii, 112.

[62] Brushaber v. Union Pac. R. Co., 240 U. S. 1, 36 Sup. Ct. 236, 60 L. Ed. 493, L. R. A. 1917D, 414, Ann. Cas. 1917B, 713; Stanton v. Baltic Min. Co., 240 U. S. 103, 36 Sup. Ct. 278, 60 L. Ed. 546. And see Dodge v. Osborn, 43 App. D. C. 144, affirmed 240 U. S. 118, 36 Sup. Ct. 275, 60 L. Ed. 557.

§ 56. Retrospective Operation of Statute

On general principles and irrespective of explicit constitutional limitations, a statute imposing an income tax may subject to taxation the income of the citizen for the whole of the current year in which the statute is passed, that is, not only so much of the income as accrued from the date of the enactment of the law to the end of the year, but also that portion which accrued or was earned from the beginning of the year to the date of the law. For the year's income is treated and considered as one entire thing, not as made up of several portions or items. And hence, although the statute might be called retrospective in its operation upon a part of the first year's income, it is not retrospective in such a sense as to render it unconstitutional.[63]

But special considerations affect the validity of the federal income tax law in this particular. Until the adoption and promulgation of the Sixteenth Amendment, Congress had no rightful power to tax incomes unless on condition that the tax should be apportioned among the several states. Hence if the act of 1913 had attempted to tax the whole of the citizen's income for that year, it would have included some gains and profits which, at the time they were acquired, and when alone they could be described as "income," were not subject to the taxing power of Congress, except on the condition mentioned. Hence it was provided that "for the year ending December 31st, 1913, said tax shall be computed on the net income accruing from March 1st to December 31st, 1913, both dates inclusive, after deducting five-sixths only of the specific exemptions and deductions herein provided for." And although the statute was enacted in October of 1913, and was thus made to apply to income accruing as far back as March 1st, it was held that the fact that it was retroactive to this extent did not impair its constitutional validity.[64] And in a case where the fiscal year for a firm of which the plaintiff was a member began before the income tax law of 1913 went into effect, but there was no showing that

[63] State v. Bell, 61 N. C. 76; State v. Frear, 148 Wis. 456, 134 N. W. 673, 135 N. W. 164, L. R. A. 1915B, 569, 606, Ann. Cas. 1913A, 1147; Drexel v. Commonwealth, 46 Pa. 31; Stockdale v. Insurance Companies, 20 Wall. 323, 22 L. Ed. 348; Schuylkill Nav. Co. v. Elliott, 21 Int. Rev. Rec. 342, Fed. Cas. No. 12,497. And see Billings v. U. S., 232 U. S. 261, 34 Sup. Ct. 421, 58 L. Ed. 596; Locke v. New Orleans, 4 Wall. 172, 18 L. Ed. 334; People v. Spring Valley Hydraulic Gold Co., 92 N. Y. 383. But compare Merchants' Ins. Co. v. McCartney, 1 Low. 447, Fed. Cas. No. 9,443.

[64] Brushaber v. Union Pac. R. Co., 240 U. S. 1, 36 Sup. Ct. 236, 60 L. Ed. 493, L. R. A. 1917D, 414, Ann. Cas. 1917B, 713; Tyee Realty Co. v. Anderson, 240 U. S. 115, 36 Sup. Ct. 281, 60 L. Ed. 554; Edwards v. Keith (D. C.) 224 Fed. 585.

during that part of the year before the law went into effect any
profits had been earned, it was held that, without such a showing,
the plaintiff could not object that income taxes were assessed on
the entire profits earned, on the ground that part of the taxes were
based on income earned before the statute became operative.[65]

§ 57. Objections to Mode of Enactment of Statute

In regard to the federal corporation tax law of 1909, it appeared
that the bill, introduced in and passed by the House of Representatives, was a general bill for the collection of revenue, including, as one of its features, a plan of inheritance taxation, and that
this part was stricken out by the Senate and the corporation tax
substituted. And it was argued that this rendered the act invalid,
since the Constitution provides that all bills for the raising of revenue shall originate in the House of Representatives. But the
court held otherwise, in view of the further provision of the Constitution that the Senate may propose or concur with amendments
to revenue bills as well as other bills.[66] This decision would be
equally applicable to any amendments or substitutions in an income tax law which the Senate might originate, if they were accepted by the House, or the bill, in its final form, duly passed by
both houses.

§ 58. Objections to Administrative Provisions of Act

Statutes providing for the taxation of incomes have often been
subjected to severe criticism on the ground that they confide too
much authority and discretion to executive and administrative
officers, in regard to the settlement of matters of detail, to the construction of the machinery necessary for the operation of the law,
and to the making of rules and regulations for its enforcement. But
it may now be regarded as a settled principle of constitutional law
that, although a legislative body cannot delegate its power to make
laws, yet, having enacted statutes, it may invest executive officers
or boards or commissions created for the purpose with authority
to make rules and regulations for the practical administration of
such statutes in matters of detail and to enforce the same, and also
to determine the existence of the facts or conditions on which the
application of the law depends. And "there is a marked and increasing tendency to leave more and more of what may be called
the detail of legislation to such officers and commissions, the legislature settling the general policy and outline of the laws on a
given subject, and confiding to administrative agencies the work

[65] Cohen v. Lowe (D. C.) 234 Fed. 474.
[66] Flint v. Stone Tracy Co., 220 U. S. 107, 31 Sup. Ct. 342, 55 L. Ed. 389,
Ann. Cas. 1912B, 1312.

of erecting the machinery necessary for their practical operation and their application in particular cases." [67]   For this reason it is held that no valid objection to the federal income tax law can be based upon the authority which it intrusts to the Commissioner of Internal Revenue, with respect to prescribing forms and making rules and regulations on various matters of administration, more especially as it does not go nearly so far in this regard as some of the earlier acts of Congress on the same subject, which were never successfully challenged on this ground. [68]   And there is no want of due process of law in those provisions of the act, and of the Revised Statutes, which make an appeal to the Commissioner of Internal Revenue, after payment of the tax, and his refusal to refund it, prerequisites to the maintenance of a suit to recover the tax on the ground of its having been erroneously or illegally assessed and collected. [69]

Objection is also made to those provisions commonly found in income tax laws which require the citizen to disclose the sources and amount of his income in sworn returns, which, under certain conditions, are open to the inspection of the public, or which require him to open his books and papers to the examination of the revenue officers or submit to interrogation concerning his business affairs.   Such provisions, it is argued, amount to authorizing "un-

[67] Black, Const. Law (3d edn.) pp. 96, 97, and cases there cited. See, particularly, Union Bridge Co. v. United States, 204 U. S. 364, 27 Sup. Ct. 367, 51 L. Ed. 523; Field v. Clark, 143 U. S. 649, 12 Sup. Ct. 495, 36 L. Ed. 291; Coopersville Co-operative Creamery Co. v. Lemon, 163 Fed. 145, 89 C. C. A. 595; In re Huttman (D. C.) 70 Fed. 699.

[68] Brushaber v. Union Pac. R. Co., 240 U. S. 1, 36 Sup. Ct. 236, 60 L. Ed. 493, L. R. A. 1917D, 414, Ann. Cas. 1917B, 713.

[69] Dodge v. Osborn, 240 U. S. 118, 36 Sup. Ct. 275, 60 L. Ed. 557. The methods of collection at the source, prescribed by the income tax provisions of the act of October 3, 1913 (38 Stat. at L. 166, chap. 16), are not wanting in due process of law because of the cost to which corporations are subjected by the duty of collection cast upon them, nor because of the resulting discrimination between corporations indebted upon coupon and registered bonds and those not so indebted, nor because of the discrimination against corporations which have assumed the payment of taxes on their bonds which results from the fact that some or all of their bondholders may be exempt from the income tax, nor because of the discrimination against owners of corporate bonds in favor of individuals none of whose income is derived from such property, nor because the law does not release corporate bondholders from the payment of a tax on their bonds, even after such taxes have been deducted by the corporation, if, after the deduction, the corporation should fail, nor because the payment of the tax by the corporation does not relieve the owners of bonds, the taxes on which have been assumed by the corporation, from their duty to include the income from such bonds in making a return of all income. Brushaber v. Union Pac. R. Co., 240 U. S. 1, 36 Sup. Ct. 236, 60 L. Ed. 493, L. R. A. 1917D, 414, Ann. Cas. 1917B, 713.

reasonable searches and seizures," and moreover, in view of the possible use of information thus obtained, they may compel the individual to furnish evidence against himself in a criminal proceeding. But no decision sustaining such objections as these has been found. On the contrary the courts hold that such provisions cannot be brought within the reasonable intendment of the constitutional guaranties referred to, that similar provisions are already very common in the tax laws of various states and have always been acquiesced in, or at least, not successfully attacked, and that, as to the matter of self-crimination, even if such a result could follow from the enforcement of any provision of an income tax law, it would be no ground for adjudging the whole statute unconstitutional, but only a matter to be pleaded by the individual in his own behalf when a criminal proceeding shall actually be brought against him and an attempt actually made to use against him evidence thus extorted.[70]

§ 59. Apportionment of Federal Income Tax

The United States income tax law of 1894 was adjudged unconstitutional on the ground that it was a "direct" tax within the meaning of the Constitution of the United States and yet was not "apportioned among the several states" as that instrument requires.[71] The corporation tax law of 1909 was also not apportioned among the states, but its validity was sustained by the Supreme Court, on the ground that it was not a direct tax upon the income of corporations, but an excise tax upon the conducting or carrying on of business in a corporate capacity, and that there is nothing in the Constitution requiring excise taxes to be apportioned according to population.[72] So far as regards the present income tax law, and any future law of the same character, the necessity of apportion-

---

[70] Flint v. Stone Tracy Co., 220 U. S. 107, 31 Sup. Ct. 342, 55 L. Ed. 389, Ann. Cas. 1912B, 1312; Peacock v. Pratt, 121 Fed. 772, 58 C. C. A. 48; Co-operative Building & Loan Ass'n v. State, 156 Ind. 463, 60 N. E. 146. And see Interstate Commerce Commission v. Brimson, 154 U. S. 447, 155 U. S. 3, 14 Sup. Ct. 1125, 15 Sup. Ct. 19, 38 L. Ed. 1047, 39 L. Ed. 49; In re Phillips, 10 Int. Rev. Rec. 107, Fed. Cas. No. 11,097; Perry v. Newsome, 10 Int. Rev. Rec. 20, Fed. Cas. No. 11,009; In re Lippman, 3 Ben. 95, Fed. Cas. No. 8,-382; In re Strouse, 1 Sawy. 605, Fed. Cas. No. 13,548; Matter of Meador, 1 Abb. U. S. 317, Fed. Cas. No. 9,375. But compare Boyd v. United States, 116 U. S. 616, 6 Sup. Ct. 524, 29 L. Ed. 746; In re Pacific Railway Commission, 32 Fed. 241; People v. Reardon, 197 N. Y. 236, 90 N. E. 829, 27 L. R. A. (N. S.) 141, 134 Am. St. Rep. 871; Robson v. Doyle, 191 Ill. 566, 61 N. E. 435.

[71] Pollock v. Farmers' Loan & Trust Co., 157 U. S. 429, 15 Sup. Ct. 673, 39 L. Ed. 759; s. c., 158 U. S. 601, 15 Sup. Ct. 912, 39 L. Ed. 1108.

[72] Flint v. Stone Tracy Co., 220 U. S. 107, 31 Sup. Ct. 342, 55 L. Ed. 389, Ann. Cas. 1912B, 1312; Anderson v. Morris & E. R. Co., 216 Fed. 83, 132 C. C. A. 327.

ment is dispensed with by the Sixteenth Amendment to the Constitution, which provides that "the Congress shall have power to lay and collect taxes on incomes, from whatever source derived, without apportionment among the several states, and without regard to any census or enumeration."

§ 60. Constitutional Objections to Penalties Imposed

Where the penalties imposed by any statute, to be visited upon those who may violate its provisions, are of such severity as to terrorize those coming within the terms of the law, and to deter them from bringing actions in the courts to test its validity, it is held to be unconstitutional, at least in this respect, both as depriving such persons of their property without due process of law and as denying them the equal protection of the laws. "It is unlawful to prevent or penalize the resistance of persons or corporations to laws which they may deem injurious or oppressive, by visiting them, on their attempt to do so, with such excessive and ruinous penalties or such a multiplicity of prosecutions or such danger of heavy fines and imprisonment as to intimidate them and prevent them from seeking relief in the courts; this amounts to denying the equal protection of the laws." [73] It may be gravely doubted whether these considerations are not applicable to the federal income tax law of 1916, since (to take a single illustration) a corporation which simply fails to make its return under that statute in due season is liable to a fine of as much as ten thousand dollars and also to have its assessment increased by fifty per cent. In so far, however, as the matter has yet been adjudicated, the statute has been upheld. In a case in the United States District Court for the Southern District of New York,[74] the constitutionality of the corporation excise tax law of 1909 was assailed on the ground that the penalty provided for failure to make a return (from $1,000 to $10,000) was so excessive as practically to prohibit any contest in the courts. But the court ruled otherwise. Hand, J., said: "As to the constitutionality of the act the only suggestion is that it makes reasonable contest impossible because of the penalties imposed for disobedience. Cases like Ex parte Young, 209 U. S. 123, 28 Sup.

---

[73] Black, Const. Law (3d edn.) p. 545; Ex parte Young, 209 U. S. 123, 28 Sup. Ct. 441, 52 L. Ed. 714, 13 L. R. A. (N. S.) 932, 14 Ann. Cas. 764; Mercantile Trust Co. v. Texas & P. Ry. Co. (C. C.) 216 Fed. 225; Central of Georgia R. Co. v. Railroad Commission of Alabama (C. C.) 161 Fed. 925; Consolidated Gas Co. v. New York (C. C.) 157 Fed. 849; Ex parte Wood (C. C.) 155 Fed. 190; Bonnett v. Vallier, 136 Wis. 193, 116 N. W. 885, 17 L. R. A. (N. S.) 486, 128 Am. St. Rep. 1061.

[74] United States v. Surprise Five, Ten, and Nineteen Cent Store (June, 1913), Treasury Decisions No. 1864.

Ct. 441 [52 L. Ed. 714, 13 L. R. A. (N. S.) 932, 14 Ann. Cas. 764], must not be pressed too far. In that case the penalties were not less than $5,000 for every passenger carried at more than two cents a mile. By the time the cause could be finally determined, the aggregate of fines would have destroyed the carrier. The court thought that the measures actually operated—and perhaps were designed—to prevent any contest. The penalties here are not disproportionate to an enforcement of the act, and the minimum not unreasonable for an honest contest if it involves substantial interests." But it cannot be conceded that this single decision is sufficient to set the question at rest.

CHAPTER IV

CONSTRUCTION OF STATUTES IMPOSING TAXES

§ 61. Rule of Strict Construction

It is a rule sanctioned by many authorities, and particularly with reference to the revenue laws of the United States, that a statute imposing taxes is to be construed strictly against the government and in favor of the taxpayer, and that no person and no property is to be included within its scope unless explicitly placed there by the clear language of the statute, and no heavier burdens imposed than the plain meaning of its terms will warrant.[1] "It is a general rule, in the interpretation of all statutes levying taxes or duties upon subjects or citizens, not to extend their provisions by implication beyond the clear import of the language used, or to enlarge their operation so as to embrace matters not specifically pointed out, although standing upon a close analogy. In every case, therefore, of doubt, such statutes are construed most strongly against the government and in favor of the subjects or citizens, because burdens are not to be imposed, nor presumed to be imposed, beyond what the statute expressly and clearly imports."[2] "If the consideration thus given to the case still leaves the matter in doubt, there should be applied the well-settled rule that the citizen is exempt from taxation, unless the same is imposed by clear and un-

---

[1] American Net & Twine Co. v. Worthington, 141 U. S. 468, 12 Sup. Ct. 55, 35 L. Ed. 821; Benziger v. U. S., 192 U. S. 38, 24 Sup. Ct. 189, 48 L. Ed. 331; Spreckels Sugar Co. v. McClain, 192 U. S. 397, 24 Sup. Ct. 376, 48 L. Ed. 496; Eidman v. Martinez, 184 U. S. 578, 22 Sup. Ct. 515, 46 L. Ed. 697; Parkview Building & Loan Ass'n v. Herold (D. C.) 203 Fed. 876; Mutual Benefit Life Ins. Co. v. Herold (D. C.) 198 Fed. 199; Missouri, K. & T. Ry. Co. v. Meyer (D. C.) 204 Fed. 140; U. S. v. Wigglesworth, 2 Story, 369, Fed. Cas. No. 16,690; Rice v. U. S., 53 Fed. 910, 4 C. C. A. 104; U. S. v. Watts, 1 Bond, 580, Fed. Cas. No. 16,653; Powers v. Barney, 5 Blatchf. 202, Fed. Cas. No. 11,361; Vicksburg & M. R. Co. v. State, 62 Miss. 105; Matter of Will of Vassar, 127 N. Y. 1, 12, 27 N. E. 394; Anderson v. Morris & E. R. Co., 216 Fed. 83, 132 C. C. A. 327; Forty-Two Broadway Co. v. Anderson (D. C.) 209 Fed. 991; Lott v. Ross, 38 Ala. 156; Gill v. Bartlett, 224 Fed. 927, 140 C. C. A. 405.

[2] U. S. v. Wigglesworth, 2 Story, 369, Fed. Cas. No. 16,690. And see Jones v. U. S., 49 Ct. Cl. 408.

equivocal language, and that, if there is a fair doubt as to the construction of an act imposing taxation, the doubt should be resolved in favor of those upon whom the tax is sought to be laid." [3]

Applying these principles to the specific case of income taxation, the rule may be deduced that only those persons and corporations are subject to the payment of the income tax who are specially described in the statute authorizing it or clearly within the meaning of the general terms which it employs, and that if any substantial and reasonable doubt arises as to whether any particular fund or kind or class of gain or acquisition constitutes taxable "income" within the meaning of the law, it is to be resolved in favor of the taxpayer and not in favor of the government. And so the authorities hold.[4] Thus, in regard to the federal corporation tax law of 1909, it was said that this statute, "levying as it does a tax upon the citizen, must be strictly construed; it cannot be enlarged by construction to cover matters not clearly within its import. The question is not what Congress might have done or should have done, but what it actually did do. When this is ascertained, the duty of the court is accomplished." [5] Still, where the meaning of a legislative enactment is plain, there is no room for construction, and it cannot be narrowed by a process of interpretation. And the rule that internal revenue laws should be strictly construed is after all but a rule of construction, which must yield when the intent of the statute is manifest.[6]

§ 62. Retrospective Operation Not Favored

It is also a rule in the construction of statutes, well established upon the authorities, that words in a statute ought not to be given a retrospective operation, unless they are so clear, strong, and imperative in that direction that no other meaning can be assigned to them, or unless the evident intention of the legislature cannot otherwise be satisfied; and this rule has been specifically applied in the interpretation of income tax laws.[7]

§ 63. Statutes in Pari Materia

It is a fundamental rule in the interpretation of statutes that acts in pari materia are to be read and construed together. And it has been said that this rule is specially applicable in the case of revenue laws, which, though made up of independent enactments, are re-

---

[3] Parkview Building & Loan Ass'n v. Herold (D. C.) 203 Fed. 876.

[4] Forman v. Board of Assessors, 35 La. Ann. 825; Lining v. Charleston, 1 McCord (S. C.) 345; Robson v. Regina, 4 Terr. Law Rep. (Canada) 80.

[5] Pennsylvania Steel Co. v. New York City Ry. Co., 198 Fed. 774, 117 C. C. A. 556.

[6] In re Hawley (D. C.) 220 Fed. 372.

[7] Lynch v. Turrish, 236 Fed. 653, 149 C. C. A. 649.

garded as one system, in which the construction of any separate act may be aided by the examination of other provisions which compose the system.[8] And it is not necessary to the application of this rule that the earlier act should still continue in force. Although it may have expired by its own limitation, or although it may have been expressly or impliedly repealed, still it is to be considered and read as explanatory of the later enactment.[9] It has been held, however, in one case, that where a personal tax law imposes a tax on a certain occupation, without defining it, it is doubtful whether the court, in construing it, can look to old and repealed tax laws, which define such occupation, to ascertain the legislative meaning.[10] It has been held that all the successive acts of Congress, from 1861 to 1867, imposing income taxes, are in pari materia, and are to be construed as one continuous enactment.[11] And of course this doctrine may be expanded so as to include the acts of Congress of 1894, 1909, 1913, and 1916. And it follows that it will be a legitimate mode of construing the present income tax law, in cases where its language in relation to a particular point or subject is obscure, confusing, or unintelligible, to compare it with the corresponding provisions on the same point in the earlier acts, which may be more clear and precise, and to presume that Congress intended its words to be understood in the same sense as before, unless there is such a distinct change of language as to compel the inference that a change in legislation was certainly intended.

§ 64. Associated Words and Phrases

It is another ancient and fundamental rule in the construction of statutes that the meaning of a doubtful word or phrase may be ascertained by reference to the meaning of other words or phrases with which it is associated, and that, where several things are referred to, they are presumed to be of the same class, when connected by a copulative conjunction, unless a contrary intent plainly appears. For example, all the acts of Congress on the subject of income taxation, from 1862 to the present time, have associated together the words "gains," "profits," and "income" as descriptive of the subject taxed, and the same is true of the income tax laws of some of the states. These words may be traced far back in the history of English taxation. The original income tax law of that country, enacted in 1799, imposed a tax on "income" by that name, but the acts of 1842 and 1853 introduced the associated terms "prof-

[8] U. S. v. Collier, 3 Blatchf. 325, Fed. Cas. No. 14,833.

[9] King v. Loxdale, 1 Burr. 445; Southern Ry. Co. v. McNeill (C. C.) 155 Fed. 756.

[10] Lockwood v. District of Columbia, 24 App. D. C. 569.

[11] U. S. v. Smith, 1 Sawy. 277, Fed. Cas. No. 16,341.

its and gains," whence they were apparently borrowed by Congress in framing the act of 1862, and have since persisted in use. Applying the rule above stated, we are justified in asserting the following principles as applicable to the interpretation of the phrase in question: If it is doubtful whether or not a particular fund or acquisition is taxable as "income," under the statute, it is not taxable unless it is income in the nature of "gain" or "profit." If any item is clearly included in the description of "gains" yet it is not taxable unless it is a gain in the nature of "income" or "profit." And although the disputed item may be certainly a "profit," in one sense of the word, yet it is not taxable unless it be a profit accruing by way of "gain" or "income."

§ 65. Departmental Construction

The executive and administrative officers of the government are bound to give effect to the laws which regulate their duties and define the sphere of their activities, and in so doing, they must necessarily put their own construction upon such acts. Particularly when a new statute goes into effect, if it shall be found to contain obscurities, ambiguities, or words or phrases of doubtful meaning, the necessity of carrying it into practical operation will compel these officers to resolve doubts and put an interpretation upon the statute, at least provisionally. When questions concerning the meaning or scope of the law shall have been submitted to the courts and judicially decided, the officers of the executive department will of course be bound to accept and abide by those decisions. And the officers of the United States Treasury Department feel themselves obliged to accept and defer to the opinions rendered by the Attorney General, though this may involve the reversal of their own previous rulings. But in advance of such judicial constructions or official advice, the administrative officers must interpret the statutes for themselves and to the best of their own abilities.[12] Hence it may often happen, and in connection with revenue laws no less than other classes of statutes, that the courts, when called upon to decide cases involving questions of construction, will have their attention directed to a uniform practical construction put upon such acts by the executive officers for their own guidance, and under which official action has been regulated and rights fixed. This practical construction is in no case binding on the courts. But it has come to be a well-settled rule that great weight should be given to the construction placed upon a statute whose meaning is doubtful by the department charged with its execution, and that if such construction has been made the basis of constant and uniform

[12] U. S. v. Lytle, 5 McLean, 9, Fed. Cas. No. 15,652.

practice on the part of the administrative officers, especially for a considerable period of time, and has been generally acquiesced in, not having been challenged by suit or other legal proceedings, it ought not to be departed from by the courts unless there are very strong reasons for so doing.[13] But the reasons for this rule do not rest upon any supposed authority on the part of officers to interpret the statute, but upon the practical considerations which should deter the courts from upsetting an established rule or custom. Hence, if the statute to be construed is a recent one, so that official action cannot be seriously deranged, nor private rights be very much affected, by a change in its interpretation, the mere fact that administrative officers have begun to read it in a certain way or to base their actions under it upon a certain interpretation, will have very little weight or influence with the courts.[14] And it has been held that the construction given to an internal revenue act by the Commissioner of Internal Revenue, though officially published, is not a construction of so much weight or dignity that a re-enactment of the statute subsequent to the construction is to be regarded as a legislative adoption of that construction, particularly where the result would be to raise a conflict between different parts of the statute or between a proviso and the body of the act.[15]

[13] U. S. v. Cerecedo Hermanos y Compania, 209 U. S. 337, 28 Sup. Ct. 532, 52 L. Ed. 821; Robertson v. Downing, 127 U. S. 607, 8 Sup. Ct. 1328, 32 L. Ed. 269; U. S. v. Healey, 160 U. S. 136, 16 Sup. Ct. 247, 40 L. Ed. 369; Stuart v. Laird, 1 Cranch, 299, 2 L. Ed. 115.

[14] Ewing v. Ainger, 97 Mich. 381, 56 N. W. 767; Employers' Liability Assur. Co. v. Com'rs of Insurance, 64 Mich. 614, 31 N. W. 542.

[15] Dollar Sav. Bank v. U. S., 19 Wall. 227, 22 L. Ed. 80.

CHAPTER V

WHAT CONSTITUTES TAXABLE INCOME

§ 66. General Definitions of Income

"Income" is defined as that gain which proceeds from labor, business, property, or capital of any kind, as, the produce of a farm, the rent of houses, the proceeds of professional business, the profits of commerce or of occupation, or the interest of money or stock in funds, etc.; revenue; salary; especially the annual receipts of a private person or a corporation from property.[1] It means that which comes into or is received from any business or investment of capital, without reference to the outgoing expenditures; when applied to the affairs of individuals, the term expresses the same idea that "revenue" does when applied to the affairs of a nation or state.[2] The term "income," as used in a statute providing that no income derived from property subject to taxation shall be taxed, "means the income for the year and is the result of the year's business. It is the net result of many combined influences—the use of the capital invested; the personal labor and services of the members of the firm, and the skill and ability with which they lay in, and from time to time renew, their stock; the carefulness and good judgment with which they sell and give credit; and the foresight and address with which they hold themselves prepared for the fluctuations and contingencies affecting the general commerce and business of the government. To express it in a more summary and comprehensive form, it is the creation of capital, industry, and skill."[3] Again, as this term is used in statutes relating to the nature and ownership of property, it includes the rents and profits of real estate, interest on money, dividends on stock, and other produce of personal property.[4] Particularly, when applied to a sum of money, or to money invested in public or corporate securities, income means interest.[5]

But an important distinction must be noted in the signification of this word, according as it is used in the ordinary business affairs of the community (or in statutes relating thereto) or in a tax statute. In the former case, it is understood to mean "net" income or profit; in the latter case, it is equivalent to "gross" income or "gross receipts," unless otherwise specified in the statute. Thus, it is said that the word "income," as used in commerce and trade, means the balance of gain over loss in the fiscal year or other period of computation, or it is the ultimate profit of a business or trade, ascertained by placing the sum total of gains over against

[1] Mundy v. Van Hoose, 104 Ga. 292, 30 S. E. 783; Sowards v. Taylor, 42 Ill. App. 275; Remington v. Field, 16 R. I. 509, 17 Atl. 551; Thorn v. De Breteuil, 86 App. Div. 405, 83 N. Y. Supp. 849. "Income" may be defined as the gain derived from capital, from labor, or from both combined. Connecticut General Life Ins. Co. v. Eaton (D. C.) 218 Fed. 188.

[2] Bates v. Porter, 74 Cal. 224, 15 Pac. 732; People v. Board of Sup'rs of Niagara County, 4 Hill (N. Y.) 20; Mundy v. Van Hoose, 104 Ga. 292, 30 S. E. 783.

[3] Wilcox v. Middlesex County Com'rs, 103 Mass. 544.

[4] Rev. Codes N. Dak., 1899, § 3322; Civ. Code S. Dak., 1903, § 238; Civ. Code Cal., 1903, § 748.

[5] Sims' Appeal, 44 Pa. 345; Pearson v. Chace, 10 R. I. 455.

the sum total of losses.[6] So, "the income of an estate means nothing more than the profit it will yield after deducting the charges of management, or the rent which may be obtained for the use of it. The rents and profits of an estate, the income, or the net income of it, are all equivalent expressions." [7]. So, in a statute providing that a certain railroad company shall be required to make an annual payment from its income to the sinking fund, to aid in the construction of the road, the word "income" must be construed as meaning the amount of money remaining to the corporation on making up its annual account, after deducting from all its receipts the necessary expense of repairs and management, and also the amount of interest on the debt of the commonwealth which the corporation is bound to pay in behalf of the commonwealth.[8] So in a railroad mortgage providing that, until default, the mortgagor shall remain in possession and operate the road and take the tolls, rents, and income, and apply them to the payment of current expenses, the term "income" means what is left after paying the expenses of earning income.[9]

But on the other hand, in a statute imposing taxes, "income" means gross receipts, not net profits, unless it is so specified. Whenever the law means to tax the clear profits arising from the employment of capital or otherwise, the expression used is "net income" or "net annual income." [10] And especially the phrase "whole income" means the aggregate of all receipts without any deduction for expenses or losses, that is, it means gross receipts and not net profits.[11] But if this word is associated with the term "profits," as in the phrase "gains, profits, and income," it may take color from the more restricted term and be limited by it. That is to say, in the phrase quoted, the word "income" should not be taken in its most extensive signification, but as meaning income which is in the nature of a profit, in other words, net income. But it must be admitted that there is some authority to the contrary.[12]

Unless limited by the context, however, the word "income" is one of very broad and comprehensive meaning. Thus, in a constitutional provision that no municipal corporation shall be-

[6] City of Kingston v. Canada Life Assur. Co., 19 Ontario, 453.
[7] Andrews v. Boyd, 5 Greenl. (5 Me.) 199.
[8] Opinion of Justices, 5 Metc. (Mass.) 596.
[9] Poland v. Lamoille Valley R. Co., 52 Vt. 144, 177.
[10] People v. Supervisors of New York, 18 Wend. (N. Y.) 605; Wells v. Shook, Fed. Cas. No. 17,406.
[11] Lawless v. Sullivan, 3 Can. Supr. Ct. 117.
[12] See Morton's Ex'rs v. Morton's Ex'r, 112 Ky. 706, 66 S. W. 641.

come indebted in any one year for a greater amount than its income, unless with the consent of two-thirds of the voters, the word income means income derived from any and all sources, and not that derived from taxation alone.[13] But it cannot be too strongly insisted upon that the word "income," when properly used, is applicable only to receipts in cash. When a bond which was purchased at a discount reaches par in the market, the owner cannot properly be said to have made a profit; he is in a position where he can realize a profit if he sells the bond, but not otherwise. If he sells, then the sum gained may constitute a part of his income, but it cannot be so described while he continues to hold the security. So, the farmer's crop is not his income; it is the source from which his income will be derived when it is converted into cash. So, a sum which is due as interest on a note, but which remains uncollected at the end of the year, may be reckoned as a part of the year's income, as a matter of bookkeeping, but it is not properly described as income until it is received, that is, it is "income" when it comes in, but not while it remains outstanding. This rule may perhaps be relaxed so far as to admit an exception in the case of certain items which are received as the equivalent of money and which are readily convertible into cash. And the Treasury Department rules that the exchange of interest coupons for funding bonds is a payment of interest on the bonds and the income tax should be imposed and paid upon such interest as income for the year in which it matures and such payment is made. (T. D. 2090, Dec. 14, 1914.) But the principle is, as ruled in an English case, that nothing is to be considered as income except what represents value in money, that is, either money or something that is equivalent to money because it can be converted into money and the proceeds expended in any way the recipient may please. In this case, speaking of the income tax of that country, it was said: "It is a tax on income in the proper sense of the word. It is a tax on what comes in, on actual receipts, not on what saves his pocket, but on what goes into his pocket." [14] Of course it is entirely within the power of a legislature having jurisdiction to lay an income tax to make the word "income" include items which are not at all proper to be described under that name. But then those items are taxed, not because they constitute income, but because the legislature has said that they shall be taxed. And on the other hand, when

---

[13] Lamar Water & Electric Light Co. v. City of Lamar, 128 Mo. 188, 26 S. W. 1025, 31 S. W. 756, 32 L. R. A. 157.

[14] Tenant v. Smith [1892] App. Cas. 150.

the word "income" is clearly defined in the act imposing the tax, it cannot be taken to include anything which is not within that definition.[15]

We conclude therefore that, for the purpose of an income tax, a proper definition of the word "income" would be all that a man receives in cash during the year, except such sums as are merely capital or principal in a changed form, that is, excluding sums which are merely the proceeds of some other form of capital converted into cash. This last point is emphasized in a recent decision of one of the federal courts, in which it was said: "What does the word 'income' mean? In ordinary speech, people recognize a difference between capital and income. I believe that the ordinary meaning attached to income, when it is not derived from personal exertion, is that it is something produced by capital without impairing that capital, and which leaves the property intact, and that nothing can be called income, for the purpose of this act, which takes away from the property itself. If it does, then it ceases to be income and amounts to a sale of capital assets."[16] Further, in order that money received by a particular person should constitute part of his income, it is necessary that it should belong to him and be received by him for his own use and benefit. But it is not a necessary part of the definition that he should have the right or power freely to dispose of it as he may will. Thus, money received in annual payments, and which otherwise would clearly be income, is not deprived of that character by the fact that part of it is predestined, by agreement, to be put into a sinking fund to meet obligations maturing in the future.[17] And where a traveling salesman is allowed a certain sum per month by his employers to cover his expenses, the money is properly included by the assessor as part of his taxable income.[18]

§ 67. Statutory Definitions of Income

The income tax act now in force carefully defines taxable income for its own purposes. In the provisions relating to the individual taxpayer, we find the following: "Subject only to such exemptions and deductions as are hereinafter allowed, the net income of a taxable person shall include gains, profits, and income derived

[15] City of New Orleans v. Hart, 14 La. Ann. 803; City of New Orleans v. Fassman, 14 La. Ann. 865.

[16] Sargent Land Co. v. Von Baumbach (D. C.) 207 Fed. 423.

[17] Nizam State Ry. Co. v. Wyatt, L. R. 24 Q. B. Div. 548.

[18] In re Assessment of Taxes, 16 Hawaii, 796.

from salaries, wages, or compensation for personal service of whatever kind and in whatever form paid, or from professions, vocations, businesses, trade, commerce, or sales, or dealings in property, whether real or personal, growing out of the ownership or use of or interest in real or personal property, also from interest, rent, dividends, securities, or the transaction of any business carried on for gain or profit, or gains or profits and income derived from any source whatever." (Act Cong. Sept. 8, 1916, § 2a [U. S. Comp. St. 1916, § 6336b].) But some kinds or items of income (which otherwise would be taxable) are exempted from the tax, the provision being as follows: "The following income shall be exempt from the provisions of this title: The proceeds of life insurance policies paid to individual beneficiaries upon the death of the insured; the amount received by the insured, as a return of premium or premiums paid by him under life insurance, endowment, or annuity contracts, either during the term or at the maturity of the term mentioned in the contract or upon the surrender of the contract; the value of property acquired by gift, bequest, devise, or descent (but the income from such property shall be included as income); interest upon the obligations of a State or any political subdivision thereof or upon the obligations of the United States or its possessions or securities issued under the provisions of the Federal farm loan Act of July seventeenth, nineteen hundred and sixteen; the compensation of the present President of the United States during the term for which he has been elected, and the judges of the Supreme and inferior courts of the United States now in office, and the compensation of all officers and employees of a State, or any political subdivision thereof, except when such compensation is paid by the United States Government." (Idem, § 4 [U. S. Comp. St. 1916, § 6336d].) Finally, before fixing the amount of income on which the tax is to be paid, the individual taxpayer is entitled to claim certain deductions, for the expenses of his business, for interest paid on his indebtedness, for taxes paid, for uncompensated losses sustained, for bad debts written off as worthless, and for the depreciation of property (Idem, § 5a [U. S. Comp. St. 1916, § 6336e]); and he is allowed a "credit" for such portion of his income (up to $20,000) as consists of dividends received on corporate stock (Idem, § 5b); and he is allowed a personal exemption of a certain minimum amount of income on which the tax does not fall. (Idem, § 7a [U. S. Comp. St. 1916, § 6336g].)

In the case of corporations, they are taxable "upon the total net income received in the preceding calendar year from all sources," after making the deductions specifically allowed by the statute. (Idem, §§ 10, 12 [U. S. Comp. St. 1916, §§ 6336j, 6336l].)

§ 68. "Income," "Profits," and "Gains" Compared

"Profit" is the gain made on any business or investment when both the receipts and expenditures are taken into consideration.[19] It is the amount of acquisition beyond expenditure, the excess of value received for producing or selling over and above cost.[20] It represents the net gain made from an investment, or from the prosecution of any business, after the payment of all expenses incurred.[21] In the common acceptation of the term, "profit" is the benefit or advantage remaining after all costs, charges, and expenses have been deducted, because until then, and while anything remains uncertain, it is impossible to say whether or not there has been a profit.[22] Or, according to a fuller description given by the Supreme Court of California, the word "profits" signifies an excess of the value of returns over the value of advances; the excess of receipts over expenditures; that is, net earnings. In commerce it means the advance in the price of goods sold beyond the cost of purchase. In distinction from the wages of labor, it is well understood to imply the net return to the capital or stock employed after deducting all the expenses, including not only the wages of those employed by the capitalist, but the wages of the capitalist himself for superintending the employment of his capital stock. Profits are divided by writers on political economy into gross and net; the former being the entire difference between the value of advances and

[19] Providence Rubber Co. v. Goodyear, 9 Wall. 788, 19 L. Ed. 566; People v. San Francisco Sav. Union, 72 Cal. 199, 13 Pac. 498; Taylor v. Harwell, 65 Ala. 1; Mayer v. Nethersole, 71 App. Div. 383, 75 N. Y. Supp. 987.

[20] Mundy v. Van Hoose, 104 Ga. 292, 30 S. E. 783; Curry v. Charles Warner Co., 2 Marv. (Del.) 98, 42 Atl. 425; Bates v. Porter, 74 Cal. 224, 15 Pac. 732; People v. Niagara County Sup'rs, 4 Hill (N. Y.) 20.

[21] Goodhart v. Pennsylvania R. Co., 177 Pa. 1, 35 Atl. 191, 55 Am. St. Rep. 705. "Profits must be taken to mean that which the mine-owner in any given year puts into his pocket, or could, if he chose, put into his pocket, minus the expenditure. He cannot go back and take into account the profit and loss account for a series of previous years. Thus, if a man works his mine at a loss for ten years, and in the eleventh year makes a profit over expenditures, he cannot set off against that profit the antecedent expenses and losses during the years in which he worked at a loss. It would be impracticable to do so. Income taxes upon profits could not be assessed without going into an inquiry embracing the whole history of the particular undertaking from its inception." Broughton & Plas Power Coal Co. v. Kirkpatrick, L. R. 14 Q. B. Div. 491.

[22] Mackey v. Millar, 6 Phila. (Pa.) 527.

(84)

the value of returns, and the latter so much of this diference as arises exclusively from the capital employed. Profits cannot consist of earnings never yet received.[23] So, the term "profits" as used in a statute imposing a tax of five per cent on all profits of railroad and canal companies, refers to the profits arising from the operation of the railroad or canal, but without deduction of interest paid to its bondholders or dividends paid to its stockholders, that is, the excess of receipts over expenses of operation.[24] But the surplus earnings of a corporation over and above all expenses are taxable as "profits," notwithstanding that it is required by law to appropriate all such surplus to a particular purpose (as, to a sinking fund) and to no other.[25]

It is said, and with truth, that this term is often used as synonymous with "income" and as meaning the same thing, and particularly where the two words are coupled in the same phrase.[26] And one court has remarked that, when they are thus joined together, there is no difference in the meaning of the words, and the use of them both is only due to a lawyer-like fondness for using several words where one would be sufficient.[27] But this is scarcely correct. There is a substantial difference in the meaning of the two words. And it is more accurate to say that, when they are joined together in the same phrase, the word "profits" is used to particularize and point out one kind of income, or income derived from a particular source; and it will generally be found that their joinder is easily explained from their correlation with other descriptive words in the same sentence, as, for example, where "gains" may be correlated with "sales or dealings in property," "income" with such words as "salaries" and earnings from "professions and vocations," and "profits" with "business, trade, and commerce." Besides, "income" is clearly a word of larger import than "profits." The former term may very properly include such items as the rent of houses, interest on investments, the earnings of a professional man, or the salary of an officer of a corporation, but none of these could with any propriety be called "profits." In effect, the latter term is more appropriately confined to gains resulting from the operations of

---

[23] People v. San Francisco Sav. Union, 72 Cal. 199, 13 Pac. 498.

[24] Sioux City & P. R. Co. v. U. S., 110 U. S. 205, 3 Sup. Ct. 565, 28 L. Ed. 120.

[25] Mersey Docks & Harbour Board v. Lucas, 51 Law J. Q. B. 114, 1 Tax Cas. 385, affirmed L. R. 8 App. Cas. 891.

[26] Bates v. Porter, 74 Cal. 224, 15 Pac. 732; Burt v. Rattle, 31 Ohio St. 116, 130.

[27] In re Clark, 62 Hun, 275, 17 N. Y. Supp. 93.

trade or commerce, and especially from mercantile or manufactur-' ing business or transportation. Moreover, it is important not to lose sight of the distinction that, while "income" means that which comes in or is received from any business or investment of capital, without reference to the outgoing expenditures, "profit" means the gain which is made upon any business or investment when both receipts and payments are taken into account.[28]

It is not quite so easy to account for the use of the word "gain" in conjunction with the two other terms which we have been considering. But it may probably be said that when a tax law employs the phrase "gains, profits, and income," to describe what is taxable, the term "gains" is inserted out of abundant caution, and intended to include an acquisition of the taxpayer which is not to be described as a "profit," and which might not be included in the term "income" if that word were taken in a narrow sense. Properly speaking, "gain" means that which is acquired or comes as a benefit,[29] and in a statute laying an income tax it may mean money received within the year which is not the fruit of a business transaction nor of the labor or exertion of the individual, but something arising from fortuitous circumstances. or conditions which he does not control. In this signification, the term would include money received as a legacy or money won on a wager.

§ 69. Income Derived from "Any Source Whatever"

It should be noticed that the act of Congress directs that the net income of taxable persons shall include, besides several enumerated sources of revenue, "gains or profits and income derived from any source whatever." It is probable that the latter phrase is to be taken in a wide and general sense, and not as being in any way limited by the enumeration preceding it. This question arose recently in Virginia, where the classification under the schedule authorizing income taxes first provides for the taxation of incomes from certain specified sources, and then for the taxation of "all other gains and profits derived from any source whatever." In defense to an action by the state against a certain attorney at law, to recover a tax on his income derived from the practice of his profession, it was contended that the clause quoted came within the doctrine of "ejusdem generis," and therefore must .be limited to incomes derived from sources of the same kind as those enumerated in the previous clauses of the schedule, and that it did not include incomes

---

28 In re Murphy, 80 App. Div. 288, 80 N. Y. Supp. 530.
29 Thorn v. De Breteuil, 86 App. Div. 405, 83 N. Y. Supp. 849.

from licensed professions, trades, or businesses.` But the Supreme Court of the state held that this broad language would be in a large measure nullified by limiting its operation to income derived not from "any source whatever," but only from sources similar to those embraced in the enumerated classes; and it was held to apply to the professional incomes of lawyers as well as to those specifically enumerated.[30]

§ 70. Change or Substitution of Capital Distinguished

Both in popular and legal parlance, "income" is distinguished from "capital" or "principal;" and in the tax laws the word "income" is used in contradistinction to property and invested capital, and it does not include receipts from the conversion, without profit, of property into money, or vice versa, or any receipts involved in a transaction which is properly speaking a replacement of capital or a substitution of capital in one form for capital in another form.[31] Thus, for instance, a lumber company, in its return of net income for taxation, is entitled to deduct, as capital assets, the market value of the standing timber from which the lumber sold during the year was manufactured, for that portion of the money received for the lumber which represents the value of the timber is not income, but a replacement of capital.[32] On the same principle, a sum of money received from a railroad company in payment of damages for a part of a person's land taken by the railroad for its use is not income; it is a substituted capital.[33] And where one sells real property on terms contemplating the payment of a certain sum at once, and the remainder in equal semiannual installments extending over a period of several years, the installments are not gains or profits, but the replacement of capital, and they are not subject to taxation under the income tax, nor is the debtor authorized to deduct from them for the tax.[34] So, where the purchase price of property is payable in a number of annual installments, each including not only a proportionate part of the actual price but also a sum as interest on the unpaid installments, the part which represents capital must be separated from that which rep-

[30] Commonwealth v. Werth, 116 Va. 604, 82 S. E. 695, Ann. Cas. 1916D, 1263.

[31] Von Baumbach v. Sargent Land Co., 219 Fed. 32, 134 C. C. A. 649; Biwabik Min. Co. v. U. S. (C. C. A.) 242 Fed. 9.

[32] Mitchell Bros. Co. v. Doyle (D. C.) 225 Fed. 437.

[33] Gibson v. Cooke, 1 Metc. (Mass.) 75.

[34] Foley v. Fletcher, 3 Hurl. & N. 769.

employer, is taxable as a part of his income.[46]   Thus the pay of an army officer on the retired list is "income" and is taxable as such.[47]   And in respect to a salary derived from any source, it is immaterial that its amount is uncertain or varies from time to time, or that it depends on the extent of the services actually rendered or the amount of business done, or that it may include commissions on sales.[48]   A locomotive engineer who earns more than the statutory minimum is taxable, although he is not paid a fixed salary but so much for every mile run.[49]   It is ruled by the Treasury Department that a person receiving an annual salary, and, in addition, a percentage commission on all sales, the exact amount due on account of commissions not being determinable until a month or more after the close of the year in which the commissions were earned, at which time both his salary for the preceding year and his commissions are paid to him, should return as income, for the year in which payment was made, the aggregate amount received on account of salary and commissions.   And where an employee is paid a sum equal to two years' salary on condition that he surrender his contract of employment, such sum should be reported by him on his annual return as income.   And where a service and payment period is divided by the end of a taxable year, the compensation for the period so divided at the end of the year will be accounted for in the return for the year in which payment is made and received.   But where the service is of such a nature as to be compensated by fee, or such that no portion of the amount becomes due until the service is completed, then the total amount of the compensation should be included in the return for the year in which the compensation is received.   (T. D. 2090, Dec. 14, 1914.)

In regard to allowances made to a salaried officer, in addition to his salary, to cover subsistence, traveling expenses, quarters, and the like, the Treasury Department rules that where an individual is furnished living quarters in addition to his salary, the rental value thereof is to be regarded a part of his compensation and is taxable as income; that the difference between the amount received as mileage and the amount of actual necessary expenses in-

---

[46] White v. Koehler, 70 N. J. Law, 526, 57 Atl. 124.

[47] In re Ward [1897] 1 Q. B. 266.

[48] In cases where officers or employees of a corporation are paid a stated salary, to which is added a percentage of the profits of the corporation, as compensation for services rendered, the company must report the amount of such combined payments made during the year, that the income tax may be assessed thereon.   (T. D. 2152, Feb. 12, 1915.)

[49] Attorney General v. Ostrum [1904] App. Cas. 144.

curred on a journey must be returned as income; that the difference between the amount received as a per diem allowance in lieu of subsistence while traveling under orders and the amount of actual necessary expense incurred is also returnable as income; and the same rule is applied to commutation of quarters and the money equivalent of quarters furnished in kind; but that amounts paid by the government, in the nature of reimbursement for subsistence and other items of actual expense incurred while absent on business for the government, are not required to be returned as income. (T. D. 2090, Dec. 14, 1914.)

It should also be observed that although a particular corporation may be of such a character as to be exempt from the income tax, yet the salaries which it pays to its officers or employees are not for that reason exempt, but are taxable to them as income. (T. D. 2090, Dec. 14, 1914.) For this reason, the salary received by the rector of a church or by a professor in a college is not exempt, though the corporation paying the salary is exempt.

§ 76. Insurance Agents' Commissions

The commissions retained by an insurance agent out of premiums paid on the policies which he writes for his company are part of his taxable income, and this applies to a commission so retained by the agent on his own life insurance policy. (T. D. 2137, Jan. 30, 1915.) An agent's commissions on renewal premiums on insurance are income when received, and income for the period in which received. (T. D. 2011, July 28, 1914.) In a case in which this subject was considered it appeared that, by the contract between an insurance company and an agent, he was to receive as compensation for soliciting insurance certain specified percentages of the premiums paid on policies written through his solicitation for the first and subsequent years for 20 years from the date of each policy, the contract providing that the commissions should accrue only as the premiums were paid to the company, and that the liability for any particular commission should terminate if the policy ceased to be in force. It was held that the specified percentages of premiums for the second and subsequent years of the life of policies, issued prior to the enactment of the income tax law, constituted income which accrued when such premiums were paid, and were taxable as such. It was also held that the liability of the agent's percentage of such premiums to the income tax was not affected by the fact that the agent hired subagents and maintained an office force, and that his percentage to some extent represented merely

(93)

deferred returns, which he had already anticipated and partially expended for office expenses.[50]

§ 77. Earnings from Professions and Trades

The earnings of professional men, such as lawyers, physicians, surgeons, clergymen, engineers, architects, authors, actors, singers, and others derived from their professional employment, constitute taxable income, if sufficient in amount to come within the terms of the statute, even though not specifically mentioned in it. Thus, a lawyer's professional earnings are taxable as income, and it is not a case of double taxation though he is also compelled to pay a license fee for the privilege of practising his profession.[51] So, the income of a clergyman or minister includes not only his fixed salary, but also occasional fees received for weddings, funerals, masses, and other professional services, though not outright donations from his parishioners or others. (T. D. 2090, Dec. 14, 1914.) And in all ordinary cases, whatever accrues to the taxpayer as compensation for his personal exertion or endeavor will be taxable as income, no matter what may be the nature of his employment or pursuit. In an English case, it was held that betting on horse races, when carried on systematically and annually and as the person's chief or only way of gaining money, is a "vocation" within the income tax law, and he must pay on his winnings, if any.[52]

§ 78. Pensions, Subsidies, and Gifts

Under the English law it is held that the pension of a retired judge or other public officer, though voted annually by the legislative authority, is taxable as income.[53] But a pension not granted by the government, but by a private individual or society, as a purely voluntary gift, and without any legal claim upon the donor, in recognition of meritorious past services or for other such reasons, is not a "profit or gain arising from any kind of property" or from "any profession, trade, employment, or vocation," and is therefore not assessable as income of the recipient.[54] On the other hand, it was held that, where a corporation establishes a pension or benefit fund for its employés, requiring each of them to become a

[50] Edwards v. Keith (D. C.) 224 Fed. 585, affirmed 231 Fed. 110, 145 C. C. A. 298.
[51] Commonwealth v. Werth, 116 Va. 604, 82 S. E. 695, Ann. Cas. 1916D, 1263.
[52] Partridge v. Mallandaine, L. R. 18 Q. B. Div. 276.
[53] Ex parte Huggins, L. R. 21 Ch. Div. 85.
[54] Turner v. Cuxon, L. R. 22 Q. B. Div. 150.

subscriber and to contribute a certain percentage of his salary, but contributions are returnable (except where forfeited for fraud or dishonesty) either by way of a superannuation benefit, or in a lump sum with interest in case of death or retirement, the full salaries of the employés accrue to them and are assessable for the income tax, and not merely the amount received after deducting such contributions.[55] On similar principles it is held that a gift of money, raised by voluntary subscriptions, and made annually to a minister of religion by his congregation, is assessable as income, because made to him as a minister and in respect to the discharge of his duties in that office, which is an "employment" within the meaning of the statute.[56] But where a curate receives from a religious society a grant in money, renewable annually at discretion and on certain conditions, and the grant is in recognition of faithful services as a clergyman, but not in respect of the particular curacy which he holds, it is held that it is not taxable as income.[57] So where a portion of a collection made in church was given by way of an "Easter offering" to the incumbent of the parish by reason of his office, but the gift would not have been made had not the recipient, besides being the incumbent, also been poor, it was held that the money was not given as an additional remuneration for services, but on account of personal poverty, and was therefore not taxable.[58]

According to the doctrine of the English cases, a subsidy paid annually by a government is taxable as income of the recipient. This was ruled in a case where a company undertook to construct a railroad in Brazil under a government guaranty of seven per cent interest on the capital raised and devoted to the building of the road, and it was held taxable on the money received from the government.[59]

The federal income tax law includes "the income from, but not the value of, property acquired by gift, bequest, devise, or descent." And under this provision it is ruled that, where the monthly salary of an officer or employé is paid for a limited period after his death

---

[55] Hudson v. Gribble [1903] 1 K. B. 517, 4 Tax Cas. 522.

[56] In re Strong, 15 Scotch Law Rep. 704, 1 Tax Cas. 207; Blakiston v. Cooper [1909] App. Cas. 104; Herbert v. McQuade [1902] 2 K. B. 621, 4 Tax Cas. 489; Cooper v. Blakiston [1909] App. Cas. 104, 5 Tax Cas. 347.

[57] Turner v. Cuxon, L. R. 22 Q. B. Div. 150.

[58] Turton v. Cooper, 5 Tax Cas. 138. But see Cooper v. Blakiston [1909] App. Cas. 104, 5 Tax Cas. 347.

[59] Blake v. Imperial Brazilian Ry., 2 Tax Cas. 58. And see Pretoria-Pietersburg R. Co. v. Elgood, 98 Law T. 741.

to his widow, in recognition of the services rendered by her husband, but without the rendition of any services by the widow, such payment is a gratuity and exempt from the income tax. It is also ruled that if property acquired by gift, bequest, etc., is sold at a price greater than the appraised value at the time the property was acquired, the gain in value is income and is subject to the tax. (T. D. 2090, Dec. 14, 1914.) It should also be observed that this provision of the statute applies only to the case of individual taxpayers, not to corporations. Consequently, the value or amount of a gift, bequest, or devise to a corporation, is not exempt but is taxable as income of the corporation for the year in which it is received. (Idem.)

§ 79. Judgments for Money

No decisions have been found bearing on the question whether a judgment for money, the amount of which is paid to the creditor within the taxing year, is to be reckoned a part of his "income" for that year. If the cause of action were an injury to property or contract rights, it might be considered as, in some sense at least, a replacement of capital. If it were for services rendered, the amount of the judgment would clearly be "compensation," or even "salary" or "fees," though recovered by suit. But a judgment in an action of tort, as, for example, defamation of character or negligence causing personal injuries, would never be regarded as a part of one's income in the common acceptation of the term, and should not be brought within even the most extensive terms of the statute, since a broad and liberal construction in favor of the government is not the rule in such cases, but the reverse. But the Treasury Department rules that a sum of money received as the result of a suit or compromise for "pain and suffering" is to be accounted such income as would be taxable under the provisions of the law, since it includes "gains or profits and income derived from any source whatever." An amount thus received would be in its nature similar to an amount paid to a person insured by an accident insurance policy on account of an accident sustained. (T. D. 2135, Jan. 23, 1915.) And payments made to an injured employee by a corporation under the accident compensation laws in force in several of the states are held to constitute taxable income of the employee. (T. D. 2570, Nov. 6, 1917.)

§ 80. Proceeds of Life and Accident Insurance Policies

The income tax law specifically exempts "the proceeds of life insurance policies paid to individual beneficiaries upon the death of the insured," and also "the amount received by the insured, as a return of premiums paid by him under life insurance, endowment, or annuity contracts, either during the term or at the maturity of the term mentioned in the contract, or upon the surrender of the contract." (Act Cong. Sept. 8, 1916, § 4 [U. S. Comp. St. 1916, § 6336d].) But as to accident insurance, the ruling of the Treasury Department is as follows: "Money paid to a person insured by an accident insurance policy, on account of accidents sustained, is returnable as gross income by the insured person. The proceeds of accident insurance policies paid upon the death of the person insured to the beneficiaries is to be treated like the proceeds of life insurance policies." (T. D. 2135, Jan. 23, 1915.)

§ 81.　Legacies and Inheritances

The income tax act of 1916 expressly excludes from the taxable income of an individual "the value of property acquired by bequest, devise, or descent, but the income from such property shall be included as income." It is ruled that "the general policy of the law and the rule of interpretation require that legacies in all cases, unless clearly inconsistent with the intention of the testator, should be held to be vested rather than contingent; and where there is a vested interest, the income from such interest, whether distributed or not, is subject to the tax; and when in the hands of fiduciaries, they are required to account for and pay the tax thereon." (T. D. 2090, Dec. 14, 1914.) A legatee is required to return as income the full amount of interest received by him on a bond, notwithstanding the fact that a part of the first coupon, payable after he had received it, had been added to the bond and included in the gross estate of the decedent, thereby becoming subject to the estate-tax law. (T. D. 2570, Nov. 6, 1917.)

§ 82.　Products of Farming and Stock-Raising

The profit derived by a farmer or stock-raiser from the sale of the products of the farm or ranch, that is, the amount received on such sales less the cost of production, constitutes income taxable under the statute now in force.[60] But so much of the produce of a farm as is directly used and consumed by the farmer and his family is not to be reckoned as a part of his income, even though it might have been sold, if not so used, and a profit derived from it.[61]

---

[60] In re Laupahoehoe Sugar Co., 18 Hawaii, 206.

[61] Robertson v. Pratt, 13 Hawaii, 590; People v. Purdy, 58 Hun, 386, 12 N. Y. Supp. 307.

And grain or other crops or live stock remaining in the producer's possession and unsold at the end of the year are not to be reckoned as a part of the year's income. This is to be inferred from the fact that those statutes which have dealt specifically with the matter have not directed that the term "income" should include the amount of crops raised, etc., or the value of such productions, but only the "amount of sales" thereof after making the proper deductions.[62] But aside from this consideration, the rule is deducible from the general principle that a law taxing income does not apply to anything of value which, if sold, is capable of producing income, but which, remaining unsold, is to be regarded as principal or at most as a source of income.

The Treasury Department has issued a detailed set of regulations upon the subject of "income from farms and allowable deductions." These are as follows:

The term "farm" as herein used embraces the farm in the ordinarily accepted sense, plantations, ranches, stock farms, dairy farms, poultry farms, fruit farms, truck farms, and all lands used for similar purposes; and for the purposes of this decision, all persons who cultivate, operate, or manage farms for gain or profit. either as owners or tenants, are designated as "farmers."

All gains, profits, and income derived from the sale or exchange of farm products, whether produced on the farm or purchased and resold by the farmer, shall be included in the return of net income for the year in which the products were actually marketed and sold; and all allowable deductions, including the legitimate expense incident to the production of that year or future years, may be claimed in the return of income for the tax year in which the right to such deductions shall arise, although the products to which such expenses and deductions are incidental may not have been sold or exchanged for money, or a money equivalent, during the year for which the return is rendered.

Rents received in crop shares shall likewise be returned as of the year in which the crop shares are reduced to money or a money equivalent, and allowable deductions, likewise, shall be claimed in the return of income for the tax year to which they apply, although expenses and deductions may be incident to products which remained unsold at the end of the year for which the deductions are

62 See, for example. Acts Virginia 1902-3-4, c. 148, p. 155, as amended by Acts 1908, c. 10, p. 20; Act Cong. June 30, 1864, 13 Stat. 223 (the civil war income tax law.)

claimed. When farm products are held for favorable market prices, no deduction on account of shrinkage in weight or physical value, or losses by reason of such shrinkage or deterioration in storage, shall be allowed.

Cost of stock purchased for resale is an allowable deduction under the item of expense, but money expended for stock for breeding purposes is regarded as capital invested, and amounts so expended do not constitute allowable deductions except as hereinafter stated.

Where stock has been purchased for any purpose, and afterwards dies from disease or injury, or is killed by order of the authorities of a state or the United States, and the cost thereof has not been claimed as an item of expense, the actual purchase price of such stock, less any depreciation which may have been previously claimed, may be deducted as a loss. Property destroyed by order of the authorities of a state or of the United States may, in like manner, be claimed as a loss; but if reimbursement is made by a state or the United States, in whole or in part, on account of stock killed or property destroyed, the amount received shall be reported as income for the year in which reimbursement is made.

The cost of farm machinery is not an allowable deduction as an item of expense, but the cost of ordinary tools may be included under this item.

Under the deduction for "a reasonable allowance for the exhaustion, wear, and tear of the property arising out of its use or employment * * *," there may be claimed a reasonable allowance for depreciation on farm buildings (other than a dwelling occupied by the owner), farm machinery, and other physical property, including stock purchased for breeding purposes; but no claim for depreciation on stock raised or purchased for resale will be allowed.

Farmers who keep books according to some approved method of accounting, which clearly show the net income, may prepare their returns from such books, although the method of accounting may not be strictly in accordance with the provisions of this decision.

A person cultivating or operating a farm for recreation or pleasure, on a basis other than the recognized principles of commercial farming, the result of which is a continual loss from year to year, is not regarded as a farmer. In such cases, if the expenses incurred in connection with the farm are in excess of the receipts therefrom, the entire receipts from sale of products may be ignored in rendering a return of income, and the expenses incurred being regarded as personal expenses will not constitute allowable deductions in the return of income derived from other sources. (T. D. No. 2153, February 4, 1915.)

§ 83. Produce of Mines and Oil and Gas Wells

The owners of mines producing coal, gold, silver, or other minerals, or of nitrate beds or other similar natural deposits, or of oil or natural gas wells, are assessable for the income tax upon the net profits realized by the sale of their products in each year.[63] The argument has sometimes been advanced that as minerals in place constitute a part of the realty, and as the extraction of any given quantity leaves the investment of the owner worth just so much the less, the sale of mineral products should be regarded as a sale of capital assets, and not as income. Thus, in a case in Pennsylvania, an oil company, having all its capital invested in oil-producing property, and paying dividends entirely out of the products of its oil wells, resisted payment of an income tax assessed against it, claiming that it could have no taxable net income until the proceeds of its business had repaid all the capital invested, since, in view of the depletion of its sources of revenue, its dividends paid included not only earnings but also a portion of its capital returned in this way to the stockholders. But the court refused to accept this view, holding that all the income received by the company from its works, after deducting the operating expenses, was net income and taxable as such.[64] Moreover, this doctrine is well w..h-in the analogy and the reason of the well-known rule that in the case of mining companies, quarry companies, and the like, which have what is called a "wasting property," the payment of dividends to the stockholders out of the amount realized on the sale of their products is not regarded as an impairment of capital, nor are such companies required to create a sinking fund, out of earnings, before declaring dividends, to offset the gradual depletion of the property in which the capital is invested.[65]

[63] Stratton's Independence v. Howbert, 231 U. S. 399, 34 Sup. Ct. 136, 58 L. Ed. 285; Alianza Co. v. Bell [1906] App. Cas. 18; Rhymney Iron Co. v. Fowler [1896] 2 Q. B. 79, 3 Tax Cas. 476; Knowles v. McAdam, L. R. 3 Ex. Div. 23, 1 Tax Cas. 161; Arizona Copper Co. v. Smiles, 29 Scotch Law Rep. 134, 3 Tax Cas. 149; Stevens v. Durban-Roodepoort Gold Min. Co., 5 Tax Cas. 402; U. S. v. Nipissing Mines Co. (D. C.) 202 Fed. 803; Commonwealth v. Ocean Oil Co., 59 Pa. 61. See, also, Treasury Decisions Nos. 1754 and 1755.

[64] Commonwealth v. Ocean Oil Co., 59 Pa. 61. Compare Sargent Land Co. v. Von Baumbach (D. C.) 207 Fed. 423.

[65] People v. Roberts, 156 N. Y. 585, 51 N. E. 293; Excelsior Water & Min-

But there is a decision that where iron mines are located in a district where the mining is done by simple quarrying after the overlying surface has been stripped off, and the quantity of the ore in the ground can be measured with substantial accuracy, the selling price of ore mined and sold in any year, so far as it represents the actual value to the mining company of the ore in the ground on the date of the taking effect of the statute, is not income, whether the value of the company's interest in the ore in the ground is based upon the amount paid therefor, or upon a subsequent appreciation of its market value before the taxing law went into effect.[66]

But here, as in the case of agricultural products discussed in the preceding section, the measure of taxable net income is not the amount or value of the products of the year's operation, but the net proceeds of sales, and hence there should not be included any ores or other products remaining unsold at the close of the year. And conversely, the year's income is not measured by the year's production. For irrespective of the time when the particular ores were brought to the surface, their proceeds are taxable as income of the year in which they are sold. Nor should the estimate of income be made to include any part of the products of mines or wells which is used by the owner in the heating, lighting, or operation of his own plant, or otherwise consumed in aid of production. There is one decision which apparently contravenes this last statement. Under a state statute imposing a percentage tax on the "gross receipts from total production" of coal and other minerals, it was held that a railroad company is subject to the tax on coal mined by it on its properties, though the coal is not sold but used in the operation of the road.[67] But the court felt compelled to adopt this conclusion by a consideration of the context and the necessity of bringing the different provisions of the act into harmony and effective operation.

§ 84. Profits of Business or Trade

The income tax law specifies, among the sources of taxable income, profits arising from "business, trade, commerce, or sales." And the words "business" and "trade" are constantly associated in similar taxing statutes. These two words, when thus found in

ing Co. v. Pierce, 90 Cal. 131, 27 Pac. 44; Lee v. Neuchatel Asphalt Co., L. R. 41 Ch. Div. 1.

[66] Biwabik Min. Co. v. U. S. (C. C. A.) 242 Fed. 9.

[67] Missouri, K. & T. Ry. Co. v. Meyer (D. C.) 204 Fed. 140.

association, take color from each other. But even as thus limited, the term "business" is a word of very wide import and embraces everything about which a person can be employed, or which he can pursue as an occupation and for profit.[68] It implies, however, continuity of action or effort, and does not include an isolated act or operation, when transactions of the same sort do not constitute the person's vocation,[69] and probably it should not be so extended as to include illicit pursuits, such as keeping a gaming house or selling liquor without a license.[70] In construing the corporation tax law of 1909, the Supreme Court of the United States, not meaning to enumerate all possible kinds of "business," but with reference to the facts in the group of cases before it, said: "We think it clear that corporations organized for the purpose of doing business, and actually engaged in such activities as leasing property, collecting rents, managing office buildings, making investments of profits, or leasing ore lands and collecting royalties, managing wharves, dividing profits, and in some cases investing the surplus, are engaged in business within the meaning of this statute, and in the capacity necessary to make such organizations subject to the law." [71] And in the same case it was specifically held that a company owning and leasing taxicabs and collecting rents therefrom was engaged in business within the meaning of the statute. "Trade" is a term more particularly applied to the operations of commerce, and especially to the buying and selling of commodities or the traffic, sale, or barter of goods. But it is legitimately capable

---

[68] People v. Com'rs of Taxes, 22 How. Prac. (N. Y.) 143.

[69] People v. Commissioners of Taxes, 23 N. Y. 242; Parkhurst v. Brock, 72 Vt. 355, 47 Atl. 1068; Delaware & H. Canal Co. v. Mahlenbrock, 63 N. J. Law, 281, 43 Atl. 978, 45 L. R. A. 538; Cooper Mfg. Co. v. Ferguson, 113 U. S. 727, 5 Sup. Ct. 739, 28 L. Ed. 1137; Anderson v. Morris & E. R. Co., 216 Fed. 83, 132 C. C. A. 327. But the doing of a single act of business may constitute the doing of business, when accompanied by a purpose to perform other like acts of business. Dayton & W. Traction Co. v. Gilligan (U. S. Dist. Ct. S. D. Ohio, W. D., 1914) T. D. No. 2000.

[70] Odell v. City of Atlanta, 97 Ga. 670, 25 S. E. 173; Walsch v. Call, 32 Wis. 159.

[71] Flint v. Stone Tracy Co., 220 U. S. 107, 31 Sup. Ct. 342, 55 L. Ed. 389, Ann. Cas. 1912B, 1312. But where a corporation was organized to own the stock of a mining company, and had no assets except such stock, a small sum in bank, office furniture, etc., and did nothing but to receive the dividends from the operating company and distribute them as such among its own stockholders, it was held not to be "doing business" within the meaning of the corporation tax law of 1909, and therefore not subject to the tax. U. S. v. Nipissing Mines Co., 206 Fed. 431, 124 C. C. A. 313.

of a wider meaning, and may be so intended when used in a tax statute and in connection with "business." Thus, an English decision holds that the ownership and employment of vessels, which are employed in the transportation of merchandise for hire, is a "trade" or concern in the nature of a trade, within the meaning of an act imposing taxes.[72] So in a case in North Carolina, construing a provision of the constitution authorizing the legislature to tax "trades, professions, franchises, and income," it was said that the word "trade" is employed in its broadest signification, and comprehends, not only all who are engaged in buying and selling merchandise, but all whose occupation or business it is to manufacture and sell the products of their plants, and includes in this sense any employment or business embarked in for gain or profit.[73]

§ 85. Carrying on Several Lines of Business

If a person or corporation carries on, at the same time, several different lines or branches of business, the resulting income is to be assessed and taxed as an entirety, and not as so many separate incomes from the different kinds of business.[74] But this rule applies only in cases where each branch or department of the business is wholly owned and operated by the taxable person or corporation. If any is owned and operated jointly with another person or corporation, it must be segregated and separately assessed. Thus, in an English case, it appeared that the corporation in question originally owned one steamship and derived its income from the operation of the vessel as a carrier of freight. Afterwards it acquired a very large interest, but not quite the entire ownership, in a second steamship, taking over the management and keeping the accounts thereof. It claimed to be assessed on the average of the profits derived from the two ships in one sum. But it was held that the second ship was a concern carried on by two or more persons jointly, and therefore its profits must be separately assessed.[75] So, under the corporation excise tax law of 1909, it was ruled that railroad companies operating leased or purchased lines must include all receipts derived therefrom in their return of net income. (T. D. 1742, par. 8.)

[72] Attorney General v. Borrodaile, 1 Price, 148.

[73] State v. Worth, 116 N. C. 1007, 21 S. E. 204.

[74] Last v. London Assur. Corp., L. R. 12 Q. B. Div. 389, 2 Tax Cas. 100; Scottish Union & N. Ins. Co. v. Smiles, 26 Scotch Law Rep. 330, 2 Tax Cas. 551. But see Brown v. Watt, 23 Scotch Law Rep. 403, 2 Tax. Cas. 143.

[75] Farrell v. Sunderland Steamship Co., 88 Law T. 741, 4 Tax Cas. 605.

§ 86. Profits of Mercantile Business

In so far as the income tax falls upon the profits of a merchant, the amount of it is not dependent on or estimated by the amount of his gross sales or gross receipts, but the taxable income is that derived from sales of goods made in excess of their cost, after deducting from the income or profits the expenses and other items allowed by the statute.[76] The deductions ordinarily allowed include interest on borrowed capital, taxes paid, losses incurred which are not compensated by insurance or otherwise, bad debts written off, and depreciation of property. Besides, the statutes allow a deduction of "necessary expenses actually paid in carrying on the business." These expenses, in the case of ordinary mercantile business, will include such items as the prime cost of goods, salaries and wages of employés, freight, advertising, insurance, and the like. But it must be observed that the income from a mercantile business, under the tax law, is not merely the profit arising from the sale of that particular stock of goods which the merchant had on hand at the beginning of the tax year, but it is the net profit arising from the whole year's commercial dealings in the goods handled by the merchant, no matter how often, in the course of the year, his stock may have been depleted, wholly or in part, and renewed.[77]

§ 87. Profits from Unauthorized Business

It is held that where a state tax is laid upon the gross receipts or the net income of corporations, or upon the volume of business transacted by them as measured by such receipts or income, it may include and apply to receipts by the company derived from a business beyond its charter powers or in which it had no authority to engage.[78] And so, it was ruled that a corporation cannot escape payment of United States internal revenue taxes on the ground that the business in which it is engaged, or from which its income or profits are derived, is unauthorized by its charter or by the laws of the state, or is otherwise ultra vires.[79] It is undoubtedly proper to apply these rulings to the assessment of the federal income tax.

[76] Millar v. Douglass, 42 Tex. 288.

[77] Wilcox v. Middlesex County Com'rs, 103 Mass. 544.

[78] People v. Roberts, 32 App. Div. 113, 52 N. Y. Supp. 859, affirmed 157 N. Y. 677, 51 N. E. 1093.

[79] Salt Lake City v. Hollister, 118 U. S. 256, 6 Sup. Ct. 1055, 30 L. Ed. 176.

§ 88. Income from Partnership Business

The profit accruing from one's share in the business conducted by a partnership is a part of his income.[80] The net earnings of the partnership constitute income of the firm so long as they remain in the possession or to the credit of the firm as such. But when a proportionate part is drawn out and paid over to an individual partner, it becomes and constitutes a part of his private income. And although an interest in the stock in trade of a partnership or in the business which it conducts may represent an investment of capital, and therefore be "principal" or "capital" of the partner, it does not follow that his share of the earnings is impressed with the same character. On the contrary, the dividends of a partnership in which a decedent was interested, and which was continued after his death, have been held not to constitute a part of the corpus of his estate, any more than interest on money constitutes a portion of the principal invested; but such dividends are income and go to the life tenant or beneficiary under a trust.[81] It is true, however, that it would be unjust and double taxation to assess a partnership upon its income derived from its business, and then to tax each partner for his share of the profits as constituting his individual income. But the act of Congress does not tax partnerships as such, but only the partners in their individual capacity.

As to the undivided earnings of a partnership, it is true that they properly constitute income of the firm, but not of the individual partners. Nevertheless, the act of Congress subjects them to taxation in the names of the partners. The provision is as follows: "Persons carrying on business in partnership shall be liable for income tax only in their individual capacity, and the share of the profits of the partnership to which any taxable partner would be entitled if the same were divided, whether divided or otherwise, shall be returned for taxation and the tax paid under the provisions of this title. * * * And such partnership, when requested by the Commissioner of Internal Revenue, or any district collector, shall render a correct return of the earnings, profits, and income of the partnership, except income exempt under section four of this act, setting forth the item of the gross income and the deductions and credits allowed by this title, and the names and addresses of the individuals who would be entitled to the net earnings, profits,

[80] In re Rogers, 37 Misc. Rep. 54, 74 N. Y. Supp. 829; In re Slocum, 169 N. Y. 153, 62 N. E. 130.

[81] Heighe v. Littig, 63 Md. 301, 52 Am. Rep. 510.

and income, if distributed." (Act Cong. Sept. 8, 1916, § 8e [U. S. Comp. St. 1916, § 6336h].) On the subject the Treasury Department rules as follows: "The character of partnership profits divisible between persons has no reference to any character which, as income accruing to the partnership, it may have borne prior to receipt by the partnership. It is therefore held that income received from a partnership cannot be traced to its source behind the partnership for the purpose of claiming individual exemption. It is held that the income from a partnership accrues to the individual partner at the time his distributive interest is determined and reducible to possession. In the returns of income made by individuals for the calendar year, therefore, there should be included such income accruing from the business of partnerships for their business years as may have been definitely ascertained by means of a book balance, whether distributed or not. In other words, members of partnerships are required to make returns of income like other individuals for the calendar year, and should include in their returns the net proceeds of their interest in partnership profits ascertained at the end of the business year falling within the calendar year for which the individual return is being rendered." (T. D. 2090, Dec. 14, 1914.)

§ 89. Profits on Sale of Real Estate

Where a parcel of real estate is sold for a price above its cost, the difference is not properly "income" of the vendor. It is more correctly described as an increase of capital assets. But it is certainly a "gain" or "profit" and falls within the meaning of either of those terms as used in the income tax law. The ruling of the Treasury Department on this point is as follows: "Gains and profits resulting from a real estate transaction are subject to the income tax in so far as they represent actual net income for the year in which the transaction occurred. The amount of income to be returned for the purpose of the income tax, in the case of the sale of capital assets, is the amount received upon the sale of the property in excess of its original cost. In determining the amount of income to be accounted for on this basis, the corporation [vendor] will consider mortgages, mortgage notes, or any other credits received in payment of the property as though they were cash, and if it should occur that the purchaser of any of the property should later default in payment, the corporation will be entitled to take credit as a loss for the amount of loss actually sustained by reason of the default. In determining the cost of the property for the purpose of arriving at the profit realized upon the sale, it will be permissible for the corporation to add to the initial cost such carrying charges as interest, taxes, insurance, etc., provided such carrying charges have not been deducted from net income which the corporation may have had and returned for years subsequent to January 1, 1909 [now March 1, 1913], and prior to the date of the sale of the property." (T. D. 2137, Jan. 30, 1915.)

It has been usual in income tax laws to set a limitation upon the time elapsing between the purchase and sale of the property, since land is often held for long periods, and in ordinary cases the increase in its value may be supposed to have been gradually accruing during the entire time. Moreover, the unrestricted jurisdiction of Congress over the taxation of incomes does not antedate March 1, 1913. Accordingly the statute provides that, "for the purpose of ascertaining the gain derived from the sale or other disposition of property, real, personal, or mixed, acquired before March 1, 1913, the fair market value or price of such property as of March 1, 1913, shall be the basis for determining the amount of such gain derived." (Act Cong. Sept. 8, 1916, § 2c [U. S. Comp. St. 1916, § 6336b].) The clause quoted is applicable in the case of individual taxpayers; but the same provision is later made in the case of corporations. (Idem., § 10, last paragraph [U. S. Comp. St. 1916, § 6336j].)

The act of Congress also contains the following very ambiguous clause: "The net income of a taxable person shall include gains, profits, and income derived from * * * sales or dealings in property, whether real or personal, growing out of the ownership or use of or interest in real or personal property." (Act Cong. Sept. 8, 1916, § 2a.) This has not been authoritatively construed. The term "dealings" has a definite meaning in law. It does not apply to the operations of one who buys to keep, though he may afterwards sell, but to the buying of any kind of property or commodity for the purpose of selling again at a profit, and that, not merely on a single occasion, but as an occupation or pursuit. In other words, "dealing" in any article is making successive purchases and sales of it as a business.[12] And the construction which the English

---

[12] See Clifford v. State, 29 Wis. 327; Saunders v. Russell, 10 Lea (Tenn.) 293; Bates v. Bank of Alabama, 2 Ala. 451; Buckley v. Briggs, 30 Mo. 452; Norris v. Commonwealth, 27 Pa. 494; Overall v. Bezeau, 37 Mich. 506; State v. Barnes, 126 N. C. 1063, 35 S. E. 605; Vernon v. Manhattan Co., 17 Wend. (N. Y.) 524; Goodwin v. Clark, 65 Me. 280.

courts have put upon the income tax law of that country excludes the profit arising from a single sale of land, while including profits derived from buying and selling realty as a business.[88]   But it seems probable that the intention of Congress was to tax not only profits arising from dealing in real estate as a business, but also the profit accruing on a single or isolated sale, or on sales not frequent enough to constitute dealing in it, and that the words "sales" and "dealings" were placed in juxtaposition to mark this distinction; and that this is the understanding of the revenue officers is apparent from the regulation quoted above.

§ 90.   Profits on Sales of Securities

In the general law (apart from matters of taxation) an addition to one's wealth obtained by selling stocks, bonds, or other securities or investments at a price above their cost is not "income" but an appreciation of capital.   Nor is it profit in the ordinary or commercial sense.   Profit is the acquisition of gain above expenditures arising from some transaction or operation, and does not include premiums received on the sale of securities.[84]   In the English law of taxation, money gained by selling securities at an advance over their cost is not reckoned as income, except in cases where the person pursues the buyi. ; and selling of securities as a business or occupation.[85]   So, where one buys a doubtful debt and recovers a larger sum than he paid for it, the gain is not profit in the sense of the income tax law, unless the purchaser is making a trade of buying such debts.[86]   But on the other hand, where a company is empowered by its charter to vary its investments, and generally to sell or exchange any of its assets, the net gain by realizing investments at larger prices than were paid for them constitutes profit chargeable with the income tax.[87]   But under the act of Congress, which makes taxable income include gains or profits arising from "sales or dealings in property, whether real or personal," it would appear that the sum gained on even a single sale of stock, or of a

[88] Tebrau Rubber Syndicate v. Farmer, 5 Tax Cas. 658.

[84] Cross v. Long Island Loan & Trust Co., 75 Hun, 533, 27 N. Y. Supp. 495; In re Graham's Estate, 198 Pa. 216, 47 Atl. 1108; Smith v. Hooper, 95 Md. 16, 51 Atl. 844, 54 Atl. 95; Eley's Appeal, 103 Pa. 300.

[85] Californian Copper Syndicate v. Harris, 6 Fraser, 894, 5 Tax Cas. 159; Tebrau Rubber Syndicate v. Farmer, 5 Tax Cas. 658.

[86] Assets Co. v. Inland Revenue [1897] W. N. 144.

[87] Scottish Investment Trust Co. v. Forbes, 31 Scotch Law Rep. 219, 3 Tax Cas. 231.

bond or other security, would be assessable. So far as concerns the decisions under the corporation excise tax law of 1909, they appear to sustain this view.[88] Under the income tax laws of 1861 to 1870, it was held that a bona fide exchange of stocks for other property, however much to the apparent advantage of the owner of the stocks, was not a sale thereof from which a profit was derived liable to taxation as income. But a transfer of stocks for a promissory note, which is collectible, or an exchange thereof for land, followed by a sale of such land within the year, whether for cash or collectible promissory notes, was considered equivalent to a sale of such stock for so much cash.[89]

§ 91. Increase in Value not Realized by Sale

In the law of trusts, an increase in the market value of securities of any kind held as investments is not accounted a part of the income of the same. Certainly, so long as the increase in value is not realized by a sale of the securities, it is merely an accretion to capital.[90] So, under the act of Congress of 1864, imposing a tax on "gains, profits, and income," it was held that a mere increase in the market value of securities does not come within the definition of any one of those terms, and specifically, that the word "gains," as used in the statute means such gains or profits as may be realized from a business transaction begun and completed during the preceding year.[91] It has also been more than once decided that an increase in the book value of the assets of a corporation, by a reappraisement or revaluation of property, does not constitute any part of the gross amount of its "income received within the year."[92] These decisions, it is believed, must prevail against the regulation made by the Treasury Department under the corporation tax law of 1909, continued under the income tax act of 1913, and apparently never rescinded, that "in the case of changes in book values of

[88] Cleveland, C., C. & St. L. Ry. Co. v. U. S. (C. C. A.) 242 Fed. 18. Compare Gauley Mountain Coal Co. v. Hays, 230 Fed. 110, 144 C. C. A. 408; U. S. v. Guggenheim Exploration Co. (D. C.) 238 Fed. 231.

[89] U. S. v. Smith, 1 Sawy. 277, Fed. Cas. No. 16,341.

[90] In re Vedder, 2 Con. Sur. 548, 15 N. Y. Supp. 798; In re Gerry, 103 N. Y. 445, 9 N. E. 235; Jennery v. Olmstead, 36 Hun (N. Y.) 536; In re Proctor, 85 Hun, 572, 33 N. Y. Supp. 196; Linsly v. Bogert, 87 Hun, 137, 33 N. Y. Supp. 975; In re Thomson's Estate, 11 Pa. Co. Ct. R. 198.

[91] Gray v. Darlington, 15 Wall. 63, 21 L. Ed. 45.

[92] Baldwin Locomotive Works v. McCoach, 221 Fed. 59, 136 C. C. A. 660, affirming (D. C.) 215 Fed. 967; Industrial Trust Co. v. Walsh (D. C.) 222 Fed. 437.

capital assets resulting from a reappraisement of property, the consequent gains or losses shall be computed for the return in the manner prescribed in the case of the sale of capital assets," and "in cases wherein there is an annual adjustment of book values of securities, real estate, and like assets, and the increases and decreases in values, thus indicated, are taken up on the books and reflected in the profit and loss account, such readjusted values will be taken into account in making the return of annual net income." (Internal Revenue Regulations No. 33, art. 111.)

§ 92. Uncollected Interest and Accounts

It has been an unsettled question whether a person's income for a given year should be held to include interest on securities accruing within the year but remaining uncollected at its close, and promissory notes and due-bills taken in discharge of a pre-existing indebtedness, but not paid within the year in which they are given, and the price of goods sold within the year, evidenced by book entries, but not received in cash. It was ruled that the amount of a promissory note taken in 1871 on the sale of a patent right, but not due until 1872, and paid in the latter year, was not taxable as income of the former year.[93] But in another case it was said that promissory notes, book accounts, and the like, due during a given year, may or may not be income of that year. This depends on their value intrinsically or their convertibility into money, property, or available assets. If they have only a nominal, and not a real value or convertible quality, and a man has realized nothing from them, and therefore does not return them as a part of his income, because he honestly believes that they are not real gains or profits, he cannot be convicted of making a false return.[94] And in construing the corporation excise tax law of 1909, it was held that the word "income," as there used, meant that which has "come in" or which has been already received, and that the net income so taxable should be determined on a cash basis, as distinguished from a revenue basis, and hence, in the case of an insurance company, did not include uncollected and deferred premiums or interest accrued and due but not actually received.[95]

The officers of the Treasury Department construed the income

[93] U. S. v. Schillinger, 14 Blatchf. 71, Fed. Cas. No. 16,228.

[94] U. S. v. Frost, 9 Int. Rev. Rec. 41, Fed. Cas. No. 15,172.

[95] Mutual Benefit Life Ins. Co. v. Herold (D. C.) 198 Fed. 199; Connecticut General Life Ins. Co. v. Eaton (D. C.) 218 Fed. 188; Insurance Co. of North America v. McCoach (D. C.) 218 Fed. 905.

tax act of 1913 as including interest on notes, bonds, and other evidences of debt accrued during the year, but not collected, that is, falling due within the year but remaining unpaid at the end of the year, provided that the account for such interest was considered good and collectible. And in the same manner they ruled that the year's income, for the purposes of the tax, includes fees, emoluments, charges, or accounts for services rendered by lawyers, physicians, and other professional men, provided they were earned within the year, although, at the close of the year, they remain in the form of unpaid bills, so only that they are considered good and collectible. But this ruling was not accepted by the courts. On the contrary, it was decided that such unpaid items are not taxable as part of the year's income, and it was said: "No instructions of the Treasury Department can enlarge the scope of this statute so as to impose the income tax upon unpaid charges for services rendered, and which, for aught anyone can tell, may never be paid." [96] Other decisions are to the same effect. In one it is said that "income" means what has come in; it means the receipt of actual cash, as opposed to contemplated revenue due but unpaid.[97] In another, it was ruled that interest accrued but not payable, and interest accrued but not paid, secured by mortgages drawing interest, are not "surplus profits" of a corporation.[98] In another case, it was held that a tax directed to be levied and collected for and during a certain year on the amount of all interest or coupons paid on the bonds of certain corporations "whenever and wherever the same shall be payable," did not cover interest earned during the year, but payable afterwards.[99] In still another decision we find the court saying: "It seems almost to border upon absurdity to speak of income as including that which has not been received, and what in the ordinary uncertainties of business may never be received. How can it be affirmed of unpaid interest that it will ever be paid, or, if so, when? The same is true of uncollected and deferred premiums. It is manifestly impossible to tell when, if ever, they will be paid. They are neither receipts nor income until paid." [100]

[96] Edwards v. Keith, 231 Fed. 110, 145 C. C. A. 298.

[97] Maryland Casualty Co. v. U. S. (Ct. Cl.) T. D. March 1, 1917, p. 32.

[98] People v. San Francisco Sav. Union, 72 Cal. 199, 13 Pac. 498.

[99] U. S. v. Indianapolis & St. L. R. Co., 113 U. S. 711, 5 Sup. Ct. 716, 28 L. Ed. 1140.

[100] Mutual Benefit Life Ins. Co. v. Herold (D. C.) 198 Fed. 199.

But whatever uncertainty there may have been on this point, it would seem that the question is definitely settled by the wording of the present income tax law, which, in its very first and dominating section, imposes the tax on "net income received in the preceding calendar year." The money due on uncollected accounts and unpaid bills and interest, cannot, by any distortion of language, be said to have been "received."

§ 93. Profit to Accrue on Uncompleted Contracts

In construing the corporation tax law of 1909, which laid a tax measured by the "entire net income received from all sources," the officers of the Treasury Department ruled that "net income on uncompleted contracts may be estimated on the basis of the percentage of the work completed as compared with the contract price of the whole work." (T. D. 1742, par. 88.) This ruling is believed to be wholly indefensible, on the grounds stated in the preceding section. Later, it was ruled that "where the service is of such a nature as to be compensated by fee, or of such a nature that no portion of the amount becomes due until the service is completed, then the total amount of the compensation should be included in the return for the year in which the compensation is received." (T. D. 2090, Dec. 14, 1914.) And a further ruling is as follows: "In the case of a large contracting company, which has numerous uncompleted contracts which probably, in some cases, run for periods of several years, there does not appear to be any objection to such corporation preparing its return in such manner that its gross income will be arrived at on the basis of completed work—that is to say, on jobs which have been finally completed and payments made during the year in which the return is made. If the gross income is arrived at in this method, the deductions from gross income should be limited to the expenditures made on account of such completed contracts." (T. D. 2161, Feb. 19, 1915.)

§ 94. Profits from Sale or Lease of Patent Rights

The Commissioner of Internal Revenue ruled that, under the corporation tax law of 1909, receipts from the sale of patent rights are to be included in taxable income, and also that royalties received on patent rights (presumably either on the sale or lease of such rights or on the use of the patented article) are also to be reckoned and reported as income, though an allowance would be made for depreciation of patents expiring during the year. (T.

D. 1742, pars. 46, 61.) As to royalties on sale or lease, the case is clear, but not so as to receipts from the sale of patents or patent rights. One who buys a patent or rights under a patent, and then sells it at an advanced price, may be said to have made a "profit" which should be taxable as a part of his income. But where the patentee sells (for example) his rights under the patent in foreign countries, it would rather seem to be a conversion of capital assets into the form of money than the receipt of income.

§ 95. Annuities

Under the federal income tax law, an annuity is regarded and treated as taxable income, whether it be created by grant, by testamentary trust, or by the contract of an insurance company. The Treasury Department rules that the amount paid under a life insurance, endowment, or annuity contract is not income when returned to the person making the contract, either upon the maturity or surrender of the contract; but the amount by which the sum received exceeds the sum paid and coming into the hands of the person making the contract and payment is income. (T. D. 2090, Dec. 14, 1914, as amended by T. D. 2152, Feb. 12, 1915.) Under the income tax law in Hawaii, it is held that the tax on an annuity paid out of income derived from property held in trust is assessable against the annuitant, and not against the trustee, but that surplus income arising from property held in trust, and accumulating in the hands of the trustee, pursuant to the terms of a will, is not taxable until the time arrives for its distribution.[101] In a Scotch case, where a husband and wife separated, and the husband by deed bound himself to make a payment of a free yearly allowance of a thousand pounds to the wife, it was held that he was bound to deduct the income tax from the payments so made, which implies, of course, that the annuity or allowance so paid to the wife was taxable to her as income.[102]

§ 96. Alimony

Alimony received by a divorced wife is regarded as within the income tax law, and she must include it in her return of income for taxation, provided it is sufficient in amount, together with any other income she may have, to exceed the amount of the personal exemption. On the other hand, it is ruled that the payment of ali-

[101] Wilder v. Hawaiian Trust Co., 20 Hawaii, 589.
[102] Dalrymple v. Dalrymple, 4 Fraser, 545.

BL.FED.TAX.—8

mony by the husband is a "personal expense" to him, and therefore he is not allowed to deduct the amount of it in making his own return for taxation. (T. D. 2090, Dec. 14, 1914.)

§ 97. Interest on Government Bonds

The federal statute now in force provides that "the following income shall be exempt from the provisions of this title, * * * interest upon the obligations of the United States (but, in the case of obligations of the United States issued after September 1st, 1917, only if and to the extent provided in the act authorizing the issue thereof) or its possessions, or securities issued under the provisions of the Federal Farm Loan Act of July 17th, 1916." (Act Cong. Sept. 8, 1916, § 4, as amended by Act Cong. Oct. 3, 1917, § 1200.) This provision is equally applicable in the case of corporations as in the case of individual owners of government bonds. Further the Act of Congress authorizing the first so-called "Liberty Loan" of 1917 provides that the principal and interest of those bonds shall be exempt "from all taxation, except estate or inheritance taxes, imposed by authority of the United States or its possessions." (Act Cong. April 24, 1917.) As to the second issue of "Liberty" bonds, the provision is that they shall be "exempt, both as to principal and interest, from all taxation now or hereafter imposed by the United States, any state, or any of the possessions of the United States, or by any local taxing authority, except (a) estate or inheritance taxes, and (b) graduated additional income taxes, commonly known as surtaxes, and excess profits and war-profits taxes, now or hereafter imposed by the United States, upon the income or profits of individuals, partnerships, associations, or corporations. The interest on an amount of such bonds and certificates the principal of which does not exceed in the aggregate $5,000, owned by any individual, partnership, association, or corporation, shall be exempt from the taxes provided for in subdivision (b) of this section." (Act Cong. September 24, 1917, § 7.) Under the corporation excise tax law of 1909, it was ruled that interest on United States bonds must be included in estimating the net income of corporations; but this was because that statute imposed a tax, not on the property of the corporation nor directly upon its income, but upon the privilege of carrying on business in a corporate capacity, the net income being used only as a measure of the tax in each particular case. (T. D. 1742, par. 37. And see 28 Opin. Atty. Gen. 138.)

(114)

§ 98. Dividends on Corporate Stock

Whatever the taxpayer may actually receive from a corporation, by way of dividends on the shares of its stock which he owns, constitutes a part of his income and will be taxable as such.[103] But a "dividend" properly so called is a distribution to stockholders of the whole or a part of the current earnings or profits of the corporation, and not a distribution of capital assets. Dividends received by a stockholder from the conversion into money and distribution in a subsequent year of property owned by the corporation on March 1, 1913 (the effective date of the income tax law of that year), and which was on that date worth the amount subsequently realized therefor, is not "income" accruing during the year of the distribution, and is not taxable under the act.[104] A distribution of capital assets is, from the point of view of stockholders, a replacement of their capital, except in the few exceptional cases where it is permissible for a corporation to divide current receipts among its stockholders, although the property in which the capital is invested is correspondingly depleted, as in the case of mining and quarry companies.[105]

Where a statute taxing incomes lays its burden upon both individuals and corporations, it is usual to provide that the individual taxpayer may deduct from his return of income for taxation the amount of any dividends received by him from corporations which are subject to the tax. This is provided in the federal income tax law, so far as concerns incomes which are subject to the "normal" tax only, though returns of incomes which are subject to the supertax must include corporate dividends. However, dividends received from corporations which are not subject to the income tax (that is, corporations which are specifically exempted from it) do not come within this rule, and are not deductible from the taxpayer's return of income. (T. D. 1857.) Dividends declared and paid by a foreign corporation which derives its entire income from business

---

[103] Van Dyke v. City of Milwaukee, 159 Wis. 460, 146 N. W. 812, 150 N. W. 509; Magee v. Denton, 5 Blatchf. 130, Fed. Cas. No. 8,943.

[104] Lynch v. Hornby, 236 Fed. 661, 149 C. C. A. 657.

[105] Reed v. Head, 6 Allen (Mass.) 174; Harvard College v. Amory, 9 Pick. (Mass.) 446. Dividends declared by a going corporation, such as a mining company, will be conclusively presumed, for the purpose of income taxation as against stockholders, to have been made and declared from net earnings or profits, so that it cannot be claimed, to avoid the income tax, that the dividends were really declared from the capital. Van Dyke v. City of Milwaukee, 159 Wis. 460, 146 N. W. 812, 150 N. W. 509.

done wholly within the United States, and pays an income tax to the federal government, should be treated in the same manner as dividends from domestic corporations. (T. D. 2090, Dec. 14, 1914.)

For the purpose of the income tax, it is immaterial whether a corporate dividend is declared and paid as a regular dividend (that is, regular in respect either to its periodicity or its amount) or as an extra dividend or a bonus in cash.[106] It is ruled that extraordinary dividends declared by a corporation, and not shown by the stockholder to be a distribution of capital assets instead of profits. are taxable against the stockholder.[107] In construing the act of 1913, the Treasury Department rules that dividends are to be returned as "income for the year in which such dividends were received, without regard to the period in which the profits or surplus were earned or the period during which they were carried as surplus or undivided profits in the treasury or on the books of the corporation." (T. D. 2274, Dec. 22, 1915.) But the act now in force provides that the term "dividends" shall be held to mean any distribution made by a corporation out of the earnings or profits accrued since March 1, 1913, and payable to its shareholders whether in cash or stock. (Act Cong. Sept. 8, 1916, § 31, as amended by Act Cong. Oct. 3, 1917, § 1211.) The Treasury ruling above quoted was made before the enactment of the act of 1916, and is clearly superseded by it.[108] The statutory provision (as amended) last above quoted continues thus: "Any distribution made to the shareholders or members of a corporation, joint-stock company or association, or insurance company, in the year 1917, or subsequent tax years, shall be deemed to have been made from the most recently accumulated undivided profits or surplus, and shall constitute a part of the annual income of the distributee for the year in which received, and shall be taxed to the distributee at the rates prescribed by law for the years in which such profits or surplus were accumulated by the corporation, joint-stock company, association, or insurance company, but nothing herein shall be construed as taxing any earnings or profits accrued prior to March first, 1913, but such earnings or profits may be distributed in stock dividends or otherwise, exempt from the tax, after the distribution of earnings and profits accrued since March first, 1913, has been made. This subdivision

---

[106] Lord v. Brooks, 52 N. H. 72.

[107] Southern Pac. Co. v. Lowe (D. C.) 238 Fed. 847.

[108] See Lynch v. Turrish, 236 Fed. 653, 149 C. C. A. 649; Lynch v. Hornby, 236 Fed. 661, 149 C. C. A. 687.

shall not apply to any distribution made prior to August sixth, 1917, out of earnings or profits accrued prior to March first, 1913."

The rule as to the taxability of dividends is not restricted to dividends declared and paid by corporations truly so called, but extends also to any distribution of profits among the members of an unincorporated society, syndicate, pool, trust, or other joint enterprise. For instance, where an investment is made in an unincorporated association organized to deal in land as a commodity, and profits are realized from the business, which are divided among the members, with no impairment of the principal, such profits are personalty, representing income, and go to the life tenant under the will of one of the members.[109]

The income tax law does not allow a corporation which owns stock in another corporation to deduct the amount of dividends received on such stock from its return of income, this privilege being restricted to individual taxpayers. (T. D. 2137, Jan. 30, 1915.) It was also held under the former act that dividends paid direct to the stockholders of a railroad corporation, which had leased all its property, must be deemed income of the railroad company and would be taxable as such.[110] When a dividend has been declared and is immediately payable, so that the stockholder can have it on demand, it is to be reckoned as a part of his income for the year, though it has not actually come into his hands as yet in the form of cash.[111] A dividend is none the less taxable income of the stockholder because it was declared and paid out of reserves previously set aside to meet depreciation and depletion of property, and was represented to the stockholders as a distribution of capital assets. (T. D. 2540, Oct. 10, 1917.)

§ 99. Same; Stock Dividends

According to the weight of authority, where a dividend is declared by a corporation on its capital stock, payable in new stock certificates based on accumulated but undivided profits, it is received as "income" by the stockholders, and not as capital, and is taxable as income, since the substance and intent of such a transaction is the distribution of earnings, and it does not result in any actual addition to capital, for although the nominal amount of the

[109] In re Thomson's Estate, 153 Pa. 333, 26 Atl. 652.

[110] Rensselaer & S. R. Co. v. Irwin (D. C.) 239 Fed. 739.

[111] Magee v. Denton, 5 Blatchf. 130, Fed. Cas. No. 8,943. And see T. D. 2048, Nov. 12, 1914.

corporation's capital stock is thereby increased, yet the corporation actually has neither more property nor more capital. Further, even if a stock dividend is not technically a "dividend" received from the corporation, it represents "gains, profits, and income" within the meaning of the income tax law. And where a stock dividend is declared and paid, the fact that the market value of the stockholder's aggregate holdings is no greater than it was before, because the stock dividend has correspondingly lessened the value of his original stock, does not prove that the stock dividend is not "income" and taxable as such, since this may be true in the case of a cash dividend.[112] This is also the position taken by the Treasury Department. (T. D. 2274, Dec. 22, 1915.)

§ 100. Accumulated or Undivided Profits of Corporations

A stockholder's distributive share in the undivided profits or accumulated earnings of a corporation are taxable to him under the federal income tax law, but only in cases where his income, including such items, is large enough to be subject to the supertax, and only in cases where the device of a corporation, accumulating its profits instead of dividing them, is resorted to for the purpose of evading the tax. The provision is as follows: "For the purpose of the additional tax, the taxable income of any individual shall include the share to which he would be entitled of the gains and profits, if divided or distributed, whether divided or distributed or not, of all corporations, joint-stock companies or associations, or insurance companies, however created or organized. formed or fraudulently availed of for the purpose of preventing the imposition of such tax through the medium of permitting such gains and profits to accumulate instead of being divided or distributed; and the fact that any such corporation, joint-stock company or association, or insurance company, is a mere holding company. or that the gains and profits are permitted to accumulate beyond the reasonable needs of the business, shall be prima facie evidence of a fraudulent purpose to escape such tax; but the fact that the gains and profits are in any case permitted to accumulate and become surplus shall not be construed as evidence of a purpose to escape the said tax in such case unless the Secretary of the Treasury shall certify that in his opinion such accumulation is unreasonable for the purposes of the business. When requested by the Commissioner of Internal Revenue, or any district collector of in-

[112] Towne v. Eisner (D. C.) 242 Fed. 702.

ternal revenue, such corporation, joint-stock company or association, or insurance company shall forward to him a correct statement of such gains and profits and the names and addresses of the individuals or shareholders who would be entitled to the same if divided or distributed." (Act Cong. Sept. 8, 1916, § 3 [U. S. Comp. St. 1916, § 6336c].) This provision "imposes no duty on the taxpayer to ascertain his distributive interest in the undivided surplus of corporations for the purpose of making return of the amount, in addition to the amount of dividends declared on his stock, unless the Secretary of the Treasury has certified that, in his opinion, such accumulation is unreasonable for the purposes of the business." (T. D. 2135, Jan. 23, 1915.)

From the fact that this provision applies only "for the purpose of the additional tax" it may be inferred that Congress did not regard a stockholder's interest in the undivided earnings or surplus of the corporation as taxable income in ordinary cases or under ordinary conditions. But the attempt has sometimes been made, under other statutes, to tax such interest as income. Thus, the United States income tax law of 1870 provided that, "in estimating the gains, profits, and income of any person, there shall be included * * * the share of any person of the gains and profits, whether divided or not, of all companies or partnerships." And there is a Canadian decision to the effect that the undivided profits of a corporation, or a portion of its profits derived from the employment of capital and annually carried into a reserve fund, may be "income" for the purposes of a testamentary trust, by which it was provided that the trustee might make advances to the beneficiaries "out of income." [113] But this is contrary to all the weight of authority.[114] In several of the cases on the subject, it is said that the word "income" is not broad enough to include things not separated in some way from the principal. It is not synonymous with "increase." The value of corporate stock may be increased by good management, prospects of business, and the like, but such increase is not income. It may also be increased by the accumulation of a surplus fund. But so long as that surplus is retained by the corporation, either as a surplus or as increased stock, it can in no proper sense be called income. It may become income-producing, but it is not

[113] Worts v. Worts, 18 Ontario, 332.

[114] Van Dyke v. City of Milwaukee, 159 Wis. 460, 146 N. W. 812, 150 N. W. 509; Board of Revenue of Montgomery County v. Montgomery Gas Light Co., 64 Ala. 269; Chicago, B. & Q. R. Co. v. Page, 1 Biss. 461, Fed. Cas. No.

income.[115] Thus, where the profits of a manufacturing or banking corporation have been accumulating for many years, until the market value of the stock is more than double its original price, and the owner dies, directing the "income" of his estate to be applied to particular objects, these extraordinary accumulations are as much a part of his capital as any other portion of his estate, and must therefore be regarded, not as income, but as part of the principal from which the future income is to arise.[116] This subject has been fully and conclusively discussed by the United States Supreme Court in the following terms: "Money earned by a corporation remains the property of the corporation, and does not become the property of the stockholders, unless and until it is distributed among them by the corporation. The corporation may treat it and deal with it either as profits of its business or as an addition to its capital. Acting in good faith and for the best interests of all concerned, the corporation may distribute its earnings at once to the stockholders as income; or it may reserve a part of the earnings of a prosperous year to make up for a possible lack of profits in future years; or it may retain portions of its earnings, and allow them to accumulate, and then invest them in its own works and plant, so as to secure and increase the permanent value of its property. Which of these courses shall be pursued is to be determined by the directors, with due regard to the condition of the company's property as a whole; and, unless in case of fraud or bad faith on their part, their discretion in this respect cannot be controlled by the courts, even at the suit of owners of preferred stock, entitled by express agreement with the corporation to dividends at a certain yearly rate in preference to the payment of any dividend on the common stock, but dependent on the profits of each particular year, as declared by the board of directors. Reserved and accumulated earnings, so long as they are held and invested by the corporation, being part of its corporate property, it follows that the interest therein, represented by each share, is capital, and not income of that share, as between the tenant for life and remainderman, legal or equitable thereof." [117]

2,668; Lauman v. Foster, 157 Iowa, 275, 135 N. W. 14, 50 L. R. A. (N. S.) 531; Tubb v. Fowler, 118 Tenn. 325, 99 S. W. 988.

[115] Spooner v. Phillips, 62 Conn. 62, 24 Atl. 524, 16 L. R. A. 461; Mills v. Britton, 64 Conn. 4, 29 Atl. 231, 24 L. R. A. 536; Smith v. Hooper, 95 Md. 16, 51 Atl. 844, 54 Atl. 95.

[116] Earp's Appeal, 28 Pa. 368.

[117] Gibbons v. Mahon, 136 U. S. 549, 10 Sup. Ct. 1057, 34 L. Ed. 525.

§ 101. Same; Additional Tax on Corporation

The revenue act of 1917 lays an additional tax on corporations in respect to undistributed earnings. Amending section 10 of the act of September 8, 1916, by adding a new subdivision, it provides: "In addition to the income tax imposed by subdivision (a) of this section, there shall be levied, assessed, collected, and paid annually an additional tax of ten per centum upon the amount, remaining undistributed six months after the end of each calendar or fiscal year, of the total net income of every corporation, joint-stock company or association, or insurance company, received during the year, as determined for the purposes of the tax imposed by such subdivision (a), but not including the amount of any income taxes paid by it within the year imposed by the authority of the United States. The tax imposed by this subdivision shall not apply to that portion of such undistributed net income which is actually invested and employed in the business or is retained for employment in the reasonable requirements of the business or is invested in obligations of the United States issued after September first, 1917: Provided, that if the Secretary of the Treasury ascertains and finds that any portion of such amount so retained at any time for employment in the business is not so employed or is not reasonably required in the business, a tax of fifteen per centum shall be levied, assessed, collected, and paid thereon. The foregoing tax rates shall apply to the undistributed net income received by every taxable corporation, joint-stock company or association, or insurance company in the calendar year 1917 and in each year thereafter, except that if it has fixed its own fiscal year under the provisions of existing law, the foregoing rates shall apply to the proportion of the taxable undistributed net income returned for the fiscal year ending prior to December thirty-first, 1917, which the period between January first, 1917, and the end of such fiscal year bears to the whole of such fiscal year." (Act Cong. Oct. 3, 1917, § 1206.)

The Treasury Department has ruled that the earnings of a corporation used to purchase preferred stock for cancellation are "retained for employment in the reasonable requirements of the business" and are therefore not taxable. Also that Liberty loan bonds of the second series bearing interest at the rate of 4 per cent per annum, and which have been issued in exchange for the 3½ per cent Liberty loan bonds, are "obligations of the United States issued after September 1, 1917," and are not subject to the tax; and current earnings invested in 3½ per cent Liberty loan bonds will

(121)

not be subject to the tax upon undistributed net income of corporations, if thus employed in the business or retained for employment in the reasonable requirements of the business. (T. D. 2570, Nov. 6, 1917.)

§ 102. Right to Subscribe for New Stock of·Corporation

It is a familiar rule in the law of corporations that when a company issues new stock (or stock previously held in reserve in the treasury), it must first be allotted to the existing stockholders, each being entitled to take his proportionate share at a price fixed. This price is usually and properly the par value of the stock, and if its market value is greater, a considerable advantage may accrue to the shareholder, who may either take his new stock and sell it at a premium or sell his right of subscription for it, and indeed the sale of these "rights" is a common occurrence on the stock exchanges. The courts all hold that the gain realized by a stockholder, either from a sale of the privilege or from its exercise and the subsequent sale of the stock at a profit, is capital or principal in his hands and not a part of his income.[118]

§ 103. Sale and Distribution of Assets of Corporation

·A distribution among stockholders of the assets of a corporation, upon its dissolution or preparatory to dissolution, is a return of capital, at least to the extent of the original investment, and not in any sense income in their hands.[119] Thus, a fund resulting from sales of materials, manufactured articles, products from the land, or the general personal property of a corporation, all indicating a final winding up of its business, cannot be called income of the stockholders when apportioned among them.[120] And where a corporation sells part of its original franchise and property, and distributes the proceeds of the same as a dividend among its stockholders, such dividend is to be regarded, as between a life tenant and remainderman of part of the stock, as capital and not as in-

---

[118] Lauman v. Foster, 157 Iowa, 275, 135 N. W. 14, 50 L. R. A. (N. S.) 531; Brinley v. Grou, 50 Conn. 66, 47 Am. Rep. 618; Moss' Appeal, 83 Pa. 264, 24 Am. Rep. 164; Biddle's Appeal, 99 Pa. 278; In re Thomson's Estate, 153 Pa. 333, 26 Atl. 652. But compare Wiltbank's Appeal, 64 Pa. 256, 3 Am. Rep. 585.

[119] Lynch v. Turrish, 236 Fed. 653, 149 C. C. A. 649; In re Thomson's Estate, 153 Pa. 333, 26 Atl. 652.

[120] Gehr v. Mont Alto Iron Co., 174 Pa. 430, 34 Atl. 638.

come.[121] And so, where a company owning large tracts of land, but not engaged in the business of buying and selling land, from time to time disposes of part of its holdings, and divides the proceeds among its stockholders, the money so obtained is not income.[122]

§ 104. Profit Accruing to Corporation from Sale of Capital Assets

From the point of view of laying the income tax on a corporation, while it is true that the conversion of any portion of its capital assets into other forms of property, or into cash, may be regarded as a replacement of capital, rather than as income, yet if the sale of such assets results in an increase in the aggregate amount of capital, the difference or profit may be regarded as income. Thus, where a bridge belonging to a private corporation was declared a county bridge (that is, taken under the power of eminent domain and made the property of the county), and the damages awarded, which were in excess of the capital stock, were divided among the shareholders in proportion to the number of their shares, it was held that the excess of the award so distributed over the amount of the capital stock represented a profit which the company had made in its business, and was taxable as such for state purposes.[123]

[121] Vinton's Appeal, 99 Pa. 434, 44 Am. Rep. 116.
[122] Stevens v. Hudson's Bay Co., 101 Law T. 96.
[123] Matson's Ford Bridge Co. v. Commonwealth, 117 Pa. 265, 11 Atl. 813.

CHAPTER VI

PERSONS AND CORPORATIONS SUBJECT TO INCOME TAX

§ 105. Residents

Every person residing within the United States, whether he is an American citizen or an alien, is subject to the federal income tax, and to the extra "war income tax" imposed by the act of 1917. The distinction drawn by the statute is not between American citizens and aliens. It is between residents of the United States (whether citizens or not) and nonresident aliens. And a secondary distinction is made between "citizens" and nonresident aliens, so that an American citizen is taxable in that character, although he may reside abroad. He passes into the other class only when he becomes an "alien" and a "nonresident" at the same time. And the Treasury Department rules that "determination by the State Department of the right to registry is not conclusive upon the Treasury in fixing citizenship for income-tax purposes; and it is

(124)

held that the native and naturalized status remains unless changed by affirmative action or forfeited by overt act." (T. D. 2135, Jan. 23, 1915.)

§ 106. Residents Deriving Income from Abroad

Under the law, persons residing within the United States are required to pay the tax upon "the entire net income received from all sources," which includes foreign investments and business as well as domestic. Under similar provisions in the corporation excise tax law of 1909, it was ruled that American corporations should include in their returns not only the income derived from the business carried on within the confines of the United States, but income received from business transacted in any foreign country as well. (T. D. 1742, par. 9.) It is undoubtedly within the competence of the government to tax its resident citizens upon their income derived from foreign investments, the domicile of the taxpayer giving jurisdiction for this purpose, although the situs of his investments may be in a foreign country.[1] This is also the law in England. Thus, a corporation organized in that country and maintaining a head office there, where its directors meet and administer its general affairs, and to which its revenues are remitted, is assessable for the income tax in England, though all its profits are derived from plantations, mines, or other enterprises conducted in foreign countries.[2] And so, dividends declared by a foreign corporation and payable at its agency in London, on shares owned by a British citizen and resident, are taxable as part of his income.[3]

§ 107. Domestic Corporations with Foreign Branches or Agencies

Where a domestic corporation has established branch offices or agencies for the transaction of its business in foreign countries, the profits accruing at such branches or agencies are part of the in-

---

[1] Memphis & C. R. Co. v. U. S., 108 U. S. 228, 2 Sup. Ct. 482, 27 L. Ed. 711; U. S. v. Bennett, 232 U. S. 299, 34 Sup. Ct. 433, 58 L. Ed. 612; Darnell v. Indiana, 226 U. S. 390, 33 Sup. Ct. 120, 57 L. Ed. 267; Kirtland v. Hotchkiss, 100 U. S. 491, 25 L. Ed. 558; Liverpool & London & Globe Ins. Co. v. Bennett [1912] 2 K. B. 41.

[2] Cesena Sulphur Co. v. Nicholson, L. R. 1 Ex. Div. 428; Imperial Continental Gas Ass'n v. Nicholson, 37 Law T. 717, 1 Tax Cas. 138; Scottish Mortgage Co. v. McKelvie, 24 Scotch Law Rep. 87, 2 Tax Cas. 165.

[3] Gilbertson v. Fergusson, L. R. 7 Q. B. Div. 562, 1 Tax Cas. 501.

come of the corporation, and will be taxable at its domicile. Thus, "a domestic corporation doing the greater part of its business in the United States, and having its principal place of business in this country, and transacting business in Porto Rico through a branch office, is required to report in its return of annual net income its entire earnings from all sources, including those arising and accruing to the branch in Porto Rico or elsewhere. The return of such corporation will be made to the collector of internal revenue of the district in this country in which is located its principal place of business." (T. D. 2137, Jan. 30, 1915.)

But it is important to distinguish this case from the case where two companies, one domestic and the other foreign, are really independent of each other, though constituent members of a pool or trust, or united in interest through one owning stock of the other, interlocking directorates, and so on. Thus, in an English case, it appeared that a company was formed in England for the purpose of bringing under a single control all the manufacturers of a particular kind of photographic camera. To do this, the company acquired 98 per cent of the stock of an American company, and retained the services of the manager of the American business. The remaining shareholders of the American company were independent of the English company. The English company, by power of attorney, appointed the American manager its proxy to vote for it at meetings of the American company. The two companies bought and sold goods to each other in the ordinary way. On this state of facts it was held that the business of the American company was not the business of the English company, so as to be assessable for income tax in England, the control exercised by the English company being the control of the stockholders only.[4] But on the other hand, a contrary decision was made in the case of an English company formed for the purpose of acquiring breweries in the United States, because it was shown that the English directors exercised effective and constant control over the business. The operations connected with the manufacture and sale of the beer took place in the United States, and were carried on by an American committee of management appointed by the company. This committee were in constant correspondence with the board of directors in England, and the general meetings of the company were held in England, where the company's books were kept, except those relating to business carried on in the United States. The

4 Kodak Limited v. Clark [1901] 2 K. B. 879, 4 Tax Cas. 549.

dividends were declared in England by the company in general meeting. Only a portion of the profits made was remitted to England, the amount needed for the dividends payable to American shareholders being retained in America for distribution. It was held that the business of the company was carried on in England, and that the company was there assessable to income tax upon the whole of the profits made, whether remitted to England or not.[5]

But in view of the fact that the income tax laws affect only "income received" by the person or corporation, it is important to inquire more closely whether profits earned at the foreign branches or agencies of a domestic corporation are taxable as a part of its income if they are not remitted in money to the home office, but retained abroad for payment of dividends, investment, or other purposes. On this question there are no American decisions. The English cases are numerous and instructive, but not entirely harmonious. At first, it was the disposition of those courts to regard the tax as falling only on profits actually received in cash. Thus, in a leading case it appeared that a company was formed in England to acquire certain brewing businesses in the state of New York, and as the law of that state would not permit a foreign corporation to own and carry on a brewery there, an American company was formed, the whole of the shares of which were taken by the English company, except seven shares which were held by the directors of the American company. So much of the profit was sent over to the English company in London as was required for distribution in dividends to such of its shareholders as resided in England, but the shareholders resident in America received their dividends there out of profits retained in America for that purpose. It was held that the income tax was chargeable only on the profits received in England by the English company.[6] Another case concerned a life insurance company established in Scotland and carrying on business abroad. The business

---

[5] Frank Jones Brewing Co. v. Apthorpe, 4 Tax Cas. 6; Apthorpe v. Peter Schoenhofen Brewing Co., 80 Law T. 395, 4 Tax Cas. 41.

[6] Bartholomay Brewing Co. v. Wyatt [1893] 2 Q. B. 499, 3 Tax Cas. 213. And see Stanley v. The Gramophone & Typewriter Limited [1908] 2 K. B. 89, 5 Tax Cas. 358; Gresham Life Assur. Soc. v. Bishop [1902] App. Cas. 287, reversing [1901] 1 K. B. 153, 4 Tax Cas. 464; Nobel Dynamite Trust Co. v. Wyatt [1893] 2 Q. B. 499, 3 Tax Cas. 224; Goerz v. Bell [1904] 2 K. B. 136; Scottish Widows Fund Life Assur. Soc. v. Farmer [1909] Sess. Cas. 1372; Pommery v. Apthorpe, 56 Law J. Q. B. 155; Crookston Bros. v. Furtado, 48 Scotch Law Rep. 134, 5 Tax Cas. 602.

was managed by directors, who had the power of accepting risks, but all investments abroad had to be sanctioned at the head office. Remittances in cash of interest received abroad were not made, and remittances out of the receipts abroad of interest and premiums were made only as required by the general policy of the company. At a quinquennial valuation, and in the yearly statements of accounts, the whole of the receipts abroad, including the interest on investments abroad, was brought into account in the division of the profits of the company. It was held that the interest received abroad and invested or applied abroad was not "received" in Scotland, so as to be taxable there.[7]

But other cases, including some of the later decisions, have evolved the rule that income may be "constructively received," so as to be taxable, if it is entered on the books of the company as cash, or locally applied or invested by direction of the head office. Thus, an English insurance company with branches in India was in the receipt of certain interest moneys, paid in India, from investments there and in the colonies. This interest was applied in India towards the payment of the various obligations of the company arising for settlement in India, including losses under its policies, and was not remitted in money to England, but it was treated in the company's accounts as if it had been so remitted. It was held that the interest was constructively received in England and was therefore taxable.[8] In another case it appeared that an insurance company was organized in England, and had its head office and directorate there, but also carried on business in certain foreign countries, and by the laws of those countries it was required, as a condition to the right to do business there, to deposit certain sums of money with government officials and to invest the money in accordance with local laws. In addition to this, the company also voluntarily invested abroad certain other sums representing accumulated profits of its business. Both classes of investments yielded interest, which was received by the company abroad, but was not remitted to England. It was held that the company was taxable in England on the income consisting of such

---

[7] Standard Life Assur. Co. v. Allan, 38 Scotch Law Rep. 628, 4 Tax Cas. 446.

[8] Universal Life Assur. Soc. v. Bishop, 68 Law J. Q. B. 962, 4 Tax Cas. 139. And see Scottish Provident Inst. v. Allan, 38 Scotch Law Rep. 874, 4 Tax Cas. 409; San Paulo Ry. Co. v. Carter [1895] 1 Q. B. 580, 3 Tax Cas. 344, affirmed [1896] App. Cas. 31; Grove v. Elliots, 3 Tax Cas. 481.

interest from both classes of investments.[9] Again, an English corporation had its head office in London, where meetings of the directors and shareholders were held, and from whence the affairs of the company were directed and managed. The company carried on the business of banking in London, Mexico, and Lima. At the branch offices it transacted all ordinary banking business, and in London it transacted the London business of the branches, but not the business of current banking accounts. It was held that the whole profits were chargeable for the income tax, whether remitted to England or not.[10] But this doctrine has not met with universal acceptance. In a case arising in Scotland, it was shown that a Scotch insurance company lent out sums of money at interest in Australia, and that the interest accruing was not remitted to Great Britain in forma specifica, but was retained abroad and invested there, but it was entered in the revenue account of the company as received. On this state of facts it was held that interest not received in Great Britain was not assessable for the income tax, and that the facts in the case did not show a constructive remittance.[11]

§ 108. Domestic Corporations Operating Exclusively Abroad

When the corporation excise tax law of 1909 was in force, a question arose as to the liability of a corporation organized under the laws of New Jersey, but which did business exclusively in Cuba. An assessment was made against this company, which it at first refused to pay, alleging, under the advice of counsel, that it was not liable to taxation under the act of 1909, because its business was transacted wholly in a foreign country and it had no assets in America, its property being within the jurisdiction of Cuba, its stockholders living there, and its income being spent and invested there. It was firmly maintained by the Internal Revenue Bureau that the company was liable for the tax notwithstanding these facts, but the question did not reach the courts, as the company finally receded from its contention and paid the amount assessed against it with the penalty and interest. (T. D. No. 1863.)

---

[9] Liverpool, L. & G. Ins. Co. v. Bennett [1911] 2 K. B. 577. And see Norwich Union Fire Ins. Co. v. Magee, 3 Tax Cas. 457.

[10] London Bank of Mexico v. Apthorpe [1892] 2 Q. B. Div. 378, 3 Tax Cas. 143.

[11] Forbes v. Scottish Provident Inst., 33 Scotch Law Rep. 228, 3 Tax Cas. 433.

§ 109. American Citizens Residing Abroad

American citizens who take up a residence abroad, whether temporary or permanent, and whether from choice or for business purposes (including diplomatic and consular officers) remain liable for the income tax. Theoretically such persons are taxable upon their entire net income (above the statutory exemption) no matter how or whence derived. But it seems an extreme exercise of the taxing power to impose the income tax upon citizens permanently domiciled abroad in respect to income or earnings wholly derived from sources located in the foreign country. This has been authoritatively declared to be the manifest purpose of Congress in the enactment of the statute now in force. "It may not be doubted," says the United States Supreme Court, "speaking in a general sense, that the taxing power, when exerted, is not usually applied to those, even albeit they are citizens, who have a permanent domicile or residence outside of the country levying the tax. Indeed, we think it must be conceded that the levy of such a tax is so beyond the normal and usual exercise of the taxing power as to cause it to be, when exerted, of rare occurrence and in the fullest sense exceptional. This being true we must approach the statute for the purpose of ascertaining whether its provisions sanction such rare and exceptional taxation. * * * As illustrative and throwing light on the real question for decision, action taken by Congress in exerting its taxing power is at least worthy of note. For instance, the provisions of the income tax law of 1864 expressly extended that tax to those domiciled abroad, and a like purpose is beyond doubt expressed in the income tax of 1913." [12] The language of the statute would therefore apply, for example, to the case of an American residing abroad and deriving his income from investments made abroad, or receiving a salary from a foreign government or from a foreign corporation. But it is not easy to see how payment of the tax could be enforced in such cases. Persons in this situation are expected to file their income-tax returns in the United States, and provision has been made for giving them some indulgence in respect to the time for payment of the tax. On so much of their income as accrues and is payable within the United States, the collection of the tax is not a matter of difficulty, but otherwise it would appear that the generality of the language of the statute must be restricted by the necessities of the case.

Again, if the act of Congress should be enforced to its fullest ex-

---

[12] U. S. v. Goelet, 232 U. S. 293, 34 Sup. Ct. 431, 58 L. Ed. 610.

tent in such cases, it would bear very heavily upon those of our citizens who may be living in a foreign country which also imposes a tax upon incomes. For instance, an American citizen residing in Paris would be liable to be taxed by the French government upon his entire income (in the character of a resident alien) and by the United States government upon the same income, in the character of a citizen residing abroad. It has been suggested that matters of this kind could be regulated by treaty between the two countries. But in the meantime, the Treasury Department has ruled that American citizens residing abroad are not relieved from liability to taxation under the Act of Congress by reason of the fact that they are also subject to the income tax laws of another country. (T. D. 2152, Feb. 12, 1915.)

§ 110. Resident Aliens

To be subject to the income tax in its full extent, it is not necessary that a person should be a citizen of this country. The tax is imposed on "every individual, a citizen or resident of the United States." But the important distinction is between resident aliens and nonresident aliens, for the former are taxed upon their "entire net income received from all sources," while the latter are taxed upon their "entire net income received from all sources within the United States." It is within the authority of the government to tax the income of foreigners resident within its territory, and the inclusion of such a provision in the income tax law does not render it unconstitutional or in any way invalid.[18]

In view of the important distinction above mentioned, the Treasury Department has made a ruling that "residence" is "that place where a man has his true, fixed, and permanent home and principal establishment, and to which, whenever he is absent, he has the intention of returning, and indicates permanency of occupation as distinct from lodging or boarding or temporary occupation." Accordingly, it is held that where an alien is permanently located in the United States, whether for business purposes or otherwise, and has his principal business establishment here, and is here permanently occupied or employed, even though his domicile may be in a foreign country, he is within the definition of a "resident of the United States." On the other hand, aliens who are physically present in the United States, but are only temporarily resident or employed here, as, for a season or other similarly definite term, and

---

[18] Moore v. Miller, 5 App. D. C. 413.

who have the expectation or intention of leaving the United States upon the termination of the employment, or accomplishment of the purpose, which necessitated their presence here, are "nonresident" aliens. (T. D. 2242, Sept. 17, 1915.)

These rules, as specially applicable to matters of taxation, may be illustrated by the following cases: In a late case in Iowa, it was held that one who, after living continuously for many years in the same house, starts on a tour of the world, leaving the house in charge of a care-taker, remains a "resident" of the state and city where his house is, for purposes of taxation, during his absence from the country, even though he may intend, on his return, to remove to another state.[14] In England it is held that a master mariner, trading between an English port and various foreign ports, who maintains a home for his family in the English port, is liable for the income tax on his salary, notwithstanding the fact that he is abroad for much the greater part of the year, and that most of his salary is earned on the high seas and not in England.[15] In another English case it appeared that an American citizen had for the last twenty years lived on board his own yacht, which was anchored in tidal navigable waters in England, obtaining his provisions and necessaries from the nearest village. The yacht had always been kept fully manned and ready to go to sea at any moment. It was held that the owner was a person "residing in the United Kingdom" within the income tax act, and was assessable accordingly.[16] A similar decision was made in the case of an American citizen, having no place of business in Great Britain, but who rented a house and shooting rights in Scotland, where he spent about two months continuously in each year, accompanied by his valet, as he had no family. His house in New York was always kept in readiness for his return, but so was the house in Scotland, which was kept furnished and ready for his occupation at any time. It was held that he was a person "residing in the United Kingdom" for the purposes of the income tax.[17] So, where a merchant carried on business in Italy, where he ordinarily resided, but also owned a residence in England, where he dwelt with his family several months in the year, it was held that he was a

[14] Barhydt v. Cross, 156 Iowa, 271, 136 N. W. 525, 40 L. R. A. (N. S.) 986, Ann. Cas. 1915C, 792.

[15] In re Young, 12 Scotch Law Rep. 602, 1 Tax Cas. 57; Rogers v. Inland Revenue, 16 Scotch Law Rep. 682, 1 Tax Cas. 225.

[16] Brown v. Burt, 81 Law J. K. B. 17.

[17] Cooper v. Cadwalader, 5 Tax Cas. 101.

resident of England, and liable to taxation on the profits of the business carried on abroad.[18]

§ 111. Nonresident Aliens

Within the contemplation of the income tax law, nonresident aliens are those who are not citizens of the United States and who do not have a permanent residence here. An American woman who marries a foreigner takes the nationality of her husband and therefore cannot claim the specific exemption allowed by the act. (T. D. 2090, Dec. 14, 1914.)

The present income tax law imposes the tax on nonresident aliens in respect to "the entire net income received in the preceding calendar year from all sources within the United States, including interest on bonds, notes, or other interest-bearing obligations of residents, corporate or otherwise." This is a change from the language of the law as originally enacted in 1913, which laid the tax on "the entire net income from all property owned and of every business, trade, or profession carried on in the United States by persons residing elsewhere." Under the act of 1913, the officers of the Treasury at first decided that interest on bonds of domestic corporations and dividends on stock of such corporations, owned by nonresident aliens, were not subject to the income tax, whether such bonds or stock were physically located within the United States or not.[19] But this decision was afterwards reversed, in view of certain remarks of the Supreme Court in the Brushaber case,[20] and it was decided that income accruing to nonresident aliens in the form of interest on the bonds of domestic corporations, or dividends on their stock, was subject to the tax. (T. D. 2313, March 21, 1916.) This last ruling would clearly seem to be correct under the present phraseology of the statute. It was likewise held that royalties paid to nonresident aliens under an agreement of purchase of certain patent rights, the payments being based on the quantity of goods produced by the use of such patents, were income accruing to such aliens by reason of property owned or business carried

[18] Lloyd v. Sulley, 21 Scotch Law Rep. 482, 2 Tax Cas. 37.

[19] T. D. 2017, Aug. 25, 1914; T. D. 2162, Feb. 24, 1915. But a federal court held that the income tax act of 1913 did impose a tax on the income from corporate stocks and bonds owned by a nonresident alien, when the stock certificates and bonds were kept in this country by an agent, who collected the income thereon for the owner. De Ganay v. Lederer (D. C.) 239 Fed. 568.

[20] Brushaber v. Union Pac. R. Co., 240 U. S. 1, 36 Sup. Ct. 236, 60 L. Ed. 493, Ann. Cas. 1917B, 713, L. R. A. 1917D, 414.

on in the United States, and therefore taxable. (T. D. 2137, Jan. 30, 1915.) But compensation paid to a nonresident alien for services rendered in a foreign country, including a per diem allowance for business and travel expenses, is not subject to the income tax. (T. D. 2152, Feb. 12, 1915.) And salary received by a foreign employee of a domestic corporation for services rendered entirely in a foreign land is not subject to deduction and withholding of the tax at the source. (T. D. 2090, Dec. 14, 1914.)

An English decision holds that, where all the trading of non-resident aliens is done, their sales made, and their profits earned, in the country where they live, they cannot be taxed in England on account of profits simply because they have an agent in England, or even a partner, to buy domestic goods for them and ship the same for sale abroad.[21] But upon the construction of the corporation tax law of 1909, an opinion was given by the Attorney General to the effect that foreign steamship companies engaged in the business of transporting passengers and freight between ports in this country and foreign ports, and maintaining freight and passenger agencies in this country, were subject to the tax; and whereas it was contended that a part of the business of such companies was the transportation of goods shipped from this country for foreign trade, and that such business could not constitutionally be taxed, the opinion was given that a tax imposed upon an exporter of merchandise, as an incident to his business, is not a tax upon the exported article, as an export, and hence not forbidden by the Constitution. (28 Opin. Atty. Gen. 211.) But a foreign steamship company having no office in the United States, and whose vessels only occasionally touch at American ports, was not regarded as doing business within this country, within the meaning of that act. (T. D. 1742, par. 21.)

It should further be observed that nonresident aliens are not entitled to claim the specific or personal exemption of $3,000 or $4,000, as the case may be, but are taxable upon the whole of their income in so far as the same is derived from sources within the United States; that they are subject to the surtax or additional tax, the same as citizens (but not to the extra or "war income tax" imposed by the act of 1917); and that the "responsible heads, agents, or representatives of such nonresident aliens, who are in charge of the property owned or business carried on or capital invested, shall make full and complete return of said income and shall

21 Sulley v. Attorney General, 5 Hurl. & N. 711.

pay the tax." (T. D. 2013, Aug. 12, 1914; T. D. 2109, Dec. 28, 1914; T. D. 2313, Mar. 21, 1916.)

§ 112. Taxability of Foreign Governments

In 1916, the Treasury Department put forth a ruling to the effect that a foreign government was liable to the federal income tax on any income it received from sources within the United States, including interest on bonds of American corporations or individuals, and including dividends on the stocks of American corporations, and that returns must be made and the tax paid by local representatives, just as in the case of individual nonresident aliens. (T. D. 2425, Dec. 28, 1916.) This ruling became a matter of serious importance when the government of Great Britain, under the financial exigencies of the Great War, found it necessary to acquire by purchase or hypothecation large quantities of American securities then held by British subjects, and it was proposed to tax the income therefrom. But an amendment to the income tax law effected by the Act of Congress of October 3, 1917, provides that "nothing in section two of the act approved October 3, 1913, or in this title, shall be construed as taxing the income of foreign governments received from investments in the United States in stocks, bonds, or other domestic securities, owned by such foreign governments, or from interest on deposits in banks in the United States of moneys belonging to foreign governments."

§ 113. Salaried Officers

Attention was given in an earlier section of this book to the constitutional validity of income taxation as applied to the salaries of federal and state officers; and it was there shown that, although the United States cannot tax the salary of a state officer, or vice versa, yet, in the absence of explicit constitutional restrictions, there is nothing to prevent Congress from taxing the compensation of the officers of the federal government, or to prevent a state from taxing the salaries of its own officers or those of its municipalities.[22] This is in accordance with the rules prevailing in other countries where income tax laws are in force. Thus, in Canada, a government official or employé is taxable on his income received in the form of a salary.[23] It was held in Ontario that the income of an officer of the House of Commons of the Dominion of Canada could not

[22] Supra, § 50.

[23] Abbott v. City of St. John, 40 Can. Sup. Ct. 597, 12 Ann. Cas. 821; Robson v. Regina, 4 Terr. L. R. 80.

be taxed by a provincial legislature or by a municipality of the province.[24] But this was overruled by the Supreme Court of Canada, which held that any civil or other officer of the Dominion might be lawfully taxed in respect to his income as such by the municipality in which he resides.[25] And the highest court in England has ruled that an officer of the Commonwealth of Australia who resides in Victoria and receives his salary in that state, is liable to be assessed in respect of his official salary for an income tax imposed by the legislature of Victoria.[26]

But laws of this kind are construed with strictness, and the salary attached to a public office is not to be brought within the reach of the income tax without explicit language to that effect. Thus it was ruled, in an early case in South Carolina, that the salaries of public officers are not liable to be taxed under an ordinance imposing a tax on all profit or income arising from the "pursuit of any faculty, profession, occupation, trade, or employment." [27] And the court in Virginia decided that, when the tax is laid upon salary or compensation for services, received by any person in the employment of a corporation, it will be held not to include the salary paid to a minister of the Gospel by the church or congregation of which he has charge, for it must be understood that the legislature meant only secular employment.[28] But the modern statutes employ language broad enough to cover all kinds of remuneration for services rendered by employés, however denominated. Thus, the act of Congress applies to "income derived from salaries, wages, or compensation for personal service of whatever kind and in whatever form paid." And the Wisconsin statute, in defining "income," includes "all wages, salaries, or fees derived from services." The tax commission of that state explains that "fees derived from services would not include the fees belonging to the state or any political subdivision. For example, if a sheriff receives a salary and turns over the fees received by him in his official capacity to the county, they would not be reckoned as income. If he receives the fees in lieu of salary, such fees would constitute income." In this connection it is also necessary to remark that, although a corporation may be exempt from taxation, in respect to its own income,

---

[24] Leprohon v. Ottawa, 2 Ont. App. 522.

[25] Abbott v. City of St. John, 40 Can. Sup. Ct. 597, 12 Ann. Cas. 821.

[26] Webb v. Outrim [1907] App. Cas. 81, 7 Ann. Cas. 84.

[27] City Council v. Lee, 1 Treadw. (S. C.) 57.

[28] Plumer v. Commonwealth, 3 Grat. (Va.) 645.

as being a religious, charitable, or educational institution, it does not follow that its employés are likewise exempt. Thus, the salary of a professor in a college is not exempt from the income tax, though the revenue of the college may be exempt.[29] The act of Congress of 1916 contains a provision that "nothing in this section shall be held to exclude from the computation of the net income the compensation paid any official by the governments of the District of Columbia, Porto Rico, and the Philippine Islands or any political subdivision thereof," in other words, the salaries of these officers are subject to the income tax.

§ 114.   Bankrupt and Insolvent Persons and Companies

It may seem an anomaly to speak of a bankrupt or insolvent person being subject to the income tax, but it was evidently in the contemplation of Congress, in enacting the law of 1916, that such cases might arise, as witness the provision that the penalty for non-payment shall not be exacted "from the estates of insane, deceased, or insolvent persons." It is a general rule of law that a bankrupt's estate is not withdrawn from taxation by the proceedings in bankruptcy, but remains subject to taxation in the hands of his trustee.[30] And it was ruled under the corporation excise tax law of 1909 that, where a corporation subject to the tax had gone into bankruptcy, the return of net income was to be made by the trustee in bankruptcy.[31] So, where an assignee for the benefit of creditors carries on the business of the assignor, and makes a profit, it is subject to the income tax. For it is not necessary that a business should be carried on for the purpose of making a profit for the owner; it is none the less carried on because the object is to earn a larger dividend for creditors.[32] The same principle would apply to a corporation in the hands of a receiver. It is true that a contrary doctrine prevailed under the corporation tax law of 1909, but that was only because the tax was not laid on the income of the corporation, but on the privilege of doing business in a corporate capacity. Hence it was held that receivers of an insolvent corporation, duly appointed by a court of equity, which corporation was not doing business when the act was passed, and had done no business since, were not within the act, and not required to make re-

---

[29] Union County v. James, 21 Pa. 525.
[30] In re Crowell (D. C.) 199 Fed. 659.
[31] T. D. 1742, par. 7.
[32] Armitage v. Moore [1900] 2 Q. B. 363, 4 Tax Cas. 199.

turns or pay taxes on the income realized by them while acting as officers of the court and under its direction.[33] But the act of Congress now in force imposes, not an excise tax on corporate business, but a tax on all incomes. Still, there is a decision of an inferior federal court that where receivers, through whom the court took possession of the property of an insolvent railroad, operated the road, funds in their hands, being the net proceeds from the operation of the road over and above expenses and authorized expenditures, are not subject to the income tax as "net earnings," and no return thereof should be made.[34]

§ 115. Estates of Decedents and Dissolved Corporations

The death of a taxpayer does not exempt his income from taxation for the current year, but his estate, in the hands of his executor or administrator, is liable for the tax on so much of the income of the year as accrued prior to the day of his death,[35] and in addition, as the statute provides, "income received by estates of deceased persons during the period of administration or settlement of the estate, shall be subject to the normal and additional tax and taxed to their estates." The same principle applies upon the dissolution of a corporation. But it was held that a corporation which had continued in business through a calendar year could not evade liability for the tax imposed by the Act of Congress of 1909, by dissolving before the time when it was required to make a return and have the tax assessed, but that the officers of the corporation still had the authority, and it was their duty, to make and render the return.[36]

§ 116. Partnerships

A partnership, as distinct from the individuals composing it, is not subject to the income tax. The provision of the statute is that "persons carrying on business in partnership shall be liable for income tax only in their individual capacity, and the share of the

[33] Pennsylvania Steel Co. v. New York City Ry. Co., 198 Fed. 774, 117 C. C. A. 556; U. S. v. Whitridge, 231 U. S. 144, 34 Sup. Ct. 24, 58 L. Ed. 159.

[34] Equitable Trust Co. v. Western Pac. Ry. Co. (D. C.) 236 Fed. 813.

[35] Mandell v. Pierce, 3 Cliff. 134, Fed. Cas. No. 9,008. The income tax act of 1913, which was approved October 3d of that year was held to apply to the estate of one who died in July of the same year, since it was made so far retroactive as to cover all income received after March 1st. Brady v. Anderson, 240 Fed. 665, 153 C. C. A. 463.

[36] U. S. v. General Inspection & Loading Co. (D. C.) 192 Fed. 223.

profits of the partnership to which any taxable partner would be entitled if the same were divided, whether divided or otherwise, shall be returned for taxation and the tax paid under the provisions of this title: Provided, that from the net distributive interests on which the individual members shall be liable for tax, normal and additional, there shall be excluded their proportionate shares received from interest on the obligations of a state or any political or taxing subdivision thereof, and upon the obligations of the United States and its possessions, and that, for the purpose of computing the normal tax, there shall be allowed a credit for their proportionate share of the profits derived from dividends."   This proviso was probably introduced into the act of 1916 in consequence of a ruling of the Treasury Department, made under the corresponding provisions of the act of 1913, to the effect that a partner's share of the profits made by his firm was "income derived from the partnership as the source, whatever its character may have been when it accrued to the partnership itself," and that consequently each partner was taxable on his entire share of the firm's profits, without deduction, although those profits may have been composed in part of interest on state or municipal bonds or dividends on corporate stock.   (T. D. 2337, June 1, 1916.)

The Treasury regulations relative to partnerships are as follows: "Individual members of a partnership are liable for income tax upon their respective interests in the net earnings of the partnership, and are required to include said net earnings in their personal returns.   Partnerships are not subject, as partnerships, to the income tax, and are required to make statements of their income and earnings as partnerships only when requested to do so by the Commissioner of Internal Revenue or the collector of internal revenue for the district in which said partnership has its principal place of business, and when such a statement is required, as aforesaid, the said statement shall give a complete and correct report of the gross income of the said partnership and also a complete account of the actual legitimate annual expenses of conducting the business of said partnership (not including living and personal expenses of the partners) and the net profits and the name and address of each of the members of said partnership and their respective interests in the net profits thus reported.

"The net annual income of a partnership, when apportioned and paid to the members thereof, shall be returned by each individual partner receiving same, in his annual return of net income, and the tax shall be paid thereon by said individual partner, as required by law.

"When the annual income of a partnership is not distributed and paid to the members thereof, the respective interest of each member in said profits shall be ascertained, and the individuals entitled thereto shall include the said amount in their annual return as part of their gross income, the same as if said profits had been distributed and paid to them.

"Undivided annual net income of partnerships thus returned by the individual members thereof, upon which the tax shall have been paid, shall not, when said profits are actually distributed and paid to the partners, be again included in their annual return as a part of their gross income.

"Foreign partnerships or firms, all the members of which are both citizens or subjects and residents of a foreign country, which are the owners of bonds and mortgages or deeds of trust or other similar obligations, including equipment trust agreements, receivers' certificates, and stocks, of corporations, joint-stock companies or associations, and insurance companies, organized or doing business in the United States, may file with the debtor or withholding agent, with their coupons or orders for registered interest, or orders for other income derived from property or investments in the United States, certificate and notice of ownership, setting forth the facts as to nonresidence and alienship, and the debtor or withholding agent shall not withhold any part of their said income.

"Where a foreign partnership or firm is composed of both nonresident foreigners and citizens of the United States, or foreigners resident in the United States or its possessions, the certificate or ownership shall show this fact, and the name and legal address of each member of said partnership, who is a citizen of the United States, or who is a foreigner residing in the United States or its possessions, shall be given on the said certificate, and no part of said income shall be withheld by the paying agent." (T. D. 1905, Nov. 28, 1913; T. D. 1957, March 12, 1914.)

§ 117. Limited Partnerships

Under the laws of some of the states (for example, Pennsylvania) limited partnership associations may be organized which possess all the essential privileges and powers of corporations, including the right to transact business under a name indicating rather a corporate existence than an association of partners, as, by the use of the word "Company" in the name, provided that the name shall also include the word "Limited," the right to sue and be sued in that name, the right to fix the limit of its own existence, within certain bounds, and to have a capital stock divided into shares. The members of such an association are not individually liable for its debts, and the shares or interests in it are transferable by the owner, provided that the transferee must either be elected to membership by the remaining members or bought out. Under the corporation excise tax law of 1909, which required payment of the tax from "every corporation, joint stock company or association," the opinion was given by the Attorney General, and followed by the officers of the treasury department, that such a limited partnership was within the meaning of the act, and was liable to the tax if organized for profit and having a capital stock represented by shares, although no certificates of stock were issued.[37] And the Treasury Department has ruled that these organizations are not exempt from the income tax in the character of partnerships, but subject to it in the character of "associations." The ruling is as follows: "Limited partnerships are held to be associations within the meaning of the federal income tax law. The profits of limited partnerships making returns in the same manner as corporations make returns will be treated the same as dividends of corporations and will be returned in the returns of individuals in the same manner as are dividends upon the stock of corporations; that is to say, the dividends received from such limited partnerships will not be subject to the normal tax in the hands of the members of the partnership receiving the same." (T. D. 2137, Jan. 30, 1915.)

§ 118. Corporations

The present statute lays the income tax, subject to certain enumerated exceptions, on "every corporation, joint stock company or association, or insurance company, organized in the United States, no matter how created or organized," and also upon similar companies "organized, authorized, or existing under the laws of any foreign country," in so far as the latter transact business or have capital invested in the United States. (Act Cong. Sept. 8, 1916, § 10 [U. S. Comp. St. 1916, § 6336j].) The rule that a corporation is an

---

[37] 28 Opin. Atty. Gen. p. 189. And see Liverpool Ins. Co. v. Massachusetts, 10 Wall. 566, 19 L. Ed. 1029; Moorhead v. Seymour (City Ct. N. Y.) 77 N. Y. Supp. 1050. Compare Chapman v. Barney, 129 U. S. 677, 9 Sup. Ct. 426, 32 L. Ed. 800.

artificial entity distinct from its stockholders is a fiction of law, which is recognized by the courts for some purposes and disregarded for others; and hence, where a railroad corporation leased its property and franchises for the whole term of its charter, the fact that the lessee paid the rent, not to the lessor entity, but directly to its stockholders and bondholders, was held not to prevent the rent so paid from being subject to taxation.[88]

A question as to the course to be pursued by a corporation so recently organized that it has not yet been in business for a full year when the time arrives for making the annual return has been thus resolved by the Treasury Department: "A corporation organized during the year should render a sworn return on the prescribed form, covering that portion of the year (calendar or fiscal) during which it was engaged in business or had an income accruing to it." (Internal Revenue Regulations No. 33, art. 84.) There is also a ruling that "corporations which have applied for and never received charters, or corporations which have received charters and never perfected their organizations, transacted no business, and had no income whatever from any source, may, upon presentation of these facts to the collector of internal revenue, be relieved from the necessity of making returns of annual net income, so long as they remain in this unorganized condition." (T. D. 2152, Feb. 12, 1915.)

§ 119. Same; Change of Name of Corporation.

It has been ruled that "the mere change in name does not constitute a new corporation. If the business was continuous throughout the year, with no change in management or operation other than the change of name, the return should be made covering the business transacted throughout the year, such return to be made by the corporation in the name which it bears at the end of the year, with a notation on the return to the effect that the name had been changed, giving both the old and new names. If, however, a distinct new corporation was organized to take over the property of the old, both corporations will be required to make separate returns covering the periods of the year during which they were respectively in charge of the business." (T. D. 2137, Jan. 30, 1915.)

§ 120. Foreign Corporations

Foreign corporations engaged in business within the United States are subject to the income tax on the amount of net income

88 Anderson v. Morris & E. R. Co., 216 Fed. 83, 132 C. C. A. 327.

(142)

accruing to them from business transacted and capital invested in the United States. (Act Cong. Sept. 8, 1916, § 10 [U. S. Comp. St. 1916, § 6336j].) They are also required to make proper income tax returns at the place where their principal business within the United States is located. (Idem., § 13, par. b [U. S. Comp. St. 1916, § 6336m].) But they are not subject to having any part of their income withheld by a debtor or withholding agent, that is, they are exempt from the process of collection at the source. (T. D. 1916, Dec. 5, 1913.) Within the meaning of the term "foreign corporations" as used in the act of Congress, and as defined by the Treasury Department, are included both municipal and private corporations organized under the laws of any country foreign to the United States. (T. D. 2006, July 16, 1914.)

It cannot be doubted that the United States government has lawful power to impose the income tax on all such foreign organizations in so far as they avail themselves of the benefit and protection of our laws to derive a revenue from capital invested or business operations carried on within our borders.[39] The method of calculating the taxable income of such foreign companies has been thus prescribed: "For the purpose of the tax, the net income of such foreign organizations shall be ascertained by deducting from the gross income arising, received, or accruing from business done and capital invested in this country the deductions enumerated in the act, which deductions shall be limited to expenditures or charges actually incurred in the maintenance and operation of the business transacted and capital invested in the United States, or, as to certain charges, such proportion of the aggregate charges as the gross income from business done and capital invested in the United States bears to the aggregate income within and without the United States. In other words, the deductions from the gross income of a foreign corporation doing business in this country should, as nearly as possible, represent the actual expenses and authorized charges incident to the business done and capital invested in this country, and must not comprehend, either directly or indirectly, any expenditures or charges incurred in the transaction of business or the investment of capital without the United States." (Internal Revenue Regulations No. 33, par. 157.)

39 See People v. Equitable Trust Co., 96 N. Y. 387.

§ 121. Same; Doing Business by Local Agents

As to foreign corporations doing business in the United States through local agents or other representatives, the Treasury Department has made the following ruling: "The federal income tax law provides that the normal tax imposed by it shall be levied, assessed, and collected upon the entire net income arising and accruing to foreign corporations from business transacted or capital invested in this country. Such a corporation may transact business or have capital invested in this country through and by an agent as completely as if it were transacting the business or investing the capital direct from its home office or through a duly established branch office in the United States. An agent who is doing business in this country, buying and selling certain products of the foreign corporation, is to all intents and purposes a branch of the foreign corporation, as through and by him the foreign corporation is transacting business in this country. The buying and selling of a product in this country through a local agency or a branch for and on behalf of a foreign corporation is clearly transacting business in this country within the meaning of the federal income tax law, and any net income arising and accruing because of the business so transacted will be held to be subject to the tax imposed by the federal income tax law, and every foreign corporation carrying on business in the manner indicated will be required to make a return of annual net income covering the business so transacted." (T. D. 2137, Jan. 30, 1915.) And later, a question having arisen as to the liability of a foreign corporation which merely sent a representative to this country to solicit business for it, such person having authority to receive and forward orders but not to fill them, the following ruling was made: "When a foreign corporation sends a representative to this country to solicit business, the merchandise thus sold to be shipped direct to the consignee, it will be held that such corporation is transacting business in this country. The fact that the solicitor or representative has only a mailing address in this country is immaterial, he is none the less an agent of the foreign corporation. To the extent that he sells in this country goods or merchandise for the foreign corporation, to that extent the foreign corporation is transacting business in the United States, and the net income arising and accruing to the corporation by reason of the business so transacted will be subject to the income tax imposed by section 2, act of October 3, 1913. (See §§ 257, 266.) Any foreign corporation transacting business in this country in the manner hereinbefore indicated will make a return of annual net income to the collector of the district in which its representative has his mailing address, showing in such return the net income accruing to it from the business so transacted." (T. D. 2161, Feb. 19, 1915.)

§ 122. Same; Dutch Administration Offices

The following is a ruling or regulation made by the Treasury Department on this subject: Dutch Administration Offices being nonresident alien corporations not engaged in business or trade in the United States, and not having an office or place of business therein, and said Dutch Administration Offices being the registered owners of stock of domestic or other resident corporations in the United States, are prima facie liable for the normal income tax on income derived from dividends upon the capital stock or from the net earnings of the aforesaid domestic or other resident corporations in the United States and to having the tax deducted and withheld from such income under section 13 (f), act of September 8, 1916. (U. S. Comp. St. 1916, § 6336m.)

It appearing that the Dutch Administration Offices, while the registered owners of stock as aforesaid, are not the actual owners thereof, but that they have issued their bearer certificates, with coupons attached, against said stock, and that the dividends on said stock are collected for the account of the holders of said bearer certificates and that the relation sustained by said Dutch Administration Offices to the said bearer certificate holders is that of agent, for the purposes of administration the Dutch Administration Offices may appoint an agent in the United States and give notice of that fact by filing in duplicate with each corporation issuing the stock so held by said Dutch Administration Offices, a notice in substantially the following form:

You are hereby advised that ――――――――――――――,
                 (Name and address of Dutch Administration Office)
the registered owner of stock in ――――――――――, has appointed
                 (Issuing corporation)
―――――――――――――――――, whose address is
      (Name of agent)
as its agent in the United States.

Upon receipt of notice as aforesaid, debtor or issuing corporations in the United States may pay over to said Dutch Administration Offices or their agent in the United States all dividends, without withholding any tax, and shall forward to the Commissioner of Internal Revenue one copy of the said notice of the appointment of the agent in the United States. It will be necessary to file this notice but once, unless there shall be a change of agent, when a similar notification should be given.

When it shall appear that the Dutch Administration Offices have an agent in the United States and when, because of that showing, dividends of domestic or other resident corporations in the United States shall have been paid to them without withholding of tax, said Dutch Administration Offices, through their agent in the United States, will be required to make returns of income and pay tax on all dividends received except such as shall be shown to have been received by them for the account of nonresident alien individuals. This showing shall be made by way of certificate No. 1087, prescribed by T. D. 2382, and all such certificates shall be attached to the return when filed. The form of return for reporting tax withheld from dividends will be prescribed by the Commissioner of Internal Revenue.

Where the normal tax has heretofore been withheld from Dutch Administration Offices which, under the foregoing, would not have been withheld if they had had an agent in the United States, they may, through an agent to be appointed by them in the United States, file with the Commissioner of Internal Revenue at Washington, a statement in which shall be set out—

(a) The name and address of the Dutch Administration Office which is the registered owner of stock of domestic corporation, and the fact that it is the registered but is not the actual owner of such stock.

(b) The name and address of each corporation in which stock is so held; the amount of dividend paid by each corporation; the amount of tax withheld by each corporation.

(c) The names and addresses of the actual owners of the stock; the amount of stock owned by each; amount of dividend payable to each. The showing called for in this paragraph (c) shall be made by attaching to the statement certificates, Form 107, prescribed by T. D. 2382.

When it shall appear by such statement and showing that tax has been withheld in excess of liability of the Dutch Administration Offices for tax, this office will give the necessary instructions to the withholding agent to release and pay over the amount of tax withheld in excess. (T. D. No. 2386, Oct. 19, 1916.)

§ 123. Public Service Corporations

The various kinds of corporations now commonly classed under this designation are not exempt from the income tax. The at-

(146)

tempt was made to withdraw them from the operation of the corporation tax law of 1909, on the ground that they exercised a delegated authority from the states which created them and bore such a relation to the general public as to make their functions quasi-governmental in character. But this contention was denied by the Supreme Court and the other federal courts,[40] and their reasoning and conclusions are just as applicable to the income tax law as to the statute of 1909. But it should be observed that the act of 1916 expressly disclaims any intention on the part of Congress to subject to the operation of the income tax any part of the revenues of a state or of a municipal corporation, whether derived from "the exercise of any essential governmental function" or from "any public utility." (Act Cong. Sept. 8, 1916, § 11, par. b [U. S. Comp. St. 1916, § 6336k].)

§ 124. Unincorporated Associations

The income tax law couples with the word "corporations" in describing those subject to the tax, the term "joint stock companies or associations." This term describes an anomalous kind of body, a hybrid in the law, occupying a position midway between a corporation and a partnership. A joint stock company or association is a body of persons united and acting together without a charter (or without being incorporated under a general law), but upon the methods and forms used by incorporated bodies for the prosecution of some common enterprise. Such an association possesses a common capital contributed by the members composing it, such capital being commonly divided into shares, of which each member possesses one or more, and which are transferable by the owner. It usually transacts business under a company name, by which, under the laws of some states, it may sue and be sued, and its affairs are generally administered by a board of managers or directors. But it differs from a corporation proper, both in the fact that it is not a legal entity separate and distinct from the members composing it, and also in the fact that all the members are personally liable for its debts.[41] A company or association of this

[40] Flint v. Stone Tracy Co., 220 U. S. 107, 31 Sup. Ct. 342, 55 L. Ed. 389, Ann. Cas. 1912B, 1312; Union Hollywood Water Co. v. Carter, 238 Fed. 329, 151 C. C. A. 345.

[41] See Allen v. Long, 80 Tex. 261, 16 S. W. 43, 26 Am. St. Rep. 735; Adams Express Co. v. Schofield, 111 Ky. 832, 64 S. W. 903; Kossakowski v. People, 177 Ill. 563, 53 N. E. 115; Lyon v. Denison, 80 Mich. 371, 45 N. W. 358, 8 L. R. A. 358; Sanford v. Board of Sup'rs of New York, 15 How. Prac. (N. Y.) 172;

kind may be formed and exist at common law. But the statutory law of some of the states (but not all) also authorizes the organization of such associations, or confers upon them more or. less of the characteristics and privileges of a corporation. In some cases these statutes go so far in this direction that the only practical difference between a corporation, properly so called, and a joint stock company organized under the state law is that, in the latter case, the stockholders remain personally liable for the debts. The federal corporation tax law of 1909 applied to "every corporation, joint stock company or association organized for profit and having a capital stock represented by shares, organized under the laws of the United States or of any state or territory." And the federal Supreme Court held that real estate trusts created by deed, for the purpose of purchasing, improving, holding, or selling lands and buildings for the benefit of the shareholders, which are not organized under any statute of the state where they are formed, and do not derive any benefit or privilege from any such statute, and which are not intended to have perpetual duration, but are limited by their terms to a fixed period, were not subject to the federal tax.[42]

On the other hand it has been held by a Circuit Court of Appeals that an unincorporated joint-stock company organized in New York, which operates an express business, its shares being transferable and its property being vested in trust for the association in five directors, enjoys such privileges under the statutes of New York as to be taxable as a joint-stock association existing under the laws of that state, under Corporation Excise Tax Law of 1909, providing that every corporation, joint-stock company or association, organized for profit and having a capital stock represented by shares, now or hereafter organized under the laws of any state, shall be subject to a special excise tax, since under the statutes of the state the association is endowed with capacities and attributes not possessed by a partnership at common law, it being practically a "corporation" by New York law, despite the absence of the important corporate attribute of limited liability.[43]

But it is important to notice that the act of 1916 is made applicable to "every corporation, joint stock company or association organized in the United States, no matter how created or organ-

In re Jones, 28 Misc. Rep. (N. Y.) 356, 59 N. Y. Supp. 983; Lane v. Albertson, 78 App. Div. 607, 79 N. Y. Supp. 947.

[42] Eliot v. Freeman, 220 U. S. 178, 31 Sup. Ct. 360, 55 L. Ed. 424.

[43] Roberts v. Anderson, 226 Fed. 7, 141 C. C. A. 121.

ized." In view of the decision above referred to, this change of language must be considered highly significant, and manifests an intention on the part of Congress to apply the tax to all kinds of joint stock companies or associations, whether organized in accordance with the law of any given state or merely with such powers and characteristics as they may possess at common law. And the Treasury department has ruled that: "It is immaterial how such corporations are created or organized. The terms 'joint-stock companies' or 'associations' shall include associates, real estate trusts, or by whatever name known, which carry on or do business in an organized capacity, whether organized under and pursuant to State laws, trust agreements, declarations of trusts, or otherwise, the net income of which, if any, is distributed, or distributable, among the members or share owners on the basis of the capital stock which each holds, or, where there is no capital stock, on the basis of the proportionate share of capital which each has invested in the business or property of the organization, all of which joint-stock companies or associations shall, in their organized capacity, be subject to the tax imposed by this act." (Internal Revenue Regulations No. 33, art. 79.)

§ 125. Same; Unincorporated Private Banking Associations

The following rulings of the Treasury Department are applicable to organizations of this class: "Private banks which have the form of corporate organizations, elect officers and a board of managers, have a distinctive name, a fixed situs, and distribute their net earnings upon the basis of the amount of capital invested by the members or owners, are held to be associations within the meaning of the federal income tax law, and in their organized capacity should make returns of annual net income and pay any income tax thereby shown to be due. The holders of the stock or the owners of the bank will be exempt from the normal tax to the extent of the dividends or earnings which they receive from such private banks as make returns in their organized capacity and pay income tax in accordance therewith. The individual owners of the bank will not be required to return as income for the purpose of the normal tax any dividends or earnings received from the private bank which pays the tax on its net earnings, but for the purpose of the supertax the dividends will be returned as income by the individual stockholders or owners. When it can be clearly shown that a private bank is owned by one man, it is evident that such bank is not an association within the meaning of the federal income tax law, and that therefore such bank will not be required to make a return such as corporations and associations are required to make, but the individual owner, if he has a net income of $3,000 or more, will be required to make a return, showing in such return the income which he receives not only from the bank but from all other sources." (T. D. 2137, Jan. 30, 1915.)

Later, and perhaps because the foregoing regulation had been misunderstood, the Treasury Department promulgated this further ruling: "In the case of private banks which have the form of corporations and which are held to be associations within the meaning of the federal income tax law, it is not the purpose of this office to assess the income tax against such banking associations and then also against the individual members of the association. Income which the members of the association receive from the bank because of their investments therein will be considered dividends, and for the purposes of the normal tax these dividends will not be required to be returned by the individual members receiving them, but if any individual member of the association have an income, including the dividends, of more than $20,000, the dividends in that case must be returned as income for the purposes of the additional or supertax." (T. D. 2152, Feb. 12, 1915.)

§ 126. Inactive Corporations and Holding Companies

A corporation which has an income, from whatever source derived, is not exempt from the income tax simply because it is not actively engaged in business or because it is merely a holding company. This tax (unlike the capital-stock tax or the corporation excise tax of 1909) is not laid on profits derived from business or on the franchise of doing business in a corporate form. It is a tax on "total net income received from all sources." The only exception to this rule is that prescribed in the statute itself, namely, in favor of a "corporation or association organized for the exclusive purpose of holding title to property, collecting income therefrom, and turning over the entire amount thereof, less expenses, to an organization which itself is exempt from the tax imposed by this title." (Act Cong. Sept. 8, 1916, § 11a, par. 12 [U. S. Comp. St. 1916, § 6336k].) As to others, the Treasury Department has ruled that "parent, holding, or other corporations must include in their gross income, and cannot deduct therefrom, any dividends or share of earnings which they may receive from a subsidiary, related, or any other corporation. The fact that the parent or holding company owns all the stock of the subsidiary company is imma-

(150)

terial, and will not warrant such parent company in omitting or deducting dividends from gross income." (T. D. 2090, Dec. 14, 1914.) A further ruling is as follows: "In a case wherein a holding company actually takes up each month on its books its proportionate share of the earnings of the underlying companies, such holding company will be required to include in its gross income the amounts thus taken up, regardless of the fact that the same may not have been actually paid to it in cash. The fact that the underlying companies credit to the holding company the amount of earnings to which it is entitled on the basis of the stock it holds, together with the fact that the holding company takes up on its books the amount thus credited, renders it incumbent upon the holding company to return these amounts as income, regardless of the fact that the underlying companies needed these earnings and used them in making extensions and improvements and in furtherance of their business. Expenditures for such extensions and improvements, being chargeable to the property account of the subsidiary companies, are not deductible from the gross income, and will therefore not have the effect to reduce the earnings to their respective shares of which the stockholders are entitled." (T. D. 2137, Jan. 30, 1915.)

§ 127. Lessor Corporations

The Treasury Department has ruled that "a railroad company operating leased or purchased lines shall include all receipts derived therefrom [in its own annual return] and if bonded indebtedness of such lines has been assumed, such operating company may deduct the interest paid thereon to an amount not exceeding one-half of the sum of its interest-bearing indebtedness and its paid-up capital stock outstanding at the close of the year." But "corporations operating leased lines should not include the stock of the lessor corporation in their own statement of capital stock outstanding at the close of the year. The indebtedness of such lessor corporations should not be included in the statement of the indebtedness of the lessee, unless the lessee has assumed the same. Each leased or subsidiary company will make its own separate return, accounting therein for all income which it may have received by way of dividends, rentals, interest, or from any other source." (Treasury Regulations No. 33, arts. 81, 82.)

§ 128. Corporations Fraudulently Formed to Evade Tax

In view of the fact that corporations, under the income tax law of 1916, are subject only to the so-called "normal" tax of one per cent, however great may be their earnings or profits while the individual taxpayer whose income exceeds $20,000 is subjected to an increasingly heavy "additional" tax, the device might easily have occurred to wealthy individuals and estates to reduce the burden of their taxes by the simple expedient of incorporating themselves. But this was met by a clause in the act providing that the additional tax shall be levied on and paid by individuals on their share of undivided or undistributed profits of any corporation or similar organization, which was formed or fraudulently availed of for the purpose of avoiding the tax by means of allowing gains and profits to accumulate, instead of being distributed. And the fact that the corporation is "a mere holding company" is made prima facie evidence of such fraudulent purpose. (Act Cong. Sept. 8, 1916, § 3 [U. S. Comp. St. 1916, § 6336c].) It will be observed that only the additional tax is referred to in this provision, for the reason that the normal tax of one per cent would be collected directly from the corporation on the basis of its net income. Whether such a device would have been effective in the absence of a statutory prohibition may well be doubted. There are decisions to the effect that individuals cannot escape liability before the law, whether for taxes or in respect to other matters, by forming a corporation which they absolutely control and which is their mere alter ego, so that, while the corporation is nominally an independent entity, they are its "mind, hands, and pockets," or by pretending that the profits and earnings on which the government seeks to lay a tax belong to a corporation, which is really no more than a shadow of themselves.[44]

§ 129. Corporations of Philippines and Porto Rico

The income tax law provides that "the provisions of this title shall extend to Porto Rico and the Philippine Islands: Provided, that the administration of the law and the collection of the taxes imposed in Porto Rico and the Philippine Islands shall be by the appropriate internal-revenue officers of those governments, and all revenues collected in Porto Rico and the Philippine Islands thereunder shall accrue intact to the general governments there-

[44] See In re Kornit Mfg. Co. (D. C.) 192 Fed. 392; Credit Mobilier of America v. Commonwealth, 67 Pa. 233.

of, respectively: Provided further, that the jurisdiction in this title conferred upon the district courts of the United States shall, so far as the Philippine Islands are concerned, be vested in the courts of the first instance of said islands: And provided further, that nothing in this title shall be held to exclude from the computation of the net income the compensation paid any official by the governments of the District of Columbia, Porto Rico, and the Philippine Islands, or the political subdivisions thereof." (Act Cong. Sept. 8, 1916, § 23 [U. S. Comp. St. 1916, § 6336v].) And the Treasury Department rules that corporations whose business is done wholly in Porto Rico and the Philippines, even though incorporated in the United States, are resident corporations of those possessions, and will make returns and pay the income tax to the collectors of internal revenue having jurisdiction there. (T. D. 2090, Dec. 14, 1914.)

§ 130. Insurance Companies

The act of Congress expressly applies to "every insurance company" organized in the United States, or organized under the laws of a foreign country and doing business in the United States. But as to mutual insurance companies, special rules are provided for ascertaining their taxable net income. In the case of mutual life insurance companies, it is enacted that they "shall not include as income in any year such portion of any actual premium received from any individual policy holder as shall have been paid back or credited to such individual policy holder, or treated as an abatement of premium of such individual policy holder, within such year." This provision was doubtless inserted in the act in view of the decisions which had been made on this point under the corporation excise tax law of 1909. That statute allowed insurance companies to deduct from their returns of income for taxation "sums other than dividends paid within the year on policy and annuity contracts." And it was held that the word "dividends" was here used in its popular sense as representing profits, and that so-called dividends of a mutual company doing business on the level premium plan, consisting merely of the portion of the loading of the premium charged in excess of the cost of insurance and returned annually to the policy holders after the first year, so far as the same were used to reduce subsequent premiums, were not income received and not subject to the tax. At the same time it was held that this rule does not apply to a dividend declared in the case of a full-paid participating policy, wherein the policy holder has no

(153)

further premium payments to make, which dividend constitutes a participation in the profits and income of the invested funds of the company.[45]

In the case of mutual fire insurance companies (and some others) "requiring their members to make premium deposits to provide for losses and expenses," it is provided that they "shall not return as income any portion of the premium deposits returned to their policy holders, but shall return as taxable income all income received by them from all other sources plus such portions of the premium deposits as are retained by the companies for purposes other than the payment of losses and expenses and reinsurance reserves." And in the case of mutual marine insurance companies, they "shall include in their return of gross income gross premiums collected and received by them less amounts paid for reinsurance, but shall be entitled to include in deductions from gross income amounts repaid to policy holders on account of premiums previously paid by them and interest paid upon such amounts between the ascertainment thereof and the payment thereof." (Act Cong. Sept. 8, 1916, § 12a, par. 2 [U. S. Comp. St. 1916, § 6336l].)

On this subject the Treasury Department has made the following ruling: "It would appear from this provision of the law that all assessments received by a mutual fire insurance company and not returned to the policy holders, but retained for purposes other than paying losses and expenses incurred during the year for which the return is made and for such reinsurance reserves as the laws of the state require, are taxable income. Therefore if mutual fire insurance companies retain out of moneys received on account of assessments an amount in excess of the losses, expenses, and reinsurance reserves of any particular year, that excess, plus amounts

---

[45] Connecticut Mut. Life Ins. Co. v. Eaton (D. C.) 218 Fed. 206; Mutual Benefit Life Ins. Co. v. Herold (D. C.) 198 Fed. 199, affirmed, 201 Fed. 918, 120 C. C. A. 256. And see New York Life Ins. Co. v. Styles, L. R. 14 App. Cas. 381, 59 Law J. Q. B. 291. But compare Last v. London Assur. Corp., L. R. 10 App. Cas. 438. In the latter case it appeared that a life insurance company issued "participating policies" at an increased premium, according to the terms of which, at the end of each five year period, the gross profits of such policies were dealt with as follows: Two-thirds were returned by way of bonus of abatement of premiums to the holders of such policies then in force, and the remaining one-third went to the company, which bore the whole expense of the business, the portion remaining after payment of expenses constituting the only profit available for dividends among the shareholders. It was held that the two-thirds returned to policy holders were "annual profits or gains" and assessable for the income tax.

received from interest, dividends, or any other source, will be considered net income, upon which the tax will be assessed. The above quoted provision of the law as construed by this office applies to all mutual fire insurance companies, regardless of the fact that some of them may not be primarily organized for profit." (T. D. 2161, Feb. 19, 1915.)

(155)

CHAPTER VII

EXEMPTIONS AND EXCEPTIONS

§ 131. Obligations and Revenues of United States, Its Possessions and Agencies

It is explicitly provided by the income tax act of 1916 (as amended in 1917) that certain kinds of income shall be exempt from the provisions of the statute, including "interest upon the obligations of the United States (but, in the case of obligations of the United States issued after September first, 1917, only if and to the extent provided in the act authorizing the issue thereof) or its possessions, or securities issued under the provisions of the Federal Farm Loan Act of July 17, 1916." (Act Cong. Sept. 8, 1916, § 4, as amended by Act Cong. Oct. 3, 1917, § 1200.) There is also a provision that, among the classes of corporations which shall be entirely exempt from the payment of the income tax, shall be included "Federal land banks and national farm-loan associations, as provided in § 26 of the act approved July 17, 1916." (Act Cong. Sept. 8, 1916, § 11a [U. S. Comp. St. 1916, § 6336k].) It is also to be noted that

(156)

the act authorizing the first "Liberty Loan" of 1917 expressly exempts both principal and interest of the bonds from all taxation imposed by the United States or its possessions, "except estate or inheritance taxes." (Act Cong. April 24, 1917.) The exemption enjoyed by the second issue of "Liberty" bonds is not so broad. It provides that they shall be exempt "from all taxation now or hereafter imposed by the United States, any state, or any of the possessions of the United States, or by any local taxing authority, except (a) estate or inheritance taxes, and (b) graduated additional income taxes, commonly known as surtaxes, and excess profits and war-profits taxes, now or hereafter imposed by the United States, upon the income or profits of individuals, partnerships, associations, or corporations. The interest on an amount of such bonds the principal of which does not exceed in the aggregate $5,000, owned by any individual, partnership, association, or corporation, shall be exempt from the taxes provided for in subdivision (b) of this section." (Act Cong. Sept. 24, 1917, § 7.)

The government's own revenues are naturally exempt from all taxation. This would appear to be too clear for argument. But the point might be of practical importance in its application to the case of a federal officer receiving fees for services, or a postmaster taking in money from the sale of stamps. If the receipts of the office (or fees) constitute the officer's compensation, they are part of his private income and may be taxable; but if he is paid a salary and required to turn in the fees or receipts of his office to the Treasury, such moneys are public revenues and not taxable.

§ 132. Revenues of States and Municipalities

It is not within the constitutional authority of Congress to lay the burden of federal taxation upon the revenues of a state or a municipal corporation, at least in so far as the same are raised by the ordinary methods of state and local taxation, or accrue from property owned or money invested by a state. Thus, it has been held that the word "corporation," in an internal revenue law, does not include a state, so that a railroad wholly owned by a state, managed by state agents, and the profits of which form a part of the revenue of the state, is not liable to taxation under such law.[1] So also, a municipal corporation is, at least in its political aspects, a portion of the sovereign power of the state, or a depository thereof, and therefore is not subject to taxation by Congress upon its mu-

---

[1] Georgia v. Atkins, 35 Ga. 315, Fed. Cas. No. 5,350.

nicipal revenues.[2] But the exemption of a state from taxation extends no further than the functions belonging to a state in its ordinary capacity, the exemption of sovereignty being limited by the attributes of sovereignty. Hence if a state unites in one undertaking an exercise of the police power with a commercial business,—as in the case of the South Carolina dispensary law, where regulation of the sale of intoxicating liquors was effected by the state itself engaging in the business and monopolizing the traffic,—the United States cannot be compelled to aid the operation of the police power by foregoing its right to lay an impost or excise tax on the business part of the transaction. And hence, the agents of the state government employed in the operation of the dispensary law were held liable to pay the internal revenue tax imposed by the act of Congress.[3] And the Supreme Court of the United States has also ruled that a municipal corporation engaged in the business of distilling spirits is subject to internal revenue taxation under the laws of the United States, whether its acts in that respect are or are not ultra vires.[4] It was probably with a view to just such cases as these that Congress, in the income tax law of 1916, has expressly disclaimed the intention to apply the statute to the revenues of states or municipal corporations, the provision being that "there shall not be taxed under this title any income derived from any public utility or from the exercise of any essential governmental function accruing to any state, territory, or the District of Columbia, or any political subdivision of a state or territory, nor any income accruing to the government of the Philippine Islands or Porto Rico, or of any political subdivision of the Philippine Islands or Porto Rico." (Act Cong. Sept. 8, 1916, § 11b.)

It was ruled by the officers of the Treasury Department that a municipal corporation which owns and operates its own waterworks, or a plant for the production and distribution of gas or electric light to its citizens, was not subject to the corporation tax under the Act of Congress of 1909, although it makes and collects fixed charges for the service so rendered and derives a profit therefrom. But this was on the explicit ground that a municipality is not a corporation "organized for profit" or one "having a capital stock represented by shares", within the language of that statute. (T. D. 1634.)

[2] U. S. v. Baltimore & O. R. Co., 17 Wall. 322, 21 L. Ed. 597.

[3] South Carolina v. U. S., 199 U. S. 437, 26 Sup. Ct. 110, 50 L. Ed. 261, 4 Ann. Cas. 737.

[4] Salt Lake City v. Hollister, 118 U. S. 256, 6 Sup. Ct. 1055, 30 L. Ed. 176.

§ 133. Interest on State and Municipal Bonds

Although the statute explicitly provides that "interest upon the obligations of a state or any political subdivision thereof" shall be "exempt from the provisions of this title" (Act Cong. Sept. 8, 1916, § 4 [U. S. Comp. St. 1916, § 6336d]), there was at first a good deal of hesitation on the part of banks and other collecting agencies as to receiving such items for collection, when unaccompanied by ownership certificates, without deducting the normal tax.   The Treasury Department found it necessary to issue a ruling that "the income derived from the interest upon the obligations of a state, county, city, or any other political subdivision thereof, or upon the obligations of the United States or its possessions, is not subject to the income tax, and a certificate of ownership in connection with the coupons or registered interest orders for such interest will not be required."   (T. D. 1892, Nov. 6, 1913.)   And again: "The income derived in the shape of interest from the obligations, general or special, of any state, or of any county, municipality, or taxing district therein, shall be exempt from the collection of the income tax at the source, whether the payment of such obligation is provided for by general or local taxation or out of a general, special, or separate fund."   (T. D. 1922, Dec. 24, 1913.)

§ 134. Political Subdivisions of State

The present income tax law, following in this respect the language of the act of 1913, provides that "interest upon the obligations of a state or any political subdivision thereof" shall be exempt.   The phrase "political subdivision" is not entirely new in the law.   As a general rule, a "political subdivision" of a state is a certain defined territory within the state, together with its inhabitants, organized for the public advantage and not in the interest of any particular individuals or classes, the chief design of which is the exercise of governmental functions, and to which is committed either generally or with reference to certain specific purposes the power of local self-government, including the power of taxation, to be exercised within the territory by the qualified electors for the benefit of the people residing within it.[5]   Quite early in the history of the income tax law, it became necessary for the officers of the Treasury department to interpret this clause of the statute with reference to interest on the bonds issued by ir-

[5] See Smith v. Howell, 60 N. J. Law, 384, 38 Atl. 180; State v. Englewood Drainage Com'rs, 41 N. J. Law, 154; Allison v. Corker, 67 N. J. Law, 596, 52 Atl. 362, 60 L. R. A. 564.

rigation districts and reclamation districts in some of the western states, and they held that such districts were not political subdivisions of the state creating them.[6] But the question was referred to the Attorney General, who gave an opinion to the effect that special assessment districts created under the laws of the several states for public purposes, such as the improvement of streets and public highways, the provision for sewerage, gas, and light, and the reclamation, drainage, or irrigation of bodies of land within such special assessment districts, when such districts are for public use, are political subdivisions of the state. In deference to this opinion, the Treasury department revoked its former ruling and made a decision that the term "political subdivision" of a state "includes special assessment districts or divisions of a state created by the proper authority of the state acting within its constitutional powers and under its general laws, for the purpose of carrying out a portion of those functions of the state which by long usage and inherent necessities of government have always been regarded as public. Levee and school districts, when lawfully created under the authority of the state, and which are authorized by the laws of the state to levy a tax to meet the obligations of such districts, are also held to be political subdivisions of a state." (T. D. 1946, Feb. 10, 1914.)

§ 135. Public Utilities Owned by States or Municipalities

If income accrues to any state or to any political subdivision of a state from the operation of any "public utility," it is expressly excepted from the income tax, and this provision is made broad enough to include the territories, the District of Columbia, the government of the Philippine Islands, and that of Porto Rico. It was probably in the mind of Congress to exempt municipal corporations from the tax when they take upon themselves for the benefit of their citizens such services as are usually performed by various kinds of public service corporations, as, for instance, in the case of a gas plant or waterworks owned and operated by the municipality. If it were not for this provision in the statute, it might be thought that, in such cases, a municipal corporation was engaged in a purely business enterprise, distinct from its governmental functions, and therefore should be subject to the tax. But the statute goes further than this. It also provides that if any state, territory, district, or political subdivision, prior to the passage

[6] T. D. 1910, Dec. 4, 1913.

of the act, shall have contracted in good faith with any person or corporation to acquire, construct, operate or maintain a public utility, the tax shall not be levied on that part of the income from the public utility which accrues to the state, municipality, etc., although the person or corporation contracted with is not relieved from the payment of the tax upon that portion of the income which accrues to him or it under the contract.[7] It is to be noted, however, that this will not apply to any contracts entered into since the passage of the act. Aside from such a provision, it appears that a public enterprise conducted by a municipality and a private corporation jointly or in partnership could not escape taxation on account of the interest of the municipality in it. Thus, a gas company was held taxable under the income tax law of 1862, although its board of trustees or directors was elected by the council of the city in which its operations were carried on, under an ordinance to that effect, and though the greater part of its capital was raised by means of loans guaranteed by the city or for which the direct obligations of the city were issued, and though the ordinance creating it provided that the property and works might be taken over by the city at any time on certain conditions.[8] The Treasury department rules that where a municipality purchases a public utility subject to a mortgage, the mortgage retains its original character, even though the municipality assumes the mortgage indebtedness and pays the interest thereon; therefore the indebtedness secured by such mortgage is not an obligation of the municipality, within the meaning of the income tax law. (Treasury Decision No. 2090, December 14, 1914.)

§ 136. Corporations Specifically Exempted

The corporation excise tax law of 1909 applied to corporations "organized for profit and having a capital stock represented by shares." This raised the question whether companies not "organized for profit" were taxable or exempt under the act of 1913, and the argument that they were exempt received a certain plausible

---

[7] An individual who enters into a contract with a state, or any political subdivision thereof, for the construction of a public highway, is held not to be an officer or employee of the said state or a political subdivision thereof, and therefore the amounts received by him from the state or a political subdivision thereof, under the terms of the contract, are not exempt from tax under the provisions of the Federal income tax law, and should be included in any return of annual net income he may be required to render. (T. D. 2152, Feb. 12, 1915.)

[8] City of Philadelphia v. The Collector, 5 Wall. 720, 18 L. Ed. 614.

support from the fact that the same phrase, "not organized for profit," occurred in that clause of the act of 1913 which specifically excepted certain kinds of companies from its operation. But a more careful construction shows that the phrase in question was meant to be restricted to those organizations named immediately before it, such as chambers of commerce, boards of trade, and civic leagues or organizations, and was not applicable to corporations in general or to the other classes of corporations mentioned in that part of the statute. As to any particular kind of corporation, therefore, its taxable status depends solely upon whether or not it is within the classes exempted by name or description in the Act of Congress, not upon the question whether or not it is organized or operated for profit. (T. D. 2152, Feb. 12, 1915.) For these reasons the Treasury Department held, under the act of 1913, that co-operative dairies, mutual telephone companies, local, mutual, or farmers' insurance companies and other like organizations, were subject to the income tax, although not organized or conducted with a view to making a profit. (T. D. 1933, Jan. 12, 1914; T. D. 1996, June 15, 1914.) But the present statute expressly exempts any "farmers' or other mutual hail, cyclone, or fire insurance company, mutual ditch or irrigation company, mutual or co-operative telephone company, or like organization of a purely local character, the income of which consists solely of assessments, dues, and fees collected from members for the sole purpose of meeting its expenses." (Act Cong. Sept. 8, 1916, § 11a, subd. 10 [U. S. Comp. St. 1916, § 6336k]).

§ 137. Same; Claiming and Proving Exempt Character

All kinds of corporations claiming to be exempt as coming within the excepting clauses of the act may be called upon by the local collector or by the Commissioner of Internal Revenue to establish their right to the exemption claimed, by affidavit or otherwise. And in this case, the regulations provide, "it will not be sufficient merely to declare that they are exempt, but they must show the character and purpose of the organization, the manner of distributing the net income, if any, or that none of the net income inures to the benefit of any private stockholder or individual. In the absence of such a showing, such organizations may at any time be required to make returns of annual net income, or disclose their books of account to a revenue officer for examination, in order that the status of the company may be determined." (Internal Revenue Regulations No. 33, art. 88.) And it is also provided by regulation that "any corporation, concerning whose status under the law there is any doubt, or which does not clearly come within one or another of the classes of those specifically enumerated as exempt, should file a return (in blank if desired) and attach thereto a statement setting out fully the nature and purpose of the organization, the source of its income and what disposition is made of it, and particularly of any surplus." (Id., art. 91.) But in cases where corporations have, by affidavit or otherwise, "clearly established the fact and satisfied collectors of internal revenue that they are exempt from the requirements of the federal income tax law, or are defunct, dissolved, or obsolete, and are no longer carrying on any business and have no property or income, returns will not be required of them after such condition has been clearly established. But one showing of this character as to each such particular corporation will be required, unless it shall later appear that any such corporation shall have such income within the meaning of the law as brings it within its requirements." (T. D. 2137, Jan. 30, 1915.)

§ 138. Corporation Owned by Exempt Organization

The Treasury Department has ruled that: "A stock corporation all of whose stock is owned by a corporation or association organized and operated exclusively for religious, charitable, scientific, or educational purposes, no part of whose net income inures to the benefit of any member, stockholder, or individual, is required, under the provisions of the federal income tax law, to make a return of annual net income and pay the income tax. The fact that all of the stock of a corporation, except shares qualifying the directors, is owned by a corporation which itself comes within the class specifically enumerated as exempt, does not relieve the first-named corporation from liability under the income tax law. The liability of a .corporation to the requirements of the federal income tax law is not contingent upon the ownership of its stock." (T. D. 2137, Jan. 30, 1915.) But this ruling, made under the act of 1913, has been materially limited by the provision in the act of 1916 which exempts from taxation the income received by any "corporation or association organized for the exclusive purpose of holding title to property, collecting income therefrom, and turning over the entire amount thereof, less expenses, to an organization which itself is exempt from the tax imposed by this title." (Act Cong. Sept. 8, 1916, § 11a, subd. 12.) And it should be observed that, although a particular corporation may be exempt from the income tax, such as a religious society or a college, it does not follow that salaries which it pays to its officers or employés are equally exempt. On the contrary, they are taxable, although the corporation is not required to deduct and withhold for the tax. (T. D. 2090, Dec. 14, 1914.)

§ 139. Close Corporations

There is a Treasury ruling that "a corporation formed as a family affair to hold property together, and not to sacrifice in selling, does not come within the class of corporations specifically enumerated as exempt from the requirements of the federal income tax law, and it is required to make a return of annual net income, showing therein all income arising and accruing to it from all sources, and to pay any income tax shown by such return to be due." (T. D. 2137, Jan. 30, 1915.)

§ 140. Agricultural and Horticultural Organizations

Following the language of the act of 1909, the income tax act of 1916 specifically exempts from its operation "agricultural or horticultural organizations." This phrase has not been judicially construed by the courts, but several rulings of the Treasury Department have indicated its meaning, as viewed by the officers charged with the administration of the law. Agricultural organizations, it was ruled, do not come within the statutory exemption, unless their chief object is the promotion or advancement of agricultural interests, and no part of the income inures to the benefit of their stockholders. "A corporation engaged in agricultural, horticultural, or similar pursuits, evidently for profit, is not, within the meaning of the law, such an agricultural or horticultural association as is specifically enumerated as exempt from the requirements of the act cited. Corporations, to come within the exempted class, must be such associations as, by. means of exhibits, contests, awards, and premiums, are designed to encourage better production of agricultural or horticultural products, not themselves engaged in agricultural or horticultural pursuits, such as county fairs and like organizations of a quasi public character, whose income, derived from gate receipts, entry fees, donations, etc., is used to meet the necessary expenses of the association, the payment of premiums, making improvements, etc., no part of which income inures to the benefit of any private stockholder or individual. A corporation engaged in the business of raising stock or poultry, or growing grain, fruits, or other products of this character, is an agricultural or horticultural society only in the sense that it indicates the kind of business in which it is engaged. If the business of the corporation so engaged is so carried on that its income inures or may inure to the benefit of its stockholders, it will be held to be a corporation organized for profit, and, regardless of the fact that it may be engaged in agricultural or horticultural pursuits, it must make returns of annual net income for each calendar year, and pay any special excise tax to which such returns may show it to be liable." [*] Thus, fruit growers' associations whose purpose is to promote the mutual benefit of their members in growing, harvesting, and marketing their products, and which are not organized for profit and have no capital stock represented by shares, and whose income is derived wholly from membership fees, dues, and assessments to meet necessary expenses, are not liable to the tax. But on the other hand, corporations owning sugar or other plantations and disposing of the products thereof, are not entitled to the exemption simply in view of the nature of their business. And corporations engaged in growing fruits, vegetables, and like products for profit, and which distribute such profits among their members on the basis of the capital invested, are liable to the statute and must make returns and pay the taxes if any are found to be due. (Treasury Decisions, No. 1742, pars. 23, 29, 30.) But note that the present statute specifically exempts any "farmers', fruit growers', or other like association, organized and operated as a sales agent for the purpose of marketing the products of its members and turning back to them the proceeds of sales, less the necessary selling expenses, on the basis of the quantity of produce furnished by them." (Act Cong. Sept. 8, 1916, § 11a, subd. 11.)

§ 141. Labor Organizations

A specific exemption is made in the federal income tax law in favor of "labor organizations." This phrase is not elsewhere defined in the act, but the intention of Congress in this behalf is plainly indicated by the events of political history and the trend of legislation in recent years. The term "labor," as here used, evidently cannot be taken in the rather wide sense given to it in some other phrases familiar in the law, such as "work and labor," "common labor," "worldly labor," and the like. But the organizations referred to are those associations of mechanics and artisans, and even of unskilled laborers, which are formed for the purpose of the mu-

[*] Treasury Decisions No. 1737.

tual advantage and protection of their members, for enforcing the regulations which they prescribe with reference to the conditions and hours of labor and the rate of wages, and other such objects, and which are commonly called "trades unions" or "brotherhoods," "federations," "guilds," or "unions" of the mechanics employed in any given trade or craft.

§ 142. Fraternal Orders and Benefit Societies

There is a specific exemption in the income tax law in favor of any "fraternal beneficiary society, order, or association, operating under the lodge system or for the exclusive benefit of the members of a fraternity itself operating under the lodge system, and providing for the payment of life, sick, accident, or other benefits to the members of such society, order, or association or their dependents." (Act Cong. Sept. 8, 1916, § 11a, subd. 3.) As here used, the word "lodge" means the meeting place (and hence the meeting itself or the aggregate of the members) of a secret society or fraternity.[10] Such bodies are very numerous in the United States, and for the most part they combine with their social, moral, or philanthropic objects the grant of pecuniary relief to sick or disabled members and to the families of deceased members. On this subject it has been remarked; "It is noteworthy that while the phrase 'fraternal beneficial' is used in the connection above shown to designate a particular kind of societies or associations that may be incorporated, yet it was not thought necessary to otherwise define the descriptive phrase thus employed. We must accordingly assume that the words 'fraternal beneficial' were used in their ordinary sense, to designate an association or society that is engaged in some work that is of a fraternal and beneficial character. According to this view, a fraternal beneficial society would be one whose members have adopted the same or a very similar calling, avocation, or profession, or who are working in unison to accomplish some worthy object, and for that reason have banded themselves together as an association or society to aid and assist one another, and to promote the common cause. The term 'fraternal' can properly be applied to such an association, for the reason that the pursuit of a common

[10] State v. Farmers' & Mechanics' Mut. Aid Ass'n, 35 Kan. 51, 9 Pac. 956. "A society or association operating under the lodge system is considered to be one organized under a charter, with properly appointed or elected officers, with an adopted ritual or ceremonial holding meetings at stated intervals, and supported by fees, dues, or assessments." Internal Revenue Regulations No. 33, art. 89.

object, calling, or profession usually has a tendency to create a brotherly feeling among those who are thus engaged. It is a well known fact that there are at the present time many voluntary or incorporated societies which are made up exclusively of persons who are engaged in the same avocation. As a general rule, such associations have been formed for the purpose of promoting the social, moral, and intellectual welfare of the members of such associations and their families, as well as for advancing their interests in other ways and in other respects." [11]

But many fraternal orders or associations are in fact but mutual insurance associations, their revenues being derived from entrance fees, membership dues, and occasional assessments levied on the members, and expended (over and above the cost of management and other small necessary expenses) in the payment of sick, accident, and death benefits. The officers of the treasury department have ruled that such an association, if it does not "operate under the lodge system," is simply an insurance company and subject to the tax, notwithstanding that all its funds are derived from membership fees and assessments and expended in the payment of such benefits.[12] A similar decision was made by a federal court in construing a state statute relating to insurance companies, which, in one section, provided that the term "insurance company" should not apply to "secret or fraternal societies, lodges, or councils which are under the supervision of a grand or supreme body, and secure members through the lodge system exclusively." It was said: "We think the association comes within the provisions of the Kentucky statute just cited; for, while it has among its purposes the promotion of acquaintance and friendship among traveling men, and to obtain for them better railroad rates and hotel accommodations, it may be said to be its principal purpose to provide a benefit fund for members in case of death or accident. This fund is derived from dues, and when depleted is replaced by assessment upon members. The certificate of membership provides for payment of a specific sum for death by accident. Provisions are made for enforcing and collecting the payment of dues. We think this association comes under the Kentucky statute, unless it is within the

---

[11] National Union v. Marlow, 74 Fed. 775, 21 C. C. A. 89.

[12] Treasury Decisions No. 1738. There is no exemption in the income tax law in favor of insurance companies other than fraternal beneficiary societies operating under the lodge system. Commercial Travelers' Life & Accident Ass'n v. Rodway (D. C.) 235 Fed. 370.

exception embodied in section 641 of the statutes. We find nothing in the organization of a secret or fraternal character. We do not find the supervision of a grand or supreme body and members secured by the lodge system exclusively. Not all commercial travelers may become members entitled to the benefits of the insurance. An application is required, setting forth the willingness of each applicant to submit to a physical examination, and waiving all provisions of law now existing or that may hereafter exist preventing any examining or attending physician from disclosing any information acquired while acting in a professional capacity or otherwise, or rendering him incompetent to testify as a witness in any way whatever. The 'benefits' are stated at a fixed amount in case of death, and certain specific sums for various injuries. It is evident that persons not answering these questions satisfactorily, though otherwise eligible, would be rejected as members. We do not discover in this association the features which characterize associations which the statute exempts from its provisions." [13]

§ 143. Religious, Charitable, and Benevolent Associations

The act of Congress also exempts any "corporation or association organized and operated exclusively for religious, charitable, scientific, or educational purposes, no part of the net income of which inures to the benefit of any private stockholder or individual." The rules with reference to the exemption of such associations from the burdens of ordinary taxation have been well worked out by the courts, and will generally be found applicable in the case of the special tax here under consideration. Specifically with regard to the corporation excise tax of 1909, it was ruled that a charitable institution was exempt whether it was supported by voluntary contributions or by state appropriations. (T. D. No. 1742, par. 4.) In England the rule has been stated that, in the income tax law, the words "charitable purposes" are to be interpreted, not according to their popular meaning, but according to their technical legal signification, though it was held in the same case that the phrase would include a home or asylum for the maintenance of single persons and widows belonging to the Moravian brotherhood.[14] And it is a general rule, in the construction of exemptions from taxation that the word "charity" is not to be restricted to the relief of the sick or poor, but extends to any form

---

13 Corley v. Travelers' Protective Ass'n. 105 Fed. 854, 46 C. C. A. 278.
14 Income Tax Com'rs v. Pemsel [1891] App. Cas. 531, 3 Tax Cas. 53.

of philanthropic endeavor or public beneficence.[15] And even under the more restricted form of exemption under the tax laws of some of the states, extending to "public" charities, or "institutions, of purely public charity," it is held that the term "public" is not equivalent to "universal." The exemption would not apply to a charity limited to a certain class of privileged individuals. But on the other hand, it need not be open to all persons alike, for the "public" to which it administers relief may be limited to the inhabitants of a given city or other place, or may be restricted to the sufferers from particular diseases or forms of need, or with reference to nationality, color, or religious connections.[16] Also, it is a well-recognized rule that an institution such as a hospital or asylum does not lose its character as a "charitable institution" because it receives pay patients, or in other words requires those of sufficient pecuniary ability to pay for the accommodation and treatment which they receive, if the income thus derived is not distributed among the corporators or stockholders, but applied exclusively to the purposes of the institution, and if, at the same time, poor or indigent patients are received and treated without charge.[17] But an English decision holds that if a hospital takes paying patients at remunerative prices, and applies its surplus income to the extension and improvement of the hospital buildings,

[15] See Gerke v. Purcell, 25 Ohio St. 229; Cleveland Library Ass'n v. Pelton, 36 Ohio St. 253; State v. Academy of Science, 13 Mo. App. 213; Massachusetts Society v. Boston, 142 Mass. 24, 6 N. E. 840. In England, on the question whether the income from an endowment is exempt as devoted to a "charitable purpose," the test is whether such income is "given in trust to be expended in assisting people to something considered by the donor to be for their benefit, and which assistance the donor intends shall be given to people who, in his opinion, cannot without such assistance, by reason of poverty, obtain that benefit, and where the intention of the donor is to assist such poverty as the substantial cause of his gift." Queen v. Com'rs of Income Tax, L. R. 22 Q. B. Div. 296, 308; In re Duty on Bootham Ward Strays, 60 Law J. Q. B. 612.

[16] Bangor v. Masonic Lodge, 73 Me. 428, 40 Am. Rep. 369; Burd Orphan Asylum v. School Dist., 90 Pa. 21; Hebrew Orphan Asylum v. New York, 11 Hun (N. Y.) 116; Income Tax Com'rs v. Pemsel [1891] App. Cas. 531, 3 Tax Cas. 53; Hastings v. Long, 11 Pa. Dist. R. 70.

[17] State v. Board of Assessors, 52 La. Ann. 223, 26 South. 872; Hennepin County v. Brotherhood of Gethsemane, 27 Minn. 460, 8 N. W. 595, 38 Am. Rep. 298; Philadelphia v. Pennsylvania Hospital, 154 Pa. 9, 25 Atl. 1076; Cawse v. Nottingham Lunatic Asylum [1891] 1 Q. B. 585, 60 Law J. Q. B. 485; Blake v. London, 18 Q. B. Div. 437. But see Needham v. Bowers, L. R. 21 Q. B. Div. 437, 2 Tax Cas. 360.

the surplus is profit and assessable for the income tax.[18] The business of maintaining a cemetery, from which revenues are derived in the form of cash for the sale of grave-sites or burial lots and annual dues or assessments upon lot-owners for the care of the grounds, is not a charity, and a corporation owning and conducting the cemetery is taxable on the income derived from it.[19] But the federal income tax law of 1916 contains a specific exemption in favor of any "cemetery company owned and operated exclusively for the benefit of its members." And on this the Treasury Department remarks that "the provisions of the law clearly indicate that companies which operate cemeteries for profit are liable to the tax. The status of cemetery associations under the law will therefore depend upon the character and purpose of the organization and what disposition is made of the income." (Internal Revenue Regulations No. 33, art. 90.)

§ 144. Educational and Scientific Institutions

The act of Congress exempts corporations organized for "scientific or educational purposes." It has been held that a provision of an income tax law exempting from its operation private schools, colleges, and other educational institutions does not make an illegal discrimination such as to render the law invalid as to other corporations or persons upon whom the tax is imposed.[20] But it seems clear that a private school, in which tuition fees are charged, and from which a revenue is derived over and above the expenses, would not be exempt under the provisions quoted, since the statute applies only to educational institutions "no part of the net income of which inures to the benefit of any private stockholder or individual." On the other hand, the exemption is apparently broad enough to include various kinds of institutions which derive their current revenues partly from endowment funds and partly from small charges to the public for admission to their buildings or

[18] St. Andrew's Hospital v. Shearsmith, L. R. 19 Q. B. Div. 624, 2 Tax Cas. 219. And in general, if a charitable, religious, or philanthropic organization incidentally to its main enterprises engages in such a business as printing and selling books, its profits therefrom are chargeable with the income tax. Religious Tract & Book Soc. v. Forbes, 33 Scotch Law Rep. 289, 3 Tax Cas. 415; Trustees of Psalms & Hymns v. Whitwell, 3 Tax Cas. 7.

[19] Paddington Burial Board v. Com'rs of Inland Revenue, L. R. 13 Q. B. Div. 9, 2 Tax Cas. 46; Paisley Cemetery Co. v. Reith, 35 Scotch Law Rep. 947, 4 Tax Cas. 1; Edinburgh Southern Cemetery Co. v. Kinmont, 2 Tax Cas. 516.

[20] Peacock v. Pratt, 121 Fed. 772, 58 C. C. A. 48.

for the use of their privileges, such as art galleries, museums of curiosities or antiquities, academies of the fine arts, institutions for the exhibition of objects illustrating the natural sciences, public libraries, and the like. In the general law of taxation, and with reference to exemptions, there has been much doubt as to whether such institutions could be classed as "schools," "institutions of learning," "purely. public charities," or the like.[21] But under the income tax laws, the test is in the question whether or not they are conducted for profit, or whether or not any part of the income is distributed to the proprietors, corporators, or shareholders as a gain or profit. And on the analogy of many similar cases, it would seem that the mere fact of admission fees being charged would not make them institutions conducted for profit, if the revenue so obtained is applied to the up-keep or expansion of the institution, rather than to the benefit of any private person interested in it.

§ 145. Building and Loan Associations

The federal income tax is not to be levied upon any "domestic building and loan association and co-operative banks without capital stock organized and operated for mutual purposes and without profit." Under substantially similar language in the act of 1913 and the corporation excise tax law of 1909, it was ruled by the Treasury Department that "building and loan associations are not exempt if they loan money to others than their members, thus doing a business similar to that engaged in by banks and trust companies. It is also held that building and loan associations

[21] Academy of Fine Arts v. Philadelphia County, 22 Pa. 496; Gerke v. Purcell, 25 Ohio St. 229; Salem Lyceum v. Salem, 154 Mass. 15, 27 N. E. 672; Mercantile Library Co. v. Philadelphia, 14 Pa. Co. Ct. R. 204; Cleveland Library Ass'n v. Pelton, 36 Ohio St. 253; Philadelphia Library Co. v. Donohugh, 12 Phila. (Pa.) 284; Manchester v. McAdam [1896] App. Cas. 500. In England, it has been held that a corporation founding and maintaining a free public library was not a "literary or scientific institution" within the meaning of the exemption clauses in the income tax law. Andrews v. Mayor of Bristol, 61 Law J. Q. B. 715. Also it was held by the court of Queen's Bench, under the exemption of income from property devoted to the "promotion of education, literature, science, or the fine arts," that the property of an institution of civil engineers was not entitled to exemption, because it was appropriated and applied not for the promotion of general education or science, but for the promotion of a particular branch of knowledge in order to enable the members of the institution to practice with more success their own profession. In re Duty on Estate of Institution of Civil Engineers, L. R. 19 Q. B. Div. 610. But this decision was reversed on appeal, in Commissioners of Inland Revenue v. Forrest, L. R. 15 App. Cas. 334.

which receive sums of money on deposit, which is not in payment
of stock, and on which the depositor receives a fixed rate of interest, regardless of the earnings of the association, are conducting
a business similar to a banking business, and are therefore subject
to the special excise tax on corporations and should be required to
make a return showing their net income." [22] It was likewise held
that such associations, providing for the loaning of funds to non-
members, for issuing preferred or guarantied interest-paying stock,
and allowing directors to cancel outstanding certificates of general
stock not borrowed upon, paying the holder the book value of
stock canceled, thereby being authorized to retire any and all stock
in their discretion, are not exempt from the tax.[23] But both the
ruling of the Treasury department and the decision cited have
been overruled by later decisions of the federal courts. The present doctrine is that neither the loaning of money to non-members
nor the issuance of prepaid stock bearing a fixed dividend is sufficient to take the association out of the benefit of the exemption.
In one of the cases so holding it was held that a building association is not excluded from the benefit of the exemption, as not
being "organized and operated exclusively for the mutual benefit
of its members," because it issues both prepaid and installment
stock, the prepaid stock being entitled to a fixed dividend, payable,
however, only out of earnings of the association.[24] And in another
case it was held that the fact that building and loan associations
organized under the laws of Ohio are authorized to borrow money
from, and loan money to, those who are not members does not deprive them of the quality of mutuality, nor place them on a par
with banking corporations, nor deprive them of the benefit of the
exemption from the income tax.[25]

§ 146. Mutual Savings Banks

Exemption from the federal income tax is also extended to any
"mutual savings bank not having a capital stock represented by
shares." Whether or not an institution exercising some of the
functions of a bank is to be classed as a "savings bank," "savings

[22] T. D. No. 1655.

[23] Pacific B. & L. Ass'n v. Hartson (D. C.) 201 Fed. 1011.

[24] Herold v. Parkview B. & L. Ass'n, 210 Fed. 577, 127 C. C. A. 213, affirming Parkview B. & L. Ass'n v. Herold (D. C.) 203 Fed. 876.

[25] Central Bldg., Loan & Sav. Co. v. Bowland (D. C.) 216 Fed. 526. And see
Wilson v. Parvin, 119 Fed. 652, 56 C. C. A. 268; People v. Preston, 140 N.
Y. 549, 35 N. E. 979, 24 L. R. A. 57.

institution," or "savings association," must be determined not by the name which it assumes or by which it is chartered, but by its organization, powers, and mode of doing business, as provided in its articles of incorporation.[26] And the phrases above quoted do not apply to every bank merely because it receives deposits of savings. The kind of associations intended by the law are those which are operated exclusively for the mutual benefit of the depositors, who alone—and not any stockholders or proprietors—are entitled to participate in the profits. Such associations are authorized under the laws of numerous states, as for example, Massachusetts, where they are thus described: A savings bank, as existing in this state, subject to the general laws, is an institution for the purpose of receiving deposits for the benefit of depositors, investing the same, accumulating the profits or interest thereof, paying such profits or interest to the depositor, or retaining the same for his greater security. There is no capital stock, and no stockholders who are entitled to receive profits from the business; but its affairs are administered by a board of trustees, the securities in which the deposits shall be invested are prescribed by law, and the conduct of its affairs is under the supervision of a public officer.[27] So, in New Jersey, it is said that a savings bank is a quasi charitable and purely benevolent institution, its only object being the safe keeping and provident investment of the funds of the depositors. The members of the corporation have no property interest in its funds, of which they are by law constituted the managers and guardians. The depositors, who alone are beneficially interested, have no voice in the management, nor even in the selection of the persons to whom the management is intrusted. Savings banks have no capital stock. They are incorporated and organized, not for the benefit of the corporators, but solely for the advantage of their depositors.[28]

§ 147. Civic Organizations and Chambers of Commerce

Specific exemption from the income tax is granted to any "business league, chamber of commerce, or board of trade, not organized for profit and no part of the net income of which inures to the benefit of any private stockholder or individual," and also to any "civic league or organization not organized for profit but operated exclusively for the promotion of social welfare." A board of trade,

[26] State v. Lincoln Sav. Bank, 14 Lea (Tenn.) 42.
[27] Commonwealth v. Reading Sav. Bank, 133 Mass. 16, 43 Am. Rep. 495.
[28] Barrett v. Bloomfield Sav. Inst., 64 N. J. Eq. 425, 54 Atl. 543.

as the term is used in America, is an organization of the principal merchants, manufacturers, tradesmen, etc., of a city, for the purpose of furthering its commercial interests, encouraging the establishment of manufacturers, promoting trade, securing or improving shipping facilities, and generally advancing the prosperity of the place as an industrial and commercial community. Exactly similar organizations are sometimes called "chambers of commerce," and the two terms are frequently stated to be synonymous. But more strictly speaking, one of the objects of a chamber of commerce is to promote convenience or facility in buying, selling, and exchanging commodities. If these commodities include stocks, bonds, and other securities, the body practically fulfills the functions of a stock exchange. And in fact, in some cities, the stock exchange is officially denominated the "chamber of commerce" or the "board of trade." If, in this sense, it is organized for profit, or has a net income which inures to the benefit of the members, it is clearly not within the exemption, but is subject to taxation under the act.

§ 148. Incorporated Clubs

Under the income tax law of 1913, incorporated clubs, organized for social purposes or for sport, and not eleemosynary or educational in character nor in the nature of benefit or insurance societies, were not specifically exempted; and the presumption was that such a club was liable to the income tax if it derived a revenue from membership dues, rent of rooms, profits of restaurant or bar, etc., and had any net income after paying expenses and deducting the other items allowed by the statute. This was the position taken by the English courts in applying the income tax law of that country.[29] And the Treasury Department made the following ruling: "All clubs are not exempt from the provisions of the income tax law, even though not operated for profit. A club desiring to be registered as an exempt organization should file with the Commissioner of Internal Revenue a copy of its charter, or an affidavit of its principal officer, setting forth the nature of its organization, the purpose for which organized, the source if any from which it derives income, and the disposition made of such income as is received by it, for consideration and determination as to whether or not it comes within the class of organizations held to be exempt under the provisions of the income tax law." (T. D. 2090, Dec. 14,

[29] Carlisle & S. Golf Club v. Smith [1912] 2 K. B. 177; Grove v. Young Men's Christian Ass'n, 88 Law T. 696, 4 Tax Cas. 613.

1914.) But the present statute declares that the income tax shall not be levied on any "club organized and operated exclusively for pleasure, recreation, and other non-profitable purposes, no part of the net income of which inures to the benefit of any private stockholder or member." (Act Cong. Sept. 8, 1916, § 11a, par. 9 [U. S. Comp. St. 1916, § 6336k].)

§ 149. Federal Land Banks

Exemption from the income tax is granted by the act of 1916 to the banks and associations organized under the Federal Farm-Loan Act of July 17, 1916 (§ 26) as follows: to the federal land banks and the national farm-loan associations absolutely, and to the joint-stock land banks as to income derived from bonds or debentures of other joint-stock land banks or of any federal land bank, belonging to such joint-stock land bank. (Act Cong. Sept. 8, 1916, § 11a, pars. 13, 14.)

§ 150. Proceeds of Life Insurance Policies

Money received from a life insurance company in settlement of a claim under a policy for the death of the assured would probably have to be reckoned as part of the "income" of the beneficiary or recipient, if not specifically exempted. But in pursuance of a humane and wise policy, the income tax laws have generally provided for the exemption of such funds. The act of Congress excepts from the description of taxable income the proceeds of life insurance policies paid upon the death of the person insured, without any limitation as to the amount, and also "the amount received by the insured, as a return of premium or premiums paid by him under life insurance, endowment, or annuity contracts, either during the term or at the maturity of the term mentioned in the contract, or upon the surrender of the contract." (Act Cong. Sept. 8, 1916, § 4 [U. S. Comp. St. 1916, § 6336d].) Attention should also be given to the following ruling of the Treasury Department: Dividends paid on life insurance policies that have not matured, whether such dividends are drawn in cash by the insured or applied to the reduction of the annual premium due, are not considered items of taxable income under the law, and should be excluded from a return of income. Dividends from paid-up policies, however, are considered income to the recipient, and must be included in the annual return of income whenever the taxpayer's income, including such dividends, is in excess of $20,000. They are considered the same as dividends or net earnings from corporations subject to a like tax, and may, therefore, be excluded from a return of income in cases where the income is subject to the normal tax of 1 per cent only. (T. D. 2137, Jan. 30, 1915.)

It should be observed, however, that the exemption only applies to life insurance policies. Money received by the insured himself under an accident policy would undoubtedly be subject to the income tax, since in theory it merely takes the place of what he would have earned during the period of his disability. But an endowment insurance contract whereby, in consideration of an annual premium, one hundred pounds is payable on the death of the insured within fifteen years, and two hundred pounds if he is alive at the end of that period, is an "insurance on his life" within the meaning of the income tax law.[30]

§ 151. Exemption of Fixed Amount of Income

All income tax laws have wholly exempted incomes below a certain fixed minimum, and allowed the deduction of a like amount from incomes large enough to be subject to the tax. The object is to relieve from the burden of this tax those persons whose annual earnings or gains are no more than sufficient to maintain a decently comfortable existence, and to permit persons of larger means to deduct a sum which may represent the ordinary living expenses of the average family, so that the tax may not fall upon the necessaries of life or a reasonable share of its comforts, but only upon superfluous income. As corporations and partnerships have no corresponding expenses, they are not entitled to the exemption of a fixed sum.

The provision of the income tax law of 1916, as amended by Act Cong. October 3, 1917, § 1203, is that, for the purpose of the normal tax only, and as applied only to citizens or residents of the United States, each taxable person each year shall be entitled to an exemption of $3,000 of income otherwise taxable, with an additional exemption of $1,000 "if the person making the return be the head of a family, or a married man with a wife living with him, or a married woman with a husband living with her." The Treasury Department defines the term "head of a family" as "a person who actually supports and maintains one or more individuals who are closely connected with him by blood relationship, relationship by marriage or by adoption, and whose right to exercise family control and provide for these dependent individuals is based upon some moral or legal obligation." (T. D. 2427, Dec. 26, 1916.) But it would be unsafe to rely implicitly upon this definition. It is prob-

---

[30] Gould v. Curtis [1912] 1 K. B. 635.

ably much too narrow. The phrase "head of a family" is a familiar one in the homestead laws and other statutes of many states, and has been construed very frequently by the courts, and authorities are not wanting to give it a much more liberal construction than that set up by the federal revenue officers.

It is also provided that in no event shall this additional exemption of $1,000 be deducted by both a husband and wife, and only one deduction of $4,000 shall be made from the aggregate income of both husband and wife when living together. In the case of guardians or trustees making the returns for their wards or beneficiaries, the personal exemption may be claimed in the return as to income derived from the property of which such guardian or trustee has charge, in favor of each ward or cestui que trust, but in no event shall a ward or cestui que trust be allowed a greater personal exemption than $3,000, or, if married, $4,000, from the amount of net income received from all sources. Also it is provided that "there shall be allowed an exemption from the amount of the net income of estates of deceased citizens or residents of the United States during the period of administration or settlement, and of trust or other estates of citizens or residents of the United States, the income of which is not distributed annually or regularly under the provisions of subdivision 'b' of section two, the sum of $3,000."

Those having dependent children are granted a further exemption as follows: "If the person making the return is the head of a family, there shall be an additional exemption of $200 for each child dependent upon such person, if under eighteen years of age, or if incapable of self-support because mentally or physically defective, but this provision shall operate only in the case of one parent in the same family."

This personal exemption can be claimed only once by the same individual with reference to the same year's income. That is, if his income exceeds the amount at which the supertax begins, he cannot deduct $3,000 (or $4,000) a second time, for the purpose of estimating the income chargeable with such supertax, after having deducted it for the purpose of the normal tax.[81] And the exemption cannot be claimed at all by a nonresident alien having an income taxable in this country. Objections have been made to the constitutional validity of that part of the statute which allows the

---

81 Cohen v. Lowe (D. C.) 234 Fed. 474.

personal exemption, but they have not been sustained by the courts.[32]

§ 152. Treasury Regulations as to Husband and Wife

With reference to the joint exemption allowed to husband and wife, and the method of making returns and claiming the exemption, the Treasury department has made the following regulations:

"Every single person and every married person not living with husband or wife in the sense below defined who has a net income exceeding $3,000 per annum is liable to pay the normal income tax under this law, but in making return for such tax may claim an exemption of $3,000 from their total net income.

"Husband and wife living together are entitled to an exemption of $4,000 only from the aggregate net income of both, which may be deducted in making the return of such income for taxation. However, when the husband and wife are separated and living permanently apart from each other, each shall be entitled to an exemption of $3,000.

"If the husband and wife not living apart have separate estates, the income from both may be made on one return, but the amount of income of each, and the full name and address of both, must be shown in such return.

"The husband, as the head and legal representative of the household and general custodian of its income, should make and render the return of the aggregate income of himself and wife, and for the purpose of levying the income tax it is assumed that he can ascertain the total amount of said income.

"If a wife has a separate estate managed by herself as her own separate property and receives an income of $3,000 or over, she may make return of her own income, and if the husband has other net income, making the aggregate of both incomes more than $4,-000, the wife's return should be attached to the return of her husband, or his income should be included in her return, in order that a deduction of $4,000 may be made from the aggregate of both incomes. The tax in such case, however, will be imposed only upon so much of the aggregate income of both as shall exceed $4,000.

"If either husband or wife separately has an income equal to or in excess of $3,000, a return of annual net income is required

[32] Brushaber v. Union Pac. R. Co., 240 U. S. 1, 36 Sup. Ct. 236, 60 L. Ed. 493, L. R. A. 1917D, 414, Ann. Cas. 1917B, 713; Robertson v. Pratt, 13 Hawaii. 590.

under the law, and such return must include the income of both, and in such case the return must be made even though the combined income of both be less than $4,000.

"If the aggregate net income of both exceeds $4,000, an annual return of their combined incomes must be made in the manner stated, although neither one separately may have an income of $3,-000 per annum. They are jointly and separately liable for such return and for the payment of the tax.

"The single or married status of the person claiming the specific exemption shall be determined as of the time of claiming such exemption if such claim be made within the year for which return is made, otherwise the status at the close of the year." (T. D. 1923, Dec. 27, 1913.)

Also the following additional regulations have been prescribed: "Where either dies during the year, having a net taxable income of $3,000 or more, a return of income should be made by the executor or administrator of the deceased as of the date of his death, and the executor or administrator may claim an exemption of $4,000. The survivor, when making a return at the end of the year for the entire year, will be allowed the applicable exemption for the single or married status existing at the close of the year.

"The regulations of the department requiring the incomes of husband and wife to be combined and authorizing the aggregate exemption of $4,000 from such combined income, are applicable for the purpose of the normal tax only. The additional tax, or surtax, imposed by the act will be computed on the basis of the separate income of each individual; that is, on the amount of each individual's income in excess of the minimum amounts upon which the surtax at the graduated rates is to be calculated." (T. D. 2090, Dec. 14, 1914.)

"A husband who has a wife and children whom he supports, but who is living apart from his wife under an agreement to do so, there being no judicial decree of separation, is entitled only to the specific exemption of $3,000.

"In the return, if the amount of income necessitates one, the decedent's specific exemption for the entire year ($4,000) should be claimed. The widow is required to file a return on Form 1040, revised, in her own behalf if her entire income for the calendar year during which her husband died amounted to $3,000 or more, and should claim a specific exemption of $3,000 if not in a married status, living with a husband, on December 31 of that year.

"Unless the wife has a separate estate which requires her to file a separate return of income or to join with her husband in a return which shall set forth her income separately, a husband having a taxable income of his own should include in his return the income accruing to the wife from the sale of special magazine articles. If neither has a net income of $3,000 or more, but together they have an aggregate net income exceeding $4,000, a return of the joint income is required to be filed by either the husband or wife, and the income derived by the wife as above set forth should be included in such return. The actual proceeds coming into the wife's possession during the tax year constitute the income to be included, and not the amounts estimated upon acceptance prior to publication and payment." (T. D. 2135, Jan. 23, 1915.)

"The specific exemption of $4,000 may be claimed in the separate return of either husband or wife, the other claiming no exemption, or may be prorated between the two. The separate incomes of husband and wife should not be combined in a return of income for the purpose of assessing the additional or surtax." (T. D. 2137, Jan. 30, 1915.)

§ 153. Exemptions Under War Income Tax

What is said in the preceding sections as to the personal exemption refers only to what may be called the regular or permanent income tax, that is, the tax imposed by the act of Sept. 8, 1916. In addition to this tax (not in substitution for it) another specific tax, called the "war income tax," is imposed by the Act of Congress of October 3, 1917, § 3. And as to this war income tax, the amount of the personal exemption allowed is $1,000 in the case of unmarried persons (instead of $3,000) and $2,000 in the case of heads of families or married persons living together (instead of $4,000), and a return is required in the case of incomes of $1,000 or over in the case of unmarried persons, and $2,000 or over in the case of married persons.

(180)

CHAPTER VIII

DEDUCTIONS AND CREDITS IN COMPUTING TAXABLE INCOME

§ 154. Expenses of Business

The federal income tax law allows the individual taxpayer to deduct from his return of net income "the necessary expenses actually paid in carrying on any business or trade, not including personal, living, or family expenses." (Act Cong. Sept. 8, 1916, § 5a [U. S. Comp. St. 1916, § 6336e].) In the case of domestic corporations it allows the deduction of "all the ordinary and necessary expenses paid within the year in the maintenance and operation of its business and properties." (Id., § 12a [U. S. Comp. St. 1916, § 6336].) In the case of foreign corporations, there may be deducted "all the ordinary and necessary expenses actually paid within the year out of earnings in the maintenance and operation of its business and property within the United States." (Id., § 12b.)

As to the individual taxpayer, it is evident that he cannot deduct so much of his current income as he has spent in the satisfaction of his personal wants or desires or in the support and maintenance of his family. The "instructions" issued by the Treasury Department state that "expenses for medical attendance, store accounts, family supplies, wages of domestic servants, cost of board, room, or house rent for family or personal use, are not expenses that can be deducted from gross income. In case an individual owns his own residence, he cannot deduct the estimated value of his rent." It is held in England that the hire of a domestic servant is not a necessary expense in carrying on business.[1] But a parish minister may deduct the cost of keeping a horse and carriage as part of the necessary expenses of his avocation.[2]

§ 155. Same; Investment of Capital Assets Distinguished

In computing allowable deductions, a distinction is to be made between expenditures which are in the nature of an investment of capital assets and those which are properly described as current expenses. Thus, in the case of a manufacturing establishment, the

---

[1] Bowers v. Harding, 1 Q. B. 560, 3 Tax Cas. 22.
[2] Jardine v. Inland Revenue [1907] Sess. Cas. 77.

purchase and renewal of the machinery necessary for the operation of the plant would be regarded as an investment of capital, and could not be deducted as an item of expense. This was brought out in an English case, where a corporation, with a view to extending its business, opened a factory and installed machinery, but subsequently closed it, removed a portion of the machinery, and re-opened the factory on a smaller scale, and thereby lost a portion of the original expenditure. It was held that this was a loss of capital, and that no deduction could be allowed therefor in assessing its income for taxation.[3] On the other hand, where a plantation is set out with rubber trees, some of which have reached the age of producing, but others not, the expense of cultivating, weeding, and caring for those portions of the estate not yet in bearing is a proper deduction, and as it is an annually recurring expense, it is prima facie not capital expenditure, but income expenditure, and so deductible.[4] So, where the business is one which is carried on in an office, whatever constitutes permanent equipment might be regarded as an investment of capital, but whatever is currently consumed or used up in the ordinary business of the office would come under the description of expense. Thus, the ordinary expenditures made by an insurance company for the renewal of office furniture and other such perishable equipment does not constitute an addition to its assets, but is a deductible expense of maintenance and operation.[5]

§ 156. Same; Expense of Beginning or Engaging in Business

If the law of the state or a municipal ordinance requires the payment of an annual license fee or occupation tax, as a condition to the right to carry on the particular business, it is a part of the necessary and proper expense thereof, and deductible as such.[6] So, where an employee is required to furnish a bond and pay the premium thereon himself, as a necessary incident of his employment, the premium so paid will constitute an allowable deduction for him in computing his net income. (T. D. 2090, Dec. 14, 1914.) But it has been ruled that the organization expenses of a corporation, such as fees of attorneys or accountants and fees paid to state authorities prior to or coincident with the securing of a charter and incor-

---

[3] Smith v. Westinghouse Brake Co., 2 Tax Cas. 357.

[4] Vallambrosa Rubber Co. v. Farmer [1910] Sess. Cas. 519.

[5] Mutual Benefit Life Ins. Co. v. Herold (D. C.) 198 Fed. 199.

[6] Kane v. Schuylkill Fire Ins. Co., 199 Pa. 205, 48 Atl. 989.

poration of the company, are not deductible as "ordinary and necessary expenses of maintenance and operation," but constitute a capital investment, representing the cost of the charter or franchise, which is an intangible asset of a more or less permanent character and often of substantial value. (T. D. 2499, June 11, 1917.) And in an English case, where the taxpayer claimed a deduction for necessary expenses incurred in carrying on his business as a surveyor, being the cost of books and instruments used by him, it was held that the deduction could not be allowed.[7]

§ 157. Same; Expense of Earning or Collecting Income

The expense of collecting income, where it consists of rent or other such items, may be deducted, where the usual and ordinary course of managing the business is to employ an agent or other collector, though it may be otherwise in regard to what may be called "optional expenses of collection," which might be looked on as something of a luxury, as where the income could be collected without incurring any such expense, but the owner prefers to employ some one to collect it.[8] The Treasury Department has ruled that a fiduciary, receiving or collecting income for the beneficiary may deduct "commissions for the collection of rents" as a necessary expense in managing the estate or trust. (T. D. 1943, Feb. 4, 1914.) And the same rule applies to any person who holds rented property as an investment. (T. D. 2090, Dec. 14, 1914.) But there is also a ruling that expenses incurred in earning income which is not subject to the tax do not constitute allowable deductions in computing income from other sources which are taxable under the law. (T. D. 2137, Jan. 30, 1915.)

§ 158. Same; General Costs of Business

A ruling has been made that "expenses of operation and maintenance shall include all expenditures for material, labor, fuel, and other items entering into the cost of the goods sold or inventoried at the end of the year, and all other expenses incurred in the operation of the business, except such as are required by the act to be segregated in the return." (Internal Revenue Regulations No. 33, art. 114.) And "in ascertaining expenses proper to be included in the deductions to be made under the item of expenses, corporations carrying materials and supplies on hand for use should include in

---

[7] In re Assessment of Taxes, 16 Hawaii, 796.

[8] Stevens v. Bishop, L. R. 20 Q. B. Div. 442. And see Duke of Norfolk v. Lamarque, L. R. 24 Q. B. Div. 485.

such expenses the charges for materials and supplies only to the amount that the same are actually disbursed and used in operation and maintenance during the year for which the return is made." (Id., art. 123.) In an English case, where part of the business taken over by a company consisted of unexecuted contracts, it was held that the price paid for such contracts was not a proper deduction from the profits arising from their performance.[9] It can hardly be doubted that the cost of advertising should be accounted an "ordinary and necessary expense," in view of the conditions under which all modern business is transacted.[10] But "sums of money expended for lobbying purposes and contributions for campaign expenses are not an ordinary and necessary expense in the operation and maintenance of a corporation, and therefore are not deductible from gross income." (T. D. 2137, Jan. 30, 1915.) And a charge entered upon the books of a corporation (in whatever form as a matter of bookkeeping) because of the sale of an issue of its bonds at less than their par value, to the extent of the difference between the amount received and the nominal value of the bonds is not a part of its "expenses actually paid within the year," to be deducted from gross income in its tax return.[11]

§ 159. Same; Manufacturing Costs

A manufacturing corporation may include as an element of the cost of manufactured products the cost of the raw material, the cost of the labor of the men who actually work on such products, and the cost of supervisory or "unproductive" labor, such as that of foremen and overseers. Overhead charges, included as a part of the expense of operating the business, may include the salaries of officers, clerks, and such other office expenses as do not have to do directly with the manufacture of the product. (T. D. 2152, Feb. 12, 1915.) But a corporation cannot include, as an overhead charge and so a part of the expenses of the business, interest paid on its indebtedness, because such payments are separately deductible under another head. And it cannot take into account, as a part of the cost of manufacturing, any possible earnings, that is, earnings which might accrue on its capital or investment had such capital been so placed as to earn a given rate of interest. (T. D. 2137, Jan. 30, 1915.)

[9] City of London Contract Corp. v. Styles, 2 Tax Cas. 239.
[10] Foster v. Goddard, 1 Black (U. S.) 506, 17 L. Ed. 228.
[11] Baldwin Locomotive Works v. McCoach, 221 Fed. 59, 136 C. C. A. 660, affirming (D. C.) 215 Fed. 967.

§ 160. Same; Legal Expenses

Money paid to an attorney at law for his professional services in advising concerning legal problems which arise in the course of the business conducted, and in drawing such papers as require legal skill and knowledge, may justly be treated as a part of the "expenses" of the business.[12] And the same is true in regard to the costs and expenses of prosecuting or defending suits at law, when litigation becomes a necessary incident of the business, either for the recovery of debts or the repulse of unjust claims.[13] The Treasury Department rules, however, that the costs of administering an estate, such as court costs, fees of attorneys, and the like, which are chargeable against the estate as an entirety, and diminish the corpus of it in the hands of the executor or administrator, are not to be deducted as "expenses." On the other hand, expenses incurred by an executor or administrator incidentally to the administration, and arising from the nature of the property and the details of its business management, such as salaries, wages, rentals, and repairs, which reduce the income accruing to the beneficiaries, but not the estate itself, are deductible expenses. (T. D. 2090, Dec. 14, 1914; T. D. 2135, Jan. 23, 1915.)

§ 161. Same; Contributions to Indemnity Fund

In an English case, it appeared that a colliery company was a member of a "coal owners' association," to which it paid an annual subscription based on its output of coal. The object of the association was to pay to its members an indemnity in the event of deficiency or stoppage of output caused by strikes or other such interferences. The company contended that the subscription made for this purpose was a kind of insurance and therefore deductible as an expense of its business. But the court held otherwise, and refused to permit it as a deduction in estimating the profits of the company for income taxation.[14] But this decision was "distinguished" in a later case, not very easy to reconcile with it. It appeared that the company in question was a member of an association of manufacturers, which was mainly formed for the purpose of keeping up prices. Under the rules and pooling arrangements of the association, the members were entitled each to a fixed propor-

---

[12] Brady v. Dilley, 27 Md. 570.

[13] Babbitt v. Selectmen of Savoy, 3 Cush. (Mass.) 530; Scofield v. Moore. 58 Hun, 601, 11 N. Y. Supp. 303.

[14] Rhymney Iron Co. v. Fowler [1896] 2 Q. B. 79, 3 Tax Cas. 476.

tion of all orders received, and any member invoicing more than its proportion must pay a fixed sum per ton on the excess to the pool account, which was distributed among those members which had invoiced less than their proportions. It was held that the net payments made by the company to the association (including a share of administration expenses) in excess of those received from the association by the company, were an admissible deduction for the purpose of arriving at the company's taxable profits.[18]

§ 162. Same; Contributions to Bank Guaranty Fund

The Treasury Department has made the following ruling:

"Banking corporations which, pursuant to the laws of the states in which they are doing business, are required to set apart, keep, and maintain in their banks the amount levied and assessed against them by the state authorities as a "depositors' guaranty fund," may deduct from their gross income in their returns of annual net income the amount so set apart each year to this fund, provided that such fund is set aside and carried to the credit of the state banking board, or other duly authorized state officer, and may be withdrawn upon demand by such board or state officer to meet the demands of these officials in reimbursing depositors in insolvent banks, and provided further that no portion of the amount thus set aside and credited is returnable under the existing laws of the state to the assets of the banking corporation. In such cases the amount of the guaranty fund thus levied against the banking corporation and so set apart, kept and maintained is no longer an asset of the bank, but is in the nature of a tax "imposed by authority of the state," and as such is deductible from the gross income of the banking corporation." (T. D. 2152, Feb. 12, 1915.)

§ 163. Same; Reserves to Meet Liabilities

It has been ruled by the Internal Revenue Bureau that "where, pursuant to the consistent practice of the corporation, or pursuant to the requirements of some federal, state, or municipal supervising authority, corporations set up and maintain reserves to meet liabilities, the amount of which and the date of payment or maturity of which is not definitely determined or determinable at the time the liability is incurred, it will be permissible for the corporations to deduct from their gross income the amounts credited

[18] Guest, Keen & Nettlefolds, Ltd., v. Fowler [1910] 1 K. B. 713, 5 Tax Cas. 511.

to such reserves each year, provided that the amounts deductible on account of the reserves shall approximate as nearly as can be determined the actual amounts which experience has demonstrated would be necessary to discharge the liabilities incurred during the year and for the payment of which additions to the reserves were made; and provided, if it shall be found that the amount credited to any such reserve is in excess of the reasonable or probable needs of the corporation to meet and discharge the liabilities for which the reserve is credited, the excess of such reserve over and above the reasonable or probable needs for the purpose indicated shall be at once disallowed as a deduction and restored to income for the purpose of the tax; and provided further, that in no event will sinking funds or other reserves set up to meet additions, betterments, or other capital obligations constitute allowable deductions from gross income. This ruling contemplates that the income and authorized deductions shall be computed and accounted for on the same basis and that the same practice shall be consistently followed year after year. Amounts paid in discharge of any liability or obligation for which a reserve has been set up, as hereinbefore outlined, will, when paid, be charged to the reserve created to meet it in so far as such reserve is sufficient to meet the liability, provided always that the liability is of a character which constitutes an allowable deduction within the meaning of the law. If upon investigation it shall be found that returns made upon the basis of accruals and reserves do not reflect the true net income, the corporation so failing in this way to return the true net income will not thereafter be permitted to make its returns upon any basis other than that of actual receipts and disbursements. The reserves contemplated by the foregoing ruling are those reserves only which are set up to meet some actual liability incurred, the amount necessary to discharge which can not at the time be definitely determined, and do not contemplate reserves to meet losses contingent upon shrinkage in values, losses from bad debts, capital investments, etc., which losses are deductible only when definitely determined as the result of a closed or completed transaction and are charged off." (T. D. 2433, Jan. 8, 1917.)

§ 164. Same; Wages and Salaries

Wages and salaries paid to clerks, servants, agents, salesmen, managers, superintendents, officers, and other employees of the individual or corporate taxpayer are deductible from income as a necessary expense of conducting the business.[16]　But this applies only to the compensation of those who are employed in the conduct of the business from which the income is derived. The wages of domestic servants, for instance, are classed as "family or living expenses," for which no deduction is allowed.[17]　It is immaterial whether the compensation of an employee is paid in the form of a fixed annual or monthly wage or in the form of a commission on sales or business transacted. The Treasury Department rules that commissions allowed to salesmen, although paid in stock, may be deducted as an expense of the business, if so charged on the books at the actual value of the stock. (Internal Revenue Regulations No. 33, art. 117.)　And if commissions are paid to salesmen in cash, as a part of the expense of conducting the business, they are allowable deductions to the employer, as is also the amount which corporations actually advance to their traveling salesmen for so-called "spending money" or "treating money," if shown to be a part of the expense of selling the product of the corporation, and if actually expended for the purpose indicated.　(T. D. 2090, Dec. 14, 1914.)　But where one company buys the business of another and agrees to employ the latter's general manager at a fixed annual salary, but with the privilege of commuting such salary by paying him a gross sum and taking 'his agreement not to enter the employ of any other company, and does so commute, the payment so made is part of the consideration of the transfer of the business, and therefore capital expenditure, and not a deductible expense.[18]

It should also be observed that the individual taxpayer cannot escape paying the income tax, or reduce its burden, by paying himself a salary for his own services in supervising and conducting his own business, and then deducting the amount of it from the income which the business yields. It has been held that where testamentary trustees receive annually the income of property and distribute it among the beneficiaries, the whole of such income is taxable, without deduction of the expenses incurred in the management or administration of the trust.[19]　And the same principle applies in the case of a corporation, where practically the whole of

---

[16] Dunwoody v. U. S., 22 Ct. Cl. 269, 278; Foster v. Goddard, 1 Black (U. S.) 506, 17 L. Ed. 228.

[17] Bowers v. Harding, 1 Q. B. 560, 3 Tax Cas. 22.

[18] Royal Ins. Co. v. Watson [1897] App. Cas. 1, 3 Tax Cas. 500.

[19] Aikin v. Macdonald's Trustees, 32 Scotch Law Rep. 85, 3 Tax Cas. 306.

the stock is owned by one person, or by two former partners who have simply incorporated their business.[20]

It has been ruled that salaries paid to an officer who is a stockholder, to constitute an allowable deduction, must be a reasonable and fair compensation, without regard to the amount of stock which such officer may hold, and not dependent upon the profits of the corporation or varying as profits vary, and such salaries must have been authorized by the board of directors and made a matter of record on the books of the corporation. (T. D. 1742, par. 81; T. D. 2152, Feb. 12, 1915.) And "amounts paid as compensation or additional compensation to officers or employees, which amounts are based upon the stock holdings of such officers or employees, are held to be dividends, and although paid in lieu of salaries or wages, are not allowable deductions from gross income." (Internal Revenue Regulations No. 33, art. 119.)

§ 165. Same; Contributions to Religious and Charitable Purposes

Rulings and decisions under the income tax law previous to 1917 were to the effect that money or any other thing of value disposed of by way of gift, donation, or endowment should not be deducted or made the basis of a deduction from the income of persons or corporations in their tax returns under the income tax law; and that money paid out by a corporation for charities was not a part of its expenses which might be deducted from gross income.[21] But the amendatory act of October 3, 1917, (§ 1201,) introduced a modification of this rule, which, however, is applicable only in the case of citizens or residents of the United States, excluding, therefore, both corporations and nonresident aliens. It is provided that "contributions or gifts actually made within the year to corporations or associations organized and operated exclusively for religious, charitable, scientific, or educational purposes, or to societies for the prevention of cruelty to children or animals, no part of the net income of which inures to the benefit of any private stockholder or individual, to an amount not in excess of fifteen per centum of the taxpayer's taxable net income as computed without the benefit of this paragraph," may be deducted from the return of net income. But "such contributions or gifts shall be allowable as deductions only if verified under rules and regulations prescribed by

20 Jacobs & Davies, Inc., v. Anderson, 228 Fed. 505, 143 C. C. A. 87.
21 Baldwin Locomotive Works v. McCoach (D. C.) 215 Fed. 967.

the Commissioner of Internal Revenue, with the approval of the Secretary of the Treasury."

§ 166.　Same; Gifts, Charities, Pensions to Employees

As applied to voluntary payments or presents by a corporation to its employees, the rule is that amounts paid for pensions to retired servants, or to their families or others dependent upon them, or paid on account of injuries received by employees, are proper deductions as expenses of the business, but that gifts or gratuities to employees in the service of a corporation are not deductible. (T. D. 2152, Feb. 12, 1915; T. D. 1742, par. 64.) But it is also ruled that "donations by corporations which legitimately represent a consideration for a benefit flowing directly or indirectly to the corporation as an incident of its business are allowable deductions from gross income in ascertaining net income subject to the income tax; as, donations to a hospital, upon consideration that employees of the corporation are to have a ward for their use in case of accident or illness. The absence of consideration moving in some form to the corporation will make a contribution a mere gratuity; and gratuities are not allowable deductions in a return of income by corporations." (T. D. 2090, Dec. 14, 1914.) But there is a decision in an English case that voluntary contributions made by a minister towards the stipend of his assistant minister are not an allowable deduction, although it was necessary for him to supplement the stipend in this way in order to secure a competent assistant.[22] A problem of more difficulty was presented in a case where S., a manufacturing corporation, entered into an agreement with W., another manufacturing company, in the same line of business, whereby, in return for the right to nominate a majority of the directors of W., the S. company undertook to pay to W. each half year such a sum as might be necessary to make up any deficit in the dividend on W.'s preferred stock. As this was done for business reasons, and to promote the trade of S., it was held not to be a charity, but a subsidy granted for trade purposes, and therefore was considered properly deductible, under the head of "expenses," for the purpose of the income tax.[23]

§ 167.　Same; Traveling Expenses

The expenses of a journey may be included in the "necessary and ordinary expenses" of carrying on a given business, where the

[22] Lothian v. Macrae, 22 Scotch Law Rep. 219, 2 Tax Cas. 65.
[23] Moore v. Stewarts & Lloyds, Ltd., 8 Fraser, 1129.

journey is made as a necessary incident of the business or is otherwise undertaken directly for its expansion or advantage, as, where a traveling salesman is allowed his expenses on the road, where the business of an individual necessarily requires him to move from place to place, where a buyer for a store is sent to a distant market to replenish the stock, or where an officer of a corporation travels on its necessary and proper errands.[24] But traveling expenses are not deductible where they are incurred merely for the comfort or convenience of the person concerned. Thus, a public officer, whose duties are to be performed in one place, but who chooses to reside in another, is not entitled to deduct, for the purpose of the income tax, his expenses incurred in going to and fro between the two places.[25] And where the directors of a corporation travel from their places of residence to the place of meeting of the company, their traveling expenses are not an allowable deduction.[26] But it is at least doubtful whether hotel bills and other items of personal expenditure can be brought under the description of "traveling expenses" in any case where such expenses might constitute a proper deduction from income. The precise question has not arisen under the income tax laws, but analogous cases are not wanting. Thus, in a contract of employment of a traveling salesman for a certain salary per annum and an allowance for expenses not to exceed a certain sum per day, the word "expenses" was construed as not including the living expenses of the salesman.[27] And a similar decision was made in a case in Ohio, on the construction of a statute allowing to a county commissioner his "reasonable and necessary expenses actually paid in the discharge of his official duties." It was held that this meant official expenses only, as distinguished from those which pertained to the commissioner's personal comfort and necessities. The court said that, for his personal expenses of any kind, he could claim nothing beyond his per diem compensation and mileage; and it was a fair inference that, if it had been intended to reimburse him for board or traveling expenses in addition to mileage, when traveling on county business, the legislature would have expressed that intention in plain terms.[28]

24 See Jardine v. Inland Revenue [1907] Sess. Cas. 77.
25 Cook v. Knott, 2 Tax Cas. 246.
26 Revell v. Directors of Elworthy Bros., Ltd., 3 Tax Cas. 12.
27 Dowd v. Krall, 32 Misc. Rep. 252, 65 N. Y. Supp. 797.
28 Richardson v. State, 66 Ohio St. 108, 63 N. E. 593.

§ 168. Same; Cost of Insurance

Premiums paid for policies of fire insurance, when written on any building in which the business is carried on, or on a stock in trade, or the unfinished products of a factory, or on office furniture and fixtures, are deductible as an expense of carrying on the business.[29] It is, in fact, a general principle of law that the cost of insurance is properly included under the head of "expenses" in almost any connection in which that term can be used.[30] The Treasury Department rules that premiums paid for insurance on property which is not occupied by the owner as a dwelling, but is rented or leased to secure an income, constitute allowable deductions in computing his net income. But premiums paid on life insurance by the insured cannot be deducted. (T. D. 2090, Dec. 14, 1914.) But where, under a life insurance policy, the insurer advances the annual premium to the assured as a loan on the security of the policy, and gives him a receipt for the premium as "paid," the assured is not entitled to deduct the amount of the premium from his gross income, for it is not in fact "paid by him." [31] And funds set aside by a corporation as a reserve for insuring its own property cannot be claimed as a deduction, though any loss actually sustained and charged to such fund may be deducted. (Internal Revenue Regulations No. 33, art. 122.)

§ 169. Same; Insurance on Lives of Officers, Employees, or Partners

It was the view of the Treasury Department that premiums paid on life insurance taken out by a partnership upon the lives of individual members of the firm constituted an allowable deduction in ascertaining the net earnings of the firm; and that where corporations paid premiums on policies insuring, in favor of the corporations, the lives of officers or others, such premiums might properly be deducted from the gross income of the corporations. (T. D. 2090, Dec. 14, 1914.) But this rule has been changed by the act of October 3, 1917, which adds several new sections to the income tax act of 1916, and among them one to be numbered section 32, which provides: "Premiums paid on life insurance policies covering the lives of officers, employees, or those financially interested

---

[29] Society of Writers to the Signet v. Inland Revenue, 24 Scotch Law Rep. 27, 2 Tax Cas. 257.

[30] Foster v. Goddard, 1 Black (U. S.) 506, 17 L. Ed. 228; Bridge v. Bridge, 146 Mass. 373, 15 N. E. 899.

[31] Hunter v. King [1904] App. Cas. 161.

BL.FED.TAX.—13

in any trade or business conducted by an individual, partnership, corporation, joint-stock company or association, or insurance company, shall not be deducted in computing the net income of such individual, corporation, joint-stock company or association, or insurance company, or in computing the profits of such partnership for the purposes of subdivision (e) of section nine."

§ 170. Same; Rent of Land, Buildings, or Equipment

The act of Congress now in force allows corporations to deduct under the head of expenses "rentals or other payments required to be made as a condition to the continued use or possession of property to which the corporation has not taken or is not taking title, or in which it has no equity." (Act Cong. Sept. 8, 1916, § 12a [U. S. Comp. St. 1916, § 6336*l*].) Although this is not repeated in the provisions relating to individual taxpayers, it seems clear that, in the case of any business conducted on leased premises, the rent is a "necessary expense" of the business. A corporation is entitled to deduct the entire amount of rent which it pays for the building in which its business is carried on, although part of the building is used as a dwelling for the manager of the business.[32] But only the actual rent paid, or the actual rental value of the premises, can be thus deducted, and not the additional expense which may be incurred in the purchase of a lease for a term of years. Thus, where leasehold premises are purchased and used for trade purposes, the deduction from the assessment on the trade profits in respect to such premises must be limited to the existing annual value thereof, whatever may have been the premium originally paid, that is, the tenant is only entitled to deduct the annual rent, and not to amortize the premium by distributing it over the years yet to run.[33] So, a brewer paying a premium for a lease of a public house, for the purpose of letting it to a tenant under a covenant to buy beer brewed by him, is not entitled to a deduction on account of the gradual exhaustion of the premium.[34]

That rent paid for personal property, as well as for land, may be an expense of the business in which it is employed, appears from a case in Pennsylvania, where it was held that compensation for the use of rolling-stock or other equipment which is hired, and not owned, by a railroad company, is certainly a part of the expense of the business which it transacts, and is therefore a part

[32] Russell v. Town & County Bank, L. R. 13 App. Cas. 418.
[33] Gillatt v. Colquhoun, 2 Tax Cas. 76.
[34] Watney v. Musgrave, L. R. 5 Ex. Div. 241, 1 Tax Cas. 272.

of the operating expenses of the road.[35]   In line with these decisions, it is ruled by the Treasury Department that payments measured by a fixed percentage on the stock of a railroad corporation, whose lines are leased by another railroad corporation, and which rent is payable by the lessee directly to the stockholders of the lessor corporation, have, under the income tax law, with respect to the corporation paying such sums, the status of a rental payment.   In such cases there are two corporations involved, the lessor and the lessee, one the rent payer and the other the rent receiver.   To the lessee, rental payments are an expense of operation; to the lessor, the rentals are an income.   A contract which provides that the rentals shall be paid to a third party, not a party to the contract, does not change the character of the payment, nor relieve the lessor from liability to tax on the rental income which the lessee pays to it or to such third party.   The income of the third party, the stockholder, is dividends on the stock which he holds in the lessor company.   Dividends cannot be paid unless the lessor has an income out of which to pay them.   Hence the lessor company is required under the law to return as income the rentals which the lessee is required to pay.   In paying direct to the stockholders, the lessee is acting as the agent of the lessor, and the amounts received by stockholders are, in effect and in fact, dividends received out of the earnings of the lessor.   (T. D. 2090, Dec. 14, 1914.)   The English law does not permit the deduction, as an expense of business, of royalties paid for the use of a patent.[36]

§ 171. Same; Mining Operations

The rule is settled in England that the cost of sinking a pit or shaft on a coal or iron mining property, to open up new seams or deposits, is an expenditure of capital and properly chargeable to that account, and cannot be regarded as an ordinary expense of the business, so as to be deductible from income for the purpose of estimating the taxable net income.[37]   And a tenant of minerals, though he may be under a constant vanishing expense in sinking new pits as the old ones become exhausted, is not entitled, in com-

---

[35] Commonwealth v. Philadelphia & E. R. R., 164 Pa. 252, 30 Atl. 145.

[36] Lanston Monotype Corp. v. Anderson [1911] 2 K. B. 1019.

[37] In re Addie & Sons, 12 Scotch Law Rep. 274, 1 Tax Cas. 1.   But see Morant v. Wheal Grenville Min. Co., 71 Law T. 758, holding that the question of whether the cost of sinking a shaft by a mining company is a capital expenditure or a working expenditure, or partly the one and partly the other, is a question of fact to be decided on the circumstances of each case.

puting his profits for the assessment of the income tax, to deduct
from the gross profits a sum estimated as representing the amount
of capital expended in making bores and sinking pits which have
become exhausted by the year's work.[88]   But in construing and
applying the corporation tax act of Congress of 1909, the Commissioner of Internal Revenue made a regulation that the cost of drilling wells, by natural-gas companies, might be charged to expense
account, rather than investment account, and so allowed in their
returns.   It was said: "The cost of drilling gas wells has been
held by competent authorities as properly chargeable to either investment or expense.   While it is preferred that the cost of drilling
wells be charged to investment, the general custom of producers of
natural gas in charging the cost of drilling to expense will be recognized, and returns of net income may be made in accordance
therewith.   Each return of annual net income should in such case
state that the expense of drilling gas wells has been charged to expense.   All other expenditures in tangible property in development
work shall be chargeable to capital assets."   But the Commissioner
also ruled that, in the case of petroleum producing properties, the
cost of drilling and equipping new producing wells should be considered and treated as an addition to capital investment account,
but that the expense of drilling holes which proved to be dry might
be charged to profit and loss.   (T. D. Nos. 1754, 1755.)

§ 172.   Same; Judgments

If a judgment is recovered against the taxpayer (whether an individual or a corporation) and paid within the year for which the
return is to be made, the question whether it is deductible as an
"ordinary and necessary expense" should be determined by reference to the cause of action on which it was recovered.   If the claim
was for goods sold, money had and received, services rendered, or
otherwise founded on contract or quasi contract, it should be easy
to determine whether the plaintiff's demand arose out of or was
incident to the conduct of the defendant's business, and if so, the
change in its form, from a disputed claim to a judgment, should not
affect the question of its allowance as a deduction.   But in the
case of a judgment for a tort, the matter is not so clear.   So far as
the authorities go, they may be said to favor the rule that if the
tort was committed directly in the course of the business operations of the defendant, or the circumstances constituting it were

[88] Coltness Iron Co. v. Black, L. R. 6 App. Cas. 315.

(196)

such as might ordinarily arise in the prosecution of that business, then the payment of the damages (whether by settlement out of court or after judgment) may be regarded as an "expense" of the business. But if the tort had no connection with the business carried on, and did not arise out of its usual or ordinary conduct, it cannot be considered as an expense of that business. And this would naturally apply also to torts having also a criminal aspect, such as libel or slander or assault and battery. Thus it was ruled, under the corporation tax law of 1909, that amounts paid on account of injuries received by employés in the course of their employment would be proper deductions as ordinary and necessary expenses of the business.[39] And in an English case, the Lord Chancellor gave as an illustration of an allowable deduction "losses sustained by a railway company in compensating passengers for accidents in traveling."[40] So again, a decision in Massachusetts holds that the "operating expenses" of a railroad company should be construed to include a claim for damages done to property by the railroad company in negligently running a train at a highway crossing.[41] But on the other hand, where a brewery company owned an inn, which was carried on by a manager as a part of its business, and a customer sleeping in the inn was injured by the fall of a chimney, which accident was attributable to the negligence of the company's servants, and he recovered a judgment for damages, it was held that the amount thereof could not be deducted in estimating the balance of profits for the purpose of the income tax, the loss not being connected with or arising out of the trade, and not being money wholly or exclusively laid out for the purposes of the trade.[42] And in the case in which this decision was made, a further illustration was given, as follows: "If a man kept a grocer's shop, for keeping which a house is necessary, and one of the window shutters fell upon and injured a man walking in the street, the loss thereby arising to the grocer ought not to be deducted" from net taxable income.

§ 173. Repairs, New Buildings, and Improvements

The cost of repairs to property such as may be necessary to restore dilapidation or to keep it in serviceable and efficient condition for the purpose of the business in which it is employed, is plainly

[39] T. D. No. 1742, par. 64.
[40] Strong & Co. v. Woodifield [1906] App. Cas. 448.
[41] Smith v. Eastern R. Co., 124 Mass. 154.
[42] Strong & Co. v. Woodifield [1906] App. Cas. 448.

deductible as an ordinary and necessary expense of the business, or of the maintenance and operation of the business or property, as these terms are used in the income tax law.[43] Thus, amounts expended by a business corporation in enlarging or making improvements in its office or premises, not in the nature of permanent improvements to the property, but to facilitate the transaction of a growing business, may be deducted as necessary expenses of the business.[44] But if a corporation has been allowed a deduction for repairs to, and renewals of, its machinery and other appliances, sufficient to cover the actual loss by wear and tear, it cannot be allowed a further deduction for estimated depreciation of its plant; in other words, it cannot "get deduction for deterioration twice over." [45] But "repairs" do not include new constructions. And the income tax laws generally provide that no deduction shall be allowed to the taxpayer for money laid out in the cost of new buildings, permanent improvements, or betterments, made to increase the value of his property or estate.[46] This is in accordance with general principles of law. Thus, in estimating the profits of the business of a partnership, it is error to include among the expenditures such amounts as have been expended in permanent improvements to the real estate of the firm. Such improvements must be regarded as an investment of capital.[47] So, a corporation purchasing gas works in a defective structural condition is not entitled to deduct, in making its return of income for taxation, sums set aside annually out of the profits to be expended in future years on restoring the plant and apparatus.[48] And a railway company is not entitled to deduct from its profits sums expended in improv-

[43] Grant v. Hartford & N. H. R. Co., 93 U. S. 225, 23 L. Ed. 878.
[44] Connecticut Mut. Life Ins. Co. v. Eaton (D. C.) 218 Fed. 206.
[45] Caledonian Ry. Co. v. Banks, 18 Scotch Law Rep. 85, 1 Tax Cas. 487.
[46] "Amounts expended in additions and betterments which constitute an increase in capital investment are not a proper deduction." Internal Revenue Regulations No. 33, art. 118. Additional machinery installed in a sugar mill is a "betterment," notwithstanding the fact that it is necessary in order to keep the plantation up to its former efficiency. In re Income Tax Appeal Cases, 18 Hawaii, 596. But the provision that no deduction shall be made for new buildings or improvements "made to increase the value of any property or estate" does not imply that deduction may be made for all amounts so paid out which do not in fact increase the value of the property. Hawaiian Commercial & Sugar Co. v. Tax Assessor, 14 Hawaii, 601, 28 Ann. Cas. 980.
[47] Braun's Appeal, 105 Pa. 414.
[48] Clayton v. New Castle-Under-Lyme Corp., 2 Tax Cas. 416.

ing a section of the line so as to bring it up to the standard of the
main line, nor the cost of the extra weight of heavy rails and other
equipment substituted for lighter ones.[49] In Hawaii, it is held that
the cost of a replacement may be allowed as a deduction if the old
article is practically but not totally abandoned, and that expenditure
for a steel and concrete bridge to replace a wooden one is deducti- ·
ble as a replacement only up to the cost of a new bridge like the
old one; beyond that it is a "betterment." [50] Under a previous income tax law, it was held that where a railroad company replaces
an old and worn-out bridge by another of like dimensions and materials, the outlay may be described as "repairs"; but if the old
bridge is replaced by a new one of much more costly and valuable
type, as, stone instead of wood, its cost may be charged as "expenses" of the company's business.[51] Under the corporation excise tax law of 1909, the following points were decided by a federal court: (1) A railroad company cannot claim deductions for
amounts expended in adding to its property or equipment or in
improving its property, such as expenditures for new or extended
sidings or spur tracks, or for building new stations and new shops,
installing new machinery, or making additions to its rolling stock
or other equipment. (2) "Maintenance" means the upkeep or pres-
ervation of the condition of the property to be operated, and does
not include additions to the equipment or to the property, or improvements of the former condition of the road. (3) Where old
rails are replaced with new and heavier rails, and wooden bridges
and culverts with concrete and steel bridges and culverts, a deduction from gross income is allowable to the extent of the cost of
renewals with like kind and quality of materials, but the amount
by which the actual expenditure exceeds the cost of such renewal
or replacement is not an allowable deduction.[52]

§ 174. Same; By Tenant or Lessee Corporation

It has been ruled that the cost of erecting a building, if included
in the terms of a lease under which the property is held by a corporation, is a proper deduction from its return of income for taxa-

[49] Highland Ry. Co. v. Balderstone, 26 Scotch Law Rep. 657, 2 Tax Cas. 485.

[50] In re Income Tax Appeal Cases, 18 Hawaii, 596.

[51] Hartford & N. H. R. Co. v. Grant, 9 Blatchf. 542, Fed. Cas. No. 6,159.

[52] Grand Rapids & I. Ry. Co. v. Doyle (U. S. Dist. Ct., W. D. Michigan, S. D.) — Fed. —, T. D. No. 2210.

tion, but should be prorated according to the time fixed by the lease. (T. D. 1742, par. 51.) And the same principle is expressed in more general terms in the following ruling of the Treasury Department: "In the case of corporations which occupy leased premises under a lease contract which requires such corporation to make all necessary repairs or improvements, which repairs or improvements revert to the owner of the fee at the expiration of the lease, the tenant corporation is entitled to charge the cost of all such repairs and improvements to the expense of doing business. This expense of improvements, somewhat permanent in character, should, however, be prorated over the number of years constituting the term of the lease, and the amount deductible from gross income of each year would be the aliquot part of the cost of such repairs and improvements." (T. D. 2137, Jan. 30, 1915.)

§ 175. Interest on Indebtedness

In the case of the individual taxpayer, the present income tax law allows him to deduct "all interest paid within the year on his indebtedness, except on indebtedness incurred for the purchase of obligations or securities the interest upon which is exempt from taxation as income under this title." (Act Cong. Sept. 8, 1916, § 5a, as amended by Act Cong. October 3, 1917.) In the case of a corporation, the deduction may cover "the amount of interest paid within the year on its indebtedness (except on indebtedness incurred for the purchase of obligations or securities the interest upon which is exempt from taxation as income under this title) to an amount of such indebtedness not in excess of the sum of (a) the entire amount of the paid-up capital stock outstanding at the close of the year, or, if no capital stock, the entire amount of capital employed in the business at the close of the year, and (b) one-half of its interest-bearing indebtedness then outstanding: Provided, that for the purpose of this title preferred capital stock shall not be considered interest-bearing indebtedness, and interest or dividends paid upon this stock shall not be deductible from gross income: Provided further, that in cases wherein shares of capital stock are issued without par or nominal value, the amount of paid-up capital stock, within the meaning of this section, as represented by such shares, will be the amount of cash or its equivalent paid or transferred to the corporation as a consideration for such shares." (Act Cong. Sept. 8, 1916, § 12a, as amended by Act Cong. October 3, 1917.)

(200)

The amount paid for accrued interest on securities purchased is properly deductible as a payment of interest,[53] except of course in the case specially denounced by the statute, where one incurs indebtedness or pays interest on the acquisition of securities (such as government or municipal bonds) which are exempt from the income tax. And in a case where a corporation which did a brokerage business was in the habit of buying securities for its customers, who paid only a part of the purchase price and paid interest on the balance to the corporation, and the company, in turn, would not pay in full for the securities so purchased, but only a part, and would pay interest on the balances which it owed, it was held that the interest received by the corporation from its customers should be included in its return as income, but that the interest which it paid on its purchases of securities was an allowable deduction in the character of interest on its indebtedness.[54]

Nothing can be deducted under this head, except what is strictly and properly to be described as "interest." Assessments laid by a corporation on its capital stock, and paid by the stockholder are regarded as an investment of capital on his part, and do not constitute an allowable deduction in the return of the stockholder. (T. D. 2090, Dec. 14, 1914.) In an English case, where a mining company borrowed money to be employed in its business, and covenanted to pay interest thereon annually and also to repay the capital with an additional bonus of ten per cent, it was held that the bonus paid could not be claimed as a deduction in estimating the assessable profits of the company.[55] So, where a mortgage company raises money on an issue of debentures, and lends the money at a higher rate of interest, a commission paid to brokers and other expenses incurred in raising the money cannot be deducted from its assessment.[56] And where a company is empowered by statute to raise money upon mortgage for the purpose of carrying out a government contract, but is required by the same act to establish a sinking fund for the extinction of the mortgage debt, and a sum is to be set aside for payment into the sinking fund out of each quarterly payment received under the contract or out of other money belonging to the company, the sums so set aside are not

---

[53] People v. Davenport, 30 Hun (N. Y.) 177.

[54] Altheimer & Rawlings Inv. Co. v. Allen (U. S. Dist. Ct. Mo.) —— Fed. ——, T. D. 2441, Feb. 15, 1917.

[55] Arizona Copper Co. v. Smiles, 29 Scotch Law Rep. 134, 3 Tax Cas. 149.

[56] Texas Land & Mtg. Co. v. Holtham, 3 Tax Cas. 255.

(201)

allowable as a deduction in arriving at the company's taxable profits.[57]

§ 176. Same; Interest on Bank Deposits

Under the English law money paid in the form of interest on deposits by a company doing a banking business, or a loan and discount business, is not deductible from its assessment for the income tax.[58] But it is otherwise under the act of Congress now in force, since it explicitly provides that, "in the case of a bank, banking association, loan or trust company, interest paid within the year on deposits or on moneys received for investment and secured by interest-bearing certificates of indebtedness issued by such bank, banking association, loan or trust company" may be deducted. In a case arising under this provision, it appeared that a corporation was engaged in the business of selling to investors so-called debenture bonds and guaranteed real estate securities, the former of which were its own obligations, with interest coupons payable to bearer and underwritten by a trust company, with which it deposited as collateral security farm mortgages payable to itself, and bearing a higher rate of interest than the bonds, and the latter being obligations payable to itself, bearing its guaranty and secured by farm mortgages, to which were attached interest coupons at the rate agreed upon with the purchaser, the corporation retaining separate obligations of the mortgagor securing additional interest. The difference in the interest rates thus paid and received represented the gross profit of the corporation on those two classes of transactions. Held that though the corporation was chartered as a bank, yet the interest paid on such obligations cannot be treated as interest paid on deposits which a banking company may deduct from its gross income, the transaction in no way being a banking transaction.[59] There is also a decision that, where depositors in a savings bank do not receive a fixed rate of interest independently of what the bank itself may make or lose in lending their money, but receive a share of such profits as the bank may find that it has made, by lending their money, after deducting expenses, such share of the profits is a "dividend" within the meaning

[57] City of Dublin Steam Packet Co. v. O'Brien, 6 Tax Cas. 101, following Mersey Docks & Harbour Board v. Lucas, 2 Tax Cas. 25.

[58] Mersey Loan & Discount Co. v. Wootton, 2 Tax Cas. 316.

[59] Middlesex Banking Co. v. Eaton, 233 Fed. 87, 147 C. C. A. 157, affirming (D. C.) 221 Fed. 86.

of the income tax law, and not "interest," and hence not deductible as interest paid on deposits.[60]

§ 177. Same; Bank Discounts and Bond Discounts

It is held in England that where a mercantile company, in order to be able to pay cash for goods purchased and thereby secure them at a better price than if bought on credit, borrows money on short time paper from bankers, the interest on such banking loans is not a proper deduction for the purpose of the income tax.[61] But the officers of the Treasury, under the act of 1909, held that discounts, other than bank discounts on notes executed by the corporation, should be segregated from the interest item on the return, and should be included under the heading of expenses. (T. D. 1742, par. 90.) In Wisconsin, the state tax commission rules that "discounts on obligations incurred but not discharged within the year would not come under the head of interest paid. When the interest is deducted from a loan in advance, such interest cannot be said to be 'paid' until the note is paid."

There is also a ruling of the Treasury Department that "in the case of a corporation selling its own bonds at a discount, the amount of the discount should be prorated over the life of the bonds, and the proportionate part of such discount applicable to each year during the life of the bonds constitutes an allowable deduction from the gross income of such year. The deduction from gross income in the case of twenty-year bonds would be one-twentieth of the aggregate amount of the discount on the bonds sold." (T. D. 2137, Jan. 30, 1915.) But this is squarely opposed to a decision by a United States circuit court of appeals.[62]

§ 178. Same; Computation of Deductible Interest for Corporations

With reference to the capital stock of a corporation, as part of the measure of the indebtedness for which it may claim a deduction with respect to interest paid, it has been ruled that the full amount of the stock as represented by the par value of the shares issued is to be regarded as the paid-up capital stock, except when such stock is assessable on account of deferred payments, in which case the amount actually paid on such shares will constitute the

---

[60] Cary v. Savings Union, 22 Wall. 38, 22 L. Ed. 779.

[61] Anglo-Continental Guano Works v. Bell, 70 Law T. (N. S.) 670, 3 Tax Cas. 239.

[62] Baldwin Locomotive Works v. McCoach, 221 Fed. 59, 136 C. C. A. 660.

(203)

actual paid-up capital, and that capital stock includes both preferred and common stock, but not surplus and undivided profits.
(T. D. 1742, pars. 15–17.)   There is also a ruling that "the amount
received by a corporation for the original issue and sale of its
capital stock is held to be the capital of the corporation. In cases
where the stock, as originally issued, is sold at a price greater or
less than the par value, neither the premium nor the discount will
be taken into account in determining the net income of the corporation for the year in which the stock is sold. That is purely
a capital transaction, and the income is neither increased nor decreased by reason of the sale, per se, of the stock at a price greater
or less than its par value."   (T. D. 2090, Dec. 14, 1914.)

On the general subject, the regulations issued by the Treasury
Department are as follows: It is held that in the case of a corporation having capital stock this deductible interest is interest
actually accrued and paid within the year on an amount of indebtedness not exceeding the paid-up capital stock outstanding at the
close of the year, increased by the addition thereto of one-half the
interest-bearing indebtedness outstanding at the close of the year.

The qualifying phrase, "outstanding at the close of the year,"
appearing in the foregoing quotation, is held to apply to both paid-
up capital stock and indebtedness, and "one-half the sum of" quali-
fies only the indebtedness, which indebtedness, like the paid-up
capital stock, is required by the law to be reported, in making return of annual net income, as outstanding at the close of the year.

If no indebtedness is outstanding at the close of the year, the
maximum deduction allowable on account of interest paid will
be the amount of interest actually accrued and paid on an amount
of indebtedness not exceeding at any time within the year the
entire paid-up capital stock outstanding at the close of the taxable
year; that is, in such case, the paid-up capital stock outstanding at
the close of the year measures the highest amount of indebtedness
upon which deductible interest can be computed.

For the purpose of an allowable deduction, interest on the
maximum amount of indebtedness, determined in the manner above
indicated, can be computed upon such amount only for the time
during which such amount of indebtedness is not in excess of the
paid-up capital stock, increased by one-half the sum of the interest-
bearing indebtedness outstanding at the close of the year.

In any event, the amount of interest, in order to constitute an
allowable deduction, must not only be within the limit of the law

as herein defined, but must have actually accrued and been paid within the year for which the return is made.

In cases where no capital stock exists, the limitation as to deduction is confined to interest actually paid on an amount of indebtedness not exceeding at any time during the year the capital employed in the business at the close of the year. (T. D. 1960, March 18, 1914.)

There was also a ruling that interest on portions of bonded or other indebtedness bearing different rates of interest may be deducted from gross income, provided the aggregate amount of such indebtedness does not exceed the paid-up capital stock plus half the bonded debt. (T. D. 1742, par. 67.) An opinion was given by the Attorney General, on the construction of the corporation excise tax act of 1909, that, in ascertaining the net income of a corporation for taxation under that act, the business of the corporation being holding and dealing in real estate, interest on an indebtedness assumed by the corporation and secured by mortgage on a property which it acquires, can be deducted only to an amount not exceeding interest at a corresponding rate on the amount of its paid-up capital stock. For by assuming the indebtedness, the corporation makes it "its" indebtedness, and the limitation of the statute applies. But where such a corporation takes title to real property subject to a mortgage, but does not assume the indebtedness secured thereby, the interest on such indebtedness may be deducted from its gross income, without limitation as to the amount of its paid-up capital stock, because the indebtedness in this case is not "its" indebtedness, but the interest payment is a "charge required to be made as a condition to the continued use or possession of property." [63] And substantially the same view of the statute was taken by the lower federal courts in a case of some prominence,[64] in which it appeared that the complainant was a corporation organized to build and rent a building in New York City. It had a paid-up capital of $600 and a bonded debt of nearly five millions, secured by mortgage, and during the year for which it was sought to be taxed it had no net income after deducting the interest on its bonded debt from its gross income. The Commissioner allowed it to deduct only "interest paid within the year on bonded indebtedness not exceeding the paid-up capital stock." But it was

[63] 28 Opin. Atty. Gen. p. 198.

[64] Anderson v. Forty-Two Broadway Co., 213 Fed. 777, 130 C. C. A. 338, affirming Forty-Two Broadway Co. v. Anderson (D. C.) 209 Fed. 991.

held that the interest on the whole amount of the bonded debt was deductible as "necessary expenses paid, including charges such as rentals or franchise payments required as a condition to the continued use of the property." For if the company had not paid the interest on its bonds, the mortgage would have been foreclosed and the property lost to it. But this decision was reversed on review by the Supreme Court. It was held that when a corporation has deducted interest on its debt to the extent allowed by that specific clause of the statute which relates to the deduction of interest paid, it cannot have an allowance or deduction of any additional amount of interest paid under the description of "ordinary and necessary expenses." [65] In this connection also it is important to notice that the present income tax law (differing from the act of 1909), under the head of "ordinary and necessary expenses paid," allows the deduction of "rentals or other payments required to be made as a condition to the continued use or possession of property to which the corporation has not taken or is not taking title, or in which it has no equity." (Act Cong. Sept. 8, 1916, § 12a [U. S. Comp. St. 1916, § 6336*l*].)

§ 179. Same; Interest on Debt Secured by Collateral

The statute further provides that "in the case of indebtedness wholly secured by property collateral, tangible or intangible, the subject of sale or hypothecation in the ordinary business of such corporation, joint-stock company or association, as a dealer only in the property constituting such collateral, or in loaning the funds thereby procured, the total interest paid by such corporation, company, or association within the year on any such indebtedness may be deducted as a part of its expenses of doing business, but interest on such indebtedness shall only be deductible on an amount of such indebtedness not in excess of the actual value of such property collateral." (Act Cong. Sept. 8, 1916, § 12a, as amended by Act Cong. October 3, 1917.)

The ruling of the Treasury Department on the subject is as follows: "As used in the act, the expression 'collateral the subject of sale,' etc., refers to physical or tangible property bound for the performance of certain covenants or payment of certain obligations, and which physical or tangible property is the subject of sale in the ordinary business of a corporation owning the same. Where such corporation is, as a matter of its ordinary business, engaged in

[65] Anderson v. Forty-Two Broadway Co., 239 U. S. 69, 36 Sup. Ct. 17, 60 L. Ed. 152.

buying and selling, or dealing in such property, the interest actually paid within the year on indebtedness wholly secured by such collateral may be allowably deducted from gross income as an expense of doing business, without regard to the limit of deductible interest as otherwise provided by the statute. The corporation must be organized and operated for the purpose of buying, selling, and dealing in the particular kind of property which becomes the collateral in question, and the particular property pledged for the debt upon which the interest is paid must be the 'subject of sale in the ordinary business of the corporation.' Real estate mortgaged, and the property of corporations organized for and engaged in the business of buying, selling, and dealing in real estate, warehouse receipts representing property the subject of sale in the ordinary business of the corporation owning the same, and which warehouse receipts are pledged as collateral for such corporation's own debt, are examples where the interest paid will be deductible as a business expense and not be subject to the statutory limitation as to interest deduction." (T. D. 2090, Dec. 14, 1914.) It is to be borne in mind, however, that as the statute stands at present, it permits the "collateral" spoken of to be either tangible or intangible property. Another ruling was made with special reference to real estate collateral as follows: Real estate to constitute collateral within the meaning of this clause of the law must be such real estate as is in fact the subject of sale in the ordinary business of the corporation. If the corporation whose ordinary business is the purchase and sale of real estate has an office building under mortgage, which office building is not subject to sale in the ordinary business of the corporation, the interest paid on such mortgage will not be deductible under item 4 of the return form (1031), but in that case would be deductible under item 6 (a) of the return form to an amount not in excess of the limit fixed by the law as set out in said item. (T. D. 2137, Jan. 30, 1915.)

But a proviso added by the act of 1917 to the statutory provision on this subject is that, "in the case of bonds or other indebtedness, which have been issued with a guaranty that the interest payable thereon shall be free from taxation, no deduction for the payment of the tax herein imposed, or any other tax paid pursuant to such guaranty, shall be allowed." (Act Cong. Oct. 3, 1917, § 1207.)

§ 180. Taxes Paid

Both individual taxpayers and domestic corporations are permitted to deduct "taxes paid within the year imposed by the authority

(207)

of the United States (except income and excess profits taxes) or of its territories or possessions, or any foreign country, or by the authority of any state, county, school district, or municipality, or other taxing subdivision of any state, not including those assessed against local benefits," and the provision is the same in favor of foreign corporations, except that the taxes must have been "paid within the United States." (Act Cong. Sept. 8, 1916, §§ 5, 12, as amended by Act Cong. Oct. 3, 1917.) Under the income tax law as originally enacted in 1913, the privilege of deducting taxes imposed by a foreign government was granted to domestic corporations, following the English practice,[66] but not to individual taxpayers. (T. D. 2090, Dec. 14, 1914.) As to foreign corporations, it will be noticed that the provision quoted does not contemplate the prorating of any taxes paid by such a company to its home government. In other words, it is not allowed to deduct (on account of its American business) any portion of the taxes it may have paid outside the United States. The income tax paid by either an individual or corporation in any one year was originally deductible from the return of that year's income, but this is now expressly forbidden. It is ruled that taxes paid by a tenant to his landlord are considered as additional payment for rent, and are deductible as an expense of carrying on business. (T. D. 2090, Dec. 14, 1914.)

Funds set aside by a corporation out of its current earnings as a reserve for the payment of accruing taxes, or taxes which have accrued but which have not yet been paid, cannot be allowed as a deduction, since the statute specifically provides that only such sums as are "paid" within the year for taxes can be deducted. (T. D. 1742, par. 77; Internal Revenue Regulations No. 33, art. 156.) And where the state law provides that stockholders in banking corporations shall be assessed and taxed upon the value of their shares of stock therein, and that the bank shall collect the tax and pay over the amount to the proper local authorities, this does not convert the tax into a tax upon or against the bank itself. Hence if a bank pays the taxes assessed upon its shareholders, but neglects or omits to collect the sums so paid from the several stockholders, or to reimburse itself by deducting such sums from their dividends, it will not be entitled to claim a deduction thereof in its income tax return under the heading of taxes paid.[67] But this rule

66 Stevens v. Durban-Roodepoort Gold Min. Co., 5 Tax Cas. 402.

67 Eliot Nat. Bank v. Gill, 218 Fed. 600, 134 C. C. A. 358, affirming (D. C.) 210 Fed. 933; National Bank of Commerce v. Allen, 223 Fed. 472, 139 C. C.

does not operate to prevent banking corporations from deducting from their gross income any state tax imposed against the corporation itself, as an excise or franchise tax, that is, a tax which the corporation is required to pay to the state in order that it may transact business within the state. (T. D. 2152, Feb. 12, 1915.) Customs duties paid on the importation of goods from abroad may be classed as "taxes" for the purposes of this statute, but if an importing merchant has included such duties in estimating the cost of the goods, for the purpose of computing his profits on their sale, he will not be entitled to deduct them from his net income as taxes. (T. D. 1742, par. 74; Internal Revenue Regulations No. 33, art. 155.) As to legacy or inheritance taxes, they are probably to be included under the broad general term "taxes" in the income tax law, but the point is not entirely free from doubt.[68] The Treasury Department has ruled that taxes paid by a corporation pursuant to a contract guaranteeing that the interest payable on its bonds or other indebtedness shall be free from taxes are not allowable to it as a deduction. (Internal Revenue Regulations, No. 33, art. 153.) On this subject the general regulation is as follows: "The contract between the issuing corporation and the bondholder whereby the bonds are guaranteed to be tax free is a contract in which this office in the administration of the Federal income tax law can have no concern. Each corporation must account for, in its return of annual net income, all income which it receives from all sources. Interest received by a corporation on bonds which it holds, whether they are guaranteed to be tax free or not, must be included in the income of the corporation receiving the same and so accounted for in its return of annual net income. In other words, the corporation receiving the income must pay the tax upon the same, if it have a net income subject to tax, and the matter of complying with the covenant of the bond is a matter to be adjusted between the debtor corporation of the bondholder." (T. D. 2137, Jan. 30, 1915.)

A. 20, affirming (D. C.) 211 Fed. 743; First Nat. Bank v. McNeel, 238 Fed. 559, 151 C. C. A. 495; Northern Trust Co. v. McCoach (D. C.) 215 Fed. 991.

[68] In New York it is held that the federal inheritance tax to be paid under the war revenue act of 1898 was not to be deducted from the valuation of an estate for the purpose of a state transfer or inheritance tax, because it was not a tax on property but one against the legatee and payable out of his legacy. In re Gihon's Estate, 169 N. Y. 443, 62 N. E. 561. But a contrary decision has been made in Massachusetts. Hooper v. Bradford, 178 Mass. 95, 59 N. E. 678.

§ 181. Same; Credit for Excess Profits Tax

As stated in the preceding section, the income tax law of 1916, as amended by the act of 1917, allows the deduction of "taxes paid within the year, except income and excess profits taxes." Yet the same statute which introduced the amendment excluding excess profits taxes from the allowable deductions (Act Cong. Oct. 3, 1917) also added to the income tax law a new section (§ 29) which provides that "in assessing income tax, the net income embraced in the return shall also be credited with the amount of any excess profits tax imposed by Act of Congress and assessed for the same calendar or fiscal year upon the taxpayer, and in the case of a member of a partnership, with his proportionate share of such excess profits tax imposed upon the partnership." It is difficult to reconcile these contradictory enactments. But the apparent meaning is this: That, in making up his income tax return, the taxpayer is not allowed to deduct any excess profits tax which he paid during the year covered by the return, but he is entitled to credit himself (or to be credited) with the amount of any excess profits tax which is assessed against him, and which he has paid or expects to pay within the year in which the return is filed.

§ 182. Losses Uncompensated

The individual taxpayer is allowed to deduct "losses actually sustained during the year, incurred in his business or trade, or arising from fires, storms, shipwreck, or other casualty, and from theft, when such losses are not compensated for by insurance or otherwise." (Act Cong. Sept. 8, 1916, § 5a [U. S. Comp. St. 1916, § 6336e].) And a corporation may deduct "all losses actually sustained and charged off within the year and not compensated for by insurance or otherwise." (Idem., § 12a [U. S. Comp. St. 1916, § 6336l].) The apparent purpose is to include only those losses which are incident to the business out of which the taxable income is produced, or such as involve the destruction or impairment of property employed, or capital invested, in that business. Thus, it is ruled that a loss sustained on a single sale of real estate is not deductible, unless the dealing in real estate is the business of the person concerned, because otherwise it cannot be said to have been incurred in trade. (T. D. 1989, June 2, 1914.) The general regulation on this subject is as follows: "Loss, to be deductible must be an absolute loss, not a speculative or fluctuating valuation of continuing investment, but must be an actual loss, actually sustained and ascertained, during the tax year for which the deduction is

(210)

sought to be made; it must be incurred in trade and be determined and ascertained upon an actual, a completed, a closed transaction. The term 'in trade,' as used in the law, is held to mean the trade or trades in which the person making the return is engaged; that is, in which he has invested money otherwise than for the purpose of being employed in isolated transactions, and to which he devotes at least a part of his time and attention. A person may engage in more than one trade, and may deduct losses incurred in all of them, provided that in each trade the above requirements are met. As to losses on stocks, grain, cotton, etc., if these are incurred by a person engaged in trade to which the buying and selling of stocks, etc., are incident as a part of the business, as by a member of a stock, grain, or cotton exchange, such losses may be deducted. A person can be engaged in more than one business, but it must be clearly shown in such cases that he is actually a dealer, or trader, or manufacturer, or whatever the occupation may be, and is actually engaged in one or more lines of recognized business, before losses can be claimed with respect to either or more than one line of business, and his status as such dealer must be clearly established." (T. D. 2090, Dec. 14, 1914.) In further explanation of these matters, the Treasury Department has also made the following statements: "A person may have more than one business in the sense of being engaged in more than one trade, and may deduct losses incurred in all of them, provided that in each trade it can be clearly shown that he is actually a dealer, or trader, or manufacturer, or whatever the occupation may be. Neither the investment by an individual of money in the stock of a company, nor the employment by the company of his services in any official capacity can serve to make the business in which the company was engaged a matter of his individual trade. A loss is none the less actual because the individual cannot divest himself of the possession of worthless stock by sale, but that condition alone does not give the loss in question such a character as appears to the Department to have been contemplated by the income tax law." (T. D. 2135, Jan. 23, 1915.)

The law and practice in England correspond rather closely with our own in this particular. Thus, it is said: "Only such losses can be deducted as are connected with, in the sense that they are really incidental to, the trade itself. They cannot be deducted if they are mainly incidental to some other vocation or fall on the trader in some other character than that of trader. The nature of the trade is to be considered," so that a taxpayer is not allowed to

(211)

deduct a loss which he has sustained in being compelled to pay a judgment recovered against him in an action of tort, where the circumstances of the tort were not an incident of his business.[69] Under the English law, it is also held that one who carries on two lines of business cannot deduct a loss sustained in one from the profits made in the other.[70] But in this respect the American practice is more liberal. A loss sustained by the embezzlement of funds by an employé is clearly incurred in trade or sustained in connection with the income-producing business, and therefore may be deducted.[71]

It will be observed that losses cannot be deducted if compensated for by insurance or otherwise. But by a reasonable construction of the statute we should conclude that a loss partially compensated for if otherwise deductible, might be deducted to the extent of the excess of loss over insurance or other compensation received. The ruling of the Treasury Department is that the deduction for loss "must be based upon the difference between the cost value and salvage value of property or assets, including in the latter value such amount, if any, as has in the current or previous years been set aside and deducted from gross income by way of depreciation, and has not been paid out in making good such depreciation." (Internal Revenue Regulations No. 33, art. 124.) And a corporation cannot deduct losses which have been made good by contributions from its stockholders.[72] Further, the loss must have been "actually sustained within the year." Under these terms, it is considered that reserves set aside to take care of anticipated or probable losses cannot be deducted. (Internal Revenue Regulations No. 33, art. 126.) And so, where one makes an unfortunate investment, giving too high a price for property, and makes such profit as he can from it for a time, then realizes that the possibilities of the property are exhausted, and writes it off on his books as a total loss, it cannot be deducted as a loss actually sustained at the time of writing it off; for the loss was incurred at the beginning.[73] And a claimed loss cannot be regarded as a loss sustained during a particular year because it was written off on the books in that year, nor does it become an actual loss by the mere act of writing off that sum to

69 Strong & Co. v. Woodifield [1906] App. Cas. 448.
70 Brown v. Watt, 23 Scotch Law Rep. 403, 2 Tax Cas. 143.
71 U. S. v. Central Nat. Bank (D. C.) 10 Fed. 612.
72 Columbia Conduit Co. v. Commonwealth, 90 Pa. 307.
73 In re Pacific Guano & Fertilizer Co., 16 Hawaii, 552.

the account of profit and loss.[74] It has also been said: "District irrigation bonds as a rule, if not always, are a lien upon the real estate affected by the irrigation project, and until the corporation has taken such steps as are necessary to protect its rights and enforce the collection of the bonds, it does not appear that the corporation would be warranted in writing out of its assets and deducting from income, as a loss, the face value or any other arbitrarily ascertained amount representing a loss or shrinkage in the value of such bonds." (T. D. 2152, Feb. 12, 1915.)

§ 183. Same; Shrinkage in Value of Securities

It is the opinion of the Treasury Department that a diminution in the value of one's intangible property, caused by shrinkage in the market value of stocks or bonds, is not deductible in the taxpayer's return of income, either under the head of "depreciation" or that of "losses." The following ruling has been made: "Bonds and securities are not subject to wear and tear within the meaning of the Federal income tax law, and therefore depreciation does not apply to any shrinkage in their value. Shrinkage in the value of securities as such does not constitute a loss actually sustained within the year, the amount of which is definitely ascertained. Therefore, under the rules of this office and consistent with the provision of the law, a shrinkage in the value of bonds or like securities does not constitute an allowable deduction from gross income either as loss or depreciation. The fact that bonds and similar securities were written off at the direction of the Comptroller of the Currency or the state banking department is not material. A mere book entry does not constitute either a loss or gain for the purpose of the income tax. The fact that bonds were written off does not. necessarily imply that they are a total loss, nor is this act a conclusive proof that any loss occurred during the year for which the return is made. Losses of this character are only ascertainable when the securities mature, are disposed of, or canceled." (T. D. 2152, Feb. 12, 1915.)

§ 184. Same; Discarding, Abandonment, or Removal of Property

Loss due to the voluntary abandonment or removal of buildings, etc., incident to the making of improvements, is either a proper charge to the cost of new additions or to depreciation already provided, as the facts may indicate, but in no case is it a proper de-

---

[74] In re Hackfeld & Co., 16 Hawaii, 559.

duction in determining net income, except as it may be reflected in a reasonable amount allowable as a deduction for depreciation. (T. D. 1742, par. 93.) Thus, the value of sugar mills, buildings, and a plantation railroad, discarded on account of the erection of a larger mill at a different place and the construction of a different railroad connected therewith, is not a "loss incurred in trade," and cannot be deducted in ascertaining taxable net income; and the loss of an old mill in good condition, by its voluntary abandonment, because of the erection of a larger mill at a different place, is not an "expense" within the meaning of the income tax law.[75] And the cost of replacing a steamship which has become unserviceable by reason of her condemnation by the federal inspectors is not a "loss" to be deducted from income.[76]

§ 185. Same; Losses Not Connected With Business or Trade

In addition to the deduction for losses of the kind discussed in the preceding sections, the present statute, unlike the income tax act of 1913, allows the individual taxpayer to make a deduction, "in transactions entered into for profit but not connected with his business or trade, the losses actually sustained therein during the year, to an amount not exceeding the profits arising therefrom." (Act Cong. Sept. 8, 1916, § 5a, subdiv. 5 [U. S. Comp. St. 1916, § 6336e].) This was evidently intended to cover the case where a person occasionally or incidentally engages in a transaction out of which he expects to make a profit, but aside from his regular trade or occupation, as, for instance, where one buys a piece of real property or some shares of stock, not to hold permanently, but to sell again, and sustains a loss when he parts with the property. Such a loss would not have been deductible under the act of 1913, because it was not "incurred in trade." Seeking a construction of that act, the following question was propounded to the Treasury Department: "A person not a recognized or licensed dealer in stocks and bonds makes $5,000 profit during the year on a stock purchase and sale, and makes a loss during the same year on a stock purchase and sale of $4,000. Is it correct to return this difference of $1,000 in gains, or should the entire $5,000 be returned as gain?" The answer was: "This office holds that the profit of $5,000 is income to be included in a return of income, and that the

[75] Hawaiian Commercial & Sugar Co. v. Tax Assessor, 14 Hawaii, 601, 28 Ann. Cas. 980.

[76] In re Wilder's Steamship Co., 16 Hawaii, 567.

$4,000 is not such a loss as may be deducted in a return of income, for the reason that it is not incurred in trade." (T. D. 2135, Jan. 23, 1915.) But a different rule would apply under the present statute.

§ 186. Debts Written Off as Worthless

The income tax law allows the individual taxpayer to deduct from his return of income "debts due to the taxpayer actually ascertained to be worthless and charged off within the year." (Act Cong. Sept. 8, 1916, § 5a.) There is no similar allowance to corporations. But under the corporation excise tax law of 1909, containing a provision for deducting uncompensated losses, it was ruled that bad debts, if charged off on the company's books during the year, were proper deductions, though, if such debts were subsequently collected, they must be accounted for as income. (T. D. 1742, par. 75.) And it is reasonable that a similar construction should be applied to the act now in force. Under the income tax law of 1913, the following ruling was made: "Debts arising from unpaid wages, salaries, rents, and items of similar taxable income due and payable on or after March 1, 1913, will not be allowed as general deductions under paragraph B. of the income tax law unless the income which they represent has been included in a return of gross income for the year in which the deduction as a bad debt is sought to be made or in a previous year and the debts themselves have been actually ascertained to be worthless and charged off. All debts representing amounts that became due and payable prior to March 1, 1913, and not ascertained to be worthless prior to that date, whether representing income or a return of capital, are held to be allowable deductions under paragraph B of the law in a return of income for the year in which they are actually ascertained to be worthless and are charged off." (T. D. 2224, July 13, 1915.)

Under the former income tax laws it was held that a merchant, in making his statement of income, was entitled to deduct from his gross profits the bad debts made during the year to which the statement related, or such as appeared to be uncollectible at the end of that year, but not debts which became worthless after the expiration of that year, although before the date of the return.[77]

The term "debts" should not be taken in its broadest sense. It is a term capable of a wide variety of meanings. But considering the connection in which it is found and the general purpose of the

[77] U. S. v. Mayer, Deady, 127, Fed. Cas. No. 15,753.

statute, it is apparent that it includes only such debts as arise in or are connected with the business of the year, or, in other words, debts which, if they had been paid, would have constituted a part of the year's taxable income. Money owing to one may constitute a part of his capital, so that its payment would not swell his income, but only change the form of the capital. In this case, if it should prove uncollectible, it would not constitute a proper deduction. Thus, in an English case, it appeared that the company in question carried on the business of zinc smelting, and for this purpose it required large quantities of "blende." To supply the blende a new company was formed, which from time to time received assistance from the smelting company in the form of advances on loan. The new company proving unsuccessful and going into liquidation, the amount due from it to the smelting company was written off as a bad debt. But it was held that the advances were an investment of capital, and that the loss was not deductible in estimating the profits of the company for assessment under the income tax.[78] On the other hand, where a brewing company made loans to its customers on the security of public houses, and if the security did not realize the amount of the loan, the company wrote off the loss as a bad debt, it was held that, in arriving at its profits for assessment to income tax, the company was entitled to deduct the amount of such losses as worthless debts.[79]

§ 187. Depreciation of Property; Statutory Provision

In the case of both individual taxpayers and corporations, the income tax law provides for the deduction from their returns of gross income of "a reasonable allowance for the exhaustion, wear and tear of property arising out of its use or employment in the business or trade." (Act Cong. Sept. 8, 1916, §§ 5, 12 [U. S. Comp. St. 1916, §§ 6336e, 6336l].) It is only under this description, and as thus limited, that a deduction can be allowed on account of the depreciation of property. And according to the plain import of these terms, an allowance for depreciation can be claimed only in respect to tangible property which is directly employed in the production of the income taxed, such as buildings, machinery, furniture and fixtures, ships, vehicles, rolling stock and roadbed, and the like. For the language of the act only applies to property which is "used" or "employed" in business or trade, and which, in

78 English Crown Spelter Co. v. Baker, 99 Law T. 353, 5 Tax Cas. 327.
79 Reid's Brewery Co. v. Male [1891] 2 Q. B. 1, 3 Tax Cas. 279.

the process of such use, is subject to "exhaustion" or "wear and tear."

§ 188. Same; Treasury Regulations

The regulations made by the Treasury Department on the general subject of the allowance for depreciation are as follows:

"The deduction for depreciation should be the estimated amount of the loss, accrued during the year to which the return relates, in the value of the property in respect of which such deduction is claimed, that arises from exhaustion, wear and tear, or obsolescence out of the uses to which the property is put, and which loss has not been made good by payments for ordinary maintenance and repairs deducted under the heading of expenses of maintenance and operation. This estimate should be formed upon the assumed life of the property, its cost, and its use. Expenses paid in any one year in making good exhaustion, wear and tear, or obsolescence in respect of which any deduction for depreciation is claimed must not be included in the deduction for expense of maintenance and operation of the property, but must be made out of accumulated allowances, deducted for depreciation in current and previous years.

"The depreciation allowance, to be deductible, must be, as nearly as possible, the measure of the loss due to wear and tear, exhaustion, and obsolescence, and should be so entered on the books as to constitute a liability against the assets of the company, and must be reflected in the annual balance sheet of the company. The annual allowance deductible on this account should be such an amount as that the aggregate of the annual allowances deducted during the life of the property, with respect to which it is claimed, will not, when the property is worn out, exhausted, or obsolete, exceed its original cost.

"Incidental repairs which neither add to the value of the property nor appreciably prolong its life, but keep it in an operating condition, may be deducted as expenses.

"Depreciation set up on the books and deducted from gross income can not be used for any purpose other than making good the loss sustained by reason of the wear and tear, exhaustion, or obsolescence of the property with respect to which it was claimed. If it develops that an amount has been reserved or deducted in excess of the loss by depreciation, the excess shall be restored to income and so accounted for.

"If any portion of the depreciation set up is diverted to any purpose other than making good the loss sustained by reason of depreciation, the income account for the year in which such diversion takes place must be correspondingly increased.

"When an amount sufficient to return this capital has been secured through annual depreciation deductions no further deduction on this account shall be allowed. For the purpose of increasing the deduction on this account no arbitrary increase in values shall • be made, unless such increase in value shall be returned as income for the year in which the increase in value was taken up on the books." (Internal Revenue Regulations No. 33, arts. 129–140.)

A further regulation was also made, as follows:

"This office has fixed no definite rates by which an allowable deduction on account of depreciation in the value of any class of property subject to wear and tear is to be computed. The rule which this office has established and which is very generally followed by corporations contemplates that an allowable depreciation deduction within the meaning of the Federal income tax law shall be computed upon the basis of the cost of the property and the probable number of years constituting its life. The life of property necessarily depends upon its character, the uses to which it is put, and the conditions under which it is used. These elements being taken into consideration, corporations should, as a result of experience and observation, very closely approximate the number of years constituting the life of the property and upon this basis determine the rate of depreciation which annually occurs." (T. D. 2152, Feb. 12, 1915.)

§ 189. Same; Rulings and Decisions

Depreciation is a well-known and important item in all modern corporation accounting. And in estimating the net profits of any business, this item must be reckoned with, either by figuring a corresponding reduction in the value of capital assets, by the creation of a surplus or reserve fund for the eventual replacement of the plant or such portions of it as will become exhausted, or by the expenditure of current earnings in the restoration of machinery or other property which has been impaired or has deteriorated by use.[80] In the latter case, there is no shrinkage in the value of assets, but there is an annual expenditure over and above the ordinary operating expenses. And under the income tax law, it is ruled

---

[80] The Treasury ruling on this subject is that "the corporation will be allowed the usual depreciation of its machinery, equipment, etc., such depreciation to be determined on the basis of the cost and estimated life of the property with respect to which the depreciation is claimed." Internal Revenue Regulations No. 33, art. 143.

that depreciation, to be an allowable deduction in the return of annual net income of a corporation, must be charged off on the ledger of the corporation, so as to show a reduction in its capital assets to the extent of the depreciation claimed. In other words, if a corporation expends money in repairing or replacing depreciated property, it may claim an allowance therefor under the head of repairs or expenses of the business, but in that case will not be entitled to claim also for depreciation.[81] The question of what is a "reasonable allowance" for depreciation is one depending on the circumstances of each particular case, and if the amount of the tax to be paid is brought into litigation, it is to be determined as a question of fact on the evidence.[82]

The application of a general rule of this kind to a concrete case is well illustrated in a Scotch case, which concerned the method of figuring the deduction to be allowed for annual wear and tear of such a piece of property as a steamship. It was said that the proper method is to take the average life of such a property (here estimated at 22 years) and over that period spread the whole original cost, allowing for each year a deduction equivalent to the quotient obtained by dividing such cost by such number of years, without taking into account the value of the use of the money so annually allowed by way of deduction, or considering what the owner may do with it. The method pursued by the commissioners of inland revenue in this case was to calculate the sum which, being allowed annually and placed at interest, would amount to the original cost of the vessel at the end of the 22 years, thus in effect requiring the owner to establish a sinking fund and keep it invested, or to amortize the value of his property by the growth of a fund for its replacement. But this the court held to be incorrect.[83]

If an allowance for depreciation can be applied to anything else than the tangible property employed in the business, a question arises concerning shrinkage in the market value of stocks, bonds, and other investments. As above stated, the statute now in force would exclude such a case if read literally. The Treasury Department takes the view that a deduction for shrinkage in the value of securities cannot be claimed under the head of "depreciation," but

[81] T. D. 1742, par. 83.

[82] U. S. v. Nipissing Mines Co. (D. C.) 202 Fed. 803.

[83] Leith, Hull & Hamburg Steam Packet Co. v. Inland Revenue, 1 Sess. Cas. Scotch (1899) 1117. Further as to the allowance for depreciation in the case of steamships, see Cunard S. S. Co. v. Coulson [1899] 1 Q. B. 865.

that depreciation in the book value of capital assets, representing an actual shrinkage, may be deducted as a "loss." (T. D. 2005, July 8, 1914; Internal Revenue Regulations No. 33, art. 134.)

It has been ruled that "good will does not represent a value attaching to physical property, and it is an intangible asset whose value, separate and apart from the business with which it is connected, is not capable of determination. For the purpose of the income tax, it is capable of neither appreciation nor depreciation. Hence an amount claimed to represent its decline in value is not an allowable deduction from gross income in computing the tax liability of an individual or corporation." (T. D. 2137, Jan. 30, 1915.)

If costumes purchased by actors and actresses are used exclusively in the production of a play, and are not adapted for occasional personal use, and are not so used, a deduction may be claimed on account of such depreciation in their value as occurs during the year, on account of wear and tear arising from their use in the productions of the play or their becoming obsolete at the close of the production. (T. D. 2090, Dec. 14, 1914.) Depreciation of farm buildings, other than a dwelling occupied by the owner, actually sustained within the year, in excess of repairs made, will be considered an allowable deduction. (Idem.)

The English income tax law provides that where full effect cannot be given to the deduction for wear and tear in any given year, owing to the profits chargeable with the income tax being less than the deduction, that part of the deduction to which effect has not been given shall, for the purpose of making the assessment for the following year, be added to the amount of the deduction for wear and tear in that year.[84] In a late case, upon the assessment of the profits of plaintiff's ships for income tax, it was admitted that, prior to the year of assessment, plaintiff had received allowances for depreciation of the ships by wear and tear of an amount aggregating at least 96 per cent of their prime cost, and that, at the time of the assessment, the break-up value of the ships was more than 4 per cent, and that in one instance plaintiff had received more than 100 per cent of the original cost. Nevertheless it was held that the commissioners were bound to allow a just and reasonable deduction for depreciation during the year of assessment.[85]

---

[84] See Scottish Shire Line v. Inland Revenue [1912] Sess. Cas. 1108.
[85] Hall v. Rickman, 94 Law T. 224.

§ 190. Same; Rented Real Estate

In the case of an income derived from the rent of a building—such as a dwelling, an apartment house, a hotel, a store, or an office building—it should be observed that a claim should not be allowed both for repairs and for depreciation, if the repairs make good the depreciation. And it is only the building which can depreciate in the sense of the income tax law, since that alone is subject to "wear and tear." On this point the Treasury Department has ruled as follows: "Real estate, as such, and as distinct from the improvements thereon, is not reduced in value by reason of wear and tear, and it therefore follows that the allowance contemplated by depreciation in the case of real estate corporations does not apply to the ground, but is intended to measure the decline in the value of the improvements, which decline in value is due to wear and tear of such improvements. In determining the cost of the real estate, in most cases no segregation is made of the cost of buildings as separate and distinct from the cost of the grounds upon which such buildings stand. In such cases, where the actual cost of the buildings or improvements at the time they were taken over by the corporation cannot be definitely determined, it will be sufficient for the purpose of determining the rate of depreciation to be used in computing the amount which will be deductible from gross income to estimate the actual value of the buildings or improvements as of [the date when the law took effect], provided such buildings were in existence at that time, and provided that the value placed upon such buildings shall not be in excess of the cost of such buildings, less an amount measuring the depreciation which had previously been sustained." (T. D. 2137, Jan. 30, 1915.)

This subject has also been discussed in an important and well-considered decision of a federal court, from which we quote as follows: "The plaintiff was allowed 3 per cent for depreciation on an apartment house owned by him. The burden is on him to show that the depreciation so allowed was too small. This allowance is for the wear and tear suffered by the building during the tax year, which means the physical deterioration that the building suffered during that period. It does not take into account depreciation in value due to a loss of rental value because of the construction of more modern buildings with improved facilities, or due to a change in the neighborhood. It is to be based on the life of the building, in the sense of the number of years the building would remain in a condition to be habitable for the uses for which it was constructed and used, and which was in the instant case for an

apartment house, and not merely the number of years it would
stand without being condemned and torn down. The annual depreciation would be an amount represented by a fraction having
one, the tax year, for the numerator and the number of years, representing the ascertained life of the building, as the denominator.
This assumes that there would be an average deterioration suffered
each year during the life of the building, and that the plaintiff
would keep the building in good repair during the life of it. This
the law exacts of him. Upon these assumptions, and giving this
meaning to the words of the statute, 'a reasonable allowance for
the exhaustion, wear, and tear of the property arising out of its
use or employment in the business,' the amount of the deduction
allowed by the government to the plaintiff on this account is deemed to be reasonable." [86]

§ 191. Same; Obsolescence

The question of allowing for depreciation in the case of property which though not physically impaired has become obsolete is
one of great difficulty. Undoubtedly a business property diminishes in value unless it is kept up to the standard of efficiency set
by new inventions, new appliances, and new methods, since it cannot otherwise successfully compete with its better-equipped rivals.
And in a broad sense, this is clearly "depreciation." But it is not
depreciation by reason of "wear and tear," or by reason of its use
in the business. And so the decisions under income tax laws, in
so far as they have adverted to this point, tend to the application of a stricter rule. Thus, in an English case it was held that
depreciation on account of wear and tear does not include the loss
on apparatus which is discarded because it has become old-fash-
ioned or obsolete, as in the case where a street railway company
changes its motive power from horse power to electric power, and
thereupon is obliged to take up and cast aside the rails in use,
which, though not worn out, cannot be used for the new track.[87]
So again, under the English statute, which allows a deduction for
"diminished value by reason of wear and tear during the year of
any machinery or plant," it was ruled that the owners of a ship
engaged in trade were not entitled to a deduction for depreciation
in the value of their vessel caused by the building of ships of a
better construction or better equipped, though this circumstance

[86] Cohen v. Lowe (D. C.) 234 Fed. 474.
[87] London County Council v. Edwards, 5 Tax Cas. 383.

rendered their own property less desirable for the use of charterers and so diminished its earning power.[88] And it has been ruled that depreciation cannot be claimed in respect to an apartment house because its rental value diminishes, in consequence of the competition of newer and more desirable apartments, or because of a change in the character of the neighborhood, making it less attractive to tenants.[89] On the other hand, the Treasury Department (perhaps somewhat inadvisedly) has ruled that a depreciation allowance may be claimed for "obsolescence out of the uses to which the property is put." (Internal Revenue Regulations No. 33, art. 129.)

§ 192. Same; Reserves for Depreciation

In England, it is held that where a company sets aside out of its net profits, and before making dividends, a sum of money to be held as a reserve fund against depreciation of buildings, plant, and machinery, this amount cannot be deducted in making return for the income tax.[90] But the rule is otherwise in the United States. The Treasury Department at first ruled that the investment of depreciation reserve funds in the concern's own plant, in the way of additions and extensions, was a diversion of such reserve funds from their proper use (making good actual deterioration), and amounted to an investment of capital, and would also indicate that the amounts set aside on account of depreciation were unreasonably great. (T. D. 2137, Jan. 30, 1915.) But on further consideration, it was ruled that reserves for depreciation and depletion are proper deductions from gross income, if reasonable, and are not to be disallowed because converted into other forms of assets. It was said: "The essential requirements of this provision are that the amount deductible on account of depreciation shall be charged off and shall be a reasonable allowance, that is, an amount sufficient to make good the loss due to these causes. The phrase 'charged off' contemplates that the reasonable allowance deducted from gross income on account of depreciation or depletion shall be credited to appropriate reserve accounts and carried as a liability against the assets, to the end that when the total of these credits equals the capital investment account, no further deductions on these accounts will be allowed. While the presumption is that amounts

[88] Burnley Steamship Co. v. Aikin, 31 Scotch Law Rep. 803, 3 Tax Cas. 275.

[89] Cohen v. Lowe (D. C.) 234 Fed. 474.

[90] Forder v. Handyside, L. R. 1 Ex. Div. 233.

credited to these accounts will be used to make good the loss sustained either through a renewal or replacement of the property or a return of capital there is no requirement of law that the funds represented by these reserve liabilities shall be held intact or remain idle against the day when they may be used in making good the depreciation of the property with respect to which the deduction is claimed or in restoring the capital invested in the depleted assets. The conversion of the depreciation reserve into tangible assets will not constitute such a diversion as would deny the corporation the right of deduction provided in all cases that the deduction claimed in the return is a reasonable allowance, that is, a fair measure of the loss due to exhaustion, wear, and tear of property growing out of its use, and is charged off or so entered on the books as to constitute a liability against the assets with respect to which the depreciation deduction is claimed." (T. D. 2481, April 10, 1917.)

§ 193. Same; Depreciation Allowance in Case of Trust Estates

On this subject, the regulation of the Treasury Department is as follows: "In the case of a trust estate where the terms of the will or trust or the decree of a court of competent jurisdiction provide for keeping the corpus of the estate intact and where physical property forming a part of the corpus of such estate has suffered depreciation through its employment in business this office will permit a deduction from gross income for the purpose of caring for this depreciation, where the deduction is applied or held by the fiduciary for making good such depreciation. No depreciation deduction will be permitted by fiduciaries otherwise than as here provided. Fiduciaries should set forth in connection with their returns the provision of the will or trust or decree requiring such depreciation deduction where any exists, or that actual depreciation occurs, the amount thereof, and that the same has been or will be preserved and applied as such.

"The intent and purpose of this regulation is to deny to fiduciaries the right of claiming a deduction for depreciation in returns for the income tax of beneficiaries when, in fact, no depreciation reserve is established nor is authorized to be established, but the amount claimed as a deduction for depreciation is actually paid to the beneficiary as income.

"All amounts paid by fiduciaries to beneficiaries of trust estates from the income of such trust estates are held to be distributions of income and will be treated for income-tax purposes in accordance with the provisions of the law and regulations applicable to the income of such beneficiaries.

"Nothing in this regulation shall be construed to deny the right of trustees to make deductions from gross income for expenses actually incurred for repairs and such other necessary expenses other than betterments as may be required to preserve the corpus of the estate in accordance with the facts, actual application, or reservation of the necessary amounts or proper provisions of the trust, the requirements of law, or the order of a court of competent jurisdiction." (T. D. 2267, Nov. 5, 1915.)

§ 194. Same; Depreciation of Patents

That species of property which is represented by the ownership of a patent is subject to depreciation both on account of the limited time during which the monopoly may be enjoyed and on account of the fact that, at any time, the patenting of new inventions or improvements may render the original machine, process, or other thing covered by the patent more or less obsolete. Accordingly the Treasury department has prescribed special rules for calculating the amount of depreciation allowable for this kind of property with reference to the income tax. It is provided that "the deduction claimed for exhaustion of the capital assets as represented by patents to be made in the return of annual net income of a corporation for any given year shall be one-seventeenth of the actual cost of such patents reduced to a cash basis. Where the patent has been secured from the government by a corporation itself, its cost would be represented by the various government fees, cost of drawings, experimental models, attorneys' fees, etc. Where the patent has been purchased by the corporation for a cash consideration, the amount would represent the cost. Where the corporation has purchased a patent and made payment therefor in stocks or other securities, the actual cash value of such stocks or other securities at the time of the purchase will represent the cost of the patent to the corporation." "With respect to the depreciation of patents, one-seventeenth of the cost is allowable as a proper deduction each year until the cost of the patent has been returned to the corporation. Where the value of a patent has disappeared through obsolescence or any other cause, and the fact has been established that the patent is valueless, the unreturned cash investment remaining in the patent may be claimed as a total loss and be deducted from gross income in the return of annual net income for the year during which the facts as to obsolescence or loss shall be established, such unreturned cash value to be fixed in accordance with the proportion that the number of years which the patent still has to run bears to the full patent period of seventeen years." (Internal Revenue Regulations No. 33, arts. 137, 138.)

§ 195. Depletion of Ores in Mines

It has been a vexed question whether or not a company engaged in the business of mining coal, ores of gold or silver, or other natural deposits, should be allowed to deduct from its income as returned for assessment, under the head of depreciation, an amount representing the diminution in the value of its property caused by the extraction of ores during the year. The weight of authority (before the enactment of the present income tax law) was to the effect that this was not permissible.[91] Under the income tax act of 1913, there was included, under the head of allowance for depreciation, "in the case of mines, a reasonable allowance for depletion of ores and all other natural deposits, not to exceed five per centum of the gross value at the mine of the output for the year for which the computation is made." In execution of this provision, the Treasury Department prescribed elaborate instructions for the computation of this depreciation allowance. (Internal Revenue Regulations No. 33, art. 142; T. D. 1755.) But these are now obsolete, because a different rule is established by the present statute. It declares that the taxpayer (whether an individual or a corporation) may deduct from his income as returned for taxation, "(a) in the case of oil and gas wells, a reasonable allowance for actual reduction in flow and production, to be ascertained not by the flush flow, but by the settled production or regular flow; (b) in the case of mines, a reasonable allowance for depletion thereof, not to exceed the market value in the mine of the product thereof which has been mined and sold during the year for which the return and computation are made, such reasonable allowance to be made in the case of both (a) and (b) under rules and regulations to be prescribed by the Secretary of the Treasury: Provided, that when the allowances authorized in (a) and (b) shall equal the

---

[91] Von Baumbach v. Sargent Land Co., 242 U. S. 503, 37 Sup. Ct. 201, 61 L. Ed. 460; Stratton's Independence v. Howbert (D. C.) 207 Fed. 419; Commonwealth v. Ocean Oil Co., 59 Pa. 61; Allanza Co. v. Bell [1906] App. Cas. 18. Compare Forty Fort Coal Co. v. Kirkendall (D. C.) 233 Fed. 704; U. S. v. Nipissing Mines Co. (D. C.) 202 Fed. 803; Knowles v. McAdam, L. R. 3 Ex. Div. 23, 1 Tax Cas. 161.

capital originally invested, or in case of purchase made prior to March 1, 1913, the fair market value as of that date, no further allowance shall be made." (Act Cong. Sept. 8, 1916, §§ 5, 12 [U. S. Comp. St. 1916, §§ 6336e, 6336l].)

In pursuance of the authority thus granted, the Treasury Department has made and promulgated the following set of regulations: "Ownership of the mine content at the time for which the computation is made is an essential prerequisite to an allowable deduction. The paragraphs above quoted authorize, in the case of mines, two classes of deductions to take care of the wasting of assets, namely, (a) depreciation, (b) depletion. Depreciàtion comprehends loss due to exhaustion, wear, and tear of physical property, other than natural deposits, and the annual allowance contemplated by this title on this account will be ascertained by spreading ratably the cost of the property over the probable number of years constituting its life. In determining the amount of depreciation deductible in the case of buildings, the cost or value of the land upon which the buildings are situated will be excluded and will not be considered as part of the original capital to be extinguished through depreciation deductions. The amount to be taken care of through depreciation deductions, applicable to physical property other than natural deposits, will always be the capital invested in it and not a value which may be arbitrarily fixed as of March 1, 1913, or as of any other date.

"In case of mines, (other than oil and gas wells) if the property was acquired prior to March 1, 1913, the amount of invested capital which may be extinguished through annual depletion deductions from gross income will be the fair market value of the mine property as of March 1, 1913. The value contemplated herein as the basis for depletion deductions authorized by this title must not be based upon the assumed salable value of the output under current operative conditions, less cost of production, for the reason that the value under such conditions would comprehend the earning capacity of the property. Neither must the value determined as of March 1, 1913, be speculative, but must be determined upon the basis of the salable value en bloc as of that date of the entire deposit of minerals contained in the property owned, exclusive of the improvements and development work; that is, the price at which the natural deposits or mineral property as an entirety in its then condition could have been disposed of for cash or its equivalent. The value en bloc having been thus ascertained, an estimate of the number of units (tons, pounds, etc.) should be made. The en bloc value divided by the estimated number of units in the mine or mining property will determine the per unit value, which, multiplied by the number of units mined and sold during any one year, will determine the sum which will constitute an allowable deduction from the gross income of that year on account of depletion.

"Deductions computed on a like basis may be made from year to year during the ownership under which the value was determined, until the aggregate en bloc value as of March 1, 1913, of the mine or mineral deposits shall have been extinguished, after which no further deduction on account of depletion with respect to this property will be allowed to the individual or corporation under whose ownership the en bloc value was determined. The precise detailed manner in which the estimated fair market value of mineral deposits as of March 1, 1913, shall be made must naturally be determined by each individual or corporation interested, and who is the owner thereof, upon such basis as must not comprehend any operating profits, the estimate in all cases to be subject to the approval of the Commissioner of Internal Revenue.

"Every individual or corporation claiming and making a deduction for depletion of natural deposits shall keep an accurate ledger account, in which shall be charged the fair market value as of March 1, 1913, or the cost, if the property was acquired subsequent to that date, of the mineral deposits involved. This account shall be credited with the amount of the depletion deduction claimed and allowed each year, to the end that when the credits to the account equal the debits no further deduction for depletion with respect to this property will be allowed. The value determined and set up as of March 1, 1913, or the cost of the property if acquired subsequent to that date will be the basis for determining the depletion deduction for all subsequent years during the ownership under which the value was fixed, and during such ownership there can be no revaluation for the purpose of this deduction if it should be found that the estimated quantity of the mineral deposit was understated at the time the value was fixed or at the time the property was acquired.

"In cases wherein the quantity of the mineral deposit in the mine prior to March 1, 1913, can not be estimated with any degree of accuracy, it will be necessary, if depletion deductions are to be availed of, for the individual or corporation owning the deposits, with the best information available, to arrive at the fair market value of the property as of March 1, 1913, that is, its fair cash value en bloc if such value is believed to be other than its original cost, which value, during the period of the ownership under which it was determined, shall be final, and shall be charged to the property account as hereinbefore indicated, and then, on the basis of the most probable number of units in the property, the per unit value shall be determined as the basis for computing annual depletion allowances, this method and allowances to be continued until, but not beyond, the time when the value as of March 1, 1913, shall have been extinguished. The original cost of the mineral deposit may be taken as the basis for computing annual depletion deductions if the fair market value as of March 1, 1913, as hereinbefore required, can not be ascertained otherwise, allowance being made for minerals which may have been removed prior to that date. In cases wherein a mineral property was acquired subsequent to March 1, 1913, the same rule for computing the annual depletion deduction will apply, except that in such case the basis of the computation will be the actual cost rather than the value as of March 1, 1913.

"The foregoing rules apply to owners in fee of mines and mining properties, and do not contemplate that an individual or corporation operating a mine under lease on a royalty basis shall be entitled to any deduction for depletion. If, however, the lessee, in addition to royalties, paid or pays a stipulated sum for the right to explore, develop, and operate a mine, the amount so paid may be ratably distributed over the life of the lease or the probable life of the mine under ordinary operating conditions, and the lessee may deduct annually as a rental payment an aliquot part of the amount of the bonus so paid until such amount has been extinguished.

"To the return made pursuant to the above rule there should be attached a statement setting out (1) whether the operator is a fee owner or lessee; (2) in the case of a fee owner, (a) the fair market value of the mineral deposits as of March 1, 1913, if the property was acquired prior to that date, (b) the cost of the mineral property if acquired subsequent to that date; (3) the method by which the value as of March 1, 1913, was determined in case the property was acquired prior to that date; (4) the estimated quantity in units in the mine as of March 1, 1913, or at the date of purchase if acquired subsequent to that date; (5) the number of units removed and sold during the year for which the return was made; and (6) any other data which would be helpful in determining the reasonableness of the depletion deduction claimed in the return. In the case of a lessee, the statement should show (a) the amount of the bonus or other payment made for the right to operate the mine; (b) the period covered by the lease." (T. D. 2446, Feb. 7, 1917.)

§ 196. Same; Oil and Gas Wells

The provision of the statute as to the allowance of a deduction for depletion in the case of these properties is that there may be claimed, "in the case of oil and gas wells, a reasonable allowance for actual reduction in flow and production, to be ascertained not by the flush flow, but by the settled production or regular flow, provided that when the allowance authorized shall equal the capital originally invested, or in case of purchase made prior to March 1, 1913, the fair market value as of that date, no further allowance shall be made." (Act Cong. Sept. 8, 1916, §§ 5, 12.) For carrying this provision into effect, the Treasury Department has made the following regulations: "The purpose of this provision is to afford a means whereby the individual or corporation owning oil or gas producing properties may, during the period of operation, deduct from gross income the cost of, or capital actually invested in, the natural deposits if the investment was made subsequent to March 1, 1913, or the fair market value as of March 1, 1913, if purchased prior to that date, the measure of the deduction being the reduction in the flow and production. The annual deduction authorized by the above-quoted provision must be reasonable, and not in excess of such a percentage of the cost or value, as the case may be, and as herein defined, of the oil or gas producing properties as is indicated by the reduction in the original flow or settled production of one year as compared with that of the preceding year. For the purpose of this deduction note may be taken of the reduction in flow and production of such individual wells as were producing oil or gas during or at some time within the year, of groups of wells or of all wells in the field or territory embraced in the same ownership. If tested by the aggregate flow of all of the wells in the field or territory owned by an individual or corporation, and new wells shall have been developed during the year, it is possible that at the end of the year there will have been no reduction in flow and production, in which case, under the specific provision of the law hereinbefore quoted, and under which the depletion deduction is measured by the reduction in flow and production, there can be no deduction for depletion. Hence, in the case of a field or territory in course of development, or in which new wells are being drilled, if the depletion deduction is to be availed of in the returns of annual net income, each individual well, or possibly each group of wells in operation at the beginning of, or brought in during, the year, if the flow and production of the group of wells is so assembled as to be tested, must be tested at the end of the year in order that the decline in the flow and production may be determined.

"New wells or new groups of wells brought in during the year may be tested as soon as they have reached the stage of settled production or regular flow, and then again at the end of the year. The decline in flow and production, if any, as indicated by these tests, will be reduced to a percentage basis, and a like percentage of the capital invested in the oil or gas property (exclusive of machinery, equipment, etc.) will constitute an allowable deduction from the gross income of the year on account of depletion. Thus, if the decline in the flow and production during the year of, say, 10 wells, costing $100,000, has been 5 per cent, as compared with the production and flow as indicated by a test made at the beginning of the period, then 5 per cent of $100,000, or $5,000, will, for the year for which the computation is made, constitute an allowable depletion deduction in favor of the individual or corporation owning and operating the property.

"If the wells are not so situated that their flow and production may be assembled in order to test and ascertain the reduction in the output as a basis for computing depletion, it will be necessary for the corporation or individual owning the property and claiming a depletion deduction to take an accurate gauge of the production and flow of each well at a certain same period of each year, and by comparing this gauge with that of the previous year determine the percentage by which the production and flow has been reduced. This having been done as to all of the wells in operation, an average percentage rate of reduction in flow and production will be ascertained and this rate will be applied to the capital invested; that is, the value of the oil or gas property as of March 1, 1913, or the cost of the same if acquired subsequent to that date, for the purpose of determining the amount which may be allowably deducted from gross income by such owning individual or corporation on account of depletion.

"In case of a field or territory fully developed and in which no new wells are being drilled, a comparison of the quantity of oil or gas produced during the year for which the computation is made with the quantity produced during the last preceding year, will disclose the reduction, and the percentage thus indicated of the reduction in flow and production of such field will be the measure of the depletion deduction to be taken by the owner with respect to the capital invested in such field.

"Notwithstanding the fact that the drilling of new wells may offset the reduction in the production and flow of the older wells in the field not fully developed, the provision of the law hereinbefore quoted does not authorize, and this office can not permit, a depletion deduction to be taken so long as the flow and production of the unit, be it a well or group of wells or the entire territory, is as great during the year for which the return is made as it was for the year immediately preceding.

"Illustrating in a general way the above rule as applied to a field or territory the case may be taken of an oil property in which the capital invested, either actual cost or fair market value, as the case may be, is $500,000 and the production during the year for which the return is made was 47,500 barrels, and for the year immediately preceding 50,000 barrels. This would indicate a reduction in production of 2,500 barrels, or a decline of 5 per cent. Applying this rate to the capital ($500,000) the individual or corporation owning the property would be entitled to deduct from gross income as depletion for the year for which the return is made the sum of $25,000, that is, 5 per cent of the invested capital. The depletion deduction in all cases until the capital invested is extinguished will be such a percentage of the unextinguished capital as the reduction in flow or production of one year is a percentage of the flow or production of the previous year.

"The estimate of the fair market value of gas and oil properties as of March 1, 1913, on which depletion deductions are based shall be the price at which the property as an entirety might have been sold for cash or its equivalent as of that date. The value hereinbefore contemplated must naturally be determined by each individual or corporation interested and who is the owner of the property upon such a basis as will not comprehend any operating profits, the estimated value in all cases to be subject to the approval of the Commissioner of Internal Revenue.

"Every individual or corporation entitled to a deduction for depletion on account of reduction in flow or production of oil or gas shall keep an accurate ledger account, in which shall be charged the fair market value as of March 1, 1913, or the cost, if the property was acquired subsequent to that date, of the property whose value declines with the removal of the natural deposits. This account shall be credited with the amount of the depletion deduction claimed and allowed each year, to the end that, when the credits to the account equal the debits, no further deduction for depletion with respect to this property and the capital invested in it will be allowed.

"The value determined and set up as of March 1, 1913, or the cost of the property if acquired subsequent to that date, will be the basis for determining the depletion deduction for all subsequent years during the ownership under which the value was fixed, and during such ownership there can be no revaluation for the purposes of this deduction if it should be found that the estimated quantity of oil or gas contained in the property was understated at the time the value was fixed or at the time the property was acquired.

"The provision of the law authorizing the depletion deduction, designed as it is to provide a means whereby the invested capital of an individual or corporation may not be subject to the tax imposed by this title, does not apply to individuals or corporations who are operating oil or gas properties under lease, since in those cases the operator has no capital invested in such properties. By capital invested, as herein used, is meant the fair market value of the properties as of March 1, 1913, if acquired prior to that date, or their actual cost if acquired subsequent to that date, as it relates to the owner in fee of the properties. Lessees, however, will be permitted to deduct from gross income each year a reasonable allowance for depreciation, which depreciation applies to the physical property, including rigs, tools, machinery of all kinds, pipes, casing, and other equipment necessary to the operation of the wells or field. If lessees, in order to secure the right to enter upon, explore, develop, or operate gas or oil properties, paid or shall pay a bonus in addition to royalties, the amount of such bonus so paid may be ratably distributed over the life of the lease or over the productive life of the property, and the lessee may deduct annually as a rental payment an aliquot part of the amount of the bonus so paid until such amount has been extinguished.

"The incidental expenses of drilling wells, that is, such expenses as are paid for wages, fuel, repairs, etc., which do not necessarily enter into and form a part of the capital invested or property account, may, at the option of the individual or corporation owning and operating the property, be charged to property account sub-

ject to depreciation or be deducted from gross income as an operating expense. If, in exercising the option, the operating individual or company charges the expense of drilling wells to property
account, the same may be taken into account in determining a reasonable allowance for depreciation during each year until the property account thus augmented has been extinguished through annual depreciation deductions, after which no further deduction on
this account will be permitted. The cost of drilling dry or non-
productive wells may be deducted from gross income as a loss.

"To each return made by an individual or corporation owning
and operating oil or gas properties there should be attached a
statement showing (1) (a) the fair market value of the property
(exclusive of machinery, equipment, etc.) as of March 1, 1913, if
acquired prior to that date, or (b) the actual cost of the property if
acquired subsequent to that date; (2) how the fair market value
of the property as of March 1, 1913, was ascertained; (3) the
quantity of oil or gas produced during the year for which the return was made; (4) the quantity produced during the year immediately preceding; (5) how the depletion deduction claimed in
the return was computed, whether upon the decline in flow and
production of individual wells, groups of wells, or the entire field;
and (6) any other data which would be helpful in determining
the reasonableness of the depletion deduction claimed in the return.

"If the operator is a lessee that fact should be stated and an explanation given as to the basis and property upon which any depreciation deduction is claimed, it being understood, as hereinbefore
indicated, that depreciation relates to the loss due to the use, wear,
and tear of physical property, and that the lessee is not entitled
to any deduction for the depletion or exhaustion of the oil or gas
deposits, but may deduct annually as a rental payment an aliquot
part of any bonus paid for the right to enter upon, explore, develop, and operate oil or gas territory, as well as the royalty payments made to the lessor for the oil or gas removed from such
property, provided the entire proceeds from the oil or gas produced during the year are returned in the gross income of the operator.
The above rule for computing allowable depletion deductions being set out in the law, no deduction on this account will be allowed if computed upon any basis other than that authorized by the
law and further amplified in this decision." (T. D. 2447, Feb. 8,
1917.)

(234)

§ 197. Depreciation of Timber Lands

In regard to an allowance for depreciation or depletion of the value of lands chiefly or solely valuable for the timber upon them, the ruling of the Treasury Department is as follows: "Corporations owning tracts of timber lands and removing therefrom and selling, or otherwise disposing of the timber will be permitted to deduct from their gross income on account of depreciation or depletion an amount representing the original cost of such timber, plus any carrying charges that may have been capitalized or not deducted from income. The purpose of the depreciation or depletion deduction is to secure to the corporation, when the timber has been exhausted, an aggregate amount which, plus the salvage value of the land, will equal the capital actually invested in such timber and land." (Internal Revenue Regulations No. 33, art. 139.) The decisions of the courts, in so far as they touch this subject, appear to be in accord with the principles set forth in the regulation.[92]

§ 198. Amortization of Bonds

Closely connected with the subject of depreciations is the rule or principle of the amortization of various forms of securities, and particularly corporate bonds. This principle is well explained by a court in New York, as follows: "It is a common matter with bankers and dealers in stocks to compute, by the aid of tables, what the actual income is of a stock running a certain definite time, for which a certain premium is paid. The actual income is plainly less than the amount yearly received, because the premium paid must be so distributed, in the calculation, over the time the stock has to run, that the owner at the end of the time will have his original investment unimpaired. Otherwise, though he may not notice this, he will have been gradually impairing his capital, in fact, using it up in the form of income. The rule is that so much out of the moneys received annually on these bonds shall be treated as income as, according to the computations and tables above mentioned, they are found to produce. The residue belongs to principal, and annually added thereto will make up for the gradual depreciation which must come as the bonds approach maturity, and will keep the fund unimpaired when they are paid off." [93] Thus, if a trustee under a will, who holds a fund in trust to pay the income to a person during his life, with remainder over, makes an invest-

---

[92] Doyle v. Mitchell Bros. Co., 235 Fed. 686, 149 C. C. A. 106.
[93] People v. Davenport, 30 Hun (N. Y.) 177.

ment in bonds, which are payable at a day certain and are bought at a premium, he is not obliged to pay the entire net income to the tenant for life, but is entitled to deduct such an amount from the actual interest received on each bond as will, by successive deductions, make good to the capital the amount of the premium paid upon the original purchase of the bond, without regard to the market value of the bond at the time of making such deductions.[94] But the rule is otherwise under the income tax law. In returning the interest on bonds as income for taxation, the bondholder cannot annually deduct therefrom a pro rata share of the premium paid in purchasing the bonds.[95]

But the Treasury Department rules that, "with respect to bond issues, where such bonds are disposed of for a price less than par and are redeemable at par, it is held that, because of the fact that such bonds must be redeemed at their face value, the loss sustained by reason of their sale for less than their face value may be prorated by the issuing corporation in accordance with the life of the bond." (Internal Revenue Regulations No. 33, art. 135.) It is explained that the intention of this ruling "is to allow corporations selling their own bonds at a discount to prorate the discount over the life of the bonds and to deduct from gross income each year an aliquot part of the discount determined in accordance with the number of years which the bonds have to run from the date of issue. This clause is not to be considered, however, as permitting corporations which had sold bonds issued prior to 1909 at a discount, and had at that time charged the entire amount of the discount into profit and loss, to take up such discount and prorate it over the life of the bonds for the purpose of deducting an aliquot part of such discount from the income of current years and thus reduce the taxable income." (T. D. 2161, Feb. 19, 1915.)

§ 199. Dividends from Corporations Subject to Tax

In order to avoid double taxation, it is customary for income tax laws to allow the deduction of dividends received from corporations liable to the tax, or which have been assessed for it. The act of Congress of 1916, as applied to the individual taxpayer, requires him to show in his return dividends received from corporations,

---

[94] New England Trust Co. v. Eaton, 140 Mass. 532, 4 N. E. 69, 54 Am. Rep. 493.

[95] T. D. 2161, Feb. 19, 1915. The same rule is applied in Wisconsin under the income tax law of that state. Van Dyke v. City of Milwaukee, 159 Wis. 460, 146 N. W. 812, 150 N. W. 509.

but then allows a "credit" therefor, in so far as concerns his liability to the "normal" income tax only. The provision is as follows: "For the purpose of the normal tax only, the income embraced in a personal return shall be credited with the amount received as dividends upon the stock or from the net earnings of any corporation, joint-stock company or association, trustee, or insurance company, which is taxable upon its net income." (Act Cong. Sept. 8, 1916, § 5b [U. S. Comp. St. 1916, § 6336e].) The same credit is allowed in the case of nonresident aliens. (Id., § 6b [U. S. Comp. St. 1916, § 6336f].) No such credit is allowed to corporations owning stock in other corporations and receiving dividends thereon.

In the year 1917, several corporations declared dividends which were not payable or paid in cash, but were paid by distributing among their stockholders proportionate amounts of the bonds issued under the Act of Congress of April 24, 1917, the so-called "Liberty Loan" bonds. These bonds are expressly exempt from all taxation, national, state, or local, except estate or inheritance taxes. A question having arisen as to whether a stockholder thus receiving one or more of these bonds by way of a dividend would have to include them in his taxable income for the year, the matter was referred to the Attorney General, who returned an opinion that they must be so returned, on the ground that the income tax "is upon the income itself as an entirety and not upon the specific articles into which this income is finally transmuted. When these bonds, therefore, are used as a medium of payment, whether in the discharge of a private debt or a corporate dividend, the profit or gain to the recipient is nevertheless subject to income tax." (T. D. 2512, June 8, 1917.)

§ 200. Special Rules as to Insurance Companies

The income tax act of 1916 allows a deduction, in the case of insurance companies, of "sums other than dividends paid within the year on policy and annuity contracts." This covers the ordinary outgo of an insurance company in the way of payments of losses under its policies and periodical payments made to beneficiaries under annuity contracts. Under this head, together with that of "losses uncompensated," according to the regulations of the Treasury Department, "the insurance company may take credit for all losses actually sustained during the year and not compensated by insurance or otherwise, including losses resulting from the sale or maturity of securities or other assets, as well as decreases by adjustment of book values of securities, in so far as such decreases represent actual declines in values which have taken place during the year for which the return is made; also losses from agency balances, or other accounts, charged off as worthless; losses by defalcation; premium notes voided by lapse, when such notes shall have been included in gross income. Credit will be taken for all death, disability, or other policy claims, including fire, accident, and liability losses, matured endowments, annuities, payments on installment policies, surrender values, and all claims actually paid under the terms of policy contracts. Salvage need not be included in gross income if deducted in ascertaining the net amount paid for losses under policy contracts." (Internal Revenue Regulations No. 33, art. 147.)

On the meaning of the word "dividends," as used in the statutory provision above quoted, an instructive decision was rendered by the Supreme Court of Kentucky. It appeared in this case that an insurance company, in its policy, stipulated for a premium larger than was actually needed to carry the risk insured against under ordinary conditions, but which might be needed under extraordinary conditions, and, in order to provide in advance against such a contingency, collected as premium for the first year the full amount stipulated for, setting aside so much thereof as was overpayment as a guaranty against misfortune, and then, for the premiums for the succeeding years, did not collect the entire amount stipulated for, because of the sufficiency of the overpayment of the first year's premium to guard against additional risks, but designated the part not collected from the policy holder as a "dividend." It was held that the company was not liable to taxation on the entire premiums stipulated for in the policy, but only for the amount actually collected, for the part of such premiums designated by the company as a dividend was not in fact a dividend, but merely an overcharge which was never collected from the policy holder, and hence was not received by the company as "cash or otherwise" within the terms of the statute.[96] There is also a decision of a federal court, applicable in the case of a life insurance company which, although a stock company, conducts a mutual department, but collects premiums from the participating policy holders on the level premium plan, and at the end of the year, when the cost of carrying the policy has been ascertained, credits

---

[96] Mutual Benefit Life Ins. Co. v. Commonwealth, 128 Ky. 174, 107 S. W. 802.

the policy holder with the excess paid, which he may have applied in reduction of the next premium, to purchase additional insurance, to shorten the premium-paying period of his policy, or to accelerate its maturity in the case of an endowment policy. It was held that the surplus so applied is not a "dividend" within the meaning of the statute, but represents nothing more than the excess of loading of the premium, which is returnable in some form to the policy holder.[97]

§ 201. Same; Mutual Companies

Special provisions are made by the income tax law for companies doing business on the mutual plan. In the case of mutual life insurance companies, they "shall not include as income in any year such portion of any actual premium received from any individual policy holder as shall have been paid back or credited to such individual policy holder, or treated as an abatement of premium of such individual policy holder, within such year." In the case of mutual fire, employers' liability, workmen's compensation, and casualty insurance companies, "requiring their members to make premium deposits to provide for losses and expenses," they "shall not return as income any portion of the premium deposits returned to their policy holders, but shall return as taxable income all income received by them from all other sources, plus such portions of the premium deposits as are retained by the companies for purposes other than the payment of losses and expenses and reinsurance reserves." As to mutual marine insurance companies, the direction is that they "shall include in their return of gross income gross premiums collected and received by them, less amounts paid for reinsurance, but shall be entitled to include in deductions from gross income amounts repaid to policy holders on account of premiums previously paid by them and interest paid upon such amounts between the ascertainment thereof and the payment thereof." (Act Cong. Sept. 8, 1916, § 12a, par. 2 [U. S. Comp. St. 1916, § 6336l].)

§ 202. Same; Reserve Funds

The statute also allows insurance companies to deduct "the net addition, if any, required by law to be made within the year to reserve funds." (Act Cong. Sept. 8, 1916, § 12a.) And it provides that "in the case of assessment insurance companies, whether do-

[97] Connecticut General Life Ins. Co. v. Eaton (D. C.) 218 Fed. 188.

mestic or foreign, the actual deposit of sums with state or territorial officers pursuant to law, as additions to guarantee or reserve funds, shall be treated as being payments required by law to reserve funds." (Id., § 12c.) The regulation of the Treasury Department on this point is as follows: "The reserve funds of insurance companies to be considered in computing the deductible net addition to reserve funds are held to include only the reinsurance reserve and the reserve for supplementary contracts required by law in the case of life insurance companies, the unearned premium reserves required by law in the case of fire, marine, accident, liability, and other insurance companies, and only such other reserves as are specifically required by the statutes of a State within which the company making the return is doing business. The reserves used in computing the net addition must not include the reserve on any policies the premiums on which have not been accounted for in gross income. For the purpose of this deduction, the net addition is the excess of the reserve at the end of the year over that at the beginning of the year and may be based upon the highest authorized reserve required by any State in which the company making the return does business." (Internal Revenue Regulations No. 33, art. 147d.)

It has recently been decided by the Supreme Court of the United States that fire insurance companies are not "required by law" (at least in Pennsylvania) to hold a reserve against unpaid losses, and consequently are not exempt from taxation on funds passed to a reserve account for that purpose, and that the words "reserve funds," as used in the income tax law, have reference to the funds ordinarily held by insurance companies as against the contingent liability on outstanding policies.[98] There is also a decision of the Court of Claims that only the net addition to reserve funds required by state statutes is deductible from the gross income of insurance companies, and that unless some state law is pointed out which justifies it, they cannot claim exemption in respect to funds passed to a reserve established to secure payments of taxes, salaries, brokerage, and agents' commissions.[99]

---

[98] McCoach v. Insurance Co. of North America, 244 U. S. 585, 37 Sup. Ct. 709. 61 L. Ed. 1333, reversing Insurance Co. of North America v. McCoach, 224 Fed. 657, 140 C. C. A. 167, which had reversed the judgment in the same case in the District Court, 218 Fed. 905.

[99] Maryland Casualty Co. v. U. S. (Ct. Cl.) reported in Treasury Decisions, March 1, 1917.

§ 203. Same; Unearned Premiums

Aside from the matter of reserve funds required by law, it has been a vexed question whether or not an insurance company could claim a deduction in respect to premiums covering a risk which extends beyond the end of the fiscal year. In an English case, a fire insurance company set up a claim to deduct a portion of its premium receipts for the year, representing the unearned or unexhausted portion of such premiums, where it remained liable on the policies for one or several years longer. The company contended that such a deduction should be allowed to it either as a fixed percentage of the total premium receipts (suggesting one-third as a proper proportion), or else to the extent of the amount which it would cost to reinsure its unexpired risks. But the court held otherwise. Conceding that it would be impossible to ascertain the true net profits of an insurance company in this situation with such mathematical accuracy as to do perfect and absolute justice, it was held that the fair and proper method is to take on the one side the whole receipts, and on the other side the whole expenditure and disbursements, for the given year, the balance remaining being, for the time at least, net profits on which the income tax should be assessed. This being done year by year, there is an absolute balancing of accounts; and if any wrong is done by losses afterwards occurring in respect of premiums on which, as profits, the income tax has been assessed and paid, it will be taken into consideration in the ensuing year.[100] And later an exactly similar decision was rendered by the Court of Appeal.[101] But only four years afterwards, the same court ruled that the profits of a fire insurance company, for the purpose of the income tax, are not to be computed by merely deducting the total of losses and disbursements for the year from the total premium receipts for the same period, but allowance must be made for outstanding policies at the end of the year, or for the unearned portion of premiums received, which may be done by deducting a fair and reasonable percentage of the year's premium receipts.[102] Substantially the same view was taken by the internal revenue officers in construing the act of Congress of 1909, for it was ruled that unearned premiums set aside by insurance companies as reserves should not be included as income until earned, unless the same should be entered on the ledger as income during the year in which they were received. (T. D. 1742, par. 70.)

[100] Imperial Fire Ins. Co. v. Wilson, 35 Law T. 271, 1 Tax Cas. 71.

[101] General Accident Co. v. McGowan [1908] App. Cas. 207, 5 Tax Cas. 308.

[102] Sun Insurance Office v. Clark [1912] App. Cas. 443.

§ 204. Rules as to Foreign Corporations

As foreign corporations are taxed, under the income tax law, only upon so much of their income as they receive from "all sources within the United States," so their allowable deductions are correspondingly restricted. Thus, the item of "expenses" will cover only expenditures in the maintenance and operation of the business and property within the United States. So "losses" must be "actually sustained within the year in business conducted by it within the United States." As to deducting interest paid by a foreign company, the rule prescribed is that it may claim a deduction for interest on its indebtedness, to an amount of such indebtedness not exceeding that portion of its paid-up capital stock (plus one-half the sum of its bonded debt) which may be regarded as invested or employed in this country, which is to be ascertained by taking the ratio between "the gross amount of its income for the year from business transacted and capital invested within the United States" and "the gross amount of its income derived from all sources within and without the United States." As to taxes paid, a foreign corporation is allowed to deduct "taxes paid within the year imposed by the authority of the United States or its territories or possessions, or under the authority of any state, county, school district, or municipality, or other taxing subdivision of any state, paid within the United States, not including those assessed against local benefits." (Act Cong. Sept. 8, 1916, § 12b.)

§ 205. Bookkeeping to Show Deductions

The regulations prescribed by the Treasury Department, with reference to corporations, provide that: "It is immaterial whether the deductions (except for taxes and losses) are evidenced by actual disbursements in cash, or whether evidenced in such other way as to be properly acknowledged by the corporate officers and so entered on the books of the corporation as to constitute a liability against the assets of the corporation making the return. Deductions for taxes, however, should be the aggregate of the amounts actually paid, as shown on the cash book of the corporation. Deductions for losses should be confined to losses actually sustained and charged off during the year and not compensated by insurance or otherwise. Except as the same may be modified by the provisions of the act, limiting certain deductions and authorizing others, the net income as returned for the purpose of the tax should be the same as that shown by the books or the annual balance sheet." (Internal Revenue Regulations No. 33, art. 158.) Another and later ruling is to the effect that corporations keeping books in accordance with standard systems of accounting, or in conformity with the requirements of some federal, state, or municipal authority having supervision over them, may make their returns on the basis on which their books are kept, provided the books so kept and the returns so made reflect the true net income of the corporation for each year.   (T. D. 2433, Jan. 8, 1917.)

(243)

CHAPTER IX

COLLECTION OF INCOME TAX AT THE SOURCE

§ 206. Explanation of Terms

The theory of "collection at the source" is that the government enforces payment of the income tax (in certain limited fields) not directly from the person who receives the income and is therefore liable for it, but indirectly, by exacting its payment, before the income reaches his hands, from the person who is to pay it to him. In other words, if A. is to receive from B. a payment which is in the nature of income and is subject to the tax, the government does not leave it to A. to account for the payment in its annual return and thereafter pay the tax on it in due season, but requires B. to deduct from the payment, at the time of making it, the amount due as income tax and pay it directly to the proper revenue officer. Persons who are in the position of B. are denominated by the Treasury regulations "debtors." It is of course to be understood that not all persons who are debtors to others, or who have payments to make to others, are within this technical designation. It applies only to those classes of persons who are described in the statute as charged with the duty of deducting and paying over the income tax, and then only in respect to such classes of payments as come within its terms. But the word "debtors" is applied by the government officers to all who come within this limited description. The term "withholding agents" is sometimes synonymous with "debtors" and sometimes has a wider meaning. For a "debtor" may appoint a fiscal or other agent to perform the duties imposed upon him with respect to the income tax, and then the latter is called a "withholding agent." The "source" is defined as the place where the income originates and is payable.

§ 207. Effect of Amendments of 1917

The provisions for collection at the source in the income tax law of 1913 and the amendatory act of 1916 were drastic and far-reaching, embracing almost every conceivable kind of income, provided it exceeded $3,000 in any taxable year, and interest on corporate securities and on foreign obligations without regard to the amount, and applying to citizens of the United States as well as to aliens and to both domestic and foreign corporations. These provisions brought forth a mass of regulations and rulings of the Treasury Department, and of official forms, which were intricate, confusing, and sometimes contradictory.

When the revenue act of 1917 was before Congress, it was proposed by the Senate to abolish altogether the system of collection at the source, but this was opposed by the House. Various compromises were effected in the conference committee, and these were written into the bill and finally accepted by both houses. The effect is very greatly to restrict this method of collecting the tax. As the law now stands, this method of requiring the deduction and paying over of the tax by the payer of the income is confined to three cases:

First, the case of income payable to a nonresident alien individual. Here collection at the source applies to income derived from "interest, rent, salaries, wages, premiums, annuities, compensation, remuneration, emoluments, or other fixed or determinable annual or periodical gains, profits, and income," but not including dividends from corporations.

Second, the case of income derived from "interest upon bonds and mortgages, or deeds of trust or other similar obligations of corporations." This applies whether the income is payable to a nonresident alien individual or to an individual citizen or resident of the United States. But it applies only "if such bonds, mortgages, or other obligations contain a contract or provision by

(245)

which the obligor agrees to pay any portion of the tax imposed by this title upon the obligee or to reimburse the obligee for any portion of the tax or to pay the interest without deduction for any tax which the obligor may be required or permitted to pay thereon or to retain therefrom under any law of the United States."

Third, the case of interest on bonds and mortgages or deeds of trust or similar obligations of domestic corporations, when owned by "nonresident alien firms, copartnerships, companies, corporations, joint-stock companies or associations, and insurance companies, not engaged in business or trade within the United States and not having an office or place of business therein." In this case, the tax is apparently to be collected at the source without regard to the presence or absence of a tax-free covenant in the bond or other obligation.

In all of the three foregoing cases, collection at the source is applied only to the "normal" income tax, not to any amount payable as an "additional" or surtax.

The Act of Congress of October 3, 1917, imposing supplementary or "war" income taxes provides that they shall be assessed, collected and paid in the same manner as the similar taxes under the act of September 8, 1916, but that "the provisions of subdivision (c) of section nine of such act, as amended by this act, requiring the normal tax of individuals on income derived from interest to be deducted and withheld at the source of the income shall not apply to the new two per centum normal tax prescribed in section one of this act until on and after January first, 1918, and thereafter only one two per centum normal tax shall be deducted and withheld at the source under the provisions of such subdivision (c), and any further normal tax for which the recipient of such income is liable under this act or such act of September 8, 1916, as amended by this act, shall be paid by such recipient." (Act Cong. Oct. 3, 1917, § 3.)

§ 208. Interest on Corporate Bonds and Similar Obligations

Before the amendment of 1917, the law required the income tax to be deducted and withheld from "interest upon bonds and mortgages, or deeds of trust or other similar obligations of corporations." The act of 1917 repeats this provision, but restricts it to cases in which the bonds or mortgages contain a "tax free" covenant, that is, one requiring the obligor to pay the full sum of the interest without deduction for any tax. As to the kind of securities included in the description of "similar obligations," the Treasury Department rules that this term embraces equipment trust agreements and receivers' certificates. And generally, it means obligations of corporations which, though not bonds or mortgages or deeds of trust, are similar in form or purpose, or in being extended beyond the time of ordinary bankable commercial paper. Temporary receipts issued pending the preparation and issue of bonds or interest notes stand in the place of the latter, and when an interest period intervenes and receipts are presented for indorsement thereon of a payment of interest, the tax should be deducted, if the obligation is within the statute. A simple promissory note, not exceeding a year in time, is not "similar" to bonds, etc., and the tax is not deductible, except when it is payable to a nonresident alien, in which event another provision of the statute applies. Scrip certificates issued by a corporation to its stockholders in lieu of dividends, bearing interest and redeemable at a specified time not later than a year from the date of issue, are not corporate obligations similar to bonds, and are not subject to deduction for the income tax. (T. D. 2090, Dec. 14, 1914; T. D. 2152, Feb. 12, 1915.)

When the interest on corporate obligations is evidenced by detachable coupons, the income tax is to be deducted when these are presented for payment. When the interest is registered, the Treasury rules that the obligor company should deduct the normal income tax before sending out checks for such interest to the registered owners, or before paying the interest on interest orders signed by the registered owners of the bonds. When bonds, under a provision to that effect contained in them, are retired, not on an interest day, but within an interest period, and prior to the expiration of the full term of the bond, the deduction for income tax should cover that part of the interest period affected between the beginning of such period and the date of retirement of the bonds. (T. D. 2090, Dec. 14, 1914.)

It will be observed that all this applies only to interest upon bonds or similar obligations made by corporations. Where interest, whether on bond and mortgage or on any other obligation, is payable by an individual, it does not come within this class. And where an individual issues coupon bonds secured by a mortgage on real estate, and subsequently a corporation purchases the real estate, and assumes (as between the mortgagor and itself) the payment of the bonds and coupons, the situation is not changed. The corporation acquires only the mortgagor's equity of redemption and his possession; the property is the security, and the character of the bond obligation remains unchanged and as created, even though the corporation is to pay all interest and eventually the mortgage. There will therefore be no withholding of the income tax by the corporation as against the owners of the bonds. (T. D. 2090, Dec. 14, 1914.)

When a corporation is required to deduct and pay over the income tax on its interest payments, the tax is not thereby laid on the corporation, but it is and remains a tax on the creditor; the corporation is merely made use of as a convenient means of collecting the tax.[1]

§ 209.   Certificates of Ownership

Though individuals subject to the income tax are entitled to a specific exemption of $3,000 or $4,000 as the case may be (or of $1,000 or $2,000 in respect to the supplementary war income tax) the act of 1916 made no clear provision for their claiming or obtaining this exemption in respect to income derived from interest on corporate securities, since, as to such items, the tax is deductible at the source without regard to the amount of the interest. The amendatory act of 1917, however, provides that the income tax shall be deducted from such interest payments "unless the person entitled to receive such interest shall file with the withholding agent, on or before February first, a signed notice in writing claiming the benefit of an exemption." (Act Cong. Sept. 8, 1916, as amended by Act Cong. Oct. 3, 1917, § 1205.) For the double purpose of securing reliable information as to the securities owned by individuals and the income derived from them, and of providing a method of claiming the exemption, the Treasury Department has provided for "certificates of ownership," which are to accompany coupons or orders for registered interest when the same are presented for payment or deposited in bank for collection. Such a certificate sets forth the name of the corporation paying the interest, a description of the bonds, giving name of issue and rate of interest, the date of maturity of the interest, the amount of interest, the total exemption to which the payee or depositor is entitled under the act of Congress, and the "amount of exemption now claimed" or else a statement that the owner "does not now" claim the exemption. The certificate further sets forth that the signer is the owner of the bonds described, and bears his signature and address, with the date. These certificates may be obtained from the internal revenue officers, and are commonly supplied by the banks.

---

1 U. S. v. Railroad Co., 17 Wall. 322, 21 L. Ed. 597.

In case corporate securities are owned jointly by several persons, the certificate of ownership may be signed by one of the owners, and the names, addresses, and proportion of ownership of each of the joint owners will be indorsed on the back of the certificate. Where the securities belong to a partnership, it is not regarded by the revenue officers as a case of joint ownership, as here described, but a separate form of certificate has been provided for this case.

If the owner of a bond of the kind made subject to this provision of the statute omits to attach his certificate of ownership to coupons deposited for collection, the Treasury regulations provide that the first bank or collecting agency receiving the coupons shall deduct and withhold the amount of the income tax and report and pay it to the Treasury. At the same time the bank will make its own certificate, reciting the facts, and acknowledging responsibility for the deduction of the income tax, which certificate will accompany the coupons to the debtor corporation in order that the tax may not be again withheld if the coupons should pass through the hands of other banks or collecting agencies. (T. D. 2135, Jan. 23, 1915.)

§ 210.   Substitute Certificates by Bank or Collecting Agency

A Treasury regulation provides that responsible banks, bankers, and other collecting agents receiving coupons for collection with certificates of ownership attached may either present the coupons with the certificates of ownership attached to the debtor corporation (that is, send them through the channels of collection with the owner's certificate attached until they reach the place of payment), or, at the option of the bank or collecting agent, the owners' certificates may be detached from the coupons and forwarded to the Commissioner of Internal Revenue; but in the latter case, the bank or collecting agent will substitute for the owner's certificate, and attach to the coupons in lieu thereof, its own certificate, containing essentially all the data appearing in the owner's certificate, except the name of the owner. It is understood that this permission was given in view of many remonstrances made by persons who objected to giving information as to their ownership of bonds to all the chain of banks through whose hands their coupons might pass in the ordinary processes of collection. Banks or other collecting agents who thus substitute their own certificates for the owners' certificates are required to keep a complete record of all such transactions and substitutions of certificates, showing all the original certificates for which their own have been substituted. (T. D. 1903, Nov. 28, 1913.)

§ 211. Payments to Nonresident Aliens

The income tax law provides that the tax shall be deducted and withheld by certain classes of persons (including partnerships and corporations) who have the "control, receipt, custody, disposal, or payment" of certain kinds of income accruing to nonresident alien individuals. The persons and corporations intended are described as "including lessees, or mortgagors of real or personal property, trustees acting in any trust capacity, executors, administrators, receivers, conservators, employers, and all officers and employees of the United States," the last phrase meaning disbursing officers and paymasters. The kinds of income affected are described as "interest, rent, salaries. wages, premiums, annuities, compensation, remuneration, emoluments, or other fixed or determinable annual or periodical gains, profits, and income, other than income derived from dividends on capital stock or from the net earnings of a corporation, joint-stock company or association, or insurance company, which is taxable upon its net income as provided in this title." (Act Cong. Sept. 8, 1916, § 9b, as amended by Act Cong. Oct. 3, 1917.) From this it appears that three things are requisite in order to require or authorize the deduction of the income tax from a payment of the kind mentioned. First, it must be a fixed or determinable payment; that is, not uncertain, fluctuating, or contingent, but definitely settled both as to liability and as to amount, the amount being either stipulated at a fixed sum or determinable by mere calculation. Second, the income must be annual or periodical; that is, it must accrue to the taxpayer in pursuance of some contract, engagement, or trust providing for annual or other periodical payments, and not for payments when and as the occasion may arise or at uncertain intervals. Third, the income must accrue to a nonresident alien individual, which excludes all American citizens, all resident aliens, and all foreign partnerships and corporations. But there is no limitation as to the amount of the income. Under the former law, it must exceed $3,000 before the tax became deductible. But the present statute requires the deduction of the tax from any payment (if of the kind included) to a nonresident alien, without regard to the amount.

§ 212. Same; Rents

The Treasury Department has ruled that real estate agents are not required to deduct and withhold the income tax from rents collected by them, as that duty devolves upon the tenant. But this probably will not hold good under the statute as it now stands, restricting the matter of collecting the tax at the source to cases where the recipient of the income is a nonresident alien. For, aside from the fact that the tenant may not always be aware of the fact that his landlord is such an alien, a real estate agent, with whom alone the tenant deals, is certainly a person "having the receipt, custody, and payment of rent." Further rulings of the Treasury on the subject of withholding by tenants were to the effect that, where a tenant rents two pieces of property from the same owner, the tenant should combine the payments and deduct and withhold the income tax. Where a board of education for a school district rents property, it is regarded as a tenant and should withhold the tax. A lessee paying rent under a lease from two or more individuals must make deductions from all payments to individuals, and he should ascertain in what proportion the rent is divided. The withholding should be made from the income of the individuals, and not from the aggregate amount paid. The situation is not different if the lessors are husband and wife, if their individual interests are separate. The situation is not changed if, by instruction, the actual payments of rent are made to one lessor, the payments to be distributed by him. Where notes are given in payment of rent, the lessee's obligation to withhold is not altered. The obligation is the same as in the case of cash rental, the withholding occurring at the time the notes are given, and not at their maturity. (T. D. 2090, Dec. 14, 1914.)

If rented property is in the hands of an executor, trustee, or receiver, representing the estate which owns it, another rule comes into play, and he will be chargeable with the collection of the income tax in the character of a fiduciary. On the relative rights and duties of landlords and tenants with respect to the income tax, some of the English cases are instructive.[2] Thus, in an action to recover rent in arrear, the tenant may deduct or offset the amount he has paid for taxes due on the property, and presumably also any sum he has paid on account of the owner's income tax.[3] But if the tenant pays the tax and omits to deduct it in his next payment of

---

[2] See Hancock v. Gillard, 76 Law J. K. B. 20.

[3] Philips v. Beer, 4 Camp. 266; Tinckler v. Prentice, 4 Taunt. 549.

rent, he cannot afterwards recover the amount as money paid for the use of the landlord.[4] Thus, where a tenant of land, during a course of twelve years, pays to the collector of taxes the landlord's property tax, and also the full rent as it becomes due, to the landlord, without claiming any deduction on account of the tax so paid, he cannot recover back from the landlord in an action against him any part of the tax so paid, both because his paying the full amount when he might have deducted is a voluntary payment, and because such an arrangement smacks of fraud on the revenue laws, since, if the tenant had deducted each year, as the law intends, the landlord would probably have raised the rent.[5] But an agreement that if the tenant will continue to pay his rent in full without deduction in respect of the landlord's tax paid by him, the latter will (at some future time) repay to the tenant all sums which he has paid or shall pay for the taxes, is not invalid as being contrary to the provisions of the statute.[6]

§ 213. Same; Payments of Interest

As to the deduction of the income tax from payments made as interest, it is requisite, under this part of the statute, that the obligation on which the interest accrues, should be that of an individual, as distinguished from a corporation. Under the English law, the income tax must be deducted from payments of "yearly interest." But it is held that where a banker makes a short term loan, for anything less than a year, the case does not come within the statute and the borrower is not to deduct for the income tax.[7] And interest accruing by force of law on a judgment is not "yearly interest" from which the income tax is to be deducted.[8] But interest on a mortgage which is calculable by the year is "yearly interest," although it is payable in a lump sum at an uncertain date, as, on the death of the mortgagor, so that when it is paid, the mortgagor's executor is to deduct the income tax.[9] When interest is payable on purchase money on a sale by order of court, the purchaser must

---

[4] Cumming v. Bedborough, 15 Mees. & W. 438.

[5] Denby v. Moore, 1 Barn. & Ald. 123.

[6] Lamb v. Brewster, L. R. 4 Q. B. Div. 607.

[7] Goslings v. Sharpe, L. R. 23 Q. B. Div. 324, 2 Tax Cas. 450. In England, in respect to dealings between merchants, discounting bills and the like, and in loans made for short periods, the income tax is not deducted by the one having to make the payment. Mosse v. Salt, 32 Beav. 269.

[8] In re Cooper [1911] 2 K. B. 550.

[9] In re Craven's Mortgage [1907] 2 Ch. 448.

pay the full purchase money and interest into court, without deduction for the income tax; but he must apply for the deduction when the money is paid out of court, and such an application would ordinarily be granted, although of course the court could not be subjected to any penalty for not allowing the deduction.[10] In paying a creditor who has proved in an administration proceeding on a bill of exchange, the practice is to deduct the income tax from the interest.[11] A person who has omitted to avail himself of the privilege conferred upon him by the income tax law of deducting and retaining income tax out of payments of yearly interest on money which he makes, may perhaps recover the amount which he should have deducted, from the person on whose behalf the income tax was paid, but he cannot claim a return of such income tax from the revenue officers.[12]

§ 214. Same; Royalties

Royalties are plainly included in the comprehensive terms of the act of Congress, and are specially enumerated in the Treasury regulations as being subject to deduction at the source. Payments on such accounts may be contingent on the amount of sales, business transacted, etc., but are "fixed or determinable" if the amount is ascertainable by mere computation. In an English case it appeared that, by an agreement between plaintiffs and defendants, the latter had the exclusive right of manufacturing and selling articles made by a secret process, and were to pay to the plaintiffs for forty years eight per cent on the gross receipts from such sales. The plaintiffs resided abroad and were foreigners, and before paying the amount payable to them under the agreement, the defendants deducted the income tax payable in respect of the amount due under the agreement. It was held that the income tax was rightly deducted.[13]

§ 215. Same; Annuities

Annuities are among the kinds of payments specified in the act of Congress, from which the income tax must be deducted and withheld in case the beneficiary is a nonresident alien. An English decision holds that, where the purchase price of land is payable

[10] Holroyd v. Wyatt, 1 De G. & Sm. 125; Humble v. Humble, 12 Beav. 43; Bebb v. Benny, 1 Kay & J. 216.

[11] Dinning v. Henderson, 3 De G. & Sm. 702.

[12] De Peyer v. King, 100 Law T. 256.

[13] Delage v. Nugget Polish Co., 92 Law T. 682.

in several annual installments, the debtor is not to deduct for income tax, as such payments are not income at all, but replacements of capital; but where a person who owned real estate, leased to a tenant at a fixed annual rental, sold the property to the tenant, no sum being fixed on as the price of the property, but the tenant agreeing to pay to the grantor annually during his life a sum equal to the rent which he had been paying, it was held that this was an annuity, and one from which the income tax should annually be deducted and withheld.[14]

§ 216. Same; Note Given for Rent or Interest

If a note has been given in payment of interest, rents, or other income taxable under this part of the statute, the maker of the note is to be regarded as the "debtor" or the "source," and is under the duty of withholding the income tax from the amount thereof on paying it at maturity. But if any person has purchased or discounted such a note, and has omitted, in acquiring it from the previous holder, to make a deduction or allowance for the tax, it is held that such purchaser can look for relief only to the person from whom he got the note, and the debtor, that is, the maker of the note, will none the less be required to deduct and withhold the tax at the maturity of the note, and this rule obtains although there was nothing on the face of the note to show that it was for interest or rent, or otherwise as the case might be. (T. D. 1891, Nov. 3, 1913.)

§ 217. Foreign Interest and Dividends

In the case of interest on the bonds of any foreign government, corporation, or individual, and interest upon foreign mortgages and other like obligations, and also dividends from foreign corporations, the income tax act of 1916 required the tax to be deducted from the amount, when the same was paid in the form of a coupon, check, or bill of exchange. But this was explicitly repealed by the act of 1917, which substitutes for it a provision requiring persons and companies engaging in the business of making foreign collections to be licensed, and (under regulations to be prescribed by the Commissioner of Internal Revenue) to furnish the government with such "information" as to their collections as will enable the internal revenue officers to identify the American holders of foreign securities and the extent of their holdings. (Act Cong. Oct. 3, 1917, § 1205, amending Act Cong. Sept. 8, 1916,

---

[14] Chadwick v. Pearl Life Assur. Co., 74 Law J. K. B. 671.

§ 9f.) It was held, however, under the former statute, that where interest on bonds of a foreign corporation is payable at its fiscal agency in the United States, or, at the option of the holder, within or without the United States, the collection of the interest is to be treated as a domestic transaction, not as a foreign collection. (T. D. 1992, June 4, 1914.)

§ 218. Licenses for Foreign Collections

Persons, firms, or corporations undertaking as a matter of business or for profit the collection of foreign interest or dividends, such as described in the preceding section, are required to obtain a license therefor from the Commissioner of Internal Revenue, and "shall be subject to such regulations enabling the government to obtain the information required under this title" as the Commissioner shall prescribe. Failure to obtain the license or to comply with the regulations is declared to be a misdemeanor and is punishable, for each offense, by a fine not exceeding $5,000, or imprisonment for not more than one year, or both in the discretion of the court. Regulations of the Treasury Department under the similar provisions of the act of 1916 were to the following effect: Such persons and corporations must make application for such licenses to the collector of internal revenue of the proper district, but without being previously notified by him, and ignorance of the law will be no excuse for failure to obtain a license or to observe the regulations relative to such collections. "The collector of internal revenue, on receipt of such application, shall satisfy himself that the person, firm, or corporation making application is considered to be of good character and business standing, and may require that he or they shall be able to show a financial rating in one or more of the recognized mercantile agencies of the United States, equal to at least one-tenth of the estimated annual amount of collections of foreign income as stated in the application. The collector of internal revenue, having thus satisfied himself of the business and financial reliability of the person, firm, or corporation making application for license, may issue the license without requiring a bond for the faithful performance of duty and compliance with the law and regulations." In cases where the applicant fails to satisfy the collector on these points, he may either refuse to issue a license, or grant one upon the filing of a surety bond satisfactory to the Commissioner of Internal Revenue in a penal sum equal to two per cent of the estimated amount of collections stated in the application, but the penal sum of such bond is not to be less than

$1,000, nor more than $100,000. When a bond is required, it is to be executed in duplicate and one filed in the office of the collector of internal revenue and the other with the Commissioner of Internal Revenue. The license may be issued without cost to the applicant, and shall continue in force until the 1st of January of the next year, when it must be renewed or a new bond furnished, and failure to give or renew the bond will automatically revoke the license. In cases where licenses are issued without a bond, the collector shall, at stated yearly periods, inquire into and satisfy himself of the financial responsibility of the licensee. When any person, firm, or corporation has branch offices, and desires to collect foreign items through such branch offices, the application for license or licenses shall be made (and bond furnished, when a bond is required) by the applicant through its principal office for its branch offices. And in such cases the bond shall be based on the total amount of such foreign business transacted by both the home office and its branch office or offices. (T. D. 1909, Nov. 28, 1913.) It was also prescribed that "all persons licensed shall keep their records in such manner as to show from whom every such item has been received, and such records shall be open at all times to the inspection of internal revenue officers." (T. D. of Oct. 25, 1913.)

§ 219. Fiduciaries

Under this general term are included guardians, trustees, executors, administrators, agents, receivers, conservators, and all other persons who hold in trust an estate of another person. These fiduciaries are required to make annual income tax returns for their beneficiaries. They are also regarded as the "source" for purposes of collecting the income tax on such parts of the income of their beneficiaries as are subject thereto, and are charged with the duty of withholding it and paying it over to the government. And in case the property of the estate, or part of it, consists of bonds or similar obligations of corporations, the fiduciary may file a notice, claiming exemption from having the tax deducted, with the debtor, that is, the debtor corporation, and upon receipt of such notice, the debtor corporation will refrain from withholding any part of the interest due on such bonds, on account of such income tax, and will not be held liable to the government for it. (T. D. 1906, Nov. 28, 1913.)

The Treasury department explains that the term "fiduciary" is one "which applies to all persons or corporations that occupy positions of peculiar confidence toward others, such as trustees, executors, or administrators, and a fiduciary, for income tax purposes, is any person or corporation that holds in trust an estate of another person or persons. There may be a fiduciary relationship between an agent and a principal; but the word 'agent' does not denote a fiduciary within the meaning of the income tax law." (T. D. 2090, Dec. 14, 1914.) "An agent having entire charge of property with authority to effect and execute leases with tenants entirely on his own responsibility, and without consulting his principal, paying taxes and expenses and all other charges in connection with the property out of funds in his hands from collection of rents, merely turning over the net proceeds from the property periodically to his principal, by virtue of authority conferred upon him by a power of attorney, is not a fiduciary within the meaning of the income tax law." (T. D. 2135, Jan. 23, 1915.) But the responsible heads, agents, or representatives of nonresident aliens, who are in charge of property owned, business carried on, or capital invested in the United States, are required to make returns of the income therefrom and pay the tax thereon. (T. D. 2090, Dec. 14, 1914.) It is also ruled that a fiduciary relation cannot be created by a power of attorney. "A person acting under a power of attorney in the management of property, having no title thereto, but with full power and authority to deal with the property as he sees fit, is under no obligation to render returns as a fiduciary. A power of attorney does not constitute a fiduciary relationship within the meaning of the income tax law, and in all cases where no legal trust has been created in the estate controlled by the agent and attorney, the liability under the law rests with the principal." (T. D. 2137, Jan. 30, 1915.)

§ 220. Kinds of Income Not Taxable at Source

The following varieties of income have been specified by the Treasury department as not subject to the process of deducting and withholding the income tax at the source of payment, although most of them are not subject to the tax at all, under the provisions of the statute:

1. Dividends on the capital stock or from the net earnings of corporations. These, it will be remembered, are not taxable at all, unless the total income (including them) is large enough to be subject to the surtax, and the provision for collection at the source does not apply to the surtax.

2. Proceeds of life insurance policies paid upon the death of the assured, or payments made by or credited to the assured on life in-

surance, endowment, or annuity contracts, upon the return thereof to the insured at the maturity of the term mentioned in the contract, or upon the surrender of the contract.

3. Income of an individual which is not fixed or certain, or payable at stated periods, or is indefinite or irregular as to amount or time of accrual. (See the next section.)

4. The value of property acquired by gift, bequest, devise, or descent.

5. Interest upon the obligations of a state, or any political subdivision thereof, and upon the obligations of the United States or its possessions.

6. Certain salaries, including that of the present President of the United States during the term for which he has been elected, that of the judges of the federal courts now in office, "and the compensation of all officers and employees of a state or any political subdivision thereof, except when such compensation is paid by the United States government." And to the foregoing should be added:

7. Interest on bank deposits or certificates of deposit.

8. Interest represented by coupons or registered interest on the obligations of corporations which matured and were payable before March 1, 1913, though presented for payment at a later date.

§ 221. Indeterminate, Non-Periodical, or Fluctuating Income

So much of a person's income as is not fixed or certain, and not payable at stated periods, or is indefinite or irregular as to the amount or the time of accrual, is not subject to have the income tax withheld at the source, even in the case of nonresident aliens, to whom alone this provision of the statute is now applicable. The Treasury Department rules that "incomes derived from the following professions and vocations come under this head: Agents compensated on the commission basis, lawyers, doctors, authors, inventors, and other professional persons whose income is irregular and indefinite." (Treasury ruling of Oct. 31, 1913.) The following regulation will be applicable to the case of American firms or corporations paying salaries to nonresident alien agents or representatives: "If an employee's total compensation, salary; and bonus is fixed, determined, and paid to him at one time, withholding should occur at that time, and both the company's withholding return and the employee's individual return of income for the year in which the amount is thus determined and paid should take consideration of the item. It follows that where a part of the compensation is in the form of a salary payable monthly, and a part in the form of a bonus not fixed and determined until on or after January 1 of the year following that in which the services were rendered, the two parts of any one year's compensation cannot be considered together for the purposes of withholding the tax and making return, but the fixed salary of one year should be considered together with the bonus received on or after January 1 of that year." (T. D. 2135, Jan. 23, 1915.)

§ 222. Income of Partnerships and Corporations

Partnerships as such are not subject to the income tax, are not required to make returns, unless specially called for, and are not subject to have any part of their income deducted at the source. But the Treasury department requires them to make proof of their exempt character, by filing a certificate of ownership with coupons or interest orders from corporate bonds, signed either in the firm's name by one member of the partnership or by each individual member of the firm, and when this is done, the tax will not be withheld by the debtor corporation with respect to the income represented by such coupons or orders. Also a form of exemption certificate has been provided for the use of firms and organizations claiming exemption from withholding at the source on income other than that derived from corporate bonds.

Domestic corporations of all kinds, whether subject to the income tax or exempt from it, are not within the terms of the statute relating to collection and deduction at the source. But when collecting interest on the bonds of other corporations, represented by coupons or interest orders, they are required to accompany the same by certificates of ownership, in order to establish their right to receive payment of the whole amount without deduction for the tax.

But as to "nonresident alien firms, copartnerships, companies, corporations, joint-stock companies or associations, and insurance companies, not engaged in business or trade within the United States and not having any office or place of business therein," a special provision is made, and the requirements as to deducting and withholding the income tax are made applicable to so much of their income as is derived from "interest upon bonds and mortgages or deeds of trust or similar obligations of domestic or other resident corporations, joint-stock companies or associations and insurance companies." (Act Cong. Sept. 8, 1916, § 13e, as amended by Act Cong. Oct. 3, 1917, § 1208.)

§ 223. Interest on Bank Deposits

By a regulation of the Treasury department, "banks, bankers, trust companies, and other banking institutions receiving deposits of money are not required to withhold at the source the normal income tax of one per cent on the interest paid, or accrued or accruing, to depositors, whether on open accounts or on certificates of deposit; but all such interest, whether paid, or accrued and not paid, must be included in his tax return by the person or persons entitled to receive such interest, whether on open account or on certificate of deposit." (T. D. 1893, Nov. 6, 1913.)

§ 224. Claiming Exemptions

A citizen or resident of the United States, who is alone entitled, as the law now stands, to the benefit of the personal exemption of a fixed minimum of income, and who would be deprived of the benefit of it if the tax were deducted and withheld at the source upon those items of income which are now subject to such deductions in the case of citizens and residents, namely, interest on corporate securities having a tax-free covenant, may secure the benefit of his exemption by claiming it from the corporation paying the interest. For the law provides that there shall be no deduction of the tax in such cases if "the person entitled to receive such interest shall file with the withholding agent, on or before February first, a signed notice in writing claiming the benefit of an exemption under section seven of this title." (Act Cong. Sept. 8, 1916, § 9c, as amended by Act Cong. Oct. 3, 1917, § 1205.)

§ 225. Credit for Source Collections in Personal Returns

Each taxable person, making his own income tax return, is entitled to a "credit," that is, a deduction from the amount of taxable net income shown by the return, "as to the amount of income, the normal tax upon which has been paid or withheld for payment at the source of the income under the provisions of this title." (Act Cong. Sept. 8, 1916, § 5c [U. S. Comp. St. 1916, § 6336e].) And in the case of a nonresident alien individual, he "shall receive the benefit of the deductions and credits provided for in this section," that is, deductions for expenses, interest paid, taxes, losses, etc., and credits for income consisting of dividends on corporate stock and for income upon which the normal tax has been deducted and withheld at the source, "only by filing or causing to be filed with the collector of internal revenue a true and accurate return of his total income, received from all sources, corporate or otherwise,

(260)

in the United States, in the manner prescribed by this title; and in case of his failure to file such return, the collector shall collect the tax on such income, and all property belonging to such non-resident alien individual shall be liable to distraint for the tax." (Act Cong. Sept. 8, 1916, § 6c, as amended by Act Cong. Oct. 3, 1917, § 1202.)

§ 226. Personal Liability of Debtors or Withholding Agents

Persons, firms, and corporations having the control, receipt, custody, disposal, or payment of interest, rent, salaries, wages, premiums, annuities, compensation, remuneration, emoluments, or other fixed or determinable annual or periodical gains, profits, and income of a nonresident alien individual (other than dividends on corporate stock) are not only required to deduct and withhold from payments so to be made a sum sufficient to pay the normal income tax, and pay over the same to the proper federal officers, but they are also made personally liable for the tax so to be paid by them for others. (Act Cong. Sept. 8, 1916, § 9b, as amended by Act Cong. Oct. 3, 1917, § 1205.) This provision for personal liability apparently does not apply to the case of corporations required to deduct and withhold the income tax from payments of interest on their bonds. But undoubtedly they become debtors to the government for the amount they are required to withhold and pay over, and on general principles of law, their liability is not that of an ordinary debtor, but that of a tax debtor, which may be enforced by the processes appropriate for the collection of taxes. Thus, in England, it is held that if official liquidators, such as receivers, trustees in bankruptcy, or assignees for creditors, pay away all the assets of the corporation or estate without making provision for a debt due to the government in respect to the income tax, they are guilty of misapplying the assets, and are personally responsible for the debt, and payment of it may be enforced by attachment.[15] So, in a case arising under the earlier income tax laws of this country, where a railroad company paid to the holders of its bonds the entire amount of semi-annual interest accruing thereon for a certain half-yearly period, it was held that the internal revenue officers rightly assessed against the company itself a tax upon the amount so paid equal to the amount of the income tax thereon.[16]

[15] In re Watchmakers' Alliance, 5 Tax Cas. 117.

[16] Lake Shore & M. S. R. Co. v. Rose, 95 U. S. 78, 24 L. Ed. 376. And see Stockdale v. Insurance Co., 20 Wall. 323, 22 L. Ed. 348.

§ 227. Exempt Corporations Required to Act as Withholding Agents

Under the income tax law of 1913, it was ruled that the various classes of corporations or associations which were specifically exempted from the operation of the law, were exempted not only from the payment of the tax on their own incomes, but also from every obligation and requirement imposed by any part of the law. Hence they were not required to act or perform any duty as withholding agents. (T. D. 1967, March 25, 1914.) But this was because of the specific provision that nothing contained in the act should apply to them. But the act of 1916 (§ 11a) is differently expressed. It provides that "there shall not be taxed under this title any income received by" any of the exempt corporations; and the Treasury Department rules that such corporations or organizations are required to answer under all the other provisions of the statute as to withholding and making returns of taxes withheld. (T. D. 2407, Dec. 4, 1916.)

(262)

CHAPTER X

INCOME TAX RETURNS

§ 228. Taxpayers Required to Make Returns

The income tax law requires a true and accurate return of income to be made by every citizen of the United States of lawful age, whether residing at home or abroad, and by all resident aliens, provided that in the one case or the other they have a net income of $3,000 or more for the taxable year. And for the purpose of the supplementary or "war" income tax, such a return is to be made by every such person having a net income of $1,000 or over, if unmarried, or of $2,000 or over if married. (Act Cong. Sept. 8, 1916, § 8b; Act Cong. Oct. 3, 1917, § 3.) In the case of a nonresident alien individual deriving an income from property owned or a business, trade, or profession carried on in the United States, the provision is that such a person shall not receive the benefit of the deductions and credits allowed (for expenses of carrying on business, interest paid, taxes, losses, etc.) except by "filing or causing to be filed with the collector of internal revenue a true and accurate return of his total income, received from all sources, corporate or otherwise, in the United States." (Act Cong. Sept. 8, 1916, § 6c, as amended by Act Cong. Oct. 3, 1917, § 1202.) This return must be made without regard to the amount of the income, since nonresident aliens are not allowed the specific exemption of a minimum amount of income. It may be made for the alien by an agent or other proper representative in the United States. (T. D. 2402, Nov. 29, 1916.)

Special provision is made by the statute for persons subject to the tax, but who are physically unable to make the required return, on account of minority, insanity, absence from the country, or serious illness. In this case the return may be made by an agent, the latter "assuming the responsibility of making the return and incurring penalties provided for erroneous, false, or fraudulent returns." (Act Cong. Sept. 8, 1916, § 8b [U. S. Comp. St. 1916, § 6336h]; T. D. 1892, Nov. 6, 1913.) In case of the death of a person whose net income for that part of the year during which he lived was $3,000 or more, a return is to be made by his executor or administrator. (Internal Revenue Regulations No. 33, art. 17.) A personal return is not required in cases where the individual's tax liability has been or is to be paid at the source. That is, when he is liable for the normal tax only, and his entire net income is subject to withholding, no personal return is required. But if his net income, not taking into account his specific exemption, includes items that are not subject to withholding, a return is required though no tax may be due. (T. D. 2135, Jan. 23, 1915.)

As to corporations, the requirement is that a return shall be made by "every corporation, joint-stock company or association, or insurance company subject to the tax herein imposed," including foreign corporations doing business in the United States.

§ 229. Returns by Guardians, Trustees, and Other Fiduciaries

The amended income tax law provides that "guardians, trustees, executors, administrators, receivers, conservators, and all persons, corporations, or associations, acting in any fiduciary capacity, shall make and render a return of the income of the person, trust, or estate for whom or which they act, and be subject to all the provisions of this title which apply to individuals. Such fiduciary shall make oath that he has sufficient knowledge of the affairs of such person, trust, or estate to enable him to make such return and that the same is, to the best of his knowledge and belief, true and correct, and be subject to all the provisions of this title which apply to individuals: Provided that a return made by one of two or more joint fiduciaries filed in the district where such fiduciary resides, under such regulations as the Secretary of the Treasury may prescribe, shall be a sufficient compliance with the requirements of this paragraph: Provided further that no return of income not exceeding $3,000 shall be required except as in this title otherwise provided." (Act Cong. Sept. 8, 1916, § 8c, as amended by Act Cong. Oct. 3, 1917, § 1204.) It is also provided that all persons, firms, and corporations, "in whatever capacity acting," that is, whether acting in a fiduciary capacity or not, "having the control, receipt, custody, disposal, or payment of interest, rent, salaries, wages, premiums, annuities, compensation, remuneration, emoluments, or other fixed or determinable annual or periodical gains, profits, and income of any nonresident alien individual, other than income derived from dividends on capital stock" of taxable corporations, shall deduct and withhold a sum sufficient to pay the normal income tax, "and shall make return thereof on or before March first of each year." (Act Cong. Sept. 8, 1916, § 9b, as amended by Act Cong. Oct. 3, 1917, § 1205.)

It is held by the Treasury Department that the income tax due from a deceased person is a debt against the estate in the hands if his executor or administrator, and it has been prescribed by regulations that the executor or administrator shall file a return for the decedent, in order that the amount due the government from his estate may be determined and paid. (T. D. 2152, Feb. 12, 1915.) As to trustees more properly so called, the rulings of the Treasury embrace the following points: The annual return of the fiduciary must contain the name and address of each of the beneficiaries for whom he acts if there are more than one, and the share of the income to which each may be entitled, and the amount of exemption claimed, the amount of income on which the fiduciary is liable for the income tax, and the amount of tax (if any) withheld. The creator of the trust in each instance being the same person, and the trustee in each instance being the same, the trustee should make a single return for all of the trusts in his hands, notwithstanding the fact that they may arise from different instruments; but where a trustee holds trusts created by different persons, though for the benefit of the same beneficiaries, he should make a separate return for each trust. (T. D. 2137, Jan. 30, 1915.) But these provisions refer only to the income accruing and payable through the particular fiduciary making the return, not to any income of the beneficiary derived from other sources. But they apply to the income accruing in the hands of the fiduciary whether or not it was dis-

(265)

tributed and paid over to the beneficiaries during the year. (T. D. 1906, Nov. 28, 1913.)

"The income of trust estates, as any other income, is subject to the income tax. When such income is received annually by a beneficiary of an estate the fiduciary will withhold the normal tax due and subject to withholding by him. Any part of the annual income of trust estates not distributed becomes an entity, and, as such, is liable for the normal and additional tax, which must be paid by the fiduciary. When the beneficiary is not in esse and the income of the estate is retained by the fiduciary, such income will be taxable to the estate as for an individual and the fiduciary will pay the tax, both normal and additional. When the beneficiary receives a part only of the income to which he is entitled from the estate and the balance is retained by the fiduciary the normal tax will be withheld on the income paid to the beneficiary and the amount of such income retained by the fiduciary will be treated as income taxable to the estate for both the normal and additional tax, which tax will be paid by the fiduciary. When the gross net income not distributed and remaining in the hands of a fiduciary is less than $20,000 the estate will be listed as a beneficiary, and only the normal income tax will be assessable and such tax will be paid by the fiduciary. When the gross net income not distributed and remaining in the hands of a fiduciary exceeds $20,000 such income is subject to both the normal and additional tax, and the estate will be listed as a beneficiary and both the normal and additional tax will be paid by the fiduciary." (T. D. 2231, July 26, 1915.)

In the case of joint fiduciaries, either may execute the return, and if the fiduciary is a corporation, the return may be signed and executed by its president, secretary, or treasurer. These returns are required to be verified by affidavit. The fiduciary's return is to be filed with the collector of internal revenue for the district where the fiduciary resides, if he has no other place of business, otherwise in the district in which he has his principal place of business. If the return is not duly made, notice of failure to make the return will be served on the fiduciary, but the person so notified may file evidence with the collector that the return was filed with some other collector, or (if the fact be so) that his beneficiary did not receive an income subject to the tax during the year. Fiduciary agents, in addition to the annual return of income required by these regulations, are also required to make an annual list return, similar to that exacted from withholding agents, when payments of income in excess of $3,000 have been made to any beneficiary. The penalty imposed upon a fiduciary who neglects or refuses to make the required income tax return is the same as that prescribed in the case of a similar default on the part of an individual taxpayer, that is, a fine of from $20 to $1,000.

§ 230. Form and Contents of Returns

The income tax law provides that returns of individuals shall be "in such form as the Commissioner of Internal Revenue, with the approval of the Secretary of the Treasury, shall prescribe, setting forth specifically the gross amount of income from all separate sources, and from the total thereof deducting the aggregate items of allowances herein authorized." (Act Cong. Sept. 8, 1916, § 8b [U. S. Comp. St. 1916, § 6336h].) It is to be noted that regulations made by the Commissioner pursuant to statutory authority, with the approval of the Secretary, in respect to the assessment and collection of internal revenue taxes, have the force of statutes; and the acts of the Commissioner are presumed to be the acts of the Secretary.[1] In pursuance of the foregoing authorization, the officers mentioned have prescribed an official form for individual taxpayers' returns. This form does not require any mention to be made of income derived from state, municipal, or other non-taxable bonds, although the language of the statute, "income from all separate sources," would be broad enough to include it. Although income consisting of dividends on corporate stock is not subject to the normal tax, its amount must be stated in the return; and the act provides that "for the purpose of the normal tax only, the income embraced in a personal return shall be credited with the amount received as dividends upon the stock or from the net earnings of any corporation, joint-stock company or association, or insurance company which is taxable upon its net income." (Act Cong. Sept. 8, 1916, § 5b [U. S. Comp. St. 1916, § 6336e].)

All individual returns are required to be verified by oath or affirmation. The oath may be taken before a collector or deputy collector of internal revenue. But this is not obligatory. Any officer authorized by law to administer oaths may take the affidavit. But the Treasury Department rules that if the verification is made before a justice of the peace or a magistrate not using a seal, a certificate of the clerk of a court of record as to the authority of such officer to administer oaths should be attached to the return. A re-

[1] In re Huttman (D. C.) 70 Fed. 699.

turn of income rendered by an individual residing abroad may be acknowledged before any duly appointed officer of the country in which he resides authorized to administer oaths and use a seal. If a return is executed in a state before a notary who is not required by the laws of the state to use a seal, and none is used, the notary should file with the Commissioner of Internal Revenue the certificate of an officer possessing a seal, showing that he is duly commissioned and authorized to administer oaths, otherwise the certificate will not be recognized. Returns acknowledged before commanding officers of naval vessels while at sea or in foreign ports will be accepted, but not returns executed before a summary court officer of the army. (T. D. 2090, Dec. 14, 1914.)

Private corporations and others desiring to have the prescribed forms printed for themselves may do so, if they will strictly observe the official requirements as to size, print, and contents of the forms. (T. D. 1939, Jan. 28, 1914.)

§ 231. Returns by Husband and Wife

The act of Congress treats husband and wife as separate and distinct taxpayers, each of whom, without reference to the other, is required to make a return and pay the tax if he or she has a sufficient income. And the language of the statute shows that it was within the contemplation of Congress that both a husband and wife might be separately taxable, or that either, without the other, might be taxable. But as to the matter of exemptions, a married pair living together may claim an exemption greater by $1,000 than that allowed to an unmarried person, presumably on account of the greater expenses of family life. This additional exemption, however, cannot be claimed by both the husband and the wife. It may be claimed by a married man, living with and supporting his wife, provided that she herself has not a taxable income. Or it may be claimed by a married woman, with a husband living with her, where she has a taxable income and he has not. But if both have taxable incomes, apparently one only can claim the additional exemption. So far the statute is reasonably intelligible. But its meaning is much clouded by the addition of the provision that "only one deduction of $4,000 shall be made from the aggregate income of both husband and wife when living together." Apparently the intention is that if either of the spouses (whether the husband or the wife) has an income large enough to be taxable, while the other has a separate and independent income not large enough to be taxable, both incomes shall be added together and included in the return to be made by the taxable person, and thereupon a total deduction of $4,000 may be made from the aggregate amount of income so included.

The regulations of the Treasury Department provide that "if the husband and wife, not living apart, have separate estates, the income from both may be made on one return, but the amount of income of each and the full name and address of both must be shown in such return." An official form for a joint return by husband and wife has been prescribed. The same Treasury regulation above referred to continues as follows: "The husband, as the head and legal representative of the household and general custodian of its income, should make and render the return of the aggregate income of himself and wife, and for the purpose of levying the income tax it is assumed that he can ascertain the total amount of said income. If a wife has a separate estate managed by herself as her own separate property, and receives an income of more than $3,000, she may make return of her own income, and if the husband has other net income, making the aggregate of both incomes more than $4,000, the wife's return should be attached to the return of her husband, or his income should be included in her return, in order that a deduction of $4,000 may be made from the aggregate of both incomes. The tax in such case, however, will be imposed only upon so much of the aggregate income of both as shall exceed $4,000. If either husband or wife separately has an income equal to or in excess of $3,000, a return of annual net income is required under the law, and such return must include the income of both, and in such case the return must be made even though the combined income of both be less than $4,000. If the aggregate net income of both exceeds $4,000, an annual return of their combined incomes must be made in the manner stated, although neither one separately has an income of $3,000 per annum. They are jointly and separately liable for such return and for the payment of the tax. The single or married status of the person claiming the specific exemption shall be determined as of the time of claiming such exemption if such claim be made within the year for which return is made, otherwise the status at the close of the year." (T. D. 1923, Dec. 27, 1913.)

§ 232. Returns by Partnerships

Partnerships as such are not subject to the income tax nor required to make regular annual returns, since the income which each partner may derive from the firm's business is supposed to be included in his personal return. But, presumably as a means of furnishing the revenue officers with more accurate information in regard to such sources of income, the statute provides as follows: "Such partnership, when requested by the Commissioner of Internal Revenue or any district collector, shall render a correct return of the earnings, profits, and income of the partnership, except income exempt under section four of this act [this relates to interest on government, state, and municipal bonds and other items exempt from the income tax] setting forth the item of the gross income and the deductions and credits allowed by this title, and the names and addresses of the individuals who would be entitled to the net earnings, profits, and income, if distributed." (Act Cong. Sept. 8, 1916, § 8e [U. S. Comp. St. 1916, § 6336h].) And the Treasury Regulation prescribes that, "when such a statement is required, it shall give a complete and correct report of the gross income of the said partnership, and also a complete account of the actual legitimate annual expenses of conducting the business of said partnership (not including living and personal expenses of the partners) and the net profits, and the name and address of each of the members of said partnership and their respective interests in the net profits thus reported." (T. D. 1905, Nov. 28, 1913.)

§ 233. Returns by Corporations

Annual income tax returns are required by the act of Congress to be made by "every corporation, joint-stock company or association, or insurance company, subject to the tax herein imposed." (Act Cong. Sept. 8, 1916, § 13b [U. S. Comp. St. 1916, § 6336m].) A corporation which is specifically exempted from the operation of the income tax law is not required to make any return.[2] Contrary rulings under the corporation excise tax law of 1909 were based on the fact that the tax was laid only upon the income of the corporation in excess of $5,000 a year, and that it would be improper to allow a corporation to decide for itself whether or not it was liable to the tax and to make or withhold a return accordingly.[3] The Treasury Regulations recognize the non-liability of exempt corporations with respect to making returns; but they also hold that every corporation not specifically enumerated as exempt

[2] Com'rs of Inland Revenue v. Incorporated Council of Law Reporting, 22 Q. B. Div. 291, 3 Tax Cas. 105.
[3] U. S. v. Acorn Roofing Co. (D. C.) 204 Fed. 157; U. S. v. Military Construction Co. (D. C.) 204 Fed. 153.

must make the return, whether or not it has any income liable to the tax, and whether or not it is subordinate to or controlled by another corporation. (Internal Revenue Regulations No. 33, art. 80.) A company newly organized or chartered is required to make a return covering that portion of the year during which it has been engaged in business or has had an income accruing to it. (Idem. art. 84.) A corporation organized and transacting no business within the calendar year of its organization must nevertheless make and file a return on the basis of the calendar year, unless such corporation shall designate a fiscal year other than the calendar year in the manner authorized. The duty to make a return depends upon corporate existence, and not upon the receipt of income. (T. D. 2090, Dec. 14, 1914.) "All corporations having an existence as such during all or any portion of.a year, unless coming within the classes specifically enumerated as exempt, are required to make returns. Dissolved corporations whose fiscal year corresponds with the calendar year will make returns covering the period from January 1 to the date of dissolution, and corporations having a fiscal year other than the calendar year will make returns covering the period from the beginning of the fiscal year to the date of dissolution." (T. D. 2090, Dec. 14, 1914.)

As to the contents of the returns to be made by corporations, the law provides that they shall contain "such facts, data, and information as are appropriate, and, in the opinion of the Commissioner, necessary to determine the correctness of the net income returned and to carry out the provisions of this title." The return should show that it is filed in the district "in which is located the principal office of the corporation, where are kept its books of account and other data from which the return is prepared." Hence a company which has its factory, mill, or other operating plant at one place, but maintains a head office or executive office at another place, where its financial and other records are kept, should designate the latter and not the former as its principal office.[4] As a necessary item of the information required, the return should show the "amount of paid-up capital stock outstanding." And the revenue officers rule that in cases where the capital stock is issued payable in installments or upon assessment, only so much of the capital as has been actually paid in upon such installments or assessments should be reported under this item. And the company

---

[4] See Burdick v. Dillon, 144 Fed. 737, 75 C. C. A. 603; In re Marine Machine & Conveyor Co. (D. C.) 91 Fed. 630.

should not include unissued or treasury stock, but only such stock as has actually been issued and for which payment has been received; or in case no stock is issued, there should be reported the amount of capital actually employed in the business and property of the corporation.

The War Revenue Act of October 3, 1917, provides (but only for the purpose of the supplementary or "war" income tax therein levied on corporations) that corporations "shall be credited with the amount received as dividends upon the stock or from the net earnings of any other corporation, joint-stock company or association, or insurance company, which is taxable upon its net income as provided in this title." (§ 4.) For the purpose of the regular or ordinary income tax, corporations are not allowed to make a deduction for such dividends received by them, and therefore the amount thereof must be shown in the return.

Under the income tax law, systems and methods of corporation bookkeeping and financial accounting become important, not only that companies may be able to make up their annual returns in accordance with the forms and regulations prescribed, but also in order that the revenue officers may be able to probe and verify the items returned if in doubt as to their correctness. The Treasury Department advises companies concerned that it does not require the use of any particular system of bookkeeping or accounting, but that the business transacted by corporations must be so recorded that each item set forth in the return may be readily verified by an examination of the books of account, and that ordinarily the books of a corporation are assumed to reflect the facts as to its earnings, income, etc., and will be taken as the best guide in computing its taxable income. But, with certain necessary exceptions, the net income disclosed by the books and verified by the annual balance sheet, or the annual report to stockholders, should be the same as that returned for taxation. And further, "in order that certain classes of corporations may arrive at their correct income, it is necessary that an inventory, or its equivalent, of materials, supplies, and merchandise on hand for use or sale at the close of each calendar year shall be made, in order to determine the gross income or to determine the expense of operation. A physical inventory is at all times preferred, but where a physical inventory is impossible, and an equivalent inventory is equally accurate, the latter will be acceptable. An equivalent inventory is an inventory of materials, supplies, and merchandise on hand taken from the books of the corporation." (Internal Revenue Regulations No. 33, arts. 182, 183, 161.)

The return of a corporation is required to be executed and verified by "the president, vice president, or other principal officer, and by the treasurer or assistant treasurer." But in cases where the company has no officer called "treasurer," the return may be signed by any officer holding an equivalent position, as, for instance, the cashier of a bank. It is conceived that the spirit and purpose of the statute and of the regulations are fully met where the return is verified by two officers of the company, one being its principal administrative officer and the other its chief financial officer. These officers do not execute the return in the name of the corporation, but in their own names individually, and hence the seal of the corporation is not required to be affixed.

§ 234. Same; Parent and Subsidiary Companies

In regard to the returns to be made by these classes of corporations, attention should be given to the following rulings of the Treasury Department: "Under the provisions of the federal income tax law and the regulations of this department, every corporation, joint-stock company or association, and every insurance company, regardless of its relation to another corporation, is held to be a separate and distinct entity and unless it comes within the class of organizations specifically enumerated in the act as exempt must make a separate and distinct return, complete in every detail. If the subsidiary companies of any parent corporation making a return in any particular district have their principal places of business in the same district, such corporations will be listed by the collector of that district and will be required to make separate returns as above indicated. If, however, the subsidiary companies keep separate books of account and have their principal accounting offices in other districts, returns of such corporations will be made to the collector of internal revenue of the district in which they have such principal offices." (T. D. 2137, Jan. 30, 1915.)

"In the case of parent corporations owning all or practically all of the stock of subsidiary companies, it is held that both corporations are separate and distinct entities and that each must make true and accurate returns, accounting for, in detail, their separate gross income and deductions therefrom, and each such company will be required to pay the income tax on the net earnings shown by such return. It is not sufficient for the purpose of the income tax law that the parent company shall report the gross income of

BL.FED.TAX.—18

the subsidiaries and deduct from such gross income the expenses of such subsidiaries. The net earnings of the subsidiary companies turned over to the parent company are dividends within the meaning of the law and as such dividends are not deductible from gross income, the parent company must pay income tax on its net income notwithstanding the fact that the earnings out of which the dividends were paid had been subject to tax as against the subsidiary companies." (T. D. 2137, January 30, 1915.)

"The fact that a corporation maintains a number of subsidiary corporations for the purpose of protecting brands, trade marks, and trade names is immaterial. The liability to make returns attaches to each subsidiary company by reason of the fact that it is a separate and distinct entity. If such subsidiary companies actually have no net income or earnings and no expenses of operation, and the earnings accrue direct to the parent company, which company also pays direct the operating expenses of the subsidiaries, that fact must be clearly set out in the returns of the subsidiaries. In any event subsidiary corporations cannot escape liability to make returns. If, however, the subsidiary concerns are mere partnerships or branches of the parent company, and not incorporated organizations, then these subsidiary concerns will not be required to make returns of annual net income, but all of their earnings and expenses will be taken up and accounted for in the returns of the parent company or corporation." (T. D. 2161, February 19, 1915.)

§ 235. Same; Designation of Fiscal Year

The law gives to corporations the privilege of designating for themselves a "fiscal year" or consecutive twelve-months period, which may be other than the calendar year, for the purpose of keeping their accounts and computing their income, and of making their returns on the basis of such fiscal year, instead of the calendar year. On this subject the Treasury Department has made the following rulings: To obtain this privilege the corporation must designate the last day of the month selected as the month in which its fiscal year shall close as the day of the closing of its fiscal year, and not less than thirty days prior to the date on which its annual return is to be filed, it must give notice in writing to the collector of internal revenue of the district in which its principal business office is located of the day it has thus designated as the closing of its fiscal year. It must then make its return of income "at the close of each such fiscal year," and the tax will be payable within 105 days after the date on which it is required to file its return.

But in the absence of such designation and notice of the closing of the fiscal year, corporations will be required to make their returns and have the tax computed upon the basis of the net income for the calendar year. The designation and notice cannot be retroactive. If it shall appear in any case that returns have been made to the collector on the basis of a fiscal year not designated as above provided, the corporations making such returns will be advised that such returns cannot be accepted, but must be made to cover the business of the calendar year. (T. D. 1897, Nov. 14, 1913.) A fiscal year must be so designated that the return made on this basis will not comprehend a period greater than twelve consecutive months. (T. D. 2001, June 22, 1914.) That portion of the year preceding the beginning of an established fiscal year is held to be a fractional part of the calendar year, and as the return of a calendar year is not required to be filed until on or before the first day of March next following, there is no provision of law whereby the return covering a fraction of a calendar year is required to be filed earlier than "on or before" the next first day of March, though it is preferred that the return for this fraction shall be filed as early as possible after the close of the period. (T. D. 2029, Oct. 24, 1914.) In the case of new corporations, if they shall file or shall have filed within the prescribed time a notice designating the last day of some month as the close of the fiscal year, such corporations will be permitted to make their returns as of the period ended with the date designated, provided the period intervening between the date of organization of the corporation and the date designated as the close of its fiscal year does not exceed 12 months. If such period does exceed 12 months, the corporation will make a return for the portion of the calendar year preceding the beginning of the fiscal year, which return must be filed on or before the 1st day of March next following the calendar year of which it is a part. (T. D. 2137, Jan. 30, 1915.)

It is also to be observed that the amendments introduced into the income tax act of 1916 (§ 8c) by the Act of Oct. 3, 1917 (§ 1204) give to partnerships the same privilege of fixing and making returns upon the basis of their own fiscal year that is accorded to corporations.

§ 236. Information Returns

The Act of October 3, 1917, amending the existing income tax law by adding three new sections numbered 26, 27, and 28, requires returns to be made by various persons and companies, which are not meant to be used as a basis for computing and assessing the tax on the person or company making the return, but to furnish the revenue officers with accurate information concerning the holders of corporate stock and securities, the recipients of fixed salaries and of rents and various other kinds of income, and concerning profits made in stock exchange transactions, in order that those officers may thus be enabled to "check up" the returns made by the receivers of such income, and determine whether the whole amount of the tax due from them has been paid. As this system is commonly called that of "information at the source," we have described these returns as "information returns." These provisions of the statute are as follows:

"Every corporation, joint-stock company or association, or insurance company subject to the tax herein imposed, when required by the Commissioner of Internal Revenue, shall render a correct return, duly verified under oath, of its payments of dividends, whether made in cash or its equivalent or in stock, including the names and addresses of stockholders and the number of shares owned by each and the tax years and the applicable amounts in which such dividends were earned, in such form and manner as may be prescribed by the Commissioner of Internal Revenue, with the approval of the Secretary of the Treasury." (§ 26.)

"Every person, corporation, partnership, or association, doing business as a broker on any exchange or board of trade or other similar place of business shall, when required .by the Commissioner of Internal Revenue, render a correct return, duly verified under oath, under such rules and regulations as the Commissioner of Internal Revenue, with the approval of the Secretary of the Treasury, may prescribe, showing the names of customers for whom such person, corporation, partnership, or association has transacted any business, with such details as to profits, losses, or other information which the Commissioner may require, as to each of such customers, as will enable the Commissioner of Internal Revenue to determine whether all income tax due on profits or gains of such customers has been paid." (§ 27.)

"All persons, corporations, partnerships, associations, and insurance companies, in whatever capacity acting, including lessees or mortgagors of real or personal property, trustees acting in any trust capacity, executors, administrators, receivers, conservators, and employers, making payment to another person, corporation, partnership, association, or insurance company, of interest, rent, salaries, wages, premiums, annuities, compensation, remuneration, emoluments, or other fixed or determinable gains, profits, and income (other than payments described in sections 26 and 27) of $800 or more in any taxable year, or, in the case of such payments made by the United States, the officers or employees of the United States having information as to such payments and required to make returns in regard thereto by the regulations hereinafter provided for, are hereby authorized and required to render a true and accurate return to the Commissioner of Internal Revenue, under such rules and regulations and in such form and manner as may be prescribed by him, with the approval of the Secretary of the Treasury, setting forth the amount of such gains, profits, and income, and the name and address of the recipient of such payment: Provided, that such returns shall be required, regardless of amounts, in the case of payments of interest upon bonds and mortgages or deeds of trust or other similar obligations of corporations, joint-stock companies, associations, and insurance companies, and in the case of collections of items (not payable in the United States) of interest upon the bonds of foreign countries and interest from the bonds and dividends from the stock of foreign corporations by persons, corporations, partnerships, or associations, undertaking as a matter of business or for profit the collection of foreign payments of such interest or dividends by means of coupons, checks, or bills of exchange. When necessary to make effective the provisions of this section, the name and address of the recipient of income shall be furnished upon demand of the person, corporation, partnership, association, or insurance company paying the income. The provisions of this section shall apply to the calendar year 1917 and each calendar year thereafter, but shall not apply to the payment of interest on obligations of the United States." (§ 28.)

§ 237. Time for Filing Returns

The time for filing an income-tax return, under the federal statute, is the first day of March in each year, the return relating to the income of the preceding calendar year, that is, the year ending on the thirty-first of December preceding. This applies alike to individuals and corporations, except that the latter are permitted to designate a fiscal year of their own, which may not be coterminous with the calendar year, and be taxed upon the income of such fiscal year, and in this case the return is to be made within sixty days after the close of such fiscal year. It is also provided that when the neglect of any taxpayer (individual or corporate) to file the return at the time prescribed is due to "sickness or absence," the collector of internal revenue "may allow such further time, not exceeding thirty days, for making and filing the return as he deems proper." (Rev. St. § 3176, as amended by Act Cong. Sept. 8, 1916 [U. S. Comp. St. 1916, § 5899].) Also "the Commissioner of Internal Revenue shall have authority to grant a reasonable extension of time, in meritorious cases, for filing returns of income by persons residing or traveling abroad who are required to make and file returns of income and who are unable to file said returns on or before March first of each year." (Act Cong. Sept. 8, 1916, § 8b [U. S. Comp. St. 1916, § 6336h].)

It has been ruled by the Treasury Department that where a corporation makes its return in due time, but it is returned for corrections, and a correct return is afterwards filed, though after the appointed day, the corporation is not to be regarded as delinquent, and the penalty for neglecting or refusing to make a return will not attach. (T. D. No. 1711.) And if a return is made out and deposited in the mails, properly addressed, and with postage paid, in ample time, in due course of the mails, to reach the office of the collector before the expiration of the time limited, its actual failure to arrive in time will not subject the taxpayer to a penalty. (Internal Revenue Regulations No. 33, art. 174.) If the last day for filing a return shall fall upon a Sunday or a holiday, the return may be made to the collector on the next following business day. (Idem, arts. 175, 176.) The acceptance by the Commissioner of a return filed after the proper time does not amount to a waiver of the penalty already incurred for delay in filing it. He is bound to accept the return, though late, since it must in any case serve as the basis of the assessment to be made, but when it is filed after the proper day, he accepts it only for that purpose, and not as made in compliance with the law.[5]

§ 238. Same; Tentative Returns

The Treasury Department has made the following ruling:

"In cases wherein foreign corporations or domestic corporations doing business in foreign countries are unable to assemble their data in time to make their returns of annual net income within the prescribed time, it will be permissible for such corporations upon a showing of this fact to file with the collector of internal revenue a tentative return in which there shall be approximated, as

---

[5] U. S. v. Surprise Five, Ten and Nineteen Cent Store (U. S. Dist. Ct. S. D. N. Y.) T. D. No. 1864.

nearly as possible the actual business transacted during the year. This tentative return will be substituted by a true and accurate return as soon as the necessary data to make such true and accurate return shall be available. Collectors of internal revenue are authorized to grant an extension of time not in excess of 30 days from the date when returns are due, such extension to be granted only in cases wherein the neglect to file the return within the prescribed time was due to the sickness or absence of an officer whose signature to the return was necessary. Foreign corporations or domestic corporations doing business in foreign countries cannot be granted an extension of time merely for the reason that they are unable to assemble their data to make the return within the prescribed time. In all such cases, liability to the penalty of the act can be obviated only by filing a tentative return as hereinbefore indicated." (T. D. 2137, Jan. 30, 1915.)

§ 239. Where Returns are to be Filed

The statute requires the return of an individual taxpayer to be filed with the collector of internal revenue "for the district in which such person has his legal residence or principal place of business, or if there be no legal residence or place of business in the United States, then with the collector of internal revenue at Baltimore, Maryland." (Act Cong. Sept. 8, 1916, § 8b.) In the case of corporations, "the return shall be made to the collector of the district in which is located the principal office of the corporation, where are kept its books of account and other data from which the return is prepared, or in the case of a foreign corporation, to the collector of the district in which is located its principal place of business in the United States, or if it have no principal place of business, office, or agency in the United States, then to the collector of internal revenue at Baltimore, Maryland." (Act Cong. Sept. 8, 1916, § 13b [U. S. Comp. St. 1916, § 6336m].) The Treasury Department has also made a regulation that "in the case of domestic corporations whose books of account and other data are kept in foreign countries, the returns should be made to the collector of internal revenue of the district in which they have branch offices in this country, if they have such branch offices. Otherwise, the return of annual net income of such corporations should be made to the collector of the district in which are located the statutory offices of the corporations." (T. D. 2137, Jan. 30, 1915.) It has been ruled that returns filed with a deputy collector of internal revenue are regarded as having been filed with the collector. (T. D.

1742, par. 40.) And that foreign corporations having several branch offices in the United States should each designate one of such branches as its principal office, and should also designate the proper officers to make the required return. (Idem, par. 11.)'

§ 240. Publicity or Inspection of Returns

The income tax act of 1916 (following exactly the provisions of the act of 1913), in so far as it relates to corporations, provides that, when the assessment shall have been made, the returns shall be filed in the office of the Commissioner of Internal Revenue, "and shall constitute public records and be open to inspection as such: Provided that any and all such returns shall be open to inspection only upon the order of the President, under rules and regulations to be prescribed by the Secretary of the Treasury and approved by the President." It also contains a provision apparently intended to aid in the administration of the revenue laws of such states as may lay a tax on incomes, concurrently with the federal statute, by throwing open to their officers, under proper restrictions, the facts in the possession of the federal officers concerning taxable corporations. This provision is as follows: "That the proper officers of any state imposing a general income tax may, upon the request of the governor thereof, have access to said returns or to an abstract thereof, showing the name and income of each such corporation, joint stock company, association, or insurance company, at such times and in such manner as the Secretary of the Treasury may prescribe." The substantive part of this enactment was taken from the corporation tax law of 1909, and the proviso from an amendatory act of 1910. In pursuance thereof, regulations were prescribed by the Secretary of the Treasury July 28, 1914, and approved by the President, and the latter issued an executive order of the same date putting them in force. These regulations may be epitomized as follows: The returns of all corporations shall be open to the inspection of the proper officers and employés of the Treasury Department, and of the officers and employés of other departments of the government, but in the latter case only on a written application, signed by the head of the department, setting forth the reasons for making it, and addressed to the Secretary of the Treasury. But if inspection of the return of any corporation is desired for the purpose of using the return (or information derived from it) in any legal proceeding, or if inspection is desired by any official of any state or territory, then the application must first be referred to the Attorney General, and, if recommended by him, transmitted to the Secretary of the Treasury. Any bona fide stockholder may be permitted to inspect the return made by his own corporation, on satisfactory proof of his ownership of stock in it, and on application to the Secretary of the Treasury showing good and sufficient cause. But the granting of such an application is in the discretion of the Secretary, and permission granted cannot be delegated or transferred to another person. The returns of certain corporations may be inspected by any person, on written application to the Secretary of the Treasury, setting forth briefly and succinctly the facts necessary to enable him to act upon the request. These are (a) companies whose stock is listed upon any duly organized and recognized stock exchange within the United States; (b) corporations whose stock is advertised in the press or offered to the public by the corporation itself for sale. It will be observed that there is no similar provision in the statute concerning the returns made by individual taxpayers, and these apparently are not public records nor open to inspection by any one or on any conditions.

To the limited extent to which statutes of this character authorize the publication or inspection of taxpayers' returns, it is held that they do not violate the constitutional prohibitions against unreasonable searches and seizures.[6] But aside from statutory authorization, the courts have shown great reluctance to force the disclosure of matters contained in such essentially confidential documents, even when desired in the interests of public justice. Thus, in England, it is held that a court will not compel the tax officers to produce or exhibit documents in their possession (such as a taxpayer's return) for use in litigation or for the use of a receiver, when it is stated that such a course would be prejudicial and injurious to the public service and interests.[7] And in the United

[6] Flint v. Stone Tracy Co., 220 U. S. 107, 31 Sup. Ct. 342, 55 L. Ed. 389, Ann. Cas. 1912B, 1312.

[7] In re Joseph Hargreaves, Ltd. [1900] 1 Ch. 347, 4 Tax Cas. 173. But in another case it is said that, notwithstanding the oath administered to a collector of taxes, that he will not disclose anything he learns in that capacity, except with the consent of the commissioners or by virtue of an act of Parliament, he is bound, when subpœnaed as a witness, to give evidence of all facts within his knowledge touching the matter in question. Lee v. Birrell, 3 Camp. 337. And in an action for slander, whereby it is alleged the plaintiff's business was injured, the defendant may obtain by subpœna, and put in evidence, the plaintiff's income tax returns for the period covered, in order to contradict the plaintiff's evidence, or that of his books, as to the alleged decline of his business. Macdonald v. Hedderwick, 3 Fraser, 674. Compare, however, Gray v. Wyllie, 6 Fraser, 448.

States the rule is even more strict. For it is held competent for the Secretary of the Treasury to make a regulation (as has been done) forbidding collectors of internal revenue to produce the records of their offices or furnish copies thereof for the use of third persons, or for use as evidence in behalf of litigants in any court, or to allow the use of official papers in their custody for any other purpose than that of aiding in the collection of the revenues of the United States, and forbidding them to "testify as to facts contained in the records or coming to their knowledge in their official capacity." And neither a state nor a state court, even in a criminal proceeding, has any power to require a collector to violate the regulation, nor to punish him for contempt because of his refusal to produce or put in evidence the records of his office, or to testify as to their contents. And if a state court undertakes thus to punish a collector for such refusal, by attachment as for contempt, he will be released by the federal courts on habeas corpus.[8] It is evident, therefore, that so far as concerns the use of income tax returns as evidence in any court, their production cannot be forced except by the consent of the United States. Congress naturally has supreme authority in this matter, and it has, as above stated, declared such returns to be public records. But it has delegated to the executive officers the duty of prescribing the conditions under which such returns may be inspected. And the regulations thereupon made appear to contemplate and sanction the use of income tax returns as evidence in courts of justice to a limited extent, but only with the approval of the high officers of the Treasury Department, and not on the initiative of collectors of internal revenue, and not in obedience to the writ of subpœna. For the regulations provide for the following three cases: First, if the return of a corporation (not of an individual taxpayer) is desired to be used in any legal proceedings other than those to which the United States is a party (that is, in private litigation or proceedings by a state or municipality), or to be used in any manner by which any information contained in the return could be made public, the application for permission to inspect such return or to furnish a certified copy thereof shall be referred to the Attorney General, and if recommended by him transmitted to the Secretary of the Treasury. Second, all returns, whether of persons or corporations, may be furnished, either in the

---

8 Boske v. Comingore, 177 U. S. 459, 20 Sup. Ct. 701, 44 L. Ed. 846; In re Lamberton (D. C.) 124 Fed. 446; Stegall v. Thurman (D. C.) 175 Fed. 813; In re Weeks (D. C.) 82 Fed. 729; In re Huttman (D. C.) 70 Fed. 699; In re Comingore (D. C.) 96 Fed. 552. Contra, see In re Hirsch (C. C.) 74 Fed. 928.

original or by certified copies, for use in any legal proceedings before any United States grand jury or in the trial of any cause to which both the United States and the person or corporation rendering the return are parties, either as plaintiff or defendant, providing such return would constitute material evidence in the proceeding or trial; but this can be done only with the approval of the Secretary of the Treasury. Third, in any case arising in the collection of the income tax, the Commissioner of Internal Revenue may furnish for use to the proper officer either the original or certified copies of returns, without the approval of the Secretary of the Treasury. Further it is provided that "in no case shall any collector, or any other internal revenue officer outside of the Treasury Department in Washington, permit to be inspected any return, or furnish any information whatsoever relative to any return or any information secured by him in his official capacity relating to such return, except in answer to a proper subpœna in a case to which the United States is a party." And "returns of individuals are under no conditions to be made public, except where such publicity shall result through the use of such returns in any legal proceedings in which the United States is a party."

§ 241. Penalties for Divulging Information

To encourage frank and full disclosures by taxpayers, and to remove as far as possible the inquisitorial features of such a law, the income tax statutes denounce very heavy penalties upon the officers charged with the assessment and collection of the tax if they shall divulge or make known (except to the limited extent authorized by the statute) the return of any taxpayer or its items or details. The act of Congress also forbids these officers to permit any person to see or examine any return or any copy thereof or any book containing any abstract or particulars thereof; and also provides that it shall be unlawful for any person to print or publish in any manner whatever not provided by law, any income return or any part thereof, or the amount or source of income, profits, losses, or expenditures appearing in any income return. Any violation of these provisions is declared a misdemeanor, and the punishment prescribed is a fine not exceeding $1,000, or imprisonment not exceeding one year, or both, and in addition, if the offender is an officer or employé of the United States, dismissal from office and perpetual incapacity for holding any office under the government. (Rev. St. § 3167, as amended by Act Cong. Sept. 8, 1916 [U. S. Comp. St. 1916, § 5887].)

§ 242. Proceedings in Case of Refusal or Neglect to File Return

Under the income tax law, where a taxable person or corporation refuses or omits to make the required return, the return is to be made by the collector or deputy collector of internal revenue according to the best information which he can obtain, including that elicited on his examination of witnesses and of books and papers, and on his own view and information. And any return so made and subscribed by a collector or deputy collector shall be prima facie good and sufficient for all legal purposes. (Rev. St. § 3176, as amended by Act Cong. Sept. 8, 1916 [U. S. Comp. St. 1916, § 5899].) But if any person liable to pay an income tax, and failing to make the required return, shall consent to disclose the particulars of any business or occupation liable to pay such tax, it shall be the duty of the collector or deputy collector to make up the return, which being distinctly read and consented to, and verified by oath or affirmation by the person liable to make such return, the same may be received as the return of such person. (Rev. St. § 3173, as amended by Act Cong. Sept. 8, 1916 [U. S. Comp. St. 1916, § 5896].) There is also another provision of the act of Congress, applicable, it would seem, to cases where a taxable person has attempted to evade the law by omitting to make any return, and where the collector, at the time the return was due, had no knowledge of the case or suspicion as to the proposed evasion. This clause provides that in case of the refusal or neglect to make a return "the Commissioner of Internal Revenue shall, upon the discovery thereof, at any time within three years after said return is due, make a return upon information obtained as provided for in this section or by existing law, and the assessment made by the Commissioner of Internal Revenue thereon shall be paid by such person or persons upon notification of the amount of such assessment." (Act Cong. Sept. 8, 1916, §§ 9a, 14a [U. S. Comp. St. 1916, §§ 6336i, 6336n].)

As a general principle of law, it is held, if the taxpayer refuses to give in his income to the assessor, it is the duty of the assessor to ascertain its amount by inquiry or otherwise, to the best of his information and judgment; and if, in discharging this duty, acting in good faith, the assessor fixes the amount of such income at a larger sum than it in fact amounted to, and assesses it at the sum thus ascertained by him, such assessment is legal, notwithstanding the mistake or overstatement, and the collection of the tax so assessed, by the tax collector, is also legal.[9] And in making his estimate of

---

[9] Lott v. Hubbard, 44 Ala. 593.

the value of property for the purpose of the income tax (as, for instance, in determining the rental value of the taxpayer's residence) the assessor is not bound to accept and follow the valuation placed on the same property by any other assessor for the purposes of any other tax.[10] It should also be observed that an assessment for the income tax cannot be impeached collaterally or re-examined in any collateral proceeding. It may be subject to appeal or review, but cannot be revised in any other mode than the special statutory mode provided for that purpose. Hence a proof in bankruptcy by a collector of taxes, in respect of arrears due under an assessment for the income tax, cannot be expunged on the ground that the debtor had not received the income or made the profits so assessed.[11]

§ 243. Same; Examination of Books, Papers, and Witnesses

It is provided in the Revised Statutes, as amended by the act of Congress of 1916, that if any person shall refuse or neglect to make the required return, on notice and demand, or shall render a return which, in the opinion of the collector, is false or fraudulent or contains any undervaluation or understatement, "it shall be lawful for the collector to summon such person, or any other person having possession, custody, or care of books of account containing entries relating to the business of such person, or any other person he may deem proper, to appear before him and produce such books, at a time and place named in the summons, and to give testimony or answer interrogatories, under oath, respecting any objects liable to tax or the returns thereof. The collector may summon any person residing or found within the state in which his district lies; and when the person intended to be summoned does not reside and cannot be found within such state, he may enter any collection district where such person may be found and there make the examination herein authorized. And to this end, he may there exercise all the authority which he might lawfully exercise in the district for which he was commissioned." And in another part of the statute, it is provided that "jurisdiction is hereby conferred upon the district courts of the United States for the district within which any person summoned under this section to appear to testify or to produce books shall reside, to compel such attendance, production of books, and testimony by appropriate process." (Rev. St. § 3173 [U. S.

[10] Walker v. Brisley, 4 Tax Cas. 254.
[11] Calvert v. Walker [1899] 2 Q. B. 145, 4 Tax Cas. 79.

Comp. St. 1916, § 5896].) And another federal statute provides that "every collector, deputy collector, and inspector is authorized to administer oaths and to take evidence touching any part of the administration of the internal revenue laws with which he is charged, or where such oaths and evidence are authorized by law to be taken." (Rev. St. § 3165 [U. S. Comp. St. 1916, § 5885].)

§ 244. Same; Constitutional Validity

The courts have sustained the constitutionality of provisions in former internal revenue laws closely similar to those just cited.[12] In one of the cases the court remarked that both acts of congress and of state legislatures conferred not only upon legislative committees, but also upon various officers, the high power to send for persons and papers to be examined in furtherance of a stated purpose, and this had been for so long a time acquiesced in that it was now scarcely worth while to debate the question seriously; and whereas it may conceded that no extraordinary power is granted by our law for any other reason than necessity, the court thought there was both a necessity and a propriety in the provision here made for the proper enforcement of the internal revenue laws.[13] This view derives considerable support also from the decision of the Supreme Court sustaining the validity of that part of the Interstate Commerce Act which gives to the Interstate Commerce Commission the power to require the attendance of witnesses and the production of books and papers.[14] Also there are decisions of the state courts to the effect that there is no violation of the constitutional provision against unreasonable searches and seizures by a statute giving to revenue officers the right to examine books and papers of taxpayers for the purpose of properly listing and assessing their taxable property.[15] It is true that if such compulsory submission to interrogation, or compulsory production of books and papers, were required directly in a criminal prosecution or in a quasi-criminal proceeding to forfeit property or collect penalties, it might be regarded as an invasion of the person's constitutional right to avoid criminating himself. There is no lack of authorities

12 In re Phillips, 10 Int. Rev. Rec. 107, Fed. Cas. No. 11,097.

13 Perry v. Newsome, 10 Int. Rev. Rec. 20, Fed. Cas. No. 11,009.

14 Interstate Commerce Commission v. Brimson, 154 U. S. 447, 155 U. S. 3, 14 Sup. Ct. 1125, 15 Sup. Ct. 19, 38 L. Ed. 1047, 39 L. Ed. 49.

15 Co-operative Bldg. & Loan Ass'n v. State, 156 Ind. 463, 60 N. E. 146; Washington Nat. Bank v. Daily, 166 Ind. 631, 77 N. E. 53; In re Conrades, 112 Mo. App. 21, 85 S. W. 150.

so holding.[16] But these cases are probably to be distinguished on the ground that an investigation merely to determine the extent of a person's taxable income is not criminal or penal, nor even, when conducted by a collector of taxes, a judicial investigation at all. And whereas it may be contended that information elicited by this investigation might be used against the person in a subsequent prosecution, as, for instance, for perjury, it must be answered that, even in a proceeding of this kind, it is the privilege of the witness to refuse to answer any question on the ground that it might criminate him. It was so held in the case concerning the powers of the Interstate Commerce Commission in this regard.[17] And in an earlier case under the internal revenue law, where a person liable for taxes refused to produce his books of account, when summoned to do so, on the ground that a criminal proceeding had been commenced against him for making a false return, and that he could not produce the books or give evidence without criminating himself, it was held that he must bring the books containing entries relating to his business before the assessor, and must then be asked to exhibit any entry relating to a particular point to be named, and if he should then say that he could not do so without criminating himself, he would be protected from exhibiting it.[18]

§ 245. .Same; Jurisdiction of Courts to Enforce Obedience

The provision of the income tax law giving to the federal district courts jurisdiction to compel the attendance of witnesses before the collector, or the production of books, or the giving of testimony, by appropriate process, is not unconstitutional as imposing on the judicial tribunals duties which are not judicial in their nature.[19] For the object of the proceeding in court under this provision is not to punish the witness for contempt of the order of the collector summoning him to appear and testify, because there is no such

[16] Boyd v. U. S., 116 U. S. 616, 6 Sup. Ct. 524, 29 L. Ed. 746; In re Pacific Railway Com'n (C. C.) 32 Fed. 241; People v. Reardon, 197 N. Y. 236, 90 N. E. 829, 27 L. R. A. (N. S.) 141, 134 Am. St. Rep. 871; Robson v. Doyle, 191 Ill. 566, 61 N. E. 435; Weeks v. U. S., 232 U. S. 383, 34 Sup. Ct. 341, 58 L. Ed. 652, L. R. A. 1915B, 834, Ann. Cas. 1915C, 1177.

[17] Interstate Commerce Commission v. Brimson, 154 U. S. 447, 155 U. S. 8, 14 Sup. Ct. 1125, 15 Sup. Ct. 19, 38 L. Ed. 1047, 39 L. Ed. 49.

[18] In re Lippman, 3 Ben. 95, Fed. Cas. No. 8,382. Compare In re Phillips, 10 Int. Rev. Rec. 107, Fed. Cas. No. 11,097.

[19] Interstate Commerce Commission v. Brimson, 154 U. S. 447, 155 U. S. 8, 14 Sup. Ct. 1125, 15 Sup. Ct. 19, 38 L. Ed. 1047, 39 L. Ed. 49.

thing as contempt of an administrative officer. But the object is to make an order, on cause shown, or in the absence of cause shown against it, requiring the witness to obey the summons of the collector, and then he may be punished, if he still refuses, not for disobeying the order of the collector, but for disobeying the order of the court.[20]

§ 246. Same; Authority of Officers; Scope of Examination

The provision of the statute that "it shall be lawful" for the collector to summon witnesses before him or require the production of books and papers does not make it obligatory on him to take this course. If he can obtain the necessary information in other ways, he is at liberty to do so.[21] It should be observed that a deputy collector may exercise this power as well as the collector; his authority is the same.[22] But whereas the collector is given authority to "summon" persons before him to give evidence, Congress, in using this term, "did not contemplate it to be of the legal dignity of a writ or other judicial process, but simply a notice, and similar in its nature to a summons issued by an overseer of roads requiring persons to attend, with the necessary implements, and to work on the public highway." [23] This notice or summons may be delivered personally, but it should in all cases give the person concerned a reasonable time to comply. In one of the cases, a supervisor of internal revenue entered a bank conducted by a firm and demanded to see their books and papers. The members of the firm, doubting his right to such inspection, asked time to consult their counsel. This was refused, and on their failure to produce their books, the supervisor served them with a summons requiring them to appear before him at his office in that city instanter on the same day. He had no regular office in that city, and no place was specified in the summons. The firm then consulted their counsel, and though he was somewhat in doubt, he advised them to submit to the inspection. They then sought the supervisor to apprise him of their consent, but were unable to find him, and he left the town the same

---

[20] In re Kinney (D. C.) 102 Fed. 468.

[21] Bailey v. New York Cent. & H. R. R. Co., 22 Wall. 604, 22 L. Ed. 840.

[22] Landram v. U. S., 16 Ct. Cl. 74. As to the powers of the deputy collector, see Act Cong. Feb. 8, 1875 (Comp. St. 1916, § 5849), which provides that "each such deputy shall have the like authority in every respect to collect the taxes levied or assessed within the portion of the district assigned to him which is by law vested in the collector himself."

[23] Matter of Meador, 1 Abb. U. S. 317, 326, Fed. Cas. No. 9,375.

night. It was held that the firm were not unreasonable in asking a short time to consult their counsel, that a compliance with the summons according to its terms was manifestly impossible, and that they should not be punished as for a contempt.[24]

It appears to be the intention of the act, though the language is far from clear, that the taxpayer may be interrogated by the collector concerning every point relating to the sources and extent of his income, or as to exemptions or deductions claimed by him, and that the mere production and submission of his books and accounts will not necessarily end the investigation if the collector is not satisfied with what he finds there. Indeed such examinations may be chiefly necessary in the case of persons who have kept no books at all, or whose accounts are fragmentary and uninforming. It has been decided that the person summoned must not only produce his books, but must submit to an examination and testify concerning entries in them.[25] But since the language of the act of Congress gives the collector power to require persons to attend before him "to give testimony or answer interrogatories under oath respecting any objects liable to tax or the returns thereof," it certainly seems to be within the lawful power of the collector to put the taxpayer through an examination as grilling and complete as an examination in bankruptcy or in proceedings supplementary to execution. But all this does not deprive the witness of his constitutional rights. He may offer proper objections to any question or to the examination of any book or paper, either on constitutional grounds, on the ground that the matter is beyond the powers of the collector to inquire into, or on the ground of a lack of relevancy or materiality.[26] And after an assessment has been made and the tax paid, the collector has no power to summon the taxpayer before him for this purpose. This is only to be done before the assessment is made, and is in aid of the making of a correct assessment.[27]

Under former internal revenue laws, it was held that the only books which the collector had the right to examine were those of the person whose assessment was in question, not those of third

[24] U. S. v. Fordyce, 13 Int. Rev. Rec. 77, Fed. Cas. No. 15,130.

[25] In re Strouse, 1 Sawy. 605, Fed. Cas. No. 13,548; Matter of Meador, 1 Abb. U. S. 317, Fed. Cas. No. 9,375. As to the right of the collector to enter premises for the purpose of examining articles claimed to be therein subject to the tax, see U. S. v. Mann, 95 U. S. 580, 24 L. Ed. 531.

[26] Interstate Commerce Commission v. Brimson, 154 U. S. 447, 155 U. S. 3, 14 Sup. Ct. 1125, 15 Sup. Ct. 19, 38 L. Ed. 1047, 39 L. Ed. 49.

[27] In re Brown, 3 Int. Rev. Rec. 134, Fed. Cas. No. 1,977.

persons who had had dealings with him. Thus, a corporation was not bound to produce and submit its books to the collector on an inquiry into the income of one of its stockholders.[28] But the terms of the present statute are so broad that it is believed this rule could not now apply. The collector is now given power to summon, not only the person whose return is in question, but "any other person having possession, custody, or care of books of account containing entries relating to the business of such person, or any other person he may deem proper." It appears that he has practically unlimited power to interrogate all persons who have had business dealings with the taxpayer, or made payments to him, or who are supposed to have any information about his income, or its origin or amount, and also to inspect the books of any person if they contain entries relatihg to the disputed income.

The fact that national banks are subject to inspection and examination by the bank inspectors does not exempt them from being called upon to allow inspection of their books on the part of revenue officers.[29]

§ 247. Penalties for Failure to Make Returns

It is provided: "That any person, corporation, partnership, association, or insurance company, liable to pay the tax, to make a return, or to supply information required under this title, who refuses or neglects to pay such tax, to make such return, or to supply such information at the time or times herein specified in each year, shall be liable, except as otherwise specially provided in this title, to a penalty of not less than $20 nor more than $1,000." (Act Cong. Sept. 8, 1916, § 18, as amended by Act Cong. Oct. 3, 1917.) This, it will be observed, covers the case of corporations as well as individual taxpayers. Yet an unrepealed clause of the act of 1916 provides that "if any of the corporations, joint-stock companies or associations, or insurance companies aforesaid shall refuse or neglect to make a return at the time or times hereinbefore specified in each year, or shall render a false or fraudulent return, such corporation, joint-stock company or association, or insurance company shall be liable to a penalty of not exceeding $10,000: Provided that the Commissioner of Internal Revenue shall have authority, in the case of either corporations or individuals, to grant a reasonable extension of time in meritorious cases, as he may deem proper."

[28] In re Chadwick, 1 Low. 439, Fed. Cas. No. 2,570.
[29] United States v. Rhawn, 11 Phila. 521, Fed. Cas. No. 16,150.

(Act Cong. Sept. 8, 1916, § 14c [U. S. Comp. St. 1916, § 6336n].) In addition, the law provides that "in case of any failure to make and file a return or list within the time prescribed by law or by the collector, the Commissioner of Internal Revenue shall add to the tax fifty per centum of its amount, except that, when a return is voluntarily and without notice from the collector filed after such time and it is shown that the failure to file it was due to a reasonable cause and not to willful neglect, no such addition shall be made to the tax." (Rev. St. § 3176, as amended by Act Cong. Sept. 8, 1916 [U. S. Comp. St. 1916, § 5899].) But there is also a provision in the war revenue act of 1917, which is clearly applicable to the supplementary or "war" income tax which it levies, though not to the regular or ordinary income tax. It is as follows: "Whoever fails to make any return required by this act or the regulations made under authority thereof within the time prescribed, or who makes any false or fraudulent return, and whoever evades or attempts to evade any tax imposed by this act, or fails to collect or truly to account for and pay over any such tax, shall be subject to a penalty of not more than $1,000, or to imprisonment for not more than one year, or both, at the discretion of the court, and in addition thereto a penalty of double the tax evaded, or not collected, or accounted for and paid over, to be assessed and collected in the same manner as taxes are assessed and collected, in any case in which the punishment is not otherwise specifically provided." (Act Cong. Oct. 3, 1917, § 1004.)

§ 248. Penalties for False or Fraudulent Returns

For false or fraudulent income tax returns, the United States statute prescribes the following penalties:

If an individual taxpayer "makes any false or fraudulent return or statement with intent to defeat or evade the assessment required" by the statute, he shall be guilty of a misdemeanor, and be punished by a fine not exceeding $2,000, or imprisonment for not more than one year, or both, in the discretion of the court, with the costs of prosecution. And in addition, the amount of the tax assessed upon him shall be increased by the addition of one hundred per cent. (Act Cong. Sept. 8, 1916, § 18; Rev. St. § 3176, as amended [U. S. Comp. St. 1916, §§ 6336q, 5899].)

If the return made by or on behalf of a corporation is false or fraudulent, as above defined, the officers of the corporation signing and verifying it are liable to the same punishment as above prescribed for individuals, and the assessment shall likewise be in-

(291)

creased by the addition of one hundred per cent of its amount, and further, by the explicit language of the statute, the corporation itself shall be liable to a penalty of not more than $10,000. (Act Cong. Sept. 8, 1916, §§ 14c, 18; Rev. St. § 3176, as amended [U. S. Comp. St. 1916, §§ 6336n, 6336q, 5899].)

In regard to the validity of these various penalties, there can be little room for dispute. Courts have often sustained them in the case of general taxes, and, specifically with reference to an income tax, it has been held that the imposition of an addition of 100 per cent as a penalty for making a false or fraudulent return is not unconstitutional.[30] It has also been held that an assessor of internal revenue, on ascertaining that the return made by a taxpayer was false and fraudulent, has power to reassess the tax and add the penalty, notwithstanding that the taxpayer has already paid the amount first assessed against him on his original return.[31] But the penalty of 100 per cent cannot be lawfully collected if the reassessment of the tax includes any sum not legally taxed, and there must first be an inquiry and a determination that the omission was false and fraudulent.[32]

In regard to the meaning of the terms employed in this part of the statute, there is a distinction to be taken between "false" and "fraudulent" returns. Fraud implies an intention to deceive or mislead. But a return which is simply incorrect is "false," though made in good faith and under a mistake of law.[33] And under the former income tax laws it was held that the addition of 100 per cent to the tax was authorized for an untrue return, although the return was not willfully false.[34] But the language of the present statute apparently reverses this rule, and authorizes the imposition of penalties only in cases where the return is both "false" and "fraudulent." For, as to the penalty for false swearing, it is denounced against any person who "makes any false or fraudulent return with intent to defeat or evade the assessment," and a false return made with intent to defeat or evade the assessment is necessarily fraudulent also. And as to the addition of the penalty of 100 per cent, this is authorized "in case a false or fraudulent return is willfully made," and of course a false return made willfully

---

[30] Doll v. Evans, 9 Phila. 364, Fed. Cas. No. 3,969.

[31] Doll v. Evans, 9 Phila. 364, Fed. Cas. No. 3,969.

[32] Michigan Cent. R. Co. v. Slack, Holmes, 231, Fed. Cas. No. 9,527.

[33] Eliot Nat. Bank v. Gill, 218 Fed. 600, 134 C. C. A. 358; National Bank of Commerce v. Allen, 223 Fed. 472, 139 C. C. A. 20.

[34] German Sav. Bank v. Archbold, 15 Blatchf. 398, Fed. Cas. No. 5,364.

is fraudulent also. It may be stated therefore that no penalty attaches to the making of a return which is incorrect in fact, but made in good faith and with no fraudulent intention, except that the amount of taxable income shown, if understated, may be increased by the collector to the proper figure on notice, hearing, and proof.

In regard to the manner of enforcing the penalties, it is ruled that the penalty imposed on a corporation for failing to make the required return is to be recovered by a civil action (not by indictment in a criminal proceeding), in which the amount of the penalty will be determined by the court, within the limits stated, after a verdict for the plaintiff.[35] But it is not within the jurisdiction of a court to modify a penalty prescribed for making a false return, its discretion being confined to the limits marked out for it by the law.[36]

Intentional falsehood in the verified return is also a criminal offense. It is believed that the penalties of perjury as at common law would attach to such false swearing, unless the statute expressly declares the offense to be a misdemeanor or expressly prescribes a punishment in the nature of a fine. For it has been decided that, although an act imposing a tax on incomes makes no provision for compelling a person to make oath to his return, yet if it permits him to do so, and he avails himself of the privilege, and makes a false return, he is guilty of perjury.[37] But the present act of Congress explicitly declares this offense to be a misdemeanor, and prescribes the punishment, viz., a fine not to exceed $2,000 or imprisonment for not more than one year, or both in the discretion of the court. Where two persons composing a partnership make and sign, in their partnership name, a false return to the collector of internal revenue, they may be jointly indicted therefor.[38]

§ 249.　Returns of Withholding Agents

The persons and corporations who are described in the Treasury regulations as "debtors" and "withholding agents" are required to make monthly and annual list returns. These terms do not include fiduciaries, such as trustees, guardians, executors, or the like, nor do they include employers, lessees, mortgagors and others who are required to deduct the income tax from fixed periodical payments

[35] T. D. No. 1740.
[36] Lord Advocate v. McLaren, 42 Scotch Law Rep. 762, 5 Tax Cas. 110.
[37] U. S. v. Smith, 1 Sawy. 277, Fed. Cas. No. 16,341.
[38] U. S. v. McGinnis, 1 Abb. U. S. 120, Fed. Cas. No. 15,678.

to be made by them to nonresident aliens. Both of these classes of persons are required to make annual returns, but separate regulations have been prescribed for them and forms provided for their use. "Debtors," as the term is used by the Internal Revenue officers with reference to the income tax, are corporations and other similar organizations which are required by the statute to deduct and pay over the income tax on interest due on their bonds or other similar obligations, and the term "withholding agents" is applied either generally to those who are described as "debtors," or more particularly to banks or other collecting agencies which are required by the regulations to deduct and pay over the income tax on coupons or orders for registered interest on such bonds or similar obligations, when they are not accompanied by certificates of ownership, and on foreign interest or dividends. The monthly returns are required to contain a list of all coupon or interest payments made on which the income tax was deducted and withheld, and also the name and address in full of the owners of the bonds, the amount of the income, amount of exemption claimed, amount of income on which the withholding agent is liable for the tax, and the amount of tax withheld. The annual returns are summaries of the monthly returns. Instructions and regulations for the preparation and return of these monthly and annual lists have been prescribed by the Treasury department and special forms provided for them. It should be noted that whereas the regulations originally directed that the monthly returns should be verified by affidavit, and the forms were drawn accordingly, this requirement has since been indefinitely "waived" as to the monthly list, though not as to the annual returns. No penalties are prescribed for the neglect or failure to render these returns. They are not required or even mentioned in the act of Congress itself, and although the general authority given to the officers of the Treasury department to make regulations for the collection of the tax would undoubtedly cover this case, yet those officers would not have authority to prescribe penalties not included in the statute. For it is a general principle of constitutional law that, while the legislative body may secure obedience to the rules and regulations made by administrative officers under such a grant of authority, by declaring their violation to be a punishable offense, yet no such power resides in the officers who make the rules.[39]

[39] Johnson v. U. S., 26 App. D. C. 128.

CHAPTER XI

ESTATE TAX; TEXT OF ACT OF CONGRESS

§ 250. Definitions of Terms

When used in this title, the term "person" includes partnerships, corporations, and associations; the term "United States" means only the States, the territories of Alaska and Hawaii, and the District of Columbia; the term "executor" means the executor or administrator of the decedent, or, if there is no executor or administrator, any person who takes possession of any property of the decedent; and the term "collector" means the collector of internal revenue of the district in which was the domicile of the decedent at the time of his death, or, if there was no such domicile in the United States, then the collector of the district in which is situated the part of the gross estate of the decedent in the United States, or, if such part of the gross estate is situated in more than one district, then the collector of internal revenue at Baltimore, Maryland. (Act Cong. Sept. 8, 1916, § 200 [U. S. Comp. St. 1916, § 6336½a].)

§ 251. Rates of Tax

A tax (hereinafter in this title referred to as the tax) equal to the following percentages of the value of the net estate, to be determined as provided in section 203 (U. S. Comp. St. 1916, § 6336½d), is hereby imposed upon the transfer of the net estate of every decedent dying after the passage of this act, whether a resident or nonresident of the United States:

One and one-half per centum of the amount of such net estate not in excess of $50,000;

Three per centum of the amount by which such net estate exceeds $50,000 and does not exceed $150,000;

Four and one-half per centum of the amount by which such net estate exceeds $150,000 and does not exceed $250,000;

Six per centum of the amount by which such net estate exceeds $250,000 and does not exceed $450,000;

Seven and one-half per centum of the amount by which such net estate exceeds $450,000 and does not exceed $1,000,000;

Nine per centum of the amount by which such net estate exceeds $1,000,000 and does not exceed $2,000,000;

Ten and one-half per centum of the amount by which such net estate exceeds $2,000,000 and does not exceed $3,000,000;

Twelve per centum of the amount by which such net estate exceeds $3,000,000 and does not exceed $4,000,000;

Thirteen and one-half per centum of the amount by which such net estate exceeds $4,000,000 and does not exceed $5,000,000;

Fifteen per centum of the amount by which such net estate exceeds $5,000,000. (Act Cong. Sept. 8, 1916, § 201, as amended by Act Cong. March 3, 1917, § 300.)

§ 252. War Estate Tax

That in addition to the tax imposed by section two hundred and one of the Act entitled "An Act to increase the revenue, and for other purposes," approved September eighth, nineteen hundred and sixteen, as amended—

(a) A tax equal to the following percentages of its value is hereby imposed upon the transfer of each net estate of every decedent dying after the passage of this Act, the transfer of which is taxable under such section (the value of such net estate to be determined as provided in Title II of such Act of September eighth, nineteen hundred and sixteen):

One-half of one per centum of the amount of such net estate not in excess of $50,000;

One per centum of the amount by which such net estate exceeds $50,000 and does not exceed $150,000;

One and one-half per centum of the amount by which such net estate exceeds $150,000 and does not exceed $250,000;

Two per centum of the amount by which such net estate exceeds $250,000 and does not exceed $450,000;

Two and one-half per centum of the amount by which such net estate exceeds $450,000 and does not exceed $1,000,000;

Three per centum of the amount by which such net estate exceeds $1,000,000 and does not exceed $2,000,000;

Three and one-half per centum of the amount by which such net estate exceeds $2,000,000 and does not exceed $3,000,000;

Four per centum of the amount by which such net estate exceeds $3,000,000 and does not exceed $4,000,000;

Four and one-half per centum of the amount by which such net estate exceeds $4,000,000 and does not exceed $5,000,000;

Five per centum of the amount by which such net estate exceeds $5,000,000 and does not exceed $8,000,000;

Seven per centum of the amount by which such net estate exceeds $8,000,000 and does not exceed $10,000,000; and

Ten per centum of the amount by which such net estate exceeds $10,000,000.   (Act Cong. Oct. 3, 1917, § 900.)

§ 253. Value of Gross Estate, How Determined

The value of the gross estate of the decedent shall be determined by including the value at the time of his death of all property, real or personal, tangible or intangible, wherever situated:

(a) To the extent of the interest therein of the decedent at the time of his death which after his death is subject to the payment of the charges against his estate and the expenses of its administration and is subject to distribution as part of his estate.

(b) To the extent of any interest therein of which the decedent has at any time made a transfer, or with respect to which he has created a trust, in contemplation of or intended to take effect in possession or enjoyment at or after his death, except in case of a bona fide sale for a fair consideration in money or money's worth. Any transfer of a material part of his property in the nature of a final disposition or distribution thereof, made by the decedent within two years prior to his death without such a consideration, shall, unless shown to the contrary, be deemed to have been made in contemplation of death within the meaning of this title; and

(c) To the extent of the interest therein held jointly or as tenants in the entirety by the decedent and any other person, or deposited in banks or other institutions in their joint names and payable to either or the survivor, except such part thereof as may be shown to have originally belonged to such other person and never to have belonged to the decedent.

For the purpose of this title stock in a domestic corporation owned and held by a nonresident decedent shall be deemed property within the United States, and any. property of which the decedent has made a transfer or with respect to which he has created a trust, within the meaning of subdivision (b) of this section, shall be deemed to be situated in the United States, if so situated either at the time of the transfer or the creation of the trust, or at the time of the decedent's death. (Act Cong. Sept. 8, 1916, § 202 [U. S. Comp. St. 1916, § 6336½c].)

§ 254. Net Value of Estate; How Determined

For the purpose of the tax the value of the net estate shall be determined—

(a) In the case of a resident, by deducting from the value of the gross estate—

(1) Such amounts for funeral expenses, administration expenses. claims against the estate, unpaid mortgages, losses incurred during the settlement of the estate arising from fires, storms, shipwreck, or other casualty, and from theft, when such losses are not compensated for by insurance or otherwise, support during the settlement of the estate of those dependent upon the decedent, and such other charges against the estate, as are allowed by the laws of the jurisdiction, whether within or without the United States, under which the estate is being administered; and

(2) An exemption of $50,000;

(b) In the case of a nonresident, by deducting from the value of that part of his gross estate which at the time of his death is situated in the United States that proportion of the deductions specified in paragraph (1) of subdivision (a) of this section which the value of such part bears to the value of his entire gross estate, wherever situated. But no deductions shall be allowed in the case of a nonresident unless the executor includes in the return required to be filed under section two hundred and five the value at the time of his death of that part of the gross estate of the nonresident not situated in the United States. (Act Cong. Sept. 8, 1916, § 203 [U. S. Comp. St. 1916, § 6336½d].)

(298)

§ 255.   Time for Payment; Discount for Prepayment; Penalty for Delinquency

The tax shall be due one year after the decedent's death. If the tax is paid before it is due, a discount at the rate of five per centum per annum, calculated from the time payment is made to the date when the tax is due, shall be deducted. If the tax is not paid within ninety days after it is due, interest at the rate of ten per cent per annum from the time of the decedent's death shall be added as part of the tax, unless because of claims against the estate, necessary litigation, or other unavoidable delay, the collector finds that the tax cannot be determined, in which case the interest shall be at the rate of six per cent per annum from the time of the decedent's death until the cause of such delay is removed, and thereafter at the rate of ten per cent per annum. Litigation to defeat the payment of the tax shall not be deemed necessary litigation. (Act Cong. Sept. 8, 1916, § 204 [U. S. Comp. St. 1916, § 6336½e].)

§ 256.   Notice of Appointment of Executor; Returns; Assessment

The executor, within thirty days after qualifying as such, or after coming into possession of any property of the decedent, whichever event first occurs, shall give written notice thereof to the collector. The executor, shall also, at such times and in such manner as may be required by the regulations made under this title, file with the collector a return under oath in duplicate, setting forth (a) the value of the gross estate of the decedent at the time of his death, or, in case of a nonresident, of that part of his gross estate situated in the United States; (b) the deductions allowed under section two hundred and three; (c) the value of the net estate of the decedent as defined in section two hundred and three; and (d) the tax paid or payable thereon; or such part of such information as may at the time be ascertainable and such supplemental data as may be necessary to establish the correct tax.

Return shall be made in all cases of estates subject to the tax or where the gross estate at the death of the decedent exceeds $60,-000, and in the case of the estate of every nonresident any part of whose gross estate is situated in the United States. If the executor is unable to make a complete return as to any part of the gross estate of the decedent, he shall include in his return a description of such part and the name of every person holding a legal or beneficial interest therein, and upon notice from the collector such person shall in like manner make a return as to such part of the gross estate. The Commissioner of Internal Revenue shall make all assessments of the tax under the authority of existing administrative special and general provisions of law relating to the assessment and collection of taxes. (Act Cong. Sept. 8, 1916, § 205 [U. S. Comp. St. 1916, § 6336½f].)

§ 257. Collector to Make Return in Certain Cases

If no administration is granted upon the estate of a decedent, or if no return is filed as provided in section two hundred and five, or if a return contains a false or incorrect statement of a material fact, the collector or deputy collector shall make a return and the Commissioner of Internal Revenue shall assess the tax thereon. (Act Cong. Sept. 8, 1916, § 206 [U. S. Comp. St. 1916, § 6336½g].)

§ 258. Payment of Tax by Executor

The executor shall pay the tax to the collector or deputy collector. If for any reason the amount of the tax can not be determined, the payment of a sum of money sufficient, in the opinion of the collector, to discharge the tax shall be deemed payment in full of the tax, except as in this section otherwise provided. If the amount so paid exceeds the amount of the tax as finally determined, the Commissioner of Internal Revenue shall refund such excess to the executor. If the amount of the tax as finally determined exceeds the amount so paid the commissioner shall notify the executor of the amount of such excess. From the time of such notification to the time of the final payment of such excess part of the tax, interest shall be added thereto at the rate of ten per centum per annum, and the amount of such excess shall be a lien upon the entire gross estate, except such part thereof as may have been sold to a bona fide purchaser for a fair consideration in money or money's worth.

The collector shall grant to the person paying the tax duplicate receipts, either of which shall be sufficient evidence of such payment, and shall entitle the executor to be credited and allowed the amount thereof by any court having jurisdiction to audit or settle his accounts. (Act Cong. Sept. 8, 1916, § 207 [U. S. Comp. St. 1916, § 6336½h].)

§ 259. Proceedings to Compel Payment of Tax

If the tax herein imposed is not paid within sixty days after it is due, the collector shall, unless there is reasonable cause for further delay, commence appropriate proceedings in any court of the United States, in the name of the United States, to subject the property of the decedent to be sold under the judgment or decree of the court. From the proceeds of such sale the amount of the tax, together with the costs and expenses of every description to be allowed by the court, shall be first paid, and the balance shall be deposited according to the order of the court, to be paid under its direction to the person entitled thereto. If the tax or any part thereof is paid by, or collected out of that part of the estate passing to or in the possession of, any person other than the executor in his capacity as such, such person shall be entitled to reimbursement out of any part of the estate still undistributed or by a just and equitable contribution by the persons whose interest in the estate of the decedent would have been reduced if the tax had been paid before the distribution of the estate or whose interest is subject to equal or prior liability for the payment of taxes, debts, or other charges against the estate, it being the purpose and intent of this title that so far as is practicable and unless otherwise directed by the will of the decedent the tax shall be paid out of the estate before its distribution. (Act Cong. Sept. 8, 1916, § 208 [U. S. Comp. St. 1916, § 6336½i].)

§ 260. Tax as Lien on Estate

Unless the tax is sooner paid in full, it shall be a lien for ten years upon the gross estate of the decedent, except that such part of the gross estate as is used for the payment of charges against the estate and expenses of its administration, allowed by any court having jurisdiction thereof, shall be divested of such lien.

If the decedent makes a transfer of, or creates a trust with respect to, any property in contemplation of or intended to take effect in possession or enjoyment at or after his death (except in the case of a bona fide sale for a fair consideration in money or money's worth) and if the tax in respect thereto is not paid when due, the transferee or trustee shall be personally liable for such tax, and such property, to the extent of the decedent's interest therein at the time of such transfer, shall be subject to a like lien equal to the amount of such tax. Any part of such property sold by such transferee or trustee to a bona fide purchaser for a fair consideration in money or money's worth shall be divested of the lien and a like lien shall then attach to all the property of such transferee or trustee, except any part sold to a bona fide purchaser for a fair consideration in money or money's worth. (Act Cong. Sept. 8, 1916, § 209 [U. S. Comp. St. 1916, § 6336½j].)

§ 261. Exemption of Decedents in Military or Naval Service

That the tax imposed by this title shall not apply to the transfer of the net estate of any decedent dying while serving in the military or naval forces of the United States, during the continuance of the war in which the United States is now engaged, or if death results from injuries received or disease contracted in such service, within one year after the termination of such war. For the purposes of this section the termination of the war shall be evidenced by the proclamation of the President. (Act Cong. Oct. 3, 1917, § 901.)

§ 262. Penalties

Whoever knowingly makes any false statement in any notice or return required to be filed by this title shall be liable to a penalty of not exceeding $5,000, or imprisonment not exceeding one year, or both, in the discretion of the court.

Whoever fails to comply with any duty imposed upon him by section two hundred and five, or, having in his possession or control any record, file, or paper, containing or supposed to contain any information concerning the estate of the decedent, fails to exhibit the same upon request to the Commissioner of Internal Revenue or any collector or law officer of the United States, or his duly authorized deputy or agent, who desires to examine the same in the performance of his duties under this title, shall be liable to a penalty of not exceeding $500, to be recovered, with costs of suit, in a civil action in the name of the United States. (Act Cong. Sept. 8, 1916, § 210 [U. S. Comp. St. 1916, § 6336½k].)

§ 263. Other Laws Made Applicable

All administrative, special, and general provisions of law, including the laws in relation to the assessment and collection of taxes, not heretofore specifically repealed are hereby made to apply to this title so far as applicable and not inconsistent with its provisions. (Act Cong. Sept. 8, 1916, § 211 [U. S. Comp. St. 1916, § 6336½l].)

(302)

§ 264. Regulations by Commissioner of Internal Revenue

The Commissioner of Internal Revenue, with the approval of the Secretary of the Treasury, shall make such regulations, and prescribe and require the use of such books and forms, as he may deem necessary to carry out the provisions of this title.   (Act Cong. Sept. 8, 1916, § 212 [U. S. Comp. St. 1916, § 6336½m].)

CHAPTER XII

ESTATE TAX; REGULATIONS AND DECISIONS

§ 265. Nature and Validity of Tax

The tax imposed by Title II of the Act of Congress of September 8, 1916, called the "estate tax," corresponds in some measure to the inheritance taxes levied by some of the states; but it is not a tax on the distributive shares of those who benefit by a testator's will or by the administration of an intestate estate, nor is it a tax on the bulk or corpus of the estate. It is not a tax on property at all. It is an excise tax on the transfer or transmission of property from a decedent to his heirs or to those who take under his will.[1] Hence it cannot be held unconstitutional on the ground that it is a direct tax, nor for want of uniformity because it exempts estates under a certain value, nor as the exercise of a power which belongs exclusively to the states.[2] It differs materially, however, from the tax imposed by the Act of 1898. For example, personal property in the United States, passing under the will of a nonresident alien executed in New York during a temporary sojourn there, was held not subject to the inheritance tax imposed by that statute.[3] But the present tax falls upon the transfer of the net estates of decedents dying after the date of its enactment, whether residents or nonresidents of the United States, provided of course, in the latter case, that there is taxable property of the estate situated within the United States.

§ 266. Territory for Levy of Tax

The term "United States," as used in the act, includes only the states, the territories of Alaska and Hawaii, and the District of Columbia. "The tax is not imposed in Porto Rico or the Philippine Islands, but under the definitions in the title, the property in the United States of deceased residents of the islands is taxable as the property of nonresidents." (Treasury Regulations No. 37, art. 2, T. D. 2378.)

§ 267. Rates of Tax

Since the original estate-tax act of September 8, 1916, was amended (in respect to the rate of the tax) by the act of March 3, 1917, and again by that of October 3, 1917, the officers of the Internal Revenue bureau have published the following authoritative statement and table:

In view of the fact that this is the second amendment providing increased rates over those contained in the original act, it is deemed advisable, in order to secure uniformity in results and avoid con-

---

[1] United States v. Priest (D. C.) 210 Fed. 332; In re Bierstadt's Estate, 99 Misc. Rep. 457, 163 N. Y. Supp. 1104.

[2] High v. Coyne (D. C.) 93 Fed. 450.

[3] Moore v. Ruckgaber, 184 U. S. 593, 22 Sup. Ct. 521, 46 L. Ed. 705.

fusion, that the following tabulation be brought specially to the attention of those officers whose duties include the computation of taxes upon the net estates of decedents.

Rates of taxation upon net estates

	Date of death.		
	Sept. 9, 1916, to Mar. 2, 1917, inclusive.	Mar. 3, 1917, to Oct. 3, 1917, inclusive.	On and after Oct. 4, 1917.
	Per cent.	*Per cent.*	*Per cent.*
Net estate not exceeding $50,000.....	1	1½	2
Net estate $50,000 to $150,000.......	2	3	4
Net estate $150,000 to $250,000.......	3	4½	6
Net estate $250,000 to $450,000......	4	6	8
Net estate $450,000 to $1,000,000....	5	7½	10
Net estate $1,000,000 to $2,000,000...	6	9	12
Net estate $2,000,000 to $3,000,000..	7	10½	14
Net estate $3,000,000 to $4,000,000..	8	12	16
Net estate $4,000,000 to $5,000,000..	9	13½	18
Net estate $5,000,000 to $8,000,000..	10	15	20
Net estate $8,000,000 to $10,000,000..	10	15	22
Net estate exceeding $10,000,000.....	10	15	25

§ 268. What is Included in Gross Estate

For the purpose of this tax, the gross estate of a decedent includes "the entire estate of every kind, real, personal, and mixed, tangible and intangible property, coming into the hands of executors or administrators, or such as would legally come into their charge if executors or administrators were appointed, and which property would be subject to charges against the estate, expenses of administration, and distribution to the heirs or legatees. This would include insurance, not payable directly to a beneficiary named in the insurance contract, but passing as a part of the administered estate. It would also include the good will of the decedent's business if such good will possessed an actual monetary value." (Treasury Regulations No. 37, art. 4, T. D. 2378.)

§ 269. Same; United States Bonds

Under the federal inheritance tax law of 1898, it was held that United States bonds included in a legacy or distributive share of a decedent's estate were not exempt from the tax on the transmission of such property by reason of the declaration in the federal statutes and on the face of the bonds that they are exempt from taxation, since the tax was not on the bonds, but on the right of transfer by will or intestate succession.[4] For the same reason, the Solicitor of Internal Revenue has given an opinion, applicable to the act of 1916, that the value of government bonds, though they are not taxable, cannot be excluded from the gross or the net estate of a decedent in determining the amount due as a tax under this statute. (T. D. 2449, Feb. 13, 1917.) And it should be noted that the bonds of the first and second "Liberty Loan" of 1917 are expressly made subject to "estate or inheritance taxes."

§ 270. Same; Property Passing Under Power of Appointment

Where a decedent exercises a general power of appointment as donee under the will of a prior decedent, the property so passing is a portion of the gross estate of the decedent appointor. Where property is transferred by a special or limited power of appointment, the question of taxability will depend upon the terms of the instrument by which the donee of the power (the appointor) acts. The facts in every such case should be fully reported to the Commissioner, in order that a decision as to tax liability may be made. (T. D. 2477, April 7, 1917.)

§ 271. Property Transferred in Contemplation of Death

The gross estate also includes "all property transferred by decedent during his lifetime, but in contemplation of, or intended to take effect at, his death. This includes not only property transferred by an instrument effecting a final disposition at the transferror's death, but transfers of any kind, including gifts and sales that were not bona fide, i. e., made for an adequate consideration in money or money's worth, where it can be established that such transfers were made in contemplation of death. The law provides not only that all such transfers of any portion of decedent's property shall be included in the gross estate, but that all such transfers of material value made within two years prior to death shall be presumed to have been made in contemplation of death, and the burden of proving that they were not made in such contemplation and securing their exemption from the tax is placed upon the beneficiary. Wherever, therefore, a collector or agent shall have knowledge of such a gift, sale, or other transfer, he shall require that it be returned as a part of the decedent's gross estate. All

[4] Murdock v. Ward, 178 U. S. 139, 20 Sup. Ct. 775, 44 L. Ed. 1009.

executors or administrators having knowledge of such transfers as are described in this paragraph are required by the law to set forth the facts upon their return of the estate." (Treasury Regulations No. 37, art. 4, T. D. 2378.) And later rulings of the Treasury Department state explicitly that the return must show every gift or transfer of material value made or effected by the decedent within two years prior to the day of his death. With the return may be submitted such evidence as the estate elects to submit showing whether the gift or transfer was made in contemplation of death, and the question of taxability will be ruled upon by the Commissioner before the assessment against the estate is confirmed. Every gift or transfer made in contemplation of, or intended to take effect at, death must be returned, regardless of the date when made. (T. D. 2513, July 16, 1917.)

§ 272. Same; Investigation of Transfers

"If, in the case of transfers made more than two years prior to decedent's death, the executors or administrators shall not include the value of the transfers upon the return of the estate, collectors shall not add such value to the gross estate until a thorough investigation has been made, all the facts have been ascertained, and the collector shall have satisfied himself that the transfers were actually made with a view of providing for the beneficiary after or because of decedent's death." (Treasury Regulations No. 37, Art. IV, T. D. 2378.)

§ 273. Same; Material Transfers Within Two Years of Death

"In the case of transfers made within two years prior to decedent's death, it should be noted that if such transfers were made in contemplation of death they are to be included in the gross estate regardless of their value. It is only where the value is a 'material part' of decedent's whole estate that the presumption is that they were made in contemplation of death. Where, therefore, an executor has made return and the collector finds that transfers of material value made within two years prior to decedent's death have been omitted, the collector shall require the executor to amend the return by including such transfers in the gross estate, unless the executor shall file conclusive evidence that the transfers were not made in contemplation of death." (Treasury Regulations No. 37, art. 4, T. D. 2378.)

Some decisions rendered under similar but earlier acts of Congress may here be cited, as helpful in the interpretation of the present statute. It was held, for instance, that a deed of gift to a son, though made as an advancement, and as such chargeable against his ultimate share of the father's estate under a will existing at the time of the deed, was a "succession" under the act of Congress of 1864, as a conveyance "without adequate and valuable considera- tion," and was therefore taxable.[5] But a deed from a mother to her sons conveying land "for and in consideration of love and af- fection, and for the further consideration of the assistance they have rendered me since the death of my husband" is not a deed of gift made without valuable and adequate consideration, in such sense that the grantees would take the succession subject to the inheritance tax.[6] In another case, the testator, his son, and several others formed a partnership to engage in banking for ten years The articles provided that the death of one or more of the part- ners, so long as three members of the firm survived, should not work a dissolution, and that in consideration of mutual stipulations and valuable considerations received by the testator from the other par- ties to the contract, on testator's death, his share in the cap- ital and profits of the firm should become absolutely vested in his son as his property. It was held that the son acquired a vested interest in his father's interest in the partnership property under the partnership agreement, by a grant based on a sufficient con- sideration, which was defeasible only on the survivorship of the testator beyond the partnership period, and hence such interest, having vested in possession independent of testator's will, was not subject to taxation under the act of Congress of 1898, laying an inheritance tax.[7]

§ 274. Property Owned Jointly

"Decedent's share in joint bank accounts or in any other prop- erty owned by decedent jointly with another or with others as tenants in entirety" should be included in the gross estate. "Only such part of such property as can be shown never to have been owned by the decedent can be excluded from his gross estate." (Treasury Regulations No. 37, Art. IV, T. D. 2378.) It is also ruled by the Treasury Department that household effects and like personal property used by husband and wife jointly in the marriage relation are presumed to be the property of the husband,

---

[5] U. S. v. Banks (D. C.) 17 Fed. 322.
[6] U. S. v. Hart (C. C.) 4 Fed. 292.
[7] Blair v. Herold (O. C.) 150 Fed. 199.

and in the absence of sufficient evidence to rebut this presumption, they must be returned as part of his gross estate. (T. D. 2529, Oct. 4, 1917.)

§ 275. Decedent's Interest in Community Property

"Under the Texas law, all property earned by a husband or wife during the period of their marriage is community property and owned jointly. The death of either does not affect the interest owned by the survivor; that is, this interest does not pass by inheritance. The public records in such cases may, however, be misleading because any conveyance, legally made to both, is apt to be recorded in the name of one, usually the husband. As a matter of fact, however, there is a legal presumption that the whole property conveyed to either is community, without reference to the manner of its acquisition. However, if property were purchased by the separate property or means of either, or were received by either as an inheritance, such property would not be community, but would be individual property, without reference to the manner in which the deed of conveyance is stated. Notwithstanding this, however, under the presumption of the Texas law, it would have to be considered community property until facts otherwise were developed." In the case of the estate in question, "the revenue agent reported as belonging to the estate of the deceased husband the entire property, which the public records showed as in his name. The widow, who is also administratrix, stated to the agent that the entire property so treated by the agent as the gross estate of the deceased husband was in fact community property, but up to this time she has submitted no evidence substantiating this contention. While, for the purposes of local administration, a presumption would be created by the local law in favor of the widow's contention in this case, such a presumption does not rest in her favor so far as any responsibility or duty that may be imposed upon her by federal law is concerned. No state statute of this character has any modifying effect whatever upon the explicit terms of a federal taxing act. The Act of Congress of September 8, 1916, creates its own presumptions and defines explicitly the terms under which exemption from tax may be claimed." Under section 202 of the Act (U. S. Comp. St. 1916, § 6336½c), "there is required to be included in the gross estate of a decedent all the interest held jointly or as tenants in the entirety by the decedent and another person, 'except such part thereof as may be shown to have originally belonged to such other person and never to have belonged to the decedent.' Under this paragraph of the taxing act, wherever the public records show property in the name of the decedent, the presumption is that it was the sole property of the decedent, and the burden of proving that another person owned, prior to the decedent's death, any interest therein is not upon the government, but is upon the estate. You will note the extremely limiting terms of the paragraph quoted above, and that it must be shown that any part of the property to be excluded from the gross estate must have actually belonged in the first instance to a person other than the decedent and that it has never been owned by the decedent. If, under the Texas law, property conveyed to a husband or wife during their marriage is taken by each in entirety and in such a manner that it could not be contended that any specific part of it belonged to either, but that each was the owner of all, and upon the death of either no new interest or title vested in the survivor, as is the case in some states, the government, under a strict and technical interpretation of paragraph C of section 202, would perhaps be justified in demanding that the whole of the property thus owned be included as a portion of the gross estate of the decedent. This, however, does not seem to have been the intent of Congress, and it has heretofore been ruled in a similar case that one-half of the property thus owned jointly should be returned as a portion of the gross estate of the decedent husband or wife as the case might be." (T. D. 2450, February 14, 1917.)

§ 276. Gross Estate Where No Executor Appointed

In the case of property of a decedent for whose estate no executor or administrator has been appointed, all the property and interests of the decedent, including the interests described in § 253, supra, will be aggregated to determine the gross estate. (Treasury Regulations No. 37, Art. V, T. D. 2378.)

§ 277. Situs of Property of Nonresident Decedents

In the case of nonresident decedents, stock owned in a domestic corporation is to be treated as a part of the gross estate in the United States, Hawaii, or Alaska. Also property transferred by a nonresident decedent in contemplation of death (as such transfers are above described) and property in which he had a joint interest will be treated as part of the gross estate in the United States, Hawaii, and Alaska, if their situs was in the United States, Hawaii, or Alaska, either at the time of making a transfer thereof or at the time of decedent's death. (Treasury Regulations No. 37, Art. VI, T. D. 2378.) Bonds of domestic corporations owned by a nonresident decedent are returnable as a portion of his gross estate only in case they are physically situated within the United States, etc., at the time of his death. If neither the decedent's domicile nor the physical situs of his property was within the United States, there is no jurisdiction to tax it. But bonds owned by a resident are taxable wherever they may be situated at the time of his death. (T. D. 2530, Oct. 4, 1917.)

§ 278. Income and Appreciation During Settlement

Estimation of the gross estate of a decedent must be based on the value of the property at the time of his death, and income earned after that date and during the settlement of the estate, and appreciation in values during the period of administration, are not to be returned for the purpose of the estate tax. (T. D. 2406, Dec. 2, 1916, rescinding a contrary rule originally made in Treasury Regulations No. 37, Art. VII.) On the same principle, where a decedent owned stock in a corporation, the entire amount of any dividend declared prior to the day of his death should be included in the amount of his gross estate, whether received before or after that day. But with regard to interest on bonds a different rule applies, and actual interest accrued up to the day of the decedent's death, but not after, is to be included in the gross estate. (T. D. 2483, April 20, 1917.)

§ 279. Deductions to Determine Net Estate

For the purpose of determining the taxable net estate, the Act allows certain deductions to be made from the gross estate, including amounts for funeral expenses, legitimate expenses of administration, valid claims against the estate, unpaid mortgages, losses incurred during the settlement of the estate if not compensated by insurance or otherwise, the support during the settlement of the estate of persons dependent upon the decedent, "and such other charges against the estate as are allowed by the laws of the jurisdiction under which the estate is being administered." The Treasury Department rules that the concluding part of this sentence limits all the preceding clauses, and hence that there cannot be deducted from the gross estate, in determining the net estate liable to the tax, any funeral or other expenses or any losses or charges which were in excess of the amounts allowable under the laws of the local jurisdiction as credits to executors or administrators in their accounts in the probate court. (T. D. 2453, March 7, 1917.) Amounts paid to states on account of inheritance, succession, or legacy taxes are not "such other charges against the estate as are allowed by the laws of the jurisdiction," and accordingly are not deductible in arriving at the amount of the federal estate tax. (T. D. 2524, Sept. 10, 1917, revoking T. D. 2395.) But it has been ruled that the executor or administrator may deduct "such other legal charges against the gross estate as may be allowed in a court of competent jurisdiction."

In regard to the deduction for unpaid mortgages, it is ruled that "only such mortgages as were existent and unpaid at the time of decedent's death" can be deducted. "If in returning the gross estate only the net value to the estate of the mortgaged property is reported, the value of the mortgages cannot be deducted, as, obviously, this would effect a double deduction." (Treasury Regulations No. 37, art. 8, T. D. 2378.) But the rule now is that mortgages on the decedent's property should be shown in the return under the heading of "deductions," and the full value of the mortgaged realty should be shown under the item "gross estate." And a similar rule applies to hypothecated personalty. (T. D. 2513, July 16, 1917.)

A deduction may be made for "losses of the estate arising during the legal period of administration and caused by fires, storms, shipwreck, or other unavoidable accident, or by theft. Only the net loss, after all compensation from insurance or otherwise has been credited, can be deducted."

An allowance for the support of decedent's dependents during the legal period of administration "cannot be an arbitrary estimate, but must be limited to the amount actually paid by the executors or administrators to such persons as were dependent upon the decedent for support at the time of his death." (Treasury Regulations No. 37, Art. VIII, T. D. 2378.) In order to justify such deduction there must be (1) a bona fide disbursement by the executor in money (2) for the support of those actually dependent upon the decedent. Though money may be actually expended for their support, it is not deductible if they had sufficient means of their own; and (3) the amount must be authorized by the local law for that specific purpose, but not necessarily the maximum amount so authorized. (T. D. 2531, Oct. 4, 1917.)

§ 280. Specific Exemption of $50,000

In the case of the estates of all residents, an exemption of $50,-000 is allowed in determining the value of the net estate for taxation. But in the case of nonresidents' estates no such exemption is allowed, the only allowable deductions from the gross estate being a certain proportion of such charges and losses as are allowed the estates of residents. (Treasury Regulations No. 37, Art. III, T. D. 2378.)

§ 281. Deductions in Case of Estates of Nonresidents

In the case of a nonresident decedent, deductions may be made for funeral expenses, costs of administration, valid claims and charges against the estate, unpaid mortgages, losses during administration, and the support of dependents, as in the case of residents, but not to the whole extent of such costs and charges, but to the extent of such a proportion of them as exists between the value of the entire gross estate and the value of that part of it which is in the United States, including Alaska and Hawaii. For instance, if ten per cent of the entire gross estate is situated in the United States, ten per cent of the total of such costs and charges may be deducted. (Treasury Regulations No. 37, Art. IX, T. D. 2378.) Furthermore, the law specifically provides that if any deductions whatever are to be allowed from the gross estate of a nonresident decedent, the return filed by the executor or administrator must show not only the value of the gross estate situated in the United States, but also the value of all the property and interests of the decedent, wherever situated.

§ 282. Notice to be Filed by Executors

Within thirty days after the issuance by the court of letters testamentary or letters of administration, a formal notice of such issuance must be filed by the executor or administrator with the collector of internal revenue of the district in which the decedent was a resident at the time of his death. (Treasury Regulations No. 37, Art. X, T. D. 2378.)

§ 283. Notice to be Given by Others than Executors

Within thirty days after the death of a decedent whose estate is taxable, the thirty-day notice must be filed by others than executors or administrators, as follows:'

(1) By the surviving husband or wife, as the case may be, for

one-half the value at the decedent's death of any community property owned by the decedent and the survivor.

(2) By the first taker after the decedent of any of the decedent's real property, where this passes, in accordance with the local law, directly to the heirs of the decedent.

(3) By donees who have received within two years prior to the decedent's death any gift of material value from the decedent, or who have received at any time whatever gifts made by decedent in contemplation of, or intended to take legal effect at, his death.

(4) By trustees holding property conveyed during lifetime by the decedent in contemplation of death or with intent to provide for others than decedent at or after decedent's death, regardless of the date of the instrument making the conveyance, or the date of possession by the trustee, or the date of vesting of the right of survivors to possession or enjoyment at or after decedent's death.

(5) By fiduciaries holding property of any kind jointly or in entirety for the decedent and another or others.

(6) By any other person or corporation holding at, or taking immediately upon decedent's death any property included in the gross estate (as defined in the Act), which property may not be taken in charge by the decedent's executor or administrator, if any. (T. D. 2454, Feb. 28, 1917.) "Any person coming into possession, prior to the issuance of letters to executors or administrators, of any property of the decedent, shall, within thirty days from the day of acquiring possession, file a similar notice with the collector." (Treasury Regulations No. 37, Art. X, T. D. 2378.)

§ 284. Duty of Beneficiaries as to Notice

Beneficiaries coming into possession of any property of a decedent, where no executor or administrator of the decedent's property is acting, and beneficiaries coming into possession of any property of a decedent prior to the appointment of executors or administrators, are required, where the estate would be subject to taxation, to file the thirty-day notice and the return required by the Act. (T. D. 2372, Sept. 25, 1916.) And in the case of an estate where no executor or administrator comes at any time into charge of the property, the burden of filing the notice is placed by law upon the individual beneficiaries. Each such beneficiary having reason to believe that the total property of the decedent exceeds the gross value of $60,000 or the net value of $50,000, must file the thirty-day notice with the collector within thirty days after coming into possession of any portion of the property.

§ 285. Notice by Corporate Transfer Agents and Registers of Bonds

The duties of corporate transfer agents, registers of bonds, and paying agents, and of corporations performing for themselves the duties customarily performed by such agents, with reference to this tax, are defined as follows:

(1) Where the transfer of stock or bonds or payment of dividends or interest theretofore the legal property of a decedent, whether a resident or a nonresident, is made to or upon the order of an executor or administrator acting under letters granted in the United States, Hawaii, or Alaska, the corporate agent or officer will not be required to file the thirty-day notice, make return, or pay tax.

.(2) The thirty-day notice is required to be filed whenever a corporation, its transfer agent, register, or paying agent is called upon to make a transfer of stock or bonds, or to pay interest or dividends, to any person succeeding in right thereto a stockholder or bondholder who, since September 8, 1916, has died domiciled outside the United States, Hawaii, or Alaska, unless such successor in interest is an executor or administrator of the nonresident decedent acting under letters granted within the United States, Hawaii, or Alaska.

(3) The thirty-day notice will show the name and address at the time of death of the nonresident decedent, a description and valuation of the property to be transferred or paid, and the name, designation (executor or other) and address of the person to whom transfer or payment is made, and will be signed by the proper officer or agent of the corporation.

(4) This notice must be filed for dividends declared prior to the day of death and for interest payable after death to the extent of the portion accrued to the day of death.

(5) If this notice be filed as required either within thirty days from death or immediately upon receipt of the order for transfer or payment, the transfer or payment need not be postponed. The collector, immediately upon receipt of the notice, will communicate with the foreign executor or succeeding party in interest, advising of the requirements of the estate-taxing Act and furnishing a blank form for the making of the return. If, within the legal period, the tax is not paid, proceedings will be instituted under section 208 of the Act (U. S. Comp. St. 1916, § 6336½i) for the sale of the property and the satisfaction of the tax.

(316)

(6) In every case, immediately upon receipt of the thirty-day notice herein referred to, the collector will notify the commissioner of the facts, so that from a record kept in the commissioner's office it may be determined whether property of the nonresident is located in more than one collection district. (T. D. 2490, May 14, 1917.)

§ 286. Notice and Return in Case of Nonresidents' Estates

The thirty-day notice is required to be filed for all property of every kind located or legally situate in this country (including Hawaii and Alaska) by those agents or representatives, donees, transferees, trustees, or fiduciaries of a decedent dying domiciled abroad, whether alien or citizen of the United States. The notice must be filed within thirty days from decedent's death with the collector of internal revenue in whose district the property within this country is situate, unless the local agent, etc., having the property in charge knows that there is other property of decedent located in another collection district, in which case the notice is to be filed with the collector of internal revenue at Baltimore, Maryland. If it is not possible for the local agent, representative, etc., to file the notice within thirty days from the death of the nonresident, the penalty denounced in the Act will not be asserted if the notice is filed within thirty days from the day upon which the local agent, etc., receives information of the nonresident decedent's death.

In due time, if the administrator or executor of the nonresident decedent has failed to file a return and pay the tax due, the collector will require such return and tax payment from the local agent, representative, etc. No deductions whatever from the gross estate will be allowed in such a case unless all the property of the nonresident decedent is shown to be located in this country and it is established that all has been returned for estate tax. Where there is more than one holder in this country of decedent's property, the collector will aggregate the separate returns.

Under no circumstances may the local agent, representative, etc., release to a foreign administrator or executor or a foreign beneficiary of the decedent any property within this country at the time of decedent's death until either (1) the tax due because thereof has been paid, or (2) ancillary letters have been taken out in this country or otherwise provision has been made by the estate for the satisfaction of the tax lien resting upon the decedent's property in this country. When such ancillary letters have been taken out or such provision has been made, the local agent, representative, etc., shall immediately inform the collector fully as to the facts. An administrator or executor acting in a foreign country will not be recognized as relieving others in charge or possession of a decedent's property from responsibility for satisfying the requirements of the taxing act, unless and until he has made return and tendered payment of all tax due. The penalty denounced in section 210 of the Act (U. S. Comp. St. 1916, § 6336½k) will be asserted against every agent, representative, etc., in this country releasing to a foreign administrator or executor or beneficiary of the decedent the property within this country, except where the requirements of this regulation have been complied with.

The above regulation fully applies to transfer agents of corporate stock or bonds, receiving into possession for transfer purposes such personalty of a nonresident decedent. The transfer shall not be effected or the stock or bonds released to the foreign administrator or executor or the succeeding beneficiary until the transfer agent shall have been fully assured either that the tax due has been paid or that ancillary letters have been taken out in this country or provision otherwise made for the satisfaction of the tax lien against the estate. This ruling applies also to safe-deposit companies, warehouses, and similar custodians of property in this country of a nonresident decedent, to brokers holding as collateral securities belonging to a nonresident decedent, to banking institutions holding money of nonresident decedents on deposit or for any specific purpose, such as the purchase of goods, so long as the title rests in the nonresident decedent, his estate or his heirs, and to debtors in this country of nonresident decedents. It does not apply to carriers of property of a nonresident decedent while such property is in their charge for the purpose of transit. (T. D. 2454, Feb. 28, 1917.)

§ 287. Collectors to Inform Executors as to Beneficiaries

Whenever a collector, in the case of a given estate, receives the notice from a beneficiary, and there are administrators or executors acting, he shall promptly inform the executors or administrators of the beneficiary's name and address, in order that the executor or administrator, in compliance with the provisions of the Act, may ascertain such facts with regard to the property possessed by the beneficiary as the executor or administrator is required to show upon his return.

§ 288. Returns by Executors or Administrators

A return of the gross and net estate must be filed with the collector by the executor or administrator within one year after the decedent's death and before distribution or tax payment is made. All information called for upon the blank return must be given. The values of securities must be stated. The highest selling price of stocks and bonds on the day of the death fixes the value to be returned; or if no sale was made, then the highest price bid. If the stocks and bonds are not listed on the market, the executor · may put upon them, from the best evidence he possesses a value which he deems to be the true value as of the day of the decedent's death. (T. D. 2513, July 16, 1917.)

§ 289.   Same; Tentative Returns

If the administration of the estate, at the expiration of the statutory year, is in such incomplete condition that correct information as to the value of the net estate cannot be given, a tentative return · may be filed showing an estimate of the gross and net estate and the tax due, and such estimated tax may be paid at the time the return is filed. The return must be made and filed with the collector in duplicate, one copy to be retained by the collector and one forwarded by him to the commissioner. Where a tentative return has been filed, a final and complete return must be made on or before the date of final payment of the tax in full. Wherever there is a partial payment of tax in advance, a tentative return must be filed before the collector will accept the partial payment. ('Treasury Regulations No. 37, Art. XIII, T. D. 2378.) The Treasury Department has also made the following ruling on the subject of tentative returns: "Section 207 of the Act (U. S. Comp. St. 1916, § 6336½h) relates primarily to the payment of the tax and not to the filing of the return, and it contemplates that if, at the time the tax is due, it is impossible, because of delay in administration, for an exactly accurate return to be made, a tentative return may be filed and the tax shown thereon to be due may be tentatively accepted by the collector. Neither section 205 (U. S. Comp. St. 1916, § 6336½f) nor section 207 contemplates that at any time return may be filed and tax paid without a reasonably approximate determination of the facts relating to the gross estate and the separate legal deductions. Therefore, when application is made to collectors for authority to file returns within one year from the death of the decedent whose estate is being returned, collectors will require that such tentative return be based upon determined or accurately determinable values of gross estate and items of deductions, and if the estate in question has not reached such a state of

(319)

settlement that a reasonably accurate return can be made, advance payment of tax will not be accepted." (T. D. 2415, December 14, 1916.)

§ 290. Place for Filing Returns

If the decedent maintained more than one residence, his principal residence, that is, the place of his actual domicile, will determine the internal revenue district in which the return must be filed and the tax paid. If the decedent was a nonresident and his sole property within the United States (including Hawaii and Alaska) was stock or bonds of an American corporation, the return should be filed with the collector in whose district the head office of the corporation is located, unless the estate has a representative in this country having the stocks or bonds in charge, in which case the return may be filed with the collector in whose district the representative has his office. (T. D. 2513, July 16, 1917.)

§ 291. Value of Estate as Determining Necessity of Return

In the case of the estates of residents, neither the thirty-day notice nor the return can be required except where the gross estate, as defined in the law and regulations, exceeds $60,000, or the net estate, computed in accordance with the law and regulations, exceeds $50,000. Wherever either of these conditions exists, the thirty-day notice and the return must be filed. But a return is required to be made of the estate of every nonresident leaving property in the United States, Alaska, or Hawaii, without regard to the amount of property so left. (Treasury Regulations No. 37, Arts. XIV, XV, T. D. 2378.)

§ 292. When Beneficiaries must File Notice and Return

In the case of estates having no executors or administrators, or where any part of the gross estate passes other than in charge of executors or administrators, the Act places upon the separate beneficiaries the precise duties with regard to the filing of the thirty-day notice and the return and the payment of the tax that are otherwise imposed on the executors and administrators. Each such beneficiary is as fully liable to all the penalties provided in the Act as is the executor or the administrator. Where the property is held for the beneficiary by guardians, trustees, or fiduciaries, the thirty-day notice and the return may be executed by such representatives of the beneficiary. (Treasury Regulations No. 37, Art. XVI, T. D. 2378.)

(320)

§ 293. When Collectors Make Final Return

Each beneficiary making return for any part of the estate is required by the law to give all the information possible regarding any part of the estate. The final and complete return in cases where no executor or administrator acts, will be compiled by the collector from the several returns of the individual beneficiaries. After having determined in this manner the total gross and net estate, the rate of tax, and the proportionate amount due from each beneficiary, the collector shall notify each beneficiary accordingly, and will enter upon the assessment list the amount of tax apportionable to each. Where a return is materially false or incorrect, or where no return is filed, the collector or his deputy, after investigation, shall make the return, and the commissioner shall assess the tax thereon. Whenever a beneficiary files with the collector in whose district he resides a notice of the receipt of property which discloses that the decedent was resident at the time of death in another collection district, the collector receiving the notice shall forward it to the proper collector and shall promptly inform the beneficiary as to the collection district in which return is required to be made and tax paid. (Treasury Regulations No. 37, Arts. XVII–XIX, T. D. 2378.)

§ 294. Penalties

Two separate penalties are provided in connection with the thirty-day notice and the return. (1) For a false statement knowingly made in a notice or return the penalty is a fine not to exceed $5,000, or imprisonment not exceeding one year, or both. (2) For failure, whether through neglect or otherwise, to file the notice or the return at the times required, a penalty of not exceeding $500, to be recovered with costs of suit in a civil action in the name of the United States. (Treasury Regulations No. 37, Art. XXI, T. D. 2378.)

§ 295. Payment of Tax; Discount for Advance Payment

The tax is due and payable one year from the day of decedent's death. Discount at the rate of 5 per cent per annum is allowed for payment in advance. Thus, if the tax is paid two months before the due date, a discount of one-sixth of 5 per cent of the total tax shown by the return as due is allowed. (Treasury Regulations No. 37, Art. XXII, T. D. 2378.) The discount should be computed on the basis of the actual number of days between the date of payment and the due date. Care should be taken to determine the number of days remaining in the month during which the payment is made and count forward actual days to the due date. Executors in computing the discount will use as the date of payment the date when such payment will actually be placed in the collector's hands, as the statute fixes that as the date of payment regardless of the date of remittance or mailing. Where executors file a return and request the collector to advise them of the amount of tax due less discount, the collector should compute the discount to some future date, advising the executor of the amount necessary to satisfy the tax on the date named, making it clear that the computation is based on the presumption that the money will be in the collector's hands on that date. Where executors file a tentative return and ask permission to make a partial payment of the tax due, specifying a certain amount, provided the discount on this amount is allowed, collectors may accept such partial payments and report the same as advance payments. The present worth of such payments must be computed in order to determine how much of the tax is discharged. The computations in such case should be filed with the tentative return, in order that when a complete or fiscal return is filed, the balance of the tax due can readily be determined. (T. D, 2497, June 4, 1917.)

§ 296. Advance Payment Relieving from Interest

Where, prior to the final settlement of an estate, the collector has accepted a tax payment which he deems sufficient fully to cover the estate's liability, such payment shall relieve from the accruing of further interest until such time, if ever, as it may be determined that the payment was insufficient. The collector shall then notify the persons liable for the additional tax, and interest at the rate of 10 per cent per annum shall run upon the due tax from the date of the collector's notice and demand until the date of payment of the entire additional tax due. (Treasury Regulations No. 37, Art. **XXV**, T. D. 2378.)

§ 297. Suit for Overdue Taxes

The law makes two provisions with regard to taxes delayed in payment beyond the due date. (1) Where the delay exceeds 60 days beyond the due date, if the collector has reason to believe the payment is being arbitrarily withheld, or the government is in danger of loss thereby, he shall report the facts to the commissioner, and, with the approval of the commissioner, he shall then proceed in accordance with section 208 (U. S. Comp. St. 1916,

§ 6336½i) to report the facts to the United States attorney in order that action may be brought to subject the property of the decedent to be sold under judgment of the United States court. (2) Where the tax is delayed in payment more than 90 days after the due date, interest begins to run at the rate of 10 per cent per annum and is computed from the day of the decedent's death to the day of payment. Provision is made, however, that if after investigation the collector determines the cause of the delay to be unavoidable, either because of necessary litigation or other condition beyond the control of those responsible for the payment of the tax, and the true tax cannot therefore be determined, the interest shall be at the rate of 6 per cent instead of 10 per cent per annum, running, nevertheless, from the date of decedent's death. The tax may be paid to the collector or his deputy. The collector will issue a receipt in duplicate. (Treasury Regulations No. 37, Arts. XXIII, XXIV, T. D. 2378.)

§ 298. Examination of Records and Documents

Under section 210 of the Act (U. S. Comp. St. 1916, § 6336½k), the commissioner, or any collector or law officer, or his authorized deputy or agent, has authority to examine any record, file, or paper containing, or supposed by the official to contain, any information regarding the estate of a decedent. Refusal to exhibit, upon the official's request, any such record, file, or paper renders the person having the custody of the same liable to a penalty of not exceeding $500, recoverable, with costs, in a civil action in the name of the United States. Before proceeding to report any such case to the United States attorney, the collector or agent should submit all the facts to the commissioner for advice. (Treasury Regulations No. 37, Art. XXVIII, T. D. 2378.)

§ 299. Abatement and Refund

The present regulations regarding abatement and refund claims will apply. Attention is called, however, to the provision of section 207 (U. S. Comp. St. 1916, § 6336½h), that where a tentative payment of tax is made, sufficient in the judgment of the collector at that time to cover all tax liability of the estate, and later it is found that there has been an overpayment, refund of the excess shall be made. This would apply regardless of whether the claim were filed within two years of date of tax payment. (Treasury Regulations No. 37, Art. XXIX, T. D. 2378.)

§ 300. Exemption of Estates of Persons in Military Service

The amendment incorporated in the act of Congress of October 3, 1917, exempts from the additional or supplementary estate tax imposed by that act the transfer of the net estate of any decedent dying while serving in the military or naval forces of the United States during the war with Germany, or if death results from injuries received or disease contracted in such service within one year after the termination of the war. But this exemption does not affect the operation of the original estate tax act or the amendment thereto of March 3, 1917, in its application to the transfers of the estates of the decedents above mentioned. Hence the net estates of the military and naval decedents specified are taxable at the rates imposed by the act of September 8, 1916, as amended by that of March 3, 1917. (T. D. 2535, Oct. 9, 1917.)

(324)

CHAPTER XIII

EXCESS PROFITS TAX

§ 301. Nature and Theory of Tax

The first excess profits tax levied by authority of federal law was that imposed by Title II of the act of Congress of March 3, 1917. This was a tax on domestic corporations and partnerships and on foreign corporations and partnerships doing business in the United States, and the rate was "eight per centum of the amount by which the net income exceeds the sum of $5,000 and eight per centum of the actual capital invested." But the present statute (Title II of the act of Congress of October 3, 1917) is wider in its application, as it includes individuals as well as partnerships and corporations, and is based upon a different theory as to what constitutes "excess profits." Stated in the most broad and general terms, this theory is that business enterprises of all sorts are now making greater profits

(325)

than they made during the three years immediately preceding the beginning of the present war. And it is upon this excess of profits, over those earned during normal times of peace, that the tax falls. Thus—restricting the illustration to the case of a domestic corporation carrying on business on invested capital—its profits for the taxable year having been determined, it is entitled to make certain deductions from that sum before the tax attaches. First, its average annual profits for the three years 1911, 1912, and 1913 will be ascertained and estimated as a percentage of the average amount of capital invested in its business during the same years. It will then be entitled to deduct from its profits for the taxable year the same percentage of its capital invested in the business for the taxable year—not necessarily the same sum or amount of profits,— "but not less than seven or more than nine per centum of the invested capital for the taxable year." This means that the corporation will be entitled to deduct as much as seven per cent of its present invested capital, whether or not its profits during the three years named averaged as much as seven per cent of the capital then invested; but on the other hand, though the profits of those years may have averaged more than nine per cent on its present capital, it will not be allowed to deduct more than nine per cent. And second, and in addition to the deduction just explained, a domestic corporation will be entitled to deduct the sum of $3,000 from its net income for the taxable year, and a domestic partnership or a citizen or resident of the United States may deduct $6,000, though no such deduction in cash is allowed to a foreign corporation or partnership or a nonresident alien individual. And all "net" earnings over and above these stated deductions will be regarded as "excess profits" and will be subject to the tax.

It is extremely unlikely that objections to this tax on constitutional grounds could be sustained. Though the precise subject has never been adjudicated, there is a decision of the Supreme Court which might serve as a precedent. It was held that the special excise tax imposed on the business of sugar refining by the war revenue act of 1898, to be measured by gross annual receipts in excess of a named sum, was not a direct tax, which would have to be apportioned among the several states, but an excise tax imposed by Congress under its power to lay and collect excises, as to which the only restriction is that they must be uniform throughout the United States. (Spreckels Sugar Refining Co. v. McClain, 192 U. S. 397, 24 Sup. Ct. 376, 48 L. Ed. 496.)

§ 302.　Definition of Terms.

That part of the revenue act of 1917 which imposes the excess profits tax begins with the following definitions of terms: The term "corporation" includes joint-stock companies or associations and insurance companies. The term "domestic" means created under the law of the United States or of any state, territory, or District thereof, and the term "foreign" means created under the law of any other possession of the United States or of any foreign country or government. (Corporations of Porto Rico or the Philippines or the Virgin Islands would therefore be classed as "foreign.") The term "United States" means only the states, the territories of Alaska and Hawaii, and the District of Columbia. The term "taxable year" means the twelve months ending December 31st, except in the case of a corporation or partnership which has fixed its own fiscal year, in which case it means such fiscal year. The first taxable year shall be the year ending December 31st, 1917, except that in the case of a corporation or partnership which has fixed its own fiscal year, it shall be the fiscal year ending during the calendar year 1917. If a corporation or partnership, prior to March 1st, 1918, makes a return covering its own fiscal year, and includes therein the income received during that part of the fiscal year falling within the calendar year 1916, the tax for such taxable year shall be that proportion of the tax computed upon the net income during such full fiscal year which the time from January 1st, 1917, to the end of such fiscal year bears to the full fiscal year. (It is to be noted that, except in so far as concerns designated fiscal years, this tax is retroactive, since it is based upon the income of the year 1917, though the act was not passed until October 3d of that year.) The term "prewar period" means the calendar years 1911, 1912, and 1913, or, if a corporation or partnership was not in existence, or an individual was not engaged in a trade or business, during the whole of such period, then as many of such years during the whole of which the corporation or partnership was in existence, or the individual was engaged in the trade or business. The terms "trade" and "business" include professions and occupations. (Hence, in the case of individuals, the tax will fall upon salaries [except those of public officers] and upon professional earnings if in excess of the statutory exemption. And note that another provision of the act declares that "all the trades or businesses in which a corporation or partnership is engaged shall be treated as a single trade or business, and all its income from whatever source derived shall be deemed to be received from such trade or business.") The term "net income" means, in the case of a foreign corporation or partnership or a nonresident alien individual, the net income received from sources within the United States. (Act Cong. Oct. 3, 1917, § 200.)

§ 303. Rate of Tax

The statute declares that the excess profits tax shall be "in addition to the taxes under existing law and under this act." Hence it is to be observed that the excess profits tax is not a substitute for any other tax, but is cumulative or supplementary to income taxes and all other taxes to which companies or partnerships or individuals may be already subject or may become subject under other provisions of the revenue act of 1917.

The provision is that "in addition to the taxes under existing law and under this act, there shall be levied, assessed, collected, and paid for each taxable year upon the income of every corporation, partnership, or individual, a tax (hereinafter in this title referred to as 'the tax') equal to the following percentages of the net income:

Twenty per centum of the amount of the net income in excess of the deduction (determined as hereinafter provided) and not in excess of fifteen per centum of the invested capital for the taxable year;

Twenty-five per centum of the amount of the net income in excess of fifteen per centum and not in excess of twenty per centum of such capital;

Thirty-five per centum of the amount of the net income in excess of twenty per centum and not in excess of twenty-five per centum of such capital;

Forty-five per centum of the amount of the net income in excess of twenty-five per centum and not in excess of thirty-three per centum of such capital; and

Sixty per centum of the amount of the net income in excess of thirty-three per centum of such capital." (Act Cong. Oct. 3, 1917, § 201.)

§ 304. "Engaged in Business;" Various Kinds of Business Combined for Purposes of the Tax

The statute likewise provides that "for the purpose of this title every corporation or partnership, not exempt under the provisions of this section shall be deemed to be engaged in business, and all the trades and businesses in which it is engaged shall be treated as a single trade or business, and all its income from whatever source derived shall be deemed to be received from such trade or business." (Act Cong. Oct. 3, 1917, § 201.) As this is specifically limited to corporations and partnerships, it would appear not to apply to individuals. If an individual draws several salaries from different sources, or is engaged in several occupations or pursuits (not having capital invested in any), the question may be raised whether his receipts from any one given source must exceed the statutory exemption of $6,000 before they become subject to the tax, or whether his receipts from all different sources may be aggregated for the purpose of the tax, and all in excess of $6,000 be subject to it.

§ 305. Exempt Corporations and Incomes

"This title shall apply to all trades or businesses of whatever description, whether continuously carried on or not, except (a) in the case of officers and employees under the United States, or any state, territory, or the District of Columbia, or any local subdivision thereof, the compensation or fees received by them as such officers or employees." (The tax is therefore to be assessed against all salaries in excess of $6,000, except those of senators and representatives in Congress and other officers and employees of the United States or of states, territories, or municipalities.)

"(b) Corporations exempt from tax under the provisions of section eleven of the act of September 8, 1916, as amended by this act, and partnerships and individuals carrying on or doing the same business, or coming within the same description." (The reference here is to the income tax act. See § 11 of this book. The corporations exempted from the income tax, and therefore from the excess profits tax also, include agricultural and horticultural organizations, labor organizations, fraternal orders and benefit societies, religious, charitable, benevolent, educational, and scientific associations and institutions, building and loan associations, mutual savings banks, mutual insurance and telephone companies, certain kinds of holding companies, civic organizations and chambers of commerce, and federal land banks. For a discussion of these corporations and their exemption, see §§ 136–149 of this book. Note that the present statute contains a like exemption in favor of partnerships and individuals in the same kind of business or coming within the same description.)

"(c) Incomes derived from the business of life, health, and accident insurance combined in one policy issued on the weekly premium payment plan." (Act Cong. Oct. 3, 1917, § 201.) It should be added that incomes of individuals from their investments (other than capital invested in their own business) are not subject to the

(329)

tax nor to be included in computing taxable profits. For the tax falls only upon profits from a "trade" or "business," including professions and occupations; and the provision of the preceding section that "all income from whatever source derived shall be deemed to be received from such trade or business" is applicable only to corporations and partnerships.

It is also provided that "the tax shall not be imposed in the case of the trade or business of a foreign corporation or partnership or a nonresident alien individual, the net income of which trade or business during the taxable year is less than $3,000." (Act Cong. Oct. 3, 1917, § 202.)

§ 306. Deductions Allowed

The provision of the statute is that, "for the purpose of this title the deduction shall be as follows, except as otherwise in this title provided:

(a) In the case of domestic corporations, the sum of (1) an amount equal to the same percentage of the invested capital for the taxable year which the average amount of the annual net income of the trade or business during the prewar period was of the invested capital for the prewar period (but not less than seven or more than nine per centum of the invested capital for the taxable year) and (2) $3,000;

(b) In the case of a domestic partnership or of a citizen or resident of the United States, the sum of (1) an amount equal to the same percentage of the invested capital for the taxable year which the average amount of the annual net income of the trade or business during the prewar period was of the invested capital for the prewar period (but not less than seven or more than nine per centum of the invested capital for the taxable year) and (2) $6,000;

(c) In the case of a foreign corporation or partnership or of a nonresident alien individual, an amount ascertained in the same manner as provided in subdivisions (a) and (b), without any exemption of $3,000 or $6,000.

(d) If the Secretary of the Treasury is unable satisfactorily to determine the average amount of the annual net income of the trade or business during the prewar period, the deduction shall be determined in the same manner as provided in section two hundred and five." (Infra, § 309.) (Act Cong. Oct. 3, 1917, § 203.)

(330)

§ 307. Deduction Allowed Where Business Not Carried on Through One Prewar Year

"If a corporation or partnership was not in existence, or an individual was not engaged in the trade or business, during the whole of any one calendar year during the prewar period, the deduction shall be an amount equal to eight per centum of the invested capital for the taxable year, plus, in the case of a domestic corporation, $3,000, and in the case of a domestic partnership or a citizen or resident of the United States, $6,000." (Act Cong. Oct. 3, 1917, § 204.)

§ 308. Case of Successor to Business Previously Carried On

"A trade or business carried on by a corporation, partnership, or individual, although formally organized or reorganized on or after January 2d, 1913, which is substantially a continuation of a trade or business carried on prior to that date, shall, for the purposes of this title, be deemed to have been in existence prior to that date, and the net income and invested capital of its predecessor prior to that date shall be deemed to have been its net income and invested capital." (Act Cong. Oct. 3, 1917, § 204.)

§ 309. Deduction Allowed Where Business was Unprofitable During Prewar Period

In order to equalize the tax, and that it may not bear too heavily upon a business which yielded no profit or only a small profit during the prewar period, the act makes the following provision: "If the Secretary of the Treasury, upon complaint, finds either (1) that during the prewar period a domestic corporation or partnership, or a citizen or resident of the United States, had no net income from the trade or business, or (2) that during the prewar period the percentage, which the net income was of the invested capital, was low as compared with the percentage, which the net income during such period of representative corporations, partnerships, and individuals, engaged in a like or similar trade or business, was of their invested capital, then the deduction shall be the sum of (1) an amount equal to the same percentage of its invested capital for the taxable year which the average deduction (determined in the same manner as provided in section two hundred and three [§ 306, supra] without including the $3,000 or $6,000 therein referred to) for such year of representative corporations, partnerships, or individuals, engaged in a like or similar trade or business, is of their average invested capital for such year plus (2) in the case

(331)

of a domestic corporation $3,000, and in the case of a domestic partnership or a citizen or resident of the United States $6,000." (Act Cong. Oct. 3, 1917, § 205.)

§ 310. Percentage of Net Income to Invested Capital How Determined

It is provided that "the percentage which the net income was of the invested capital in each trade or business shall be determined by the Commissioner of Internal Revenue, in accordance with regulations prescribed by him, with the approval of the Secretary of the Treasury. In the case of a corporation or partnership which has fixed its own fiscal year, the percentage determined by the calendar year ending during such fiscal year shall be used." (Act Cong. Oct. 3, 1917, § 205.)

§ 311. Assessment of Tax; Claim for Abatement

Still referring to the case of a trade or business which yielded little or no profit during the prewar period (§ 309, supra), the law provides: "The tax shall be assessed upon the basis of the deduction determined as provided in section two hundred and three [that is, the tax shall be assessed against the particular company, partnership, or individual upon the same general basis that is prescribed for all subject to the tax, and without reference to exceptional circumstances] but the taxpayer claiming the benefit of this section may at the time of making the return file a claim for abatement of the amount by which the tax so assessed exceeds a tax computed upon the basis of a deduction determined as provided in this section [that is, a deduction computed by comparison with the average deduction allowed to representative corporations, partnerships, or individuals engaged in a like or similar trade or business.] In such event, collection of the part of the tax covered by such claim for abatement shall not be made until the claim is decided, but if in the judgment of the Commissioner of Internal Revenue, the interests of the United States would be jeopardized thereby he may require the claimant to give a bond in such amount and with such sureties as the commissioner may think wise to safeguard such interests, conditioned for the payment of any tax found to be due, with the interest thereon, and if such bond, satisfactory to the commissioner, is not given within such time as he prescribes, the full amount of tax assessed, shall be collected and the amount overpaid, if any, shall upon final decision of the application be re-

(332)

funded as a tax erroneously or illegally collected." (Act Cong. Oct. 3, 1917, § 205.)

§ 312. Net Income of Corporation How Ascertained

"For the purposes of this title the net income of a corporation shall be ascertained and returned (a) for the calendar years 1911 and 1912, upon the same basis and in the same manner as provided in section thirty-eight of an act entitled 'An act to provide revenue, equalize duties, and encourage the industries of the United States, and for other purposes,' approved August fifth, 1909, except that income taxes paid by it within the year imposed by the authority of the United States shall be included; (b) for the calendar year 1913, upon the same basis and in the same manner as provided in section II of the act entitled 'An act to reduce tariff duties and to provide revenue for the government, and for other purposes,' approved October third, 1913, except that income taxes paid by it within the year imposed by the authority of the United States shall be included, and except that the amounts received by it as dividends upon the stock or from the net earnings of other corporations, joint-stock companies or associations, or insurance companies, subject to the tax imposed by section II of such act of October third, 1913, shall be deducted; and (c) for the taxable year upon the same basis and in the same manner as provided in Title I of the act entitled 'An act to increase the revenue and for other purposes,' approved September eighth, 1916, as amended by this act, except that the amounts received by it as dividends upon the stock or from the net earnings of other corporations, joint-stock companies or associations, or insurance companies subject to the tax imposed by Title I of such act of September eighth, 1916, shall be deducted." (Act Cong. Oct. 3, 1917, § 206.)

The act of August 5, 1909, above referred to as the guide for computing the net income of corporations for the years 1911 and 1912, was the act which imposed a special excise tax on corporations, the subject of the tax being the franchise or privilege of doing business in a corporate capacity, though it was measured by the net income. The thirty-eighth section of that act provided as follows: "Such net income shall be ascertained by deducting from the gross amount of the income of such corporation, joint stock company or association, or insurance company, received within the year from all sources, (first) all the ordinary and necessary expenses actually paid within the year out of income in the maintenance and operation of its business and properties, including all charges

such as rentals or franchise payments, required to be made as a
condition to the continued use or possession of property; (second)
all losses actually sustained within the year and not compensated
by insurance or otherwise, including a reasonable allowance for
depreciation of property, if any, and in the case of insurance companies the sums other than dividends, paid within the year on policy and annuity contracts and the net addition, if any, required
by law to be made within the year to reserve funds; (third) interest actually paid within the year on its bonded or other indebtedness
to an amount of such bonded and other indebtedness not exceeding the paid-up capital stock of such corporation, joint stock company or association, or insurance company, outstanding at the close
of the year, and in the case of a bank, banking association, or trust
company, all interest actually paid by it within the year on deposits; (fourth) all sums paid by it within the year for taxes imposed under the authority of the United States or of any state or
territory thereof, or imposed by the government of any foreign
country as a condition to carry on business therein; (fifth) all
amounts received by it within the year as dividends upon stock of
other corporations, joint stock companies or associations, or insurance companies, subject to the tax hereby imposed." The foregoing was applicable only to domestic corporations. But as to foreign corporations, the same deductions were allowed, except that
the deductible "expenses" and "losses" must have been incurred
in the course of the business carried on within the United States or
its territories, and that, in the case of a foreign company, the deduction for interest paid was not to be measured by reference to
the whole of its paid-up capital stock, but to "the proportion of
its paid-up capital stock outstanding at the close of the year which
the gross amount of its income for the year from business transacted and capital invested within the United States and any of its
territories, Alaska, and the District of Columbia bears to the gross
amount of its income derived from all sources within and without the United States."

The act of October 3, 1913, referred to above as the basis for computing the net income of corporations for the calendar year 1913,
was the general income tax act of that year. The deductions which
it allowed, for the purpose of ascertaining the taxable net income
of a corporation, were substantially similar to those allowed by the
act of 1909, above quoted, except that it was permitted to make a
deduction for interest paid on its indebtedness "to an amount of

such indebtedness not exceeding one-half of the sum of its interest-bearing indebtedness and its paid-up capital stock outstanding at the close of the year." Under the act of 1913, however, a corporation was not allowed to deduct sums which it had received in the form of dividends on the stock of other corporations. But under the express language of the act now under consideration, it will be allowed to deduct such dividends in figuring its income for the year 1913, for the purpose of the excess profits tax. On the other hand, it cannot deduct the amount paid for federal income taxes, which was before permitted.

To ascertain the net income of a corporation for the taxable year, the computation must be made, as above directed, on the basis and in the manner prescribed by the act of September 8, 1916. This is the general income tax law now in force, and it is printed in full in the first chapter of this book, the method of computing the net income of corporations being prescribed in § 12. But it is to be noted that the excess profits tax act allows the deduction of dividends received from other corporations, which is not permitted under the income tax law.

§ 313. Net Income of Partnerships and Individuals How Ascertained

"The net income of a partnership or individual shall be ascertained and returned for the calendar years 1911, 1912, and 1913, and for the taxable year, upon the same basis and in the same manner as provided in Title I of such act of September 8th, 1916, as amended by this act [this is the general income tax law now in force, printed in full in the first chapter of this book, and the method of computing taxable net income is prescribed in § 5, supra, which embodies § 5 of the act] except that the credit allowed by subdivision (b) of section five of such act shall be deducted. [The "credit" here spoken of is for income received in the form of dividends on corporate stock.] There shall be allowed (a) in the case of a domestic partnership the same deductions as allowed to individuals in subdivision (a) of section five of such act of September 8, 1916, as amended by this act; and (b) in the case of a foreign partnership the same deductions as allowed to individuals in subdivision (a) of section six of such act as amended by this act." (Act Cong. Oct. 3, 1917, § 206.) The deductions above spoken of as allowable in the case of a foreign partnership are those allowed by the income tax law to a nonresident alien individual. (See § 6, supra.)

§ 314. Meaning of "Invested Capital"

The statute defines this term in the following language: "As used in this title, the term 'invested capital' for any year means the average invested capital for the year, as defined and limited in this title, averaged monthly. As used in this title 'invested capital' does not include stocks, bonds (other than obligations of the United States), or other assets, the income from which is not subject to the tax imposed by this title, nor money or other property borrowed, and means, subject to the above limitations:

(a) In the case of a corporation or partnership: (1) Actual cash paid in, (2) the actual cash value of tangible property paid in other than cash, for stock or shares in such corporation or partnership, at the time of such payment (but in case such tangible property was paid in prior to January first, 1914, the actual cash value of such property as of January first, 1914, but in no case to exceed the par value of the original stock or shares specifically issued therefor), and (3) paid in or earned surplus and undivided profits used or employed in the business, exclusive of undivided profits earned during the taxable year: Provided, that (a) the actual cash value of patents and copyrights paid in for stock or shares in such corporation or partnership, at the time of such payment, shall be included as invested capital, but not to exceed the par value of such stock or shares at the time of such payment, and (b) the good will, trade marks, trade brands, the franchise of a corporation or partnership, or other intangible property, shall be included as invested capital if the corporation or partnership made payment bona fide therefor specifically as such in cash or tangible property, the value of such good will, trade mark, trade brand, franchise, or intangible property, not to exceed the actual cash or actual cash value of the tangible property paid therefor at the time of such payment; but good will, trade marks, trade brands, franchise of a corporation or partnership, or other intangible property, bona fide purchased prior to March third, 1917, for and with interests or shares in a partnership or for and with shares in the capital stock of a corporation (issued prior to March third, 1917), in an amount not to exceed, on March third, 1917, twenty per centum of the total interests or shares in the partnership or of the total shares of the capital stock of the corporation, shall be included in invested capital at a value not to exceed the actual cash value at the time of such purchase, and in case of issue of stock therefor not to exceed the par value of such stock;

(b) In the case of an individual, (1) actual cash paid into the

(336)

trade or business, and (2) the actual cash value of tangible property paid into the trade or business, other than cash, at the time of such payment (but in case such tangible property was paid in prior to January first, 1914, the actual cash value of such property as of January first, 1914), and (3) the actual cash value of patents, copyrights, good will, trade marks, trade brands, franchises, or other intangible property, paid into the trade or business, at the time of such payment, if payment was made therefor specifically as such in cash or tangible property, not to exceed the actual cash or actual cash value of the tangible property bona fide paid therefor at the time of such payment.

In the case of a foreign corporation or partnership or of a nonresident alien individual, the term 'invested capital' means that proportion of the entire invested capital, as defined and limited in this title, which the entire net income from sources within the United States bears to the entire net income." (Act Cong. Oct. 3, 1917, § 207.)

The Treasury Department has made the following ruling: "Investments in obligations of the United States, including Liberty bonds of both the first and second issues, made by a corporation or partnership from capital, surplus, or undivided profits will be included in invested capital for the purpose of computing the deduction and rate of taxation under the excess profits tax law; but undivided profits earned during the taxable year cannot be included in invested capital." (T. D. 2541, Oct. 20, 1917.)

§ 315.　Same; Reorganization, Consolidation, or Change of Ownership After March 3, 1917

"In case of the reorganization, consolidation or change of ownership of a trade or business after March third, 1917, if an interest or control in such trade or business of fifty per centum or more remains in control of the same persons, corporations, associations, partnerships, or any of them, then in ascertaining the invested capital of the trade or business no asset transferred or received from the prior trade or business shall be allowed a greater value than would have been allowed under this title in computing the invested capital of such prior trade or business if such asset had not been so transferred or received, unless such asset was paid for specifically as such, in cash or tangible property, and then not to exceed the actual cash or actual cash value of the tangible property paid therefor at the time of such payment." (Act Cong. Oct. 3, 1917, § 208.)

§ 316. Tax on Profits of Trade or Business Without Invested Capital

It is further provided by the statute that "in the case of a trade or business having no invested capital or not more than a nominal capital, there shall be levied, assessed, collected, and paid, in addition to the taxes under existing law and under this act, in lieu of the tax imposed by section two hundred and one (supra, § 303), a tax equivalent to eight per centum of the net income of such trade or business in excess of the following deductions: In the case of a domestic corporation $3,000, and in the case of a domestic partnership or a citizen or resident of the United States $6,000; in the case of all other trades or business, no deduction." (Act Cong. Oct. 3, 1917, § 209.) Since an earlier provision of the act declares that the terms "trade and business" shall include professions and occupations, it is evidently the intention of this section to lay the excess profits tax on every individual who derives an income in excess of $6,000 from any trade, business, profession, or occupation which he pursues without an investment of capital in it, or with only a nominal investment of capital. Officers of the United States and of states and municipalities are expressly excepted from the tax, whether in receipt of a salary or compensated by fees (supra, § 305), whence it is apparent that all other salaried men whose compensation is more than $6,000 a year must pay a tax of eight per cent on the excess.

§ 317. Deduction Allowed Where Invested Capital Cannot be Satisfactorily Determined

"If the Secretary of the Treasury is unable in any case satisfactorily to determine the invested capital, the amount of the deduction shall be the sum of (1) an amount equal to the same proportion of the net income of the trade or business received during the taxable year as the proportion which the average deduction (determined in the same manner as provided in section two hundred and three [supra, § 306] without including the $3,000 or $6,000 therein referred to) for the same calendar year of representative corporations, partnerships, and individuals, engaged in a like or similar trade or business, bears to the total net income of the trade or business received by such corporations, partnerships and individuals, plus (2) in the case of a domestic corporation $3,000, and in the case of a domestic partnership or a citizen or resident of the United States $6,000. For the purpose of this section, the proportion between the deduction and the net income in each trade or business shall be determined by the Commissioner of Internal Revenue in accordance with regulations prescribed by him, with the approval of the Secretary of the Treasury. In the case of a corporation or partnership which has fixed its own fiscal year, the proportion determined for the calendar year ending during such fiscal year shall be used." (Act Cong. Oct. 3, 1917, § 210.)

§ 318. Returns by Foreign and Domestic Partnerships

The act requires that "every foreign partnership having a net income of $3,000 or more for the taxable year, and every domestic partnership having a net income of $6,000 for the taxable year, shall render a correct return of the income of the trade or business for the taxable year, setting forth specifically the gross income for such year, and the deductions allowed in this title. Such returns shall be rendered at the same time and in the same manner as is prescribed for income-tax returns under Title I of such act of September eighth, 1916, as amended by this Act." (Act Cong. Oct. 3, 1917, § 211.) It will be observed that the succeeding section of the statute makes all of the provisions of the income tax law, in so far as relates to returns and payment of the tax, applicable to the excess profits tax. The reason for making this special provision as to returns by partnerships is that they are not required to make returns for the purpose of the income tax unless "requested" by the Commissioner of Internal Revenue or a district collector. See, supra, § 8.

§ 319. Administrative Provisions; Returns; Payment of Tax; Penalties

The provision of the statute is that "all administrative, special, and general provisions of law, including the laws in relation to the assessment, remission, collection, and refund of internal revenue taxes not heretofore specifically repealed, and not inconsistent with the provisions of this title are hereby extended and made applicable to the provisions of this title and to the tax herein imposed, and all provisions of Title I of such act of September eighth, 1916, as amended by this act, relating to returns and payment of the tax therein imposed, including penalties, are hereby made applicable to the tax imposed by this title." (Act Cong. Oct. 3, 1917, § 212.) The act referred to is the income tax act now in force, as amended by the present statute. The provisions with regard to returns by individuals and corporations may be seen at large in §§ 8 and 13, supra. The time for payment of the tax is in all cases "on or before the fifteenth day of June" in each year, except where a corporation has legally designated its own fiscal year, in which case it has 105 days after the date for making its return in which to pay the tax. Supra, §§ 9, 14. On the general subject of income tax returns, see, supra, §§ 228–249. As to penalties for failure to make returns and for false and fraudulent returns, see, supra, §§ 247, 248.

§ 320. Commissioner to Make Regulations and Require Information

"The Commissioner of Internal Revenue, with the approval of the Secretary of the Treasury, shall make all necessary regulations for carrying out the provisions of this title, and may require any corporation, partnership, or individual, subject to the provisions of this title, to furnish him with such facts, data, and information as in his judgment are necessary to collect the tax imposed by this title." (Act Cong. Oct. 3, 1917, § 213.)

§ 321. Repeal; Munition Manufacturers' Tax

The original excess profits tax is repealed by the following provision: "That Title II (sections two hundred to two hundred and seven inclusive) of the act entitled 'An act to provide increased revenue to defray the expenses of the increased appropriations for the army and navy, and the extensions of fortifications, and for other purposes,' approved March third, 1917, is hereby repealed. Any amount heretofore or hereafter paid on account of the tax imposed by such title II, shall be credited towards the payment of the tax imposed by this title, and if the amount so paid exceeds the amount of such tax the excess shall be refunded as a tax erroneously or illegally collected." (Act Cong. Oct. 3, 1917, § 214.)

In 1916, a tax was imposed by act of Congress upon all manufacturers of munitions, at the rate of twelve and one-half per cent upon their entire net profits. The tax was to be in force until one year after the termination of the present war. But the present statute reduces the rate of this tax to ten per cent, and makes it expire by limitation on January 1, 1918. (Act Cong. Oct. 3, 1917, § 214.)

(340)

CHAPTER XIV

CAPITAL STOCK TAX

§ 322. Nature and Incidence of Tax

This is a special tax imposed on corporations by Title IV, § 407, of the Act of Congress of September 8, 1916 (U. S. Comp. St. 1916, §§ 5980a–5980i). It was not repealed by the War Tax Act of 1917. It is imposed upon corporations "organized in the United States for profit and having a capital stock represented by shares" and upon corporations "organized for profit under the laws of any foreign country and engaged in business in the United States." It is measured, in the case of domestic corporations, by the "fair average value of the capital stock for the preceding year," and in the case of foreign corporations, by the amount of "capital actually invested in the transaction of its business in the United States." It is described as a "special excise tax with respect to the carrying on or doing business." It is thus very similar to the tax on corporations imposed by the act of 1909, or to occupational taxes upon individuals, except that it is estimated on the basis of the value of the capital stock, instead of by the amount of income, or instead of being a fixed annual sum. The corporation excise tax law of 1909 was held valid and constitutional, as against the objection that it imposed a direct tax not apportioned among the states;[1] and undoubtedly the same principle would support the present statute.

§ 323. Tax on Domestic Corporations

The language of the statute as applied to domestic corporations is as follows: "Every corporation, joint-stock company or 'association, now or hereafter organized in the United States for profit and having a capital stock represented by shares, and every insurance company, now or hereafter organized under the laws of the United States, or any State or Territory of the United States, shall pay annually a special excise tax with respect to the carrying on or doing business by such corporation, joint-stock company or association, or insurance company, equivalent to 50 cents for each $1,000 of the fair value of its capital stock and in estimating the value of capital stock the surplus and undivided profits shall be included: Provided, That in the case of insurance companies such deposits and reserve funds as they are required by law or contract to maintain or hold for the protection of or payment to or apportionment among policyholders shall not be included. The amount of such annual tax shall in all cases be computed on the basis of the fair average value of the capital stock for the preceding year: Provided, That for the purpose of this tax an exemption of $99,000 shall be allowed from the capital stock as defined in this paragraph of each corporation, joint-stock company or association, or insurance company: Provided further, That a corporation, joint-stock company or association, or insurance company, actually paying the tax imposed by section three hundred and one of Title III of this Act shall be entitled to a credit as against the tax imposed by this paragraph equal to the amount of the tax so actually paid: And provided further, That this tax shall not be imposed upon any corporation, joint-stock company or association, or insurance company not engaged in business during the preceding taxable year, or which is exempt under the provisions of section eleven, Title I, of this Act."

§ 324. Tax on Foreign Corporations

As applied to foreign corporations, the provision of the statute is as follows: "Every corporation, joint-stock company or association, or insurance company, now or hereafter organized for profit under the laws of any foreign country and engaged in business in the United States shall pay annually a special excise tax with re-

[1] Stratton's Independence v. Howbert (D. C.) 207 Fed. 419.

(342)

spect to the carrying on or doing business in the United States by such corporation, joint-stock company or association, or insurance company, equivalent to 50 cents for each $1,000 of the capital actually invested in the transaction of its business in the United States: Provided, That in the case of insurance companies such deposits or reserve funds as they are required by law or contract to maintain or hold in the United States for the protection of or payment to or apportionment among policyholders, shall not be included. The amount of such annual tax shall in all cases be computed on the basis of the average amount of capital so invested during the preceding year: Provided, That for the purpose of this tax an exemption from the amount of capital so invested shall be allowed equal to such proportion of $99,000 as the amount so invested bears to the total amount invested in the transaction of business in the United States or elsewhere: Provided, further, That this exemption shall be allowed only if such corporation, joint-stock company or association, or insurance company makes return to the Commissioner of Internal Revenue, under regulations prescribed by him with the approval of the Secretary of the Treasury, of the amount of capital invested in the transaction of business outside the United States: And provided further, That a corporation, joint-stock company or association, or insurance company actually paying the tax imposed by section three hundred and one of Title III of this Act shall be entitled to a credit as against the tax imposed by this paragraph equal to the amount of the tax so actually paid: And provided further, That this tax shall not be imposed upon any corporation, joint-stock company or association, or insurance company not engaged in business during the preceding taxable year, or. which is exempt under the provisions of section eleven, Title I, of this Act."

§ 325. Corporations Which are Exempt

The corporations which are specifically exempted from this tax are the same that are exempted from the payment of the income tax. (See, supra, §§ 136–149.) It should be observed, however, in the case of this tax as well as the income tax, that the exemption of agricultural and horticultural organizations applies only to those corporations that are engaged in that business merely for the general welfare and benefit of the public, such as agricultural or horticultural fairs; but a corporation engaged in general farming, raising cattle, or any agricultural business for profit, is liable to the tax the same as any other corporation. (T. D. 2417, Dec. 16, 1916.) Further, the capital stock tax does not fall upon a corporation unless it is "organized for profit." And there may be corporations which would be free from the tax on this ground, though not mentioned by name among those exempt from the income tax. And again, in the case of a domestic corporation, it is requisite to its liability to this tax that it should have a "capital stock represented by shares." Hence mutual insurance companies and all other associations not having such a capital stock so represented will be exempt. (Treasury Regulations No. 38, T. D. 2383.) And it will be noticed that any domestic corporation with a capital less than $99,000 is exempt from the tax, though not necessarily from the duty of making a return. And such corporations are exempt as were not "engaged in business during the preceding taxable year." As to corporations which are in the hands of receivers, it is ruled that they will not be required to make a return for the capital stock tax, unless the receivership terminates before the close of the taxable period, nor will corporations now operating under their own corporate management, but which were in the hands of receivers during the preceding taxable year, be required to file a return. (T. D. 2424, Dec. 30, 1916.) It was also held under the corporation excise tax law of 1909, which was expressed in identical language in this respect, that real estate trusts created by deed, for the purpose of purchasing, improving, holding, or selling lands and buildings for the benefit of the shareholders, but not organized under any statute of the state where they are formed, and not deriving any benefit or privilege from any such statute, and which are not intended to have perpetual duration, but are limited by their terms to a fixed period, were not subject to the federal tax.[2]

§ 326. What Corporations Required to Make Returns

Under the regulations of the Treasury Department, every corporation, joint-stock company or association, and insurance company, organized in the United States for profit and having a capital stock issued and outstanding, represented by shares of the market value of $75,000 or over, and not exempt, is required to make a return on Form 707, irrespective of the par value of its capital stock unless such corporation, etc., was not engaged in business during the preceding taxable year. (It has been explained that the reason for requiring returns from companies whose stock has a market value of $75,000 or over, although the fair value of their stock may not exceed $99,000, the exemption allowed by law, was to leave the final determination of the question of tax liability of

---

[2] Eliot v. Freeman, 220 U. S. 178, 31 Sup. Ct. 360, 55 L. Ed. 424.

the company for the collector or the Commissioner of Internal Revenue. T. D. 2417, Dec. 16, 1916.) As to foreign companies, the regulation is that "every corporation, joint-stock company or association, or insurance company, organized for profit under the laws of any foreign country, and engaged in business in the United States, shall make return on Form 708, irrespective of the amount of capital employed either at home or in this country in the transaction of its business." (Treasury Regulations No. 38, Art. III, T. D. 2383.)

§ 327. "Engaging in Business" as a Prerequisite to Liability

Since this is described by the statute as "a special excise tax with respect to the carrying on or doing business" by the corporation, it follows that it is a condition precedent to liability to the tax that the corporation in question should have been engaged in business during the preceding taxable (fiscal) year. But this does not mean that it must have been engaged in business during the entire year, but at some time in the course of the year, and the length of time has no bearing upon the amount of tax due. That is to be found by ascertaining the actual average market value of the stock of the company. (T. D. 2423, Dec. 30, 1916.) If the corporation was engaged in business for any length of time, even one day, it is required to file a return, and, if liable, pay the tax. There is no relation between the amount of tax payable and the length of time during which the company was so engaged in business. (T. D. 2417, Dec. 16, 1916.) Such was also the decision of the courts under the corporation excise tax act of 1909, which was exactly similar in this respect.[3]

§ 328. What Constitutes Carrying On or Doing Business

The corporation tax law of 1909, like the present capital stock tax, imposed a tax on all corporations organized for profit and having a capital stock represented by shares, and, as in the present case, the tax was levied "with respect to the carrying on or doing business" by such corporations. The decisions rendered under the former statute are therefore fully applicable to the present law. And first, it was held that, to be subject to the tax, the corporation must not only be organized for the purpose of doing business, but must also be actually engaged in that business; it was not enough that it should have been organized for the transaction of some or

---

[3] Blalock v. Georgia Ry. & Electric Co., 228 Fed. 296, 142 C. C. A. 588, Ann. Cas. 1917A, 679.

various kinds of business, but it was not subject to the tax if it abstained from doing any business.[4] And as to the discontinuance of a business once begun, it was said that the true test to determine whether a corporation is "engaged in business" is whether it is continuing the body and substance of the business for which it was organized, and in which it set out, or whether it has substantially retired from it and turned it over to another. If the latter appears, then its tax-exempt status must be determined by the further query whether it had during the critical period done only such acts as are properly and normally incidental to the status of a mere lessor of its property, or whether it had exercised its peculiar corporate franchise outside of and beyond the fair scope of that status.[5]

§ 329. Same; Mining Operations

Certain mining companies sought to avoid liability to taxation under the act of 1909, on the plea that their operations did not constitute "carrying on or doing business," but were merely the transformation of one form of property (ores in place) into another form of property (money). But the Supreme Court held otherwise. "It is not correct, from either the theoretical or the practical standpoint, to say that a mining corporation is not engaged in business, but is merely occupied in converting its capital assets from one form into another. The sale outright of a mining property might be fairly described as a mere conversion of the capital from land into money. But when a company is digging pits, sinking shafts, tunneling, drifting, stoping, drilling, blasting, and hoisting ores, it is employing capital and labor in transmuting a part of the realty into personalty and putting it into marketable form. The very process of mining is, in a sense, equivalent in its results to a manufacturing process. And however the question shall be described, the transaction is indubitably 'business' within the fair meaning of the act."[6]

§ 330. Same; Lessor Corporations

A corporation organized for the purpose of owning and renting an office building, but which had wholly parted with the manage-

---

[4] Emery, Bird, Thayer Realty Co. v. U. S. (D. C.) 198 Fed. 242. And see Wilkes-Barre & W. V. Traction Co. v. Davis (D. C.) 214 Fed. 511.

[5] Traction Cos. v. Collectors of Internal Revenue, 223 Fed. 984, 139 C. C. A. 360.

[6] Stratton's Independence v. Howbert, 231 U. S. 399, 34 Sup. Ct. 136, 58 L. Ed. 285.

ment and control of the property, and by the terms of a reorganization had disqualified itself from any activity in respect to it, its sole authority being to hold the title subject to a lease for 130 years, and to receive and distribute the rentals which might accrue under the terms of the lease, or the proceeds of any sale of the land, if it should be sold, was held not subject to the corporation excise tax laid by the act of 1909, because not "doing business" within the meaning of the law.[7] And so, where a corporation with general business powers amended its articles so as to limit its activities to the mere ownership and rental of certain property occupied and used by its stockholders as a department store, and applied the entire rent, first to the payment of interest on mortgage liens, and then to the payment of dividends to stockholders, it was not "doing business" and not taxable under that act.[8] And generally, a railroad, electric, gas, industrial, or manufacturing corporation, which has leased its property to another similar company, the lessee continuing the operation of the business, and the lessor merely taking such action from time to time as is necessary to continue its corporate existence, and to receive and distribute its rentals, is not doing business so as to render it subject to the tax.[9] And where this situation occurs, it is immaterial that one of the purposes for which the lessor corporation was organized, as stated in its charter, was to "lease" property which it might acquire or construct, if, by such a lease, it puts the property out of its control and thereafter transacts no similar business.[10] And a company is not engaged in business, within the meaning of the law, if, after renting its entire property, it retains a franchise of corporate existence, and is ready to resume possession at the expiration of the lease, and to exercise its franchise of eminent domain when required by the

[7] Zonne v. Minneapolis Syndicate, 220 U. S. 187, 31 Sup. Ct. 361, 55 L. Ed. 428. And see Abrast Realty Co. v. Maxwell (D. C.) 206 Fed. 333; U. S. v. Emery, Bird, Thayer Realty Co., 237 U. S. 38, 35 Sup. Ct. 499, 59 L. Ed. 825.

[8] Maxwell v. Abrast Realty Co., 218 Fed. 457, 134 C. C. A. 255.

[9] McCoach v. Continental Passenger Ry. Co., 233 Fed. 976, 147 C. C. A. 650; New York Mail & Newspaper Transp. Co. v. Anderson, 234 Fed. 590, 148 C. C. A. 356; Miller v. Snake River Valley R. Co., 223 Fed. 946, 139 C. C. A. 426; New York Cent. & H. R. R. Co. v. Gill, 219 Fed. 184, 134 C. C. A. 558; Jasper & E. Ry. Co. v. Walker, 238 Fed. 533, 151 C. C. A. 469; State Line & S. R. Co. v. Davis (D. C.) 228 Fed. 246; Waterbury Gas Light Co. v. Walsh (D. C.) 228 Fed. 54; Public Service Gas Co. v. Herold (D. C.) 227 Fed. 496; Cambria Steel Co. v. McCoach (D. C.) 225 Fed. 278; Public Service Ry. Co. v. Herold (D. C.) 219 Fed. 301.

[10] Public Service Ry. Co. v. Herold, 229 Fed. 902, 144 C. C. A. 184.

lessee.[11] And it has been held that the acquisition of property by the lessor company by purchase and condemnation, pursuant to the request and direction of the lessee, which property was paid for with money furnished by the lessee and was immediately delivered into the possession of the lessee and used by it in operating the business under the terms of the lease, was not such a doing of business as made the lessor liable for the payment of the tax.[12]

But on the other hand, a corporation is engaged in business and liable to the tax where, after leasing all its property, it affirmatively exercises its power for the acquisition of additional franchise rights,[13] or exercises its reserved power to extend its business at the lessee's request,[14] or exercises its corporate powers to increase its estate by the issuance and sale of bonds.[15] And realty corporations organized for and actively engaged in such activities as handling large tracts of land owned by them, leasing and selling parcels thereof, disposing of stumpage, seeing that their lessees under mining leases live up to their contracts, and distributing the proceeds of such activities among their stockholders, are engaged in business within the meaning of the taxing act.[16]

§ 331. Same; Holding Companies

The lower federal courts held that a holding company, which was not engaged in business for itself, but confined its activities to the receipt and distribution of the profits turned over by its subsidiaries, was not subject to the excise tax imposed by the act of 1909, since it was not "carrying on or doing business." [17] But the Treasury Department declares that it has "never acquiesced" in these decisions, and holds that a holding company, organized in the United States for the purpose of acquiring and holding capital stock of subsidiary companies, and actually engaged in holding such stock, voting thereon, receiving dividends thereon, and distributing money among its own shareholders, is engaged in business, within the

[11] McCoach v. Minehill & S. H. R. Co., 228 U. S. 295, 33 Sup. Ct. 419, 57 L. Ed. 842.

[12] Lewellyn v. Pittsburgh, B. & L. E. R. Co., 222 Fed. 177, 137 C. C. A. 617; New York Cent. & H. R. R. Co. v. Gill, 219 Fed. 184, 134 C. C. A. 558.

[13] Public Service Ry. Co. v. Herold (D. C.) 227 Fed. 490.

[14] Public Service Ry. Co. v. Moffett (D. C.) 227 Fed. 494.

[15] Public Service Electric Co. v. Herold (D. C.) 227 Fed. 486.

[16] Von Baumbach v. Sargent Land Co., 242 U. S. 503, 37 Sup. Ct. 201, 61 L. Ed. 460.

[17] U. S. v. Nipissing Mines Co., 206 Fed. 431, 124 C. C. A. 313; Butterick Co. v. U. S. (D. C.) 240 Fed. 539.

meaning of the act of Congress of September 8, 1916, and liable to the special excise tax on capital stock. (T. D. 2429, Jan. 4, 1917.) In a recent case it appeared that a terminal company was organized for the purpose of providing and operating a terminal for certain stated railroads, which were required to use the station to be built, and to which the capital stock of the corporation was issued, said railroads paying for the use of the terminal, which payments were part of the operating expenses of the roads, they being entitled to dividends on their stock in the corporation. The terminal company also granted concessions and licenses to others than the stock-holding railroads for the transaction of various kinds of business, and operated facilities for supplying power, light, and heat manufactured by it. It was held that the terminal company was "organized for profit," within the meaning of the taxing act, and was also engaged in business.[18]

§ 332. Same; Foreign Corporations

Where an English corporation owned timber lands in California and operated a match factory there, but sold such lands to another company, as well as its plant, the foreign company to retain title until paid in full, although it retained an attorney in California to look after its interests and an agent for the service of process, as required by the state statute, it was held that it was not thereafter "doing business" in the state so as to be liable to the corporation excise tax.[19] But on the other hand, where a Canadian corporation, whose business was the making of newspaper print paper, sent agents into the United States to solicit purchasers for its product, paying their expenses, hiring desk room in the United States, empowering the salesmen to make written contracts, in part in the United States, subject to the corporation's approval in Canada, and, when approved, to deliver the contracts, and paying rent and other items of expense by checks drawn on an American bank, where the company kept the funds which it received for goods delivered to American purchasers, and then, to perform its written contracts, shipped paper consigned to itself in the United States to different points, where it hired storage rooms, and had the paper delivered to itself at such rooms, where it stored it in its own name and at its own risk pending delivery and to meet anticipated de-

---

[18] Boston Terminal Co. v. Gill (U. S. Dist. Ct. D. Mass.) —— Fed. ——, T. D. 2428, Dec. 30, 1916.

[19] Bryant & May v. Scott (D. C.) 226 Fed. 875.

mands, it was held that such Canadian company was "doing business" within the United States, so as to be liable to the tax.[20]

§ 333. Returns by Holding Companies and Subsidiaries

Holding companies and subsidiary corporations are both required to file returns and to pay the capital-stock tax, and no deductions are allowed on the return of the holding corporation for the tax paid by a subsidiary. Subsidiary companies may compute the fair value of their capital stock by apportionment of the fair value of the total capital stock of the parent company among the various subsidiaries in proportion to the earnings. (T. D. 2503, June 25, 1917.) Where a holding company owns all the stock of several subsidiary corporations which is not listed on any exchange or which has not been sold in the last fiscal year, it has been held that the fair value of the stock of such subsidiary companies may be estimated from the market value of the total capital stock of the holding company (the parent corporation) by apportionment of the fair value of the total capital stock of the holding corporation among the subsidiary companies. This does not of course relieve the holding company from its liability to the special excise tax, the average fair value of the stock of which can probably be computed under Case I or II. (T. D. 2423, Dec. 30, 1916.)

§ 334. Regulations for Computation of Tax; Domestic Corporations

The tax on companies or associations having a capital stock represented by shares is imposed on the fair average value for the preceding year, and not on the face or par value of the capital stock. The fair value of the capital stock shall be ascertained as follows:

Case I. If the stock is listed on any exchange, its fair value will be determined by adding the quoted highest bid price for the stock on the last business day of each month during the preceding fiscal year (or if no bid price was quoted on the last day, then the latest day in the month on which a bid was quoted), and dividing by 12, the result being the average bid price per share for that year. (Treasury Regulations No. 38, Art. VI, T. D. 2383.) If the stock of the corporation is listed on an exchange or is dealt in on the New York curb, the fair value should be computed under Case I

---

[20] Laurentide Co. v. Durey (D. C.) 231 Fed. 223.

from the highest price bid on the last day of each month, or the last day of the month on which a bid was made. A corporation, if it prefers, may average the fair value throughout the entire fiscal year by showing on a statement attached to the back of the return the highest price paid for the stock on each day throughout the year. (T. D. 2503, June 25, 1917.)

Case II. If the stock is not listed on any exchange, but sales thereof have actually been made, and the price paid for the stock is known to the officer making the return, or can be discovered by him, the average price at which sales were made during the preceding fiscal year shall be the determining factor in ascertaining the fair value per share. In the foregoing two cases the actual fair value of the stock is ascertainable from the facts without the necessity of making an estimate. (Treasury Regulations No. 38, Art. VI, T. D. 2383.) Corporations estimating the value of their stock under Case II, will comply strictly with the regulations by taking the "average price at which sales were made during the preceding fiscal year," and not the average selling price per share. Thus, if 10 shares were sold at $100, and 1,000 shares were sold at $70, the average price at which sales were made would be $85. The average selling price in such a case would be $70.29, but this price will not be accepted as an average fair value. (T. D. 2423, Dec. 30, 1916.) In a case to be computed under Case II, if there have not been a sufficient number of sales of stock to establish a basis for estimating the fair value of the total capital stock, the corporation will be required to fill out Case III. (T. D. 2503, June 25, 1917.) As to both Cases I and II, and as applied to corporations having both preferred and common stock, the Treasury has ruled that the highest prices quoted and the highest sale prices of both kinds of stock should be listed, and these items multiplied by the total number of shares of each kind of stock outstanding on the return date, and added together, which will give the fair value of the total capital stock, both common and preferred, for the preceding fiscal year. (T. D. 2417, Dec. 16, 1916.)

Case III. If neither of the preceding "Cases" is applicable, the fair average value of the capital stock shall be estimated, and the surplus and undivided profits for the preceding fiscal year will be taken into consideration as required by the statute, as well as the nature of the business, its earning capacity, and average dividends paid, or profits earned, during the preceding five years. (Treasury Regulations No. 38, Art. VI, T. D. 2383.) The items of "surplus" and "undivided profits" should be the average sur-

(351)

plus and average undivided profits as shown by the books of the corporation for the preceding fiscal year. But as the fair value of the stock ascertained under this Case is only an estimate, the Internal Revenue office has permitted corporations whose fiscal years ended on December 31, 1915, or any other date, to use the figures shown by the books on that date. Any surplus or undivided profits of a corporation that is invested in bonds or other securities having no connection whatever with the actual business of the corporation should be stated on the return, and will be taken into consideration if the fair value of the stock is estimated under Case III. The "estimated earning capacity" of a corporation should be its prospective earnings for the next following year, and should be expressed in terms of percentage of the par value of the capital stock. The "average dividends paid during preceding five years" may be found by adding together all regular and extra dividends paid during the five years and dividing by 5. (T. D. 2417, Dec. 16, 1916.)

As to the "earning capacity" of the company (an item of the greatest importance in estimating the value of its stock under Case III), it is ruled that this is shown by the average percentage of profits over the five-year period. The Internal Revenue Bureau states that "it has been found upon examination of the returns of net income of a large number of different classes of corporations listed on an exchange that they earn approximately the following rates in order to make their stock worth par." The percentages given are: Banking institutions, if east of the Mississippi River, 6%, but if west of the Mississippi, 8%; railroads, electric railways, and light and power companies, 8%; mercantile companies, mining companies, industrial companies, and oil-refining companies, 10%; and oil-producing companies, 15%. But corporations which have no regular earnings, such as companies organized for the purpose of developing and selling timberland, mining property, and other real property, and corporations that have earned no profits in the past five years, or have only been engaged in business one or two years, cannot very well estimate the value of the stock from their earning capacity. They are therefore permitted to file a detailed statement, attached to the back of the return, showing their assets and liabilities outstanding on June 30, of the designated year, or at the end of their own last fiscal year, and may estimate the fair value of the stock from the book value. (T. D. 2503, June 25, 1917.)

(352)

The "book value" of stock should be estimated in the ordinary way, by adding surplus and undivided profits to par value, and this will be taken as the basis of the approximate value of the stock per share, unless, by reason of earning capacity, the real value is in excess of the book value, or unless for any reason the book value is fictitious and is shown by overestimating the value of assets. If the "average profits per share earned during preceding five years" indicate an "estimated earning capacity" in excess of the book value, the fair value of the capital stock may be based upon a reasonable return on capital invested, dependent on the hazards of the business and what prices the stock of corporations engaged in a similar character of business brings in the open market. If the book value is fictitious, and is shown by overestimating the capital assets, this fact should be fully explained, either on the return or in a statement attached thereto, and may be given allowance in determining the fair value of the stock where the "average profits" and "earning capacity" are exceedingly low. (T. D. 2423, Dec. 30, 1916.)

§ 335. Estimation of Capital, Surplus, and Profits

In computing the value of the capital stock of a corporation for the purpose of this tax, the corporation is not entitled to deduct that amount of its capital which may be invested in United States bonds issued under the act of April 24, 1917, the so-called "Liberty Loan" bonds.[21] Nor are any deductions to be allowed to corporations organized in the United States for capital invested in England, France, or other foreign countries. (T. D. 2417, Dec. 16, 1916.) And domestic insurance companies are not permitted to deduct reserves and deposits maintained or held in the United States for the protection of, or payment to, or apportionment among, policy holders, as such reserves and deposits are reflected in the fair value of the stock as computed under either of the three "Cases" prescribed by the Treasury Department. (T. D. 2503, June 25, 1917.) Where a fund accumulated by a bank was carried on its books under the head of "profit and loss" for a period of years, and was used in the bank's business like its other capital, such fund, it was held, though not technically "surplus," should be regarded as an accretion to capital, and was therefore subject to tax under the act of 1898, taxing bankers on their capital, and

---

[21] Opinion of Attorney General, T. D. 2512, June 8, 1917.

providing that, in estimating capital, "surplus" should be included.[22]

§ 336. Same; Banks and Bankers

The Treasury Department has ruled that the tax due from incorporated companies engaged in the banking business is measured by the total amount of the capital, surplus, and undivided profits used in the business, as shown by their books for the fiscal year preceding the period for which the tax is due. Money borrowed, bills payable, rediscounts, and time certificates of deposit should not be included as a portion of the capital. (T. D. 2125, Jan. 15, 1915.) It was likewise held that the "undivided profits should be figured for each business day, and the average thereof taken as the amount of undivided profits to be used in computing the tax due. In many instances it is clear that such a method would be more or less impracticable and involve too lengthy a calculation in arriving at the basis desired. Therefore, while perhaps the daily average of undivided profits, as set forth above, is the one absolutely accurate method by which to arrive at the amount to be entered into the total of capital, surplus, and undivided profits, this office will accept a return under oath from any banker where the undivided profits are computed in any manner whereby a fair and just amount is arrived at representing the average amount of the undivided profits employed by the bank during the fiscal year for which the tax is due." (T. D. 2064, Nov. 23, 1914.) The individual fair value of stocks of two banks that have a definite combined market value, but no separate value (ownership of each share of stock in one of them carrying automatically a share of stock in the other), may be ascertained by apportionment of this market value on the basis of the capital stock, surplus, and undivided profits of each corporation for the fiscal year. (T. D. 2426, Dec. 29, 1916.)

§ 337. Meaning of "Capital Stock Outstanding"

Capital stock that has once been issued by a corporation is regarded as being "outstanding," even though it is afterwards acquired by the company for value and carried on the books as "treasury stock." (T. D. 2417, Dec. 16, 1916.) If a corporation has increased or decreased its capital stock during the fiscal year, a

---

[22] Leather Manufacturers' Nat. Bank v. Treat, 128 Fed. 262, 62 C. C. A. 644.

statement should be attached to the back of the return setting forth the number of shares of stock outstanding each month, with the average fair value of the stock for that month, computed under one of the three "Cases." (T. D. 2503, June 25, 1917.)

§ 338. Computation of Tax; Foreign Corporations

The tax imposed on corporations, joint-stock companies or associations, and insurance companies, organized for profit under the laws of any foreign country and engaged in business in the United States, shall be computed upon the actual capital invested in the transaction of its business in the United States. The basis of taxation is the average amount of capital so invested during the preceding fiscal year.

The exemption from the amount of capital invested in the United States equal to the proportion of $99,000 which the amount so invested bears to the total amount invested in the transaction of business in the United States or elsewhere, shall only be allowed a company or association which makes return to the Commissioner of Internal Revenue, under these regulations, of the amount of capital invested in the transaction of business outside of the United States. Thus a foreign company or association investing part of its capital in the transaction of business in the United States shall be liable for tax in the amount of 50 cents for each $1,000 of the actual capital invested in the United States, without deduction of the said proportion of $99,000, unless it discloses in its return the amount of capital invested in the transaction of business outside of the United States. (Treasury Regulations No. 38, Art. VI, § 2, T. D. 2383.)

§ 339. Same; Foreign Insurance Companies

"After careful consideration it has been decided that the amount of capital invested in the transaction of business in the United States by foreign insurance companies is the amount of 'surplus to policy holders,' as shown by the conventional form of report to state insurance departments. Foreign insurance companies are permitted to state the amount of surplus to policy holders as shown by the report for the last fiscal year ended December 31, 1916. The only deduction allowed is the amount of deposits actually required by states in which the company is transacting business." (T. D. 2503, June 25, 1917.)

§ 340. Filing Returns; Penalty for Delinquency

The Act of Congress under which this tax is laid (Act Sept. 8, 1916, § 409 [U. S. Comp. St. 1916, § 5980k]) provides that "all administrative or special provisions of law, including the law relating to the assessment of taxes so far as applicable, are hereby extended to and made a part of this title, and every person, firm, company, corporation, or association liable to any tax imposed by this title shall keep such records and render under oath such statements and returns as shall comply with such regulations as the Commissioner of Internal Revenue, with the approval of the Secretary of the Treasury, may from time to time prescribe." As this is a "special" tax, the returns of corporations are required to be made annually in July. The law prescribing a penalty for delinquency in this respect is § 3176 of the Revised Statutes, as amended by the Act of Sept. 8, 1916, which reads as follows: "In case of any failure to make and file a return within the time prescribed by law or by the collector, the Commissioner of Internal Revenue shall add to the tax fifty per centum of its amount, except that, when a return is voluntarily and without notice from the collector filed after such time and it is shown that the failure to file it was due to a reasonable cause and not to willful neglect, no such addition shall be made to the tax. In case a false or fraudulent return is willfully made, the Commissioner of Internal Revenue shall add to the tax one hundred per centum of its amount. The amount so added to any tax shall be collected at the same time and in the same manner and as part of the tax, unless the tax has been paid before the discovery of the neglect, falsity, or fraud, in which case the amount so added shall be collected in the same manner as the tax." The Treasury Department has given notice that the 50 per cent penalty for delinquency in filing returns will be strictly enforced against corporations which fail to file returns of capital-stock tax within the time prescribed by law or by the collector. (T. D. 2503, June 25, 1917.)

§ 341. Form of Return for Domestic Corporations

The return required to be made by corporations, joint-stock companies or associations, or insurance companies, organized in the United States, is to be made on official Form No. 707, and shall set forth the following particulars: (1) Total number of shares of stock now outstanding. (2) Par value of shares. (3) Par value of total capital stock outstanding. (4) Amount of surplus. (5)

Amount of undivided profits. (6) Case I. Average market value per share during preceding fiscal year, if stock is listed on an exchange. Case II. If stock is not listed on an exchange, average market value per share computed from sales made during preceding fiscal year. Case III. If stock is not listed on any exchange and no sales have been made during preceding fiscal year, or if sales have been made and the price is unknown, the fair average value of the stock may be estimated from the following data set forth on the return: Amount of surplus, amount of undivided profits, nature of business, estimated earning capacity, average dividends per share paid during preceding five years, average profits per share earned during preceding five years. (7) Total number of shares of stock outstanding on last day of fiscal year. (8) Fair value of total capital stock for preceding fiscal year. (9) Deduction allowed by law of $99,000. (10) Amount of fair value of stock over $99,000 upon which tax should be computed. (11) Tax at rate of 50 cents per year for each full $1,000. (12) Amount of munitions tax, if any, paid under Title III of Act of September 8, 1916, since making the last previous return. (13) Amount of tax due. (Treasury Regulations No. 38, Art. IV, T. D. 2383.)

§ 342. Form of Return for Foreign Corporations

The return required to be made by foreign corporations, joint-stock companies or associations, or insurance companies, having capital invested in the transaction of their business in the United States, is to be made on the official Form No. 708, and shall set forth the following particulars: (1) Amount of capital invested in the United States. (2) Amount of capital invested in foreign countries. (3) Total amount of capital invested in the corporation, both in the United States and elsewhere. (4) Percentage of capital invested in the United States. (5) Percentage of $99,000 allowed to be deducted under the law. (6) Amount of capital upon which tax should be computed. (7) Tax at the rate of 50 cents per year for each full $1,000. (8) Amount of munitions tax, if any, paid under Title III of the Act of September 8, 1916, since making the last previous return. (9) Amount of tax due. (Treasury Regulations No. 38, T. D. 2383, Art. V.)

§ 343. Payment of Tax; Penalty

A general provision of law applicable to the tax under consideration is that "all special taxes shall become due on the first day of July in each year, or on commencing any trade or business on which such tax is imposed. In the former case the tax shall be reckoned for one year, and in the latter case it shall be reckoned proportionately from the first day of the month in which liability to a special tax commenced to the first day of July following." (Rev. St. § 3237, as superseded by Act Oct. 1, 1890, § 53 [U. S. Comp. St. 1916, § 5960].) The capital stock tax is a "special" tax, because it is specifically so denominated in the act imposing it, and it is payable in advance for a period extending from the date of taking effect of the act to the end of the fiscal year, and annually thereafter in July, the beginning of the government's fiscal year. (T. D. 2423, Dec. 30, 1916.) Upon failure to pay the tax assessed within ten days after notice and demand, a penalty of 5 per cent of the tax unpaid, and interest at the rate of 1 per cent a month until paid, will be added to the amount of the tax. (Treasury Regulations No. 38, art. 7, T. D. 2383.) Collectors may accept payment of the tax when the returns are filed as "advance collections," provided there is no question about the amount of tax due, but corporations are not required to pay the tax until after ten days' notice and demand. (T. D. 2417, Dec. 16, 1916.)

CHAPTER XV

OCCUPATION TAXES

§ 344. Statute Imposing Tax

The Act of Congress of September 8, 1916, § 407 (U. S. Comp. St. 1916, §§ 5980a–5980i), imposes special taxes upon all those who follow certain enumerated avocations. In each case the tax is a fixed sum of money and is to be paid annually. Those subject to the tax are brokers, pawnbrokers, ship brokers, customhouse brokers, proprietors of theaters, museums, and concert halls, proprietors of circuses, proprietors or agents of other public exhibitions or shows for money (not falling within the two preceding classes), and proprietors of bowling alleys and billiard rooms. It has been held that this tax is within the powers of Congress and is constitutionally valid. It is not a direct tax upon property, such as would have to be apportioned under the Constitution, but it is a franchise tax or privilege tax, and is legal and valid as laid.[1]

§ 345. Brokers

The tax upon brokers is $30 per year; and the act provides that "every person, firm, or company whose business it is to negotiate purchases of sales of stocks, bonds, exchange, bullion, coined money, bank notes, promissory notes, or other securities, for others, shall be regarded as a broker." (Act Cong. Sept. 8, 1916, § 407, par. 2.) In the first place, it is to be noticed that the term "brokers," as here defined, is limited to those who negotiate the

---

[1] Anderson v. Farmers' Loan & Trust Co. (C. C. A.) 241 Fed. 322; Real Estate Title Ins. & Trust Co. v. Lederer (D. C.) 229 Fed. 799.

purchase and sale of stocks, bonds, notes, or other securities, or
of exchange, bullion, or coined money. Under the Spanish War
Revenue Act of 1898, and also under the Act of Oct. 22, 1914, a
special tax was imposed upon a class of brokers designated as
"commercial brokers," and they were defined as persons who "negotiate sales or purchases of goods, wares, produce, or merchandise."
Brokers of this kind are not subject to the special tax under the
present statute; but the sale of certain articles on produce exchanges is subject to the stamp tax. In general, however, persons
who receive stocks and bonds for sale for others, and who also purchase and sell stocks and bonds on their own account, and lend and
advance money thereon, are liable to the brokers' tax.[2] So, proprietors of "bucket shops" who issue memoranda of their transactions in stocks, even though they sell only "futures," are taxable as
brokers. (T. D. 2046, Nov. 9, 1914.) Real estate agents engaged
in negotiating, on a commission, sales and purchases of real estate,
collecting rents, etc., do not incur liability as brokers; but if, in
connection with such business, they engage in negotiating the purchase and sale of notes, mortgages, and other securities, they are
liable to the special tax.[3]

In regard to the nature of the securities negotiated or dealt in, it
is held that bills of exchange, bonds for the payment of money,
and promissory notes are in the popular acceptation of the term
"securities" for money.[4] But the term "security dealers" in a
state statute imposing a license tax on persons so designated, does
not include the purchaser of a judgment on a note for less than its
face value.[5] Persons whose practice it is to buy up the fee-bills of
witnesses are not brokers; but an express company engaged in the
business of buying or selling foreign money or bills of exchange is
required to pay the special tax as a broker. (T. D. 2046, Nov. 9,
1914.)

In the next place, it is only when the negotiation or dealing in
stocks, bonds, etc., is the business of the person in question, his
trade, his profession, or his means of getting a livelihood, that he
becomes a broker within the meaning of the law.[6] Thus, if per-

---

[2] Peabody v. Gilbert, 5 Blatchf. 334, Fed. Cas. No. 10,868, note; Clark v.
Gilbert, 5 Blatchf. 330, Fed. Cas. No. 2,822.

[3] Rounds v. Alee, 116 Iowa, 345, 89 N. W. 1098; T. D. 2083, Dec. 8, 1914.

[4] Jennings v. Davis, 31 Conn. 139.

[5] Mace v. Buchanan (Tenn. Ch. App.) 52 S. W. 505.

[6] Warren v. Shook, 91 U. S. 704, 23 L. Ed. 421.

sons negotiate the purchase or sale of promissory notes, but if these are only occasional acts and do not constitute their regular business, they are not brokers. So a lawyer may make investments for his clients without being liable to the tax as a broker, unless he does it to such an extent that it can be called a "business." The purchase of state or municipal orders or warrants by any person does not subject him to the tax as a broker, if not done to an extent constituting it his business. And occasional transactions in the sale of sight drafts do not necessitate the payment of the special tax. Nor is the liability incurred by merchants merely because they cash checks for their customers. (T. D. 2046, Nov. 9, 1914.) For the same reason, the special tax as a broker is not required to be paid by a person because of the fact of his holding a seat on the stock exchange, if he transacts no business directly or indirectly. (T. D. 2046, Nov. 9, 1914.) And loan and mortgage companies are not liable to the tax as brokers on account of their loaning money on notes or bonds secured by mortgage or trust deed on real estate. But they become so liable if they purchase notes, bonds, or other securities, and so also if they engage in the sale of the securities on which they make their loans. (Idem.) And while a mining syndicate or other association issuing certificates of stock in a company organized by it is not required to pay the special tax as a broker therefor, a manager or other person employed by it to sell such certificates on commission is a broker and is required to pay the tax. (Idem.)

Under the Act of 1914, it was originally held by the Treasury Department that a person incurred the special-tax liability as a broker if he negotiated the purchase of stocks and bonds for himself alone. (T. D. 2249.) But this ruling was revoked (T. D. 2263, Nov. 15, 1915), and would be, of course, entirely inconsistent with the words of the present statute. There is, however, a ruling of the Treasury that a person is not to be taxed as a broker unless he negotiates purchases and sales for any and all applicants, and that if he negotiates such sales and purchases exclusively for certain persons or firms with whom he is under contract, he is to be regarded as their agent and not as a broker. (T. D. 2107, Dec. 28, 1914.)

§ 346. Pawnbrokers

The tax upon pawnbrokers is $50 per year. "Every person, firm, or company whose business or occupation it is to take or receive by way of pledge, pawn, or exchange any goods, wares, or merchandise, or any kind of personal property whatever, as security for the repayment of money loaned thereon, shall be deemed a pawnbroker." (Act Cong. Sept. 8, 1916, § 407, par. 3.) A person is not required to pay the special tax as a pawnbroker, because of rare or occasional transactions which cannot be regarded as his business or occupation. And the tax is not required to be paid for the making of loans when the chattels are not taken or received by way of pledge, pawn, or exchange. But a person using no tickets in his business, but making a pretense of buying articles which are brought to him, which he holds under a verbal agreement that the articles can be bought back again by the person selling them, on the payment of a specified bonus, is a pawnbroker and liable to the tax. (T. D. 2046, Nov. 9, 1914.) Under a state statute it has been held that two elements are required to constitute one a pawnbroker: (1) The person must be engaged in the business of receiving property in pledge for money advanced; an occasional loan will not be sufficient, but the person must so engage in the occupation that it will be known as his regular business; (2) he must be engaged in receiving property in pledge or as security for money or other thing advanced to the pawnor or pledgor.[7] But a licensed auctioneer who advances money on goods and charges commissions on such advances, has been held liable to the payment of a tax as a pawnbroker.[8]

§ 347. Ship Brokers

Ship brokers are required to pay an annual tax of $20. "Every person, firm, or company whose business it is as a broker to negotiate freights and other business for the owners of vessels or for the shippers or consignors or consignees of freight carried by vessels, shall be regarded as a ship broker under this section." (Act Cong. Sept. 8, 1916, § 407, par. 4.) In a somewhat wider sense, ship brokers have been defined as brokers who negotiate the purchase and sale of ships and the business of freighting vessels.[9] But it cannot be doubted that the purchase and sale of ships would be regarded as "other business for the owners of vessels" within the meaning of the law.

---

[7] City of Chicago v. Hulbert, 118 Ill. 632, 8 N. E. 812, 59 Am. Rep. 400.

[8] Hunt v. City of Philadelphia, 35 Pa. 277.

[9] City of Little Rock v. Barton, 33 Ark. 436.

§ 348. Customhouse Brokers

The annual tax upon customhouse brokers is $10. And it is provided that "every person, firm, or company whose occupation it is, as the agent of others, to arrange entries and other customhouse papers, or transact business at any port of entry relating to the importation or exportation of goods, wares, or merchandise, shall be regarded as a customhouse broker." (Act Cong. Sept. 8, 1916, § 407, par. 5.) Under this provision the Treasury Department has ruled that "a person or firm holding himself or itself out to the public as engaged in the occupation of a customhouse broker, either by maintaining an office or sending out literature, advertising matter, etc., is required to pay the special tax." (T. D. 2321, April 13, 1916.) Bills of sale of vessels are "customhouse papers" within the meaning of this paragraph, and one whose occupation it is, as the agent of others, to prepare such bills of sale is required to pay the tax as a customhouse broker. (T. D. 2046, Nov. 9, 1914.) Payment of the special tax by a person in his own name as a customhouse broker is sufficient to cover the business done by him at the place of business stated, whether such business is done by him on his own account or as an agent for other persons. (T. D. 2046, Nov. 9, 1914.) But if the complete business of customhouse brokers is transacted by parties at offices at different ports of one internal revenue district, a separate and distinct special tax must be paid for each of their offices. (Idem.)

§ 349. Theaters, Museums, and Concert Halls

The proprietors of these places of amusement, to which a charge for admission is made, are subjected to a special tax proportioned to the seating capacity of the place. The provision is that "proprietors of theaters, museums, and concert halls, having a seating capacity of not more than 250, shall pay $25; having a seating capacity of more than 250 and not exceeding 500, shall pay $50; having a seating capacity exceeding 500 and not exceeding 800, shall pay $75; having a seating capacity of more than 800, shall pay $100. Every edifice used for the purpose of dramatic or operatic or other representations, plays, or performances, for admission to which entrance money is received, not including halls or armories rented or used occasionally for concerts or theatrical representations, shall be regarded as a theater: Provided, that in cities, towns, or villages of 5,000 inhabitants or less, the amount of such payment shall be one-half of that above stated: Provided further, that whenever any such edifice is under lease at the passage of this act, the tax shall be paid by the lessee, unless otherwise stipulated between the parties to said lease." (Act Cong. Sept. 8, 1916, § 407, par. 6.) Where a theater increases its seating capacity during a fiscal year, it must thereupon pay the tax at the higher rate, but may be credited with the amount of the lower tax already paid. (T. D. 2117, Jan. 11, 1915.) And under similar provisions in the act of 1898, it was ruled that where theaters are entirely closed to performances during the months of July and August, and only open in the month of September, the special tax is to be reckoned from the 1st day of September to the first day of July following, at the rate based upon its seating capacity for the year beginning July 1st. (T. D. 2046, Nov. 9, 1914.) Persons are not required to pay the special tax for the mere occasional renting of their hall for public performances to dramatic companies or other persons charging entrance money therefore, but the special tax of $10 (for "other public exhibitions or shows") must be paid by such persons or companies if they give dramatic performances or other such exhibitions for money. (Idem.)

Various other rulings made by the Treasury Department under the similar language of the act of 1914 will be applicable to the present statute, if it is borne in mind that the method of evidencing the payment of the tax on theaters under the earlier statute was by the issuance to the proprietor of a "special-tax stamp," which is not now required. The following was a comprehensive ruling on the subject: "Where the owner of a building pays special tax as proprietor of a theater, covering a theater or auditorium in the building in question, the stamp secured by him will cover all dramatic or operatic or other representations, plays, or performances given in such theater or auditorium produced either by himself or under his proprietorship, or produced by others under lease of the theater or auditorium from the owner thereof. The owner may, upon application to the collector of internal revenue, have the special-tax stamp transferred to any other theater, auditorium, or airdome provided the seating capacity of the theater, auditorium, or airdome is not greater than the seating capacity indicated on the face of the special-tax stamp. Of course, if performances are continued at the building from which the stamp is transferred, a new special-tax stamp must be taken out to cover such building. Where a lessee of a theater pays special tax therefor, the special-tax stamp secured by him, if not transferred to another location, will cover performances given in the theater under the proprietorship of another who subleases the theater from the lessee. However, if the lessee sells out his lease and is no longer connected with the theater in any capacity whatsoever, his special-tax stamp will not cover performances given by the purchaser of the lease. Where two parties pay special tax and operate a theater as a partnership, upon one of the partners selling out his interest or a new partner coming into the partnership, the special-tax stamp secured by the partnership will cover performances given by the succeeding partnership. Where a hall or auditorium is maintained for public entertainment, but operatic or dramatic or other representations, plays, or performances are given therein only occasionally, for example, on an average of not exceeding twice a month, the proprietors of such hall or auditorium do not incur special-tax liability. The owners or agents of theatrical troupes traveling around the country and giving performances in halls or auditoriums for which special taxes have not been paid by the owners or lessees thereof, are required to pay special tax under the sixth subdivision of section 3 of the act aforesaid, and may have their special-tax stamps transferred from place to place upon application to the collector of internal revenue. It will suffice if the owner or agent, upon entering a collection district, files with the collector a statement as to the theaters and towns in which performances are to be given." (T. D. 2297, Feb. 11, 1916.)

§ 350. Motion-Picture Theaters and Air Domes

A theater in which moving pictures are shown is taxable as a "theater" under this provision of the statute, and not under the succeeding general clause as to "other public exhibitions and shows for money." (T. D. 2040, Nov. 3, 1914.) Under the Act of 1914, the Treasury Department at first held that "air domes" were taxable at a flat rate in the character of "other public exhibitions or shows for money," but afterwards reversed this ruling, and decided that they were taxable as "theaters" and therefore at a rate varying according to the seating capacity. Additional rulings were made as follows: "Where such air dome is adjacent to a theater, for which the special tax has been paid, and the seating capacity of the air dome does not exceed the seating capacity of the theater, and performances are not given simultaneously in the air dome and theater, the special-tax stamp secured to cover the theater will cover performances given in the air dome. Where the proprietor of a theater operates an air dome at another location, upon closing his theater he may transfer the special-tax stamp for such theater to the air dome, provided, of course, the seating capacity of the air dome does not exceed the seating capacity of the theater, and the special-tax stamp, issued to cover performances given in an air dome, may be transferred to cover a theater owned by the same party, under the above conditions." (T. D. 2217, June 11, 1915.)

§ 351. Circuses

The special tax is fixed at the rate of $100 per annum on the proprietors of circuses; and "every building, space, tent, or area where feats of horsemanship or acrobatic sports or theatrical performances not otherwise provided for in this section are exhibited, shall be regarded as a circus: Provided that no special tax paid in one state, territory, or the District of Columbia shall exempt exhibitions from the tax in another state, territory, or the District of Columbia, and but one special tax shall be imposed for exhibitions within any one state, territory, or District." (Act Cong. Sept. 8, 1916, § 407, par. 7.) According to the interpretation put upon this provision by the Treasury Department, a circus, when it goes on the road, is required to pay the special tax of $100 for the year, and if it carries any additional attractions, not covered by the general admission, but for which a separate entrance price is charged, such as "side shows" or the like, it is liable to tax at the rate of $10 per annum on each such attraction, these being "other public exhibitions or shows for money not enumerated in this section," within the subsequent clause of the statute. So, traveling carnival companies, if charging one general admission to the grounds, are required to pay a tax at the rate of $10 per annum, but must pay an additional tax at the same rate for each separate attraction for which a separate admission is charged. (T. D. 2183, March 26, 1915.) Exhibitions of feats of horsemanship, such as are seen in circuses, when they occur on race tracks, are subject to the tax of $100; but mere tests of speed of horses in racing are not regarded as "feats of horsemanship," within the meaning of this paragraph. (T. D. 2046, Nov. 9, 1914.) Variety shows, whether given at summer resorts or elsewhere, which include "acrobatic sports," come within the definition of a circus and are taxable as such. (Idem.) But the "theatrical performances" contemplated by this paragraph are only those which are given in connection with a circus. (Idem.) A show under canvas, exhibiting among other things acrobatic and athletic exercises, but no feats of horsemanship and having no menagerie, is not subject to tax as a circus, if the acrobatic exercises are so few and simple as to make it unreasonable to hold that they make the show a circus. (Idem.) And a small wagon show, having no circus feats, but only such acts as trapeze acts, wire walking, trained ponies, singing, and dancing, is not to be regarded as a circus; but it is a "public exhibition or show" within the meaning of the succeeding paragraph of the act, for which the special tax of $10 is to be paid. (Idem.)

§ 352. Other Public Exhibitions and Shows

The provision on this subject is that "proprietors or agents of all other public exhibitions or shows for money not enumerated in this section shall pay $10: Provided, that a special tax paid in one state, territory, or the District of Columbia shall not exempt exhibitions from the tax in another state, territory, or the District of Columbia, and but one special tax shall be required for exhibitions within any one state, territory, or the District of Columbia: Provided further, that this paragraph shall not apply to Chautauquas, lecture lyceums, agricultural or industrial fairs, or exhibitions held under the auspices of religious or charitable associations: Provided further, that an aggregation of entertainments, known as a street fair, shall not pay a larger tax than $100 in any state, territory, or in the District of Columbia." (Act Cong. Sept. 8, 1916, § 407, par. 8.) It has been ruled that wagon shows, dog and pony shows, and other similar exhibitions, which do not come within the definition of circuses given in the preceding paragraph of the act, are taxable at $10 per annum under this paragraph. (T. D. 2183, March 26, 1915.) And the show of a medicine vender, consisting of various athletic, humorous, and comic performances, together with an exhibition of rope walking and trapeze performances, the object being merely to attract a crowd, is liable to the tax of $10, but not to the larger tax as a circus. (T. D. 2046, Nov. 9, 1914.) And a lecturer who uses a stereopticon to illustrate his lecture and charges an admission fee, is liable to the special tax as giving a public exhibition or show for money. (Idem.) But on the other hand, amateur theatrical exhibitions, either in private houses or in licensed public halls, to which admission is charged for the payment of expenses incurred in giving the exhibition, but not for the pecuniary benefit of the performers or the manager, are not such performances as are subject to the tax. And an amateur club or association may charge admission to its performances without becoming liable to the tax, if the proceeds are not for the benefit of the club or its members, but are devoted to some charitable or public object. (T. D. 2046, Nov. 9, 1914.) In addition, the Treasury Department has ruled that the following are not subject to this special tax: Performances of elocutionists; circus performances at county fairs; merry-go-rounds; illustrated lectures given by an educational association; harvest shows; fortune telling; baseball and football games; theatrical entertainments for the benefit of the fire department; band concerts in city parks; piano lecture recitals; university exhibitions.

In respect to the exception in favor of "Chautauquas and lecture lyceums," it is ruled that a so-called "lyceum bureau" which sends out companies of artists, performers, actors, orchestras, quartets, illustrators, imitators, magicians, dramatic and operatic companies, and other entertainers, giving performances in various places, is not exempt under this clause. (T. D. 2448, Feb. 14, 1917.)

In regard to cabarets and similar places, the ruling is that concert gardens where no admission fee is charged, but where beer and other drinks are sold and shows or stage entertainments are given, are within the meaning of this paragraph and must pay the special tax; but that, on the other hand, the tax is not required to be paid by proprietors of restaurants or cafes for merely employing bands of music or orchestras to play during meal hours for the benefit of their patrons, no admission price being charged, and no performance or exhibition being given in connection therewith. (T. D. 2046, Nov. 9, 1914.)

§ 353. Bowling Alleys and Billiard Rooms

"Proprietors of bowling alleys and billiard rooms shall pay $5 for each alley or table. Every building or place where bowls are thrown or where games of billiards or pool are played, except in private homes, shall be regarded as a bowling alley or a billiard room, respectively." (Act Cong. Sept. 8, 1916, § 407, par. 9.) In regard to the exception of "private homes," it is ruled that this term is to be taken in its common or ordinary meaning, as describing an individual or family residence; and the tax is applicable to pool or billiard tables and bowling alleys in clubs, fraternity houses, lodge halls, charitable institutions, Y. M. C. A. buildings, hotels, and boarding houses. (T. D. 2462, Feb. 16, 1917.) But post exchanges, if under complete government control, are not liable to the special tax for operating billiard tables or bowling alleys. (T. D. 2439, Jan. 27, 1917.) So also, billiard and pool tables and bowling alleys are exempt when they are maintained for the use of officers and employés of state and municipal governments, provided that the amusement equipment is actually the property of the state or municipality itself, so that the tax, if laid, would fall upon the public treasury. But if the equipment belongs to and is maintained for the use of a public or quasi-public agency, such as a fire company or militia company, and the method of providing it or maintaining it is such that the tax would fall on the company or institution or on its individual members, then it is not exempt. (T. D. 2462, Feb. 16, 1917.) It is also held that in every building or place where bowls are thrown, each division or track is a separate alley, for which the special tax of $5 must be paid. (T. D. 2046, Nov. 9, 1914.) But tables for the games known as "bagatelle" and "tivoli" are not liable to the tax. (Idem.) A person who is for the time being in the possession and control of a billiard table in a place or building open to the public is prima facie the proprietor of a billiard room and liable to pay the special tax therefor, even if the general property and ultimate control of the table or place, or either of them, be in some one else.[10]

§ 354. Place of Business; Branch Offices

Under Rev. St. U. S., §§ 3234 and 3241 (U. S. Comp. St. 1916, §§ 5957, 5964), a member of a firm who has acquired all the interests of the other members of the firm in the firm assets, and succeeded to the business, may carry it on under a license issued to the firm, at a place other than the old place of business of the firm.[11] It is ruled that the broker's tax is not required to be paid for a branch office where a clerk is employed merely to receive orders and transmit them by wire to the head office. But the tax must be paid for every branch office where the employé in charge not only receives and transmits orders with the money to the main office, but also receives from the main office moneys for disbursement to customers, or keeps accounts with the customers at the branch office, or does other business with relation to the transactions of brokers at such branch office. And so, if the complete business of customhouse brokers is transacted by parties at offices at different ports of one district, a separate and distinct special tax must be paid for each of their offices. (T. D. 2046, Nov. 9, 1914.)

§ 355. Payment and Collection of Tax

The occupation taxes discussed in this chapter are all annual taxes, and each is of a fixed and invariable amount. The statute levying these taxes makes no provision as to the time of their payment, merely stating that they are "imposed annually." But there

[10] U. S. v. Howard, 13 Int. Rev. Rec. 118, Fed. Cas. No. 15,402.
[11] U. S. v. Davis (D. C.) 37 Fed. 468.

BL.FED.TAX.—24

is an applicable provision of general law, as follows: "All special taxes shall become due on the first day of July in each year, or on commencing any trade or business on which such tax is imposed. In the former case the tax shall be reckoned for one year, and in the latter case it shall be reckoned proportionately from the first day of the month in which the liability to a special tax commenced to the first day of July following." (Rev. St. U. S., § 3237, as superseded by Act Oct. 1, 1890, § 53 [U. S. Comp. St. 1916, § 5960].) As to the enforcement and collection of the tax, the statute provides that "all administrative or special provisions of law, including the law relating to the assessment of taxes, so far as applicable, are hereby extended to and made a part of this title, and every person, firm, company, corporation, or association liable to any tax imposed by this title, shall keep such records, and render, under oath, such statements and returns, and shall comply with such regulations, as the Commissioner of Internal Revenue, with the approval of the Secretary of the Treasury, may from time to time prescribe." (Act Cong. Sept. 8, 1916, § 409 [U. S. Comp. St. 1916, § 5980k].)

§ 356. Penalties

The law declares that "every person who carries on any business or occupation for which special taxes are imposed by this title, without having paid the special tax therein provided, shall, besides being liable to the payment of such special tax, be deemed guilty of a misdemeanor, and upon conviction thereof shall pay a fine of not more than $500, or be imprisoned not more than six months, or both, in the discretion of the court." (Act Cong. Sept. 8, 1916, § 408 [U. S. Comp. St. 1916, § 5980j].)

CHAPTER XVI

TAX ON FACILITIES FURNISHED BY PUBLIC UTILITIES AND ON INSURANCE

§ 357. Transportation of Property by Freight or Express

The War Revenue Act of 1917 provides that "from and after the first day of November, 1917, there shall be levied, assessed, collected, and paid (a) a tax equivalent to three per centum of the amount paid for the transportation by rail or water or by any form of mechanical motor power when in competition with carriers by rail or water of property by freight consigned from one point in the United States to another; (b) a tax of 1 cent for each 20 cents, or fraction thereof, paid to any person, corporation, partnership, or association, engaged in the business of transporting parcels or packages by express over regular routes between fixed terminals, for the transportation of any package, parcel, or shipment by express from one point in the United States to another." (Act Cong. Oct. 3, 1917, § 500.)

This is not a new tax in the history of federal legislation. Similar taxes were imposed in 1864 and again in 1898. It was held the words "express business," as used in the act of 1864 imposing a tax on persons engaged in such business, involved the idea of regularity as to route or time or both, so that the phrase would not cover what was done by a person who carried goods solely on call and at special request, and who did not run regular trips or over regular routes.[1] It will be observed that the tax laid by the present stat-

---

[1] Retzer v. Wood, 109 U. S. 185, 3 Sup. Ct. 164, 27 L. Ed. 900.

ute does not fall upon the carrier or his business, but upon the price paid to him for carriage, and only in case he is "engaged in the business" and transports express shipments "over regular routes between fixed terminals." The act of 1898 required receipts or bills of lading to be issued for shipments by freight or express, and the tax was to be paid by means of an adhesive stamp affixed thereto. The Treasury Department ruled that the tax was not applicable to "the movement of household furniture in use as such from one residence to another solely by wagon or similar road vehicle, or of trunks, hand baggage, etc., of a passenger to and from railroad depots, steamship piers, etc., or to the movement of packages and freight under contract covering any period whereby for a lump sum or an amount measured by the number or weight of packages transported, one party contracts to deliver all of the packages, or all of a certain kind of packages, which the other party may have for delivery generally or in a certain neighborhood during the period, or whereby the sole use of certain trucks, lighters, or other similar means of local transportation is obtained for a given space of time. or under contracts or agreements establishing the relationship of employer and employee, rather than that of consignee and carrier, respectively." (T. D. 2197, May 8, 1915.) But street railway companies are subject to the requirements of the law when they accept for transportation goods, parcels, and packages as a part of their regular business. (T. D. 2113, Jan. 5, 1915.) Under former statutes the use of the word "goods," as describing the kind of property for the transportation of which a tax must be paid, created an ambiguity. The Attorney General in 1898 held that, where an express company receives money for transportation, it is to be regarded as "goods," within the meaning of the act of that year. (T. D. 2051, Nov. 9, 1914.) But the present statute applies to the transportation of "property" by freight, and of "any package, parcel, or shipment by express."

§ 358. Transportation of Passengers; Reservations on Parlor and Sleeping Cars, and Vessels

The provision on this subject is that, from and after November 1, 1917, there shall be assessed and collected "a tax equivalent to eight per centum of the amount paid for the transportation of persons by rail or water, or by any form of mechanical motor power on a regularly established line when in competition with carriers by rail or water, from one point in the United States to another or to any point in Canada or Mexico, where the ticket therefor is sold or issued in the United States, not including the amount paid for commutation or season tickets for trips less than thirty miles, or for transportation the fare for which does not exceed 35 cents, and a tax equivalent to ten per centum of the amount paid for seats, berths, and staterooms in parlor cars, sleeping cars, or on vessels. If a mileage book used for such transportation or accommodation has been purchased before this section takes effect, or if cash fare be paid, the tax imposed by this section shall be collected from the person presenting the mileage book, or paying the cash fare, by the conductor or other agent, when presented for such transportation or accommodation, and the amount so collected shall be paid to the United States in such manner and at such times as the Commissioner of Internal Revenue, with the approval of the Secretary of the Treasury, may prescribe; if a ticket (other than a mileage book) is bought and partially used before this section goes into effect, it shall not be taxed, but if bought but not so used before this section takes effect, it shall not be valid for passage until the tax has been paid and such payment evidenced on the ticket in such manner as the Commissioner of Internal Revenue, with the approval of the Secretary of the Treasury, may by regulation prescribe." (Act Cong. Oct. 3, 1917, § 500.) It would appear that these provisions apply to the transportation of passengers by interurban trolley lines, at least in cases where the fare exceeds 35 cents. Under the earlier statute it was ruled that the stamp tax on bills of lading or shipping receipts did not apply to baggage received by railroad companies and carried on the same train with the owner, whether such baggage was the quantity ordinarily allowed by the rules of the railroad or was in excess of such amount. (T. D. 2051, Nov. 9, 1914.) But the ruling under the present statute is that a sum paid for the transportation of excess baggage is to be treated as part of the amount paid for the transportation of persons and therefore is subject to tax at a like rate; but no tax is imposed on an amount paid for the storage of baggage. (T. D. 2570, Nov. 6, 1917.) Additional rulings of the Treasury Department on the construction of this part of the law are as follows: The term "United States," as used in the phrase "from one point in the United States to another," means the states, the territories of Alaska and Hawaii, and the District of Columbia. The phrase "less than 30 miles" means less than 30 constructive miles in instances where two or more carriers are competing for transportation services. "Commutation or season tickets" include all tickets issued to and intended for the use of the purchaser for a certain number of trips between two given termini, whether limited or unlimited as to the time in which they are to be used; but commutation or season tickets do not include party tickets. A mileage book purchased on or after November 1, 1917, is subject to the tax upon the full purchase price at the time of purchase; and where a mileage book purchased prior to that date, is used on or after that date, the person presenting such book, whether the transportation fare to be used is more or less than 35 cents, must pay to the conductor or other agent the tax on such proportionate amount of the cost of the book as the unused mileage bears to the total mileage originally in the book. Where through transportation is paid in full, for example, from New York to Hongkong by way of Vancouver, British Columbia, the railway ticket from New York to Vancouver would be subject to tax under the present section of the law, and the steamship ticket from Vaucouver to Hongkong would be subject to the stamp tax on passage tickets. (Infra, § 395.) Where a corpse is transported under tariffs requiring one first-class ticket therefor and one first-class ticket for an attendant, under the carrier's regulations, the tax is imposed as in the case of passenger transportation on both tickets; where a corpse is transported by freight or express, the amount paid for such transportation would be subject to the tax imposed in the case of freight or express transportation. (T. D. 2570, Nov. 6, 1917.)

§ 359. Transportation of Oil by Pipe Line

The provision of the statute is that, from and after November 1, 1917, there shall be levied, assessed, collected, and paid "a tax equivalent to five per centum of the amount paid for the transportation of oil by pipe line." (Act Cong. Oct. 3, 1917, § 500.) The revenue act of 1898 imposed a tax on companies "owning or controlling any pipe line for transporting oil or other products" on their gross receipts above a certain sum, and it was held to apply only to receipts from the transportation business and to persons or companies engaged in such business; and a company engaged in the business of producing and buying natural gas, which it conveyed by means of pipes to a city, where it distributed and sold the same to consumers, was held not engaged in the business of transportation nor subject to the tax.[2]

---

[2] U. S. v. Northwestern Ohio Natural Gas Co. (C. C.) 141 Fed. 198.

§ 360. Telegraph and Telephone Messages

The act of 1917 imposes "a tax of 5 cents upon each telegraph, telephone, or radio dispatch, message, or conversation, which originates within the United States, and for the transmission of which a charge of 15 cents or more is imposed: Provided, that only one payment of such tax shall be required, notwithstanding the lines or stations of one or more persons, corporations, partnerships, or associations shall be used for the transmission of such dispatch, message, or conversation." (Act Cong. Oct. 3, 1917, § 500.) There was a provision exactly similar to this (except as to the amount of the tax) in the so-called "emergency revenue law" of October 22, 1914, and under it the Treasury Department made the following rulings: "Every company shall include in its report all taxable messages originated by it, without regard to the ownership of toll lines used in transmitting those messages. Telephone companies receiving messages to be retransmitted over the lines of a telegraph company, or telegraph companies receiving messages to be retransmitted over the line of a telephone company, will be regarded as the point where such messages originate. In such cases the company retransmitting such messages will not be required to include the same in its monthly return. Where, however, a message sent over a telephone line is received directly from the sender, the company receiving and transmitting the same will, in such case, be regarded as the point of origin, and will include all such taxable messages in its monthly return. A reversed message will be considered as originating at the point of collection." It was also ruled that messages originating at automatic telephone stations, for each of which a charge of 15 cents or more was made, are subject to the tax. "The method of collecting the tax from the senders of such messages is a matter wholly within the province of the companies receiving and transmitting the messages. All overtime telephone messages, where the additional rate is less than 15 cents, but the total charge, on account of the overtime, brings the charge to 15 cents or more, are subject to tax. Messages transmitted over private leased circuits and relating exclusively to the business for which the circuit was leased are held to be exempt from the tax. Where, however, any such leased circuit is used for the transmission of messages other than above stated, return for all such messages for which a charge of 15 cents or more would ordinarily be made must be rendered monthly by the lessee. Messages of officers and employees of the United States government on official business and like mes-

(375)

sages of state officials are exempted from the tax." (T. D. 2067, Nov. 23, 1914.) It was likewise ruled that the telegrams of foreign diplomatic officers residing in this* country were exempt. (T. D. 2051, Nov. 9, 1914.) The act of 1914 provided that "the messages or dispatches of the officers and employees of any telegraph or telephone company concerning the affairs and service of the company, and like messages or dispatches of the officials and employees of railroad companies sent over the wires on their respective railroads shall be exempt." The act of 1917 contains no such exception, but messages of the kind described will probably be exempt from the fact that the tax is not laid on messages except where "a charge of 15 cents or more is imposed." But it was ruled that telegraph messages of associated steamship lines, or fast freight lines operating over railroads, were not entitled to exemption. (T. D. 2051, Nov. 9, 1914.) The act of 1898 taxed telephone companies 1 cent on each message for which a charge of 15 cents or more was made. It was held that a company is subject to the tax on messages transmitted under contracts with its subscribers by which each pays $90 a year for the right to send not to exceed 600 local messages during the year, since one using the whole of his privilege would in effect pay exactly 15 cents for each message, and if he sent actually less than 600 messages in the year, each would cost more than 15 cents.[8]

§ 361. By Whom Tax is Payable

As to the incidence of the foregoing taxes (freight and express shipments, passenger tickets and reservations on Pullman cars and vessels, transportation of oil, and telegraph and telephone messages) the provision of the statute is that "the taxes imposed shall be paid by the person, corporation, partnership, or association paying for the services or facilities rendered." And as to the transportation of goods, "in case the carrier does not, because of its ownership of the commodity transported, or for any other reason, receive the amount which as a carrier it would otherwise charge, such carrier shall pay a tax equivalent to the tax which would be imposed upon the transportation of such commodity if the carrier received payment for such transportation: Provided, that in case of a carrier which on May 1st, 1917, had no rates or tariffs on file with the proper federal or state authority, the tax shall be computed on the basis of the rates or tariffs of other carriers for like services as ascertained and determined by the Com-

[8] New York Telephone Co. v. Treat, 130 Fed. 340, 64 C. C. A. 586.

missioner of Internal Revenue." (Act Cong. Oct. 3, 1917, § 501.) The proviso of the preceding section of the act should also be noted, to the effect that "nothing herein contained shall be construed to require the carrier collecting such tax to list separately in any bill of lading, freight receipt, or other similar document, the amount of the tax herein levied, if the total amount of the freight and tax be therein stated." Under former statutes taxing express and freight shipments, the carrier was required to issue a receipt or bill of lading and to affix thereto a revenue stamp evidencing the amount of the tax. Carriers generally required the shipper to pay for the stamp, or increased their rates to an extent sufficient to cover its cost, and the courts held that there was nothing in the statutes or in the general policy of the law to prevent this, provided the increased rates were not unreasonable,[4] and that an order made by a state railroad commission requiring express companies to pay the tax, without passing the burden of it to the shipper, was without jurisdiction and void.[5]

§ 362. What Transactions Exempt from Taxation

As to the transportation of freight and express, the law provides that "nothing in this or the preceding section shall be construed as imposing a tax upon the transportation of any commodity which is necessary for the use of the carrier in the conduct of its business as such and is intended to be so used or has been so used, or upon the transportation of company material transported by one carrier, which constitutes a part of a railroad system, for another carrier which is also a part of the same system." (Act Cong. Oct. 3, 1917, § 501.) And as to all the taxes imposed by this part of the act (including also the transportation of persons and telegraph and telephone messages) the provision is that "no tax shall be imposed upon any payment received for services rendered to the United States or any state, territory, or the District of Columbia. The right to exemption under this section shall be evidenced in such manner as the Commissioner of Internal Revenue, with the approval of the Secretary of the Treasury, may by regulation prescribe." (Act Cong. Oct. 3, 1917, § 502.)

---

[4] Crawford v. Hubbell, 177 U. S. 419, 20 Sup. Ct. 701, 44 L. Ed. 829; Trammell v. Dinsmore, 102 Fed. 794, 42 C. C. A. 623; Crawford v. Hubbell (C. C.) 89 Fed. 961; People v. Wells, Fargo & Co., 135 Cal. 503, 64 Pac. 702, 67 Pac. 895.

[5] Dinsmore v. Southern Express Co. (C. C.) 92 Fed. 714.

§ 363. Exemption of Government and State Business and Transportation

Relative to the exemption specified in the last clause of the preceding section, the Treasury Department has ruled as follows: "All shipments either by freight or express, the charges on which are paid by the United States, will be free of the tax. Shipments of government property by government officers will be made on government bills of lading. Shipments of property belonging to a state, territory, or the District of Columbia, the charges on which are paid by the state, territory, or the District of Columbia, will be made free of the tax. It will be necessary in all cases of shipments made by freight or express, where government bills of lading are not used, for the officer or employee of the United States, state, territory, or District of Columbia to satisfy the agent to whom the charges are paid that the service rendered or to be rendered is for the United States, state, territory, or District of Columbia, as the case may be, and the agent collecting the charges should note on the records of his office the name of the consignor and consignee, and indicate thereon that such shipment covered service rendered the United States, state, territory, or District of Columbia, as the case may be, and was not subject to the tax. Shipments by freight or express of property received by the United States or any state, territory, or the District of Columbia are free of the tax, provided the United States, or any state, territory, or the District of Columbia is liable for and pays the transportation charges on such shipments."

"When officers or employees of the United States, or of any state, territory, or the District of Columbia, travel on transportation requests, the transportation requests will be sufficient evidence that the tickets obtained thereon, either for transportation by rail or water, or for seats, berths, or staterooms in parlor cars, sleeping cars, or on vessels, were received from the agent without the payment of the tax. The agent of the transportation company who issues the ticket should note on the records of his office the number of the government transportation request. When travel is made by officers or employees of a state, territory, or the District of Columbia, upon transportation requests, a notation should be made on the records of the agent issuing the ticket so that a verification can be made as in case of government transportation requests." "When an officer or employee of the United States, or of a state, territory, or the District of Columbia, is traveling on official business and pays cash for his transportation or presents a mileage book purchased prior to November 1, 1917, he will give to the agent from whom tickets are obtained for transportation by rail or water, or for seats, berths, or staterooms in parlor cars, sleeping cars, or on vessels, or to the conductor or agent to whom he presents the mileage book, his cetificate stating that the service to be rendered from the place named to the place named is on account of official business and not for private purposes. Transportation agents should not accept such certificates unless the officer or employee presenting same shows satisfactory credentials. In case a ticket, obtained either on a transportation request or by purchase, and not partially used prior to November 1, 1917, is presented for travel on official business on or after November 1, 1917, a certificate made in the form indicated above should be given to the conductor to whom such ticket is first presented."

"All telegraph, telephone, or radio messages of officers and employees of the United States, or of a state, territory, or the District of Columbia, on official business, are exempt from tax, and should not be reported in the monthly return of the telegraph, telephone, or radio company. In case of a telegraph or radio message, the officer or employee sending such message should certify thereon that it is on account of official business and not for private purposes." (T. D. 2551, Oct. 22, 1917.)

§ 364. Collection of Tax and Monthly Returns

The statute provides that "each person, corporation, partnership, or association receiving any payments referred to in section 500 [namely, the section which imposes the tax on freight and express shipments, on the transportation of passengers and on reservations in parlor cars and ships, on the transportation of oil by pipe line, and on telegraph and telephone and radio messages] shall collect the amount of the tax, if any, imposed by such section from the person, corporation, partnership, or association making such payments, and shall make monthly returns under oath, in duplicate, and pay the taxes so collected and the taxes imposed upon it under paragraph two of section 501 [that is, the tax on the transportation of commodities carried free, because the carrier owns the commodity or for any other reason] to the collector of internal revenue of the district in which the principal office or place of business is located. Such returns shall contain such information, and be made in such manner as the Commissioner of Internal Revenue, with the approval of the Secretary of the Treasury, may by regulation prescribe." (Act Cong. Oct. 3, 1917, § 503.)

As similar taxes under former. statutes were generally paid by means of revenue stamps, regulations for the collection of the tax, and for returns, were not prescribed, except in the case of telegraph and telephone companies. As to these, the Treasury Department made the following rulings: "A company shall make one report and one return for the company as a whole, and not for each of its exchanges and toll stations separately; such report and return shall be made to the collector of internal revenue of the district in which the company's principal office is located. Reports and returns may be made by a company for its fiscal month or billing period, to be filed within 30 days after expiration of the fiscal month, provided full return is made for the period during which the tax is to be collected. Additions may be made any month for errors on the previous month's reports and returns. Reductions covering items reported in excess in previous months not allowable. In such cases amended returns may be filed before assessment is made, otherwise, claim for abatement or refund, as the case may be, should be filed." (T. D. 2067, Nov. 23, 1914.)

§ 365. Tax on Insurance Policies

The act provides that "from and after the first day of November, 1917, there shall be levied, assessed, collected, and paid the following taxes on the issuance of insurance policies:

(a) Life insurance: A tax equivalent to 8 cents on each $100 or fractional part thereof of the amount for which any life is insured under any policy of insurance, or other instrument, by whatever name the same is called: Provided, that on all policies for life insurance only by which a life is insured not in excess of $500, issued on the industrial or weekly payment plan of insurance, the tax shall be forty per centum of the amount of the first weekly premium: Provided further, that policies of reinsurance shall be exempt from the tax imposed by this subdivision;

(b) Marine, inland, and fire insurance: A tax equivalent to 1 cent on each dollar or fractional part thereof of the premium charged under each policy of insurance or other instrument by whatever name the same is called whereby insurance is made or renewed upon property of any description (including rents or profits), whether against peril by sea or inland waters, or by fire or lightning, or other peril: Provided, that policies of reinsurance shall be exempt from the tax imposed by this subdivision;

(c) Casualty insurance: A tax equivalent to 1 cent on each dollar or fractional part thereof of the premium charged under each policy of insurance or obligation of the nature of idemnity for loss, damage, or liability (except bonds taxable under subdivision two of Schedule A of Title VIII) [this relates to the stamp tax on bonds] issued or executed or renewed by any person, corporation, partnership, or association transacting the business of employers' liability, workmen's compensation, accident, health, tornado, plate glass, steam boiler, elevator, burglary, automatic sprinkler, automobile, or other branch of insurance (except life insurance, and insurance described and taxed in the preceding subdivision): Provided, that policies of reinsurance shall be exempt from the tax imposed by this subdivision;

(d) Policies issued by any person, corporation, partnership, or association, whose income is exempt from taxation under Title I of the act entitled 'An act to increase the revenue, and for other purposes,' approved September 8th, 1916, shall be exempt from the taxes imposed by this section." (Act Cong. Oct. 3, 1917, § 504.)

§ 366. What Policies Exempt

The policies of insurance specifically exempted from the present tax, by the provision quoted in the preceding paragraph, are those issued by companies or associations which are exempted from taxation on their incomes by the act of Sept. 8, 1916. In so far as these exempted companies or associations could be engaged in the business of insurance, they are of two classes only: First, "fraternal beneficiary societies, orders, or associations, operating under the lodge system or for the exclusive benefit of the members of a fraternity itself operating under the lodge system, and providing for the payment of life, sick, accident, or other benefits to the members of such society, order, or association or their dependents;" and second, "farmers' or other mutual hail, cyclone, or fire insurance companies, the income of which consists solely of assessments, dues, and fees collected from members for the sole purpose of meeting their expenses." It has been ruled that the exemption of policies of "mutual fire insurance companies" does not apply to policies issued by companies, otherwise mutual or co-operative, which actually obtain a profit either from premiums received from non-members or from the investment of their funds. (T. D. 2195, April 23, 1915.) But where the state law requires such companies to carry a certain amount of reserve, and directs the manner in which such reserve funds shall be invested, the policies of the company are not taken out of the exemption because of the profit which it derives from such investment of reserve funds, nor are they taken out of

the exemption because the company deposits and carries a sum of
money in a bank as a working cash balance, though the deposit
bears interest. (T. D. 2114, Jan. 5, 1915.)

§ 367. Decisions and Rulings on Taxation of Insurance

A stamp tax on policies of insurance, in so far as it imposes such
a tax on policies of marine insurance which are necessary incidents
of the business of exporting, and themselves constitute exports by
virtue of their being sent with other documents to foreign ports, is
unconstitutional, under Article I, § 9 of the Constitution, which declares that "no tax or duty shall be laid on articles exported from
any state." [6] But where a general marine policy is issued covering
successive shipments, the assured submitting to the underwriter a
declaration showing the cargo and its value when on board, on
which the underwriter issues a certificate "to cover," which the
assured sent to the consignee abroad with the other papers, such
insurance and custom of business do not constitute "exports," or
a necessary incident to the business of exporting, within the meaning of the Constitution.[7] Policies of insurance issued by foreign
companies will be subject to the tax, when written by brokers
or agents in the United States and even, it seems, when prepared
and issued in a foreign country, but delivered in the United States
and covering property in this country. (T. D. 2286, Jan. 22, 1916.)
And it has been ruled that policies of marine insurance, when issued by foreign companies having no established agencies in the
United States, are nevertheless subject to the tax when obtained
by or through insurance brokers residing in this country. (T. D.
2051, Nov. 9, 1914.) A certificate of title or search, carrying with
it a guaranty of title and assuming liability for any loss incurred
through a flaw in the title, is held by the Treasury Department to
be in the nature of an insurance, and subject to taxation for that
portion of the premium which is charged for its guaranty provision. (T. D. 2087, Dec. 11, 1914.) Under the act of 1914, which
required the tax on policies of insurance to be paid by means of
revenue stamps, some difficulty was experienced in determining the
mode of collecting the tax in the case of continuous policies and
of "open" policies, the latter being those in which the value of the
property is not fixed in advance, but is left to be ascertained at the

---

[6] Thames & Mersey Marine Ins. Co. v. U. S. (D. C.) 217 Fed. 683. And see
U. S. v. Hvoslef, 237 U. S. 1, 35 Sup. Ct. 459, 59 L. Ed. 813, Ann. Cas. 1916A,
286.

[7] Thames & Mersey Marine Ins. Co. v. U. S. (D. C.) 217 Fed. 685.

time of a loss, or in which the extent of the property insured is not determined by the policy, but other items may be added from time to time. But the Treasury Department ruled, in the case of continuous policies, that the tax accrued in proportion to the amount of the premium due and payable when issued, and that stamps should be affixed upon receipts covering the payment of subsequent payments or assessments. (T. D. 2119, Jan. 11, 1915.) And in the case of open policies, an arrangement was made by which companies might pay the tax on the monthly totals of premiums charged and collected. (T. D. 2106, Dec. 29, 1914.)

The present statute does not specifically direct that the tax on insurance policies shall be paid by the assured. But under the substantially similar provisions of the act of 1914, the Treasury Department ruled that if an insurance company insists that the assured shall pay the amount of the tax, "it is not a matter which the internal revenue laws can deal with. It is a matter between the insurance company and the policy holder." (T. D. 2068, Nov. 26, 1914.)

§ 368. Returns and Payment of Tax on Insurance

It is provided "that every person, corporation, partnership, or association issuing policies of insurance upon the issuance of which a tax is imposed by section 504, shall, within the first fifteen days of each month, make a return under oath, in duplicate, and pay such tax to the collector of internal revenue of the district in which the principal office or place of business of such person, corporation, partnership, or association is located. Such returns shall contain such information and be made in such manner as the Commissioner of Internal Revenue, with the approval of the Secretary of the Treasury, may by regulation prescribe." (Act Cong. Oct. 3, 1917, § 505.)

§ 369. Administrative and General Provisions; Penalties

The act of Congress of October 3, 1917, contains certain general or administrative provisions which are applicable to all the taxes considered in this chapter. In the first place, "all administrative, special, or stamp provisions of law, including the law relating to the assessment of taxes, so far as applicable, are hereby extended to and made a part of this act, and every person, corporation, partnership, or association liable to any tax imposed by this act, or for the collection thereof, shall keep such records, and render under oath such statements and returns, and shall comply with such regulations as the Commissioner of Internal Revenue, with the approval of the Secretary of the Treasury, may from time to time prescribe." (§ 1001.) It is likewise provided that in all cases where the method of collecting a tax imposed by the act is not prescribed, the method of its collection may be determined by the Commissioner of Internal Revenue, and that if he determines or prescribes that any particular tax shall be paid by means of stamps, all the administrative and penalty provisions of that portion of the act which relates to the stamp tax shall be applicable. (§ 1003.) The general penalty provision of the act, which applies to the several taxes considered in this chapter (since no specific penalties are prescribed with reference to them) is as follows: "That whoever fails to make any return required by this act or the regulations made under authority thereof within the time prescribed, or who makes any false or fraudulent return, and whoever evades or attempts to evade any tax imposed by this act, or fails to collect or truly to account for and pay over any such tax, shall be subject to a penalty of not more than $1,000, or to imprisonment for not more than one year, or both, at the discretion of the court, and in addition thereto a penalty of double the tax evaded, or not collected, or accounted for and paid over, to be assessed and collected in the same manner as taxes are assessed and collected, in any case in which the punishment is not otherwise specifically provided." (§ 1004.)

(384)

CHAPTER XVII

STAMP TAXES

§ 370. Statutory Provisions Levying Stamp Tax

It is provided by the act of 1917 that "on and after the first day of December, nineteen hundred and seventeen, there shall be levied, collected, and paid, for and in respect of the several bonds, debentures, or certificates of stock and of indebtedness, and other documents, instruments, matters, and things mentioned and described in Schedule A of this title, or for or in respect of the vellum, parchment, or paper upon which such instruments, matters, or things. or any of them, are written or printed, by any person, corporation, partnership, or association who makes, signs, issues, sells, removes, consigns, or ships the same, or for whose use or benefit the same are made, signed, issued, sold, removed, consigned, or shipped, the several taxes specified in such schedule." (Act Cong. Oct. 3, 1917, § 800.)

§ 371. Constitutionality of Tax

A federal stamp tax on such transactions as the sale and transfer of corporate stock is not unconstitutional as a direct tax on property, which must be apportioned among the states, but it falls within the class of "duties, imposts, and excises" which are required to be uniform throughout the United States.[1] Thus, the provision of the statute imposing a tax on each sale or agreement to sell merchandise or products on a produce exchange, and requiring the delivery of a bill or memorandum of each such sale, to be stamped in an amount equal to the tax on the sale, is not a direct tax, but is in the nature of a duty or excise tax for the privilege of doing business at such a place, graduated according to the use. and it satisfies the constitutional requirement of uniformity and is valid.[2] But it was held that the stamp tax imposed under the act of 1898 on charter parties, in its application to those which were exclusively for the carriage of cargo from state ports to foreign ports, violated the provision of the Constitution that no tax or duty shall be laid on articles exported from any state.[3]

§ 372. Time of Incidence of Tax

Where a transaction which would be subject to the stamp tax. or the written evidence of it, is completed before the day appointed for the tax to take effect, it is not subject to the tax, though operative in the future. On the other hand, though a transaction or the evidence of it may have had its inception before such appointed day, it is subject to the tax if completed afterwards. The Treas-

[1] Thomas v. U. S., 192 U. S. 363, 24 Sup. Ct. 305, 48 L. Ed. 481. And see same case below, U. S. v. Thomas (C. C.) 115 Fed. 207, for an illuminating discussion of the whole subject.

[2] Nicol v. Ames, 173 U. S. 509, 19 Sup. Ct. 522, 43 L. Ed. 786, affirming (C. C.) 89 Fed. 144.

[3] U. S. v. Hvoslef, 237 U. S. 1, 35 Sup. Ct. 459, 59 L. Ed. 813, Ann. Cas. 1916A, 286.

ury Department ruled, under earlier stamp tax acts, that bonds executed and delivered prior to the inception of the act, whether taking effect immediately or subsequent to the enforcement of the taxing act, are not subject to the tax. (T. D. 2072, Nov. 28, 1914.) But deeds executed and delivered after the date when the act becomes effective, conveying property in pursuance of a contract made prior to that time, are taxable. (T. D. 2279, Jan. 7, 1916.) So a deed delivered after the day of taking effect of the act must be stamped, though made and executed before. (T. D. 2042, Oct. 31, 1914.) And a deed executed and delivered prior to the taking effect of the act is yet subject to the stamp tax when it is offered for registration after that date, in states where, by the local law, registration is necessary to pass the title. (T. D. 2051, Nov. 9, 1914.) So, where a power of attorney to transfer a certificate of stock is dated prior to the taking effect of the act, but the name of the transferee is filled in, and the stock presented for transfer, after that date, both the power of attorney and the certificate must be stamped. (T. D. 2051, Nov. 9, 1914.)

§ 373. Bonds of Indebtedness

The provision of the statute as to instruments of this kind is as follows: "Bonds, debentures, or certificates of indebtedness issued on and after the first day of December, 1917, by any person, corporation, partnership, or association, on each $100 of face value or fraction thereof, 5 cents: provided, that every renewal of the foregoing shall be taxed as a new issue: Provided further, that when a bond conditioned for the repayment or payment of money is given in a penal sum greater than the debt secured, the tax shall be based upon the amount secured." (Act Cong. Oct. 3, 1917, Schedule A, par. 1.)

Under a similar provision in an earlier statute, it was ruled that "gold coupon notes" issued in a series by a corporation under the terms and conditions of an indenture of trust were taxable as "bonds, debentures, or certificates of indebtedness," and not as promissory notes. (T. D. 2257, Oct. 30, 1915.) The stamp tax act of 1914 did not contain the proviso found in the present act, that "every renewal" of a bond, etc., "shall be taxed as a new issue;" but it was ruled that if a new bond was executed under an agreement for renewal or extension, it must be stamped. (T. D. 2165, March 3, 1915.) Under that statute it was held that a stamp was required on the bond accompanying a mortgage. (T. D. 2060, Nov. 20, 1914.) This is perhaps doubtful under the present act, in view of the proviso in the paragraph relating to the tax on conveyances, that "nothing contained in this paragraph shall be so construed as to impose a tax upon any instrument or writing given to secure a debt." By the ordinary rules of construction, however, the effect of this proviso should be restricted to the specific instruments mentioned in the same paragraph, namely, deeds and other instruments transferring the title to realty, and on this construction, an instrument transferring the title to land not absolutely but as security for a debt (that is, a mortgage or deed of trust) would be exempt from the stamp tax, while the bond which evidences the debt secured would be taxable as a bond. Where a pledge of real estate is effected by giving a deed absolute in form and taking back a "bond to reconvey," the bond is subject to the stamp tax. (T. D. 2051, Nov. 9, 1914.) And bonds issued by individuals, accompanying mortgages on property, which contain, in addition to the promise to pay a sum of money at a stated time, penal conditions and provisions, default in any one of which would render forfeitable the mortgagor's right to the property (such as the bond executed by a shareholder in a building and loan association given in connection with a mortgage to secure a loan of money on real estate) are taxable as bonds, and not as promissory notes. (T. D. 2165, March 3, 1915.)

§ 374. Indemnity, Surety, and Other Bonds

As distinguished from bonds of indebtedness, considered in the preceding section, the stamp tax is laid on "bonds for indemnifying any person, corporation, partnership, or corporation who shall have become bound or engaged as surety, and all bonds for the due execution or performance of any contract, obligation, or requirement, or the duties of any office or position, and to account for money received by virtue thereof, and all other bonds of any description, except such as may be required in legal proceedings, not otherwise provided for in this schedule, 50 cents: Provided, that where a premium is charged for the execution of such bond the tax shall be paid at the rate of one per centum on each dollar or fractional part thereof of the premium charged: Provided further, that policies of reinsurance shall be exempt from the tax imposed by this subdivision." (Act Cong. Oct. 3, 1917, Schedule A, par. 2.)

Under a similar provision in the stamp tax act of 1914, the Treasury Department ruled that every bond and obligation in the nature thereof, without regard to form, sealed or unsealed, with or without sureties, made by any individual, firm, or corporation to indemnify any person, corporation, or other entity for loss, damage, or liability, or for the doing or not doing of anything therein specified, and all undertakings, proposals, or agreements of every character offering indemnity or guaranteeing validity to any person or thing, are subject to the 50 cent tax, except where a premium is charged for the execution of the bond, in which case the tax, and the only tax, is at the rate of one per cent of the premium charged. (T. D. 2072, Nov. 28, 1914.) Thus, an indemnity bond given by a corporation to secure payment of interest, insurance, and taxes, or for the performance of some duty, such as that of a receiver, is taxable at the rate of 50 cents, except where a premium is paid for it and the tax is measured by the amount of the premium. (T. D. 2277, Jan. 7, 1916.) A mere agreement to build a house is not taxable, but if a bond is included for the faithful performance of the work or of the contract, it is subject to the tax as a bond. (T. D. 2051, Nov. 9, 1914.) Bonds issued by guaranty companies in Canada, guarantying the fidelity of employees of individuals or corporations in the United States, if executed and delivered in Canada, are not taxable; but if they are not valid until countersigned or delivered by an agent in the United States, they should be stamped. (T. D. 2051, Nov. 9, 1914.)

On the other hand, bonds given by officers of a state or municipality for the faithful performance of their duties, and any bonds given to states or municipalities for the performance of contracts for governmental purposes, such as the construction of public buildings, or otherwise for the protection of the state or municipality in any respect, are held free from federal taxation on the broad ground that states and political subdivisions thereof are constitutionally exempt from any taxation on the part of the federal government. (T. D. 2111, Dec. 28, 1914.) And the Treasury Department ruled that this provision as to the stamp tax on bonds did not include "such documents as applications addressed to surety and fidelity companies wherein the applicant agrees to indemnify the company in case of loss under the bond applied for, agreements executed by shippers undertaking to hold railroads harmless on account of any loss occurring by reason of the payment of claims against such railroads without the presentation of original bills of lading, etc., agreements executed by depositors of banks and institutions of a similar character agreeing to hold such institutions harmless on account of the payment to depositors of sums covered by pass books or checks and drafts, etc., which have been lost, and other papers of similar character and scope which, not under seal and without sureties, impose upon those executing them no liability other than that which would be automatically imposed upon them by operation of law." (T. D. 2133, Jan. 18, 1915.)

§ 375. Bonds Given in Legal Proceedings

It was firmly held by various state courts that bonds required and given in various forms of legal proceedings (such as appeal bonds, bonds to release attachments, and the like) were not subject to the stamp tax imposed by earlier acts of Congress.[4] And this was also the view of the Treasury Department, which ruled that the stamp tax act did not apply to bonds given by court officers under the direction or authority of the court, or bonds given in cases of appeal, or bonds given by executors, administrators, guardians, and receivers (T. D. 2091, Dec. 14, 1914), nor to a bond filed by order of court to obtain a decree or order for the sale of real estate (T. D. 2051, Nov. 9, 1914), nor to bonds given in connection with seizures of goods for violation of the internal revenue laws, that is, by the person whose goods are seized to take the case into court or for the release of the goods preliminary to suit. (T. D. 2328, April 29, 1916.) And it will be observed that the present stamp tax act (in Schedule A, par. 2) expressly excepts bonds "such as may be required in legal proceedings."

§ 376. Original Issue of Capital Stock

The statute imposes a stamp tax as follows: "On each original issue, whether on organization or reorganization, of certificates of stock by any association, company, or corporation, on each $100 of face value or fraction thereof, 5 cents: Provided, that where capital stock is issued without face value, the tax shall be 5 cents per share, unless the actual value is in excess of $100 per share, in which case the tax shall be 5 cents on each $100 of actual value or fraction thereof. The stamps representing the tax imposed by this paragraph shall be attached to the stock books and not to the certificates issued." Under a similar provision in an earlier statute, the Bureau of Internal Revenue ruled that, where a company issues and sells its bonds, which are convertible at the option of the holder into stock of the company, if the certificates of stock are actually issued and then held in trust for the purchasers of bonds, to be exchanged on their demand, the transaction whereby an ex-

---

[4] Violet v. Heath, 26 Ind. 178; Depuy v. Schuyler, 45 Ill. 306; Derbes v. Romero, 28 La. Ann. 644; Sampson v. Barnard, 98 Mass. 359; Bowers v. Beck, 2 Nev. 139; McGovern v. Hoesback, 53 Pa. 176.

change of bonds for stock is effected is a "transfer" and taxable as such, and not an original issue; but if the certificates of stock are not actually issued until an owner of bonds applies for an exchange, that is an "issue" of the stock and not a transfer. (T. D. 2155, Feb. 16, 1915.) It was also ruled that a new certificate of stock issued to the holder in lieu of the original certificate, the stock remaining in his ownership, does not require a stamp (T. D. 2051, Nov. 9, 1914), and that preferred stock issued in lieu of common stock is not taxable where there is no change of ownership. (T. D. 2051, Nov. 9, 1914.) Where one owns a number of shares of stock represented by one certificate, and sells part of it to another, and thereupon the certificate is "split" by the company, and two new certificates issued, one to the purchaser and the other to the seller, the latter representing what remains of his stock, the certificate to the purchaser is to be stamped, but not that to the original holder. (T. D. 2051, Nov. 9, 1914.)

§ 377. Sales and Transfers of Capital Stock

The statute imposes a stamp tax of 2 cents on each $100 of face value or fraction thereof, "on all sales, or agreements to sell, or memoranda of sales or deliveries of, or transfers of legal title to, shares or certificates of stock in any association, company, or corporation, whether made upon or shown by the books of the association, company, or corporation, or by any assignment in blank, or by any delivery, or by any paper or agreement or memorandum or other evidence of transfer or sale, whether entitling the holder in any manner to the benefit of such stock or not." And it is provided that "where such shares of stock are without par value, the tax shall be two cents on the transfer or sale or agreement to sell on each share, unless the actual value thereof is in excess of $100 per share, in which case the tax shall be 2 cents on each $100 of actual value or fraction thereof."

There is in this provision no distinction between the stock of foreign and domestic corporations. Certificates of stock of a foreign corporation, when sold or delivered within the United States, are subject to the same tax as certificates of stock of any domestic corporation. (T. D. 2073, Nov. 23, 1914.) It was ruled under former laws that transfers of stock of building and loan associations were not subject to the stamp tax. (T. D. 2112, Dec. 31, 1914.) But this is probably not so under the present act. For although, by an earlier section, "stocks and bonds issued by cooperative building and loan associations" are declared to be exempt, this appears to apply only to the original issues of such stocks, and not to their subsequent transfer. It has been judicially decided that a "call" for stock, which contains an absolute promise to sell the stock at any time within a limited number of days at a certain price, though it may be a unilateral contract, is an "agreement to sell" within the provisions of the stamp tax act.[5] It should also be noted that transfers of stock from parties occupying fiduciary relationships, to those for whom they hold the stock in trust, are transfers subject to taxation. (T. D. 2051, Nov. 9, 1914.) Where one certificate represents several shares, the tax of 2 cents on each $100 or fraction thereof is to be reckoned on the face value of the certificate, and not on the face value of each separate share (T. D. 2051, Nov. 9, 1914), which makes an important difference where the par value of the share is less than $100.

§ 378. Same; Pledge or Loan of Stock

The act further provides: "It is not intended by this title to impose a tax upon an agreement evidencing a deposit of stock certificates as collateral security for money loaned thereon, which stock certificates are not actually sold, nor upon such stock certificates so deposited." (Act Cong. Oct. 3, 1917, Schedule A, par. 4.) On a similar principle, it has been ruled by the Treasury Department that where one merely lends certificates of stock to another, to enable him to fulfill a contract for delivery of such stock to a purchaser, and afterwards the borrower discharges his obligation to the lender by returning to him similar certificates for an equal amount of the same stock, neither transaction is subject to the stamp tax. (T. D. 2182, March 26, 1915.)

§ 379. Same; Transactions Between Broker and Customer

The same paragraph of the statute provides further that "the tax shall not be imposed upon deliveries or transfers to a broker for sale, nor upon deliveries or transfers by a broker to a customer for whom and upon whose order he has purchased same, but such deliveries or transfers shall be accompanied by a certificate setting forth the facts." (Act Cong. Oct. 3, 1917, Schedule A, par. 4.) Under an earlier act it was ruled that, where a certificate of stock assigned in blank is merely handed to a broker for the purpose of a sale, this is not a taxable transfer of it, although technically the title to the certificate might be regarded as passing temporarily to the broker. But if the certificate is actually transferred to the name

---

[5] Treat v. White, 181 U. S. 264, 21 Sup. Ct. 611, 45 L. Ed. 853.

of the broker, and the transfer is registered on the books of the company, it is taxable, even though the transfer is made merely for the purpose of a sale. (T. D. 2248, Sept. 28, 1915.) Where brokers acting in behalf of their principals buy stock and receive stamped bills of sale in their own names, they may transfer such stock on the books of the company to the names of their principals without additional stamp tax. (T. D. 2051, Nov. 9, 1914.) No tax is imposed by this section on the closing of a stock transaction caused by the margin being exhausted because of the market going against the speculator. (T. D. 2051, Nov. 9, 1914.) In a case in the federal court, it appeared that a stockbroker, by his course of business, entered into agreements with his customers to buy or sell stocks at a fixed price for future delivery. Each of such agreements was evidenced by a written memorandum properly stamped in accordance with the law. These transactions were purely speculative, conducted on margins, and no actual delivery of stocks was contemplated by the parties, but settlement was made by the payment of differences and the surrender of the written memoranda. It was held that such settlements did not involve agreements for a resale of the stocks, so as to require new memoranda to be made and stamped. And it was remarked that the courts have no authority to infer such agreements, contrary to the fact, for the purpose of extending the provisions of the statute to transactions not within its terms.[6]

§ 380.   Same; Transactions with Agents and Correspondents

In cases where a stockbroker executes orders which are sent in by agents or correspondents, the latter dealing directly with the customers, the rule as to the imposition of the stamp tax is not so clear. In one of the principal cases it appeared that the plaintiff corporation was engaged in business as a stockbroker, and that its business was transacted with numerous correspondents, on whose telegraphic orders it would report a purchase or sale, and forward the correspondent a memorandum of each purchase or sale, such as is required by the statute. The correspondents were also dealing with customers, and their orders to the plaintiff generally represented orders from their own customers, to whom they delivered a memorandum of each purchase or sale, bearing a stamp as required by the act, but stating the transaction between the correspondent and the customer only. The customer was not known or named in the transaction between the correspondent and the plaintiff. It

[6] McClain v. Fleshman, 106 Fed. 880, 46 C. C. A. 15.

was held that such transactions were transactions between principals, separate and distinct from those between the correspondents and their customers, and that the plaintiff was subject to the tax on each memorandum given thereon.[7] In another case it was held that a bucket shop which made contracts for the purchase and sale of stocks with its customers, and executed the same through pretended purchases and sales through another bucket shop, having no relation with such customers, the contract between them expressly providing that the first was not an agent of the second, was conducting a separate business, and the transactions of both concerns were subject to the stamp tax.[8] But on the other hand, in a more recent case, where plaintiff accepted purchases and sales of stocks on margins obtained from customers by various correspondents, and a stamp tax was paid on the memorandum given to the customer, it was held that the plaintiff was not bound to pay a second tax on a memorandum between it and the correspondent.[9]

§ 381. Same; Where Stamp is to be Affixed

The provision of the law in this regard is as follows: "In case of sale where the evidence of transfer is shown only by the books of the company, the stamp shall be placed upon such books; and where the change of ownership is by transfer of the certificate, the stamp shall be placed upon the certificate; and in cases of an agreement to sell, or where the transfer is by delivery of the certificate assigned in blank, there shall be made and delivered by the seller to the buyer a bill or memorandum of such sale, to which the stamp shall be affixed; and every bill or memorandum of sale or agreement to sell before-mentioned shall show the date thereof, the name of the seller, the amount of the sale, and the matter or thing to which it refers." (Act Cong. Oct. 3, 1917, Schedule A, par. 4.) Upon this it is to be remarked that, according to previous rulings of the Treasury Department, where the change of ownership is evidenced by indorsement of the certificate, the stamp should be affixed upon the certificate so indorsed, and not upon the new certificate issued by the corporation to the purchaser. (T. D. 2275, Dec. 30, 1915.) And where stock is transferred for which no certificate has been issued, and the evidence of transfer is shown only

---

[7] Municipal Telegraph & Stock Co. v. Ward (C. C.) 133 Fed. 70, affirmed 138 Fed. 1006, 70 C. C. A. 284.

[8] Eldridge v. Ward, 174 Fed. 402, 98 C. C. A. 619, affirming 155 Fed. 253.

[9] Metropolitan Stock Exchange v. Gill, 199 Fed. 545, 118 C. C. A. 19.

by the books of the company, the stamp should be placed upon such books. (T. D. 2051, Nov. 9, 1914.)

§ 382. Sales on Produce Exchange

A stamp tax is imposed "upon each sale, agreement of sale, or agreement to sell, including so-called transferred or scratch sales, any products or merchandise at any exchange, or board of trade, or other similar place, for future delivery, for each $100 in value of the merchandise covered by said sale or agreement of sale or agreement to sell, 2 cents, and for each additional $100 or fractional part thereof in excess of $100, 2 cents: Provided, that on every sale or agreement of sale or agreement to sell as aforesaid, there shall be made and delivered by the seller to the buyer a bill, memorandum, agreement, or other evidence of such sale, agreement of sale, or agreement to sell, to which there shall be affixed a lawful stamp or stamps in value equal to the amount of the tax on such sale. And every such bill, memorandum, or other evidence of sale or agreement to sell shall show the date thereof, the name of the seller, the amount of the sale, and the matter or thing to which it refers. No bill, memorandum, agreement or other evidence of such sale, or agreement of sale, or agreement to sell, in case of cash sales of products or merchandise for immediate or prompt delivery which in good faith are actually intended to be delivered shall be subject to this tax." (Act Cong. Oct. 3, 1917, Schedule A, par. 5.)

Under similar provisions in earlier statutes, the Treasury Department has ruled that, to constitute an "exchange or board of trade or other similar place," so as to subject the evidence of a sale made there to the tax, there must be more than one person, company, or partnership authorized to negotiate sales thereat; that sales of live stock at stock yards come within the law; and that sales of grain made at an exchange, and sales of grain made by brokers in their own offices, are taxable. (T. D. 2051, Nov. 9, 1914.) There is also a decision that offers to sell grain subject to deferred acceptance are taxable on the basis of the total price for which the seller agrees to sell, not on the basis of the amount the broker is to receive.[10]

§ 383. Same; Transfers to Clearing House

This section of the act of Congress also provides that "sellers of commodities described herein, having paid the tax provided by this subdivision, may transfer such contracts to a clearing house corpo-

[10] Calkins v. Smietanka (D. C.) 240 Fed. 138.

ration or association, and such transfer shall not be deemed to be a sale, or agreement of sale, or an agreement to sell within the provisions of this act, provided that such transfer shall not vest any beneficial interest in such clearing house association, but shall be made for the sole purpose of enabling such clearing house association to adjust and balance the accounts of the members of said clearing house association on their several contracts." (Act Cong. Oct. 3, 1917, Schedule A, par. 5.)

§ 384. Promissory Notes and Similar Instruments

The stamp tax is imposed on "drafts or checks payable otherwise than at sight or on demand, promissory notes, except bank notes issued for circulation, and for each renewal of the same, for a sum not exceeding $100, 2 cents, and for each additional $100 or fractional part thereof, 2 cents." (Act Cong. Oct. 3, 1917, Schedule A, par. 6.)

Promissory notes under seal are taxable the same os other promissory notes, and not as bonds. (T. D. 2051, Nov. 9, 1914.) And a written agreement signed by four persons jointly and severally promising to pay to a fifth person the sums set opposite their names, requires but a single stamp.[11] No stamp is required upon the transfer by indorsement of a promissory note. (T. D. 2051, Nov. 9, 1914.) Treasury notes issued by a foreign government, and placed for sale in this country through bankers or brokers, are not subject to the stamp tax as promissory notes. (T. D. 2180, March 26, 1915.) A promissory note drawn in a foreign country and placed in the mails in that country for delivery to a person residing in the United States is not taxable. For delivery of commercial paper is necessary for its completion, and such an instrument is delivered when placed in the mails, so that the laws of the foreign country would determine the validity of the contract, even if the instrument is made payable in the United States. On the other hand, a promissory note drawn in the United States and placed in the mails for delivery to a person residing in a foreign country, is taxable. (T. D. 2170, March 4, 1915.) Coupons or interest notes attached to and forming part of a bond or principal note are not subject to tax as promissory notes, even though they are in the form of such notes. (T. D. 2101, Dec. 24, 1914.)

In regard to instruments of an ambiguous or unusual character, it is well to remember the statement of the Supreme Court that "the liability of an instrument to a stamp duty, as well as the

11 Ballard v. Burnside, 49 Barb. (N. Y.) 102.

amount of such duty, is determined by the form and face of the instrument, and cannot be affected by proof of facts outside of the instrument itself." [12]　It has been held that a receipt for money loaned, importing an obligation to repay it, requires a stamp.[13] A receipt given by a loan company for property received as security for a debt is not a promissory note; but if the receipt includes a promise to pay a certain sum of money at a specified time, with interest, this makes it a promissory note, on which the maker could be sued at law, and therefore it is taxable. (T. D. 2170, March 4, 1915.)　In regard to the taxability of contracts for the purchase of pianos, machinery, or other merchandise, in which, among other conditions and provisions, there is included an agreement to pay the vendor a stipulated sum of money at a stated time, with interest, for value received, it is held by the Treasury Department that if this agreement is in form and effect a good and valid promissory note, upon which the maker would be liable in a suit at law, it is taxable as a promissory note under the act.　But if the contract merely provides for the payment of the purchase price in installments and enumerates the dates upon which such payments are due, stating that in default of payment the vendor may take the property, such an agreement is not a promissory note. (T. D. 2170, March 4, 1915.)

§ 385.　Same; Loans by Insurance Companies on their Policies

An important ruling by the Treasury Department under an earlier stamp-tax act was as follows: "It appears that it is the practice (in some cases required by law) for life insurance companies to make loans to persons insured therein on the security of their policies, and that while the agreements evidencing such loans are usually in the form of conventional promissory notes, they contain other provisions entirely inconsistent with the general character and functions of promissory notes and negotiable paper generally. Such agreements commonly provide that the remedy of the company, in case the loan or interest thereon be not paid when due, is to be that the amount thereof shall be deducted from the dividends due the insured on his policy, or, in some cases, that the policy shall be canceled and a paid-up policy then issued in lieu of the canceled policy in an amount to be expressed in proportion to the sum due the company on the unpaid loan and interest.　Such

[12] United States v. Isham, 17 Wall. 496, 21 L. Ed. 728.
[13] Hoops v. Atkins, 41 Ga. 109.

agreements, in the opinion of this office, are not promissory notes within the usual conception of the term or within the intent and purpose of the Act of October 22, 1914 [imposing stamp taxes], they giving to the lenders not a right to collect a sum certain and at all events, but merely a right to set off against an asset of, or a debt owing to, the insured (unpaid dividends or paid-up value of the policy) a debt owed by the assured to the company. Such agreements, this office holds, therefore, are not subject to tax as promissory notes under the act in question." (T. D. 2097, Dec. 19, 1914.)

§ 386. Same; Note with Warrant of Attorney

A provision in a note authorizing any attorney at law to appear for the maker and confess judgment against him in favor of the holder in any court, does not make it necessary to stamp the instrument as a power of attorney in addition to its taxability as a promissory note.[14]

§ 387. Same; Renewals and Extensions

A contract or agreement extending either a chattel mortgage or a mortgage of real estate is not taxable; but if such extension effects the renewal of promissory notes, either embodied in the mortgage or given in connection with it, the renewal of such notes is taxable. (T. D. 2170, March 4, 1915.) "Part payment of a note after it has become due, or payment of accrued interest after maturity, the note being allowed to run, and the holder neither losing nor postponing his right of action, is merely in the nature of a forbearance, and is not taxable as a renewal." (T. D. 2265, Nov. 22, 1915.) Where notes secured by a deed of trust are used as collateral, the deed of trust and the notes are required to be stamped, not on the basis of their face value, but on the amount for which they are pledged (that is to say, the memorandum of their pledge must be so stamped.) This pledge of notes and deed of trust does not require to be stamped again because of renewals of the notes held as collateral, if the pledge itself is not renewed. (T. D. 2051, Nov. 9, 1914.)

§ 388. Drafts, Checks, and Orders for Money

There is at present no stamp tax on ordinary drafts or on checks on banks, if they are payable at sight or on demand, as is common with such instruments. The Treasury Department ruled

14 Treat v. Tolman, 113 Fed. 892, 51 C. C. A. 522; T. D. 2081, Dec. 8, 1914.

under former laws that drafts, acceptances, overdrafts, and post-dated checks were not taxable as promissory notes, even though used in such a way as to perform some of the functions of notes. (T. D. 2170, March 4, 1915.) ·But a post-dated check would certainly be subject to the present tax, since it is "payable otherwise than at sight or on demand." In a case where a debtor placed a note due to him in the hands of defendant, a creditor, to receive the amount and take out his indebtedness, and afterwards wrote to the plaintiff, another creditor, that he should receive his debt from the proceeds of the note after defendant was paid, and the plaintiff, by direction of the debtor, showed the letter to the defendant, who promised to pay the money when received, it was held that the letter was not an order or promise to pay money or a note or an assignment, and therefore was not an instrument requiring a revenue stamp.[15] But in another case, it appeared that a mercantile company, by an arrangement with a cotton-mill company, sold goods to the employees of the latter, which paid the accounts therefor on presentation from wages due the employees. The mercantile company required each purchaser to sign an order on the mill company for the amount of his purchase, which orders, however, were not presented, but were filed and kept as vouchers by the mercantile company, which guarantied the correctness of the accounts which it presented. It was held that such orders were "orders for the payment of money" within the meaning of the revenue law and required to be stamped.[16]

§ 389. · Deeds and Other Conveyances

The stamp tax is laid upon every "deed, instrument, or writing, whereby any lands, tenements, or other realty sold shall be granted, assigned, transferred, or otherwise conveyed to, or vested in, the purchaser or purchasers, or any other person or persons, by his, her, or their direction, when the consideration or value of the interest or property conveyed, exclusive of the value of any lien or encumbrance remaining thereon at the time of sale, exceeds $100 and does not exceed $500, 50 cents; and for each additional $500 or fractional part thereof, 50 cents: Provided, that nothing contained in this paragraph shall be so construed as to impose a tax upon any instrument or writing given to secure a debt." (Act Cong. Oct. 3, 1917, Schedule A, par. 7.)

[15] Boyd v. Hood, 57 Pa. 98.
[16] Granby Mercantile Co. v. Webster (C. C.) 98 Fed. 604.

Under exactly similar language in earlier tax laws, it was ruled that a contract for the sale of real estate, which passes no title, but provides for the issuance of a deed at some future date upon the fulfillment of certain conditions, is not subject to the tax if executed by the owner of the land; and that, for similar reasons, deeds in escrow do not become subject to the tax until the final delivery is made. (T. D. 2115, Jan. 4, 1915.) A quitclaim deed given for no consideration, or for the nominal consideration of $1, for the purpose of correcting a flaw in the title, is not subject to the tax; nor a partition deed which is operative in defining boundary lines or in showing by location the interest of each tenant in common; nor deeds to burial sites, which do not convey title to land, but only a right to sepulture, to erect monuments, etc.; nor a deed executed by a debtor covering an assignment of property to a trustee to be held for the benefit of a creditor, though, if the trustee sells or conveys such property, either to the creditor or a third person, the deed executed by him is taxable. (T. D. 2115, Jan. 4, 1915.) So, deeds that are simply confirmatory, and do not vest a title not already vested, are exempt from the tax; and releases of mortgages and deeds of trust operating as mortgages are not subject to the tax, no matter in what form they are executed. (T. D. 2051, Nov. 9, 1914.) Oil leases, leases of mining property, long-term mining leases, etc., which in themselves convey no title to or interest in real property, are exempt from the tax. (T. D. 2115, Jan. 4, 1915.) But a ground-rent deed is taxable as a conveyance and not as a lease. (T. D. 2051, Nov. 9, 1914.) Deeds of conveyance executed by and between tenants in common are not taxable, but deeds of conveyance between joint tenants are subject to the tax. (T. D. 2051, Nov. 9, 1914.) And in the case of an exchange of two properties, the deeds transferring title to each are subject to the tax, which should in each case be computed on the basis of the actual value of the interest or property conveyed, the amount of any lien or encumbrance being deducted. (T. D. 2115, Jan. 4, 1915.) A deed transferring title to property to a building and loan association for the purpose of securing a loan on the property so conveyed, which property is immediately reconveyed to its owner, is not subject to the tax, nor is the deed of reconveyance. (T. D. 2115, Jan. 4, 1915.) The conveyance of a mine, though located on unpatented land (that is, on the public domain) is subject to the stamp tax. (T. D. 2051, Nov. 9, 1914.) But a deed of conveyance of real estate situated in a country that is not United States territory is not taxable, though both the grantor and grantee are citizens and residents of the United States. (T. D. 2051, Nov. 9, 1914.)

§ 390. Same; Deeds of Sheriffs and Court Officers

The fact that land is sold on execution or under decree of foreclosure, and that the deed is consequently executed by the sheriff, master in chancery, or other officer making the sale, does not exempt the conveyance from the stamp tax. Making the deed is not a judicial function, and the title to the land sold is merely conveyed to the purchaser at a judicial sale through the officer, instead of the defendant himself making the deed.[17] The purchaser at a judicial sale is entitled to a deed which will be a defense to his title in any tribunal in which it may be attacked, and hence he can compel the referee or other officer to affix thereto the proper revenue stamps.[18] And the fact that a conveyance is made by a master commissioner under a decree of foreclosure in which the priority of liens is considered and settled, and after competitive sale, does not affect the requirement that the instrument, being a "conveyance of realty," shall bear the proper documentary stamps.[19]

§ 391. Same; Consideration or Value as Measure of Tax

Since the stamp tax falls upon conveyances only "when the consideration or value of the interest or property conveyed" exceeds a certain amount, conveyances of realty to trustees or other persons without a valuable consideration are not taxable. (T. D. 2051, Nov. 9, 1914.) So, where a husband and wife make a deed to a third person, who immediately reconveys the property to the wife, no actual consideration passing in either case, neither deed requires a stamp; and a deed issued to cover a gift from husband to wife, or from parent to child, stating the consideration as "natural love and affection and $1," or a deed of land presented as a gift to a municipality, in which the consideration is stated to be the grantor's "desire to promote the public welfare," is not taxable. (T. D. 2115, Jan. 4, 1915.) But merely stating a nominal consideration in the deed will not save it from the necessity of being stamped if an actual consideration passed; but in that case the tax must be measured by the actual value of the interest or property conveyed.

[17] Crawford v. New South Farm & Home Co. (D. C.) 231 Fed. 999.
[18] Loring v. Chase, 26 Misc. Rep. 318, 56 N. Y. Supp. 312.
[19] Farmers' L. & T. Co. v. Council Bluffs Gas & Electric Light Co. (C. C.) 90 Fed. 806.

(T. D. 2115, Jan. 4, 1915.) Stock in a corporation is a valuable consideration for the transfer of real property, and a deed conveying land to a corporation for such a consideration is taxable in proportion to the value of the property conveyed. (T. D. 2278, Jan. 7, 1916.) It has been ruled, however, that where half the purchase price is paid in cash and a promissory note given for the balance, the tax on the deed is to be computed on the basis of the cash received, and the note is taxable under the provision of the statute relating to promissory notes. (T. D. 2115, Jan. 4, 1915.) The stamp tax on a deed of real property made by a sheriff or referee to the mortgagee, who bids in the property at the foreclosure sale to satisfy the mortgage lien, should be computed on the amount bid for the property, plus the costs, if paid by the purchaser. (T. D. 2159, Feb. 19, 1915.)

When property is conveyed subject to incumbrances, the tax is to be computed on the value of the interest transferred, that is, on the value of the equity of redemption or the value of the property over and above the incumbrances, not on its entire value.[20] But there is some difficulty in determining the amount of the tax where a mortgage or other lien is given back simultaneously with the deed. The statute allows the deduction of "any lien or incumbrance remaining thereon at the time of sale." And the Treasury Department has made the following ruling: "Where the purchaser receives a deed conveying the entire title to himself, even though it be received under a specific agreement that a mortgage or lien thereon will immediately ensue, unless such mortgage or lien is evidenced in the deed, as showing that its execution was a part of, or consideration in, the original sale and transfer of title, the tax to be imposed upon the deed should be computed on the entire amount of consideration given, or the value of the interest or property conveyed, and the note or notes will be subject to the tax imposed upon such instruments under the provisions of the act. In short, unless the mortgage given by a purchaser of real property, at the time of purchase, is specifically evidenced in the instrument of conveyance, the only incumbrances which may be deducted from the amount of actual consideration given, or the actual value of the interest or property conveyed, in computing the amount of tax to be imposed upon the deed, are those which rested upon the property at the time of its purchase." (T. D. 2123, Jan. 11, 1915.)

[20] Central Trust Co. v. Columbus, H. V. & T. Ry. Co. (C. C.) 92 Fed. 919.

§ 392. Parcel-Post Packages

The statute imposes "upon every parcel or package transported from one point in the United States to another by parcel post, on which the postage amounts to 25 cents or more, a tax of 1 cent for each 25 cents or fractional part thereof charged for such transportation, to be paid by the consignor. No such parcel or package shall be transported until a stamp or stamps representing the tax due shall have been affixed thereto." (Act Cong. Oct. 3, 1917, Schedule A, par. 14.)

§ 393. Custom-House Entry

The stamp tax is imposed on each "entry of any goods, wares, or merchandise at any custom-house, either for consumption or warehousing, not exceeding $100 in value, 25 cents; exceeding $100 and not exceeding $500 in value, 50 cents; exceeding $500 in value, $1." (Act Cong. Oct. 3, 1917, Schedule A, par. 8.)

§ 394. Withdrawal from Bonded Warehouse

A stamp tax of 50 cents is imposed upon each "entry for the withdrawal of any goods or merchandise from customs bonded warehouse." It is ruled that where a warehouse entry is duly stamped, and the goods covered thereby are transferred under rewarehouse entries to one or more bonded warehouses, the goods remaining continuously under the jurisdiction and control of the government, no additional stamp tax is required on such rewarehouse entries. (T. D. 35,688, Customs, Sept. 1, 1915.)

§ 395. Passage Tickets

The stamp tax is imposed on every "passage ticket, one way or round trip, for each passenger, sold or issued in the United States, for passage by any vessel to a port or place not in the United States, Canada, or Mexico, if costing not exceeding $30, $1; costing more than $30 and not exceeding $60, $3; costing more than $60, $5; Provided, that such passenger tickets, costing $10 or less, shall be exempt from taxation." It is ruled that this tax applies, if the ticket is sold in the United States, whether or not the vessel sails from an American port. It is the duty of the person selling the ticket to affix and cancel the stamp to the ticket or paper which evidences the sale, namely, the coupon or order, at the time the same is sold. Where a single ticket is issued for transportation of more than one passenger, the ticket, coupon, or order must be stamped at the proper rate for each passenger, based upon the num-

ber of passengers and the total amount paid for the transportation. (T. D. 2067, Nov. 23, 1914.) But a stamp is not required
on passage tickets issued to members of foreign embassies or lega-
tions, or to members of their households, or to consuls of foreign
countries. Nor is it required on tickets issued to government employees when traveling on official business or under conditions
which involve reimbursement by the government of their traveling
expenses; though such employees, when traveling at their own
expense, will be required to pay the tax on such tickets. (T. D.
2189, April 19, 1915.)

§ 396. Proxies

The statute (Act Cong. Oct. 3, 1917, Schedule A, par. 11) imposes
a stamp tax on each "proxy for voting at any election for officers,
or meeting for the transaction of business, of any incorporated
company or association, except religious, educational, charitable,
fraternal, or literary societies, or public cemeteries, 10 cents." The
stamp may be affixed and canceled either by the party who executes
the proxy or by the party to whom the proxy is given. (T. D. 2129,
Jan. 19, 1915.) And where proxies are sent out by corporations to
be executed and returned to the corporation or to the person named
in the instrument, such proxies may be stamped after execution
and delivery by the person receiving the same as the agent of the
person executing the proxy. (T. D. 2067, Nov. 23, 1914.) A ten-
cent stamp is required for each signature on such a proxy, if executed by several persons jointly. (T. D. 2129, Jan. 19, 1915.) It
is also ruled that directors of a corporation are "officers" within the
meaning of the act. (T. D. 2129, Jan. 19, 1915.) A power of attorney or proxy executed by a person residing in a foreign country to a person residing in this country, to vote at the election of
officers of a corporation, is taxable, since the instrument is not
operative and effective until accepted by the person in this country to whom it is issued. But such proxies issued by persons in
the United States, authorizing persons in foreign countries to vote
at corporate elections, are not taxable. (T. D. 2129, Jan. 19,
1915.)

§ 397. Powers of Attorney

The stamp tax is upon any "power of attorney granting authority to do or perform some act for or in behalf of the grantor, which
authority is not otherwise vested in the grantee, 25 cents; Provided, that no stamps shall be required upon any papers necessary to

be used for the collection of claims from the United States or from any state for pensions, back pay, bounty, or for property lost in the military or naval service, or upon powers of attorney required in bankruptcy cases." (Act Cong. Oct. 3, 1917, Schedule A, par. 12.) Under similar provisions in other acts, the Treasury Department has made numerous rulings. Thus, an assignment, for a valuable consideration, of debts, mortgages, bonds, wages, etc., ordinarily transfers to the assignee all the rights of the assignor and the remedies necessary for their enforcement, and it is held that the assignee acquires no further rights under a power-of-attorney clause in the assignment than are conveyed by the instrument itself, so that such a pro forma power of attorney is not taxable. (T. D. 2134, Jan. 23, 1915.) So, a power of sale embodied in a mortgage or deed of trust differs from a power of attorney in many respects, one of which is that the latter always creates an agency or a representative relation, whereas a mortgagee under a power of sale acts on his own behalf and for his own benefit; and hence such a power of sale is not taxable as a power of attorney. (T. D. 2196, May 3, 1915.) So the pro forma power of attorney to transfer stock on the books of the corporation, which is embodied in the assignment printed on the back of the certificate is not subject to the stamp tax. (T. D. 2085, Dec. 9, 1914.) And the appointment by a depositor of a deputy to have access to a safe-deposit box is not a power of attorney. (T. D. 2134, Jan. 23, 1915.) So a power of attorney given under a state statute which authorizes payment of a person's poll tax to be made for him by another "duly authorized by him in writing" is not subject to the tax. (T. D. 2269, Dec. 9, 1915.) A certified copy of a power of attorney, such as is required to be filed in some of the executive departments of the government by various insurance and bonding companies, is not taxable. (T. D. 2134, Jan. 23, 1915.) But the tax is on the power of attorney, not the act to be done under it or the subject to which it relates. Hence a power of attorney to sell and transfer government bonds is taxable. (T. D. 2051, Nov. 9, 1914.) But a power of attorney requires only one 25-cent stamp, though it contains a power of substitution. (T. D. 2134, Jan. 23, 1915.)

It has also been ruled that where a corporation, by resolution of its board of directors, empowers an officer thereof to sell, assign, or transfer stock or bonds standing in the name of the corporation, or to perform any act in the name of the corporation, such authority is not taxable as a power of attorney, for the reason that it is necessary for a corporation to perform its corporate acts through one of its officers. But if a person other than an officer of the corporation acting in his official capacity is given this authority, the the power of attorney so granted will require the stamp. And a general power of attorney granted by the board of directors to a person not an officer of the corporation, for the purpose of representing the corporation in transactions of a like kind and nature, such as conveying land or acknowledging deeds, is considered as specific authority for each individual transaction, and a revenue stamp is required on each instrument containing the power of attorney. (T. D. 2134, Jan. 23, 1915.)

The tax on a power of attorney is due when the instrument is executed and is made valid by acceptance, and not when the power is exercised. For this reason, a power of attorney executed by a person residing in a foreign country to a person in this country is taxable, as the instrument is not operative until accepted by the attorney in fact; and for the same reason, a power of attorney executed by a person residing in this country to a person in a foreign country is not taxable. (T. D. 2134, Jan. 23, 1915.)

The exception in the statute as to powers of attorney required in bankruptcy cases was probably inserted in view of certain decisions in the federal courts that such powers, authorizing one to appear for a creditor in bankruptcy proceedings, cast his vote, accept compositions, receive payment of dividends, and the like, were subject to the law and must be stamped.[21]

§ 398. Playing Cards

The provision of the statute is for a levy "upon every pack of playing cards containing not more than fifty-four cards, manufactured or imported, and sold, or removed for consumption or sale, after the passage of this act, a tax of five cents per pack, in addition to the tax imposed under existing law." (Act Cong. Oct. 3, 1917, Schedule A, par. 13.) The tax imposed by existing law is 2 cents per pack, without regard to price or value. This provision, it is ruled, requires that each pack of cards shall show a stamp denoting the payment of the tax, so that a dealer may not reassemble cards from packs that have paid the tax, and offer the reassembled packs for sale in new wrappings without restamping.[22]

21 In re Hawley (D. C.) 220 Fed. 372; In re Capitol Trading Co. (D. C.) 229 Fed. 806.

22 U. S. v. Neustaedter (C. C.) 149 Fed. 1010.

This additional tax on playing cards became effective on and after October 4, 1917. But the Treasury rules that the additional tax does not apply to cards manufactured and removed tax-paid prior to October 4, in the hands of jobbers and retail dealers, unless the packs to which the stamps were affixed have been broken and the cards repacked in new cases, in which event the dealer so packing the same would be liable to the tax as in the case of an original manufacturer. The following regulations on the subject have been promulgated: "Every manufacturer and importer of playing cards will render to the collector of the district wherein the factory is located a sworn inventory, in duplicate, on or before October 31, 1917, showing the number of packs of playing cards, entering separately the number of stamped and unstamped packs on hand at the beginning of business October 4, and likewise the number of attached and unattached stamps at the rate of 2 cents. These inventories may be rendered on Form 215, modified to suit the nature of the article or in typewritten form. On October 31, or within 10 days thereafter, every manufacturer or importer will render under oath, in duplicate, a return covering the period October 4 to 31, inclusive, showing the number of packs of cards manufactured or imported, the number withdrawn tax paid, the name and address of each person, firm or corporation to whom such cards may be consigned or sold, the number and total value at the rate of 2 cents of stamps affixed, and the additional tax of 5 cents per pack due thereon. This return will be rendered for each subsequent month on the last day thereof, or on or before the 10th day of the succeeding month, until the supply of stamps at the old rate on hand is exhausted. Forms for rendering these returns may be obtained upon application to the collector of the district, or manufacturers or importers, if they so desire, may make up such monthly return upon the typewriter, provided it conforms in detail with that prescribed. Collectors will carefully verify these inventories and returns and enter for assessment on their lists, Form 23, the additional tax at 5 cents shown due from manufacturers or importers until the stock of stamps at the rate of 2 cents held by the taxpayer has been exhausted. Thereafter every manufacturer and importer will be required to render such return for each month during continuance in business, but the additional tax will not be noted thereon, as all stamps purchased from the collector on and after October 4 will be sold and accounted for at the new rate. One copy of the inventory and of each monthly return will be forwarded to this office by the collector and the other copy retained in his office." (T. D. 2538, Oct. 10, 1917.)

§ 399. Instruments Exempt from Stamp Tax

"There shall not be taxed under this title any bond, note, or other instrument issued by the United States, or by any foreign government, or by any state, territory, or the District of Columbia, or local subdivision thereof, or municipal or other corporation exercising the taxing power, when issued in the exercise of a strictly governmental, taxing, or municipal function; or stocks and bonds issued by cooperative building and loan associations which are organized and operated exclusively for the benefit of their members and make loans only to their shareholders, or by mutual ditch or irrigating companies." (Act Cong. Oct. 3, 1917, § 801.)

In general, any document is exempt, the stamping of which would make it necessary that the government (national or local) should furnish or pay for the stamp. (T. D. 2073, Nov. 23, 1914.) Thus, no stamp is required upon federal or state shipments of government or state property, for which, if a stamp were issued, the federal or state government would be required to pay. (T. D. 2067, Nov. 23, 1914.) So, deeds executed by a state, county, town, or other municipal corporation are not subject to the stamp tax. (T. D. 2283, Jan. 19, 1916.) On the same principle, the bond required to be given by a liquor dealer or saloon keeper to the state or municipality, as one of the conditions of the granting of a license to him, is an instrumentality employed in the carrying on of government, and cannot be taxed by the federal government.[23] So, a notary public appointed under the laws of a state by its governor, is a state officer employed in the exercise of functions belonging to it in a governmental capacity, and a bond which he is required to execute for the faithful discharge of his duties, as a condition to his qualification, is an instrument exempt from the stamp tax.[24]

Under former stamp-tax laws "certificates" of various kinds were subject to the tax, but those intended for the use of the government and those issued for a public purpose were held to be exempt. A recital of some of these may be useful as tending to show what is an "instrument issued in the exercise of a governmental function." The Treasury Department ruled that the following were exempt: Certificates of officers of the United States or of any state or mu-

---

[23] Ambrosini v. U. S., 187 U. S. 1, 23 Sup. Ct. 1, 47 L. Ed. 49; U. S. v. Owens (D. C.) 100 Fed. 70.

[24] Bettman v. Warwick, 108 Fed. 46, 47 C. C. A. 185.

nicipality exercising the taxing power, given in the discharge of official functions necessary in carrying on the machinery of government; a certificate of a court officer under the direction and authority of the court, necessary to give effect to the court proceedings; court processes, such as writs of summons, attachment, subpœna, warrants, orders of court; returns or reports made to the government for its own use, such as income and special tax returns, applications for licenses, reports made to the Interstate Commerce Commission, reports made to the Comptroller of the Currency, and to other branches of the federal and state governments for governmental purposes or use; certificates issued at tax sales or certificates of redemption. Also certificates were held exempt which were required in the interest of the public health, safety, or welfare, such as certificates by inspectors of steam vessels, locomotives, boilers, power plants, factories, meats, food products, lading of inflammables or explosives, births, marriages, death, quarantine, health, etc.; certificates issued by health officers relative to state statutes regulating the employment of child labor; certificates given under state laws by inspectors and weighers of grain, and teachers' certificates. (T. D. 2087, Dec. 11, 1914.)

The exemption extended to co-operative building and loan associations extends only to stocks and bonds issued by such companies; all other taxable instruments which may be executed and delivered by them are subject to the tax. (T. D. 2044, Nov. 9, 1914.)

§ 400. Affixing Stamps

It is immaterial which of the parties to a written instrument affixes the revenue stamp thereto.[25] And the stamp need not be affixed before the signing or partial execution of the instrument, if it is done before the paper is issued.[26] Copies or duplicates of taxable instruments are not ordinarily required to be stamped. But if such copies or duplicates are meant to be used in business, the Treasury Department rules that they should have written or stamped upon them the words "original duly stamped" or words to that effect. (T. D. 2073, Nov. 23, 1914.) But under the Act of 1898, which imposed a stamp tax on charter parties and other papers relating to the charter of a vessel, it was held that where charter parties were executed in a foreign country and left there, but

---

[25] Adams v. Dale, 29 Ind. 273; Voight v. McKain, 2 Pittsb. (Pa.) 522.
[26] Home Title Ins. Co. v. Keith (D. C.) 230 Fed. 905.

copies were made and brought into the United States to be used in their place for the benefit of one or both of the parties, such copies were subject to the stamp tax.[27] Upon an original issue of bonds, it is a substantial compliance with the law if the stamps denoting the tax are affixed either to the bonds or to the indenture under which the bonds are issued. If the latter method is adopted, a notation of the fact should be printed or engraved on the bonds. When temporary bonds are issued the stamps should be affixed to the indenture, and a notation of that fact made on both the temporary and definitive bonds. (T. D. 2164, Feb. 20, 1915.) It should be remembered that ordinary postage stamps cannot be used for the payment of any internal revenue taxes, and that documentary and proprietary stamps cannot be used interchangeably. And "where a stamp of the proper denomination to pay the tax due on an article or document cannot be procured, two or more stamps may be used. In such case as few stamps as possible should be attached, and each stamp should be canceled in the manner provided by regulation." (T. D. 2067, Nov. 23, 1914.)

§ 401. Method of Cancellation

The law provides that "whenever an adhesive stamp is used for denoting any tax imposed by this title, except as hereinafter provided, the person, corporation, partnership, or association using or affixing the same shall write or stamp or cause to be written or stamped thereupon the initials of his or its name and the date upon which the same is attached or used, so that the same may not again be used: Provided, that the Commissioner of Internal Revenue may prescribe such other method for the cancellation of such stamps as he may deem expedient." (Act Cong. Oct. 3, 1917, § 804.) The regulations on this point made by the Bureau of Internal Revenue under the Act of 1914 were as follows: "The person using or affixing the stamp shall write or stamp thereon, with ink, the initials of his name and the date (year, month, and day) in which the same shall be attached or used, or shall, by cutting and canceling said stamp with a machine or punch, which will affix the initials and date as aforesaid, so deface the stamp as to render it unfit for reuse. The cancellation by either method should not so deface the stamp as to prevent its denomination and genuineness from being readily determined. In addition to the foregoing,

---

[27] Simpson v. Treat (C. C.) 126 Fed. 1003. See Wright v. Michigan Cent. R. Co., 130 Fed. 843, 65 C. C. A. 327.

stamps of the value of 10 cents or more shall have three parallel incisions made by some sharp instrument lengthwise through the stamp after the stamp has been attached to the document: Provided, this will not be required where stamps are canceled by perforation." (T. D. 2067, Nov. 23, 1914.)

The courts have held that a revenue stamp is effectually canceled when it is so defaced that it cannot be used a second time; [28] that the sufficiency of the cancellation of a revenue stamp is not affected by the failure to affix the initials of the party's name; [29] that a revenue stamp on a note may as well be canceled by the initials of the payee as by those of the maker; [30] and that where there are several obligors joining in a bond, it is not necessary that all of them should take part in the cancellation of the stamp (as by putting their several initials upon it), but it may be done by one of them alone.[31] Also it has been ruled that it is not the intent of the law or the regulations that the initials of an individual employee should be written upon a revenue stamp which he affixes to a document in the course of his employment, but the initials of the principal for whom he acts will be sufficient. (T. D. 2113, Jan. 5, 1915.)

§ 402. Effect of Failure to Stamp

Earlier revenue laws of the United States provided, in some cases, that a conveyance should not be placed on the record, or that other instruments should not be admitted in evidence in the courts, unless duly stamped. But the present act contains no such provision. The only consequence of the failure to affix and cancel the revenue stamp in the case of an instrument requiring one is that the person who "makes, signs, issues, or accepts" the instrument "without the full amount of tax thereon being duly paid," is guilty of a misdemeanor and subject to a fine. And it is well settled that in the absence of a statute so providing the failure to affix a revenue stamp to a taxable instrument does not render the instrument void.[32]

---

[28] Taylor v. Duncan, 33 Tex. 440.

[29] Foster v. Holley's Adm'rs, 49 Ala. 593.

[30] Schultz v. Herndon, 32 Tex. 390.

[31] Teagarden v. Garver, 24 Ind. 399.

[32] Nicol v. Ames (C. C.) 89 Fed. 144; Dowell v. Applegate (C. C.) 7 Fed. 881; Goodwine v. Wands, 25 Ind. 101; Adams v. Dale, 29 Ind. 273; D'Armond v. Dubose, 22 La. Ann. 131, 2 Am. Rep. 718; Desmond v. Norris, 10 Allen (Mass.) 250; Jacobs v. Cunningham, 32 Tex. 774.

§ 403. Penalties for Failure to Affix Stamps and Failure to Cancel

The statute declares that any person "is guilty of a misdemeanor, and upon conviction thereof shall pay a fine of not more than $100 for each offense," who does any of the following things:

"Makes, signs, issues, or accepts, or causes to be made, signed, issued, or accepted, any instrument, document, or paper of any kind or description whatsoever without the full amount of tax thereon being duly paid;

"Consigns or ships, or causes to be consigned or shipped by parcel post, any parcel, package, or article without the full amount of tax being duly paid;

"Manufactures or imports and sells, or offers for sale, or causes to be manufactured or imported and sold, or offered for sale, any playing cards, package, or other article without the full amount of tax being duly paid;

"Makes use of any adhesive stamp to denote any tax imposed by this title without canceling or obliterating such stamp as prescribed in [the act]." (Act Cong. Oct. 3, 1917, § 802.)

In addition to the foregoing, there is a special and more severe penalty provided for failure to comply with the law in respect to stamping sales and transfers of corporate stock. It is as follows: "Any person or persons liable to pay the tax as herein provided, or anyone who acts in the matter as agent or broker for such person or persons, who shall make any such sale, or who shall in pursuance of any such sale deliver any stock or evidence of the sale of any stock or bill or memorandum thereof, as herein required, without having the proper stamps affixed thereto, with intent to evade the foregoing provisions, shall be deemed guilty of a misdemeanor, and upon conviction thereof shall pay a fine of not exceeding $1,000, or be imprisoned not more than six months, or both, at the discretion of the court." (Act Cong. Oct. 3, 1917, Schedule A, par. 5.)

So also, in regard to sales on produce exchanges or boards of trade, it is provided that "any person or persons liable to pay the tax as herein provided, or anyone who acts in the matter as agent or broker for such person or persons, who shall make any such sale or agreement of sale, or agreement to sell, or who shall, in pursuance of any such sale, agreement of sale, or agreement to sell, deliver any such products or merchandise without a bill, memorandum, or other evidence thereof as herein required, or who shall deliver such bill, memorandum, or other evidence of sale, or agree-

(412)

ment to sell, without having the proper stamps affixed thereto, with intent to evade the foregoing provisions, shall be deemed guilty of a misdemeanor, and upon conviction thereof shall pay a fine of not exceeding $1,000, or be imprisoned not more than six months, or both, at the discretion of the court." (Act Cong. Oct. 3, 1917, Schedule A, par. 5.)

§ 404. Penalties for Fraudulent Removal, Reuse, or Counterfeiting of Stamps

Every person is declared "guilty of a misdemeanor, and upon conviction shall be punished by a fine of not more than $1,000, or by imprisonment for not more than five years, or both, in the discretion of the court," who does any of the following acts:

"(a) Fraudulently cuts, tears, or removes from any vellum, parchment, paper, instrument, writing, package, or article, upon which any tax is imposed by this title, any adhesive stamp or the impression of any stamp, die, plate, or other article provided, made, or used in pursuance of this title;

(b) Fraudulently uses, joins, fixes, or places to, with, or upon any vellum, parchment, paper, instrument, writing, package, or article, upon which any tax is imposed by this title, (1) any adhesive stamp, or the impression of any stamp, die, plate, or other article, which has been cut, torn, or removed from any other vellum, parchment, paper, instrument, writing, package, or article, upon which any tax is imposed by this title; or (2) any adhesive stamp or the impression of any stamp, die, plate, or other article of insufficient value; or (3) any forged or counterfeit stamp, or the impression of any forged or counterfeited stamp, die, plate, or other article;

(c) Willfully removes, or alters the cancellation, or defacing marks of, or otherwise prepares, any adhesive stamp, with intent to use, or cause the same to be used, after it has been already used, or knowingly or willfully buys, sells, offers for sale, or gives away, any such washed or restored stamp to any person for use, or knowingly uses the same;

(d) Knowingly and without lawful excuse (the burden of proof of such excuse being on the accused) has in possession any washed, restored, or altered stamp, which has been removed from any vellum, parchment, paper, instrument, writing, package, or article." And in addition it is provided that "any such reused, canceled, or counterfeit stamp, and the vellum, parchment, document, paper, package, or article upon which it is placed or impressed shall be forfeited to the United States." (Act Cong. Oct. 3, 1917, § 803.)

§ 405. Collection of Omitted Stamp Taxes

Under the War Revenue Act of 1898, it was held that a collector had no authority to demand and collect from a person the value of the stamps which would have been required had he complied with the law in regard to stamping given instruments, the only penalty for a violation of the act being by prosecution and fine, and that consequently a payment by such person, enforced by the collector under a threat of suit, was illegally exacted and might be recovered back.[33] But the present statute contains a provision that "all internal-revenue laws relating to the assessment and collection of taxes are hereby extended to and made a part of this title, so far as applicable, for the purpose of collecting stamp taxes omitted through mistake or fraud from any instrument, document, paper, writing, parcel, package, or article named herein." (Act Cong. Oct. 3, 1917, § 805c.) Among the laws thus referred to is a provision that the Commissioner of Internal Revenue "is hereby authorized and required to make the inquiries, determinations, and assessments of all taxes imposed by this title, or accruing under any former internal revenue act, where such taxes had not been duly paid by stamp at the time and in the manner provided by law, and shall certify a list of such assessments, when made, to the proper collectors respectively, who shall proceed to collect and account for the taxes and penalties so certified." Rev. St. U. S. § 3182 (U. S. Comp. St. 1916, § 5904). And under the stamp-tax act of 1914, in view of this provision, it was held proper for the Commissioner to assess, and for collectors to demand and receive, unpaid or omitted stamp taxes.[34]

§ 406. Preparation and Distribution of Stamps

The law provides that "the Commissioner of Internal Revenue shall cause to be prepared and distributed for the payment of the taxes prescribed in this title suitable stamps denoting the tax on the document, article, or thing to which the same may be affixed, and shall prescribe such method for the affixing and cancellation of said stamps in substitution for or in addition to the method pro-

---

[33] McClain v. Fleshman, 106 Fed. 880, 46 C. C. A. 15.
[34] Calkins v. Smietanka (D. C.) 240 Fed. 138.

vided in this title, as he may deem expedient." (Act Cong. Oct. 3, 1917, § 805a.) Provision is also made for the keeping of documentary stamps for sale by the various postmasters throughout the United States, and by assistant treasurers and designated depositaries of the United States. And the Secretary of the Treasury is authorized, from time to time, to make such regulations as he may find necessary to insure the safe-keeping or prevent the illegal use of all such adhesive stamps.

CHAPTER XVIII

EXCISE, COMMODITIES, AND MISCELLANEOUS TAXES

§ 407. Distilled Spirits

The war revenue act of 1917 provides that "on and after the passage of this act there shall be levied and collected on all distilled

(416)

spirits in bond at that time, or that have been or that may be then or thereafter produced in or imported into the United States, except such distilled spirits as are subject to the tax provided in section three hundred and three [infra, § 409] in addition to the tax now imposed by law, a tax of $1.10 (or if withdrawn for beverage purposes or for use in the manufacture or production of any article used or intended for use as a beverage, a tax of $2.10) on each proof gallon, or wine gallon when below proof, and a proportionate tax at a like rate on all fractional parts of such proof or wine gallon, to be paid by the distiller or importer when withdrawn, and collected under the provisions of existing law." (Act Cong. Oct. 3, 1917, § 300.) Aside from the annual license taxes on wholesale and retail liquor dealers and rectifiers of spirits, the existing tax on distilled spirits as such was $1.10 per gallon, so that, the tax of 1917 being additional and not in substitution for the existing tax, distilled spirits are now taxed at $3.20 per gallon, unless withdrawn for other than beverage purposes, in which case the tax is $2.20. Existing laws also provide for stamps for distilled spirits intended for export, and case stamps for spirits bottled in bond, at 10 cents each. It is held that the internal revenue tax on spirits becomes due as soon as the spirits are produced.[1]

§ 408. Imported Perfumes Containing Distilled Spirits

A further provision of the act of 1917 is that "in addition to the tax under existing law, there shall be levied and collected upon all perfumes hereafter imported into the United States containing distilled spirits, a tax of $1.10 per wine gallon, and a proportionate tax at a like rate on all fractional parts of such wine gallon. Such tax shall be collected by the collector of customs and deposited as internal-revenue collections under such rules and regulations as the Commissioner of Internal Revenue, with the approval of the Secretary of the Treasury, may prescribe." (Act Cong. Oct. 3, 1917, § 300.) Prior to this enactment, there was no internal revenue tax on such imported perfumes, the only "tax under existing law" being the customs duty.

§ 409. Tax on Existing Stocks of Distilled Spirits

The so-called "floor tax" on distillates imposed by the act of 1917 is found in the following provision: "Upon all distilled spirits produced in or imported into the United States upon which the tax

---

[1] United States Fidelity & Guaranty Co. v. U. S., 220 Fed. 592, 136 C. C. A. 50.

now imposed by law has been paid, and which, on the day this act
is passed, are held by a retailer in a quantity in excess of fifty gallons in the aggregate, or by any other person, corporation, partnership, or association in any quantity, and which are intended for
sale, there shall be levied, assessed, collected, and paid a tax of
$1.10 (or if intended for sale for beverage purposes or for use in
the manufacture or production of any article used or intended for
use as a beverage, a tax of $2.10) on each proof gallon, and a pro-
portionate tax at a like rate on all fractional parts of such proof
gallon: Provided that the tax on such distilled spirits in the custody of a court of bankruptcy in insolvency proceedings on June
first, 1917, shall be paid by the person to whom the court delivers
such distilled spirits at the time of such delivery, to the extent that
the amount thus delivered exceeds the fifty gallons hereinbefore
provided." (Act Cong. Oct. 3, 1917, § 303.)

The Treasury Department rules that "all distilled spirits in possession of a manufacturing chemist, pharmacist, or any other person, firm, or corporation, held for sale, although not for sale as distilled spirits, on October 4, 1917, are subject to the additional floor
tax at $1.10 or $2.10 per proof gallon, as the case may be. Distilled spirits in the possession of manufacturers on October 4, 1917,
which, in the legitimate processes of manufacture, had been rendered unfit for use as beverages, are not subject to the additional
floor tax, but the manufacturing processes must have been bona fide
and not for the mere purpose of evasion. Non-beverage distilled
spirits taxable at the rate of $2.20 per proof gallon may be used
by manufacturers of flavoring extracts where such extracts are
unfit for use as a beverage, and such extracts may in turn be used
in manufacturing beverages." (T. D. 2566, Oct. 27, 1917.)

§ 410.　Rectified Spirits and Blended Wines and Whiskies

"In addition to the tax now imposed or imposed by this act on
distilled spirits, there shall be levied, assessed, collected, and paid
a tax of 15 cents on each proof gallon and a proportionate tax at
a like rate on all fractional parts of such proof gallon on all distilled spirits or wines hereafter rectified, purified, or refined in
such manner, and on all mixtures hereafter produced in such manner, that the person so rectifying, purifying, refining, or mixing
the same is a rectifier within the meaning of section 3244, Revised
Statutes, as amended, and on all such articles in the possession of
the rectifier on the day this act is passed: Provided that this tax
shall not apply to gin produced by the redistillation of a pure spirit

(418)

over juniper berries and other aromatics. The tax imposed by this section shall not attach to cordials or liqueurs on which a tax is imposed and paid under the act approved September 8, 1916, nor to the mixing and blending of wines, where such blending is for the sole purpose of perfecting such wines according to commercial standards, nor to blends made exclusively of two or more pure straight whiskies aged in wood for a period not less than four years and without the addition of coloring or flavoring matter or any other substance than pure water and if not reduced below ninety proof: Provided that such blended whiskies shall be exempt from tax under this section only when compounded under the immediate supervision of a revenue officer, in such tanks and under such conditions and supervision as the Commissioner of Internal Revenue, with the approval of the Secretary of the Treasury, may prescribe." "Any person violating any of the provisions of this section shall be deemed to be guilty of a misdemeanor, and, upon conviction, shall be fined not more than $1,000 or imprisoned not more than two years. He shall, in addition, be liable to double the tax evaded together with the tax, to be collected by assessment or on any bond given." (Act Cong. Oct. 3, 1917, § 304.) Rectifiers of spirits are already subject to an annual license tax of $100, if they produce less than 500 barrels a year, or $200 if they produce more than 500 barrels.

The Treasury Department rules that, since this section of the act of 1917 imposes a tax on all mixtures produced in such a manner as to cause the person mixing them to be a rectifier within Rev. St. § 3244, U. S. Comp. St. 1916, § 5971 (which refers to mixing wine or spirits with any other material so as to produce a "compound liquor"), any retail liquor dealer who manufactures compound liquors in advance of sale, or except to fill bar orders after such orders have been received, will be held liable as a rectifier. (T. D. 2546, Oct. 23, 1917.)

§ 411. Beer and Other Fermented Liquors

It is enacted by the act of 1917 that "on and after the passage of this act, there shall be levied and collected on all beer, lager beer, ale, porter, and other similar fermented liquor, containing one-half per centum or more of alcohol, brewed or manufactured and sold, or stored in warehouse, or removed for consumption or sale, within the United States, by whatever name such liquors may be called, in addition to the tax now imposed by law, a tax of $1.50 for every barrel containing not more than thirty-one gallons, and at a like

rate for any other quantity or for the fractional parts of a barrel
authorized and defined by law." (Act Cong. Oct. 3, 1917, § 307.)
The previously existing tax on beer and similar brewery products
was at the same rate of $1.50 per barrel, so that such liquors are
now taxable at the rate of $3 per barrel.

§ 412. Wines, Liqueurs, and Cordials

"Upon all still wines, including vermouth, and upon all champagne and other sparkling wines, liqueurs, cordials, artificial or imitation wines or compounds sold as wine, produced in or imported
into the United States, and hereafter removed from the custom
house, place of manufacture, or from bonded premises for sale or
consumption, there shall be levied and collected, in addition to the
tax now imposed by law upon such articles, a tax equal to such
tax, to be levied, collected, and paid under the provisions of existing law." (Act Cong. Oct. 3, 1917, § 309.)

The existing taxes on these products (which are exactly doubled
by the addition of the tax imposed by the act of 1917) are as follows: On still wines, containing not more than 14 per cent of absolute alcohol, 4 cents per wine gallon; containing over 14 per
cent but not over 21 per cent of alcohol, 10 cents per wine gallon;
containing over 21 per cent but not over 24 per cent of alcohol, 25
cents per wine gallon. If such products contain over 24 per cent
of alcohol, they are classed and are taxable as distilled spirits. On
champagne and other sparkling wines, the existing tax (now doubled) is 3 cents on each half-pint or fraction thereof. The tax on
artificially carbonated wine, previously one and one-half cents per
half-pint or fraction thereof, is now 3 cents.

In addition, the act of 1917 imposes a "floor tax" on wines and
the other products mentioned in the section quoted above, as follows: "Upon all articles specified in [said section] upon which the
tax now imposed by law has been paid, and which are, on the day
this act is passed, held in excess of 25 gallons in the aggregate of
such articles and intended for sale, there shall be levied, collected,
and paid a tax equal to the tax imposed by such section." (Act
Cong. Oct. 3, 1917, § 310.)

§ 413. Grape Brandy and Wine Spirits

It is provided that "upon all grape brandy or wine spirits withdrawn by a producer of wines from any fruit distillery or special
bonded warehouse under subdivision (c) of section 402 of the act
approved September 8, 1916, there shall be levied, assessed, collected, and paid, in addition to the tax therein imposed [10 cents

(420)

per proof gallon] a tax equal to double such tax, to be assessed, collected, and paid under the provisions of existing law. Upon all sweet wines held for sale by the producer thereof on the day this act is passed, there shall be levied, assessed, collected, and paid an additional tax equivalent to 10 cents per proof gallon upon the grape brandy or wine spirits used in the fortification of such wine, and an additional tax of 20 cents per proof gallon shall be levied, assessed, collected, and paid upon all grape brandy or wine spirits withdrawn by a producer of sweet wines for the purpose of fortifying such wines and not so used prior to the passage of this act." (Act Cong. Oct. 3, 1917, §§ 311, 312.)

§ 414.   Non-Intoxicating or "Soft" Drinks, Sirups, Extracts, and Mineral Waters

The act of 1917 levies a tax upon these products (not previously taxed by the United States) in the following terms: "There shall be levied, assessed, collected, and paid (a) upon all prepared sirups or extracts (intended for use in the manufacture or production of beverages commonly known as soft drinks, by soda fountains, bottling establishments, and other similar places) sold by the manufacturer, producer, or importer thereof, if so sold for not more than $1.30 per gallon, a tax of 5 cents per gallon; if so sold for more than $1.30 and not more than $2 per gallon, a tax of 8 cents per gallon; if so sold for more than $2 and not more than $3 per gallon, a tax of 10 cents per gallon; if so sold for more than $3 and not more than $4 per gallon, a tax of 15 cents per gallon; and if so sold for more than $4 per gallon, a tax of 20 cents per gallon; and (b) upon all unfermented grape juice, soft drinks, or artificial mineral waters (not carbonated) and fermented liquors containing less than one-half per centum of alcohol, sold by the manufacturer, producer, or importer thereof, in bottles or other closed containers, and upon all ginger ale, root beer, sarsaparilla, pop, and other carbonated waters or beverages, manufactured and sold by the manufacturer, producer, or importer of the carbonic acid gas used in carbonating the same, a tax of 1 cent per gallon; and (c) upon all natural mineral waters or table waters, sold by the producer, bottler, or importer thereof, in bottles or other closed containers, at over 10 cents per gallon, a tax of 1 cent per gallon." (Act Cong. Oct. 3, 1917, § 313.)

In the interpretation of this provision of the law, the Treasury Department has made the following rulings: The act does not impose a tax upon sirups or extracts intended for use by the maker for further manufacturing purposes, nor upon extracts prepared and intended to be used for household purposes. There is no prohibition against using flavoring extracts which contain some alcohol to flavor sirups that are to be used in manufacturing soft drinks. There is no exemption in favor of carbonated beverages which are mixed and sold at soda fountains. The manufacturer of soft drinks who purchases his carbonic acid gas must pay 5 cents per pound upon the amount of gas he buys; the manufacturer of soft drinks who makes his own gas must pay 1 cent per gallon upon all soft drinks sold; the manufacturer of sirups or extracts must pay from 5 cents to 20 cents per gallon upon all sales of sirups or extracts which are intended for use in the manufacture of soft drinks. Carbonic acid gas used in drawing beer from a container is not taxable. Where concentrates or extracts are sold to be further manufactured into flavoring extracts or sirups, the person completing the manufacture is subject to the tax. Where concentrates or extracts are sold to the bottler or the manufacturer of the soft drinks, the manufacturer of the concentrates or extracts is subject to the tax. (T. D. 2570, Nov. 6, 1917.)

§ 415. Same; Returns by Manufacturers, Bottlers, and Importers

It is required that "each such manufacturer, producer, bottler, or importer shall make monthly returns under oath to the collector of internal revenue for the district in which is located the principal place of business, containing such information necessary for the assessment of the tax, and at such times and in such manner, as the Commissioner of Internal Revenue, with the approval of the Secretary of the Treasury, may by regulation prescribe." (Act Cong. Oct. 3, 1917, § 314.)

§ 416. Carbonic Acid Gas in Drums

"Upon all carbonic acid gas in drums or other containers (intended for use in the manufacture or production of carbonated water or other drinks) sold by the manufacturer, producer, or importer thereof, there shall be levied, assessed, collected, and paid a tax of 5 cents per pound. Such tax shall be paid by the purchaser to the vendor thereof and shall be collected, returned, and paid to the United States by such vendor in the same manner as provided in section five hundred and three." (Act Cong. Oct. 3, 1917, § 315.) The section referred to relates to the collection of the tax on transportation and other facilities furnished by public-service corporations. See, supra, § 364 of this volume.

§ 417.   Cigars and Cigarettes

Prior to the act of 1917, the internal revenue tax on cigars weighing more than 3 pounds per 1000 was at the uniform rate of $3 per thousand, without regard to the retail price or value of the cigars; and on cigars not weighing more than 3 pounds per 1000, the tax was at the rate of 75 cents per thousand. On cigarettes the tax was $1.25 per 1000, if they weighed not more than 3 pounds to the thousand, or $3.60, if of greater weight. To these taxes additional and graded taxes are levied by the act of 1917, as follows: "Upon cigars and cigarettes, which shall be manufactured and sold, or removed for consumption or sale, there shall be levied and collected, in addition to the taxes now imposed by existing law, the following taxes to be paid by the manufacturer or importer thereof: (a) on cigars of all descriptions made of tobacco or any substitute therefor, and weighing not more than three pounds per thousand, 25 cents per thousand; (b) on cigars made of tobacco or any substitute therefor, and weighing more than three pounds per thousand, if manufactured or imported to retail at 4 cents or more each, and not more than 7 cents each, $1 per thousand; (c) if manufactured or imported to retail at more than 7 cents each and not more than 15 cents each, $3 per thousand; (d) if manufactured or imported to retail at more than 15 cents each and not more than 20 cents each, $5 per thousand; (e) if manufactured or imported to retail at more than 20 cents each, $7 per thousand: Provided, that the word 're-tail' as used in this section shall mean the ordinary retail price of a single cigar, and that the Commissioner of Internal Revenue may by regulation require the manufacturer or importer to affix to each box or container a conspicuous label indicating by letter the clause of this section under which the cigars therein contained have been tax-paid, which must correspond with the tax-paid stamp on said box or container; (f) on cigarettes made of tobacco or any substitute therefor, made in or imported into the United States, and weighing not more than three pounds per thousand, 80 cents per thousand; weighing more than three pounds per thousand, $1.20 per thousand."

"Every manufacturer of cigarettes (including small cigars weighing not more than three pounds per thousand) shall put up all the cigarettes and such small cigars that he manufactures or has manufactured for him, and sells or removes for consumption or use, in packages or parcels containing 5, 8, 10, 12, 15, 16, 20, 24, 40, 50, 80, or 100 cigarettes each, and shall securely affix to each of said packages or parcels a suitable stamp denoting the tax thereon and shall properly cancel the same prior to such sale or removal for consumption or use, under such regulations as the Commissioner of Internal Revenue, with the approval of the Secretary of the Treasury, shall prescribe; and all cigarettes imported from a foreign country shall be packed, stamped, and the stamps canceled in a like manner, in addition to the import stamp indicating inspection of the custom-house before they are withdrawn therefrom." (Act Cong. Oct. 3, 1917, § 400.)

In pursuance of the authority above given, the Commissioner of Internal Revenue has made regulations dividing cigars which weigh more than 3 pounds per 1,000 into five classes, numbered A, B, C, D, and E, according to the price at which they are manufactured or imported to be sold, these classes corresponding exactly to the lettered subdivisions of the section above quoted. The regulations further provide: "The rate of tax to be paid on cigars weighing more than 3 pounds per 1,000 is based upon the retail price of each cigar, and it is provided that the word 'retail' shall mean the ordinary retail price of a single cigar. The ordinary retail price of a single cigar is held to be the price at which cigars are or would be sold singly. Where cigars are manufactured or imported to retail at two or three for a certain price, the rate of tax payment is determined upon the retail price at which such cigars would be sold singly. In the case of cigars which are sold only by the box and never retailed in less quantities, i. e., where the box is the unit of sale, the rate of tax to be paid thereon is to be determined by the maximum value of a single cigar, obtained by dividing the box price by the number of cigars packed therein, where the same brand of cigars is put up in different size packages. In the case of imported cigars, the importer will be required to file an affidavit with the collector of customs setting forth the necessary information with reference to the retail price of the cigars when sold singly, and the importer will be held responsible for the proper tax payment of such cigars."

"Every manufacturer or importer will be required to affix to each box or container of cigars weighing more than 3 pounds per 1000 a conspicuous label indicating by letter the clause of said section under which the cigars therein contained have been tax paid, which must correspond with the tax-paid stamp on said box or container. Such label shall be not less than one inch long nor less than three-fourths of an inch wide, and shall be affixed to the front of the box or container and shall bear the following legend: 'The contents of this box have been tax paid as cigars of Class —— as indicated by the internal revenue stamp affixed.' In each such label the class shall be indicated by letter A, B, C, D, or E, corresponding with the appropriate class."

In regard to the new sizes of packages for cigarettes and cigars authorized by the act (namely, those containing 12, 16, 24, 40, or 80), the regulations provide that "to each package or parcel there shall be affixed a suitable stamp denoting the tax thereon, which shall be canceled prior to removal for sale or consumption, under such regulations as the Commissioner of Internal Revenue shall prescribe. Such stamps shall be affixed in such a manner as to seal the package, and shall be canceled by the manufacturer writing or imprinting on each stamp his factory number, the number of the district and state, and the date of cancellation to include the month and year. In the case of importer of small cigars or cigarettes, the stamp shall be canceled by the owner or importer thereof by writing or imprinting upon the same his name and the date of cancellation to include the month and year. Stamps for the new sizes of packages for manufactured tobacco and snuff shall be affixed and canceled in the same manner as are other strip stamps for tobacco and snuff under the provisions of existing regulations." (T. D. 2569, Oct. 17, 1917.)

§ 418. Tobacco and Snuff

Prior to the act of 1917, tobacco and snuff were subject to an internal revenue tax of 8 cents a pound, to which a new and additional tax of 5 cents a pound is added by the said act, as follows: "Upon all tobacco and snuff hereafter manufactured and sold, or removed for consumption or use, there shall be levied and collected. in addition to the tax now imposed by law upon such articles. a tax of 5 cents per pound, to be levied, collected, and paid under the provisions of existing law. In addition to the packages provided for under existing law, manufactured tobacco and snuff may be put up and prepared by the manufacturer for sale or consumption in packages of the following description: Packages containing one-eighth, three-eighths, five-eighths, seven-eighths, one and one-eighth, one and three-eighths, one and five-eighths, one and seven-eighths, and five ounces." (Act Cong. Oct. 3, 1917, § 401.)

§ 419. Floor Tax on Tobacco and Cigars

In addition to the other provisions of the act of 1917, it is enacted that "there shall also be levied and collected, upon all manufactured tobacco and snuff in excess of 100 pounds, or upon cigars and cigarettes in excess of 1000, which were manufactured or imported, and removed from factory or custom-house prior to the passage of this act, bearing tax-paid stamps affixed to such articles for the payment of the taxes thereon, and which are, on the day after this act is passed, held and intended for sale by any person, corporation, partnership, or association, and upon all manufactured tobacco, snuff, cigars, or cigarettes, removed from factory or custom-house after the passage of this act, but prior to the time when the tax imposed by section four hundred or four hundred and one upon such articles takes effect [that is, thirty days after the passage of the act, or November 2, 1917] an additional tax equal to one-half the tax imposed by such sections upon such articles." (Act Cong. Oct. 3, 1917, § 403.)

§ 420. Cigarette Papers and Tubes

From and after November 2, 1917, the revenue act of that year imposes a tax on these articles in the following terms: "There shall be levied, assessed, and collected upon cigarette paper made up into packages, books, sets, or tubes, made up in or imported into the United States and intended for use by the smoker in making cigarettes the following taxes: On each package, book, or set, containing more than 25 but not more than 50 papers, one-half of 1 cent; containing more than 50 but not more than 100 papers, 1 cent; containing more than 100 papers, 1 cent for each 100 papers or fractional part thereof; and upon tubes, 2 cents for each 100 tubes or fractional part thereof." (Act Cong. Oct. 3, 1917, § 404.)

No provision having been made by statute for the collection of this tax, the Treasury Department has made the following regulations; "The taxes imposed by this section of the act accrue upon the removal of such packages, books, sets, or tubes from the place where they are made in the United States, or, if they are imported, upon withdrawal from custom-house for consumption or use. Cigarette papers made up into packages, books, or sets containing not more than 25 papers, and also cigarette tubes delivered to a duly registered manufacturer of cigarettes under conditions hereinafter stated, are exempt from tax. No provision is made by law for the exportation without the payment of tax of cigarette papers in packages, books, or sets, or of cigarette tubes." As to imported cigarette papers and tubes: "When cigarette paper made up into packages, books, or sets, or cigarette tubes are imported into the United States, the customs consumption entry or withdrawal for consumption entry shall be prepared in triplicate and shall show in detail (a) number of packages, etc., containing not more than 25 papers each; (b) number of packages, etc., containing more than 25 but not more than 50 papers each; (c) number of packages, etc., containing more than 50 but not more than 100 papers each; (d) number of packages, etc., containing —— papers each; (e) number of packages, etc., containing —— papers each; (f) number of cigarette tubes intended for use by the smoker in making cigarettes (taxable); (g) number of cigarette tubes (exempt) to be delivered to a duly registered manufacturer of cigarettes, giving name, address, factory number, district, and state of such manufacturer."

"Two copies of such customs entries will be filed with the collector of internal revenue. The internal-revenue tax on the cigarette papers in packages, books, or sets or cigarette tubes shown by such entries to be due shall be paid to the collector of internal revenue at the time the entries are filed with him. Receipts on Form 1 shall be issued until a form for the payment of such taxes can be printed and furnished to collectors. On one copy of the customs entry the collector of internal revenue will indorse a certificate under his official seal, setting forth that the internal-revenue tax on the articles described therein has been paid, naming the amount of such payment, and he will then deliver such copy, so certified, to the importer, to be filed by him with the collector of customs. The release of the articles described in the customs entry will not be made by the customs officer, in whose custody the same are, without the certificate of the collector of internal revenue, as prescribed. Report in duplicate will also be made on each importation by the collector of customs to the collector of internal revenue of the quantity imported, as ascertained on final examination. Upon such report payment of additional tax due will be required immediately. If payment in any case is in excess of the tax as ascertained from such report, claim for refund of the excess may be filed."

As to domestic manufactures: "Every person, corporation, partnership, or association making up cigarette paper into packages, books, sets, or tubes in the United States will be required to keep a book and enter therein each day the number of packages, books, or sets, and the number of papers contained therein, and the number of tubes removed for consumption or use under the several heads, as follows: (a) Containing not more than 25 papers each; (b) containing more than 25 but not more than 50 papers each; (c) containing more than 50 but not more than 100 papers each;

(d) containing ——— papers each; (e) containing ——— papers each; (f) number of packages of tubes per 100 or fractional part thereof; (g) number of cigarette tubes exempt from tax."

"A daily record will also be required to be kept of the number of cigarette tubes sold and delivered tax free to duly registered manufacturers of cigarettes, giving the name, address, factory number, the number of the district, and the State of each, and also the number of packages of cigarette tubes containing 100 tubes or fractional part thereof, and the number of tubes intended for use by the smoker in making cigarettes removed subject to tax. At the close of each month return will be required to be made from the book of the maker of cigarette papers into packages, books, sets, or tubes which will indicate the amount of tax required to be paid; and such return, with abstracts of the record of the sales and deliveries of cigarette tubes delivered to manufacturers of cigarettes and removed for use by the smoker in making cigarettes, will be sworn to and filed with the collector of internal revenue for the district on or before the 10th day of the succeeding month. Payment of the tax shown to be due will be required at the time of filing return." (T. D. 2552, Oct. 22, 1917.)

It is also ruled by the Treasury Department that closed-end tubes used in the preparation of catarrh and asthma remedies are not taxable as "cigarette tubes." (T. D. 2570, Nov. 6, 1917.)

§ 421. Time of Incidence of Tax on Tobacco and its Products

The act of 1917 provides that "sections four hundred, four hundred and one, and four hundred and four [these are the sections imposing the tax on cigars, cigarettes, tobacco, snuff, and cigarette papers, supra, §§ 417, 418, 420] shall take effect thirty days after the passage of this act: Provided that after the passage of this act and before the expiration of the aforesaid thirty days, cigarettes and manufactured tobacco and snuff may be put up in the packages now provided for by law or in the packages provided for in sections four hundred and four hundred and one." (Act Cong. Oct. 3, 1917, § 402.)

§ 422. Excise Taxes on Sales of Commodities

The revenue act of 1917 levies excise taxes on the sale of various commodities, chiefly motor vehicles, mechanical musical instruments, moving-picture films, jewelry, sporting goods, toilet articles, proprietary medicines, chewing gum, cameras, and boats. Several general rulings on the subject of this tax have been made

(428)

by the Treasury Department in response to questions propounded by interested parties. To the question "are goods manufactured in the United States and sold to persons in foreign countries subject to the tax?" the answer was given: "There is no exemption in favor of goods which are to be exported. The United States Supreme Court in numerous cases has held that such a tax does not constitute a tax on exports or on articles exported, within the meaning of the Constitution. A general tax laid on all property alike and not levied on goods in course of exportation, nor because of their intended exportation, is not within the constitutional prohibition." Turpin v. Burgess, 117 U. S. 504, 6 Sup. Ct. 835, 29 L. Ed. 988.

It was asked: "In computing the price at which goods are sold, may the usual trade discounts be deducted from the price thereof for the purpose of ascertaining the tax?" The answer was given: "The amount of tax is determined by the price at which the goods are actually sold by the manufacturer, producer, or importer. Hence discounts would be deducted from the list price."

A third question was: "Are net or gross sales to be reported? That is, may there be deducted from the sales of each month merchandise which has been sold in a previous month and which is returned during the month in which the report is made?" The Department replied: "The merchandise becomes taxable when the manufacturer parts with his title in it, and all taxable goods actually sold should be reported. However, goods which are delivered to the buyer subject to his approval or to other conditions, and the property right to them is reserved to the seller, are not to be reported until the completion of the sale."

A case stated for the consideration of the Department was as follows: "A manufacturing company disposes of a portion of its output through a selling corporation, of which it owns all the capital stock. Is the transfer by the parent company to the subsidiary a sale within the meaning of the act, subjecting the parent company to the tax?" It was ruled that "the transfer from the manufacturing corporation to the selling corporation is a sale, provided the price at which the article is sold or charged to the distributing corporation is no less than is charged to the independent outside distributors under similar conditions. The selling corporation is liable to the floor tax on all articles subject to tax which have been charged and delivered to it prior to October 4, 1917, and thereafter the manufacturing company should pay tax upon delivery of all articles to the selling corporation as upon sales, the price fixed in no case to be less than the price at which the taxable article is sold to independent distributors under similar conditions." (T. D. 2547, Oct. 22, 1917.) The word "sold" as used in this section of the law is construed to mean that a contract of sale has been entered into between vendor and vendee under the terms of which the article which is the subject of the contract becomes the property of the vendee. (T. D. 2570, Nov. 6, 1917.)

§ 423. Same; Motor Vehicles

It is provided by the act of Congress of October 3, 1917 (section 600) that "there shall be levied, assessed, collected, and paid upon all automobiles, automobile trucks, automobile wagons, and motorcycles, sold by the manufacturer, producer, or importer, a tax equivalent to three per centum of the price for which so sold." In the interpretation of this provision the Internal Revenue office has made the following rulings: "(a) Automobiles and motorcycles sold by the manufacturer to the United States Government on contract, at contract prices, are taxable under the excise-tax law; (b) a chassis is held to be an automobile and taxable as such; (c) an automobile body is not taxable as an automobile when sold alone; when sold in combination with a chassis, the tax rests upon the completed article; (d) a usable or substantially complete automobile produced by assembling certain parts of trucks and cars, either new or secondhand, is subject to tax; (e) so-called used or second-hand automobiles are not subject to tax under section 600 when sold by the manufacturer, producer, or importer, nor to tax imposed by section 602 if held and intended for sale by a wholesaler on the morning of October 4, 1917; (f) the so-called side car to be attached to a motorcycle is not taxable unless sold in combination with a motorcycle, in which case the tax attaches to the completed article." (T. D. 2570, Nov. 6, 1917.)

§ 424. Same; Mechanical Musical Instruments

A tax equivalent to three per cent of the price for which they are sold by the manufacturer, producer, or importer, and when sold by such manufacturer, producer, or importer, is imposed by the revenue act of 1917 upon "all piano players, graphophones, phonographs, talking machines, and records used in connection with any musical instrument, piano player, graphophone, phonograph, or talking machine." (Act Cong. Oct. 3, 1917, § 600b.) Machines commercially and commonly known as "dictaphones" or "dicta-

(430)

graphs," and used for dictation purposes, are not taxable as phonographs under this section of the law. (T. D. 2570, Nov. 6, 1917.)

§ 425. Same; Moving Picture Films

"Upon all moving-picture films which have not been exposed, sold by the manufacturer or importer" the statute imposes a tax "equivalent to one-fourth of 1 cent per linear foot; and upon all positive moving-picture films (containing a picture ready for projection) sold or leased by the manufacturer, producer, or importer, a tax equivalent to one-half of 1 cent per linear foot." (Act Cong. Oct. 3, 1917, § 600, c, d.) Doubt having arisen as to whether this provision was meant to tax such films every time they were sold or leased, or once for all, an opinion was given by the Commissioner of Internal Revenue, as follows: "The tax on the manufacturers of automobiles, musical instruments, sports goods, etc., imposed by the same title, has to be paid but once, and it is logical to assume that Congress intended likewise in the case of moving-picture films. It also appears that a different interpretation of the section in question would impose a greater burden than could have been intended. The language of the subdivisions imposing the tax upon the other articles mentioned differs from that concerning films, in that the tax is imposed upon the articles 'sold by the manufacturer, producer, or importer.' However, the framers of the act recognized that moving-picture films as a rule are not sold, but are merely leased or rented to exhibitors, and it was evidently in view of such practice that the language of the paragraph relating to moving-picture films was made to read 'sold or leased' instead of merely 'sold.' Accordingly, the words 'sold or leased,' as they appear in this subdivision, are construed to mean when first sold or leased, requiring the payment of the tax only once." (T. D. 2568, Oct. 30, 1917.)

§ 426. Same; Jewelry

There is imposed "upon any article commonly or commercially known as jewelry, whether real or imitation, sold by the manufacturer, producer, or importer thereof, a tax equivalent to three per centum of the price for which so sold." (Act Cong. Oct. 3, 1917, § 600e.) In regard to the incidence of this tax, the following rulings have been made by the Treasury Department: "(1) All articles which have been specifically classified as jewelry by the board of customs appraisers shall be taxed as jewelry under the present act. (2) All ornaments worn for personal adornment only are classifiable as jewelry. (3) All precious stones and pearls, both real and imitation, whether cut or uncut, which are set and ready to wear in condition sold are classifiable as jewelry and subject to tax. Precious stones cut but not set will be regarded as subject to tax when sold by the importer, or, if cutting is done in the United States, when sold by the manufacturer or dealer for whom the cutting was done. Pearls matched, drilled, and temporarily strung on silk thread, without clasps, will not be regarded as jewelry when sold to dealers for further manufacture or completion, but will be regarded as jewelry when sold to a customer for personal use, whether with or without a clasp. The same will apply to loose drilled pearls. (4) All watches not used solely for utility purposes are considered as taxable within the meaning of section 600 of the war-revenue act. This will embrace all watches worn externally for purposes of ornament and all watches intended to be carried in the pocket the outer case of which is so ornamented by the addition of jewels or other ornamentation that the value of the case is relatively disproportionate to the value of the movement. (5) As to the question of what is a retailer, it is held that a retailer who is not also a wholesaler is one who sells only to personal customers and does not solicit or seek to make sales to other dealers for resale. Any dealer who makes the sale of jewelry to other dealers for resale a substantial part of his business, or who solicits such business, will be regarded as a wholesale dealer. (6) As to the specific articles referred to by the committee, it is held that the following, when made of precious or imitation metals to be carried on the person, shall be considered as jewelry: Dorean (powder) boxes, vanity boxes, stamp boxes, match boxes, cigarette cases, cigar cases, eyeglass cases, eyeglass chains, eyeglass holders, lorgnettes, lorgnons, card cases, vinaigrettes, handkerchief holders, garters, suspenders, emblem charms, emblem pins, emblem buttons, mesh bags, memorandum books, lip-salve cases, eyebrow pencils, cigar cutters, compasses, key chains, key rings, and like articles." (T. D. 2553, Oct. 26, 1917.)

§ 427. Same; Sporting Goods and Games

The same section of the revenue act of 1917 imposes "upon all tennis rackets, golf clubs, baseball bats, lacrosse sticks, balls of all kinds, including baseballs, foot balls, tennis, golf, lacrosse, billiard and pool balls, fishing rods and reels, billiard and pool tables, chess and checker boards and pieces, dice, games and parts of games, except playing cards and childrens' toys and games, sold by the manufacturer, producer, or importer, a tax equivalent to three per centum of the price for which so sold." (Act Cong. Oct. 3, 1917, § 600f.) As concerns certain of the articles affected by this paragraph, the Treasury Department was asked for an opinion on the following question: "In the case of parts of golf clubs sold to golf professionals in the rough—that is, iron heads, wooden heads, leather straps for handles and shafts—when these separate parts are assembled by the professional and the completed club sold by him, who is the manufacturer of the golf club and when is this tax payable?" It was answered: "Iron heads, wooden heads, etc., are not golf clubs, neither are they parts of games within the meaning of the statute. The one who produces the finished product is the manufacturer and is charged with the tax." (T. D. 2547, Oct. 22, 1917.)

§ 428. Same; Toilet Articles

These are described by the statute as "all perfumes, essences, extracts, toilet waters, cosmetics, petroleum jellies, hair oils, pomades, hair dressings, hair restoratives, hair dyes, tooth and mouth washes, dentifrices, tooth pastes, aromatic cachous, toilet soaps and powders, or any similar substance, article, or preparation by whatsoever name known or distinguished, which are used or applied or intended to be used or applied for toilet purposes," and when they are "sold by the manufacturer, producer, or importer," the statute imposes a "tax equivalent to two per centum of the price for which so sold." (Act Cong. Oct. 3, 1917, § 600g.)

§ 429. Same; Proprietary and Patent Medicines

In respect to these articles, the tax is imposed upon "all pills, tablets, powders, tinctures, troches or lozenges, sirups, medicinal cordials or bitters, anodynes, tonics, plasters, liniments, salves, ointments, pastes, drops, waters (except those taxed under section three hundred and thirteen of this act [namely natural or artificial mineral waters]), essences, spirits, oils, and all medicinal preparations, compounds, or compositions whatsoever, the manufacturer or producer of which claims to have any private formula, secret, or occult art for making or preparing the same, or has or claims to have any exclusive right or title to the making or preparing the same, or which are prepared, uttered, vended, or exposed for sale under any letters patent or trade-mark, or which, if prepared by any formula, published or unpublished, are held out or recommended to the public by the makers, venders, or proprietors thereof as proprietary medicines or medicinal proprietary articles or preparations, or as remedies or specifics for any disease, diseases, or affection whatever, affecting the human or animal body." When these are sold by the manufacturer, producer, or importer, a tax is imposed equivalent to two per centum of the price for which so sold. (Act Cong. Oct. 3, 1917, § 600h.)

The revenue act of 1898 contained a clause almost exactly similar to that quoted above, and several applicable decisions of the courts were rendered under it. It was held that the medicinal preparations intended to be taxed were the more or less monopolistic or non-competitive kind, protected against imitation by patent, trade-mark, or proprietary rights, intended for self-medication, and generally accompanied by puffing inducements and unreliable statements.[2] Medicinal plasters which are in composition exactly the same as other plasters bearing the same name, put up by others and sold in competition with them, and based on the same well-known medical formulas, without any claim to special merit except with respect to the care exercised in the selection of ingredients and the manner in which they are compounded, are not "medicinal proprietary articles," within the meaning of the act. A trade-mark medicine or medicinal article, with which patent and proprietary medicines are coupled in the statute, and which is thereby subjected to the tax, must be held to be a medicine or article as to which a monopoly has been secured by means of a trade-mark or trade-name, under which it is prepared and sold; and where a trade-mark used on an article merely signifies its origin, and has no other purpose or connection with it, being used on all articles and preparations made by the manufacturers to identify the same as their product, and to give them such recommendation to the public as is afforded by their reputation, it does not render such article subject to the tax. Thus, the fact that certain medicinal plasters put up and sold by a manufacturer had printed thereon such descriptive words as "A Soothing Dressing," "Strengthening Plaster," or "Perfect Mustard," the latter being shown to mean in the trade only that it was ready for use, did not constitute such representation of merit or recommendations as to render them subject to the tax, nor were they taxable because, as to some of them, the packages bore the words "patent applied for." [3] So, plasters described

[2] Rutan v. Johnson & Johnson, 231 Fed. 369, 145 C. C. A. 363.

[3] Johnson & Johnson v. Rutan (C. C.) 122 Fed. 993.

as "dental" merely because cut into very small pieces suitable for dentists' use, are not within the tax act, nor are finger hats, nor corn or bunion plasters, the action of which, when applied, is purely mechanical and not medicinal. But plasters described as "Johnson's" or as "rheumatic" may be regarded severally as proprietary and as recommended as a remedy for rheumatism, and are taxable.[4] And a mild form of beer, containing about two per cent of alcohol, put up and sold by the manufacturers in bottles labeled "Rochester Tonic," was held subject to the tax under the act of 1898, on the ground that the use of the word "tonic" was a recommendation of it as a medicinal preparation, and that it was prepared under a secret formula; and it was held that it was not exempt from the tax imposed by this statute because the manufacturer had paid the revenue tax on it as beer before it was bottled.[5]

§ 430.   Same; Chewing Gum

The revenue act of 1917 imposes "upon all chewing gum or substitute therefor, sold by the manufacturer, producer, or importer, a tax equivalent to two per centum of the price for which so sold." (Act Cong. Oct. 3, 1917, § 600i.)

§ 431.   Same; Cameras

The same section of the same statute imposes "upon all cameras sold by the manufacturer, producer, or importer, a tax equivalent to three per centum of the price for which so sold." (Act Cong. Oct. 3, 1917, § 600j.)

§ 432.   Floor Tax on Commodities

In respect to many of the articles upon the sales of which this portion of the statute lays an excise tax—that is, automobiles and other motor vehicles, piano players and other mechanical musical instruments, jewelry, sporting goods and games, toilet articles, patent and proprietary medicines, chewing gum, and cameras—it is provided that all of such articles "which on the day this act is passed [October 3, 1917] are held and intended for sale by a person, corporation, partnership, or association, other than (1) by a retailer who is not also a wholesaler, or (2) the manufacturer, producer, or importer thereof, there shall be levied, assessed, collected, and paid a tax equivalent to one-half the tax imposed [severally]

---

[4] Johnson & Johnson v. Herold (D. C.) 161 Fed. 593.

[5] U. S. v. J. D. Iler Brewing Co., 121 Fed. 41, 57 C. C. A. 381.

upon the sale of the articles therein enumerated. This tax shall be paid by the person, corporation, partnership, or association so holding such articles. The taxes imposed by this section shall be assessed, collected, and paid in the same manner as provided in section ten hundred and two [infra, § 445] in the case of additional taxes upon articles upon which the tax imposed by existing law has been paid. Nothing in this section shall be construed to impose a tax upon articles sold and delivered prior to May ninth, 1917, where the title is reserved in the vendor as security for the payment of the purchase money." (Act Cong. Oct. 3, 1917, § 602.) The term "wholesaler" as above used does not include a retailer who occasionally sells goods to other retailers at less than retail prices, unless it appears that an effort was made to solicit such business for profit. (T. D. 2570, Nov. 6, 1917.)

§ 433. Returns and Payment of Tax on Commodities

In respect to the excise taxes on the various classes of commodities discussed in the preceding sections, it is provided that "each manufacturer, producer, or importer of any of the articles enumerated in section six hundred shall make monthly returns under oath in duplicate, and pay the taxes imposed on such articles by this title, to the collector of internal revenue of the district in which is located the principal place of business. Such returns shall contain such information and be made at such times and in such manner as the Commissioner of Internal Revenue, with the approval of the Secretary of the Treasury, may by regulations prescribe." (Act Cong. Oct. 3, 1917, § 601.) Another applicable provision of the same statute is as follows: "All administrative, special, or stamp provisions of law, including the law relating to the assessment of taxes, so far as applicable, are hereby extended to and made a part of this act, and every person, corporation, partnership, or association liable to any tax imposed by this act, or for the collection thereof, shall keep such records, and render, under oath, such statements and returns, and shall comply with such regulations as the Commissioner of Internal Revenue, with the approval of the Secretary of the Treasury, may from time to time prescribe." (Act Cong. Oct. 3, 1917, § 1001.) An itinerant manufacturer who moves from place to place and makes and sells an article subject to this tax should make returns and pay the tax to the collector of the district where the sales are made. (T. D. 2570, Nov. 6, 1917.)

§ 434.   Same; Penalty for Failure to Make Return or for False or Fraudulent Return

Applicable to the excise taxes on commodities, as well as to all other taxes imposed by the act of 1917, the following penalties are imposed: "Whoever fails to make any return required by this act or the regulations made under authority thereof within the time prescribed, or who makes any false or fraudulent return, and whoever evades or attempts to evade any tax imposed by this act, or fails to collect or truly to account for and pay over any such tax, shall be subject to a penalty of not more than $1,000, or to imprisonment for not more than one year, or both, at the discretion of the court, and in addition thereto a penalty of double the tax evaded, or not collected, or accounted for and paid over, to be assessed and collected in the same manner as taxes are assessed and collected, in any case in which the punishment is not otherwise specifically provided." (Act Cong. Oct. 3, 1917, § 1004.)

§ 435.   Where Vendee or Lessee Pays Commodities Tax

A special provision of the act of 1917 is: "That (a) if any person, corporation, partnership, or association has prior to May ninth, 1917, made a bona fide contract with a dealer for the sale, after the tax takes effect, of any article (or, in the case of moving picture films, such a contract with a dealer, exchange, or exhibitor, for the sale or lease thereof) upon which a tax is imposed under Title III, IV, or VI, or under subdivision thirteen of Schedule A of Title VIII, or under this section,[6] and (b) if such contract does not permit the adding of the whole of such tax to the amount to be paid under such contract, then the vendee or lessee shall, in lieu of the vendor or lessor, pay so much of such tax as is not so permitted to be added to the contract price. The taxes payable by the vendee or lessee under this section shall be paid to the vendor or lessor at the time the sale or lease is consummated, and collected, return-ed, and paid to the United States by such vendor or lessor in the same manner as provided in section five hundred and three." That is, he is required to make monthly returns under oath, and pay over the tax-money to the collector of internal revenue for the district

[6] Title III of the act relates to the tax on spirits, beer, wine, and other beverages. See, supra, §§ 407–416. Title IV is the title imposing the war tax on cigars, cigarettes, and tobacco. See, supra, §§ 417–420. Title VI imposes the war excise taxes on various classes of commodities. See, supra, §§ 422–431. Subdivision 13 of Schedule A of Title VIII imposes the stamp tax on playing cards. See, supra, § 398.

in which his principal place of business is located. "The term 'dealer' as used in this section includes a vendee who purchases any article with intent to use it in the manufacture or production of another article intended for sale." (Act Cong. Oct. 3, 1917, § 1007.)

§ 436. Annual Excise Tax on Yachts and Boats

As a part of the war revenue act of 1917, it is provided that "on the day this act takes effect, and thereafter on July first in each year, and also at the time of the original purchase of a new boat by a user, if on any other date than July first, there shall be levied, assessed, collected and paid upon the use of yachts, pleasure boats, power boats, and sailing boats, of over five net tons, and motor boats with fixed engines, not used exclusively for trade or national defense, and not built according to plans and specifications approved by the Navy Department, an excise tax to be based on each yacht or boat, at rates as follows: Yachts, pleasure boats, power boats, motor boats with fixed engines, and sailing boats, of over five net tons, length not over fifty feet, 50 cents for each foot, length over fifty feet and not over one hundred feet, $1 for each foot, length over one hundred feet, $2 for each foot; motor boats of not over five net tons with fixed engines, $5. In determining the length of such yachts, pleasure boats, power boats, motor boats with fixed engines, and sailing boats, the measurement of over-all length shall govern. In the case of a tax imposed at the time of the original purchase of a new boat on any date other than July first, the amount to be paid shall be the same number of twelfths of the amount of the tax as the number of calendar months, including the month of sale, remaining prior to the following July first." (Act Cong. Oct. 3, 1917, § 603.) It is held that the "user" of a boat, as the term is used in this section, means any person who purchases a vessel for his own use, as distinguished from one who buys as a dealer. (T. D. 2570, Nov. 6, 1917.)

§ 437. Importations from Virgin Islands

On this subject the provision of the statute is that "there shall be levied, collected, and paid in the United States, upon articles coming into the United States from the West Indian Islands acquired from Denmark, a tax equal to the internal-revenue tax imposed in the United States upon like articles of domestic manufacture; such articles shipped from said islands to the United States shall be exempt from the payment of any tax imposed by the internal-revenue laws of said islands: Provided, that there shall be levied, collected, and paid in said islands, upon articles imported from the United

States, a tax equal to the internal-revenue tax imposed in said islands upon like articles there manufactured; and such articles going into said islands from the United States shall be exempt from payment of any tax imposed by the internal-revenue laws of the United States." (Act Cong. Oct. 3, 1917, § 1000.)

§ 438.   War Tax on Admissions

The war revenue act of 1917 imposes a tax on admissions to places of amusement in the following terms: "That from and after the first day of November, nineteen hundred and seventeen, there shall be levied, assessed, collected, and paid (a) a tax of 1 cent for each 10 cents or fraction thereof of the amount paid for admission to any place, including admission by season ticket or subscription, to be paid by the person paying for such admission: Provided, that the tax on admission of children under twelve years of age where an admission charge for such children is made shall in every case be 1 cent; and (b) in the case of persons (except bona fide employees, municipal officers on official business, and children under twelve years of age) admitted free to any place at a time when and under circumstances under which an admission charge is made to other persons of the same class, a tax of 1 cent for each 10 cents or fraction thereof of the price so charged to such other persons for the same or similar accommodations, to be paid by the person so admitted; and (c) a tax of 1 cent for each 10 cents or fraction thereof paid for admission to any public performance for profit at any cabaret or other similar entertainment to which the charge for admission is wholly or in part included in the price paid for refreshment, service, or merchandise; the amount paid for such admission to be computed under rules prescribed by the Commissioner of Internal Revenue, with the approval of the Secretary of the Treasury, such tax to be paid by the person paying for such refreshment, service, or merchandise. In the case of persons having the permanent use of boxes or seats in an opera house or any place of amusement or a lease for the use of such box or seat in such opera house or place of amusement there shall be levied, assessed, collected, and paid a tax equivalent to ten per centum of the amount for which a similar box or seat is sold for performance or exhibition at which the box or seat is used or reserved by or for the lessee or holder. These taxes shall not be imposed in the case of a place the maximum charge for admission to which is 5 cents, or in the case of shows, rides, and other amusements, (the maximum charge for admission to which is

(439)

10 cents) within outdoor general amusement parks, or in the case of admissions to such parks.

No tax shall be levied under this title in respect to any admissions all the proceeds of which inure exclusively to the benefit of religious, educational, or charitable institutions, societies, or organizations, or admissions to agricultural fairs none of the profits of which are distributed to stockholders or members of the association conducting the same.

The term "admission" as used in this title includes seats and tables, reserved or otherwise, and other similar accommodations, and the charges made therefor." (Act Cong. Oct. 3, 1917, § 700.)

On this subject the Treasury Department rules that the tax attaches upon subscriptions to racing associations, regardless of whether or not the subscriber attends any of the meets. The association itself must pay the tax due for persons admitted free. The provision of the section which allows "bona fide employees" to be admitted tax free applies only to actual employees of the association, and not to employees of the owners of racing horses, etc. And in respect to the exemption in favor of religious and some other institutions, it is ruled that the word "proceeds," as used in this part of the section, means gross receipts less payments of proper expenses, or, in other words, net proceeds. If the net proceeds inure exclusively to the benefit of religious, educational, or charitable institutions, societies, or organizations, no tax is collectible on the admissions. (T. D. 2547, Oct. 22, 1917.)

The following rulings have also been made: "The tax on admissions is to be collected from the original vendor of the tickets on amount charged original vendee. One who rents or leases a theater outright for one or more performances must make return and pay tax, but the proprietor of the theater is required to show in his returns the dates when and the parties to whom he rents or leases his place." "The tax is computed in the case of subscription tickets upon the amount actually paid therefor." "In the case of an opera box under lease to a club, the tax shall be computed upon the basis of the price paid for the use of similar boxes by parties who pay for each performance severally. If there are no other boxes of similar size, the tax shall be computed by dividing the tax payable upon a smaller box by the number of seats in the smaller box and multiplying the tax per seat by the number of seats in the larger box. If there are no other boxes occupying a similiar position, the tax should be based upon the price of single seats in the same part of the house." "The exemption in cases where the maximum charge for admission is 5 cents does not apply to theaters where the amount charged for admission to any section or part thereof exceeds 5 cents." "Admissions charged to university and college athletic contests are subject to tax." (T. D. 2570, Nov. 6, 1917.)

§ 439. War Tax on Club Dues

It is provided that "from and after the first day of November, 1917, there shall be levied, assessed, collected, and paid a tax equivalent to ten per centum of the amount paid as dues or membership fees (including initiation fees) to any social, athletic, or sporting club or organization, where such dues or fees are in excess of $12 per year; such taxes to be paid by the person paying such dues or fees: Provided, that there shall be exempted from the provisions of this section all amounts paid as dues or fees to a fraternal beneficiary society, order, or association operating under the lodge system or for the exclusive benefit of the members of a fraternity itself operating under the lodge system, and providing for the payment of life, sick, accident or other benefits to the members of such society, order, or association or their dependents." (Act Cong. Oct. 3, 1917, § 701.)

The Treasury Department rules that "any organization which maintains headquarters for the purpose of affording its members the opportunity of informally congregating for social intercourse is a social club within the meaning of the law," and that "amounts paid prior to November 1, 1917, as club dues or admissions are not taxable under the act of October 3, 1917, regardless of the period or periods covered thereby." (T. D. 2570, Nov. 6, 1917.)

§ 440. Returns and Collection of Tax on Admissions and Club Dues

"Every person, corporation, partnership, or association (a) receiving any payments for such admission, dues, or fees shall collect the amount of the tax imposed by section seven hundred [supra, § 438] or seven hundred and one [supra, § 439] from the person making such payments, or (b) admitting any person free to any place for admission to which a charge is made, shall collect the amount of the tax imposed by section seven hundred [supra, § 438 from the person so admitted, and (c) in either case shall make returns and payments of the amounts so collected, at the same time and in the same manner as provided in section five hundred and three of this act." (Act Cong. Oct. 3, 1917, § 702.) Section 503 of the act, above referred to, provides for returns and for the collection and payment over of the tax on the transportation of freight, express matter, and passengers. See, supra, § 364.

§ 441. Tax on Opium and Other Narcotics

The internal revenue act of October 1, 1890, § 36, imposed a tax of ten dollars per pound on all "opium manufactured in the United States for smoking purposes." A later act (February 9, 1909 [U. S. Comp. St. 1916, §§ 8800, 8801]) prohibited the importation into the United States of opium for other than medicinal purposes, but it was held that this did not repeal nor in any way narrow the application of the act taxing manufactured opium.[7] But on January 17, 1914, Congress passed a new act on the subject (38 Stat. 277 [U. S. Comp. St. 1916, §§ 6287a–6287f]), which provides: "That an internal revenue tax of $300 per pound shall be levied and collected upon all opium manufactured in the United States for smoking purposes; and no person shall engage in such manufacture who is not a citizen of the United States and who has not given the bond required by the Commissioner of Internal Revenue. Every person who prepares opium suitable for smoking purposes from crude gum opium, or from any preparation thereof, or from the residue of smoked or partially smoked opium, commonly known as yen shee, or from any mixture of the above, or any of them, shall be regarded as a manufacturer of smoking opium within the meaning of this act." The statute further requires a bond in the sum of not less than $100,000, and imposes, for violations of the law, a penalty of not less than $10,000 fine, or imprisonment for not less than five years, or both. It is held that an indictment under this act cannot be sustained if it appears that the defendant has not refused to give the required bond.[8] Any process by which crude opium is converted into a product fit for smoking constitutes a "manufacture" of opium.[9] It was held under the earlier act (that of 1890) that the reconversion of the residuum of opium after smoking into a form fit for resmoking could not be considered as a manufacture of it.[10] But the rule must be different under the act of 1914, since it makes a specific reference to "the residue of smoked or partially smoked

---

[7] Marks v. U. S., 196 Fed. 476, 116 C. C. A. 250.
[8] Lee Mow Lin v. U. S., 240 Fed. 408, 153 C. C. A. 334.
[9] Marks v. U. S., 196 Fed. 476, 116 C. C. A. 250.
[10] U. S. v. Shelley, 229 U. S. 239, 33 Sup. Ct. 635, 57 L. Ed. 1167.

opium." However, merely adding water to an extract of opium which is already smokable is not a manufacture of smoking opium.[11]

· Not superseding the foregoing provisions, but supplementary to them, the so-called "Harrison Act" (Act Cong. Dec. 17, 1914 [U. S. Comp. St. 1916, §§ 6287g–6287q]) provides that "every person who produces, imports, manufactures, compounds, deals in, dispenses, sells, distributes or gives away opium or coca leaves, or any compound, manufacture, salt, derivative, or preparation thereof, shall register with the collector of internal revenue of the district his name or style, place of business, and place or places where such business is to be carried on. At the time of such registry and on or before the first day of July, annually thereafter, every person who produces, imports, manufactures, compounds, deals in, dispenses, sells, distributes, or gives away any of the aforesaid drugs shall pay to the said collector a special tax at the rate of $1 per annum." The act also provides (section 8) that "it shall be unlawful for any person not registered under the provisions of this act, and who has not paid the special tax provided for by this act, to have in his possession or under his control any of the aforesaid drugs." But it is held that this provision is applicable only to those persons who are required to be registered, viz., those who "produce, import, manufacture," etc., the drugs mentioned; so that it is not unlawful for a person not in any way engaged in or connected with the production or distribution of opium to have the drug or its derivatives in his possession, without being registered, at least if his supply was not unlawfully obtained.[12] This statute is held to be a revenue act, and so within the power of Congress to enact, although it is also intended to prevent the unauthorized dissemination of habit-forming drugs.[13]

§ 442. Tax on Oleomargarine and Adulterated Butter

Under the Oleomargarine Act of August 2, 1886, as amended by Act Cong. May 9, 1902, the following annual license or excise taxes are imposed: Manufacturers of oleomargarine, $600; wholesale dealers in oleomargarine artificially colored in imitation of butter $480; wholesale dealers in oleomargarine free from artificial coloration, $200; retail dealers in oleomargarine artificially

---

[11] Seidler v. U. S., 228 Fed. 336, 142 C. C. A. 628.

[12] U. S. v. Jin Fuey Moy, 241 U. S. 394, 36 Sup. Ct. 658, 60 L. Ed. 1061.

[13] Lowe v. Farbwerke-Hoechst Co., 240 Fed. 671, 153 C. C. A. 469.

colored in imitation of butter, $48; retail dealers in oleomargarine free from artificial coloration, $6; manufacturers of adulterated butter, $600; wholesale dealers in adulterated butter, $480; retail dealers in adulterated butter, $48; manufacturers of process or renovated butter, $50. In addition, these products are subject to excise taxation at the following rates: Domestic oleomargarine, artificially colored to look like butter, of any shade of yellow, 10 cents per pound; oleomargarine free from coloration that causes it to look like butter, of any shade of yellow, one-fourth of one cent per pound; oleomargarine imported from foreign countries, 15 cents per pound; adulterated butter, 10 cents per pound; process or renovated butter, one-fourth of one cent per pound.

The power of Congress to levy excises was not exceeded by the enactment of the statutes imposing a tax on artificially colored oleomargarine, because the imposition of such a tax may destroy or restrict the manufacture of that article; and an excise which does not conflict with any express limitation of the Constitution cannot be held invalid because the court may think the rate of taxation too high.[14] But a regulation made by the Commissioner of Internal Revenue, that butter having 16 per cent or more of moisture shall be classed as adulterated butter, was held invalid as being legislative in character and beyond the powers committed to him.[15] A dealer in adulterated butter is liable to the tax whether he "knowingly" engaged in the business or not.[16] And the statute is applicable to a manufacturer who does not make white oleomargarine, but mixes artificial coloration with it, as he thereby becomes a "manufacturer" under the act.[17] It is also held that the offense of defrauding, or attempting to defraud, the United States of the tax on oleomargarine may be committed by a corporation, as well as by an individual.[18]

§ 443. Tax on Mixed Flour

Manufacturers, packers, and repackers of mixed flour are subject, under the internal revenue laws of the United States, to an annual excise or license tax of twelve dollars. And in addition, the product itself is subject to internal revenue taxation at the

[14] McCray v. U. S., 195 U. S. 27, 24 Sup. Ct. 769, 49 L. Ed. 78, 1 Ann. Cas. 561.

[15] Henningsen Produce Co. v. Whaley (D. C.) 238 Fed. 650.

[16] C. H. Lawrence & Co. v. Seyburn, 202 Fed. 913, 121 C. C. A. 271.

[17] May v. U. S., 199 Fed. 42, 117 C. C. A. 420.

[18] U. S. v. Orr (D. C.) 223 Fed. 222.

following rates: Per barrel of 196 pounds or more than 98 pounds, 4 cents; half barrel of 98 pounds or more than 49 pounds, .2 cents;   quarter barrel of 49 pounds or more than 24½ pounds, 1 cent; eighth barrel of 24½ pounds or less, one-half of one cent. Mixed flour imported from foreign countries must pay an internal revenue tax at the foregoing rates, in addition to the import duties.

§ 444. Tax on Filled Cheese

Manufacturers of filled cheese are required to pay an annual ·excise or license tax at the rate of $400, wholesale dealers are subject to a like annual tax of $250, and retail dealers are annually taxed at the rate of $12.   In addition, the product itself is subject to an internal revenue tax at the rate of one cent per pound if of domestic production, or eight cents per pound if imported.

§ 445. Payment and Collection of Floor Taxes

This is the name given to the additional taxes imposed by the war revenue act of October 3, 1917, on commodities of certain kinds, in stock or in the hands of manufacturers or dealers and held for sale on the day after the passage of the act, and on which the internal revenue taxes under existing law had already been paid, or which were not subject to such taxation under existing law.   The commodities chiefly affected were distilled spirits and wines (supra, §§ 409, 412), cigars, cigarettes, tobacco, and snuff (supra, § 419), motor vehicles, mechanical musical instruments, jewelry, sporting goods, and games, toilet articles, patent or proprietary medicines, chewing gum, and cameras (supra, § 432).

The statute provides that "where additional taxes are imposed by this act upon articles or commodities, upon which the tax imposed by existing law has been paid, the person, corporation, partnership, or association required by this act to pay the tax shall, within thirty days after its passage, make return under oath in such form and under such regulations as the Commissioner of Internal Revenue with the approval of the Secretary of the Treasury shall prescribe.   Payment of the tax shown to be due may be extended to a date not exceeding seven months from the passage of this act, upon the filing of a bond for payment in such form and amount and with such sureties as the Commissioner of Internal Revenue, with the approval of the Secretary of the Treasury, may prescribe."   (Act Cong. Oct. 3, 1917, § 1002.)   The officers of the Treasury ruled that the articles or commodities subject to the tax "held and intended for sale on the morning of October 4, 1917, at each place of business, each warehouse, distributing depot, or storeroom, not connected with any place of business, and each manufacturer's shipping room on unbounded space, are required to be inventoried. The contents of broken packages are also required to be inventoried. Goods in transit on the date specified must be included in the inventory of the consignee if the title thereto has passed to him, and in the inventory of the consignor if shipped under such conditions that the title does not pass until delivery." (T. D. 2556, Oct. 16, 1917.) The following rulings were also made: "(1) Alcohol held on October 3, 1917, by manufacturers of proprietary medicines for use in manufacture as an ingredient in the manufacture of medicines is subject to the floor tax, unless on the day the act took effect it was in process of manufacture and had been rendered unfit for beverage purposes. (2) Where a corporation operates one or more retail stores and under the same name, but separately as far as bookkeeping and stock keeping are concerned, the corporation's inventory return of stock on hand should include only that in the wholesale department. Where the bookkeeping and stock keeping of the wholesale and retail departments of establishments are kept separate, they will be regarded as if they were separate and distinct departments, and the retail stock will not be subject to the floor tax. (3) Goods shipped and invoiced prior to October 4 are the property of the consignee and if shipped to a wholesaler are subject to the floor tax. If, however, title is reserved in the manufacturer, he is subject to the manufacturer's tax and the wholesaler is relieved from the floor tax. The time when title passes depends upon the intention of the parties. In the absence of an intention to the contrary, title is assumed to pass from the seller to the buyer upon the delivery of the goods to the carrier. (4) Where a manufacturer consigns his entire product to a retailer, retaining ownership in the same until disposed of by the retailer, the manufacturer is required to make return, under oath, of all goods sold to the retailer from and after October 4, and to enable him to do so he must secure monthly returns from the retailer of the goods sold." (T. D. 2547, Oct. 22, 1917.)

In regard to the permissible extension of the time for payment of the floor taxes, the following instructions were issued: "If payment of floor taxes due cannot be made within the time prescribed by law and surety company bonds cannot be furnished,

(446)

collectors are hereby authorized to accept settlement on the following conditions: A bond with adequate personal surety supported by other satisfactory security, conditioned in a penal sum not less than the tax due, and with the provision that not less than 20 per cent of the total amount of tax shall be paid on or before November 2, 1917, and not less than 20 per cent on or before the following dates: December 3, 1917, January 2, 1918, February 2, 1918, March 2, 1918. Collectors must approve all bonds and must exercise great caution in accepting security herein authorized before forwarding same to this office. Such bond shall be executed in duplicate in a penal sum of not less than the tax due and in no case less than $1,000." (T. D. 2557, Oct. 27, 1917.) It was also ruled that Liberty bonds of the United States, to the actual amount of the taxes due, may be deposited as security for the payment of floor taxes in lieu of surety bonds (T. D. 2537, Oct. 17, 1917), and collectors were authorized to accept, instead of the Liberty bonds themselves, a certificate of a bank or trust company, a member of the federal reserve system, that the taxpayer has deposited with it certificates of indebtedness in full payment of Liberty bond subscriptions. (T. D. 2554, Oct. 25, 1917.)

CHAPTER XIX

ASSESSMENT, PAYMENT, AND COLLECTION OF TAXES

§ 446. Assessment of Federal Taxes

In respect to all the forms of federal taxes which require an assessment as a basis for fixing the definite liability of the taxpayer, the assessment is to be made by the Commissioner of Internal Revenue. In the case of the income tax, the assessment is based primarily on the returns of the taxpayers, which, having been filed with the several collectors, are forwarded to the Bureau of Internal Revenue at Washington. The assessment lists are then sent to the several collectors, in their respective districts, that they may proceed with the collection of the tax. It is not within the duty or the authority of a collector to ascertain whether the conclusions of the assessor in any given case are correct, nor can he revise the assessments in any way, nor refuse to enforce an assessment regularly made by an assessor in the exercise of the latter's jurisdiction. The duties of a collector in the enforcement of a tax assessed are purely ministerial. He has the right to assume that the taxes assessed are due, and that all proper steps have been taken to ascertain this fact. The assessment, duly certified to him, is his authority to proceed and constitutes his protection. For the assessor acts judicially in determining what persons and things are subject to

(448)

taxation, and if the subject-matter is within his jurisdiction, a mistake as to the person or thing taxed, or an irregularity in the proceedings on his part, will not invalidate his action as assessor so far as to make the collector, who proceeds on a warrant in proper form to collect the tax a trespasser.[1]

§ 447. Increasing Amount of Taxable Income Returned

The federal income tax law provides that "if the collector or deputy collector have reason to believe that the amount of any income returned is understated, he shall give due notice to the person making the return to show cause why the amount of the return should not be increased, and upon proof of the amount understated may increase the same accordingly. Such person may furnish sworn testimony to prove any relevant facts, and if dissatisfied with the decision of the collector, may appeal to the Commissioner of Internal Revenue for his decision." (Act Cong. Sept. 8, 1916, § 19 [U. S. Comp. St. 1916, § 6336r].) This provision is applicable only when a return has been made. If the taxpayer has neglected or refused to make any return, the case is governed by other provisions of the act. The powers here specially conferred on collectors and deputy collectors cannot be exercised by mere clerks employed by the collectors.[2] An increase in the taxable income returned is not to be made until after a hearing. The collector is first to give notice to the taxpayer and summon him to show cause why his assessment should not be increased. Apparently the burden of proof in such cases is upon the government, that is, the collector. For although the taxpayer is called upon to show cause why the amount of the return should not be increased, yet the increase can only be made "upon proof of the amount understated." Under earlier internal revenue laws it was held that, if the books and accounts of the taxpayer correspond with and justify the return he has made, then the burden is on the government to establish any deficiency or understatement.[3] But on the other hand, while the taxpayer may present his affidavit to the collector stating the amount of his assessable income, and exhibit his books and accounts in support thereof, neither the affidavit nor the exhibits

---

[1] Haffin v. Mason, 15 Wall. 671, 21 L. Ed. 196; Erskine v. Hohnbach, 14 Wall. 613, 20 L. Ed. 745; Delaware R. Co. v. Prettyman, 17 Int. Rev. Rec. 99, Fed. Cas. No. 3,767.

[2] U. S. v. Rhawn, 11 Phila. 521, Fed. Cas. No. 16,150.

[3] Dandelet v. Smith, 18 Wall. 642, 21 L. Ed. 758.

will be so far conclusive as to prevent the collector from taking other evidence if he is not convinced of their correctness.[4]

§ 448. Assessment on Discovery of Delinquency or of Fraud

With respect to income taxes, the statute provides that "in cases of refusal or neglect to make such return, and in cases of erroneous, false, or fraudulent returns, the Commissioner of Internal Revenue shall, upon discovery thereof, at any time within three years after said return is due, or has been made, make a return upon information obtained as provided for in this title or by existing law, or require the necessary corrections to be made." (Act Cong. Sept. 8, 1916, §§ 9a, 14a [U. S. Comp. St. 1916, §§ 6336i, 6336n].) In another part of the act it is provided that "if any person, corporation, company, or association fails to make and file a return or list at the time prescribed by law, or makes, willfully or otherwise, a false or fraudulent return or list, the collector or deputy collector shall make the return or list from his own knowledge and from such information as he can obtain through testimony or otherwise." (Rev. St. U. S., § 3176, as amended by Act Cong. Sept. 8, 1916 [U. S. Comp. St. 1916, § 5899].) The duplication of authority and duty resulting from these concurrent provisions probably arises from the fact that the latter provision was found in a section of the Revised Statutes, which was amended and then incorporated in the income tax law, without adverting to the inconsistencies thereby introduced. On the principle of construction which requires that effect shall be given, if possible, to all the different parts and clauses of a statute, it must probably be held that the authority to take the action here described is concurrent in the Commissioner and the several collectors. But whereas the Commissioner is expressly bound by the limitation of three years, it may be doubted whether collectors are so bound, that part of the act which relates to them containing no such limitation.

When the Commissioner undertakes thus to make a return for a delinquent taxpayer, or to correct a return suspected to be false or fraudulent, the law makes no provision for notice to the person or corporation affected nor for an opportunity to satisfy the Commissioner of the truth of the matter or contest his proposed return or assessment. But it is a general principle of law that a proceeding for the assessment of property for taxation is judicial in its character, and in order to its validity the law authorizing it must provide

4 Pahlman v. Raster, 20 Wall. 189, 22 L. Ed. 342.

some kind of notice and an opportunity to be heard respecting it, before the proceeding becomes final or it will want the essential ingredient of due process of law.[5]   Besides, there must be proof or some kind of evidence, obtained by the Commissioner, or produced before him, to warrant him in fixing the amount of the taxable income of the person or corporation affected.[6]   Under former income tax laws it was held that a reassessment might be made although the return of the taxpayer was correct, and the error in the original assessment was due to the mistake of the revenue officers.[7]   But the language of the present act could hardly be stretched to that extent.

The fact that a return was made and that the tax assessed thereon was punctually paid by the taxpayer does not estop the Commissioner from taking the action contemplated in this provision of the law; but the discovery that the return was false and fraudulent opens up the whole matter and warrants him in fixing the correct amount of the tax.[8]   But he is strictly limited as to time, and can do nothing under this provision when more than three years have elapsed since the date when the return in question was due.[9]   But the corrected assessment is not required to be made within the three years.   The limitation is not on the making of the assessment, but on the discovery of the failure to make a return or of the falsity of the return made, within the three-year period.[10]   And neither the limitation contained in this part of the law nor any other statute of limitations bars an action by the United States to recover the difference between the amount of the tax levied and paid and the amount which should have been paid, if the taxpayer's return had correctly stated his net income.[11]

[5] Santa Clara County v. Southern Pac. R. Co. (C. C.) 18 Fed. 385, 9 Sawy. 165; Eaton v. Union County Nat. Bank, 141 Ind. 159, 40 N. E. 693; Central of Georgia Ry. Co. v. Wright, 207 U. S. 127, 28 Sup. Ct. 47, 52 L. Ed. 134, 12 Ann. Cas. 463.

[6] Barker v. White, 11 Blatchf. 445, Fed. Cas. No. 996.

[7] Barker v. White, 11 Blatchf. 445, Fed. Cas. No. 996; U. S. v. Black, 11 Blatchf. 538, Fed. Cas. No. 14,600.

[8] Eliot Nat. Bank v. Gill (D. C.) 210 Fed. 933; The Collector v. Beggs, 17 Wall. 182, 21 L. Ed. 624; U. S. v. Little Miami, C. & X. R. Co. (C. C.) 1 Fed. 700; Doll v. Evans, Fed. Cas. No. 3,969.   Compare In re Brown, Fed. Cas. No. 1,977; Commonwealth v. Pennsylvania Co., 145 Pa. 266, 23 Atl. 549.

[9] In re Archer, 9 Ben. 427, Fed. Cas. No. 506.   Compare Camp. Bird, Limited, v. Howbert (U. S. Dist. Ct., D. Colorado) T. D. No. 2366, Sept. 12, 1916.   See U. S. v. O'Neill (C. C.) 19 Fed. 567.

[10] Eliot Nat. Bank v. Gill (D. C.) 210 Fed. 933.

[11] U. S. v. Minneapolis Threshing Mach. Co. (D. C.) 229 Fed. 1019.

§ 449. Impeaching and Contesting Assessment

An assessment of taxes made by the Commissioner of Internal Revenue is prima facie valid and correct, but it is not conclusive or unimpeachable in any proceeding where it is directly involved. On the contrary, in a suit by the government for the amount of the tax or in any similar proceeding, it is open to the taxpayer to challenge the validity of the assessment and show illegality, want of jurisdiction, or that the assessment is excessive or incorrect, though he must assume the burden of proving these matters in order to overcome the presumption which supports the assessment.[12] And if any indistinguishable or inseparable part or proportion of an assessment of internal revenue taxes is illegal, the whole assessment is illegal.[13] But when the taxpayer has produced sufficient evidence to rebut the presumption of law as to the validity of the assessment, then the burden of proof is shifted on the government to establish its validity.[14] When the validity of the assessment comes into question only collaterally, as, for instance, in a suit against a collector to recover the value of property sold by him to enforce its collection, the rule is different. In these circumstances, the assessment cannot be impeached collaterally on account of mere mistakes, errors, or irregularities,[15] but a want of jurisdiction over the person or subject-matter, or an entire want of authority in the officer to make the assessment, may be shown against it even collaterally.[16]

§ 450. Appeal and Review of Assessment

Under the income tax law, when the collector believes that the amount of income disclosed by any return filed with him has been understated, he may, on notice, hearing, and proof, increase the amount returned to the figure which he is satisfied is correct. But his decision is not final, and provision for an appeal to a higher

---

[12] Clinkenbeard v. U. S., 21 Wall. 65, 22 L. Ed. 477; United States v. Thurber (D. C.) 28 Fed. 56: United States v. Bank of America (C. C.) 15 Fed. 730; United States v. Rindskopf, 8 Biss. 507, Fed. Cas. No. 16,166; Runkle v. Citizens' Ins. Co. (C. C.) 6 Fed. 143; United States v. Myers, 3 Hughes, 239, Fed. Cas. No. 15,846; Schmitt v. Trowbridge, Fed. Cas. No. 12,468; United States Fidelity & Guaranty Co. v. U. S., 201 Fed. 91, 119 C. C. A. 429.

[13] Hubbard v. Brainard, 35 Conn. 563.

[14] U. S. v. Rindskopf, 8 Biss. 507, Fed. Cas. No. 16,166.

[15] Kensett v. Stivers (C. C.) 10 Fed. 517; Milan Distilling Co. v. Tillson, 26 Int. Rev. Rec. 5, Fed. Cas. No. 9,539.

[16] Runkle v. Citizens' Ins. Co. (C. C.) 6 Fed. 143.

officer is made in the following terms: "Such person may furnish sworn testimony to prove any relevant facts, and, if dissatisfied with the decision of the collector, may appeal to the Commissioner of Internal Revenue for his decision, under such rules of procedure as may be prescribed by regulation." (Act Cong. Sept. 8, 1916, § 19 [U. S. Comp. St. 1916, § 6336r].) This evidently contemplates a hearing de novo before the Commissioner. In similar cases under general revenue laws, that is, where an appeal is allowed from an assessor or collector to a commissioner or a board of equalization or review, it is usual to provide that the decision of the latter shall be final. This has not been done in the statute under consideration, but it is the evident meaning of Congress that the decision of the Commissioner shall be final in so far as to preclude any further investigation by the officers acting in the assessment and collection of the tax. But such provisions in the tax laws are not understood so as to make the proceeding final in the sense of debarring an aggrieved party from the privilege of prosecuting or defending his rights in the courts.[17]

§ 451. Notice of Assessment

Under the federal income tax law, all persons and corporations against whom assessments have been made "shall be notified of the amount for which they are respectively liable on or before the first day of June of each successive year." (Act Cong. Sept. 8, 1916, §§ 9a, 14a [U. S. Comp. St. 1916, §§ 6336i, 6336n].) Assessment lists are made in duplicate in the office of the Commissioner of Internal Revenue, and one copy sent to each collector of internal revenue, covering the persons and corporations assessed in his district. Thereupon the collector carries out the provision of the statute quoted above by sending to each taxable person and corporation in his district a notice of the amount of income tax assessed against him or it, and that the same will be due and payable on or before the fifteenth day of June ensuing. This is a preliminary notice of assessment, and is not to be confused with the formal demand for payment of the tax which must follow if it is not paid by the appointed day, and which is necessary to fix the liability for the penalty and added interest, nor with the third notice (a general demand for the tax, penalty, and interest) which issues if payment is not made within ten days after service of the second

[17] See McGehee v. Mathis, 21 Ark. 40; Milan Distilling Co. v. Tillson, 26 Int. Rev. Rec. 5, Fed. Cas. No. 9,539; Corning & Co. v. U. S., 34 Ct. Cl. 271.

demand, and which is necessary to create a lien in favor of the
United States.

§ 452. Rate of Ordinary Income Tax

In the case of individuals, the rate of taxation under the act of
Congress of September 8, 1916, which imposes the ordinary, regular, or standing income tax, is two per cent on all income in excess
of the statutory exemptions and deductions. This is called the
"normal" tax. But there is an additional or surtax imposed on that
part of the individual's income which exceeds a certain amount.
This is provided for in section 1b of the act (U. S. Comp. St. 1916,
§ 6336a) as follows:

"In addition to the income tax imposed by subdivision (a) of this
section (herein referred to as the normal tax) there shall be levied,
assessed, collected, and paid upon the total net income of every individual, or, in the case of a nonresident alien, the total net income
received from all sources within the United States, an additional income tax (herein referred to as the additional tax) of one
per centum per annum upon the amount by which such total net
income exceeds $20,000 and does not exceed $40,000, two per centum per annum upon the amount by which such total net income
exceeds $40,000 and does not exceed $60,000, three per centum per
annum upon the amount by which such total net income exceeds
$60,000 and does not exceed $80,000, four per centum per annum
upon the amount by which such total net income exceeds $80,000
and does not exceed $100,000, five per centum per annum upon the
amount by which such total net income exceeds $100,000 and does
not exceed $150,000, six per centum per annum upon the amount
by which such total net income exceeds $150,000 and does not ex-
ceed $200,000, seven per centum per annum upon the amount by
which such total net income exceeds $200,000 and does not exceed
$250,000, eight per centum per annum upon the amount by which
such total net income exceeds $250,000 and does not exceed $300,-
000, nine per centum per annum upon the amount by which such
total net income exceeds $300,000 and does not exceed $500,000, ten
per centum per annum upon the amount by which such total net
income exceeds $500,000, and does not exceed $1,000,000, eleven
per centum per annum upon the amount by which such total net
income exceeds $1,000,000 and does not exceed $1,500,000, twelve
per centum per annum upon the amount by which such total net
income exceeds $1,500,000 and does not exceed $2,000,000, and

thirteen per centum per annum upon the amount by which such total net income exceeds $2,000,000."

In the case of corporations, the rate of the normal or ordinary income tax is two per cent. Deductions are allowed, but no specific exemption, and there is no surtax on corporations.

§ 453. Rate of War Income Tax

The Act of Congress of October 3, 1917, called the "War Revenue Act," also imposes taxes on incomes; and it must be carefully observed that these are not in abrogation of, or substitution for, those imposed under the act of 1916, but supplementary and additional to them. The provisions for these cumulative or additional income taxes are as follows:

"That in addition to the normal tax imposed" by the act of September 8, 1916, "there shall be levied, assessed, collected, and paid a like normal tax of two per centum upon the income of every individual, a citizen or resident of the United States, received in the calendar year 1917 and every calendar year thereafter." (Act Cong. Oct. 3, 1917; § 1.)

"That in addition to the additional tax imposed" by said act, "there shall be levied, assessed, collected, and paid a like additional tax upon the income of every individual received in the calendar year 1917 and every calendar year thereafter as follows:

One per centum per annum upon the amount by which the total net income exceeds $5,000 and does not exceed $7,500;

Two per centum per annum upon the amount by which the total net income exceeds $7,500 and does not exceed $10,000;

Three per centum per annum upon the amount by which the total net income exceeds $10,000 and does not exceed $12,500;

Four per centum per annum upon the amount by which the total net income exceeds $12,500 and does not exceed $15,000;

Five per centum per annum upon the amount by which the total net income exceeds $15,000 and does not exceed $20,000;

Seven per centum per annum upon the amount by which the total net income exceeds $20,000 and does not exceed $40,000;

Ten per centum per annum upon the amount by which the total net income exceeds $40,000 and does not exceed $60,000;

Fourteen per centum per annum upon the amount by which the total net income exceeds $60,000 and does not exceed $80,000;

Eighteen per centum per annum upon the amount by which the total net income exceeds $80,000 and does not exceed $100,000;

Twenty-two per centum per annum upon the amount by which the total net income exceeds $100,000 and does not exceed $150,000;

Twenty-five per centum per annum upon the amount by which the total net income exceeds $150,000 and does not exceed $200,000;

Thirty per centum per annum upon the amount by which the total net income exceeds $200,000 and does not exceed $250,000;

Thirty-four per centum per annum upon the amount by which the total net income exceeds $250,000 and does not exceed $300,000;

Thirty-seven per centum per annum upon the amount by which the total net income exceeds $300,000 and does not exceed $500,000;

Forty per centum per annum upon the amount by which the total net income exceeds $500,000 and does not exceed $750,000;

Forty-five per centum per annum upon the amount by which the total net income exceeds $750,000 and does not exceed $1,000,000;

Fifty per centum per annum upon the amount by which the total net income exceeds $1,000,000." (Act Cong. Oct. 3, 1917, § 2.)

Upon corporations an additional flat tax of four per cent per annum is imposed. (Act Cong. Oct. 3, 1917, § 4.)

§ 454. Time for Payment of Taxes

Corporations which exercise the privilege granted them by the federal statute of designating a fiscal year differing from the calendar year are required to pay their income taxes within 105 days after the date upon which they are required to file their returns of income for assessment. And "debtors" or "withholding agents," that is to say, those persons, firms, and corporations who are required to deduct and withhold the income tax from interest payments, rents, salaries, etc., disbursable by them, are directed to remit the sums so withheld by them for the income tax to the collector of internal revenue with their annual returns, but these returns are not to be made until the persons as against whom the income tax was so withheld shall have had time to file their claims for exemptions and deductions, which they are allowed to do not later than thirty days before the first day of March. But aside from these exceptional cases, and as establishing the general rule for individuals and corporations alike, the act provides that "all persons shall be notified of the amount for which they are respectively liable on or before the first day of June of each successive year, and said assessments shall be paid on or before the fifteenth day of June." But the penalty for delinquency applies only to "sums due and unpaid after the fifteenth day of June in any year, and for ten days after notice and demand thereof by the collector." (Act Cong. Sept. 8, 1916, §§ 9a, 14a [U. S. Comp. St. 1916, §§ 6336i, 6336n].) Under a similar provision in the corporation tax law of 1909, it was ruled that the taxes are due and payable ten days after the date of the actual mailing of the notice and demand. But where a notice so sent is not delivered in due time, by reason of delay in the mail, and satisfactory evidence of that fact is furnished, the penalty will not be collected, provided the full tax due is paid to the collector within ten days after the actual receipt of the notice. (T. D. No. 1659.) But if a notice from the collector was mailed to a delinquent taxpayer in a franked envelope, properly addressed, bearing the return address of the collector, and was not returned by the post office department, the presumption is that it was duly received.[18] In view of the fact that the short period of ten days allowed for the sending and receipt of the notice, and the remitting of the taxes thereunder, would be wholly insufficient in the case of numerous citizens who were traveling abroad or permanently resident abroad, the Treasury Department ruled that the penalty should not be considered as attaching in such cases until ten days after the time when the notice should be received by the taxpayer in the ordinary course of the mails, and that the penalty should not be enforced in such cases if it was proved that the notice was not received in due time by reason of delay in the mails. (T. D. 2028, Oct. 24, 1914.) Where a check is tendered in payment of the tax, which is not accepted as payment by the collector, and he deposits it in a bank for collection, the penalty for non-payment must be exacted, unless the collection is made and the tax turned over to the collector within ten days after mailing notice to the taxpayer. It is immaterial that the check was deposited in due time for the collection to have been made if the bank had been diligent. And the fact that the particular bank is a government depository does not make it an agency for the collection of internal revenue taxes, and therefore laches on its part in the performance of business duties, outside of its functions as such depository cannot be imputed to the government or affect its interests. (T. D. No. 1651.) As to the time for payment of federal taxes other than the income tax, the reader is referred to the chapters dealing with those taxes respectively.

[18] U. S. v. General Inspection & Loading Co. (D. C.) 204 Fed. 657.

§ 455. Demand for Payment of Tax

The provision of the income tax law for the addition of a penalty and interest to "any sums due and unpaid after the fifteenth day of June in any year and for ten days after notice and demand thereof by the collector," is construed by the Treasury Department as meaning that, while the taxpayer is supposed to have been already notified of the amount of his tax and of the day when it is due, and may, if he chooses, make payment at any time after receiving such notice, yet if the tax is not paid at the close of the day of June 15th, it then becomes necessary for the collector to send him a formal demand for payment, and thereupon the taxpayer has ten days after service of such demand in which to make his payment, and he does not become "delinquent," in the sense of being subject to any penalty, until the expiration of the ten days. (T. D. 1995, June 12, 1914; T. D. 2003, June 26, 1914.)

Provisions of this kind in a revenue law, designed for the information and protection of the citizen, and prescribed as a preliminary to the imposition of penalties upon him, are mandatory in the strictest sense, and must be strictly construed and literally followed, and if any prescribed notice or demand is omitted, the government cannot enforce its claims to any additional tax or interest.[19] Nor can any substitution be permitted. Thus, for instance, the issuance of a warrant to the collector of internal revenue taxes is not an equivalent for the demand which he is required by law to make, at least where the person taxed has had no notice of it.[20] And while the prescribed notice and demand may not be a part of the assessment, nor a condition precedent to a valid assessment, yet it is necessary by the terms of the statute before the taxpayer can be charged with the penalty and interest for delinquency, and it is also necessary before the collector can distrain for the taxes,[21] and to create and bring into operation a lien in favor of the government.[22]

§ 456. Payment and Receipt

Payment of internal revenue taxes may be made in any money which is a legal tender for that purpose. Also, by an act of Con-

[19] U. S. v. Allen (C. C.) 14 Fed. 263; Eastman v. Little, 5 N. H. 290; Dow v. Chandler, 85 Mo. 245.

[20] Brown v. Goodwin, 1 Abb. N. C. (N. Y.) 452.

[21] U. S. v. Bristow (C. C.) 20 Fed. 378; U. S. v. Pennsylvania Co. (D. C.) 27 Fed. 539.

[22] U. S. v. Pacific R. Co., 4 Dill. 71, Fed. Cas. No. 15,984.

gress, collectors are authorized to receive in payment of internal revenue taxes certified checks drawn on national and state banks and trust companies during such time and under such regulations as the Secretary of the Treasury may prescribe. (Act Cong. March 2, 1911, 36 Stat. 965 [U. S. Comp. St. 1916, § 5711].) The regulations permit the acceptance of certified checks drawn on banks and trust companies in the place where the collector has his office, and also of "out of town" checks, provided the latter can be collected without any expense to the government; but collectors are warned that if they accept any other form of exchange or security, they do so at their own peril, except perhaps in cases where the bank in which they make their deposits will accept such paper indorsed by the collector "without recourse." (T. D. 1963, March 18, 1914; T. D. 1990, June 1, 1914.)

Where a tax past due to the United States has been paid to the collector, he and his sureties are liable therefor, although the amount so paid had not then been returned to the assessor's office or passed upon by him nor had a sworn statement of the taxpayer been delivered.[23] And where an internal revenue tax is required to be paid by the "owner" of the property, it need not necessarily be paid by the owner in person. It is enough if the payment is made by him acting through some friend or agent, whether compensated or not, or by any person who will act in his behalf, and whose act is not disavowed by the owner.[24]

Upon payment of an income tax, it is made the duty of the collector to "give to the person making such payment a full written or printed receipt, expressing the amount paid and the particular account for which such payment was made; and whenever such payment is made, such collector shall, if required, give a separate receipt for each tax paid by any debtor, on account of payments made to or to be made by him to separate creditors in such form that such debtor can conveniently produce the same separately to his several creditors in satisfaction of their respective demands to the amounts specified in such receipts; and such receipts shall be sufficient evidence in favor of such debtor to justify him in withholding the amount therein expressed from his next payment to his creditor." (Act Cong. Sept. 8, 1916, § 17 [U. S. Comp. St. 1916, § 6336p].)

[23] King v. U. S., 99 U. S. 229, 25 L. Ed. 373.
[24] Bennett v. Hunter, 9 Wall. 326, 19 L. Ed. 672; U. S. v. Lee, 106 U. S. 196, 1 Sup. Ct. 240, 27 L. Ed. 171; Tracey v. Irwin, 18 Wall. 549, 21 L. Ed. 786.

§ 457. Penalty for Delinquency

Failure to pay the federal income tax when due, and for ten days after notice and demand thereof by the collector, will subject the taxpayer, whether an individual or a corporation, to a penalty of five per cent of the amount of the tax unpaid, which is to be added to that amount, together with interest at the rate of one per cent a month from the time the tax became due until it is paid. But an exception is made in favor of the estates of insane, deceased, and insolvent persons. (Act Cong. Sept. 8, 1916, §§ 9a, 14a [U. S. Comp. St. 1916, §§ 6336i, 6336n].) Also an indulgence has been granted to persons absent in foreign countries at the time for paying the tax, the provision being that the penalty and interest will not be enforced against them if they make payment within ten days (or place their remittance in the mails) subsequent to the time when the notice and demand should be received by them in the ordinary course of the mails. (T. D. 2028, Oct. 24, 1914.)

There is no constitutional objection to adding a penalty to a tax for failing to pay it at or within the appointed time.[25] And when the addition of a penalty follows automatically and as a mere matter of computation, upon the failure to pay at the proper time, its imposition is not a judicial proceeding, and if the taxpayer had notice and a hearing on the question of fixing the amount of his assessment, it is immaterial that the penalty is added without further notice or an opportunity to be heard, and he cannot complain that he is deprived of his property without due process of law.[26] But penalties are never extended by implication, and unless expressly imposed, they cannot be enforced.[27]

Whether the interest on the unpaid tax begins to run from the end of the ten days allowed for payment in the collector's demand, or relates back to the day when the tax should ordinarily have been paid is an unsettled question. It is a general rule that interest cannot be claimed on unpaid taxes until after a demand for them,[28] and that a taxpayer is not technically in default until the expiration of any period of time allowed him to make payment.[29] But the statute makes the interest run from "the time the tax became due,"

[25] De Treville v. Smalls, 98 U. S. 517, 25 L. Ed. 174. See Savings Bank v. Archbold, 104 U. S. 708, 26 L. Ed. 901.

[26] Passavant v. U. S., 148 U. S. 214, 13 Sup. Ct. 572, 37 L. Ed. 426.

[27] Elliott v. Railroad Co., 99 U. S. 573, 25 L. Ed. 292.

[28] Second & Third Street Passenger Ry. Co. v. Philadelphia, 51 Pa. 465.

[29] Harrison v. U. S., 20 Ct. Cl. 175.

and explicitly provides that assessments "shall be paid on or before the fifteenth day of June."

In the case of corporations going out of existence in the course of the year, and leaving no assets, the Treasury Department has ruled that the former officers of the corporation cannot be held individually liable for the penalty prescribed by law, nor are the individual assets of the stockholders liable. But if the corporation left assets which have been distributed among the stockholders, such assets are available for the collection of the tax, though not for the penalty.[30] It should also be observed that a pardon for offenses against the revenue laws cannot relieve the offenders from the payment of taxes.[31]

§ 458.   Lien of Taxes

An act of Congress, amending a section of the Revised Statutes, provides: "If any person liable to pay any tax neglects or refuses to pay the same after demand, the amount shall be a lien in favor of the United States from the time when the assessment list was received by the collector, except when otherwise provided, until paid, with the interest, penalties, and costs that may accrue in addition thereto upon all property and rights to property belonging to such person: Provided, however, That such lien shall not be valid as against any mortgagee, purchaser, or judgment creditor until notice of such lien shall be filed by the collector in the office of the clerk of the district court of the district within which the property subject to such lien is situated: Provided further, Whenever any state by appropriate legislation authorizes the filing of such notice in the office of the registrar or recorder of deeds of the counties of that state, or in the state of Louisiana in the parishes thereof, then such lien shall not be valid in that state as against any mortgagee, purchaser, or judgment creditor, until such notice shall be filed in the office of the registrar or recorder of deeds of the county or counties, or parish or parishes in the state of Louisiana, within which the property subject to the lien is situated." (Act Cong. March 4, 1913, amending Rev. St. U. S. § 3186 [U. S. Comp. St. 1916, § 5908].) An opinion was given by the Attorney General that this statute was applicable to the special tax on corporations imposed by the act of 1909, and if so, it would for the same reasons be applicable to the income tax law. The act impos-

[30] T. D. No. 1852.
[31] U. S. v. Roelle, Fed. Cas. No. 16,186.

ing a tax upon the devolution of estates makes special provisions for a lien for unpaid taxes thereunder, upon the gross estate of the decedent, to continue for ten years. (Act Cong. Sept. 8, 1916, § 209 [U. S. Comp. St. 1916, § 6336½j].) Under the inheritance tax law of 1898, it was held that where an executor failed to pay a legacy tax due, the government might sue him to impose a lien on the property bequeathed, if he had it in his possession, and if not, might institute proceedings against the person who had it.[32] The internal revenue tax on distilled spirits becomes due as soon as the spirits are produced, and the government has a first lien thereon until the tax is paid.[33]

It will be observed that the lien for unpaid income taxes is to date "from the time when the assessment list was received by the collector," but is created only by a neglect or refusal to pay "after demand." The explanation is that an unpaid income tax is and continues a mere personal liability of the taxpayer until its payment is demanded. A demand in due form, stating the amount of the tax, is necessary to create and bring into operation the lien. But when such a demand has been made, and payment is thereafter neglected or refused, the lien of the tax relates back to the time when the assessment list was received by the collector, though it attaches only to the property belonging to the taxpayer at the time when the demand was made.[34] The preliminary notice of assessment referred to in an earlier section is not such a demand as to lay a foundation for the lien, nor is the demand of payment of the tax which is issued upon non-payment of the tax on the day when due, for this last must give the taxpayer ten days after service to make his payment before delinquency is established, and because it cannot include any demand for penalty or interest, liability for which does not attach until delinquency. Accordingly it is the custom of the revenue officers, in case of non-payment after the ten days, to follow with a general demand for payment of the tax, penalty, and interest, which establishes the lien.[35]

Prior to the act of Congress amending the Revised Statutes in this particular, it was held that a state law requiring that all liens

[32] U. S. v. Priest (D. C.) 210 Fed. 332.

[33] United States Fidelity & Guaranty Co. v. U. S., 220 Fed. 592, 136 C. C. A. 50.

[34] U. S. v. Pacific R. R. (C. C.) 1 Fed. 97; Brown v. Goodwin, 1 Abb. N. C. (N. Y.) 452; U. S. v. Pacific R. R., 4 Dill. 71, Fed. Cas. No. 15,984.

[35] Internal Revenue Regulations No. 33, art. 197.

on real property must be recorded in order to affect third parties did not apply to tax liens in favor of the United States, and though such tax liens were not recorded, they might be enforced against the lands in the hands of purchasers for value without notice, mortgagees, and judgment creditors.[36] This is expressly changed by the amendatory act recited above. And after its enactment, collectors of internal revenue were given general instructions to file notices of such liens in the proper offices "when deemed advisable in order to protect the interests of the government," and particularly "where the collector apprehends that attempts will be made to defeat collection by transfer of property or placing incumbrances thereon, or where, from the size of the assessment or for any other reason the collector is of the opinion that such action is advisable to protect the government," and "when the tax has been paid, notice should in like manner be filed, showing satisfaction of the claim and removal of lien." (T. D. No. 1841.)

A lien for taxes does not stand upon the footing of an ordinary incumbrance, and is not displaced by a sale of the property under a pre-existing judgment or decree, unless otherwise directed by statute.[37] But it is the practice in some of the state courts that when property incumbered by a tax lien in favor of the United States is sold on execution issuing out of the state court, the government's lien must first be paid out of the proceeds of the execution sale, and its priority will be recognized in the state court.[38] The lien, however, does not come into existence unless all the prescribed steps in connection with the making of the assessment and whatever else is declared by the statute to be necessary to the fixing of liability have been duly and properly taken.[39] But the lien, once attached, cannot be waived or released by any disclaimer on the part of the collector.[40]

Under the corporation tax law of 1909, it was ruled that the assets of a corporation are subject to the lien for the payment of the tax, provided that the corporation has not been dissolved and

[36] U. S. v. Snyder, 149 U. S. 210, 13 Sup. Ct. 846, 37 L. Ed. 705; Hartman v. Bean, 99 U. S. 393, 25 L. Ed. 455; U. S. v. Turner, Fed. Cas. No. 16,548; Alkan v. Bean, 8 Biss. 83, Fed. Cas. No. 202; U. S. v. Black, 3 Brewst. (Pa.) 167.

[37] Osterberg v. Union Trust Co., 93 U. S. 424, 23 L. Ed. 964.

[38] Appeal of Dungan, 68 Pa. 204, 8 Am. Rep. 169. But compare Bosset v. Miller, 2 Woodw. Dec. (Pa.) 40.

[39] U. S. v. Pacific R. R., 1 Fed. 97.

[40] Alkan v. Bean, 8 Biss. 83, Fed. Cas. No. 202.

all its assets distributed prior to the time when the list of assessments came into the hands of the collector. And even if a corporation is dissolved before the tax falls due, so that the government cannot claim a lien on its assets, still the tax imposed may be collected by the government by pursuing the assets into the hands of the stockholders, in the same manner as any other creditor might obtain satisfaction of his debt.[41]

§ 459. Collection by Suit

The rule is thoroughly well established that an action of debt or any other proper form of proceedings may be maintained in the name of the United States for the recovery of any sum due from the defendant for internal revenue taxes.[42] It was held that in the collection of taxes imposed on corporations by the excise tax law of 1909, the government was not confined to the summary proceedings therein authorized, but that it might resort to a plenary suit; and that, where a tax of a fixed percentage, such as that imposed by the act in question, is so definitely described in the statute that its amount can be ascertained and determined on evidence by a court, a suit therefor will lie without an assessment of the tax.[43] It was also held under the same statute that indebitatus assumpsit was a proper form of action to be brought by the United States for the recovery of the tax.[44] Specially with reference to the income tax law, it must be remembered that it contains a provision that "all administrative, special, and general provisions of law, including the laws in relation to the assessment, remission, collection, and refund of internal revenue taxes not heretofore specifically repealed, and not inconsistent with the provisions of this title, are hereby extended and made applicable to the provisions of this title and to the tax herein imposed." (Act Cong. Sept. 8, 1916, § 22 [U. S. Comp. S. 1916, § 6336u].) And an almost identical provision inserted in

[41] 28 Opin. Atty. Gen. 241.

[42] Billings v. U. S., 232 U. S. 261, 34 Sup. Ct. 421, 58 L. Ed. 596; U. S. v. Chamberlin, 219 U. S. 250, 31 Sup. Ct. 155, 55 L. Ed. 204; Dollar Sav. Bank v. U. S., 19 Wall. 227, 22 L. Ed. 80; U. S. v. United States Fidelity & Guaranty Co., 221 Fed. 27, 136 C. C. A. 553; U. S. v. Bristow (C. C.) 20 Fed. 378; U. S. v. Little Miami, C. & X. R. Co. (C. C.) 1 Fed. 700; U. S. v. Pacific R. R., 4 Dill 66, Fed. Cas. No. 15,983; U. S. v. Halloran, 14 Blatchf. 1, Fed. Cas. No. 15,286; U. S. v. Washington Mills, 2 Cliff. 601, Fed. Cas. No. 16,647; U. S. v. Tilden, 9 Ben. 368, Fed. Cas. No. 16,519.

[43] U. S. v. Grand Rapids & I. Ry. Co. (D. C.) 239 Fed. 153.

[44] U. S. v. Minneapolis Threshing Mach. Co. (D. C.) 229 Fed. 1019.

the War Revenue Act of 1898, was held to confer express statutory authority for the maintenance of an action by the United States to recover the stamp taxes thereby imposed.[45] The legacy tax imposed by the act of 1898 not being a debt of the decedent's estate, it was held that the United States could not maintain an action at law to recover the same against the executor or administrator in his representative capacity.[46] But the "estates tax" law now in force provides that "if the tax herein imposed is not paid within sixty days after it is due, the collector shall, unless there is reasonable cause for further delay, commence appropriate proceedings in any court of the United States, in the name of the United States, to subject the property of the decedent to be sold under the judgment or decree of the court." (Act Cong. Sept. 8, 1916, § 208 [U. S. Comp. St. 1916, § 6336½i].)

Jurisdiction of suits by the United States for the recovery of internal revenue taxes is given to the federal district courts. The Judicial Code provides that these courts shall have "original jurisdiction of all suits of a civil nature, at common law or in equity, brought by the United States, or by any officer thereof authorized by law to sue," and specifically "of all cases arising under any law providing for internal revenue." [47] And "taxes accruing under any law providing internal revenue may be sued for and recovered either in the district where the liability for such tax occurs or in the district where the delinquent resides." [48] But a suit will not lie to recover such a tax in a district other than those mentioned, although the defendant may be found there and served with process there.[49] It is immaterial in these cases that the amount in controversy does not equal or exceed $3,000; that limitation upon the jurisdiction of the federal courts is not applicable in internal

---

[45] U. S. v. Chamberlin, 219 U. S. 250, 31 Sup. Ct. 155, 55 L. Ed. 204. But see McClain v. Fleshman, 106 Fed. 880. 46 C. C. A. 15.

[46] U. S. v. Fitts (D. C.) 197 Fed. 1007.

[47] Federal Judicial Code, 1911, § 24 (Comp. St. 1916, § 991). And see Coffey v. United States, 116 U. S. 427, 6 Sup. Ct. 432, 29 L. Ed. 681. As to the courts of the District of Columbia being "courts of the United States," see James v. United States, 202 U. S. 401, 26 Sup. Ct. 685, 50 L. Ed. 1079. As to the jurisdiction of the district court of Alaska, see McAllister v. United States, 141 U. S. 174, 11 Sup. Ct. 949, 35 L. Ed. 693.

[48] Federal Judicial Code, 1911, § 44 (Comp. St. 1916, § 1026).

[49] United States v. New York, N. H. & H. R. Co., 10 Ben. 144, Fed. Cas. No. 15,874.

revenue cases.[50] It may be doubted whether the courts of the states would have jurisdiction of suits for the recovery of these taxes. It is provided that the jurisdiction of the federal courts shall be exclusive of that of the state courts in "all suits for penalties and forfeitures incurred under the laws of the United States." [51] But a reasonable construction of this provision might lead to the conclusion that it was the intention of Congress to grant exclusive jurisdiction to the federal courts in cases where the suit was brought solely for a penalty or forfeiture, and not to include cases where the action was for the recovery of a tax, though it might incidentally include a claim for a penalty.

By way of defense to such an action, the defendant may allege and show want of jurisdiction in the assessing officers, or that the assessment was erroneous, illegal, or excessive.[52] But the government is not estopped or debarred from maintaining a suit to recover income taxes by the fact that the taxpayer made a return, on which a tax was assessed against him, and that he paid the amount of the tax, when the suit is based on the claim of the government that the amount so assessed and paid was incorrect and too small in amount.[53] But on the other hand, the defendant is entitled to a deduction of any amount admitted by the government to have been previously overpaid, even though there is no plea of set-off.[54]

It is a well-established principle that the United States is not bound by any statute of limitations, nor barred by any laches or delay of its officers, however gross, in a suit brought by it as a sovereign government to enforce a public right or to assert a public interest.[55] And this rule has been applied to suits for the

---

[50] Ames v. Hager, 36 Fed. 129, 1 L. R. A. 377.

[51] Federal Judicial Code, 1911, § 256 (Comp. St. 1916, § 1233). See United States v. Mooney, 116 U. S. 104, 6 Sup. Ct. 304, 29 L. Ed. 550.

[52] Clinkenbeard v. United States, 21 Wall. 65, 22 L. Ed. 477; United States v. Thurber (D. C.) 28 Fed. 56; United States v. Nebraska Distilling Co., 80 Fed. 285, 25 C. C. A. 418.

[53] United States v. Tilden, 9 Ben. 368, 24 Int. Rev. Rec. 99, Fed. Cas. No. 16,519; United States v. Philadelphia & R. R. Co., 123 U. S. 113, 8 Sup. Ct. 77, 31 L. Ed. 138; United States v. Little Miami, C. & X. R. Co. (C. C.) 1 Fed. 700; United States v. Hazard, Fed. Cas. No. 15,337; United States v. New York Guaranty & Indemnity Co., 8 Ben. 269, Fed. Cas. No. 15,872.

[54] Missouri R., F. S. & G. R. Co. v. United States (C. C.) 19 Fed. 66.

[55] United States v. Beebe, 127 U. S. 338, 8 Sup. Ct. 1083, 32 L. Ed. 121; United States v. Insley, 130 U. S. 263, 9 Sup. Ct. 485, 32 L. Ed. 968.

recovery of taxes.[56] But very long delay in demanding a tax or instituting proceedings for its recovery may bar an action by the government, if it is shown that the delay has prejudiced the defendant by the disappearance or loss of evidence essential to his defense.[57] And in a case where the amount of taxes assessable against a corporation was settled by agreement between the company and the assessor, and accordingly assessed and the amount paid, and nearly twelve years afterwards a suit was brought by the government on the allegation that the assessment was too low and that a further sum was due, it was held that the fact of the assessment, the payment of the tax under it, and the acquiescence of the government, for so long a period afterwards, raised a presumption that the assessment was correct, and that the money paid covered the defendant's entire liability, and that the burden was thus cast upon the government of proving, by evidence such as fully to satisfy the mind, that the assessment was erroneous.[58]

The assessment list, regular in form, makes a prima facie case for the government, and it is not necessary for it, in the first instance, to go into the particulars of the assessment, or to show that it was properly made.[59] But the assessment is not conclusive evidence. It may be attacked and controverted as excessive or illegal, in defense to the action.[60] In regard to the particulars of the income alleged to have been received by the defendant and to be subject to the tax, the burden of proof is on the government to show their existence and amount, and also, it would appear, that the exemptions and deductions claimed by the taxpayer are fictitious, exaggerated, or not allowable.[61] But when evidence for this purpose has been adduced, it is for the taxpayer to controvert it by proper proof, and if he fails to do so, a finding in favor of the Unit-

---

[56] U. S. v. Grand Rapids & I. Ry. Co. (D. C.) 239 Fed. 153; U. S. v. Tilden, 9 Ben. 368, Fed. Cas. No. 16,519.

[57] United States v. Marquette, H. & O. R. Co. (C. C.) 17 Fed. 719.

[58] United States v. Philadelphia & R. R. Co., 123 U. S. 113, 8 Sup. Ct. 77, 31 L. Ed. 138.

[59] Western Express Co. v. United States, 141 Fed. 28, 72 C. C. A. 516; United States v. Butler, Fed. Cas. No. 14,702; United States v. Cole (D. C.) 134 Fed. 697.

[60] United States v. Bank of America (C. C.) 15 Fed. 730; United States v. Rindskopf, 8 Biss. 507, Fed. Cas. No. 16,166; Runkle v. Citizens' Ins. Co. (C. C.) 6 Fed. 143.

[61] Little Miami, C. & X. R. Co. v. United States, 108 U. S. 277, 2 Sup. Ct. 627, 27 L. Ed. 724; United States v. Central Nat. Bank (D. C.) 15 Fed. 222.

ed States is justified.[62] But internal revenue regulations prescribed by the Treasury Department, for the guidance of officers in the administration of the law, have not the force of rules of evidence in actions by the government to enforce payment of the tax.[63]

§ 460. Collection by Distraint

The laws of the United States, made applicable to the collection of internal revenue taxes, provide that "if any person liable to pay any tax neglects or refuses to pay the same within ten days after notice and demand, it shall be lawful for the collector or his deputy to collect the said taxes, with five per centum additional thereto, and interest as aforesaid, by distraint and sale, in the manner hereafter provided, of the goods, chattels, or effects, including stocks, securities and evidences of debt, of the person delinquent as aforesaid." [64] Distraint is not a judicial process by which the property of a debtor can be taken for the satisfaction of a debt. but it is an executive process by which the right to seize and take property for the payment of taxes is exercised; its use does not deprive the citizen of his property without due process of law, nor otherwise contravene the constitution; summary remedies for the collection of debts due to a government have always existed.[65] And the right and duty of the collector to distrain is not suspended or in any way affected by the commencement of an action by the government to recover the same taxes.[66] A distress warrant from the Treasury is conclusive evidence of the facts recited in it and of the authority to make the levy, so far as to justify the marshal in acting under it, but the question of indebtedness may be the subject of litigation, the levy providing security for the event of the suit.[67] It is necessary, however, to the validity of a sale made on distress that the collector should strictly comply with the directions of the statute in regard to notice and demand, advertisement of the sale, and whatever else is intended for the benefit or pro-

[62] U. S. v. Cole (D. C.) 134 Fed. 697.

[63] U. S. v. Cole (D. C.) 134 Fed. 697.

[64] Rev. St. U. S., §§ 3187–3195 (U. S. Comp. St. 1916, §§ 5909–5917).

[65] Murray v. Hoboken Land & Imp. Co., 18 How. 272, 15 L. Ed. 372; Allen v. Sheridan (C. C.) 145 Fed. 963; Mason v. Rollins, 2 Biss. 99, Fed. Cas. No. 9,252; Marshall v. Wadsworth, 64 N. H. 386, 10 Atl. 685.

[66] Harding v. Woodcock, 137 U. S. 43, 11 Sup. Ct. 6, 34 L. Ed. 580.

[67] Murray v. Hoboken Land & Imp. Co., 18 How. 272, 15 L. Ed. 372.

tection of the taxpayer.[68]   State exemption laws are not applicable
to debts due by a citizen to the United States; and as concerns the
exemption of property from distraint for internal revenue taxes,
the provision of the Revised Statutes which authorizes the use of
this process also enumerates the property which shall be exempt,
and this alone applies, without regard to the laws of the particular
state.[69]   In the execution of a distraint, stock in a corporation may
be seized or levied on by the simple service of a notice on the proper officer of the corporation.[70]   It should be added that property
seized and sold by a collector, in the enforcement of the internal
revenue laws, cannot be replevied from the purchaser by the former
owner under process from a state court, and such a proceeding
will not be tolerated by a federal court, the remedy for a wrong-
ful seizure given by the statute being exclusive.[71]   Moreover, severe penalties are denounced against persons who forcibly ob-
struct or hinder collectors in the performance of their duty, or
who forcibly rescue property seized by a collector for non-payment
of taxes.[72]

§ 461.   Sale of Real Estate for Delinquent Taxes

The federal statutes also provide that "when goods, chattels, or
effects sufficient to satisfy the taxes imposed upon any person are
not found by the collector or deputy collector, he is authorized to
collect the same by seizure and sale of real estate." [73]   So far as
regards this provision, it is probably correct to say, as some of
the decisions have maintained, that no right to seize and sell land
exists until there has been a failure to find sufficient personal estate, and this fact is essential to the validity of the sale, and must be
proved, if challenged, by evidence outside the collector's deed.[74]
But the statutes also provide that the Commissioner of Internal
Revenue "may direct a bill in chancery to be filed, in a district or
circuit court of the United States to enforce the lien of the United

---

[68] State Nat. Bank v. Morrison, 1 McCrary, 204, Fed. Cas. No. 13,325; Blake
v. Johnson, 1 N. H. 91; Parker v. Rule, 9 Cranch, 64, 3 L. Ed. 658.

[69] U. S. v. Howell (C. C.) 9 Fed. 674.

[70] Miller v. U. S., 11 Wall. 268, 20 L. Ed. 135.

[71] Allen v. Sheridan (C. C.) 145 Fed. 963.

[72] Rev. St. U. S., § 3177 (U. S. Comp. St. 1916, § 5900).   See U. S. v. Ford
(D. C.) 34 Fed. 26.

[73] Rev. St. U. S., § 3196 (U. S. Comp. St. 1916, § 5918).

[74] Brown v. Goodwin, 75 N. Y. 409.   And see Mansfield v. Excelsior Refinery
Co., 135 U. S. 326, 10 Sup. Ct. 825, 34 L. Ed. 162.

States for tax upon any real estate, or to subject any real estate owned by the delinquent, or in which he has any right, title, or interest, to the payment of such tax." [75] And it is held that the remedy thus provided is cumulative, and that it is not necessary to exhaust the possible remedy against the goods and chattels of the taxpayer before resorting to a bill in equity to subject his real estate.[76] But when the United States has foreclosed a lien on realty for delinquent internal revenue taxes, and bid in the property, and seeks to maintain its title as against a vendee of the former owner, the remedy is by an action at law to recover possession, and not by a bill in equity to remove cloud on title.[77]

The Revised Statutes contain detailed and specific directions as to the procedure to be followed on a seizure and sale of land, the allowance of a right of redemption, and the deed to be given by the collector.[78] In general it may be said, according to the rule applicable to all sales for taxes, that the collector must proceed strictly in accordance with the directions of the statute, at least in so far as regards all steps to be taken for advising the taxpayer of the proceedings or otherwise intended for his benefit.[79] And the general doctrine is that the collector's deed is prima facie evidence of the facts required by the statute to be stated in it (such being the provision of the statute itself), but not of any other recitals nor of any facts not included in the deed,[80] although, under certain earlier statutes levying direct taxes, it was held that the collector's deed was prima facie evidence of the regularity of the sale and of all antecedent facts essential to its validity and to that of the purchaser's title thereunder, and could only be affected by proof that the lands were not subject to the tax, that it had been paid prior to the sale, or that the property had been redeemed.[81]

[75] Rev. St. U. S., § 3207 (U. S. Comp. St. 1916, § 5929).

[76] Mansfield v. Excelsior Refinery Co., 135 U. S. 326, 10 Sup. Ct. 825, 34 L. Ed. 162; Blacklock v. U. S., 208 U. S. 75, 28 Sup. Ct. 228, 52 L. Ed. 396; U. S. v. Curry (D. C.) 201 Fed. 371; Alkan v. Bean, 8 Biss. 83, Fed. Cas. No. 202.

[77] U. S. v. Wilson, 118 U. S. 86, 6 Sup. Ct. 991, 30 L. Ed. 110.

[78] See Rev. St. U. S., §§ 3196–3208 (U. S. Comp. St. 1916, §§ 5918–5930).

[79] Allen v. Smith, 1 Leigh (Va.) 231.

[80] Fox v. Stafford, 90 N. C. 296; Stewart v. Pergusson, 133 N. C. 276, 45 S. E. 585; Brown v. Goodwin, 75 N. Y. 409. And see Williams v. Peyton, 4 Wheat. 77, 4 L. Ed. 518.

[81] De Treville v. Smalls, 98 U. S. 517, 25 L. Ed. 174; Keely v. Sanders, 99 U. S. 441, 25 L. Ed. 327; Sherry v. McKinley, 99 U. S. 496, 25 L. Ed. 330.

§ 462. Remedies of Taxpayer Illegally Assessed; Injunction

If there are any circumstances under which an individual or corporation complaining of his or its assessment for the income tax can succeed in procuring an injunction to restrain its assessment or collection, they must be very rare and exceptional. The general rule in such cases has been thus set forth by the United States Supreme Court: When a court of equity is asked to enjoin the collection of taxes, it is essential that the case be brought within some of the recognized rules of equity jurisdiction, and neither illegality nor irregularity in the proceedings, nor error or excess in the valuation, nor the hardship and injustice of the law, provided it be constitutional, nor any grievance which can be remedied by a suit at law, either before or after the payment of the tax, will authorize an injunction against its collection; and no injunction can be granted until it is shown that all the taxes conceded to be due, or which the court can see ought to be paid, or which can be shown to be due by affidavits, have been paid or unconditionally tendered.[82] But besides this, it is explicitly provided by a law of the United States that "no suit for the purpose of restraining the assessment or collection of any tax shall be maintained in any court." [83] Hence it is held that a bill in equity will not lie to enjoin a collector of internal revenue taxes from proceeding by distraint or otherwise to collect a tax assessed by the Commissioner of Internal Revenue, although the tax is alleged in the bill to have been illegally assessed.[84] And a bill in equity filed in the Supreme Court of the District of Columbia, to enjoin the Commissioner from assessing the complainant for the "additional tax" or surtax, on the ground that that feature of the income tax law was unconstitutional, was dismissed on the ground that the complainant had an adequate remedy at law, by paying the amount of the tax under protest and suing for its recovery.[85] In other cases also

---

[82] State Railroad Tax Cases, 92 U. S. 575, 23 L. Ed. 663; Schulenberg-Boeckeler Lumber Co. v. Town of Hayward (C. C.) 20 Fed. 422; Lexington v. McQuillan's Heirs, 9 Dana (Ky.) 513, 35 Am. Dec. 159.

[83] Rev. St. U. S., § 3224 (U. S. Comp. St. 1916, § 5947).

[84] Snyder v. Marks, 109 U. S. 189, 3 Sup. Ct. 157, 27 L. Ed. 901; Shelton v. Platt, 139 U. S. 591, 11 Sup. Ct. 646, 35 L. Ed. 273; Wisconsin v. Frear, 231 U. S. 616, 34 Sup. Ct. 272, 58 L. Ed. 400; Kohlhamer v. Smietanka (D. C.) 239 Fed. 408; Cutting v. Gilbert, 5 Blatchf. 259, Fed. Cas. No. 3,519; Smith v. Com'rs of Leavenworth, 9 Kan. 296.

[85] Dodge v. Osborn, 43 App. D. C. 144, affirmed, 240 U. S. 118, 36 Sup. Ct. 275, 60 L. Ed. 557.

it has been held that even the alleged unconstitutionality of an act of Congress levying taxes furnishes no ground to enjoin their collection.[86] And the fact that a particular collector may be financially unable to respond in a suit to recover back taxes paid to him, is no justification for an injunction, since the government will assume his responsibility.[87]

As to the case where the injunction is not asked against the officers of the government, but against a corporation, to restrain it from paying an internal revenue tax, it is held that such a suit, brought by a stockholder, is not forbidden by the above quoted provision of the Revised Statutes.[88] But such a suit was held properly dismissed where the corporation made no serious defense, and there was no showing of irreparable injury, or of any effort to secure action by the corporation or its directors, other than a demand on the resident managing agent, the distance of the directors (in Alaska) from the place where the plaintiff resided, and in which the court was held, being relied on as an excuse for not making any further effort.[89]

Likewise, it is held that a bill of peace will not lie, on the theory that all persons charged with an internal revenue tax have such a unity of interest in contesting the tax that they may join as plaintiffs in a bill to restrain the assessment and collection of it, and that a determinate number of such persons may appear in the name of themselves and for the rest.[90]

§ 463. Same; Appeal; Certiorari; Mandamus

Certiorari is not a proper remedy to review an assessment made by revenue officers in so far as their proceedings thereon have been purely administrative, nor for alleged irregularities in their proceedings, or for undue or excessive assessment, nor for alleged mistakes in the manner of making the assessment.[91] But where the

[86] Delaware R. Co. v. Prettyman, 17 Int. Rev. Rec. 99, Fed. Cas. No. 3,767.

[87] Cutting v. Gilbert, 5 Blatchf. 259, Fed. Cas. No. 3,519.

[88] Brushaber v. Union Pac. R. Co., 240 U. S. 1, 36 Sup. Ct. 236, 60 L. Ed. 493, L. R. A. 1917D, 414, Ann. Cas. 1917B, 713; Stanton v. Baltic Min. Co., 240 U. S. 103, 36 Sup. Ct. 278, 60 L. Ed. 546; Pollock v. Farmers' Loan & Trust Co., 157 U. S. 429, 15 Sup. Ct. 673, 39 L. Ed. 759.

[89] Corbus v. Alaska Treadwell Gold Min. Co., 187 U. S. 455, 23 Sup. Ct. 157, 47 L. Ed. 256. And see Straus v. Abrast Realty Co. (D. C.) 200 Fed. 327. Compare State v. Frear, 148 Wis. 456, 134 N. W. 673, 135 N. W. 164, L. R. A. 1915B, 569, 606, Ann. Cas. 1913A, 1147.

[90] Cutting v. Gilbert, 5 Blatchf. 259, Fed. Cas. No. 3,519.

[91] State v. City of Elizabeth, 50 N. J. Law, 347, 13 Atl. 5.

particular matter complained of involved a determination to be made by the revenue officers in a judicial or quasi-judicial capacity, as, for instance, where it was necessary for them to decide whether the particular person, corporation, property, or income was subject to the tax or exempt from it, and generally where it is alleged that the assessment was illegal (not merely irregular or excessive), then certiorari may issue to review the action of those officers.[92] The principles were stated in a recent case in Iowa, where it was remarked that, where there is jurisdiction to assess, and the board of equalization makes an erroneous or excessive assessment, the remedy of the taxpayer is by appeal and not by certiorari; but where there is no jurisdiction to make any assessment (as in the case where the board assesses a person on intangible personal property after he has left the state and taken up a domicile elsewhere), certiorari is the proper remedy. "There is a clear distinction between a case of erroneous or over assessment, and a case of assessment without authority, as one made under an unconstitutional law, or one made of property exempt from taxation, or one of property for the assessment of which the law has made no provision."[93]

It has been ruled in some of the cases that mandamus will lie on behalf of a person illegally assessed, to compel the revenue officers to strike the assessment from the roll,[94] and that if an assessor of taxes makes an erroneously high assessment on given property, in consequence of a mistaken view of the law, and refuses to reduce it to the proper figures, on application made to him for that purpose, he may be compelled to do so by mandamus.[95] So, where the amount of an assessment has been fixed by the revenue officers having power to hear appeals and review assessments, the duty of those charged with the collection of the tax, to enter the assessment, as so fixed, is purely ministerial, and if they assume to in-

[92] Ewing v. City of St. Louis. 5 Wall. 413, 18 L. Ed. 657; Spears v. Loague, 6 Cold. (Tenn.) 420: State v. City of Elizabeth, 50 N. J. Law, 347, 13 Atl. 5; Alexandria Canal, R. & B. Co. v. District of Columbia, 5 Mackey (D. C.) 376; Wood v. District of Columbia, 6 Mackey (D. C.) 142; Le Roy v. New York, 20 Johns. (N. Y.) 430, 11 Am. Dec. 289; Baldwin v. Calkins, 10 Wend. (N. Y.) 167. See Rex v. Com'rs of Income Tax, 91 Law T. 94. Compare Degge v. Hitchcock, 229 U. S. 162, 33 Sup. Ct. 639, 57 L. Ed. 1135.

[93] Remey v. Board of Equalization, 80 Iowa, 470, 45 N. W. 899.

[94] People v. Assessors of Barton, 44 Barb. (N. Y.) 148; Smith v. King, 14 Or. 10, 12 Pac. 8.

[95] People v. Olmsted, 45 Barb. (N. Y.) 644.

crease it, and to enter the increased assessment on the books they may be compelled by mandamus to restore it to the proper amount.[96] Also the English decisions hold that, in a case where an allowance which ought to be granted is refused, mandamus lies to the commissioners of taxes requiring them to grant the allowance and to give a certificate of the allowance with an order for the payment thereof.[97] But where it is claimed that a board of assessors have assessed a particular piece of property in the name of the wrong person, the proper remedy is by certiorari to review their proceedings, and not by mandamus to compel them to correct or change the assessment list.[98] As to the allowance of an appeal or petition for review of an assessment before administrative officers, the rule is that they may be compelled by mandamus to grant an appeal if they are clearly wrong in refusing it, but that they cannot be thus constrained to decide the appeal in a particular manner, nor, having rendered a decision, to revise or reverse it.[99]

As to the common-law writ of prohibition, this remedy is given to arrest a proceeding in an inferior court in a case which is not within its jurisdiction and it is not an appropriate remedy to restrain officers charged with the assessment or collection of a tax from proceeding in the exercise of their duty, though it be alleged that the tax is invalid or the assessment illegal.[100] However, in a case in South Carolina, a corporation which claimed to be exempt from the particular tax in question, and which therefore made no return of its property, a return and assessment being made against it by the proper officer, sued for and obtained a writ of prohibition forbidding the revenue officers to proceed with the collection of the tax.[101]

---

[96] State v. Covington, 35 S. C. 245, 14 S. E. 499.

[97] Commissioners of Income Tax v. Pemsel [1891] A. C. 531; Queen v. Com'rs of Income Tax, L. R. 22 Q. B. Div. 296.

[98] People v. Gilon, 56 Hun, 641, 9 N. Y. Supp. 212.

[99] Gibbs v. Hampden County Com'rs, 19 Pick. (Mass.) 298; People v. Supervisors of Otsego County, 51 N. Y. 401.

[100] Coronado v. San Diego, 97 Cal. 440, 32 Pac. 518; Le Conte v. Town of Berkeley, 57 Cal. 269; Hobart v. Tillson, 66 Cal. 210, 5 Pac. 83; Farmers' Cooperative Union v. Thresher, 62 Cal. 407; Camron v. Kenfield, 57 Cal. 550; Talbot v. Dent, 9 B. Mon. (Ky.) 526; Cody v. Lennard, 45 Ga. 85. See State v. Commissioners of Roads, 1 Mill, Const. (S. C.) 55, 12 Am. Dec. 596.

[101] State v. Hood, 15 Rich. (S. C.) 177.

§ 464. Compromise of Penalties or of Litigation

An unrepealed act of Congress. provides "that the Commissioner of Internal Revenue, with the advice and consent of the Secretary of the Treasury, may compromise any civil or criminal case arising under the internal revenue laws instead of commencing suit thereon; and with the advice and consent of the said Secretary and the recommendation of the Attorney General, he may compromise any such case after a suit thereon has been commenced." [102] This was held applicable to the penalties imposed by the corporation tax law of 1909 for failure to file the return required of corporations. But the Commissioner of Internal Revenue instructed the collectors on this point as follows: "Particular attention is called to the fact that no solicitation of an offer should be made, and no delinquent should be induced by threats to invoke the power of the commissioner to compromise, and no assurance should be given of the probable action of the commissioner if an offer is made. But where the officers of a corporation are ignorant of a provision of law providing for a compromise of offenses against the revenues, and they desire to make an appeal for clemency in the manner provided, it is the duty of the collector to give them suitable instructions. The amount to be offered in each such case must be left to the discretion of the corporation making the offer, and in nowise should be suggested by the collector or any other revenue officer. In connection with the corporation tax law, this right of compromise extends only to the penalty prescribed under paragraph 8, and not to the tax itself, nor to the addition of fifty per cent assessed." (T. D. No. 1692.) Later rulings and regulations of the Department, applicable to the act of 1909 or to the income tax law, point out that where an offer in compromise is submitted by a delinquent taxpayer, it is a condition precedent to the adjustment of the matter involved that the return for the year in respect to which the delinquency exists should be filed. "Offers in compromise are acceptable only in cases where the corporations were delinquent in the matter of filing their returns, and cannot be considered as sufficiently satisfying the requirements of the law in cases where corporations fail or refuse to file any return whatever." (T. D. 2161, Feb. 19, 1915.) With reference to corporations and individuals who failed to file income tax returns for the year 1914, the Bureau of Internal Revenue announced that it

---

[102] Rev. St. U. S., § 3229 (U. S. Comp. St. 1916, § 5952).

would accept offers in compromise of the specific penalties in minimum amounts as follows: from individuals, $5; from corporations, $10. But where such delinquents failed to file returns for 1913 within the prescribed time, offers for 1914 delinquencies would be accepted as follows: from individuals, $7.50; from corporations, $15. (T. D. 2193, April 24, 1915.) With reference to corporations, individuals, and withholding agents who had failed to file income tax returns within the prescribed time for the year 1915 and prior years, it was announced that offers in compromise of the specific penalties would be accepted in minimum sums as follows: For the year 1914, $10 from corporations, and $5 from individuals or withholding agents; for the year 1915, $20 from corporations, and the same from individuals or withholding agents; for the years 1914 and 1915, $30 from corporations, and $25 from individuals or withholding agents. "The minimum amounts stated above apply only to those cases where there was no intention to evade the law or escape taxation." (T. D. 2311, March 23, 1916.) This last ruling was afterwards so far modified that the Bureau announced its willingness to accept offers in compromise of the specific penalty for delinquency in filing income tax returns for the year 1915 in the sum of $5 for individuals, and $10 for corporations. (T. D. 2349, July 24, 1916.)

On the application of this subject to the tax imposed by an earlier statute, the Supreme Court of the United States said: "The power intrusted by law to the Secretary was not a judicial one, but one of mercy, to mitigate the severity of the law. It admitted of no appeal to the Court of Claims, or to any other court. It was the exercise of his discretion in a matter intrusted to him alone, and from which there could be no appeal." [103] In passing upon cases submitted to him for compromise, the Secretary of the Treasury, while he is not at liberty to act from motives merely of compassion or charity, may consider not only the pecuniary interests of the government, but also take into view general considerations of justice and equity and of public policy.[104] But collectors of internal revenue have no power to make any compromise, settlement, or commutation of taxes, so as to bind or affect the government.[105]

---

[103] Dorsheimer v. U. S., 7 Wall. 166, 174, 19 L. Ed. 187.
[104] 17 Opin. Atty. Gen. p. 213.
[105] Martin's Adm'r v. U. S., 4 T. B. Mon. (Ky.) 487.

CHAPTER XX

REFUNDING AND RECOVERY OF TAXES ILLEGALLY EXACTED

§ 465.   Statutory Provisions.
466.   Abatement and Refund by Commissioner of Internal Revenue.
467.   Suit for Recovery of Taxes Paid.
468.   Same; Parties to Action.
469.   Same; Pleading and Evidence.
470.   Same; Payment of Tax Under Protest.
471.   Same; Payment Voluntary or Under Duress.
472.   Same; Appeal to Commissioner as Pre-requisite.
473.   Same; Jurisdiction.
474.   Same; Limitation of Actions.
475.   Same; Amount of Recovery; Interest; Costs.
476.   Same; Payment of Judgment; Reimbursement of Collector.
477.   Action of Tort Against Collector.

§ 465. Statutory Provisions

The acts of Congress imposing taxes do not ordinarily make specific provision for the refund or recovery of taxes illegally exacted or assessed to an excessive amount, the rights and remedies of the taxpayer in such cases being governed by the ordinary rules of law applicable in matters of taxation.   These rules, however, are prescribed in some detail in the Revised Statutes, the applicable provisions of which are incorporated in the taxing laws by some such general clause as that which is found in the income tax act of 1916, which is as follows: "All administrative, special, and general provisions of law, including the laws in relation to the assessment, remission, collection, and refund of internal revenue taxes, not heretofore specifically repealed and not inconsistent with the provisions of this title, are hereby extended and made applicable to the provisions of this title and to the tax herein imposed." (Act Cong. Sept. 8, 1916, § 22 [U. S. Comp. St. 1916, § 6336w].)

§ 466. Abatement and Refund by Commissioner of Internal Revenue

Authority for the refunding of taxes illegally exacted, or assessed and collected in a sum greater than the taxpayer should have been required to pay, is given in the following provision of the general laws relating to internal revenue: "The Commissioner of Internal Revenue, subject to regulations prescribed by the Secretary of the Treasury, is authorized, on appeal to him made, to remit, refund, and pay back all taxes erroneously or illegally assessed or collected,

(477)

all penalties collected without authority, and all taxes that appear to be unjustly assessed or excessive in amount, or in any manner wrongfully collected. Provided, that where a second assessment is made in case of a list, statement, or return which, in the opinion of the collector or deputy collector, was false or fraudulent, or contained any understatement or undervaluation, such assessment shall not be remitted, nor shall taxes collected under such assessment be refunded or paid back, unless it is proved that said list, statement, or return was not false or fraudulent, and did not contain any understatement or undervaluation." (Rev. St. U. S., § 3220, Comp. St. 1916, § 5944.) This provision is held by the Treasury Department to be applicable to the case of income taxes, and as authorizing either a claim for the abatement of an income tax alleged to have been erroneously assessed or to be excessive in amount, which may be filed before payment and before any steps are taken to collect it, or an application, after the tax has been paid, for the refunding of so much of it as is claimed to be excessive or illegal; and a claim for abatement may be made either by the withholding agent against whom the assessment was made or by the person on account of whom the taxes were withheld.[1] These two remedies should not be confused. The Treasury department has prescribed an official form and procedure for an application for abatement, and a different form and procedure for an application for refund, and these regulations have the force of law and must be followed by the applicant.[2] Also the burden is on him to produce satisfactory and sufficient evidence in support of his claim.[3]

The authority thus conferred on the Commissioner to allow a refund of a tax is exclusive,[4] and in exercising it he acts judicially. While he will naturally defer to any decisions of the courts applicable to the questions of law involved, he is not bound by the decision of any other administrative officer. Even three adverse decisions by successive Secretaries of the Treasury will not prevent the Commissioner from taking up and allowing a claim for the refund of taxes.[5] Nor can he be constrained by mandamus to grant the refund demanded. In any case where a federal officer has a discretion as to the refunding of money collected from a citizen or claimed to be due him from the government, or a quasi-judicial duty

---

[1] Internal Revenue Regulations No. 33, art. 33.
[2] Hastings v. Herold (C. C.) 184 Fed. 759.
[3] T. D. No. 1859.
[4] Boehm v. U. S., 21 Ct. Cl. 290.
[5] Sybrandt v. U. S., 19 Ct. Cl. 461.

(478)

to perform in respect to ascertaining or settling the amount, his action cannot be controlled by the writ of mandamus.[6] His decision on such a claim is in the nature of an award, and there is no appeal from it.[7] But the determination of the Commissioner rests within his own control so long as the sum which he has ordered refunded has not been paid by the government and no suit has been brought for its recovery. Until one or the other of these steps has been taken, he has power to reconsider his award and to revoke it,[8] and it seems that this step may also be taken, in the same circumstances, by the successor in office of the Commissioner who made the award.[9] But in any case where the departmental regulations require the Commissioner to transmit the claim, with his findings thereon, to the Secretary of the Treasury for the latter's consideration and advisement, the award does not become final until this step has been taken.[10]

It should be repeated that the allowance of a claim for refund by the Commissioner of Internal Revenue is not the simple passing of an ordinary claim by an ordinary accounting officer, but is in the nature of an adjudication, on which an action may be maintained, and it is conclusive unless impeached by the United States in some appropriate form.[11] It may be so impeached for fraud or mistake,[12] or for want of jurisdiction or exceeding his jurisdiction,[13] but not for error in the determination of any fact which it was his duty to determine, as, for instance, whether the claim was presented to him in due time.[14] And his decision is absolutely binding on the accounting and disbursing officers of the Treasury. They cannot question it or refuse payment of it on any ground whatever, and the claimant is not obliged to follow the award through the Treas-

[6] Kendall v. Stokes, 3 How. 87, 11 L. Ed. 506; Decatur v. Paulding, 14 Pet. 497, 599 Appx., 10 L. Ed. 559, 609; Graham v. Norton, 15 Wall. 427, 21 L. Ed. 177.

[7] First Nat. Bank of Greencastle v. U. S., 15 Ct. Cl. 228.

[8] Ridgway v. U. S., 18 Ct. Cl. 707.

[9] Stotesbury v. U. S., 23 Ct. Cl. 285.

[10] Stotesbury v. U. S., 146 U. S. 196, 13 Sup. Ct. 1, 36 L. Ed. 940; Dupasseur v. U. S., 19 Ct. Cl. 1.

[11] U. S. v. Kaufman, 96 U. S. 567, 24 L. Ed. 792; Edison Electric Illuminating Co. v. U. S., 38 Ct. Cl. 208.

[12] Edison Electric Illuminating Co. v. U. S., 38 Ct. Cl. 208.

[13] Seat v. U. S., 18 Ct. Cl. 458.

[14] First Nat. Bank of Greencastle v. U. S., 15 Ct. Cl. 225.

ury or satisfy other officials of its correctness.[15] The award of a refund establishes a liability on the part of the government upon which an action may be maintained in the Court of Claims.[16]

§ 467. Suit for Recovery of Taxes Paid

The general provisions of the United States internal revenue laws do not explicitly authorize the maintenance of a suit for the recovery back of internal revenue taxes when illegally or improperly exacted, but they do so by clear and necessary implication. For they provide for the reimbursement of a collector for "sums of money recovered against him in any court for any internal taxes collected by him;" prescribe the burden of proof in suits for the recovery of taxes assessed after the rendering of an alleged false return; forbid the maintenance of such a suit until after an appeal shall have been taken to the Commissioner of Internal Revenue: and set up a limitation of two years against "any suit or proceeding for the recovery of any internal tax." (Rev. St. U. S., §§ 3220, 3225, 3226, 3227 [U. S. Comp. St. 1916, §§ 5944, 5948–5950].) Accordingly, it is well settled by the decisions of the courts that an action at law may be maintained for the recovery back of any sum claimed to have been illegally exacted and collected by the revenue officers in payment of an internal revenue tax.[17] But no such suit lay at common law. The right to maintain it can only be deduced from and supported by the laws of the United States. And hence it can only be maintained under and in strict pursuance of those statutes, and only after full compliance with any provisions of the law which are made conditions precedent to the award of relief to the taxpayer.[18] Thus, if the law requires a return to be made for the purposes of taxation, it has been held that an action cannot be maintained by one who has made no return.[19] But probably

[15] Barnett v. U. S., 16 Ct. Cl. 515; Woolner v. U. S., 13 Ct. Cl. 355; First Nat. Bank of Greencastle v. U. S., 15 Ct. Cl. 225.

[16] City of Louisville v. U. S., 31 Ct. Cl. 1; Boehm v. U. S., 21 Ct. Cl. 290; Edison Electric Illuminating Co. v. U. S., 38 Ct. Cl. 208.

[17] Kentucky Improvement Co. v. Slack, 100 U. S. 648, 25 L. Ed. 609; Atchison, T. & S. F. Ry. Co. v. O'Connor, 223 U. S. 280, 32 Sup. Ct. 216, 56 L. Ed. 436, Ann. Cas. 1913C, 1050; U. S. v. Shipley, 197 Fed. 265, 116 C. C. A. 627; Straus v. Abrast Realty Co. (D. C.) 200 Fed. 327; Seabrook v. U. S., 21 Ct. Cl. 39.

[18] Hastings v. Herold (C. C.) 184 Fed. 759; U. S. v. Barnes, 222 U. S. 513, 32 Sup. Ct. 117, 56 L. Ed. 291.

[19] Goldsmith v. Augusta & S. R. Co., 62 Ga. 468.

this rule must be modified in the case of income taxes, for otherwise it might result in denying any relief to a taxpayer objecting to the demand for payment of an income tax precisely on the ground that his income was of such a character or amount that he was not required to make any return.

As to the ground of such an action, in the first place it is held that the collection of a tax which was not due or which was excessive is not the commission of a tort by the collecting officer, but is a taking of private property for public use without just compensation, which places upon the government a quasi contractual obligation to refund the amount collected, or the excess, as the case may be, which obligation should be discharged by the revenue officers on proper application to them, but if they will not repay the sum claimed, or contend that they have no warrant in law to do so, then the obligation resting upon the government may be enforced by the judgment of a court.[20]   Or, in some cases, the action may be maintained as for the recovery of money paid under a mistake of fact.[21]   The right of action is not restricted to cases where the plaintiff denies his liability to the payment of any tax at all, but where the revenue officers increase the amount of an assessment on the ground of fraud or omission in the return, a suit may be brought to recover back what they are alleged to have wrongfully collected in consequence of the increased assessment.[22]

Attention should be given to the following provision of the Revised Statutes: "When a second assessment is made in case of any list, statement, or return, which in the opinion of the collector or deputy collector was false or fraudulent, or contained any understatement or undervaluation, no taxes collected under such assessment shall be recovered by suit, unless it is proved that the said list, statement, or return was not false nor fraudulent, and did not contain any understatement or undervaluation." (Rev. St. U. S., § 3225 [U. S. Comp. St. 1916, § 5948].) In view of this provision, where the return of a taxpayer understated the amount for which he was subject to taxation, though it was made in good faith and without any intention to escape the payment of lawful taxes, and a second assessment was made by the Commissioner of Internal Revenue, and the tax paid thereunder, it was held that the taxpayer

---

[20] Armour v. Roberts (C. C.) 151 Fed. 846.
[21] Kahn v. Herold (C. C.) 147 Fed. 575.
[22] U. S. v. Hodson, Fed. Cas. No. 15,376.

could not recover the tax so paid in an action against the collector.[23]

No one can recover from a collector the amount of tax paid to him, and for which the plaintiff was in fact justly liable, on account of mere omissions, irregularities, or mistakes in the manner of assessment or collection.[24] Thus, where a complaining taxpayer has had a full hearing before the revenue officers, and has obtained a material abatement of a tax assessed against him, the courts will not allow him to recover against the collector because of mere irregularities in the form of the assessment or in the manner of making it, or because, in compelling payment of the tax, the collector did not conform to certain proceedings, intended to secure a full hearing to taxpayers, which the statute made it lawful but not necessary to observe before resorting to a levy on complainant's property.[25] And where one sets forth in his written protest the ground of his objection to the payment of a tax demanded of him, and thereafter brings suit for the recovery of the tax paid, he cannot recover on any other ground than that so set forth.[26] Where one seeks to recover back a tax assessed against him as a broker, under the act of Congress imposing special internal revenue taxes on such persons, and which he paid, and the ground of his action is that he was not subject to the tax, his complaint should set out the transactions on account of which the tax was assessed.[27] Where a citizen deposits money with a collector of internal revenue for a special purpose, and the latter pays it into the United States treasury on account of a tax subsequently assessed against such person, who then brings an action to recover the same, the government can set up the tax as a counterclaim, though the money was improperly paid into the treasury.[28]

§ 468.　Same; Parties to Action

An action to recover back internal revenue taxes paid may be brought by a fiduciary in behalf of his beneficiary. In a case where a federal inheritance tax was wrongfully assessed against three cestuis que trust under a will, and was jointly paid under protest

---

[23] Camp Bird, Limited, v. Howbert (U. S. Dist. Ct., D. Colorado) T. D. No. 2366, Sept. 12, 1916. And see Powell v. U. S. (C. C.) 135 Fed. 881.

[24] Schafer v. Craft (D. C.) 144 Fed. 907.

[25] Bailey v. Railroad Co., 22 Wall. 604, 22 L. Ed. 840.

[26] Davies v. Arthur, 96 U. S. 148, 24 L. Ed. 758.

[27] Haight & Freese Co. v. McCoach (C. C.) 135 Fed. 894.

[28] Howser v. U. S., 13 Ct. Cl. 284.

by the trustees, it was held that such trustees and the beneficiaries were entitled to join in a single suit against the collector of internal revenue to recover the amount paid.[29]   The remedy by suit against the collector is not exclusive.[30]   Under recent legislation of Congress a suit of this kind may be brought directly against the United States, instead of against the collector.[31]   And a cause of action to recover from a collector of internal revenue a sum alleged to have been paid to him under protest for taxes illegally exacted does not abate by his death, the action not being one of tort; but it may be continued against the estate of the deceased collector.[32] But a suit for the recovery of taxes erroneously or illegally assessed must be brought against the collector who collected the taxes, and not against his successor in office. If brought against the collector to whom the taxes were paid, the law provides that it shall not abate by the expiration of his term of office, but the court may allow it to be continued against his successor. But it must be brought originally against the original collector; it cannot be instituted in the first instance against his successor.[33]

§ 469. Same; Pleading and Evidence

In an action against a collector of internal revenue to recover back of the excise tax collected from a corporation on the ground that it was not doing business during a part of the year for which the tax was collected, allegations of the petition that there were no earnings of the corporation during that part of the year, "subject to tax," because the corporation had leased its property and turned it over to the lessee, was objectionable as a negative pregnant, from which it was to be implied that the corporation did receive an unnamed amount of income, but that, in the opinion of the pleader, such amount should be excluded from consideration in computing the amount of the tax.[34]   On the other hand, in such a suit, where the plaintiff corporation had alleged that it was not

[29] Armour v. Roberts (C. C.) 151 Fed. 846.

[30] U. S. v. Emery, Bird, Thayer Realty Co., 237 U. S. 28, 35 Sup. Ct. 499, 59 L. Ed. 825.

[31] Emery, Bird, Thayer Realty Co. v. U. S. (D. C.) 198 Fed. 242; Christie-Street Commission Co. v. U. S., 136 Fed. 326, 69 C. C. A. 464.

[32] Patton v. Brady, 184 U. S. 608, 22 Sup. Ct. 493, 46 L. Ed. 713.

[33] Philadelphia, H. & P. R. Co. v. Lederer (C. C. A.) 242 Fed. 492, affirming 239 Fed. 184; Roberts v. Lowe (U. S. Dist. Ct. S. D. New York), —— Fed. ——, T. D. No. 2394, Nov. 14, 1916.

[34] Blalock v. Georgia Ry. & Electric Co., 228 Fed. 296, 142 C. C. A. 588, Ann. Cas. 1917A, 679.

engaged in business, allegations in the affidavit of defense that the plaintiff had not in fact gone out of business, in connection with its property, nor disqualified itself from any activities under its charter in respect thereto, and was still actually engaged in the doing of business within the meaning of the statute, and in the capacity necessary to make it subject thereto, were held too general to avail the pleader, and expressive of conclusions which must be ascertained from specific facts alleged.[35]

In a suit against a collector of internal revenue to recover back taxes paid to him, the burden of proof is on the plaintiff to show that the collector is justly bound to refund the amount claimed, that the tax was illegal, or the assessment excessive, that plaintiff is within the class of persons or corporations specially exempted by the statute, or whatever else may be the groundwork of his demand.[36] Thus, in an action to recover the income tax paid by a stockholder on dividends declared by the corporation, if the plaintiff alleges that the dividends were a payment from capital and not from income, he must sustain the burden of proving it.[37] So, to recover income taxes paid under protest, on the ground that an insufficient amount was allowed for depreciation of the income-producing property, the plaintiff has the burden of showing that the amount allowed was too small.[38] In an action of this kind, the books and accounts of the taxpayer, though not necessarily conclusive for or against the government, under all circumstances, ought to be the best evidence, if kept correctly, to show whether or not there was any understatement or undervaluation in his tax return: and until it is shown that they cannot be produced, or that they do not contain the information required, resort cannot be had to the recollection or knowledge of witnesses as to circumstances bearing on the ultimate fact in issue.[39] If the plaintiff sustains the burden of proof by producing evidence, which remains uncontradicted, that his tax return was correct, as against the allegation that it was false or fraudulent or understated, it is not sufficient to defeat his recovery that a suspicion of fraud should emerge from the

[35] State Line & S. R. Co. v. Davis (D. C.) 228 Fed. 246.

[36] Bailey v. New York Cent. R. Co., 22 Wall. 604, 22 L. Ed. 840; Schafer v. Craft (D. C.) 144 Fed. 907; German Sav. & Loan Soc. v. Oulton, 1 Sawy. 695, Fed. Cas. No. 5,362.

[37] Southern Pac. Co. v. Lowe (D. C.) 238 Fed. 847.

[38] Cohen v. Lowe (D. C.) 234 Fed. 474.

[39] Bergdoll v. Pollock, 95 U. S. 337, 24 L. Ed. 512.

evidence as a whole. There must be clear, affirmative, and convincing testimony to support an allegation of fraud.[40]

§ 470. Same; Payment of Tax Under Protest

It is a general principle of law, applicable to income taxes as well as to any others, that after a taxpayer has exhausted his lawful remedies to induce the administrative officers to cancel or reduce an assessment which he considers illegal or unjust in whole or in part, he must then pay the tax, but may save his right to bring an action for its recovery by accompanying his payment with a protest, addressed to the officer charged with the collection of the tax.[41] This rule was held applicable to the corporation excise tax law of 1909, and a ruling was made that, no particular form of protest having been prescribed, any form would be sufficient if filed before the payment of the tax, and the collectors of internal revenue were specially warned that the right of protest must not be denied. In a case arising under this statute, it appeared that, the plaintiff corporation having failed to pay the tax assessed against it, a writ of distraint was issued by the collector, and, the corporation having been notified that the tax would be collected by levy, the deputy collector took from a representative of the corporation the amount of the tax, against the verbal protest of the corporate officer at the time, and a written notice of protest then served, in which the corporation denied that it was liable to the tax. It was held that the protest was sufficient to entitle the corporation to recover the amount from the collector, on its being determined that the corporation was not within the law. The court said: "Where the tax is paid under such circumstances that the terms of protest are understood and sufficiently expressed to be brought to the notice of the government, and where the levy is used merely to protect the government officer in acting under the statute, an action may be maintained to recover the tax."[42] In another case it was

[40] Hyams v. U. S. (C. C.) 139 Fed. 997.

[41] U. S. v. New York & Cuba Mail S. S. Co., 200 U. S. 488, 26 Sup. Ct. 327, 50 L. Ed. 569; Bailey v. New York Cent. & H. R. R. Co., 106 U. S. 109, 1 Sup. Ct. 62, 27 L. Ed. 81; Baltimore v. Baltimore Railroad, 10 Wall. 543, 19 L. Ed. 1043; Cutting v. Gilbert, 5 Blatchf. 259, Fed. Cas. No. 3,519; Nelson v. Carman, 5 Blatchf. 511, Fed. Cas. No. 10,103; Shaefer v. Ketchum, 6 Int. Rev. Rec. 4, Fed. Cas. No. 12,693; Robbins v. Freeland, 14 Int. Rev. Rec. 28, Fed. Cas. No. 11,886. But compare U. S. v. Hvoslef, 237 U. S. 1, 35 Sup. Ct. 459, 59 L. Ed. 813, Ann. Cas. 1916A, 286.

[42] Abrast Realty Co. v. Maxwell (D. C.) 206 Fed. 833.

said: "The case stands on a different footing from that of the illegal exaction of duties on imports. To recover these the statute makes it necessary that the party interested shall give notice in writing to the collector, if dissatisfied with his decision, setting forth distinctly and specifically the grounds of his objection thereto. No such written notice or protest is required of a party paying illegal taxes under the internal revenue laws. He must pay under protest in some form, it is true, or his payment will be deemed voluntary. But whilst a written protest would in all cases be most convenient, there is no statutory requirement that the protest shall be in writing." [43] And in another decision it was held sufficient where the taxpayer made a merely verbal protest, which the deputy collector noted on the back of the tax receipt which he gave to the taxpayer.[44] Also, where the plaintiff was a large purchaser and user of internal revenue stamps, and there was a constant dispute between it and the department as to whether certain articles which it manufactured were subject to the tax, it was held that it need not enter a formal protest every time it bought stamps in order to preserve its right to sue.[45] But where plaintiff purchased and affixed stamps to an uncompounded chemical substance, without protest or objection, until the decision of a case holding that the substance was not subject to the tax, it was held that his payment was voluntary and he could not recover the value of the stamps so used.[46]

§ 471. Same; Payment Voluntary or Under Duress

Payment of an internal revenue tax, when made without any objection or protest, is a voluntary payment, and according to the rules of law applicable to taxes in general, the sum so paid cannot be recovered back in an action against the collector, even though the tax was not due or was illegally exacted.[47] On the other hand, there is duress (actual or implied) sufficient to prevent the payment from being regarded as voluntary, when it is made under the pressure of the collector's threat to proceed at once to enforce pay-

---

[43] Wright v. Blakeslee, 101 U. S. 174, 25 L. Ed. 1048.

[44] Shaefer v. Ketchum, 6 Int. Rev. Rec. 4, Fed. Cas. No. 12,693.

[45] Johnson v. Herold (C. C.) 161 Fed. 593.

[46] Merck v. Treat, 202 Fed. 133, 122 C. C. A. 301.

[47] U. S. v. New York & Cuba Mail S. S. Co., 200 U. S. 488, 26 Sup. Ct. 327, 50 L. Ed. 569; Merck v. Treat, 202 Fed. 133, 122 C. C. A. 301; Beer v. Moffatt (D. C.) 192 Fed. 984; Newhall v. Jordan (C. C.) 149 Fed. 586; Christie-Street Commission Co. v. U. S. (C. C.) 126 Fed. 991.

ment with the penalty and interest added,[48] or when both parties understand at the time that payment must be made or the law will be enforced,[49] or when the citizen must either pay what the collector demands or go out of business,[50] or when the payment is made as the only means of acquiring possession of property,[51] or to avoid the seizure and sale of property.[52] But in general, in an action to recover back a sum paid in discharge of internal revenue taxes, the question whether the payment was made under duress is a question of fact.[53]

A more difficult question is whether the mere lodging of a formal protest is sufficient to save the payment from being treated as voluntary when there is no actual duress or threats. It has been held that it is sufficient,[54] and many cases may be found in the reports in which this course was pursued, and the subsequent suit against the collector allowed to proceed without any·such question being raised. But doubt was cast upon this point by a decision of the United States Supreme Court, in which it was said: "Generally speaking, even a protest or notice will not avail if the payment be made voluntarily, with full knowledge of all the circumstances, and without any coercion by the actual or threatened exercise of power possessed, or supposed to be possessed, by the party exacting or receiving the payment, over the person or property of the person making the payment, from which the latter has no other means of immediate relief than such payment." [55] Yet in a later decision of the same court, statements were made quite sufficient, it would appear, to neutralize those just quoted. "It is reasonable," said the court, "that a man who denies the legality of a tax should have a clear and certain remedy. The rule being established that, apart from special circumstances, he cannot interfere by injunction with the state's collection of its revenues, an action at law to recover back what he has paid is the alternative left. Of course we are speaking of those cases where the state is not put to

---

[48] Cambria Steel Co. v. McCoach (D. C.) 225 Fed. 278; Herold v. Kahn, 159 Fed. 608, 86 C. C. A. 598.

[49] Shaefer v. Ketchum, 6 Int. Rev. Rec. 4, Fed. Cas. No. 12,693.

[50] Swift Co. v. U. S., 111 U. S. 22, 4 Sup. Ct. 244, 28 L. Ed. 341.

[51] Simons v. U. S., 19 Ct. Cl. 601.

[52] Hubbard v. Brainard, 35 Conn. 563.

[53] Rutan v. Johnson & Johnson, 231 Fed. 369, 145 C. C. A. 363.

[54] Adams v. U. S., 1 Ct. Cl. 306; Schmitt v. Trowbridge, Fed. Cas. No. 12,-468.

[55] Chesebrough v. U. S., 192 U. S. 253, 24 Sup. Ct. 262, 48 L. Ed. 432.

an action if the citizen refuses to pay. In these latter he can interpose his objections by way of defense; but when, as is common, the state has a more summary remedy, such as distress, and the party indicates by protest that he is yielding to what he cannot prevent, courts sometimes, perhaps, have been a little too slow to recognize the implied duress under which payment is made. But even if the state is driven to an action, if, at the same time, the citizen is put at a serious disadvantage in the assertion of his legal, in this case of his constitutional, rights, by defense in the suit, justice may require that he should be at liberty to avoid those disadvantages by paying promptly and bringing suit on his side." [56]

§ 472. Same; Appeal to Commissioner as Prerequisite

The internal revenue laws provide that "no suit shall be maintained in any court for the recovery of any internal tax alleged to have been erroneously or illegally assessed or collected, or of any penalty claimed to have been collected without authority, or of any sum alleged to have been excessive or in any manner wrongfully collected, until appeal shall have been duly made to the Commissioner of Internal Revenue, according to the provisions of law in that regard, and the regulations of the Secretary of the Treasury established in pursuance thereof, and a decision of the Commissioner has been had therein: Provided, that if such decision is delayed more than six months from the date of such appeal, then the said suit may be brought, without first having a decision of the Commissioner, at any time within the period limited in the next section," that is to say, "within two years next after the cause of action accrued" or within one year after a decision rendered by the Commissioner.[57] This statute is mandatory, and the party aggrieved must pursue the remedy here prescribed before he can resort to a court either of law or equity for relief.[58] It was at one time held in Connecticut that this statute did not operate to pre-

[56] Atchison, T. & S. F. Ry. Co. v. O'Connor, 223 U. S. 280, 32 Sup. Ct. 216, 56 L. Ed. 436, Ann. Cas. 1913C, 1050.

[57] Rev. St. U. S., §§ 3226, 3227 (U. S. Comp. St. 1916, §§ 5949, 5950).

[58] Dodge v. Osborn, 240 U. S. 118, 36 Sup. Ct. 275, 60 L. Ed. 557; Kings County Sav. Inst. v. Blair, 116 U. S. 200, 6 Sup. Ct. 353, 29 L. Ed. 657; Cheatham v. U. S., 92 U. S. 85, 23 L. Ed. 561; Erskine v. Hohnbach, 14 Wall. 613, 20 L. Ed. 745; Public Service Gas Co. v. Herold (D. C.) 227 Fed. 496; Stuart v. Barnes (C. C.) 43 Fed. 281; Com'rs of Sinking Fund v. Buckner (C. C.) 48 Fed. 533; Magee v. Denton, 5 Blatchf. 130, Fed. Cas. No. 8,943; Hubbard v. Kelley, 8 W. Va. 46.

vent the maintenance of such suits in the courts of the state.[59] But the Supreme Court of the United States decided that it was applicable to all courts, state as well as federal.[60] Where, after the assessment of an internal revenue tax, alleged to be illegal, application is made to the Commissioner of Internal Revenue for review, and he overrules the application and refuses to abate the tax, it is held that this is a sufficient compliance with the statute, and the plaintiff is not bound, after paying the tax, to appeal again to the Commissioner as a condition precedent to his right to sue the collector for the recovery of the tax.[61] But aside from such cases, the law must be strictly complied with. A written application to the Commissioner to refund a sum exacted in payment of taxes is not the equivalent of an appeal to him from an adverse decision by the collector.[62] But though the appeal must be addressed to the Commissioner, lodging it with the proper collector of internal revenue, for transmission to the Commissioner in the usual course of business, under the requirements of the Treasury regulations, is in effect the presentation of it to the Commissioner.[63] Further, the taking of such appeal is an absolute condition precedent to the right to maintain an action, and plaintiff's failure to do so is not an objection which can be waived by the collector's entering a general appearance in the suit and omitting to plead such failure.[64] Further, the plaintiff must produce a written appeal in evidence or an authentic copy thereof, or show good cause for its absence,[65] and when he sues in the Court of Claims, it is necessary for him to produce proof not only of the appeal, but of the Commissioner's decision thereon, and a certificate indorsed on the appeal paper, "examined and rejected," signed by a person unknown to the court, and with no proof that he held any official position or what it was, and no proof that the Commissioner adopted it as his decision, is

[59] Hubbard v. Brainard, 35 Conn. 563.

[60] Collector v. Hubbard, 12 Wall. 1, 20 L. Ed. 272.

[61] Weaver v. Ewers, 195 Fed. 247, 115 C. C. A. 219; Schwarzchild & Sulzberger Co. v. Rucker (C. C.) 143 Fed. 656; San Francisco Sav. & Loan Soc. v. Cary, 2 Sawy. 333, Fed. Cas. No. 12,317.

[62] Chesebrough v. U. S., 192 U. S. 253, 24 Sup. Ct. 262, 48 L. Ed. 432.

[63] U. S. v. Savings Bank, 104 U. S. 728, 26 L. Ed. 908; Real Estate Sav. Bank v. U. S., 16 Ct. Cl. 335.

[64] De Bary v. Dunne (C. C.) 162 Fed. 961, disapproving Hendy v. Soule, 1 Deady, 400, Fed. Cas. No. 6,359.

[65] Hubbard v. Kelley, 8 W. Va. 46.

not enough.[66] And again, while a claim for the refund of taxes, before it can be put in suit, must have been rejected by the Commissioner, it is also true that this rejection must have been on the merits, and not on account of mere defect of form in making application to him or other irregularity.[67]

But all this does not make the assessment of an internal revenue tax, unappealed from, res judicata and conclusive, so as to prevent the defendant in a suit brought by the government from setting up as a defense the erroneous assessment or illegality of the tax.[68] And on the other hand, the rejection of an appeal for refund of a tax collected does not exhaust the Commissioner's authority so that he is prevented from allowing the repayment of a judgment recovered against a collector in a suit brought to recover back the same tax.[69]

§ 473. Same; Jurisdiction

If a suit for the recovery of taxes alleged to have been illegally exacted under the internal revenue laws is to be brought and prosecuted directly against the United States, it is within the jurisdiction of the Court of Claims,[70] and equally within the jurisdiction of a United States district court under the Tucker Act.[71] If the action is instituted against the collector of internal revenue to whom the taxes were paid, the proper federal district court will have jurisdiction over it, both under that provision of the statutes which invests those courts with jurisdiction of causes "arising under the laws of the United States" and under that provision which specially gives them original jurisdiction of "all cases arising under any law providing for internal revenue." [72] And under either provision, it is not required that the parties should be citizens of different states, and if the action is framed with reference to the special provision regarding actions arising under the revenue laws, the requirement

---

[66] Lauer v. U. S., 5 Ct. Cl. 447.

[67] James v. Hicks, 110 U. S. 272, 4 Sup. Ct. 6, 28 L. Ed. 144; Hicks v. James (C. C.) 4 Hughes, 470, 48 Fed. 542.

[68] Clinkenbeard v. U. S., 21 Wall. 65, 22 L. Ed. 477; Dodge v. Brady, 240 U. S. 122, 36 Sup. Ct. 277, 60 L. Ed. 560.

[69] Nixon v. U. S., 18 Ct. Cl. 448.

[70] Federal Judicial Code, 1911, § 145 (U. S. Comp. St. 1916, § 1136).

[71] Dooley v. U. S., 182 U. S. 222, 21 Sup. Ct. 762, 45 L. Ed. 1074; U. S. v. Finch, 201 Fed. 95, 119 C. C. A. 433, Ann. Cas. 1916A, 319; U. S. v. Shipley, 197 Fed. 265, 116 C. C. A. 627; Hvoslet v. U. S. (D. C.) 217 Fed. 680.

[72] Federal Judicial Code, 1911, § 24 (U. S. Comp. St. 1916, § 991).

as to the amount in controversy (which must exceed $3,000 in ordinary cases) does not apply.[73] A final judgment of a federal district court in such a case is reviewable in the circuit court of appeals, but not in the Supreme Court of the United States, except in the single case where the issue is as to the constitutional validity of the statute imposing the tax.[74]

There is nothing in the laws of the United States to prevent a state court of competent jurisdiction from taking cognizance of such an action against a collector of internal revenue. But the collector, if sued in a state court, would have the privilege of removing the cause into the federal district court. An act of Congress provides that "any civil suit commenced in any court of a state against any officer appointed under or acting by authority of any revenue law of the United States, on account of any act done under color of his office or of any such law" and "affecting the validity of any such revenue law," may, "at any time before the trial or final hearing thereof, be removed for trial into the district court next to be holden in the district where the same is pending." [75] And it has been held that an action against a collector of internal revenue to recover back taxes alleged to have been illegally or erroneously assessed by him, and paid to him under protest, is one which may be removed to the federal court under this act.[76]

§ 474. Same; Limitation of Actions

The internal revenue laws provide that "no suit or proceeding for the recovery of any internal tax alleged to have been erroneously or illegally assessed or collected, or of any penalty alleged to have been collected without authority, or of any sum alleged to have been excessive or in any manner wrongfully collected, shall be maintained in any court, unless the same is brought within two years next after the cause of action accrued," and, in connection

---

[73] Patton v. Brady, 184 U. S. 608, 22 Sup. Ct. 493, 46 L. Ed. 713; Com'rs of Sinking Fund v. Buckner (C. C.) 48 Fed. 533.

[74] Hubbard v. Soby, 146 U. S. 56, 13 Sup. Ct. 13, 36 L. Ed. 886; U. S. v. Hopewell, 51 Fed. 798, 2 C. C. A. 510; Louisville Public Warehouse Co. v. Collector of Customs, 49 Fed. 561, 1 C. C. A. 371; Federal Judicial Code, 1911, §§ 128, 238 (Comp. St. 1916, §§ 1120, 1215).

[75] Rev. St. U. S., § 643, re-enacted as section 33 of the Federal Judicial Code of 1911 (Comp. St. 1916, § 1015).

[76] Venable v. Richards, 105 U. S. 636, 26 L. Ed. 1106; City of Philadelphia v. The Collector, 5 Wall. 720, 18 L. Ed. 614; Collector of Internal Revenue v. Hubbard, 12 Wall. 1, 20 L. Ed. 272; Tennessee v. Davis, 100 U. S. 257, 25 L. Ed. 648.

with the requirement that an appeal shall first be taken to the Commissioner of Internal Revenue and decided by him, it is provided that "if such decision is delayed more than six months from the date of such appeal, then the said suit may be brought without first having a decision of the Commissioner at any time within the period limited," that is, two years.[77] It is held that the statute of limitations begins to run from the accrual of the cause of action, and its running is not suspended during the pendency of the appeal to the Commissioner.[78] But it is also a rule that the cause of action is lost unless presented to the Commissioner within two years after it accrued,[79] though, if it has been so presented by appeal, the claimant is held by some of the authorities to be entitled to two years from the date of the Commissioner's decision in which to bring his suit.[80] At any rate, this special statute of limitations, applicable only to cases under the internal revenue laws, is not repealed or superseded by the later statutes establishing generally a limitation of six years for suits against the United States.[81] And a suit for the recovery of internal revenue taxes paid, brought in the Court of Claims, is barred by the special limitation of two years, notwithstanding the fact that the general statute of limitations applicable to suits in that court allows six years.[82] In any court,

[77] Rev. St. U. S., §§ 3226–3228 (U. S. Comp. St. 1916, §§ 5949–5951).

[78] Public Service Ry. Co. v. Moffett (D. C.) 227 Fed. 494; Public Service Electric Co. v. Herold (D. C.) 227 Fed. 491; Public Service Ry. Co. v. Herold (D. C.) 219 Fed. 301; Christie-Street Commission Co. v. U. S. (C. C.) 129 Fed. 506, affirmed 136 Fed. 326, 69 C. C. A. 464.

[79] Kings County Sav. Inst. v. Blair, 116 U. S. 200, 6 Sup. Ct. 353, 29 L. Ed. 657; Public Service Ry. Co. v. Herold, 229 Fed. 902, 144 C. C. A. 184; New York Mail & Newspaper Transp. Co. v. Anderson, 234 Fed. 590, 148 C. C. A. 356. But the present income tax law contains a provision that "upon the examination of any return of income made pursuant to this title, if it shall appear that amounts of tax have been paid in excess of those properly due, the taxpayer shall be permitted to present a claim for refund thereof notwithstanding the provisions of section 3228 of the Revised Statutes." Act Cong. Sept. 8, 1916, § 14a (U. S. Comp. St. 1916, § 6336n). And in view of this, the Treasury Department rules that claims for refund may be made or reopened which had already been rejected by the Commissioner because of the statute of limitations in force at the time, provided the question involves an examination of the return. T. D. 2395, Nov. 17, 1916.

[80] Wright v. Blakeslee, 101 U. S. 174, 25 L. Ed. 1048; Cheatham v. U. S., 92 U. S. 85, 23 L. Ed. 561.

[81] Christie-Street Commission Co. v. U. S. (C. C.) 126 Fed. 991; Public Service Ry. Co. v. Herold, 229 Fed. 902, 144 C. C. A. 184.

[82] Fort Pitt Gas Co. v. U. S. (Ct. Cl.) T. D. No. 1979.

where the complaint in such an action shows that more than two years have elapsed since the cause of action accrued, the objection may be taken by demurrer,[83] and statements made by the revenue officers to the claimant, pending his appeal to the Commissioner, that the claim would be allowed, or that it had been certified favorably to the auditing office, do not raise an estoppel against the government so as to avoid the bar of the statute.[84]

As to the provision with regard to cases where the decision of the Commissioner is delayed for more than six months after the taking of the appeal to him, this will enable the claimant, at the end of the six months, to bring a suit for the recovery of the taxes without waiting any longer for a decision on his appeal.[85] And the clause has been interpreted as meaning that, when the Commissioner's decision is not made within the six months, the cause of action accrues then, at the end of the six months, and it will be barred if suit is not brought within two years from that time.[86] But the better opinion appears to be that the provision that the claimant "may" bring suit without a decision by the Commissioner, if the decision is delayed more than six months, is permissive only, and that it does not oblige the claimant to commence his suit within a maximum period of two years and six months after taking his appeal in any case, but he may, at his election, wait for the Commissioner's decision, however long it may be delayed, and if it is adverse to him, bring his suit at any time within two years after its rendition.[87]

§ 475. Same; Amount of Recovery; Interest; Costs

It is a well settled rule that, in suits against collectors of internal revenue to recover moneys alleged to have been illegally exacted in payment of taxes, and paid under protest, interest is recoverable by the successful plaintiff, without any special statutory warrant for it, and this although the judgment is not to be paid by the collector, but directly from the Treasury, for this does not make the suit formally one against the United States, notwith-

[83] Com'rs of Sinking Fund v. Buckner (C. C.) 48 Fed. 533. ·

[84] Christie-Street Commission Co. v. U. S. (C. C.) 129 Fed. 506.

[85] Coblens v. Abel, 1 Woolw. 293, Fed. Cas. No. 2,926.

[86] Schwarzchild & Sulzberger Co. v. Rucker (C. C.) 143 Fed. 656; Christie-Street Commission Co. v. U. S. (C. C.) 126 Fed. 991.

[87] Merck v. Treat, 174 Fed. 388, 98 C. C. A. 606; State Line & S. R. Co. v. Davis (D. C.) 228 Fed. 246; Arnson v. Murphy, 109 U. S. 238, 3 Sup. Ct. 184, 27 L. Ed. 920; James v. Hicks, 110 U. S. 272, 4 Sup. Ct. 6, 28 L. Ed. 144.

standing the ultimate liability of the government.[88] Ordinarily such interest will run from the date of the payment made to the collector,[89] although under some special circumstances, such as unreasonable delay in bringing suit, it may be limited to run from the date of the demand for repayment,[90] or even from the date of commencing the suit.[91] Further, if the collector brings a writ of error to review a judgment recovered against him for money exacted by and paid to him as taxes, and the appellate court affirms the judgment, it will allow interest on the judgment.[92] But where a person from whom an internal revenue tax has been illegally exacted accepts from the government, without objection, the repayment of the sum thus illegally exacted, he thereby gives up his right to sue for interest as incidental damages.[93]

When judgment goes against the collector in such a case, the court may, if it so finds, "certify that there was probable cause for the act done by the collector, or that he acted under the directions of the Secretary of the Treasury or other proper officer of the government," and in that case, "no execution shall issue against the collector, but the amount so recovered shall, upon final judgment, be provided for and paid out of the proper appropriation from the Treasury."[94] And the rule as to costs in the case of recovery of judgment against the collector for taxes illegally exacted is that costs incurred before judgment, and before the granting of this "certificate of probable cause," are properly awarded against him.[95]

[88] Billings v. U. S., 232 U. S. 261, 34 Sup. Ct. 421, 58 L. Ed. 596; National Home v. Parrish, 229 U. S. 494, 33 Sup. Ct. 944, 57 L. Ed. 1296; Erskine v. Van Arsdale, 15 Wall. 75, 21 L. Ed. 63; Redfield v. Bartels, 139 U. S. 694, 11 Sup. Ct. 683, 35 L. Ed. 310; Kinney y. Conant, 166 Fed. 720, 92 C. C. A. 410; Herold v. Shanley, 146 Fed. 20, 76 C. C. A. 478; Pennsylvania Co. for Insurances on Lives, etc., v. McClain (C. C.) 105 Fed. 367; State Line & S. R. Co. v. Davis (D. C.) 228 Fed. 246; New York Mail & Newspaper Transp. Co. v. Anderson, 234 Fed. 590, 148 C. C. A. 356.

[89] Conant v. Kinney (C. C.) 162 Fed. 581, affirmed Kinney v. Conant, 166 Fed. 720, 92 C. C. A. 410.

[90] Treat v. Taylor, 166 Fed. 1021, 91 C. C. A. 330. And see Com'rs of Sinking Fund v. Buckner (C. C.) 48 Fed. 533.

[91] Burroughs v. Abel (C. C.) 105 Fed. 366.

[92] Cochran v. Schell, 107 U. S. 625, 2 Sup. Ct. 827, 27 L. Ed. 543; Klock Produce Co. v. Hartson (D. C.) 212 Fed. 758.

[93] Stewart v. Barnes, 153 U. S. 456, 14 Sup. Ct. 849, 38 L. Ed. 781.

[94] Rev. St. U. S., § 989 (U. S. Comp. St. 1916, § 1635).

[95] Treat v. Farmers' Loan & Trust Co., 185 Fed. 760, 108 C. C. A. 98.

§ 476. Same; Payment of Judgment, Reimbursement of Collector

As stated in the preceding section, if judgment is recovered against the collector for taxes illegally exacted, but the court grants a certificate that there was probable cause for his action in making the collection, no execution shall issue against him, but the claim shall be paid out of the Treasury. But the suit is a private suit, and there is no claim against the government until this certificate has been obtained from the court, but then the government assumes a certain liability.[96] Another provision of the internal revenue laws authorizes the Commissioner of Internal Revenue, subject to regulations prescribed by the Secretary of the Treasury, to "repay to any collector or deputy collector the full amount of such sums of money as may be recovered against him in any court, for any internal taxes collected by him, with the costs and expenses of suit."[97] It is held that the Commissioner, when acting under this section, is not bound by the judgment recovered against the collector, and he is not precluded from acting because no notice was given to the government which would enable it to defend in the court where the judgment was rendered. The term "repay" in the statute does not imply that the collector must pay the judgment before the Commissioner can act. The statute is for the protection of the officer, and the damages and costs may be allowed by the Commissioner directly to the judgment creditor.[98] And where the Commissioner makes an order for the allowance of the amount of the judgment directly to the creditor, instead of to the collector, the creditor may sue on such allowance in the Court of Claims, if the collector does not object and sets up no claim himself.[99]

§ 477. Action of Tort Against Collector

An assessor of internal revenue acts judicially in determining what persons and things are subject to taxation under an act of Congress. If the subject-matter is within his jurisdiction, that is, if he is bound to inquire and determine who and what are subject to the tax, a mistake as to the person or thing taxed, or an irregularity in the proceedings on his part, will not invalidate his action

[96] White v. Arthur (C. C.) 10 Fed. 80, 20 Blatchf. 237. And see U. S. v. Sherman, 98 U. S. 565, 25 L. Ed. 235.

[97] Rev. St. U. S., § 3220 (Comp. St. 1916, § 5944).

[98] U. S. v. Frerichs, 124 U. S. 315, 8 Sup. Ct. 514, 31 L. Ed. 471; Dunnegun v. U. S., 17 Ct. Cl. 247; Nixon v. U. S., 18 Ct. Cl. 448.

[99] Nixon v. U. S., 18 Ct. Cl. 448.

as assessor so far as to make the collector, who proceeds on a warrant in proper form to collect the tax, a trespasser.[100] In a decision of the United States Supreme Court it was held that, if a collector of internal revenue has a proper warrant from the assessor for the collection of taxes specially assessed for deficiency of an original return, he cannot be sued in trespass for distraining and selling the taxpayer's property, on such person's refusal to pay the new assessment, even though such assessment may have been illegally made, for the warrant of the assessor is a justification to him.[101] And in another case in the same court it was said: "Taxes illegally exacted under the revenue laws of the United States may be recovered back, if paid under protest, in an action of assumpsit against the collector, but the person taxed cannot enjoin the collector from enforcing payment, and very grave doubts are entertained whether trespass against the collector is a proper remedy under existing laws." [102] It should also be noticed that "all property taken or detained by any officer or other person, under authority of any revenue law of the United States, shall be irrepleviable, and shall be deemed to be in the custody of the law, and subject only to the orders and decrees of the courts of the United States having jurisdiction thereof." [103] Hence even if a collector should levy upon and distrain the property of one person for payment of the tax due from another, replevin is not an available remedy for the rightful owner.[104]

---

[100] Delaware R. Co. v. Prettyman, 17 Int. Rev. Rec. 99, Fed. Cas. No. 3,767. And see Kercheval v. Allen, 220 Fed. 262, 135 C. C. A. 1; Public Service Ry. Co. v. Herold (D. C.) 219 Fed. 301; Roberts v. Lowe (D. C.) 236 Fed. 604.

[101] Haffin v. Mason, 15 Wall. 671, 21 L. Ed. 196.

[102] Barnes v. The Railroads, 17 Wall. 294, 21 L. Ed. 544.

[103] Rev. St. U. S., § 934 (U. S. Comp. St. 1916, § 1560).

[104] Treat v. Staples, Holmes, 1, Fed. Cas. No. 14,162; Brice v. Elliott, Fed. Cas. No. 1,854.

INDEX

A

AMORTIZATION OF BONDS,
   Deduction for, in computing taxable income, 198.

ANNUAL RETURNS,
   For purpose of income tax, see Returns.

ANNUITIES,
   Payment of, $800 or more a year, to be reported, 28.
   As taxable income, 95.
   To nonresident alien, collection of income tax on, 215.

ANY SOURCE WHATEVER,
   Taxability of income derived from, 69.

APARTMENT HOUSE PROPERTY,
   Allowance for depreciation in income-tax return of owner, 190.
      No deduction for obsolescence, 191.

APPEAL,
   From assessment of internal revenue taxes, 450.

APPEAL BONDS,
   Not subject to stamp tax, 375.

APPOINTMENT,
   Property passing under power of, subject to estate tax, 270.

APPORTIONMENT,
   Of federal income tax, 59.

ARCHITECTS,
   Professional earnings of, as taxable income, 77.
      When subject to excess profits tax, 316.

ARMY AND NAVY,
   Estates of persons dying in military or naval service exempt estate tax.
      261, 300.

ART GALLERIES,
   When exempt from income tax, 144.
   Exempt from excess profits tax, 305.
   Exempt from capital stock tax, 325.

ASSESSMENT,
   Of federal taxes in general, 446.
   Of income tax, how made, 9, 446.
      Conclusive on collector, 446.
      Increasing amount of taxable income returned, 447.
         Burden of proof and evidence, 447.
      On discovery of delinquency or fraud, 448.
         By Commissioner or collector, 448.
         Notice or hearing on, 448.
         Evidence, 448.

INDEX

[The figures refer to sections]

CANCELLATION,

Of internal revenue stamps, 401.
Penalty for failure to cancel, 403.
Penalty for removal or re-use of canceled stamps, 404.

CAPITAL,

Change or substitution of, distinguished from income, 70.
Invested, meaning of, in excess profits tax law, 314.
Excess profits tax on business conducted without, 316.
Indeterminable, deduction allowed in case of, 317.
Estimation of, for capital stock tax, 335.

CAPITAL ASSETS,

Of corporation, taxation of profit from sale of, 103, 104.
Change or substitution of, distinguished from income, 70.
Investment of, distinguished from expense of business, 155.

CAPITAL STOCK,

Dividends on, included in income tax returns, 8f.
See Dividends.
Amount of, to be shown in corporation income tax returns, 233.
What constitutes capital stock outstanding, 233, 337.
Stamp tax on original issue of, 376.
On sales and transfers of, 377.
Pledge of stock or loan, 378.
Transactions between broker and customer, 379.
Transactions with agents, 380.
Where stamp is to be affixed, 381.
Exemption of building and loan associations, 399.
Affixing stamps, 400.
Cancellation of stamps, 401.
Effect of failure to stamp, 402.
Penalties, 403, 404.

CAPITAL STOCK TAX,

Nature and incidence of tax, 322.
Tax on domestic corporations, 323.
Tax on foreign corporations, 324.
Corporations which are exempt, 325.
What corporations required to make returns, 326.
"Engaging in business" necessary to liability, 327.
What constitutes carrying on business, 328.
Mining operations, 329.
Lessor corporations, 330.
Holding companies, 331.
Foreign corporations, 332.
Returns by holding companies and subsidiaries, 333.
Regulations for computation of tax, 334.
Domestic corporations, 334.
Estimation of capital, surplus, and profits, 335.
Banks and bankers, 336.

BL.FED.TAX.—33

COSMETICS,

Excise tax on sales of, 428.

COST,

Of carrying on business as deductible expense, 158.
Manufacturing costs, 159.
Of incorporating company, not deductible as "expense," 156.

COSTS,

In suits for recovery of taxes illegally exacted, 475.

COUNTIES,

See Municipal Corporations.

COUPONS,

Collection of income tax on presentation of, 208.
Ownership certificates accompanying, 209.

COURTS,

District, jurisdiction of, in income tax cases, 20.
Jurisdiction of suits to compel payment of estate tax, 259.
For collection of internal revenue taxes, 459.
Suit to recover taxes illegally exacted and paid, 473.

CREDITS,

In income tax returns, for dividends received, 5b.
For tax paid or withheld at source, 5c, 225.
To nonresident alien, 6b.
In partnership returns, 8e.
For excess profits taxes assessed, 29.

CRIMINAL LAW,

Unlawfully divulging income tax returns a misdemeanor, 241.
Making false or fraudulent return a misdemeanor, 18, 248.
Failure to pay occupation tax a misdemeanor, 356.
Failure to affix or cancel revenue stamps, 403.
Fraudulent removal or re-use of revenue stamps, 404.

CROPS,

Profits on sale of, as taxable income, 82.
Products consumed by family, 82.
Crops unsold at end of year, 82.

CRUELTY TO ANIMALS,

Donations to societies for preventing, deductible in computing donor's taxable income, 165.

CUSTOMHOUSE BROKERS,

Federal occupation tax on, 348.

CUSTOMHOUSE ENTRIES,

Stamp tax on, 393.

CUSTOMS DUTIES,

When deductible from income as "taxes paid," 180.

D

DISTILLED SPIRITS,
Tax on, 407.
Imported perfumes containing, 408.
Floor tax on, 409.
Rectified spirits, 410.
Blended whiskies, 410.
Payment and collection of floor tax, 445.

DISTRAINT,
Enforcing payment of internal revenue taxes by, 460.

DISTRESS WARRANT,
To enforce payment of internal revenue taxes, 460.

DISTRICT COURTS,
Jurisdiction of, in income tax cases, 20, 245.
Of suits to compel payment of estate tax, 259.
Of suit for collection of income taxes, 459.
Of suit to recover taxes illegally exacted and paid, 473.

DISTRICT OF COLUMBIA,
Income from public utility contracts, exempt, 11b.
Salaries or compensation paid by, as taxable income, 23.
Not subject to excess profits tax, 305.
Instruments made by or to, exempt from stamp tax, 399.

DITCH COMPANIES,
Mutual, when exempt from income tax, 11.

DIVIDENDS,
Credit for amount of, in return of individual taxpayer, 5.
Payments of, to be reported by corporations, 26, 236.
Definition of, for purpose of income tax law, 31.
As taxable income, 98.
Stock dividends, 99.
Credit for, in personal income-tax returns, 199.
Dividends paid in Liberty Loan bonds, 199.
Of foreign corporations, collection of income tax on, 217.
Income of individual from, not subject to excess profits tax, 305.

DOMESTIC CORPORATIONS,
Operating abroad, taxation of incomes of, 107, 108.
Stock and bonds of, when taxable as part of nonresident deceased owner's estate, 277.
Tax on excess profits of, see Excess Profits Tax.
Returns by, for excess profits tax, 319.
Capital stock tax on, 323.
Computation of tax, 334.
Form of return for, 341.
Payment of tax, 343.

DONATIONS,

To charities, deductible, in computing taxable income, 165.
To religious, scientific, and educational purposes, 165.
To societies for prevention of cruelty to animals, 165.
In contemplation of death, effect of estate tax on, 271.

DOUBLE TAXATION,

Constitutional objections to, applied to income tax, 53, 54.

DRAFTS,

Stamp tax on, 384.

DUE PROCESS OF LAW,

Requirement of, in income taxation, 43.

DURESS,

Taxes paid under, suit to recover back, 471.

DUTCH ADMINISTRATION OFFICES,

Income tax on securities and investments of, 122.

DUTIES ON IMPORTS,

Deductible from income as "taxes paid," 180.

E

EARNINGS,

From profession or trade, as taxable income, 77.
Subject to excess profits tax, 316.

EDUCATIONAL INSTITUTIONS,

Exempt from income tax, 11, 144.
Donations to, deductible in computing taxable income, 165.
Exempt from excess profits tax, 305.
Exempt from capital stock tax, 325.

EMBEZZLEMENT,

Losses sustained by, deductible from income, 182.

EMINENT DOMAIN,

Compensation for land taken under, not income, 70.

EMOLUMENTS,

See Salaries; Wages.

EMPLOYEES,

Of state or municipality, salary of, not taxable, 50.
Salaries or wages of, as taxable income, 75.
Payments to, deductible in computing taxable income, 164.
Of federal, state, or municipal government not subject to excess profits tax, 305.
Bonds given by, subject to stamp tax, 374.
Exception as to public and municipal officers, 399.

EXCISE TAXES—Continued,
Admissions and club dues, 438, 439.
Opium and other narcotics, 441.
Oleomargarine and adulterated butter, 442.
Mixed flour, 443.
Filled cheese, 444.

EXECUTORS,
Income tax returns to be made by, 8.
Form and contents of returns, 229.
Taxation of income of estates, 115.
Duty of, in deducting and paying over income tax, 219.
Paying $800 or more to any beneficiary, to report to Internal Revenue office, 236.
Notice to be filed by, for purpose of estate tax, 256, 282.
To make returns for purpose of estate tax, 256, 288–291.
Payment of estate tax by, 258, 295.
Bonds of, not subject to stamp tax, 375.

EXEMPTIONS,
What income exempt from taxation, 4.
Allowed for purposes of normal tax, 7.
Corporations exempt from income tax, 11.
Foreign governments exempt from income tax, 30.
Constitutional validity of, 51, 52.
Under federal income tax law, 131–153.
Obligations and revenues of United States, 131.
Revenues of states and municipalities, 132.
Interest on state and municipal bonds, 133.
Political subdivisions of states, 134.
Public utilities owned by states or municipalities, 135.
Corporations specifically exempt, 136.
Claiming and proving exempt character, 137.
Corporation owned by exempt organization, 138.
Close corporations, 139.
Agricultural and horticultural organizations, 140.
Labor organizations, 141.
Fraternal orders and benefit societies, 142.
Religious, charitable and benevolent associations, 143.
Educational and scientific institutions, 144.
Building and loan associations, 145.
Mutual savings banks, 146.
Civic organizations and chambers of commerce, 147.
Incorporated clubs, 148.
Federal land banks, 149.
Proceeds of life insurance policies, 150.
Exemption of fixed amount of income, 151.
Treasury regulations as to husband and wife, 152.
Exemptions under war income tax, 153.
Claim of, where tax collected at the source, 224.
Corporations exempt from income tax not required to make returns, 233.

INDEX   525
[The figures refer to sections]

EXEMPTIONS—Continued,

Specific, under estate tax law, 280.
Soldiers and sailors, estates of, exempt from estate tax, 261.
Corporations and incomes exempt from excess profits tax, 305.
Corporations exempt from capital stock tax, 325.
　　Corporations not engaged in business, 327–331.
From tax on transportation and on telegraph and telephone messages, 362, 363.
　　Government and state business, 363.
From tax on insurance policies, 366.
From stamp tax, 399.
　　Instruments made by or to government, state, or municipal corporation, 399.
　　Stock and bonds of co-operative building and loan associations, 399.
　　Stock and bonds of mutual ditch and irrigation companies, 399.

EXPENSES,

Deductible in computing taxable estate of decedent, 279.
　　Funeral expenses, 279.
　　Costs of administration, 279.
　　Support of decedent's dependents, 279.

EXPENSES OF BUSINESS,

Deduction of, allowed, in computing net income, 154.
Investment of capital assets distinguished, 155.
Expense of beginning or engaging in business, 156.
Expense of earning or collecting income, 157.
General costs of business, 158.
Manufacturing costs, 159.
Legal expenses, 160.
Contributions to indemnity fund, 161.
Contributions to bank guaranty fund, 162.
Reserves to meet liabilities, 163.
Wages and salaries, 164.
Contributions to religious and charitable purposes, 165.
Gifts, charities, pensions to employees, 166.
Traveling expenses, 167.
Cost of insurance, 168.
Insurance on lives of officers, employees, or partners, 169.
Rent of land, buildings, or equipment, 170.
Mining operations, 171.
Judgments, 172.

EXPRESS COMPANIES,

Tax on transportation of parcels by, 357.
　　By whom tax is payable, 361.
　　What transactions exempt, 362, 363.
　　Returns and collection of tax, 364.

EXTENSION,

Of time for filing income tax returns, 237.

FORECLOSURE,

Deed given on sale under, subject to stamp tax, 390.

FOREIGN BUSINESS,

Income of Americans from, subject to tax, 106.

FOREIGN COLLECTIONS,

License for, under income tax law, 9f.
Items of, to be reported to Internal Revenue office, 236.

FOREIGN CORPORATIONS,

Liability of, to income tax, 120.
Doing business by local agents, 121.
Dutch administration offices, 122.
Deductions allowed to, in computing taxable income, 204.
Collection of income tax on interest or dividends from, 217.
Interest or dividends from, to be reported to Internal Revenue office, 236.
Tax on excess profits of, see Excess Profits Tax.
Returns by, for excess profits tax, 319.
Capital stock tax on, 324.
Computation of tax, 338.
Form of return, 342.
Payment of tax, 343.

FOREIGN GOVERNMENTS,

Not subject to income tax on American investments, 112.
Items of interest paid by, to be reported to Internal Revenue office, 236.
Bonds and other instruments of, exempt from stamp tax, 399.

FOREIGN INVESTMENTS,

Of American citizens, liable to income tax, 106.

FORTHCOMING BONDS,

Not subject to stamp tax, 375.

FRANCHISE,

Value of, included in "invested capital," 314.

FRANCHISE TAXES,

Income taxes distinguished from, 37.
Taxes on occupations as, 344.

FRATERNAL ORDERS,

Exemption of, from income tax, 11, 142.
Exempt from excess profits tax, 305.
Exempt from capital stock tax, 325.
Exempt from excise tax on membership dues, 439.

FRAUD,

In income tax returns, penalty for, 18, 248.

BL.FED.TAX.—34

H

HAIR,
Excise tax on sales of dyes, oils, dressings, and restoratives for, 428.

HEAD OF A FAMILY,
Exemption allowed to, under income tax law, 7.
Under war income tax law, 34.
Defined, by Treasury regulations, 151.
Income tax returns by, 231.

HOLDING COMPANIES,
When exempt from income tax, 11.
. When liable to income tax, 126.
Income tax returns by, 234.
Liability to capital stock tax, 331.
Returns by, for capital stock tax, 333.

HORTICULTURAL ORGANIZATIONS,
Exemption of, from income tax, 11, 140.
From excess profits tax, 305.
From capital stock tax, 325.

HOSPITALS,
Exempt from payment of income tax, 143.
Donations to, deductible in income tax return, 165.

HUSBAND AND WIFE,
Exemption allowed to, under income tax law, 7.
Under war income tax law, 34.
Regulations as to claiming exemption, 152.
Income tax returns by, 231.

I

ILLEGAL ASSESSMENT,
Remedies of taxpayer against, 462.
Injunction, 462.
Suit for recovery of taxes paid, 467.

ILLNESS,
Income tax return to be made for person disabled by, 228.

IMPROVEMENTS,
Cost of, not deductible in computing taxable income, 173.

INACTIVE CORPORATIONS,
Liability of, to income tax, 126.
To capital stock tax, 327–331.

INCOME,
Taxable, what constitutes, 66–104.
General definitions of income, 66.

INCOME TAX—Continued,

    Constitutional provisions affecting, 39, 40.
    History of federal income tax laws, 41.
    Constitutional validity of, 43-60.
    Construction of laws imposing, 61-65.
    What constitutes taxable income, 66-104.
    Persons and corporations subject to, 105-130.
    Exemptions and exceptions, 131-153.
    Deductions and credits in computing income, 154-205.
    Collection of, at the source, 206-227.
    Returns for purpose of, 228-249.

INCORPORATION EXPENSES,

    Not deductible in computing taxable income, 156.

INDEBTEDNESS,

    See Debts.

INDEMNITY BONDS,

    Stamp tax on, 374.

INDEMNITY FUND,

    Contributions to, deduction for, from taxable income, 161.

INDIVIDUALS,

    Income tax on, see Income Tax.
    Tax on excess profits of, see Excess Profits Tax.
    Computing net income of, for excess profits tax, 313.
    Returns by, for excess profits tax, 318.

INFANTS,

    Income tax returns to be made for, 228, 229.
        See also Guardians.

INFORMATION RETURNS,

    By corporations as to payment of dividends, 26, 236.
    By brokers as to stock-exchange transactions, 27, 236.
    As to payment of fixed incomes above $800 per year, 28, 236.

INHERITANCE,

    Property acquired by, as taxable income, 81.
    Taxes paid on, deductible in computing net income, 180.
    Federal estate tax, see Estate Tax.
    Taxes paid to state on, not deducted in computing taxable estate of decedent, 279.

INJUNCTION,

    To restrain collection of taxes, 462.

INSANE PERSONS,

    Making income tax returns for, 228.

INVESTED CAPITAL—Continued,
  In case of change of ownership of business, 315.
  Tax on profits of trade or business conducted without, 316.

INVESTMENTS,
  Profit on change of, when taxable as income, 90.
  Income of individual from, not subject to excess profits tax, 305.

IRRIGATION COMPANIES,
  Mutual, when exempt from income tax, 11.
    Stock and bonds of, exempt from stamp tax, 399.

IRRIGATION DISTRICTS,
  Interest on bonds of, not subject to income tax, 134.

ISSUE OF STOCK,
  In corporation, stamp tax on, 376.

J

JEWELRY,
  Excise tax on sales of, 426.
  Floor tax on existing stocks of, 432.
  Returns and payment of tax, 433.
  Penalty for failure to make return or false return, 434.

JOINT OWNERS,
  Of bonds, collection of income tax from, 209.
  Application of estate tax in case of, 274.
  Decedent's interest in community property, 275.

JOINT RETURNS,
  By husband and wife, 231.

JOINT-STOCK COMPANIES,
  Liability of, to income tax, 10, 124.
  Capital stock tax on, 323.

JOINT-STOCK LAND BANKS,
  Exemption of certain income of, from taxation, 11.

JOINT TRUSTEES,
  Making of income tax returns by, 229.

JUDGES,
  Federal, salary of, exempt from tax, 4.

JUDGMENT,
  For money, as taxable income, 79.
  Paid, when deductible in computing net income, 172.
  For amount of estate tax due and sale thereunder, 259.
  Against collector, for recovery of taxes illegally exacted, 476.

JUDICIAL SALE,

Of decedent's property, to collect estate tax, 259.
Deed given on, subject to stamp tax, 390.

JURISDICTION,

Of district courts in income tax cases, 20, 245.
Of suits to compel payment of estate tax, 259.
Of suit for collection of income taxes, 459.
Of suit to recover taxes illegally exacted and paid, **473.**

L

LABOR ORGANIZATIONS,

Exemption of, from income tax, 11, 141.
Exempt from excess profits tax, 305.
Exempt from capital stock tax, 325.

LAND,

Rent of, as taxable income, 72.
Royalty paid in lieu of rent, 73.
Rental value of residence, 74.
Profit from sale of, as taxable income, 89.
Taken under eminent domain, compensation for, not income, 70.
Rent of, deductible in computing taxable income, 170.
Sale of, to satisfy delinquent taxes, 461.

LANDLORD AND TENANT,

See Rent.

LAWYERS,

Professional earnings of, as taxable income, 77.
Fees of, deductible as expense of business, 160.
For incorporation of company, 156.
Income tax of, not collectible at source, 221.
When subject to excess profits tax, 316.

LEASE,

See Landlord and Tenant.
Of patent rights, profits from as taxable income, 94.

LEGACIES,

When taxable as income, 81.
Tax paid on, deductible in computing taxable income, 180.
Federal estate tax, see Estate Tax.
Taxes paid to state on, not deducted in computing taxable estate of decedent, 279.

LEGAL EXPENSES,

Deductible from income, for purpose of income tax, 160.

LESSEES,

Paying rent, $800 or more a year, to make reports to Commissioner of Internal Revenue, 236.

LESSOR CORPORATIONS,
>Liability to income tax, 127.
>Income tax returns by, 234.
>Liability to capital stock tax, 330.

LEVEE DISTRICTS,
>Interest on obligations of, exempt from income tax, 134.

LIBERTY LOAN BONDS,
>Exemption of, from income tax, 97.
>Status of dividends paid in, 199.
>Not exempt from estate tax, 269.
>Included in "invested capital," 314.
>Not deductible for purpose of capital stock tax, 335.

LIBRARIES,
>Public, income of, when exempt, 144.

LICENSE,
>For foreign collections, under income tax law, 9f.
>Cost of, as deductible expense in computing income, 156.
>For making foreign collections, for purpose of income tax, 218.

LIEN,
>Of estate tax on decedent's estate, 260.
>Of income tax, 458.

LIFE–INSURANCE POLICIES,
>Proceeds of, exempt from income tax, 4, 80, 150.

LIMITATION OF ACTIONS,
>Not applicable in government's suit to collect taxes, 459.
>In suit to recover back taxes paid, 474.

LIMITED PARTNERSHIP,
>Liable to income tax as a corporation, 117.

LIQUEURS,
>War revenue tax on, 412.

LIQUORS,
>See Beer; Distilled Spirits; Wines.

LIVE STOCK,
>Profits on raising and sale of, as taxable income, 82.
>Sale of, at stock yards, stamp tax on, 382.

LOAN,
>Of stock, not subject to stamp tax, 378.

LOAN ASSOCIATIONS,
>Domestic, exempt from income tax, 11, 145.
>Exempt from excess profits tax, 305.

M

MERCHANDISE,

Profits on sales of, as income, 86.

Sale of, on produce exchange, stamp tax on, 382.

MERCHANTS,

Profits or earnings of, as taxable income, 86.

MILEAGE,

Books issued for, tax on, 358.

By whom tax is payable, 361.

Collection of tax and returns, 364.

MINERAL WATERS,

War excise tax on, 414.

Returns by manufacturers and bottlers, 415.

MINES,

Profits from, as taxable income, 83.

Royalties for rent of, taxable as income, 73.

Expense of operating, deductible in computing taxable income, 171.

Deduction allowed for depletion of, 195.

Operation of, as "business" under capital stock tax, 329.

MINISTERS,

Salaries and fees of, as taxable income, 77.

When subject to excess profits tax, 316.

MINORS,

Income tax returns made for, 228, 229.

MISDEMEANORS,

Unlawfully divulging income tax returns, 241.

Making false or fraudulent income tax return, 248.

Failure to pay occupation tax, 356.

Failure to affix or cancel revenue stamps, 403.

Fraudulent removal or re-use of revenue stamps, 404.

MIXED FLOUR,

Tax on, 443.

MONEY BORROWED,

Not included in "invested capital," 314.

MORTGAGE BONDS,

Liability of, to stamp tax, 373.

MORTGAGES,

Income tax on income from, when deducted at source, 9c.

Held by nonresident aliens, collection of income tax on interest on, 211.

Foreign, collection of income tax on, 217.

License for foreign collections, 218.

Deducted in computing taxable estate of decedent, 279.

Income of individual from, not subject to excess profits tax, 305.

Not subject to stamp tax, 389.

MUTUAL SAVINGS BANKS,
> When exempt from income tax, 11, 146.
> When exempt from excess profits tax, 305.
> Exempt from capital stock tax, 325.

N

NAME OF CORPORATION,
> Effect of change of, on liability to income tax, 119.

NARCOTICS,
> Tax on manufacture and sale of, 441.

NATIONAL FARM LOAN ASSOCIATIONS,
> Exempt from income tax, 11, 149.
> Exempt from excess profits tax, 305.
> Exempt from capital stock tax, 325.

NATURAL DEPOSITS,
> Allowance for depletion of, in income tax returns, 195.

NATURAL GAS,
> Profits from wells of, as taxable income, 83.
> Deduction for depletion of, 196.

NAVY,
> Estates of persons dying in naval service exempt from estate tax, 261, 300.

NEGLECT,
> To file income tax return, proceedings in case of, 242.
>> Penalties prescribed, 247.

NET INCOME,
> Of individuals, normal and additional tax on, 1.
>> Under war revenue act, 1917, 34.
>> How determined, 2.
> Of citizen or resident of United States, 5.
> Of nonresident alien, 6.
> Of domestic corporation, 12.
> Of foreign corporation, 12.
> Deductions allowed in computing, 154–205.
> How computed for excess profits tax, 312.
>> Deductions allowed, 312.

NET VALUE,
> Of decedent's estate, for purpose of estate tax, 254.
>> Deductions allowed to be made, 279.
>> Specific exemption of $50,000, 280.
>> Deductions in case of nonresidents' estates, 281.

NEW BUILDINGS,
> Cost of, when deductible in computing taxable income, 173.

NOTICE—Continued,
> Duty of beneficiaries as to notice, 284.
> Given by corporate transfer agents, 285.
> Given by registers of bonds, 285.
> In case of nonresidents' estates, 286.

O

OATH OR AFFIRMATION,
> Income tax returns to be verified by, 230.

OBLIGATIONS,
> Of government, state, or municipality, exempt from income tax, 4, 97, 131, 133.
> See, generally, Bonds.

OBSOLESCENCE OF PROPERTY,
> Deduction for, in computing taxable income, 191.

OCCUPATIONS,
> Earnings from, as taxable income, 77.
> Classed as "trade" or "business" for purpose of excess profits tax, 302.

OCCUPATION TAXES,
> Income taxes distinguished from, 37.
> Deductible as "expense," in computing income, 156.
> Imposed by act of Congress, 344–356.
>> Brokers, 345.
>> Pawnbrokers, 346.
>> Ship brokers, 347.
>> Customhouse brokers, 348.
>> Theaters, museums, concert halls, 349.
>> Motion picture theaters and air domes, 350.
>> Circuses, 351.
>> Other public exhibitions and shows, 352.
>> Bowling alleys and billiard rooms, 353.
>> Place of business; branch offices, 354.
>> Payment and collection of tax, 355.
>> Penalties, 356.

OFFICE EXPENSES,
> Deductible in computing taxable income, 155.

OFFICERS,
> Federal and state, taxation of salaries of, 50.
> Salaries of, as taxable income, 75, 113.
> Salaries of, subject to excess profits tax, 305, 316.
>> Exemption of salaries of public officers, 305.
> Bonds given by, subject to stamp tax, 374.
>> Exception as to public officers, 399.

P

BL.FED.TAX.—35

REAL ESTATE,
    Rent of, as taxable income, 72.
        Royalty paid in lieu of rent, 73.
        Rental value of residence, 74.
    Profit from sale of, as taxable income, 89.
    Deduction for depreciation of, in computing income, 190.
    Sale of, to satisfy delinquent taxes, 461.

REAL ESTATE AGENTS,
    When subject to occupation tax as brokers, 345.

REAL ESTATE TRUSTS,
    Liability of, to income tax, 124.
        To capital stock tax, 325.

RECEIPTS,
    To be given for income tax payments, 17, 456.
    For payments of taxes on decedents' estates, 258.

RECEIVERS,
    Income tax returns to be made by, 8.
        Form and contents of returns, 229.
    Of corporations, returns by, 13c.
    Income tax on estates in hands of, 114.
    Duty of, in deducting and paying over income tax, 219.
    Paying out $800 or more to report to Internal Revenue office, 236.
    Corporations in hands of, liability to capital stock tax, 325.
    Bonds of, subject to stamp tax, 374.

RECLAMATION DISTRICTS,
    Interest on obligations of, exempt from income tax, 134.

RECORDS,
    Examination of, for purpose of estate tax, 298.

RECORDS, PHONOGRAPHIC,
    Excise tax on sales of, 424.

RECTIFIED SPIRITS,
    Tax on, 410.

REFUND,
    Of estate tax collected in excess of liability, 299.
    Of taxes illegally or excessively assessed, 466.

REFUSAL,
    To file income tax return, proceedings in case of, 242.
        Penalties prescribed, 247.

REGISTERED BONDS,
    Collection of income tax on interest on, 208.
    Registers of, to give notice for purpose of estate tax, 285.

BL.FED.TAX.—36

TIME—Continued.

> For filing income tax returns, 237.
>> Tentative returns, 238.
>> Extension of time by Commissioner, 237.
> For filing returns for excess profits tax, 318, 312.
> For payment of excess profits tax, 319.
> For filing returns for capital stock tax, 340.
> For payment of capital stock tax, 343.
> Of incidence of stamp tax, 372.

TOBACCO,

> War excise tax on cigars and cigarettes, 417.
>> On tobacco and snuff, 418.
> Floor tax on tobacco and cigars, 419.
> Time of incidence of tax, 421.
> Payment and collection of floor tax on, 445.

TOILET ARTICLES,

> Excise tax on sales of, 428.
> Floor tax on existing stocks of, 432.
> Returns and payment of tax, 433.
> Penalty for failure to make return or false return, 434.

TOILET SOAPS AND POWDERS,

> Excise tax on sales of, 428.

TOILET WATERS,

> Excise tax on sales of, 428.

TORT,

> Judgment for damages for personal injury taxable as income, 79.
>> When deductible by defendant as "expense," 172.
> Action of, against collector of internal revenue, 477.

TRADE,

> Losses incurred in, deductible, what are, 182.

TRADE MARKS,

> Value of, included in "invested capital," 314.

TRADES,

> Earnings from, as taxable income, 77.
> Include professions and occupations for purpose of excess profits tax, 302.
> Conducted without invested capital, excess profits tax on, 316.

TRANSFER AGENTS,

> Notice to be given by, for purposes of estate tax, 285.

TRANSFER OF PROPERTY,

> In contemplation of death, subject to estate tax, 271.
>> Investigation of transfers, 272.
>> Transfers within two years of death, 273.
> Stamp tax on sale or transfer of capital stock, 377.

[The figures refer to sections]

UNDIVIDED PROFITS—Continued,

Included in "invested capital," 314.
Computation of, for purpose of capital stock tax, 336.

UNIFORMITY,

Constitutional requirement applied to income taxes, 44.

UNINCORPORATED ASSOCIATION,

Income tax on profits of, when distributed to members, 98.
Liability to taxation on income, 124.

UNITED STATES,

Interest on obligations of, how far exempt from income tax, 4, 97.
Revenues and obligations of, exempt from income tax, 131.
Bonds of, not exempt from estate tax, 269.
Salaries of officers of, not subject to excess profits tax, 305.
Exempt from tax on transportation and on telegraph and telephone messages, 363.
Instruments made to or by, exempt from stamp tax, 399.
Suit against, to recover taxes illegally exacted and paid, 468.

UNITED STATES COURTS,

Jurisdiction of, in income tax cases, 20.
Of suits to compel payment of estate tax, 259.

UNIVERSITIES,

Exempt from income tax, 144.

V

VERIFICATION,

Of income tax returns, 230.
Of corporation's income tax return, 233.

VESSELS,

Tax on transportation of property by, 357.
On transportation of passengers, 358.
On staterooms reserved, 358.
By whom tax is payable, 361.
What transactions exempt, 362, 363.
Returns and collection of tax, 364.
Tax on passage tickets for foreign voyage, 395.

VIRGIN ISLANDS,

Tax on importations from, 437.

W

WAGES,

Payment of, $800 or more a year, to be reported, 28, 236.
As taxable income, 75.
Paid, deduction for, in computing taxable income, 164.
Not wages of domestic servants, 154.

WAREHOUSE ENTRIES,
    Stamp tax on, 394.

WARRANT OF ATTORNEY,
    Stamp tax on note with, 386.
    Stamp tax on powers of attorney, 397.

WAR REVENUE ACT, 1917,
    War income tax, 34.
    War estate tax, 252.
    Excess profits tax, 301.
    Tax on transportation, 357–359.
    Tax on telegraph and telephone messages, 360.
    Tax on insurance, 365.
    Stamp taxes, 370.
    Excise and commodities taxes, 407.

WEAR AND TEAR,
    Allowance for depreciation caused by, 187.

WHISKY,
    See Distilled Spirits.

WIFE,
    See Husband and Wife.

WINES,
    Blended, tax on, 410.
    War revenue tax on, 412.

WITHHOLDING AGENTS,
    Duties and liabilities of, 226.
        See Collection at the Source.
    Returns by, 249.

WITHHOLDING OF TAX AT SOURCE,
    See Collection at the Source.

WITNESSES,
    Examination of, where taxpayer neglects or refuses to file income tax return, 243.

WORTHLESS DEBTS,
    Deduction for, in computing taxable income, 186.

Y

YACHTS,
    Annual excise tax on, 436.

YEAR,
    Calendar year normal period for computing income tax, 1, 8.
    Designation of fiscal year by corporations, 10, 235.

[END]